Concepts of
Athletic Training

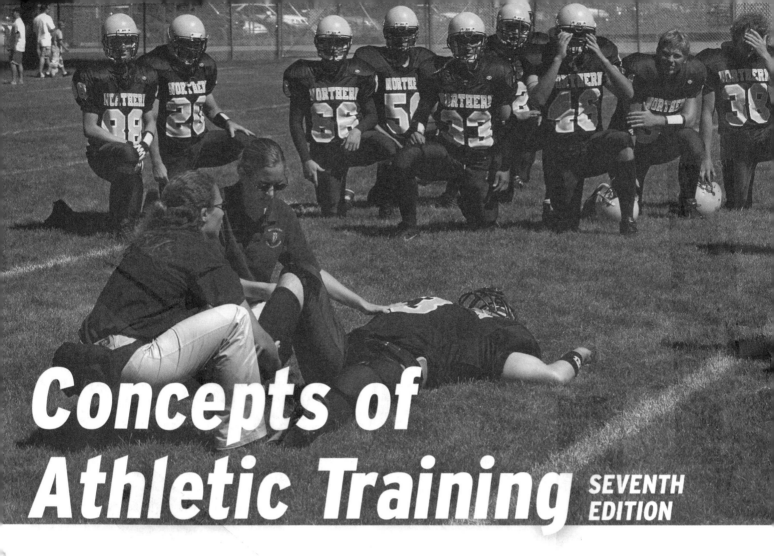

Concepts of Athletic Training SEVENTH EDITION

Ronald P. Pfeiffer, EdD (AT Ret.)
Interim Associate Dean, College of Education
Professor of Kinesiology
Executive Director, Center for Orthopaedic and Biomechanics Research (COBR)
Boise State University

Brent C. Mangus, EdD (AT Ret.)
Professor Emeritus
Department of Health and Human Performance
Texas A&M University

Cynthia A. Trowbridge, PhD, ATC, LAT, CSCS
Associate Professor and Clinical Educational Coordinator
University of Texas at Arlington

JONES & BARTLETT
LEARNING

World Headquarters
Jones & Bartlett Learning
5 Wall Street
Burlington, MA 01803
978-443-5000
info@jblearning.com
www.jblearning.com

Jones & Bartlett Learning books and products are available through most bookstores and online booksellers. To contact Jones & Bartlett Learning directly, call 800-832-0034, fax 978-443-8000, or visit our website, www.jblearning.com.

Production Credits

Executive Publisher: William Brottmiller
Publisher: Cathy L. Esperti
Acquisitions Editor: Ryan Angel
Associate Editor: Kayla Dos Santos
Production Manager: Tracey McCrea
Senior Marketing Manager: Andrea DeFronzo
Art Development Editor: Joanna Lundeen
Production Assistant: Eileen Worthley

VP, Manufacturing and Inventory Control: Therese Connell
Composition: Aptara®, Inc.
Cover Design: Kristin E. Parker
Photo Research and Permissions Coordinator: Lauren Miller
Cover Image: © Dennis MacDonald/Alamy Images
Printing and Binding: Edwards Brothers Malloy
Cover Printing: Edwards Brothers Malloy

To order this product in paperback, use ISBN: 978-1-284-03412-7

To order this product in hardcover, use ISBN: 978-1-284-06246-5

Library of Congress Cataloging-in-Publication Data
Pfeiffer, Ronald P., author.
  Concepts of athletic training.—Seventh edition / Ronald Pfeiffer, Brent Mangus, Cindy Trowbridge.
    pages cm
  Includes bibliographical references and index.
  ISBN 978-1-284-02214-8 (pbk.)—ISBN 978-1-284-12075-2 (hardcover)
  1. Athletic trainers. 2. Sports injuries. 3. Sports medicine. I. Mangus, Brent C., author.
II. Trowbridge, Cynthia A., author. III. Title.
  RC1210.P45 2015
  617.1'027—dc23
                                                      2013045773

6048

Printed in the United States of America
18 17 16 15 14   10 9 8 7 6 5 4 3 2 1

Brief Contents

Chapter 1   **The Concept of Sports Injury**   1
Chapter 2   **The Athletic Health Care Team**   23
Chapter 3   **The Law of Sports Injury**   33
Chapter 4   **Sports-Injury Prevention**   45
Chapter 5   **The Psychology of Athletes and Sports Injury**   61
Chapter 6   **Nutritional Considerations**   77
Chapter 7   **Emergency Plan and Initial Injury Evaluation**   105
Chapter 8   **The Injury Process**   119
Chapter 9   **Injuries to the Head, Neck, and Face**   135
Chapter 10   **Injuries to the Thoracic Through Coccygeal Spine**   169
Chapter 11   **Injuries to the Shoulder Region**   179
Chapter 12   **Injuries to the Arm, Wrist, and Hand**   195
Chapter 13   **Injuries to the Thorax and Abdomen**   223
Chapter 14   **Injuries to the Hip and Pelvis**   237
Chapter 15   **Injuries to the Thigh, Leg, and Knee**   249
Chapter 16   **Injuries to the Lower Leg, Ankle, and Foot**   269
Chapter 17   **Skin Conditions in Sports**   295
Chapter 18   **Thermal Injuries**   307
Chapter 19   **Other Medicinal Concerns**   321
Chapter 20   **The Adolescent Athlete: Special Medical Concerns**   337

Contents

Preface. xi
How to Use This Book! xiii
Acknowledgments. xvii

Chapter 1
The Concept of Sports Injury. 1
Major Concepts 1
Definition of Sports Injury 3
Injury Classifications. 7
   Sprains 7
   Strains. 7
   Contusions 8
   Fractures. 8
   Dislocations 10
Injury Recognition 11
Epidemiology of Sports Injury 11
Classification of Sports. 12
Extent of the Injury Problem: Some Examples. . . . 13
   Tackle Football 13
   Basketball. 14
   Baseball and Softball 15
   Wrestling. 16
   Volleyball 18
   Soccer. 18
Review Questions. 19
References 20

Chapter 2
The Athletic Health Care Team 23
Major Concepts 23
Sports Medicine. 24
Key Members of the Team. 25
Professional Settings for the Practice
   of Athletic Training. 27
   The Secondary School Setting 28
   Locating a BOC-Certified Athletic Trainer 29
Review Questions. 30
References 31

Chapter 3
The Law of Sports Injury 33
Major Concepts 33
Ethics of Sports-Injury Care 35
The Concept of Tort. 35

What Is the Physical Educator's or
   Coach's Liability? 37
Are Coaches and Physical Educators
   Protected? 39
How to Reduce the Chances of Going to Court . . 39
What Coaches or Physical Educators
   Can Do If They Get Sued 42
Role of the Athletic Trainer 42
Review Questions. 42
Recommended Reading 43
References 43

Chapter 4
Sports-Injury Prevention 45
Major Concepts 45
Causative Factors in Injury 46
Intervention Strategies. 47
   Extrinsic Factors 47
   Intrinsic Factors. 48
Injury Prevention and Conditioning 50
   Aerobic Fitness 51
   Anaerobic Fitness 51
   Muscle Strength, Power, and Endurance 52
   Flexibility. 53
   Body Composition 54
   Periodization. 55
Review Questions. 58
References 58

Chapter 5
The Psychology of Athletes
and Sports Injury 61
Major Concepts 61
Personality Variables 62
Psychosocial Variables 64
   Depression 65
   Seasonal Affective Disorder 66
Competitive Stress and the
   Child/Adolescent 66
Psychology of the Injured Athlete 68
   Recommendations 69
Eating Disorders. 69
   Anorexia Nervosa and Bulimia Nervosa 70
   Research 71
   Sport Specificity and Eating Disorders 72

Prevention. 73
Treatment 73
Review Questions. 74
References 74

Chapter 6

Nutritional Considerations 77

Major Concepts 77
Nutrients: An Overview 78
Caloric Intake (Rest + Activity) 78
Carbohydrates 79
Fats (Lipids). 81
Proteins. 83
Vitamins 84
Minerals 85
Water 86
Nutritional Knowledge of Athletes
and Coaches: What the Research Shows 86
Special Considerations. 88
Female Athletes 88
Endurance Sports 88
Wrestling. 88
Conclusions 89
Educating Athletes: What Can the Coach Do? . . . 90
General Dietary Guidelines for Athletes 91
Daily Diet: Nutritional Maintenance 91
Precompetition Diets 92
Nutrition During Competition 93
Nutrition for Post Exercise 93
Nutrition and Injury Recovery 93
Managing Body Weight. 94
Minimal Competitive Weight 95
Supplements and Ergogenic Aids 97
Nutritional Supplements. 98
Anabolic-Androgenic Products. 100
Review Questions. 101
References 102

Chapter 7

**Emergency Plan and Initial
Injury Evaluation 105**

Major Concepts 105
Emergency Team 107
Best Practices for Emergency Planning
for Athletics 107
Emergency Care Training. 107
Injury Evaluation Procedures 108
The Coach's Responsibility 108
The Evaluation Process. 108
Assessment of the Injured Athlete: Initial Check . 109
Determining Responsiveness 109
Respiratory System. 110
Circulatory System 111

Summary. 111
Assessment of the Injured Athlete:
Physical Exam. 112
Medical History. 112
Observation and Palpation. 113
Shock 114
Removal from Field/Court 114
Return to Play?. 114
The Coach's Limitations 115
Review Questions. 116
References 116

Chapter 8

The Injury Process 119

Major Concepts 119
The Physics of Sports Injury 120
The Physiology of Sports Injury 120
Inflammatory Response Phase 121
Fibroblastic Repair Phase 124
Maturation and Remodeling Phase 124
Pain and Acute Injury. 125
Intervention Procedures. 126
Cryotherapy and Thermotherapy 127
Pharmacologic Agents 129
The Role of Exercise Rehabilitation. 131
Review Questions. 132
References 133

Chapter 9

Injuries to the Head, Neck, and Face . . .135

Major Concepts 135
Anatomy Review 136
Skull 136
The Meninges. 137
The Central Nervous System 137
The Peripheral Nervous System 138
The Face. 138
The Neck (Cervical Spine). 138
Head Injuries in Sports. 138
Background Information. 138
Type and Mechanism of Injury 140
Concussion (Mild Traumatic Brain Injury) 140
Post-Concussive Syndrome 141
Second Impact Syndrome 142
Intracranial Injury 143
Cranial Injury. 144
Initial Treatment of a Suspected
Head Injury: Guidelines 144
Initial Check 145
Physical Examination 145
Cervical Spine Injuries 149
Background Information. 149
Mechanisms of Injury 151
Brachial Plexus Injuries 152

Sprains 152
Strains 153
Fractures and Dislocations 153
Initial Treatment of a Suspected
   Neck Injury: Guidelines 154
Emergency Procedures for the Treatment
   of Head and Neck Injuries in Football 156
Injuries to the Maxillofacial Region 158
Dental Injuries 159
Eye Injuries 160
Nose Injuries 162
Fractures of the Face (Non-Nasal) 164
Wounds of the Facial Region 164
Review Questions 165
References 166

Chapter 10
Injuries to the Thoracic Through Coccygeal Spine 169

Major Concepts 169
Anatomy Review of the Thoracic Spine 170
Common Sports Injuries 170
Skeletal Injuries 170
Sprains 172
Strains 172
Intervertebral Disk Injuries 172
Anatomy Review of the Lumbar
   Spine Distally to the Coccyx 173
Common Sports Injuries 173
Spondylolysis and Spondylolisthesis 173
Traumatic Fractures 175
Sprains and Strains 175
Lumbar Disk Injuries 176
Review Questions 177
References 177

Chapter 11
Injuries to the Shoulder Region 179

Major Concepts 179
Anatomy Review 180
Common Sports Injuries 183
Skeletal Injuries 183
Soft-Tissue Injuries 185
Review Questions 192
References 193

Chapter 12
Injuries to the Arm, Wrist, and Hand 195

Major Concepts 195
Anatomy Review 196
Soft-Tissue Injuries to the Upper Arm 196

Myositis Ossificans Traumatica 197
Triceps Injuries 198
Fractures of the Upper Arm 199
Elbow Injuries 201
Sprains and Dislocations 202
Fractures 203
Epicondylitis of the Elbow 204
Osteochondritis Dissecans of the Elbow 205
Contusions of the Elbow 206
Wrist and Forearm Injuries 206
Wrist Fractures 208
Wrist Sprains and Dislocations 209
Nerve Injuries to the Wrist 210
Unique Tendon Problems
   of the Wrist 212
Hand Injuries 213
Hand Fractures 213
Sprains and Dislocations of the Hand 214
Wrist and Thumb Taping 218
Review Questions 220
References 221

Chapter 13
Injuries to the Thorax and Abdomen 223

Major Concepts 223
Anatomy Review 224
Internal Organs 225
Common Sports Injuries 226
External Injuries 226
Internal Injuries 227
Review Questions 234
References 235

Chapter 14
Injuries to the Hip and Pelvis 237

Major Concepts 237
Anatomy Review 238
Common Sports Injuries 240
Skeletal Injuries 240
Soft-Tissue Injuries 244
Prevention 246
Review Questions 247
References 247

Chapter 15
Injuries to the Thigh, Leg, and Knee 249

Major Concepts 249
Anatomy Review 250
Common Sports Injuries 252
Skeletal Injuries 252

Soft-Tissue Injuries to the Thigh 253
Patellofemoral Joint Injuries 256
Patellofemoral Conditions 258
Menisci Injuries 259
Knee Ligament Injuries 260
Prevention 263
Knee Bracing 265
Review Questions 266
References 267

Chapter 16

Injuries to the Lower Leg, Ankle, and Foot 269

Major Concepts 269
Anatomy Review 270
Common Sports Injuries 273
Skeletal Injuries 273
Soft-Tissue Injuries 274
Foot Disorders 281
Preventive Ankle Taping 287
Review Questions 292
References 292

Chapter 17

Skin Conditions in Sports 295

Major Concepts 295
Wounds 296
Treatment 297
HIV/HBV and the Athlete 298
Other Skin Conditions 299
Ultraviolet Light-Related Skin Problems 299
Skin Infections 299
Wrestling and Skin Infections 304
Allergic Reactions 304
Review Questions 305
References 305

Chapter 18

Thermal Injuries 307

Major Concepts 307
Exertional Heat Illnesses 309
Dehydration 309
Heat Cramps 310
Heat Exhaustion 311
Exertional Heatstroke 311
Prevention of Exertional Heat Illnesses 312
Cold-Related Health Problems 313
Hypothermia 313
Frostbite and Frostnip 315
Cold Urticaria 316
Review Questions 318
References 319

Chapter 19

Other Medicinal Concerns 321

Major Concepts 321
Exercise and Infectious Disease 322
Respiratory Infections 322
Gastrointestinal Infections 323
Other Infectious Diseases 323
Exercise-Induced Asthma 327
The Athlete with Sickle Cell Trait 329
The Athlete with Diabetes 330
Epilepsy and Sports Participation 331
Review Questions 334
References 334

Chapter 20

The Adolescent Athlete: Special Medical Concerns 337

Major Concepts 337
Youth Sports in America 338
Factors in Youth Sports Participation 338
Epidemic of Youth Sports Injury 338
The Growing Athlete 339
Puberty 339
Growth 340
Injury Mechanisms 340
Ligament Injuries 340
Tendon Injuries 341
Growth Plate Injuries 342
Growth Cartilage 342
Contributors to Injury 343
Intrinsic Factors 344
Extrinsic Factors 344
Injury Imitators 345
Oncologic 346
Rheumatologic 346
Infectious 346
Neurovascular 346
Psychologic 346
Strength Training 346
Safety 347
Lat Pull Down 348
Bench Press 348
Military Press 348
Squats 348
Prevention of Injury 348
Preparticipation Physical Examination 348
Treatment and Rehabilitation
of Injuries 349
Stretching Programs 349
Coaching Techniques 349
Female Athletes 349
Prescription Stimulant Medications 350
Review Questions 350

x Contents

Suggested Readings 351
References 351

Appendix 1 National Athletic Trainers'
Association Position Statement: Preventing
Sudden Death in Sports. 353

Appendix 2 National Athletic Trainers'
Association Position Statement: Safe Weight
Loss and Maintenance Practices in Sport
and Exercise 387

Glossary. 411

Index 419

Appendix 1 NATA Position Statement:
Exertional Heat Illness . . . . On Web Site

Appendix 2 Weight Loss in Wrestlers. . . . On Web Site

Appendix 3 Generic First Aid Kit for
Sports Injuries (Checklist). . . . . On Web Site

Appendix 4 Equipment Fitting . . . . On Web Site

Appendix 5 CPR . . . . On Web Site

Preface

More than 3 million children under the age of 14 are injured while participating in organized school sports or playing recreationally and around 750,000 of these injuries require treatment at an emergency care facility. The good news is there are more BOC-Certified Athletic Trainers (ATs) employed in the nation's high schools than at any other time in history. However, the reality is that the majority of schools, especially middle schools, still do not employ ATs and, as a result, the coaching personnel or physical educators are likely to serve as "first responders" in the majority of sports-injury situations. Because coaches and physical educators interact with children of all ages and have teams or classes that include both pre-adolescents and post-pubescent youth, this puts considerable pressure on them to become knowledgeable on the "best practices" for prevention and management of injuries to both populations. In order to make correct decisions, these personnel must be properly trained, not only in basic first aid, but in more advanced knowledge in order to properly manage injuries that are complicated by sports equipment and personal protective equipment such as helmets, face masks, mouth guards, and other equipment.

The primary goal of this book is the prevention, care, and management of sport and physical activity related injuries. Because coaches or non-high level sports medicine professionals are most likely the first responders, the target audience for the *Concepts of Athletic Training* includes anyone planning a career as a coach, physical educator, or personal trainer. This seventh edition is also excellent for high school students or college students majoring in athletic training. The general field of sports medicine continues to be a rapidly evolving field of study. The content will form a solid foundation for more advanced studies in this exciting and constantly evolving allied health field.

New to This Edition

The authors have made every effort to update critical material throughout the text in order to make the content as current as possible. This latest edition includes considerable updates in regards to sports injury epidemiology (Chapter 1, *The Concept of Sports Injury*, *The Athletic Health Care Team* [Chapter 2]), proper prevention strategies including emergency planning (Chapter 7, *Emergency Plan and Initial Injury Evaluation*),

legal issues (Chapter 3, *The Law of Sports Injury*), pre-participation physical exams and strength training and periodization techniques (Chapter 4, *Sports-Injury Prevention*), in addition to updated information on the importance of nutrition in injury prevention (Chapter 6, *Nutritional Considerations*). Response to injury, including the coach's or physical educator's initial decisions and subsequent actions, are critical in determining the outcome of an injury; therefore, significant updates have been added to chapters that focus on injuries to the head, neck, face, mouth (Chapter 9, *Injuries to the Head, Neck, and Face*), upper and lower extremities, skin (Chapter 17, *Skin Conditions in Sports*), and the low back, thorax, and abdomen (Chapter 10, *Injuries to the Thoracic Through Coccygeal Spine* and Chapter 13, *Injuries to the Thorax and Abdomen*). Because the majority of sport- and activity-related injuries involve the musculoskeletal system, much of this text's content is devoted to the recognition, immediate care, and management of injuries such as sprains, strains, dislocations, and fractures in the extremities. In an effort to help coaches and physical educators provide proper advice for the home management of musculoskeletal injuries, Chapter 8, *The Injury Process* includes the latest information regarding the treatment of inflammation. Fortunately, only a small percentage of sports- and activity-related injuries are life threatening or result in permanent disability. However, deaths and permanent disability tragically continue to be an outcome in a small percentage of cases. Most of these injuries are related to trauma to the head and/or neck or are heat related. Detailed information on head and neck injuries, as well as prevention of heat disorders, is provided in Chapter 9, *Injuries to the Head, Neck, and Face* and Chapter 18, *Thermal Injuries*. These chapters have been updated in relation to recent publications on the recognition, treatment, and disposition of concussions, neck injuries, and heat illness. New information on cardiac concerns, diabetes, exercise-induced asthma, sickle cell crisis, and MRSA are also included in Chapter 19, *Other Medicinal Concerns* as coaches and physical educators may be the first to respond to these incidents and proper recognition and activation of an emergency action plan is essential. This newest edition also includes vital information related the psychology of sports participation and injury (Chapter 5, *The Psychology of Athletes and Sport Injury*) and includes advice on recognizing symptoms and directions for referral of youth who may be experiencing psychological issues related to sports participation, sports injury, or undue pressure from caregivers.

Because coaches and physical educators are often responsible for adolescent athletes, this latest edition continues to feature a chapter devoted to the adolescent athlete (Chapter 20, *The Adolescent Athlete: Special Medical Concerns*). The rationale for this is simple: The vast majority of school-aged athletes (grades 7–12) are, in fact, adolescents or even pre-adolescents. As such, they represent an anatomically distinct population when compared to adult athletes. These differences must be recognized and considered by coaching personnel when making decisions regarding not only injury management, but also when designing and implementing injury prevention programs.

What Is Not Included and Why

Periodically the authors are asked why our text does not include detailed information on more advanced techniques including taping/wrapping, as well as joint assessments. The answer is easy; those procedures clearly fall outside the scope of practice for a coach or physical education teacher. As we have targeted this text to those populations, we feel it would be irresponsible to introduce students to clinical skills they should not attempt to execute in the field. We also market the text to pre-athletic training majors, however, students who complete a CAATE accredited athletic training program will receive extensive training in many advanced skills by way of other, more advanced texts, as well as by way of mentoring from clinical instructors.

Conclusion

This book is an outstanding resource for students studying to become physical education teachers, coaches, and athletic trainers. Personnel charged with the responsibility of providing emergency care for athletes must be trained in the first aid procedures appropriate for sports injuries. The content of this text will provide instructors and students with a wealth of information on topics related to the care and prevention of sports injuries. The goal, of course, is to give coaching and teaching personnel the necessary knowledge and critical-thinking skills to recognize and differentiate minor from more serious sports injuries. Once decisions are made regarding the nature of the injury, appropriate first aid care and/or medical referral can be instituted.

How to Use This Book!

Major Concepts sections provide an introduction that sets the stage for each chapter and provides an overview of what is to come.

MAJOR CONCEPTS

The cornerstone of optimal management of sports- and activity-related injuries is the athletic healthcare team (AHCT), which is made up of a variety of highly trained medical and allied medical personnel as well as other professionals, and coordinates on site with nonmedical personnel including coaches, administrators, parents, and the athletes. This chapter provides an overview of the principal members of the team and reviews the evolution of the field of **sports medicine**. In addition, it describes specific services provided by the athletic healthcare team, giving special attention to the team physician and the athletic trainer who is certified by the Board of Certification, Inc. (BOC). It also outlines educational requirements for BOC certification and employment options for certified athletic trainers.

go.jblearning.com/PfeifferCWS

For a full suite of assignments and additional learning activities (indicated by the icons throughout the text), use the access code found in the front of your text. If you do not have an access code, you can obtain one at go.jblearning.com/PfeifferCWS.

This icon urges students to visit the Navigate Companion Website for additional assignments and practice activities.

What if? features are real-world scenarios that encourage students to work on critical decision-making skills. These sections provide information typically available to coaching personnel when confronted with an injury-related problem. Applications range from simple decision-making practice sessions to role-playing exercises in the classroom.

WHAT IF?

A group of parents asks you, the soccer coach at the local high school, your recommendation for the best way to provide preseason physical evaluations that are required by the state high school association. What would you recommend?

WHAT IF?

A high school senior asks you for information on the academic requirements and certification process to become an athletic trainer.

Athletic Trainers Speak Out boxes feature a different athletic trainer in every chapter who discuss an element of athlete care and injury prevention.

Athletic Trainers SPEAK Out

Courtesy of Forrest Pecha, MS, ATC, LAT, OTC, CSCS, St. Luke's Sports Medicine.

Athletic trainers have been instrumental in the prevention, diagnosis, care, and treatment of musculoskeletal injuries for athletes and active populations for decades. Athletic training forefathers logged many hours and have worked tirelessly managing the athletic sidelines to bring recognition to our profession as healthcare professionals. Today, as athletic training evolves, athletic trainers (ATs) are reaching out into a number of emerging settings and continue to provide the same level of care to patients as we have from the inception of our profession.

ATs have a background in musculoskeletal care, unique to our profession, that sets us apart from many other healthcare providers. Working as a "physician extender" is not unique to our profession; we have been working side by side with physicians through the grassroots of our profession and continue to manage athletes together in the athletic training rooms. The physician extender career setting has evolved and taken the AT from the sidelines to the physician offices. ATs have become instrumental in patient care models in the clinical setting and play an ever-growing role in today's healthcare. ATs fill many responsibilities within the physician clinic, from taking patient histories, completing physical exams and inspection, scribing for their physicians, casting, bracing, and teaching home exercises, to providing patient education, pre- and postoperative patient care, surgical assistance, and the list goes on. ATs working in this role have shown positive financial impacts to their clinics, increased clinic efficiency, and improved patient satisfaction. ATs are being sought out at an increasing pace to work in the physician clinics and be members of the healthcare team.

—Forrest Q. Pecha, MS, ATC, LAT, OTC, CSCS

Forrest Q. Pecha is the Director of Clinical Residency and Outreach at St. Luke's Sports Medicine.

Courtesy of Forrest Pecha, MS, ATC, LAT, OTC, CSCS, St. Luke's Sports Medicine.

Time Out boxes provide additional information related to the text, such as NATA Athletic Helmet Removal Guidelines, guidelines for working with an injured athlete, how to recognize the signs of concussion, and much more.

TIME OUT 2.1

Major support for the placement of BOC-certified athletic trainers in secondary schools was provided by the AMA's House of Delegates in June 1998. The AMA House of Delegates adopted the following statements as policy:

1. The AMA believes that (a) the Board of Education and the Department of Health of the individual states should encourage that an adequate Athletic Medicine Unit be established in every school that mounts a sports program; (b) the Athletic Medicine Unit should be composed of an allopathic or osteopathic physician director with unlimited license to practice medicine, an athletic health coordinator (preferably a BOC-certified athletic trainer), and other necessary personnel; (c) the duties of the Athletic Medicine Unit should be prevention of injury, the provision of medical care with the cooperation of the family's physician and others of the healthcare team of the community, and the rehabilitation of the injured; (d) except in extreme emergencies, the selection of the treating physician is the choice of the parent or guardian and any directed referral therefore requires their consent; (e) Athletic Medicine Units should be required to submit complete reports of all injuries to a designated authority; and (f) medical schools, colleges, and universities should be urged to cooperate in establishing education programs for athletic health

coordinators (BOC-certified athletic trainers) as well as continuing medical education and graduate programs in Sports Medicine.

2. The AMA urges high school administrators, athletic directors, and coaches to work with local physicians, medical societies, and medical specialty societies, as well as government officials and community groups, to undertake appropriate measures to ensure funding to provide the services of a certified athletic trainer to all high school athletes.

3. Recognizing that not all high schools have the resources to procure the services of a certified athletic trainer and further recognizing that athletic trainers cannot be present at all practices and competitions, the AMA encourages high school administrators and athletic directors to ensure that all coaches are appropriately trained in emergency first aid and basic life support.

Source: Reproduced from Lyznicki JM, Riggs JA, Champion HC. (1999). Certified athletic trainers in secondary schools: Report of the Council on Scientific Affairs, American Medical Association. J Athl Train. 34(3):272–276. Reprinted with permission.

All relevant chapters begin with an Anatomy Review to introduce body parts to students unfamiliar with human anatomy and provide a refresher for others who may have taken past anatomy courses.

ANATOMY REVIEW

The shoulder allows for a great deal of movement while at the same time providing a point of attachment for the arm to the thorax. The skeleton of the shoulder (Figure 11.1) consists of the bones of the shoulder girdle and the upper arm bone (humerus). The clavicle and the scapula make up the shoulder girdle, so named because these two bones surround (girdle) the upper thorax. The head of the humerus combines with the shallow glenoid fossa of the scapula to form the highly mobile **glenohumeral (GH) joint**, commonly known as the shoulder joint (Figure 11.2). The GH joint is provided with additional stability by a fibrocartilaginous cuplike structure known as the glenoid labrum, which is directly attached to the glenoid fossa (Gray, 1985). The labrum extends out into the GH joint, making the glenoid fossa a deeper receptacle for the head of the humerus (Snyder, Rames, & Wolber, 1991). In addition, the long-head tendon of the biceps brachii muscle is attached to the superior labrum and to the supraglenoid tubercle at the top of the GH joint. The shoulder region also includes the **acromioclavicular (AC) joint**, located between the distal end of the clavicle and the acromion of the scapula (Figure 11.2), and the **sternoclavicular (SC) joint**, located between the proximal end of the clavicle and the manubrium of the sternum (Figure 11.3). Each of these joints is held together with ligaments and joint capsules that provide stability while also allowing for necessary movement, which is quite limited.

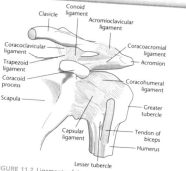

FIGURE 11.2 Ligaments of the acromioclavicular and glenohumeral joints.

shoulder girdle and the GH joint work together to move the arm. Consequently, any limitation from injury to the shoulder girdle will indirectly affect the GH joint. The muscles in the region of the shoulder can be divided into two groups—those that act on the shoulder girdle and those that act on the GH joint (Figures 11.4 and 11.5). The muscles of the shoulder girdle are the levator scapulae, trapezius, rhomboids, subclavius, pectoralis minor, and serratus anterior

Key terms are bolded within the text and defined in boxes to help students quickly identify and understand new terms.

sports medicine Branch of medicine concerned with the medical aspects of sports participation.
orthopedic surgeon Physician who corrects deformities of the musculoskeletal system.
team physician A medical doctor who agrees to provide at least limited medical coverage to a particular sports program or institution.

Each chapter closes with Review Questions that continue to engage students in a thoughtful review of important chapter material.

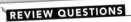

REVIEW QUESTIONS

1. Define the term *sports medicine*.
2. What is the CAQ and how does it relate to the team physician?
3. List the specific services that should be provided to the athlete by the team physician.
4. What are the six practice domains of the BOC-certified athletic trainer?
5. List several professional medical organizations that promote the study of sports medicine.
6. What has been the largest employment market for athletic trainers in recent years?
7. Briefly describe six different employment options for a BOC-certified athletic trainer in the school setting. Elaborate on the advantages and disadvantages of each option.
8. True or false: It is generally acknowledged that sports medicine services in the future will be provided by medical specialists rather than primary care physicians.
9. List the eight professional content areas that are required by CAATE for accredited curricula in athletic training.

Integrated Teaching and Learning Package:

For Instructors: Instructor resources include Instructor's Manuals, Test Banks, Lecture Outlines in PowerPoint format, and Image Banks

For Students: The Navigate Companion Website, included free with every new copy of the text, includes an interactive anatomy review, animated flashcards, crossword puzzles, scenarios, review questions, and more.

Acknowledgments

Those familiar with the previous editions of this text will note we have a new co-author, Dr. Cynthia Trowbridge, Associate Professor of Kinesiology and Clinical Education Coordinator in the Athletic Training Education Program at University of Texas, Arlington. Dr. Trowbridge has over 20 years of experience as a clinician, educator, and scholar. Along with being an exceptional writer, she brings a wealth of knowledge and experience in the profession to our team! We are indeed fortunate to have Dr. Trowbridge on-board as a co-author for the seventh edition. I'd also like to thank my other co-author, Dr. Brent Mangus, for all that he has done for nearly 20 years to ensure this book is contemporary and represents "best practices" across the seven editions. Brent's knowledge, impressive intellect, and wisdom have made the evolution of this text possible. I also want to recognize all those in the profession who have influenced me over the years. Space does not allow me to mention you all by name, but my years as a student at Central Michigan University, University of Oregon, and Brigham Young University provided me with a wealth of opportunities to be mentored by a number of outstanding and dedicated professionals. Thank you all!

—Ron Pfeiffer
Boise, ID

Reviewers

Richard A. Bingham, MS, ATC
College of Southern Idaho
Twin Falls, ID

Kimberly Calvert, MS, ATC, PES
University of Wisconsin Oshkosh
Oshkosh, WI

Bruce E. Ferguson, MS, ATC
Taft College
Taft, CA

Dave Hammons, EdD, AT
Boise State University
Boise, ID

George D. Harris, MD, MS
UMKC School of Medicine
Kansas City, MO

Kris Hinnerichs
Wayne State College
Wayne, NE

Dani Moffit, PhD, ATC
Temple University
Philadelphia, PA

Christopher Nightingale
University of Maine
Orono, ME

Patricia M. Patane, MS, ATC, PT, CSCS
Stony Brook University
Stony Brook, NY

Rebecca Lewis Schultz, PhD
University of Sioux Falls
Sioux Falls, SD

Hal Strough, PhD, ATC
The College of ST. Scholastica
Duluth, MN

Scott Sunderland, MS, ATC
Knox College
Galesburg, IL

The Concept of Sports Injury

MAJOR CONCEPTS

After reading and studying this chapter, the reader will be familiar with the scope and breadth of the topic of sports injury. This chapter discusses the most popular definitions of sports injury currently in use, along with a variety of the most commonly used medical terms related to the type and severity of injury. These terms are used throughout the remainder of the text and can also prove useful to the coach when communicating with members of the medical community about sports injuries. The last sections of the chapter introduce the concept of epidemiology as it applies to the study of sports injury. A straightforward sport classification system is introduced that is based on the relative amount of physical contact that typically occurs during the activity. This chapter concludes with specific participation and injury data from the most popular interscholastic sports in the United States.

go.jblearning.com/PfeifferCWS

For a full suite of assignments and additional learning activities (indicated by the icons throughout the text), use the access code found in the front of your text. If you do not have an access code, you can obtain one at go.jblearning.com/PfeifferCWS.

Organized competitive interscholastic high school sports continue to be extremely popular among American children. Recent research indicates that approximately 7.7 million public school children are involved in these activities annually (National Federation of State High School Associations [NFSH], n.d.). Along with modest growth in high school sports programs, there has been massive growth in the number of adolescent and pediatric-aged children playing sports outside of, or in addition to, school-sponsored programs. As a result, approximately 38 million school-aged children are involved in organized sports in the United States (Mickalide & Hansen, 2012). Although these sports may involve children as young as 5 years of age, the level of competition is often extremely high as attested by the fact that it is common for teams to travel hundreds and sometimes thousands of miles to compete in tournaments. Further, it is not uncommon for children in sports such as tennis and gymnastics to invest as much as 20 hours a week in their chosen activity (Maffulli & Caine, 2005).

With the implementation of Title IX of the Education Amendments of 1972, growth in the participation of female athletes in the United States was reported through the 1980s at 700% (Stanitski, 1989). Ironically, as a result of persistent stereotypes in both the lay and coaching communities that girls were not tough enough to play sports, many young female athletes were historically discouraged from participation. Even more disturbing is the fact that such negative stereotypes still persist in some sports organizations. Available evidence suggests that for some sports the injury rates are higher for girls, while in other sports the rates are higher for boys. High school data, for example, indicate that in sports in which both sexes compete, such as soccer and basketball, there are some differences in injury rates based on sex. For example, in basketball, girls sustain more concussions and knee injuries, while boys sustain more fractures and contusions (Borowski et al., 2008). Injury data from high school soccer show that overall the injury rates are very similar between sexes. There is a notable exception, however, in that girls are found to have a much higher rate of knee ligament sprains. The rates for complete ligament sprains in the knee requiring surgery were 13 times higher in girls than in boys (Yard, Schroder, et al., 2008). The majority of these complete ligament sprains resulted from noncontact mechanisms of injury—a phenomenon that continues to be an area of intense research within the sports medicine community. Data support the premise that with respect to severe injuries, for example, those resulting in a loss of more than 21 days of sports participation, the aggregate rate for boys' sports was higher than for girls'

(Darrow et al., 2009). However, when the data were restricted to comparisons of basketball, soccer, and baseball/softball, girls were found to have higher rates of injuries qualifying as severe. The authors of this study concluded that this finding is the result of the differences in rates of participation between girls' and boys' basketball (Darrow et al., 2009). (See **Figure 1.1** and **Figure 1.2**.)

Despite the best efforts of parents, coaches, and officials, injury continues to be an unavoidable reality for a significant number of participants. In a recent survey, youth coaches reported that at least one player on their team had suffered an injury. Of those coaches working with kids between the ages of 8 and 14 years, the most common types of injuries reported involved either wounds or bruises. Those coaches working with older players (up to 18 years of age) reported higher percentages of injuries such as fractures and concussions/head injuries. Parents reported that football produced the highest number of injuries, while swimming, softball, track, and cheerleading had the lowest number of

FIGURE 1.1 Historically, females were discouraged from sports participation based on unfounded fears of gender-based vulnerability to injury.

© Shawn Pecor/ShutterStock, Inc.

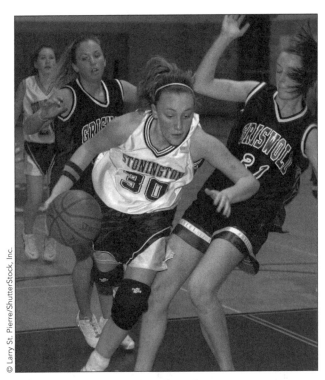

FIGURE 1.2 Although data show that in some sports females have a higher risk for some injuries compared to their male counterparts, it is also true that in other sports, rates for males are higher.

injuries. Data were also reported on the kinds of injuries that resulted in players being forced to miss a game or practice (time loss) and concluded that sprained ankles accounted for 18% of time-loss injuries (Mickalide & Hansen, 2012).

Damore and colleagues (2003) conducted research examining a broader age distribution. They studied emergency department admissions of patients ranging in age from 5 to 21 years at four hospitals for two 1-month periods (October 1999 and April 2000). They recorded a total of 1421 injuries in a group of 1275 patients in the age range of their study. Of these injuries, 41% were attributed to sports participation. The average age for such patients in their study was 12.2 years, with sprains, contusions, and fractures being the most common injuries. Males sustained more injuries (62%) to the musculoskeletal system than did their female counterparts.

Radelet and colleagues (2002) studied injuries in a population of children (1659) involved in community sports programs over the course of 2 years. Specifically, they monitored the injuries in children ranging in age from 7 to 13 years who were involved in baseball, softball, soccer, and football. An injury was defined as "requiring on-field evaluation by coaching staff, or causing a player to stop participation for any period of time, or requiring first aid during an event." They further defined an "athlete exposure" as one athlete participating in one event (game or practice). Their results, expressed as the rate of injury per 100 athlete exposures, were that soccer had the highest rate at 2.1 injuries, followed by baseball at 1.7, football at 1.5, and softball at 1.0. In all sports, there were more injuries in games than in practices, with contusions being the most common injury overall. It is also interesting to note that in soccer, there were no gender differences in injury rates.

Definition of Sports Injury

Most current definitions of sports injury incorporate the length of time away from participation (time lost) as the major determinant of injury severity. In 1982, the National Collegiate Athletic Association (NCAA) established the Injury Surveillance System (ISS), which instituted a common set of injury and risk definitions for use in tracking collegiate sports injuries. To qualify as an injury under the ISS, an injury must meet the following criteria:

1. Occurs as a result of participation in an organized intercollegiate practice or game

2. Requires medical attention by a team athletic trainer or physician

3. Results in restriction of the student athlete's participation or performance for 1 or more days beyond the day of injury (Benson, 1995)

The NCAA monitors injuries at Division I, II, and III institutions across all regions of the country and produces an annual report of the findings.

The National Athletic Trainers' Association (NATA) commissioned two national surveys of high school sports injuries, each spanning 3-year periods (i.e., 1986–1988 and 1995–1997). The injury definitions used in the NATA studies are similar to those used in the ISS because they rely on estimates of time lost from play as the indicator of injury severity (Foster, 1996).

Even though time lost is a convenient method for identifying an injury, such a definition does not lend itself to an accurate reflection of the severity of the injury. Severity of injury determinations may be made by a variety of people, including the coach, physicians or other sports medicine personnel, parents, or perhaps even the athlete. A related problem is that no standard is currently in use by all organizations monitoring sports injuries for the amount of time—hours, days, weeks, or months—that must be lost to qualify as a specific level of injury severity.

From a scientific standpoint, using the amount of time lost as a definition of sports **injury** is subject to significant error as previously described, depending on the method of data collection and injury definitions employed. However, once an injury is identified, several qualifiers are available to enable sports medicine personnel to better describe the precise characteristics of the injury. These include the type of tissue(s) involved, injury location, and timeframe of the injury, that is, either acute or chronic.

A commonly used medical classification system for injuries uses two major categories: acute and chronic. **Acute injuries** have been defined as those "characterized by a rapid onset, resulting from a traumatic event" (American Academy of Orthopaedic Surgeons [AAOS], 1991). Acute injuries are usually associated with a significant traumatic event (**Figure 1.3**), followed immediately by a pattern of signs and symptoms such as pain, swelling, and loss of function. In the case of an acute injury, **critical force** has been defined as the "magnitude of a single force for which the anatomical structure of interest is damaged" (Nigg & Bobbert, 1990). The potential for critical force, and subsequent acute injury, is clearly seen in tackle football. Estimates demonstrate that the vertebral bodies in the human cervical spine have a critical force limit of 340–455 kilograms. Researchers, using devices to simulate a typical tackle, have estimated that compressive forces acting on the cervical spine can exceed these limits (Torg, 1982).

Chronic injuries have been defined as those "characterized by a slow, insidious onset, implying a gradual development of structural damage" (American Academy of Family Physicians [AAFP], 1992). Chronic sports injuries, in contrast to acute ones, are not associated with a single traumatic episode; rather, they

FIGURE 1.4 Chronic injuries are common in high-impact sports such as running.

develop progressively over time. In many cases, they occur in athletes who are involved in activities that require repeated, continuous movements, such as in running (**Figure 1.4**). Consequently, such injuries are sometimes called overuse injuries, implying the athlete, by virtue of excessive participation, has exceeded the body's ability to recover from repeated bouts of activity. Overuse injuries in tendons occur when the workload from exercise exceeds the ability of musculotendinous tissues to recover (Hess et al., 1989). Thus, activity serves to cause a progressive breakdown of the tissue, eventually leading to failure. Common sites for overuse injuries are the Achilles tendon, the patellar tendon, and the rotator cuff tendon in the shoulder (Hess et al., 1989). The Achilles tendon is subjected to tremendous stress during running and jumping (**Figure 1.5**). Research indicates that these forces may exceed the physiologic limits of the tendon, thereby resulting in damage (Curwain & Stanish, 1984). Likewise, the patellar tendon must absorb repeated episodes of stress during sports. For instance, jumping and landing, as well as kicking a soccer ball (**Figure 1.6**), generate forces in this tendon that are many times greater than those produced during normal gait (Gainor et al., 1978). The rotator cuff tendons, specifically the supraspinatus tendon, are also vulnerable to injury from overuse. Any activity requiring repeated overhead movements of the arm,

FIGURE 1.3 Acute injury in an athlete.

FIGURE 1.5 Injuries to the Achilles tendon are common in track and field events.

FIGURE 1.7 Tennis places significant stress on the rotator cuff.

such as overhead strokes in tennis (**Figure 1.7**), places significant stress on this tendon. This is especially true during the deceleration phase of a swing or throw, after the arm has reached peak velocity. During this period of movement, muscles undergo **eccentric contraction**, a type of contraction identified as a causative factor in tendon injury (Curwain & Stanish, 1984). Such stress can cause damage in the supraspinatus tendon, resulting in a chronic injury.

DiFiori (1999) categorizes factors contributing to overuse injuries as either intrinsic—such as immature (growth) cartilage, lack of flexibility, lack of proper conditioning, psychological factors—or extrinsic, including such factors as excessive training or lack of adequate recovery, incorrect technique, and playing on uneven surfaces or surfaces that are too hard.

injury Act that damages or hurts.

acute injury Characterized by rapid onset, resulting from a traumatic event.

critical force Magnitude of a single force by which an anatomic structure is damaged.

chronic injury Characterized by a slow, insidious onset, implying a gradual development of structural damage.

eccentric contraction The simultaneous processes of muscle contraction and stretching of the muscle–tendon unit by an extrinsic force.

FIGURE 1.6 Jumping and landing, as well as kicking a soccer ball, subject the patellar tendon to stress.

Probably the most commonly used terms for differentiating tissues involved in a given injury are **soft tissue** versus skeletal tissue. Soft tissue, as a category, includes muscles, **fascia**, tendons, **joint capsules**, ligaments, blood vessels, and nerves. Most soft-tissue injuries involve contusions (bruises), sprains (ligaments/capsules), and strains (muscles/tendons). Skeletal tissue includes any bony structure in the body. Therefore, under this system, a common ankle sprain would qualify as a soft-tissue injury; a fractured wrist would be deemed a skeletal injury.

A notable exception to the general confusion in defining a sports injury has to do with injuries so severe that they are known as catastrophic. **Catastrophic injuries** often involve damage to the brain and/or spinal cord and are potentially life threatening or permanent. Another group of catastrophic injuries involves those linked to heat-related disorders. In the context of high school and college sports, catastrophic injury has been defined as "any severe injury incurred during participation in a school/college sponsored sport" (Mueller & Cantu, 2009). Research on catastrophic injuries in schools and colleges has been conducted since 1982 by the National Center for Catastrophic Sports Injury Research (NCCSIR), based at the University of North Carolina (Mueller & Cantu, 2009). Mueller and Cantu define direct catastrophic injuries as those that result directly from participation in the skills of a given sport. Indirect catastrophic injuries are those caused by systemic failure resulting from exertion while participating in a sports activity or by a complication that was secondary to a nonfatal injury (Mueller & Cantu, 2009). Given these definitions, a catastrophic injury can occur as either a direct result of participation (sustaining a neck fracture during a tackle in football) or an indirect result (suffering a systemic heatstroke during a cross-country run).

Though catastrophic sports injuries account for a small portion of all sports-related injuries, their potential for serious complications has resulted in an increased awareness by members of the sports medicine community. The most recent data available from the NCCSIR (1982–2011) indicate that the 2010 football season at the high school level produced two deaths along with 10 injuries that resulted in disability and 10 catastrophic injuries that recovered. In the college ranks for the same season, there was one death, two injuries resulting in disability, and two injuries that recovered. While it can easily be argued that these numbers are too high, they should be considered in the context that there are about 1.5 million middle and high school football participants annually in the United States. Given the large number of participants, the long-term rates of direct catastrophic injury in high school football based on rates per 100,000 participants are below 1/100,000. College football has about 75,000 participants annually in the United States, and while the rates for nonfatal and serious injuries are higher than at the high school level, they are lower than those seen in ice hockey and gymnastics. It is also notable that in all categories, there have

---

Athletic Trainers SPEAK Out

Sports-injury prevention is the cornerstone of the athletic trainer. Sports-injury prevention begins with a comprehensive sport-specific physical examination given by a qualified medical professional and continues through the selection and proper fitting of equipment and developing the physical components for sports competition. I have always said that if an athletic trainer can take an injured body part and rehabilitate that body part and individual back into full participation, then why can't an athletic trainer take an uninjured body part and individual and provide a strength and conditioning experience that brings that athlete to a top level of participation for physical activity and competition? With the knowledge, skills, and experience certified athletic trainers have in the area of athletic injury prevention, they can assist the coach and work with the athlete in flexibility, strength, plyometric, and aerobic fitness in the prevention of sports injury and in the enhancement of sports performance.

—Malissa Martin, EdD, ATC, CSCS

Dr. Martin is the director of Athletic Training Education in the Department of Health Sciences at the College of Mount St. Joseph.

been dramatic reductions in catastrophic injuries in football when compared to data from the late 1960s and early 1970s. This trend has resulted from a combination of rule changes, improved helmet standards, improved medical care of the participants, and better coaching of proper blocking and tackling techniques.

Injury Classifications

Regardless of the specific force involved in producing an injury, it is critical that all personnel involved in supervision of sports and physical activities, particularly coaches, be familiar with and fluent in the use of the basic terminology of connective-tissue injury. It is essential that personnel be able to recognize any injury, and whenever possible correctly identify it as soon after the injury occurs as possible, and then clearly describe it when communicating with other members of the sports medicine team (e.g., the team physician or athletic trainer). It is also vital that sports personnel master a vocabulary of standardized terms universal to all members of the sports medicine team. In 1968, the Committee on the Medical Aspects of Sports, a branch of the American Medical Association (AMA), published Standard Nomenclature of Athletic Injuries (SNAI). Though this text is no longer in print, it provided clearly defined, standardized terms that are still in use today and should be used by those providing care for sports injuries.

Because the vast majority of sports injuries involve damage to connective tissue, the terms that apply to these common conditions are listed hereafter. Obviously, a certain degree of variability is unavoidable in any clinical definition. However, these terms, when used properly, can greatly reduce the confusion that so often exists regarding specific injuries.

Sprains

Sprains are injuries to ligaments, which surround all synovial joints in the body. The severity of sprains is highly variable depending on the forces involved. SNAI describes three categories of sprains, based on the level of severity.

First-Degree Sprains

According to SNAI, first-degree sprains are the mildest form of sprain; only mild pain and disability occur. These sprains demonstrate little or no swelling and are associated with minor ligament damage.

Second-Degree Sprains

Second-degree sprains are more severe; they imply more actual damage to the ligament(s) involved, with an increase in the amount of pain and dysfunction. Swelling is more pronounced, and abnormal motion is present. Such injuries have a tendency to recur.

Third-Degree Sprains

Third-degree sprains are the most severe form of sprain and imply a complete tear of the ligament(s) involved. Given the extensive damage, pain, swelling, and **hemorrhage** are significant and are associated with considerable loss of joint stability.

Strains

Strains are injuries to muscles, tendons, or the junction between the two, commonly known as the musculotendinous junction (MTJ). The most common location of a strain is the MTJ; however, the exact reason for this is unknown. As is the case with sprains, there is tremendous variability in the severity of strains incurred in sports. SNAI presents three categories of strains.

First-Degree Strains

SNAI describes first-degree strains as the mildest form with little associated damage to muscle and tendon structures. Pain is most noticeable during use; mild swelling and muscle spasm may be present.

Second-Degree Strains

Second-degree strains imply more extensive damage to the soft-tissue structures involved. Pain, swelling, and muscle spasm are more pronounced, and functional loss is moderate. These types of injuries are associated with excessive, forced stretching or a failure in the synergistic action in a muscle group.

soft tissue Includes muscles, fascia, tendons, joint capsules, ligaments, blood vessels, and nerves.

fascia Fibrous membrane that covers, supports, and separates muscles.

joint capsule Saclike structure that encloses the ends of bones in a diarthrodial joint.

catastrophic injury Injury involving damage to the brain and/or spinal cord that presents a potentially life-threatening situation or the possibility of permanent disability.

sprain Injury to a joint and the surrounding structures, primarily ligaments and/or joint capsules.

hemorrhage Discharge of blood.

strain Injury involving muscles and tendons or the junction between the two, commonly known as the musculotendinous junction.

Third-Degree Strains

Third-degree strains are the most severe form and imply a complete rupture of the soft-tissue structures involved. Damage may occur at a variety of locations, including the bony attachment of the tendon (**avulsion** fracture), the tissues between the tendon and muscle (MTJ), or in the muscle itself. A defect may be apparent through the skin and will be associated with significant swelling. Obviously, this type of injury involves significant loss of function.

Contusions

In all probability, common bruises or contusions are the most frequent sports injury, regardless of activity. **Contusions** result from direct blows to the body surface that cause a compression of the underlying tissue(s) as well as the skin (O'Donoghue, 1984). They can occur in almost any activity; however, collision and contact sports such as tackle football, basketball, and baseball are more to blame in this regard. Curiously, many athletes and coaches view contusions as routine, minor injuries, but they can be serious, even life-threatening injuries when the tissues involve vital organs such as the kidneys or the brain.

Contusions are typically characterized as being associated with pain, stiffness, swelling, **ecchymosis** (discoloration), and **hematoma** (pooling of blood). If not treated properly, subsequent contusions to the same area of muscles can result in a condition known as **myositis ossificans**, which involves the development of bonelike formations in the muscle tissue.

Fractures

Fractures and dislocations represent two categories of injuries involving either bones or joints of the body. Though such injuries can occur in any activity, they are more common in collision sports in which large forces come into play. **Fractures** have been defined as "a break of a bone" (Venes & Taber, 2009). Compound fractures are potentially more serious because of the risk of infection related to the open wound. Furthermore, control of bleeding may be necessary depending on the severity and location of the wound.

Acute fractures are relatively uncommon sports injuries. When they occur, however, appropriate first aid is essential to prevent complications such as shock, excessive blood loss, or permanent damage. Fortunately, with modern diagnostic procedures, identifying traumatic fractures is relatively easy. The National Safety Council (1991) provides the following descriptions of signs and symptoms:

- *Swelling.* Caused by bleeding; it occurs rapidly after a fracture.
- *Deformity.* This is not always obvious. Compare the injured with the uninjured opposite body part when checking for deformity.
- *Pain and tenderness.* Commonly found only at the injury site. The athlete usually can point to the site of pain. A useful procedure for detecting fractures is to feel gently along the bones; complaints about pain or tenderness serve as a reliable sign of a fracture.
- *Loss of use.* Inability to use the injured part. Guarded motion occurs because movement produces pain, and the athlete will refuse to use the injured limb. However, sometimes the athlete is able to move the limb with little or no pain.
- *Grating sensation.* Do not move the injured limb in an attempt to see if a grating sensation called **crepitation** can be felt (and sometimes even heard) when broken bone ends rub together.
- *History of the injury.* Suspect a fracture whenever severe forces are involved, especially in high-risk sports such as tackle football, alpine skiing, and ice hockey. The athlete may have heard or felt the bone snap.

Fractures may also be described in terms of the specific nature of the break in the bone. The major types of traumatic fractures are shown in **Figure 1.8**.

Stress Fracture

A **stress fracture** is typically linked to sports because it develops over a relatively long time period, as opposed to other fractures caused by a single trauma. Stress fractures occur when a bone is subjected to repeated episodes of overloading (stress) that exceed its rate of recovery. In effect, the bone starts to break down and eventually begins to fail. Because stress fractures take time to develop, the signs and symptoms are easily confused with other, less serious sports-related problems. This is especially true for stress fractures of the lower leg bones, which are often confused with shin splints. Although stress fractures can occur throughout the body, the majority occur in the lower extremities. Athletes at high risk for stress fractures are those who are in poor physical condition or are overweight. However, even well conditioned participants may develop such a fracture, particularly when they have made a recent and sudden increase in the intensity of their training program. Stress fractures may even be related to diet.

The symptoms of a stress fracture are nebulous at best; nevertheless, certain factors are usually present when one is developing:

- *Pain/tenderness.* Athlete complains of pain and/or tenderness. A constant ache is not relieved with rest.

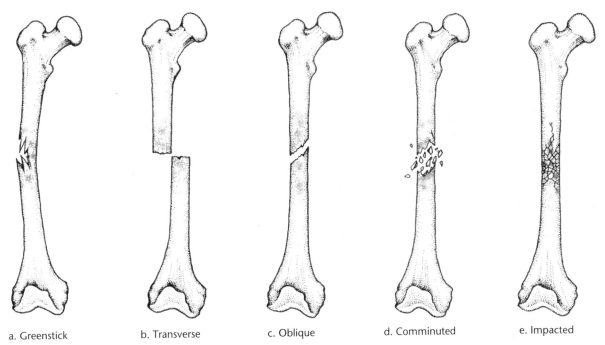

a. Greenstick   b. Transverse   c. Oblique   d. Comminuted   e. Impacted

FIGURE 1.8 Types of fractures.

- *Absence of trauma.* Suspect such a fracture when there is no history of traumatic event, yet the symptoms persist.
- *Repetitive activity.* The athlete is involved in an activity that subjects the suspect area to repeated stressful episodes.
- *Duration.* Symptoms have slowly developed over a period of days, weeks, or even months.

Stress fractures often present the physician with a difficult diagnosis because, during the initial phases, X-ray examinations may not show the fracture. In fact, it may take several weeks or longer after the onset of symptoms for the fracture to be visible on X-ray (Venes & Taber, 2009). It is this healing process, which involves the formation of hyaline cartilage around the area of the fracture, known technically as a callus, that can be seen on an X-ray and that signals that a fracture has occurred (see **Figure 1.9**). As a result, the physician must base the diagnosis on the factors listed previously. The best approach is to treat athletes as if they have a stress fracture and repeat the X-ray evaluation on a weekly or biweekly basis until a callus is seen. In difficult cases, a bone scan or magnetic resonance imaging (MRI) may be used to obtain a positive diagnosis.

Treatment of stress fractures involves rest and splinting or casting when necessary, followed by a slow, gradual return to participation. Athletes are often encouraged to maintain their fitness levels during recovery by cross training—that is, riding a stationary bike, jogging in shallow water, or swimming. All of these activities provide good stimulation of aerobic fitness while reducing stress on the skeletal system. Any program of recovery must be structured on an individual basis by the coach, athletic trainer, and physician.

avulsion Forcible tearing away or separation.

contusion Bruise or injury to soft tissue that does not break the skin.

ecchymosis Black-and-blue discoloration of the skin caused by hemorrhage.

hematoma A localized collection of extravasated blood, usually clotted, that is confined within an organ, tissue, or space.

myositis ossificans Myositis marked by ossification within a muscle.

fracture A break or crack in a bone.

crepitation Crackling sound heard during the movement of a broken bone.

stress fracture Small crack or break in a bone related to excessive, repeated overloads; also known as overuse fracture or march fracture.

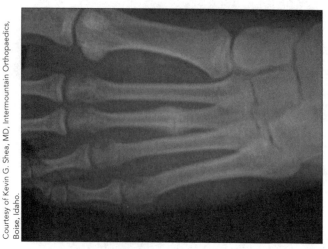

FIGURE 1.9 Stress fracture of the third metatarsal (approximately midshaft) in the left foot. Note callus formation around the site of the fracture.

Salter-Harris Fractures

A category of fractures unique to the adolescent athlete involves the epiphyseal growth plate and is known as **Salter-Harris fractures**. These fractures are classified based on the specific location of the fracture line(s) across the epiphyseal region of the bone. Five types (I, II, III, IV, V) have been identified (**Figure 1.10**):

- Type I involves a complete separation of the **epiphysis** from the **metaphysis**.
- Type II involves a separation of the epiphysis from the metaphysis as well as a fracture through a small part of the metaphysis.

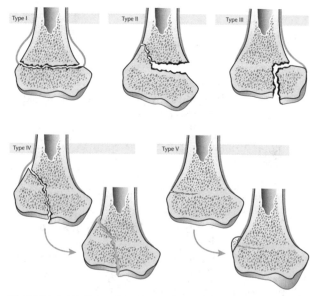

FIGURE 1.10 Salter-Harris epiphyseal fractures.

- Type III involves a fracture of the epiphysis.
- Type IV involves fracture of both the epiphysis and metaphysis.
- Type V involves a crushing injury of the epiphysis without displacement.

Salter-Harris fractures can result in long-term complications for bone growth if not cared for properly. These complications include premature closure of the growth plate or abnormal joint alignment, which can result in the possibility of different leg lengths when growth ceases. These injuries must be evaluated by a physician, who will determine the best method of management. If there is a fracture associated with displacement of the fragments, reduction is required. This may be accomplished either with or without surgical intervention, depending on the specifics of the pathology as determined by the physician.

Dislocations

Dislocations have been defined as "the temporary displacement of a bone from its normal position in a joint" (Venes & Taber, 2009). Two types of dislocations can occur, based on the severity of the injury. A **subluxation** takes place when the bones of a joint are only partially displaced. A **luxation** happens when the bones of a joint are totally displaced. In a sense, any dislocation, whether it is a subluxation or luxation, should be viewed as a severe type of sprain. Recall that sprains involve damage to the tissues surrounding joints—that is, capsules and ligaments. As such, dislocations present many of the same signs and symptoms as those seen in sprains. First aid treatment for dislocations combines care given for both sprains and fractures.

Dislocations can occur in any articulation; however, specific joints seem to be more vulnerable. Two joints in the shoulder complex, the glenohumeral and acromioclavicular joints, are injured frequently in sports such as tackle football and wrestling. The small joints in the fingers are commonly dislocated in baseball and softball. Fortunately, such dislocations are relatively easy to evaluate because their most definitive sign is deformity of the joint. Deformity is typically easily identified because the joint can be quickly compared to the same joint on the opposite side of the body or an adjacent joint such as in a finger or toe. Symptoms of dislocation include joint dysfunction, as well as the feeling of the joint having been forced out of normal position. Often the athlete reports having heard a snapping or popping sound as well. If treated properly, full recovery typically occurs. It is important to note that at no time should the coach attempt to reduce (put back in place) any dislocation, no matter how minor it may appear to be. All dislocations should be diagnosed and reduced by a physician after a complete medical evaluation.

Injury Recognition

From a practical standpoint, learning to recognize injury, regardless of the classification system used, is an essential skill to be mastered by the coach. To a great extent, the athlete's health and safety are determined by the decisions and subsequent actions of the coach, because the coach is most often the first to arrive at the scene of an injury. In addition, the dramatic increase in sports-injury litigation should serve as further incentive for coaching personnel to be prepared for emergencies. The premise that most injuries are best treated with the "run-it-off" approach is dangerous, to say the least. Today's coach should treat all possible injuries as such, until proven otherwise. It is imperative that coaching personnel develop the knowledge and skills to discriminate injuries requiring medical referral from those not necessitating such evaluation. Moreover, it should be noted that such decisions are best left to qualified health specialists, such as athletic trainers certified by the Board of Certification (BOC). Every effort should be made to have such a specialist employed, either permanently or part-time, by the school or agency sponsoring the sports program.

Epidemiology of Sports Injury

Scientific sports-injury research is a relatively recent phenomenon. The majority of the early studies, sometimes known as case-series studies, were based on information collected by medical personnel at hospitals or clinics (Walter et al., 1985). Although these data have provided valuable information, significant problems are associated with this type of data collection. Typically, only athletes with significant injuries seek medical attention at a hospital or clinic. Thus, a large number of athletes with injuries of minor to moderate severity may not be included in the study. Another problem with case-series research is the inability to accurately identify the cause or causes of a specific injury. For example, researchers at a particular clinic might conclude that

WHAT IF?

A student athlete asks you to explain the difference between a subluxation and a luxation of a joint.

less experienced athletes are more susceptible to injuries. However, without knowing the general level of experience of all athletes—injured and uninjured—it is impossible to determine what constitutes inexperience.

A better approach to sports-injury research involves the application of the principles of **epidemiology**. The science of epidemiology involves the "study of the distribution of diseases, injuries, or other health states in human populations for the purpose of identifying and implementing measures to prevent their development and spread" (Caine, Caine, & Lindner, 1996). The sports epidemiologist collects information in an effort to identify **risk factors** that may have contributed to a particular injury. Hypotheses are then developed and tested to confirm a statistical relationship. Risk factors, such as collisions in tackle football or ice hockey, may be inherent to the sport. Equipment may increase the risk of injury—for example, a safety helmet with a faulty design or a diving board set too close to the pool deck. The athlete may also possess risk factors—for example, muscle imbalances, obesity, low skill level, or any of a variety of congenital conditions.

By identifying statistical relationships between suspected risk factors and specific injuries, sports regulatory organizations can implement strategies designed to reduce or eliminate the risk of sports injuries. The incidence of spine injury in tackle football was significantly reduced by a rule change implemented in 1976 that made the practice of **spearing** (tackling and/or blocking with the head as the initial point of contact) illegal (Torg, 1982). In this case, the available data indicated that the technique of spearing placed the cervical spine (neck) of athletes at risk.

Salter-Harris fracture A category of fractures that involves the growth plate.
epiphysis Cartilaginous growth region of a bone.
metaphysis That portion of growing bone located between the shaft and the epiphysis.
dislocation The displacement of contiguous surfaces of bones comprising a joint.
subluxation Partial or incomplete dislocation of an articulation.
luxation Complete dislocation of a joint.
epidemiology The study of the distribution of disease or injury within a population and its environment.
risk factor Causative agent in a sports injury.
spearing A practice in tackle football whereby a player performs either a tackle or a block using the head as the initial point of contact.

Curiously, it was also hypothesized that improvements in helmet technology in the early 1970s may have contributed to the increase in cervical spine injury because athletes were inclined to tackle with their heads down, essentially using their head as a weapon, in the belief they would not sustain a head injury.

Since the early 1970s, several organizations in the United States have sponsored large-scale injury surveillance systems. The earliest to employ epidemiological methods was the National Athletic Injury/Illness Reporting System (NAIRS), which was instituted in 1974. More recently, the National Collegiate Athletic Association Injury Surveillance System (NCAA-ISS) and the High School Reporting Information Online (RIO) system, an Internet-based reporting system (https://highschool.riostudies.com), have established ongoing sports-injury surveillance systems. Sports organizations such as the National Football League (NFL) and the National Hockey League (NHL) conduct ongoing injury surveillance annually as well.

The National Center for Catastrophic Sports Injury Research began operation in 1982 with a focus on the documentation of catastrophic injuries at the high school and college levels (Mueller & Cantu, 1993). This center monitors catastrophic injuries in the following sports:

Baseball	Soccer
Basketball	Softball
Cross-country skiing	Swimming
Field hockey	Tennis
Football	Track
Gymnastics	Volleyball
Ice hockey	Water polo
Lacrosse	Wrestling

The primary goal of all organizations involved in sports-injury research is to identify risk factors for injury and, whenever possible, to develop and implement strategies to eliminate or reduce these risk(s). It is hoped that the information collected by these organizations will lead to continued reductions in both the frequency and severity of sports injuries.

Classification of Sports

Just as injuries can be defined and described using a variety of medical and scientific terms, sports can be classified based on their comparative risk of injury based on criteria such as the amount of physical contact between participants or the relative intensity of the activities. The American Academy of Pediatrics (AAP) classifies many popular sports into three categories based on the likelihood of collisions with participants or inanimate objects. The categories are contact/collision, limited contact, and noncontact. The first category, contact/collision, combines sports that involve intentional contact between participants such as tackle football, wrestling, martial arts, and ice hockey (collision sports) with sports such as basketball, lacrosse, and soccer, which often involve some contact between participants (contact sports), and the difference is the amount of force involved (AAP, 2001). Limited-contact sports are sports where contact between participants or with inanimate objects is "infrequent or inadvertent" (AAP, 2001). Examples of sports in this category include baseball and softball, downhill skiing, and volleyball. Noncontact sports, as the name implies, typically do not involve contact between participants. Examples of these sports include badminton, bowling, golf, and running (AAP, 2001). As such, the potential for impact-related injuries is lower in limited-contact and noncontact sports than in contact/collision sports. Note, however, that such classification systems do not imply that sports classified as something other than contact/collision are completely safe. To the contrary, not all injuries are related to the amount of physical contact between participants. For example, temperature-related injuries such as heat exhaustion and heatstroke can occur in virtually any sport when proper preventive measures are neglected. Also note that the AAP states that participation in boxing is not recommended (AAP, 1994).

Sports medicine personnel, coaches, administrators, and parents can use this information when athletes are found to have specific health-related problems during their preparticipation physical evaluations (PPE). For example, a child with a history of head injury, such as a concussion, would be identified and be required to receive a full neurological evaluation and subsequent physician's recommendation regarding continuing with competitive sports, particularly contact/collision sports. However, contrary to popular belief, noncontact sports can represent a risk to athletes as well. For example, a child with an identified, clinically significant congenital heart disorder might be advised to avoid aerobic activities such as track, swimming, and aerobic dance.

WHAT IF?

A student athlete asks you the classification of her three favorite sports, for example, softball, golf, and soccer.

Extent of the Injury Problem: Some Examples

This section presents current statistical information on injuries in six popular interscholastic sports, beginning with tackle football.

Tackle Football

Tackle football (**Figure 1.11**) continues to be popular, with an estimated 4,200,000 participants in the United States in 2012. This includes approximately 100,000 post-high school players involved in the NFL, arena and semi-pro leagues, and at the collegiate level. USA Football (the national governing body of American football at the youth and amateur levels) estimates there are 3 million youth players in the United States as well (Mueller & Colgate, 2013). The most recent data available from the National Federation of State High School Associations (NFHS) for 2011–2012 indicate that in

FIGURE 1.11 Up to 34% of participants in interscholastic tackle football can expect to be injured.

high school (grades 9–12) there were 1,095,993 participants (NFHS, n.d.).

Ramirez and colleagues (2006) conducted a 2-year study of high school football injuries that surveyed 87 schools in California. They reported an overall injury rate of 25.5 injuries for every 100 players, with the highest rates occurring during games. A study funded by the National Athletic Trainers' Association (NATA) conducted at the high school level found that 34% of the participants were injured (Powell & Barber-Foss, 1999). The NATA survey suggests that the percentage of high school–level players injured annually has dropped slightly compared with the 3-year period of 1985–1987.

More recent research conducted by Shankar and colleagues (2007) at the high school level estimates that 517,726 injuries occurred in football during the 2005–2006 season. In this study, researchers defined an injury as having occurred either in practice or a game, requiring the care of either the athletic trainer or a physician, and that was severe enough to require the athlete to miss 1 day, or more, of participation beyond the day of the injury. They defined an "athlete exposure" as participation in either a game or a practice. As such, injury rates were expressed in this study as the number of injuries for every 1000 athlete exposures. This is the most common way of expressing the rate of injury and it allows researchers to make comparisons between sources of injuries, for example, between practice and games. The majority (88.2%) of these injuries were classified as "new," meaning they were not re-injuries of previous injuries (Shankar et al., 2007). The most commonly injured areas of the body were the knee and ankle, with ligament injuries (sprains) being the most common type of injury to both joints. In all, lower extremity injuries accounted for 46.9% of all injuries. With respect to the upper extremities, the shoulder accounted for 12.4% of injuries, followed by the hand at 9.3%. The head/face and the torso/spine/neck combined for 23.1% of injuries (Shankar et al., 2007). Similar to the findings of Ramirez and colleagues (2006), Shankar and associates also found that the injury rate during games was five times the rate seen in practice. This is a sobering finding and most certainly highlights the importance of having trained sports medicine professionals present at games whenever possible.

Research examining injuries in youth football provides a wealth of information. For example, Stuart and colleagues (2002) examined the injury rates in 915 players aged 9 to 13 years distributed across 42 teams. Over the course of one season, these researchers recorded a total of 55 injuries during games. Of these, the majority were contusions (60%), with muscle strains, sprains, fractures, abrasions, and concussions accounting for 20%, 9%, 7%, 2%, and 2%, respectively. The majority of the injuries involved the lower extremities, including four fractures, all Salter-Harris type (Figure 1.10). It is interesting to note that their data also indicate a relationship between age and injury: Older players were found to be at a higher risk for injuries. In addition, the highest relative risk of injury by player position was found for running backs and quarterbacks, followed by defensive backs and then linebackers.

Malina and colleagues (2006) studied 678 players aged 9 to 14 years (PONY Football League) over two consecutive seasons. An injury was defined as "any injury that causes cessation of a player's customary participation on the day following the day of onset." BOC-certified athletic trainers were on site to record all injuries, both at home games and practices, to ensure accuracy of the data. A total of 259 injuries were recorded over two seasons, with 178 occurring in practice and the remaining 81 in games. Most injuries (64%) were minor, with moderate and major injuries at 18% and 13%, respectively. Injury rates were similar for players in the 4th and 5th grades at 13.3 and 12.9 per 1000 exposures, respectively, with rates doubling for the 7th and 8th grades at 26.1 and 27.4 injuries per 1000 exposures, respectively. It is also interesting to note that, excluding the 6th-grade cohort, game injury rates were more than double the rates seen in practice for all other grade levels. Further, the game injury rates for the 7th and 8th grades were the same as the game rates for high school participants reported by Powel and Barber-Foss (1999). However, when compared to the more recent high school data from Shankar et al. (2007), it appears that the injury rates for the youth sports players greatly exceed the rates seen at the high school level. Shankar et al. (2007) reported that practice injury rates were 2.56 injuries per 1000 exposures and 12.04 per 1000 exposures for games. These numbers are significantly lower than the rates reported by Malina et al. (2006). In aggregate, these findings reinforce the notion that coaching personnel at the youth football level must be trained in first aid and cardiopulmonary resuscitation (CPR), and whenever possible, a BOC-certified athletic trainer should be on hand for both practices and games (Powell & Barber-Foss, 1999).

Understandably, an ongoing area of concern in tackle football is the incidence of injuries involving the brain and spinal cord. Recently, Mueller and Cantu (2013) found that although there have been significant reductions in football-related fatalities and nonfatal catastrophic injuries since 1976, data for 2010 indicate there were a total of 12 cases of permanent disability (10 in high school and 2 collegiate level); seven of these injuries involved the cervical spine and five involved brain injuries. In 2006, there were four such injuries reported; however, that number jumped to 19 in 2007 (Mueller & Cantu, 2009). Earlier research on high school sports conducted by Powell and Barber-Foss (1999) indicates an increase in the reported incidence of injuries to the head/neck/spine. Specifically, the authors found that 10.3% of all the injuries reported during the 3-year period of 1995–1997 were classified as neurotrauma (injuries to the nervous system such as mild brain injury). In this category, football exceeded a number of other sports, including wrestling, baseball, soccer, and basketball.

Given the inherently violent nature of the sport, it may be impossible to eliminate head and neck injuries from football completely; however, these data certainly make it clear that more work needs to be done to implement effective strategies to reduce the incidence of serious injuries associated with football.

Basketball

Slightly fewer than 1 million high school students, boys and girls, participated in basketball programs in the United States during the 2011–2012 school year (NFHSA, n.d.). Borowski and colleagues' (2008) research is consistent with earlier work by Powell and Barber-Foss (1999). The data indicate that for both genders, basketball continues to be associated with a high percentage of injuries in the lower extremities. For example, the ankle/foot, knee, and hip/thigh/upper leg accounted for 62.8% of the injuries for both sexes (Borowski et al., 2008).

Note that the incidence of knee injuries in basketball is consistently higher for girls than it is for boys (**Figure 1.12**). In addition, girls also demonstrate

FIGURE 1.12 Basketball places the lower extremities of female players at particular risk.

a higher percentage of knee injuries requiring surgery (Powell & Barber-Foss, 1999). It is notable that Borowski and associates (2008) found that injuries to the knee were the most frequent injury requiring surgery. This finding is troubling for a number of reasons including the fact that major knee ligament injuries are typically season ending and can even jeopardize an athlete's ability to return to the sport. Aside from the financial implications, evidence suggests that for those athletes who sustain injuries to their anterior cruciate ligament (ACL), a significant percentage will go on to develop premature osteoarthritis in the knee. The data suggest that this will occur in as many as 26% of those who have surgical reconstruction of their ligament and in as many as 60% to 100% of those who do not have reconstructive surgery (Louboutin et al., 2009).

Data from the 2005–2006 season collected by the NCAA-ISS yield results similar to, but perhaps more striking than, the high school data. Female basketball players at the collegiate level were found to have injured their knees, specifically the ACL, at a much higher rate than their male counterparts did. Specifically, the women's injury rate during practice was approximately twice that seen in men's practices. The difference between female and male players' ACL injuries in games was even more striking in that the rate of ACL injury during games was three times higher for women than for men. As such, it appears that with respect to collegiate basketball, female athletes continue to exhibit a far greater risk for sustaining injuries to the ACL than do their male counterparts. Although a great deal of research has been and continues to be focused on explanations for these differences, no definitive cause has yet been identified. Research to date attempts to identify risk factors in female athletes associated with a higher risk for noncontact ACL injuries (Arendt & Dick, 1995; Griffin et al., 2000; Harmon & Ireland, 2000; Hewett, Myer, & Ford, 2006; Hewett, Ford, & Myer, 2006; Kirkendall & Garrett, 2000).

Baseball and Softball

Participation figures for the 2011–2012-season show there were 474,219 participants in baseball and 367,023 in softball at the high school level (NFHS, n.d.). The latest available injury data collected during the 2005–2007 baseball seasons demonstrate an overall injury rate of 1.26 injuries per 1000 athlete exposures (Collins & Comstock, 2008). For comparison, using the same data collection system (High School RIO) within the same time period, the overall rate of injury for boys in basketball was 1.83, soccer was 2.34, and football was 4.36 (Borowski et al., 2008; Shankar et al., 2007; Yard, Schroder, et al., 2008). As such, of the four sports described here,

baseball had the lowest overall injury rate. Of the injuries reported, sprains and strains combined for 41.1% of the injuries, with contusions and fractures making up an additional 30.3% of the total.

The body areas most commonly injured were the shoulder, ankle, and head and face combining for 43.5% of all injuries. However, despite the low overall rate of injury, this latest research also highlights the finding that 11.6% of all injuries reported resulted from being struck by a batted ball. More alarming is the finding that 48% of those injuries were to the head/face (Collins & Comstock, 2008). When compared to earlier work by Powell and Barber-Foss (1999), Collins and Comstock (2008) found that the incidence of injuries to the head and face has increased significantly as well as has the incidence of fractures. In light of these findings, the authors recommend that pitchers, infielders, and batters all wear helmets with face shields or wear mouth guards and eye protection (Collins & Comstock, 2008).

Recent injury data for high school softball is not available; however, Marshall and associates (2007) published the results of a long-term study (1988–1989 through 2003–2004) of injuries associated with collegiate-level softball. A consistent finding regardless of NCAA division was that injury rates were nearly double in games versus practice; for example, in Division 1, these rates were 4.45 per 1000 athlete exposures versus 2.98 per 1000 athlete exposures, respectively. Overall, the lower extremities accounted for 42% of all injuries, whereas the upper extremities accounted for 33%. For both games and practice, the ankle was the most commonly injured body area and the injury type in both cases was a sprain. Fixed bases played heavily into the rate of ankle injuries: Of the 9% of game-related injuries caused by contact with a fixed base, 43.3% were classified as ankle ligament sprains (Marshall et al., 2007). Many of these ankle sprains resulted from feet-first sliding when base running.

Similar to the data from baseball, Marshall and colleagues (2007) noted that being struck by a batted ball in 2003–2004 accounted for 11.8% of all game-related injuries. Of these, pitchers and batters were most commonly injured by batted balls (Marshall et al., 2007). Head injuries associated with being struck by batted balls had the highest frequency in batters and third basemen (Marshall et al., 2007). As was the case with baseball, it seems prudent that appropriate safety equipment be worn at all times by those players shown to be at risk.

Approximately 4.8 million children between the ages of 5 and 14 years play baseball, softball, or tee-ball annually (AAP, 2001). According to the AAP, perhaps as many as 8% of these children are injured each year. Of these injuries, 26% are fractures and 37% are contusions/abrasions. It is worth noting that the AAP has determined that children have an increased vulnerability to chest impacts from balls, perhaps because of the increased elasticity of the thorax in these young players (AAP, 2001). Between the years 1973 and 1995, 88 baseball-related deaths were reported in this age group. Forty-three percent resulted from direct ball impact with the chest. The AAP has made a number of recommendations designed to reduce the risk of such injuries, including the use of batting helmets and face protectors, both at bat and when on base; outfitting catchers with a helmet, face mask, and chest and neck protector; eliminating the on-deck circle; and adding protective screening around dugouts and player benches. Eye injuries are a major concern in baseball, which is the most productive sport in this regard. One-third of these injuries result from being struck by a pitched ball.

A persistent area of concern for decades has been the risk of injury to the elbow in adolescent pitchers. This fear was apparently based on the fact that many young pitchers complained of elbow pain and subsequent medical evaluation sometimes found evidence of overuse injuries in these children. It was thought that these injuries were related to throwing excessive numbers of curve balls and/or breaking pitches. Specifically, the area of concern is the medial humeral epicondyle and the muscles that attach at this location. In the adolescent elbow, these attachments represent a growth plate; as such, they may be vulnerable to the repeated stresses that pitching can generate. Adams (1965) raised serious concerns about elbow injuries among Little League pitchers. This condition, dubbed **Little League elbow**, created a considerable amount of worry among parents in the late 1960s. Two studies conducted by major medical groups published in the 1970s examined the relationship between pitching mechanics and injuries. These researchers found no relationship between pitching and elbow damage (Gugenheim et al., 1976; Larson et al., 1976). In contrast to these studies, Micheli and Fehlandt (1992) endeavored to identify what causes injuries to tendons and **apophyses** (bony attachments of tendons) in a population of 445 children aged 8 to 19 years. Their conclusion was that for boys, baseball was associated with the highest occurrence of injury. Further, softball was the fourth most commonly associated sport for injury in girls. Overall, they found that in their study group the most common injuries were to the elbow (Micheli & Fehlandt, 1992). It has also been reported that those pitching with a sidearm technique (**Figure 1.13**) are three times more likely to develop elbow problems than those who pitch using the more traditional overhand style (Stanitski, 1993).

A common assumption within the lay community is that softball pitching (so-called underhand or "windmill"

FIGURE 1.13 The correct pitching technique combined with limits on the number of pitches per week can spare Little Leaguers possible elbow damage.

© Peter Weber/ShutterStock, Inc.

style pitching) is inherently safer than overhand pitching associated with baseball. However, although it is the case that rules are in place at the amateur level in baseball that limit the total number of innings pitched, softball has no such restrictions. In fact, one study noted that female pitchers pitch in as many as six games during a weekend tournament with a total of 1200–1500 pitches pitched over 3 days (Werner et al., 2006). Pain in the **anterior** shoulder has been reported as a common symptom in softball pitchers and is associated with excessively high forces that are generated during the "windmill" style pitch, which stresses the attachment of the long head of the biceps brachii to the glenoid labrum (Rojas et al., 2009). The forces acting on the biceps brachii attachment were found to be higher than those in the overhand throw (Rojas et al., 2009). Contrary to the work cited earlier on Little League elbow, Lyman et al. (2002) did find an association between elbow pain and pitching in a group of 476 youth pitchers between the ages of 9 and 14 years. They found that as pitch count increased through the season, so did the risk of elbow pain. Fleisig and colleagues (2009) concluded that there are four factors that increase the risk of elbow injury in youth players: 1) number of pitches thrown, 2) pitching mechanics, 3) pitch type, and 4) physical condition of the player. However, it is critical to note that a number of studies that attempted to link curve balls with elbow injury failed to find a consistent link.

Wrestling

Wrestling at the high school level drew 272,149 participants during the 2011–2012 season (NFHS, n.d.). Its continued popularity is no doubt partly a result of the fact that participants are matched by body weight, thus

FIGURE 1.14 In wrestling, takedown and escape maneuvers can result in injuries.

allowing children of all body sizes to participate. However, given the nature of the sport, collisions/contact with opponents and mats do result in various injuries. In addition, joint injuries occur in takedown and escape maneuvers as well as in holds (**Figure 1.14**), which are essential parts of the sport.

Yard, Collins, and colleagues (2008) reported injury data on high school and college wrestlers for the 2005–2006 season and overall found that collegiate wrestlers are injured at a rate three times greater than their high school counterparts are. The knee is the most commonly injured body area at the collegiate level, representing 17.1% of all injuries, with shoulder strains/sprains and dislocations/subluxations combining for 16.2% of the injuries. Injuries of the head/face account for 7.4% of injuries, and concussions comprise 5.8%. At the high school level, shoulder strains/sprains account for 8.5% of injuries followed closely by ankle strains/sprains at 7.6% and knee strains/sprains at 7.0%. Curiously, concussions at the high school level accounted for 5.4% of injuries, falling within 0.4% of the collegiate percentage (Yard, Collins, et al., 2008). Injury rates were found to be much higher in

matches than in practice for both high school and collegiate participants (two and five times higher, respectively; Yard, Collins, et al., 2008).

Other injuries common to wrestling are **friction** burns to the skin, skin infections, and irritation of the outer ear (sometimes referred to as cauliflower ear). Mandatory headgear that provides ear protection, improvements in mat surfaces, and vigilant cleaning and maintenance of facilities have significantly reduced the incidence of these problems. As a result of an increase in the incidence of reported cases of skin infections caused by methicillin-resistant *Staphylococcus aureus* (MRSA) in recent years, everyone involved with the sport of wrestling, including the athletes, has become more vigilant with respect to spotting skin infections early. The available data indicate that although MRSA continues to be a threat, many other skin-related infections occur with much greater frequency. High school wrestling data, for example, list skin infections as 8.5% of all reported "injuries," with impetigo accounting for 30.0%, herpes at 20.5%, and ringworm at 20.0% (Yard, Collins, et al., 2008). The same study found that at the collegiate level, skin infections made up 20.3% of all reported "injuries." Herpes was the most common, at 47.1% of all reported skin infections, with impetigo accounting for 36.8%, tinea corporis at 7.4%, cellulitis at 5.9%, and MRSA cases at 2.9%.

At the high school level, the majority of skin infections were on the head/face and neck (Yard, Collins, et al., 2008). Many skin infections are highly contagious through direct contact with an infected person or contaminated equipment such as wrestling mats and clothing. It is critical that coaches, athletes, and support personnel such as athletic trainers remain vigilant to identify potential skin infections and treat them accordingly before they can spread to others. Athletes with active skin infections should be removed from participation and referred to a physician for diagnosis and, when necessary, treatment, and these athletes should not return to participation until cleared to return by a physician. Wrestling mats should be cleaned daily after practice with an appropriate disinfectant product designed specifically to

WHAT IF?

A parent asks you for advice about which high school sport is the safest for his daughter. Based on available data, what would you tell him?

Little League elbow Condition related to excessive throwing that results in swelling of the medial epicondyle of the elbow, that is, medial humeral epicondylitis.

apophysis Bony outgrowth to which muscles attach.

anterior Before or in front of.

friction Heat producing.

kill MRSA and other common pathogens. The position statement of the National Athletic Trainers' Association on community-acquired MRSA infections is available at http://nata.org/sites/default/files/MRSA.pdf.

Because wrestling incorporates specific weight categories, the sport has historically been plagued with problems associated with rapid and excessive weight loss by participants.

Volleyball

The sport of volleyball continues to be extremely popular at the high school level. The latest participation figures show that for the 2011–2012 season, there were 418,903 participants (NFHS, n.d.). Volleyball involves jumping, diving, and overhand arm swinging (serves and spiking) and as such qualifies as a limited-contact sport. The 1995–1997 NATA study (Powell & Barber-Foss, 1999) found that 14.9% of the volleyball participants sustained some type of participation-related injury. Of those, the majority (51.5%) were classified as sprains, which was the highest percentage of sprains for the 10 sports surveyed. Of these sprains, 41.8% involved the ankle/foot, exceeding girls' basketball in this regard for the same survey. Knee injuries in volleyball constituted 11.1% of the injuries reported in the survey (Powell & Barber-Foss, 1999).

High school data reported approximately 10 years later (2005–2008) demonstrate a strikingly similar percentage of volleyball injuries involving the ankle at 42.6%, which was about 2% less than the rate seen in girls' basketball and approximately 20% higher than that seen in girls' soccer (Swenson et al., 2009). In a study of severe injuries (resulting in a loss of more than 21 days of participation) in high school athletes, Darrow et al. (2009) reported that volleyball produced the lowest percentage of severe injuries (3.9%) of all the sports in the study that surveyed boys' football, boys' and girls' soccer, girls' volleyball, boys' and girls' basketball, boys' wrestling, boys' baseball, and girls' softball. The knee and ankle were involved in approximately 60% of the severe injuries related to volleyball, with fractures and complete and incomplete ligament tears making up more than 82% of reported events (Darrow et al., 2009).

Soccer

Soccer, commonly called football outside the United States (**Figure 1.15**), has grown in popularity throughout the United States with recent estimates of nearly 14 million participants younger than age 18. According

FIGURE 1.15 The most common injuries among soccer players involve the knee, shin, and ankle.

to the NFHS, during the 2011–2012 season, a total of 782,732 boys and girls participated in soccer programs at their respective high schools (NFHS, n.d.).

Although soccer does not involve intentional collisions between players, incidental collisions frequently occur, and as such, it is classified by the AAP as a contact/collision sport (AAP, 1994). Protective equipment is limited, with most body areas exposed to external trauma. High school data representing participation in 2005–2007 found an overall injury rate (genders combined) of 2.39 injuries per 1000 athletic exposures. This was further divided into injuries during competition, which yielded a rate of 4.77 per 1000 athletic exposures versus a rate seen in practice of 1.37 (Yard, Schroder, et al., 2008). Incomplete and complete ligament sprains along with contusions accounted for nearly 60% of all the injuries, genders combined. The lower extremities (thigh, knee, ankle) and the head/face combined for approximately 69% of the injuries. A stunning finding was that during competitions, girls sustained complete ligament sprains at a rate of 26.4 per 100,000 athlete exposures, compared to a competition rate for boys of 1.98 (Yard, Schroder, et al., 2008).

With respect to knee injuries, specifically the ACL, available data indicate that female youth participants sustain higher numbers of these injuries than their male counterparts do. Research based on youth soccer insurance claims found that female participants dramatically increased the number of claims for ACL injuries at age 14, and compared with males, females demonstrated a higher ratio of knee injury compared to all injuries and a higher ratio of ACL injury compared to all injuries (Shea et al., 2004).

A unique aspect of the game involves the skill known as heading, in which a participant contacts a ball with the head, in most cases after it has been kicked into the air. Some medical experts have hypothesized that this practice may lead to possible head injury. Historically, little reliable research has been conducted attempting to confirm this hypothesis (Jordan et al., 1996; Smodlaka, 1984). However, research examining the incidence of head injury from all causes in soccer, as well as evidence of decreased neurocognitive function, has increased significantly in recent years. Boden, Kirkendall, and Garrett (1998) examined the rate of concussions in soccer at the collegiate level and found that the majority of the concussions reported resulted from collisions with an opponent rather than from intentional heading of the ball. Although prevention of concussion must remain a priority across all sports, available data in soccer indicate that there is not much difference in the rate of concussions between boys and girls, with concussions representing about 3% of all injuries reported (Le Gall, Carling, & Reilly, 2008). Research has also shown that although heading the ball continues to result in concussion, collisions between players is the most common cause of concussion (Koutures, Gregory, & Council on Sports Medicine and Fitness, 2010). In recent years specialized helmets for soccer players have been introduced in an effort to reduce the incidence of head injury. However, data based on sound science fail to support their universal use at this time (Koutures et al., 2010).

A number of deaths and severe injuries have been related to improperly constructed movable soccer goals. For the period from 1979 to 1994, at least 21 deaths were reported; an additional 120 nonfatal injuries occurred that were directly related to movable goals (Consumer Product Safety Commission [CPSC], 1995). The majority of these injuries and fatalities occurred when the goals tipped over and struck the victims. As a result, numerous soccer organizations—such as the Federation Internationale de Football, the National Federation of State High School Associations, and the National Collegiate Athletic Association—have established strict criteria for the construction of soccer goals. In addition, the Consumer Product Safety Commission has published guidelines for the design and construction of movable soccer goals.

REVIEW QUESTIONS

1. Damore and colleagues (2003) conducted research on emergency department admissions in a population of patients ranging in age from 5 to 21 years. What percentage of these admissions was attributable to sports injuries?

2. What are the most commonly used criteria for defining a sports injury?

3. Describe briefly two major problems that arise regarding the most commonly used definitions of sports injury.

4. What are the three criteria necessary for an injury to be classified as such under the NCAA's Injury Surveillance System (ISS)?

5. Define and differentiate between acute and chronic forms of injury.

6. What constitutes a catastrophic sports injury?

7. What specific tissue types are involved in sprains and strains? How is the severity of these injuries defined?

8. What makes a stress fracture unique when compared with other types of fractures?

9. Define and differentiate between subluxation and luxation.

10. Using the sports classification system presented in this chapter, what is the classification for the sport of basketball?

11. What is the science of epidemiology?

12. According to Shankar et al. (2007), what are the most commonly injured areas of the body in tackle football?

13. True or false: According to Shankar et al. (2007), the injury rate in football practice is five times higher than in games.

14. In basketball, what injury most often results in surgery?

15. What were the conclusions of Micheli and Fehlandt (1992) regarding the relationship between elbow injuries and participation in baseball?

16. What piece of equipment related to soccer has been found to play a direct role in the majority of deaths in this sport?

REFERENCES

Adams JE. (1965). Injury to the throwing arm: A study of traumatic changes in the elbow joint of boy baseball players. *California Med.* 102:127–132.

Adirim TA, Cheng TL. (2003). Overview of injuries in the young athlete. *Sports Med.* 33(1):75–81.

American Academy of Family Physicians. (1992). *Preparticipation Physical Evaluation* (1st ed.). Chicago, Ill: American Academy of Family Physicians.

American Academy of Orthopaedic Surgeons. (1991). *Athletic Training and Sports Medicine* (2d ed.). Park Ridge, Ill: American Academy of Orthopaedic Surgeons.

American Academy of Pediatrics. (1994). Committee on Sports Medicine and Fitness. Medical conditions affecting sports participation. *Pediatrics.* 94(5):757–760.

American Academy of Pediatrics. (2001). Risk of injury from baseball and softball in children. *Pediatrics.* 107(4):782–784.

American Medical Association. (1968). *Standard Nomenclature of Athletic Injuries* (1st ed.). Chicago, Ill: American Medical Association.

Arendt E, Dick R. (1995). Knee injury patterns among men and women in collegiate basketball and soccer: NCAA data and review of literature. *Am J Sports Med.* 23(6):694–701.

Benson M. (1995). *1995–96 NCAA Sports Medicine Handbook* (8th ed.). Indianapolis, Ind: National Collegiate Athletic Association.

Boden BP, Kirkendall DT, Garrett WE Jr. (1998). Concussion incidence in elite college soccer players. *Am J Sports Med.* 26:238–241.

Borowski LA, Yard EE, Fields SK, Comstock RD. (2008). The epidemiology of US high school basketball injuries, 2005–2007. *Am J Sports Med.* 36(12):2328–2335.

Caine DJ, Caine CG, Lindner KJ (eds.). (1996). *Epidemiology of Sports Injuries.* Champaign, Ill: Human Kinetics.

Collins CL, Comstock RD. (2008). Epidemiological features of high school baseball injuries in the United States, 2005–2007. *Pediatrics.* 121(6):1181–1187.

Consumer Product Safety Commission. (1995). Guidelines for movable soccer goal safety. CPSC Document #326. Available: http://www.cpsc.gov/en/Safety-Education/Safety-Guides/Sports-Fitness-and-Recreation/Guidelines-for-Movable-Soccer-Goal-Safety/.

Curwain S, Stanish WD. (1984). *Tendinitis: Its Etiology and Treatment.* Lexington, Mass: D. C. Heath and Company.

Damore DT, Metzl JD, Ramundo M, Pan S, Van Amerongen R. (2003). Patterns in childhood sports injury. *Pediatr Emerg Care.* 19(2):65–67.

Darrow CJ, Collins CL, Yard EE, Comstock RD. (2009). Epidemiology of severe injuries among United States high school athletes: 2005–2007. *Am J Sports Med.* 37(9):1798–1805.

DiFiori JP. (1999). Overuse injuries in children and adolescents. *Phys Sportsmed.* 27(1):75–89.

Fleisig GS, Weber A, Hassell N, Andrews JR. (2009). Prevention of elbow injuries in youth baseball pitchers. *Curr Sports Med Rep.* 8(5):250–254.

Foster T. (1996, April). NATA releases results from high school injury study. *NATA News.*

Gainor BJ, Piotrowski G, Puhl JJ, Allen WC. (1978). The kick: Biomechanics and collision injury. *Am J Sports Med.* 6:185–193.

Griffin LY, et al. (2000). Noncontact anterior cruciate ligament injuries: Risk factors and prevention strategies. *J Am Acad Orthop Surg.* 8(3):141–150.

Gugenheim JJ, Agel J, Albohm MJ, Arendt EA, Dick RW, Garrett WE, Garrick JG, Hewett TE, Huston L, Ireland ML, Johnson RJ, Kibler WB, Lephart S, Lewis JL, Lindenfeld TN, Mandelbaum BR, Marchak P, Teitz CC, Wojtys EM. (1976). Little-League survey: The Houston study. *Am J Sports Med.* 4:189–199.

Harmon KG, Ireland ML. (2000). Gender differences in noncontact anterior cruciate ligament injuries. *Clin Sports Med.* 19(2):287–302.

Hess GP, Cappiello WL, Poole RM, Hunter SC. (1989). Prevention and treatment of overuse tendon injuries. *Sports Med.* 8:371–384.

Hewett TE, Myer GD, Ford KR. (2006). Anterior cruciate ligament injuries in female athletes: Part 1, Mechanisms and risk factors. *Am J Sports Med.* 34:299–311.

Hewett TE, Ford KR, Myer GD. (2006). Anterior cruciate ligament injuries in female athletes: Part 2, A metaanalysis of neuromuscular interventions aimed at injury prevention. *Am J Sports Med.* 34:490–498.

Jordan SE, Green GA, Galanty HL, Mandelbaum BR, Jabour BA. (1996). Acute and chronic brain injury in United States national team soccer players. *Med Sci Sports Exerc.* 24:205–210.

Kirkendall DT, Garrett WE Jr. (2000). The anterior cruciate ligament enigma. Injury mechanisms and prevention. *Clin Orthop.* 372:64–68.

Koutures CG, Gregory AJ, Council on Sports Medicine and Fitness. (2010). Clinical report—Injuries in youth soccer. *Pediatrics.* Available: http://pediatrics.aappublications.org/cgi/reprint/peds.2009-3009v1.

Larson RL, Singer KM, Bergstrom R, Thomas S. (1976). Little-League survey: The Eugene study. *Am J Sports Med.* 4:201–209.

Le Gall F, Carling C, Reilly T. (2008). Injuries in young elite female soccer players: An 8-season prospective study. *Am J Sports Med.* 36(2):276–284.

Louboutin H, Debarge R, Richou J, Selmi TA, Donell ST, Neyret P, Dubrana F. (2009). Osteoarthritis in patients with anterior cruciate ligament rupture: A review of risk factors. *Knee.* 16(4):239–244.

Lyman S, Fleisig GS, Andrews JR, Osinski ED. (2002). Effect of pitch type, pitch count, and pitching mechanics on risk of elbow and shoulder pain in youth baseball pitchers. *Am J Sports Med.* 30(4):463–468.

Maffulli N, Caine DJ (eds.). (2005). Epidemiology of pediatric sports injuries. Individual sports. *Med Sports Sci.* 48:1–7.

Malina RM, Morano PJ, Barron M, Miller SJ, Cumming SP, Kontos AP. (2006). Incidence and player risk factors for injury in youth football. *Clin J Sport Med.* 16(3): 214–222.

Marshall SW, Hamstra-Wright KL, Dick R, Grove KA, Agel J. (2007). Descriptive epidemiology of collegiate women's softball injuries: National Collegiate Athletic Association Injury Surveillance System, 1988–1989 through 2003–2004. *J Athl Train.* 42(2):286–294.

Micheli LJ, Fehlandt AF. (1992). Overuse injuries to tendons and apophyses in children and adolescents. *Clin Sports Med.* 11:713–726.

Mickalide AD, Hansen LM. (2012). *Coaching Our Kids to Fewer Injuries: A Report on Youth Sports Safety.* Washington, DC: Safe Kids Worldwide.

Mueller FO, Cantu RC. (1993). *National Center for Catastrophic Sport Injury Research—tenth annual report—fall 1982–spring 1992.* Unpublished manuscript. Chapel Hill, NC: University of North Carolina, Department of Physical Education.

Mueller FO, Cantu RC. (2009). *National Center for Catastrophic Sport Injury Research—twenty-sixth annual report—fall 1982–spring 2008.* Chapel Hill, NC: University of North Carolina, Department of Physical Education. Available: http://www.unc.edu/depts/nccsi/AllSport.pdf.

Mueller FO, Cantu RC. (2013). *National Center for Catastrophic Sport Injury Research—twenty-ninth annual report—fall 1982–spring 2011.* Chapel Hill, NC: University of North Carolina, Department of Physical Education. Available: http://www.unc.edu/depts/nccsi.

National Center for Catastrophic Sports Injury Research. (1982–2011). Catastrophic sports injury research: Twenty-ninth annual report. Available: http://www.unc.edu/depts/nccsi/2011Allsport.pdf.

National Federation of State High School Associations. (n.d.). 2011–12 high school athletics participation survey. Available: http://www.nfhs.org/content.aspx?id=3282.

National Safety Council. (1991). *First Aid and CPR* (1st ed.). Sudbury, Mass: Jones and Bartlett.

Nigg BM, Bobbert M. (1990). On the potential of various approaches in load analysis to reduce the frequency of sports injuries. *J Biomech.* 23(Suppl. 1):3–12.

O'Donoghue DH. (1984). *Treatment of Injuries to Athletes.* Philadelphia, Pa: W. B. Saunders.

Powell JW, Barber-Foss KD. (1999). Injury patterns in selected high school sports: A review of the 1995–97 seasons. *J Athl Train.* 34:277–284.

Radelet MA, Lephart SM, Rubinstein EN, Myers JB. (2002). Survey of the injury rate for children in community sports. *Pediatrics.* 110:e28.

Ramirez M, Schaffer KB, Shen H, Kashani S, Kraus JF. (2006). Injuries to high school football athletes in California. *Am J Sports Med.* 34:1147–1158.

Rojas IL, Provencher MT, Bhatia S, Foucher KC, Bach BR Jr, Romeo AA, Wimmer MA, Verma NN. (2009). Biceps activity during windmill softball pitching: Injury implications and comparison with overhand throwing. *Am J Sports Med.* 37(3):558–565.

Shankar PR, Fields SK, Collins CL, Dick RW, Comstock RD. (2007). Epidemiology of high school and collegiate football injuries in the United States, 2005–2006. *Am J Sports Med.* 35(8):1295–1303.

Shea KG, Pfeiffer R, Wang JH, Curtin M, Apel PJ. (2004). Anterior cruciate ligament injury in pediatric and adolescent soccer players: An analysis of insurance data. *J Pediatr Orthop.* 24:623–628.

Smodlaka V. (1984). Medical aspects of heading the ball in soccer. *Phys Sportsmed.* 12:127–131.

Stanitski CL. (1989). Common injuries in preadolescent and adolescent athletes—recommendations for prevention. *Sports Med.* 7:32–41.

Stanitski CL. (1993). Combating overuse injuries—a focus on children and adolescents. *Phys Sportsmed.* 21:87–106.

Stuart MJ, Morrey MA, Smith AM, Meis JK, Ortiguera CJ. (2002). Injuries in youth football: A prospective observational cohort analysis among players aged 9 to 13 years. *Mayo Clin Proc.* 77(4):317–322.

Swenson DM, Yard EE, Fields SK, Comstock RD. (2009). Patterns of recurrent injuries among US high school athletes, 2005–2008. *Am J Sports Med.* 37(8):1586–1593.

Torg JS. (1982). *Athletic Injuries to the Head, Neck and Face.* Philadelphia, Pa: Lea & Febiger.

Venes D, Taber CW. (2009). *Taber's Cyclopedic Medical Dictionary* (21st ed.). Philadelphia, Pa: F. A. Davis.

Walter SD, Sutton JR, McIntosh JM, Connolly C. (1985). The aetiology of sport injuries—a review of methodologies. *Sports Med.* 2:47–58.

Werner SL, Jones DG, Guido JA Jr, Brunet ME. (2006). Kinematics and kinetics of elite windmill softball pitching. *Am J Sports Med.* 34(4):597–603.

Yard EE, Collins CL, Dick RW, Comstock RD. (2008). An epidemiologic comparison of high school and college wrestling injuries. *Am J Sports Med.* 36(1):57–64.

Yard EE, Schroeder MJ, Fields SK, Collins CL, Comstock RD. (2008). The epidemiology of United States high school soccer injuries, 2005–2007. *Am J Sports Med.* 36(10):1930–1937.

The Athletic Health Care Team

MAJOR CONCEPTS

The cornerstone of optimal management of sports- and activity-related injuries is the athletic healthcare team (AHCT), which is made up of a variety of highly trained medical and allied medical personnel as well as other professionals, and coordinates on site with nonmedical personnel including coaches, administrators, parents, and the athletes. This chapter provides an overview of the principal members of the team and reviews the evolution of the field of **sports medicine**. In addition, it describes specific services provided by the athletic healthcare team, giving special attention to the team physician and the athletic trainer who is certified by the Board of Certification, Inc. (BOC). It also outlines educational requirements for BOC certification and employment options for certified athletic trainers.

go.jblearning.com/PfeifferCWS

For a full suite of assignments and additional learning activities (indicated by the icons throughout the text), use the access code found in the front of your text. If you do not have an access code, you can obtain one at go.jblearning.com/PfeifferCWS.

Effective delivery of health care to participants in sports and other physical activities is best achieved through a comprehensive team approach that includes a BOC-certified athletic trainer, a medical physician director, and emergency medical services (EMS) personnel who then work in concert with additional personnel such as school nurses, medical specialists, dentists, counselors, and others (Almquist et al., 2008). This group comprises the athletic healthcare team (AHCT) and it coordinates on site with coaches, administrators, athletes, and parents to prepare all aspects of a comprehensive medical care plan for a particular setting, typically a secondary school setting (Almquist et al., 2008).

A task force, in a publication in the *Journal of Athletic Training,* outlined in detail the critical functions of the AHCT and identified and defined the components necessary to provide medical care effectively in the secondary school setting (Almquist et al., 2008). Their article included 11 specific functions of the AHCT that are necessary to ensure that "appropriate medical coverage" is provided in this setting, such as development of a healthcare administrative system, use of preparticipation physical evaluations, promotion of safe facilities, and other critical elements (Almquist et al., 2008). A consensus statement has also been developed by this group for the National Athletic Trainers' Association (NATA, n.d.) on providing appropriate medical care. Although implementing the components outlined in this summary statement requires considerable investment of time and energy, the long-term results are improved, comprehensive healthcare services for athletes. In addition, by having such a plan in place, the school and associated personnel can reduce the likelihood of litigation associated with sports-related injuries.

Because of time constraints and the associated costs, it is not practical for a physician to be on campus daily in the high school setting to provide medical services to the athletes. As such, a cost-effective option is to employ a BOC-certified athletic trainer. An athletic trainer can be on campus on a daily basis and is in position to observe injuries as soon as they occur. This individual can serve as the "point person" in coordinating the day-to-day operation and directives of the athletic healthcare team. At the very least, in cases when an athletic trainer is not present, coaches trained in first aid and cardiopulmonary resuscitation (CPR) can, and should, provide basic first aid and life-support services to the athletes in their charge.

The AHCT should coordinate its efforts regarding injury prevention through constant dialogue regarding conditioning programs; equipment inspection, purchases, and repair; and environmental conditions. The AHCT should provide services such as preparticipation health screening, development and implementation of an emergency plan, medical supervision of practice and games/contests, injury recognition and treatment (including rehabilitation), implementation of age-appropriate and sports-specific injury prevention programs, detailed record keeping, and education programs for coaches, athletes, and, where appropriate, parents. It is also critical that the AHCT communicate with the local emergency care providers, such as paramedics or emergency medical technicians (EMTs), to plan ahead of time regarding matters such as access to game and practice facilities, practice and game schedules, and specific procedures such as helmet removal in tackle football.

Sports Medicine

Sports medicine has been defined as "a field that uses a holistic, comprehensive, and multidisciplinary approach to health care for those engaged in a sporting or recreational activity" (Dirckx, 1997). Historically, those most often associated with the practice of sports medicine have included physicians who work directly with athletes, typically **orthopedic surgeons**, and athletic trainers. As the field of sports medicine has evolved over the past several decades, a number of related professionals have been added to the list of potential practitioners in the field of sports medicine. These include primary care physicians (family practice, internal medicine, OB-GYN, pediatrics), osteopathic physicians, chiropractic physicians, sports physical therapists, sport-massage practitioners, dentists, sports psychologists, sports nutritionists, exercise physiologists, strength and conditioning coaches, and, in school settings, school nurses.

At the professional level, today's athletes may have access to a wide variety of sports medicine services. These often include comprehensive preseason physical evaluations; proper instruction on sports skills; supervision of conditioning programs; psychological assessments; nutrition education and dietary counseling; help with preventive taping, strapping, and bracing; acute injury care with medical referral; and injury rehabilitation. Sports medicine services at the interscholastic level are typically much more limited, but at the very least they include some type of required preseason physical evaluation. Additionally, an increasing number of high schools nationwide employ a BOC-certified athletic trainer. In some instances, however, in the absence of an athletic trainer, athletic events may be supervised by a medical doctor or other health professional or left up to the discretion of the coaching staff. NATA (n.d.) has published a consensus statement titled "Appropriate Medical Care for Secondary School-Age Athletes" that outlines the essential components and members of the AHCT. Historically, the medical care of professional and college athletes was traditionally provided by a physician, often an orthopedic surgeon. This was logical because many of the serious injuries sustained at this level involved bones and joints. However, with the increased popularity of sports across all age groups and a subsequent rise in demand for services, many different medical specialists now provide sports medicine services.

It is generally acknowledged that more sports medicine services in the future will be offered to the athletic community by primary care physicians (family practice, internal medicine, pediatrics). Because medical schools typically do not provide specialized training in the care of sports- and activity-related injury, additional postgraduate education is available today to qualified primary care physicians in the field of sports medicine. Sports medicine fellowships lasting a minimum of 1 year lead to an additional credential, the Certificate of Added Qualifications in Sports Medicine (CAQ). The CAQ is available to any primary care practitioner and is awarded on successful completion of the fellowship plus successful completion of an examination. The CAQ is offered annually to family physicians in conjunction with the American Board of Emergency Medicine, the American Board of Internal Medicine, and the American Board of Pediatrics (American Board of Family Medicine, 2013).

Key Members of the Team

Although each member of the AHCT is important, three are essential: the coach, the team physician, and the BOC-certified athletic trainer. Although typically not recognized as experts in sports injury, coaches are critical in the process of injury prevention and, in many cases, also function as a "first responder" when an athlete is injured. Regardless of their academic background, coaches in public schools should receive training in basic conditioning procedures, maintenance and fitting of protective equipment, first aid and CPR, operation of an automated external defibrillator (AED), and recognition and management of common sports injuries. In addition, coaches should be competent to teach correct technique of sports skills to the athletes they train. This is especially critical in contact/collision sports that are inherently more dangerous and can be made even more so by athletes performing skills incorrectly.

Although it would be ideal if all public school sports programs had a team physician and a BOC-certified athletic trainer, the reality is that in the majority of cases, the coach alone must provide basic sports medicine services to his or her athletes. Even when a school does employ an athletic trainer, it is impossible for one athletic trainer

to be physically present at all practices and games. In many high schools that employ a BOC-certified athletic trainer, there is a program for students in the school to begin learning some basic athletic training skills as well. These students, usually junior and senior level, are typically required to be certified in first aid and CPR and can serve as first responders in the absence of the athletic trainer. However, despite these efforts to provide coverage, it remains the case in many schools that when an injury occurs, the coach is often the first person on the scene of the injury and, further, must make the initial decisions regarding the status of the athlete and administer appropriate first aid procedures. Coaches must be good communicators and be willing to follow the recommendations of the athletic trainer and team physician when making decisions about an injured athlete's recovery plan and return-to-play schedule. At the same time, the athletic trainer and team physician need to include the coach and other athletic department personnel in matters such as development of the conditioning programs and the emergency plan.

According to the latest "Team Physician Consensus Statement: 2013 Update," a **team physician** must be either a medical doctor (MD) or doctor of osteopathy (DO) and hold an unrestricted license (American College of Sports Medicine [ACSM], 2013). Team physicians agree to provide (either voluntarily or for pay) at least limited medical care to a particular sports program or institution. These services range in scope from, for example, a pediatrician who volunteers to be present for home football games at the local high school, to the other end of the continuum, a nationally prominent orthopedic surgeon who contracts with a major league baseball team to serve as their team physician. The team physician must be willing to commit the necessary time and effort to provide care to each athlete and team. In addition, the team physician must develop and maintain a contemporary knowledge base of the sport(s) for which he or she is accepting responsibility. The ACSM's (2013) consensus statement also provides a detailed listing of the qualifications and responsibilities of the team physician.

sports medicine Branch of medicine concerned with the medical aspects of sports participation.

orthopedic surgeon Physician who corrects deformities of the musculoskeletal system.

team physician A medical doctor who agrees to provide at least limited medical coverage to a particular sports program or institution.

A qualified team physician has an understanding of sports injuries that most other doctors simply do not possess. Furthermore, a team physician generally knows the common risk factors regarding sports injuries, is familiar with the athletes, and should have a genuine interest in the welfare of each participant. These attributes are a great advantage to both coaches and athletes.

Acquiring the services of a team physician may not be an easy task, especially in rural communities and in situations where little or no money is available. Historically, team physicians have reported that the major reason they become involved with sports is because of a strong personal interest (Rogers, 1985). This likely remains the case today and as such, it may be possible to obtain a team physician on a volunteer basis, at least for the purposes of providing medical care at athletic events. To expect more will, in all likelihood, require that some sort of contractual payment plan be arranged. Contacting your state medical association or board may provide information on how to locate interested physicians. Also, if a college or university is nearby, its team physician may be willing to provide services to your program as well. If not, he or she may know of other physicians in the area who would be willing to do so.

A variety of continuing education programs is currently available to team physicians through workshops, seminars, and postgraduate courses offered by hospitals, medical schools, and professional groups. In addition, numerous medical organizations exist that promote the study of sports medicine through membership. These include the American Medical Society for Sports Medicine, the American Academy of Family Physicians, the American Orthopedic Society for Sports Medicine, the American College of Sports Medicine, the American Osteopathic Academy of Sports Medicine, and the American Academy of Orthopaedic Surgeons.

The general consensus within the sports medicine community about the best way to provide comprehensive medical care for student athletes (during practice and games) is to hire a BOC-certified athletic trainer who works in conjunction with a team physician. Athletic trainers are recognized allied healthcare professionals who complete a bachelor's or master's degree with extensive academic and clinical training in the broad area of the care and prevention of sports injuries. The BOC (2012b) defines athletic trainers (ATs) as "health care professionals who collaborate with physicians. The services provided by ATs comprise prevention, emergency care, clinical diagnosis, therapeutic intervention and rehabilitation of injuries and medical conditions." Including a BOC-certified athletic trainer on the high school staff can greatly enhance the overall quality of sports medicine services (**Figure 2.1**).

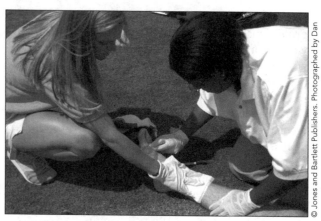

FIGURE 2.1 An athletic trainer evaluates an athlete with an acute injury.

© Jones and Bartlett Publishers. Photographed by Dan Evans Photography.

The practice domains for athletic training, as described by the BOC (2012a), are as follows:

- Injury/illness prevention and wellness protection
- Clinical evaluation and diagnosis
- Immediate and emergency care
- Treatment and rehabilitation
- Organizational and professional health and well-being
- Professional preparation

The National Athletic Trainers' Association is the national professional membership association for the profession of athletic training in the United States and was founded in 1950. Becoming a BOC-certified athletic trainer requires qualifying to sit for, and then passing, the BOC certification examination, which is Web based (completed online) and is offered five times annually in February, April, June, August, and November via a national network of computerized testing centers. To qualify to sit for the examination, you must have completed an educational program accredited as an entry-level program by the Commission on Accreditation of Athletic Training Education (CAATE). Applicants must have an endorsement on the examination application from their CAATE program director. In addition, applicants must have proof of current certification in emergency cardiac care. The *BOC Exam Candidate Handbook* is available for review and free download at the BOC website (http://bocatc.org/candidates/candidate-handbook).

Guidelines for the development and implementation of entry-level education programs in athletic training have been developed and are published by CAATE in the document titled "Standards for the Accreditation of Professional Athletic Training Programs"

(Commission on Accreditation of Athletic Training Education [CAATE], 2012). Educational programs in athletic training must be intensively reviewed for initial accreditation and continued accreditation via on-site visits and annual reports. The program review process is conducted by CAATE.

The CAATE-accredited curriculum offers specific courses designed to prepare students in essential cognitive, affective, and psychomotor domains. More than 500 specific skills have been identified and must be included in the educational program by way of classroom instruction and clinical education. Clinical education involves students acquiring skills under the direct supervision of clinical instructors in settings that are typical in the athletic training facilities located on the campus of the institution sponsoring the educational program. In addition, through formal affiliations, students may gain additional clinical experience off campus in settings such as high schools, other colleges and universities, and professional sports organizations that are located in the immediate geographic vicinity of the institution sponsoring the educational program. Entry-level athletic training education programs must incorporate competency-based classroom and clinical education experiences. CAATE-accredited programs must include formal instruction in the following "professional content" areas:

- Evidence-based practice
- Prevention and health promotion
- Clinical examination and diagnosis
- Acute care of injury and illness
- Therapeutic interventions
- Psychosocial strategies and referral
- Healthcare administration
- Professional development and responsibility

In addition to the formal instruction, students must also complete academic clinical education over the course of a minimum of 2 years and must include a component of working with patients with general medical conditions, both genders, varying levels of risk, and utilization of protective equipment (NATA, 2009).

To remain certified, an athletic trainer is required to earn continuing education units (CEUs) and report these activities to the BOC every 2 years by participating in activities such as attending professional meetings, writing articles for journals, making presentations, and enrolling in college classes that pertain to sports medicine. In addition, current certification in emergency cardiac care (ECC) must be maintained during each 2-year CEU cycle. Specifically, certification must

WHAT IF?

A high school senior asks you for information on the academic requirements and certification process to become an athletic trainer.

include knowledge of adult and pediatric CPR, AED use, second-rescuer CPR, airway obstruction, and barrier devices. Organizations providing such training that are accepted by the BOC include the American Red Cross, American Heart Association, and American Academy of Orthopaedic Surgeons. For more information regarding the BOC certification examination as well as continuing education requirements, contact the BOC (http://www.bocatc.org/contacts).

Professional Settings for the Practice of Athletic Training

Historically, the practice of athletic training was confined to the collegiate sports setting, with an emphasis on caring for injuries in tackle football. It was not until the 1970s that this situation changed significantly, as the services of athletic trainers began to be recognized as extremely valuable in the secondary school sports setting. (The secondary school setting is discussed later in this chapter.) With the growth of the field of sports medicine in the 1980s, there was a parallel growth in a new type of medical clinic in the United States known as a sports medicine clinic. These practices were typically staffed with an orthopedic surgeon and allied health personnel, including athletic trainers and physical therapists. Their patient population consisted of high school, college, and recreational athletes. Services included outpatient physical therapy, fitness evaluation and exercise prescription, lifestyle counseling, evaluation and treatment of injuries, and even sports medicine research (Weidner, 1988). Growth in the number of these clinics was characterized as explosive through the 1980s, and many athletic trainers found employment in this setting (Weidner, 1988). (See **Figure 2.2.**)

Today the types of job settings for athletic trainers have increased dramatically as the profession gains more public recognition. Growth continues in the secondary school setting, and athletic trainers continue to find employment in settings such as clinics (private and hospital-based clinics).

Growth in the number of sports medicine clinics over the past several decades has not gone unnoticed by the nation's hospitals. As such, there has been recent

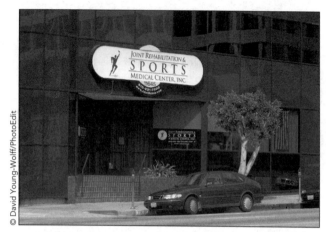

FIGURE 2.2 Growth in the number of sports medicine clinics was characterized as explosive through the 1980s.

growth in hospital-based sports medicine outpatient services. Because BOC-certified athletic trainers possess expertise in the care of those injured in sports and recreational activities, they have found employment opportunities in these new settings. Another relatively recent addition to the professional settings available to athletic trainers is the industrial/corporate setting. Major corporations have found it beneficial and profitable to employ athletic trainers to provide direct services to their employees involved in on-site health and fitness programs or in the area of ergonomics. In the most recent NATA salary survey, the average annual salary of athletic trainers employed in the corporate setting, depending on their specific duties, ranged from a low of $44,252 to a high of $61,837 (NATA, 2013). Although the corporate setting still represents a small percentage of all employment of athletic trainers, it is anticipated that placement in this venue will increase in the future.

To practice in the professional sports setting is often considered to be the dream job for many entering the profession of athletic training. Although the thrill of working with highly paid, marquee athletes may be attractive to some, there are some less attractive aspects to working in this setting. These include the tremendous pressure to win that is placed on the coaching staff that can, and often does, affect the sports medicine staff and the lack of job security associated with changes in coaching staff that occur frequently at the professional level. It is not anticipated that there will be any significant growth in employment in this setting in the near future.

The Secondary School Setting

"Why doesn't your school employ an athletic trainer?" When asked this question, most administrators respond that they cannot afford to hire such a person. This argument is no longer as valid as it once may have been. Today, schools have a variety of options available to them if they want to hire a BOC-certified athletic trainer. The most cost-effective approach appears to be employing one individual as both teacher and athletic trainer. This person is typically hired as a teacher and in addition provides athletic training services after school. Ideally, classroom loads can be adjusted to give the teacher/athletic trainer time in the afternoons or mornings to see athletes before practice. This allows an opportunity for rehabilitation, evaluation of injury recovery, counseling, and any other tasks that cannot be effectively completed otherwise. Administrators find this option to be very affordable because the teacher/athletic trainer can be given a standard teaching contract and can provide educational services to the general student population. Additional monetary stipends, often similar to those given a head coach in the same school or district, are sometimes negotiated to pay for the athletic training services provided. A recent study of salaries for 2011 found that the national average annual salary for public high school athletic trainers was $52,935 (NATA, 2013).

A less affordable but more effective option is for the school to hire a full-time athletic trainer. This individual has no formal teaching responsibilities at the school but is responsible for implementing a comprehensive sports medicine program. This can include follow-up care and rehabilitation of injured athletes during the morning hours prior to practice (during study hall, for example). In addition, the full-time athletic trainer may be able to arrange a schedule so that it more closely approximates the normal number of hours per week provided by other personnel at the school. Though this option often results in the best health care for student athletes, school districts are generally reluctant to commit to the initial financial outlay necessary to develop such a position. Given the financial realities of many school districts around the country, this option may not see significant growth in the foreseeable future.

Other options are available to schools; however, they all offer fewer services to both the school and the athletes. Some alternatives include hiring a part-time athletic trainer or a graduate student/athletic trainer if a university is located nearby, contracting to provide in-service training on various aspects of services with a local sports medicine clinic, or using a substitute teacher/athletic trainer. Though all of these options may save the school money in the short term, they obviously shortchange the student athletes with respect to the availability of sports medicine services.

Having a BOC-certified athletic trainer on staff provides many indirect benefits to the school. From a

Athletic Trainers SPEAK Out

Courtesy of Forrest Pecha, MS, ATC, LAT, OTC, CSCS, St. Luke's Sports Medicine.

Athletic trainers have been instrumental in the prevention, diagnosis, care, and treatment of musculoskeletal injuries for athletes and active populations for decades. Athletic training forefathers logged many hours and have worked tirelessly managing the athletic sidelines to bring recognition to our profession as healthcare professionals. Today, as athletic training evolves, athletic trainers (ATs) are reaching out into a number of emerging settings and continue to provide the same level of care to patients as we have from the inception of our profession.

ATs have a background in musculoskeletal care, unique to our profession, that sets us apart from many other healthcare providers. Working as a "physician extender" is not unique to our profession; we have been working side by side with physicians through the grassroots of our profession and continue to manage athletes together in the athletic training rooms. The physician extender career setting has evolved and taken the AT from the sidelines to the physician offices. ATs have become instrumental in patient care models in the clinical setting and play an ever-growing role in today's healthcare. ATs fill many responsibilities within the physician clinic, from taking patient histories, completing physical exams and inspection, scribing for their physicians, casting, bracing, and teaching home exercises, to providing patient education, pre- and postoperative patient care, surgical assistance, and the list goes on. ATs working in this role have shown positive financial impacts to their clinics, increased clinic efficiency, and improved patient satisfaction. ATs are being sought out at an increasing pace to work in the physician clinics and be members of the healthcare team.

—Forrest Q. Pecha, MS, ATC, LAT, OTC, CSCS

Forrest Q. Pecha is the Director of Clinical Residency and Outreach at St. Luke's Sports Medicine.

Courtesy of Forrest Pecha, MS, ATC, LAT, OTC, CSCS, St. Luke's Sports Medicine.

legal standpoint, the school is less vulnerable to tort claims related to sports injuries. This is because such claims are often based on the premise that the school failed to provide adequate medical care to athletes. A qualified athletic trainer also offers many unique educational opportunities for the school. For example, such a professional can teach classes in basic sports injury care, first aid and CPR, nutrition, and physical conditioning. The athletic trainer can also implement a student athletic trainer program at the school to provide educational opportunities for high school students interested in a career in sports medicine. High school student athletic trainers wishing to continue their education at the university level may qualify for scholarships or other types of financial aid. Such funds are typically made available through the sports medicine program at the sponsoring institutions. Finally, the athletic trainer can provide in-service training on various aspects of sports-injury management for the coaching staff. Obviously, the school can realize many

returns on its investment when it hires a BOC-certified athletic trainer (see **Time Out 2.1**).

BOC-certified athletic trainers signify a marked improvement in the healthcare services provided to athletes, regardless of level of competition. This is partly because of the fact that even under the best of circumstances team physicians are typically available to athletes only on a part-time basis. The BOC-certified athletic trainer can provide a direct link between the injured athlete and the appropriate medical services. In this way, the coach is relieved of much of the responsibility of providing care for the injured participants.

Locating a BOC-Certified Athletic Trainer

Once the decision is made to hire a certified athletic trainer, school administration can locate potential applicants by listing the position with the NATA's Career Center placement service. This can be accomplished

TIME OUT 2.1

Major support for the placement of BOC-certified athletic trainers in secondary schools was provided by the AMA's House of Delegates in June 1998. The AMA House of Delegates adopted the following statements as policy:

1. The AMA believes that (a) the Board of Education and the Department of Health of the individual states should encourage that an adequate Athletic Medicine Unit be established in every school that mounts a sports program; (b) the Athletic Medicine Unit should be composed of an allopathic or osteopathic physician director with unlimited license to practice medicine, an athletic health coordinator (preferably a BOC-certified athletic trainer), and other necessary personnel; (c) the duties of the Athletic Medicine Unit should be prevention of injury, the provision of medical care with the cooperation of the family's physician and others of the healthcare team of the community, and the rehabilitation of the injured; (d) except in extreme emergencies, the selection of the treating physician is the choice of the parent or guardian and any directed referral therefore requires their consent; (e) Athletic Medicine Units should be required to submit complete reports of all injuries to a designated authority; and (f) medical schools, colleges, and universities should be urged to cooperate in establishing education programs for athletic health

coordinators (BOC-certified athletic trainers) as well as continuing medical education and graduate programs in Sports Medicine.

2. The AMA urges high school administrators, athletic directors, and coaches to work with local physicians, medical societies, and medical specialty societies, as well as government officials and community groups, to undertake appropriate measures to ensure funding to provide the services of a certified athletic trainer to all high school athletes.

3. Recognizing that not all high schools have the resources to procure the services of a certified athletic trainer and further recognizing that athletic trainers cannot be present at all practices and competitions, the AMA encourages high school administrators and athletic directors to ensure that all coaches are appropriately trained in emergency first aid and basic life support.

Source: Reproduced from Lyznicki JM, Riggs JA, Champion HC. (1999). Certified athletic trainers in secondary schools: Report of the Council on Scientific Affairs, American Medical Association. *J Athl Train.* 34(3):272–276. Reprinted with permission.

by visiting the NATA website (http://www.nata.org/career-center) and following the links to the placement service. Another option is to contact universities that offer CAATE-approved curriculums in athletic training for a listing of their recent graduates. A listing of all universities with NATA-approved curricula is available at the NATA website or by contacting the NATA national office at 214-637-6282.

REVIEW QUESTIONS

1. Define the term *sports medicine*.
2. What is the CAQ and how does it relate to the team physician?
3. List the specific services that should be provided to the athlete by the team physician.
4. What are the six practice domains of the BOC-certified athletic trainer?
5. List several professional medical organizations that promote the study of sports medicine.
6. What has been the largest employment market for athletic trainers in recent years?
7. Briefly describe six different employment options for a BOC-certified athletic trainer in the school setting. Elaborate on the advantages and disadvantages of each option.
8. True or false: It is generally acknowledged that sports medicine services in the future will be provided by medical specialists rather than primary care physicians.
9. List the eight professional content areas that are required by CAATE for accredited curricula in athletic training.

REFERENCES

Almquist J, Valovich McLeod TC, Cavanna A, Jenkinson D, Lincoln AE, Loud K, Peterson BC, Portwood C, Reynolds J, Woods TS. (2008). Summary statement: Appropriate medical care for the secondary school-aged athlete. *J Athl Train.* 43(4):416–427.

American Board of Family Medicine. (2013). Certificates of added qualifications (CAQs). Available: https://www.theabfm.org/caq/index.aspx.

American College of Sports Medicine. (2013). Team physician consensus statement: 2013 update. Available: http://www.acsm.org/docs/other-documents/team_physician_consensus_statement____2013_update-24.pdf.

Board of Certification, Inc. (2012a). Defining athletic training. Available: http://bocatc.org/resources/index.php?option=com_content&task=view&id=114&Itemid=122.

Board of Certification, Inc. (2012b). What is an athletic trainer? Available: http://www.bocatc.org/public/what-is-an-athletic-trainer.

Commission on Accreditation of Athletic Training Education. (2012). Standards for the accreditation of professional athletic training programs. Available: http://caate.occutrain.net/wp-content/uploads/2013/07/2012-Standards-with-glossary-posted.pdf.

Dirckx JH (ed.). (1997). *Stedman's Concise Medical Dictionary for the Health Professions.* Baltimore, Md: Williams & Wilkins.

National Athletic Trainers' Association. (2009). Athletic training education overview. Available: http://www.nata.org/athletic-training.

National Athletic Trainers' Association. (2013). NATA 2011 athletic training salary survey results. Available: http://www.nata.org/sites/default/files/2011-AT-Salaries.pdf.

National Athletic Trainers' Association. (n.d.). Appropriate medical care for secondary school-age athletes. Available: http://www.nata.org/sites/default/files/AppropriateMedicalCare4SecondarySchoolAgeAthletes.pdf.

Rogers CC. (1985). Does sports medicine fit in the new health-care market? *Phys Sports Med.* 13(1):116–127.

Weidner TG. (1988). Sports-medicine centers: Aspects of their operation and approaches to sports-medicine care. *Athletic Training.* 23(1):22–26.

The Law of Sports Injury

MAJOR CONCEPTS

As with medicine in general, the field of sports medicine has witnessed a dramatic increase in the amount of litigation over the last decade. This chapter introduces the reader to legal terminology and outlines what constitutes the physical education teacher's, coach's, and referee's duty when working with athletes. It provides a listing of the major forms of teaching, coaching, and refereeing liability along with information on how to reduce the risk of litigation. It also presents appropriate steps to take in the event of a lawsuit and concludes with a discussion on the ethics of sports-injury care.

go.jblearning.com/PfeifferCWS

For a full suite of assignments and additional learning activities (indicated by the icons throughout the text), use the access code found in the front of your text. If you do not have an access code, you can obtain one at go.jblearning.com/PfeifferCWS.

The physical education teacher or coach is often the first on the scene when a sports injury occurs. Even referees may also be called into action due their proximity to the playing field. The physical education teacher's, coach's, or referee's decisions and actions at the time of the injury are critical to the welfare of the athlete (**Figure 3.1**). These decisions and actions are based on the standards of care that a reasonably prudent person would perform in a similar circumstance in an attempt to avoid harm to the athlete. Inappropriate or nonprudent decisions and actions may jeopardize the injured participant and lead to legal action by the athlete and/or parents or legal guardians (in the case of minors). Perhaps at no other time in the history of sports has the potential for legal action against teachers, coaches, and other sports personnel been as great as it is today. Several recent tort cases are listed in **Time Out 3.1**.

There are a number of reasons for this increase in lawsuits. According to Appenzeller (2000), one of these is the simple fact that in the United States, people have a right to sue; Americans have created a sports culture whereby athletes believe they should be able to participate without risk of injury; there is large monetary expense associated with many injuries and, as a result, those who are injured may sue to recover for medical expenses because many

FIGURE 3.1 Coaches assist an injured athlete.

insurance companies will settle out of court by opting to pay a sum of money. Another reason is the sheer number of lawyers in the United States; according to the American Bar Association there were 1,225,452 licensed lawyers practicing in 2010 (Podgers, 2011). There are also

TIME OUT 3.1

Recently Settled Cases of Negligence in Sports

Blake Hunt (Flushing, NY, 2007)

Blake Hunt, while a senior in high school, shattered the C5 vertebra in his neck when a running back's knee snapped his head backward. The injury left him paralyzed from the waist down. Hunt filed suit against the Parks Department, the Department of Education, and the Public Schools Athletic League alleging improper and inadequate supervision, officiating, and medical care. Hunt also alleged that he was too small to be competing on the field with larger players. The lawsuit was settled out of court for $8 million (Wolohan, 2010).

Mackenzie Clay (Seattle, WA, 2007)

Mackenzie Clay, while a senior wrestler in high school, suffered a spinal cord injury as a result of two wrestlers falling on him during a practice in the school's cafeteria. The injury left him in a wheelchair. Clay filed a negligence suit against the school district alleging the school's coaches lacked Washington Interscholastic Activities Association certification at the time and that they failed to use the appropriate number and size of wrestling mats for the practice. Clay received a $1 million settlement from Seattle Public Schools

and $14 million from Washington Schools Risk Management Pool, the district's insurance company (Cohen, 2009).

Antonio Reyes (Wenatchee, WA, 2011)

Antonio Reyes, at 14 years old, drowned in the deep end of the pool after a physical education (PE) class. His family filed a negligence lawsuit alleging there was not an effort to evaluate his swimming ability and there was not adequate supervision, including a certified lifeguard on duty. Wenatchee (WA) school district reached a $2 million settlement in 2012 (Popke, 2013).

Max Gilpin (Louisville, KY, 2008)

Max Gilpin, at 15 years old, died of heat stroke 3 days after a Louisville, KY, high school football practice. The family filed a negligence lawsuit against the school district and head football coach alleging reckless disregard of safety requirements. The insurers settled for $1.75 million. The head football coach also became the first coach to be charged criminally with reckless homicide and wanton endangerment. The coach was acquitted in 2009 (Beahm, 2010).

increased expectations of young athletes and parents relative to potential future financial gain of a successful sports career. If injured, affected parties may sue to recover their future financial losses. Other factors include the huge increase in the number of sports participants, increase in the severity of injuries, greater visibility of sports through the media, rising expectations regarding legal negligence, greater awareness of sports as a business due to the huge revenues of many athletic organizations, and consumer awareness about sports product manufacturing (Wong, 2010).

Ethics of Sports-Injury Care

The athlete's health and safety should be the ultimate priority for all those involved in organized sports. A coach's livelihood and career often depend on a win–loss record because sports are now viewed as a business with an increasing emphasis on winning and earning monetary rewards. In addition, athletes (and often their parents or legal guardians) will pressure coaches for an opportunity to play. Therefore, a coach may feel pressure to return an athlete to play without proper medical care or follow up.

According to the National Federation of State High School Associations (NFHS), 38 of 50 states require that coaches complete first aid certification before coaching or within 1–2 years of being appointed to a position (NFHS, n.d.). In addition, each school district often determines its own policy and may require first aid and even CPR certifications for their coaches. Unfortunately, this requirement does not indicate that coaches understand the intricacies of first aid care and the disposition of athletes after injury. Research regarding whether coaches have adequate first aid knowledge in accordance with nationally recognized guidelines has produced discouraging results (Braun et al., 2009; Dunn & Ransone, 1999; McLeod et al., 2008). Thirty-six percent of 104 California high school athletic coaches passed a first aid test based on nationally recognized guidelines (Dunn & Ransone, 1999). In Arizona, only 3% of 156 youth sports coaches (McLeod et al., 2008) passed the same first aid assessment test used by Dunn and Ransone. The positive news is that those coaches who reported first aid or CPR certification scored higher on the assessment test. Therefore, education does help. Similar results were also achieved through a study done in Michigan where only 5% of 290 coaches in youth sporting leagues passed a first aid assessment quiz (Braun et al., 2009). Overall, coaches are likely to withhold an injured young athlete from competition (Dunn & Ransone, 1999; McLeod et al., 2008); however, specific data from the Game Situation Data Sheet

(GSDS) were analyzed and it was interpreted that coaches can still be aggressive in returning injured youth to competition if the game is "on the line." Both studies (Dunn & Ransone 1999; McLeod et al., 2008) reported that when a close game was at stake, more than 50% of all surveyed coaches reported a conflict of interest when a starting player was injured and wanted to return to the game. Perhaps even more alarming was that 75% of the "first aid–knowledgeable" coaches made incorrect return-to-play decisions in high-stakes games (Dunn & Ransone, 1999). Therefore, the coach must resist the temptation to circumvent the standards of first aid care. An objective and unbiased opinion is critical when decisions are made regarding the return of an injured athlete to participation. Under no circumstance should an injured athlete be allowed to resume sports without the consent of a qualified medical professional such as a certified athletic trainer or medical doctor. Unethical behavior by a coach will in all probability be considered negligence by a court of law, so all individuals involved in the supervision or instruction of youth in sports need to understand the concepts of liability and tort law applied to sports.

The Concept of Tort

A **tort** is a private or civil wrong or injury suffered by an individual as a result of another person's conduct (Ray & Konin, 2011; Wong, 2010). There are two general categories of torts: intentional and unintentional (negligence; Wong, 2010). The difference between the two types of torts lies in the intent to harm. **Negligence** is a type of tort, defined as the failure to do what a reasonably careful and prudent person would have done under the same or like circumstances, or, conversely, it is defined as doing something that a reasonably careful and prudent person would not have done under the same or like circumstances (Ray & Konin, 2011; Wong, 2010). The conduct of a reasonable person is not always perfect, but will be considered to match the level of skills possessed by like members of the community (Wong, 2010). Therefore, a team doctor is held to different

tort A private wrong or injury, suffered by an individual as a result of another person's conduct.
negligence The failure to do what a reasonably careful and prudent person would have done under the same or like circumstances, or doing something that a reasonably careful and prudent person would not have done under the same or like circumstances.

standards of reasonable care than a coach or PE teacher. In the context of sports, an injured athlete may argue that an injury resulted from someone else's behavior—that of an opponent, an official, a PE teacher, or a coach. These torts are likely unintentional or negligence torts where there was no intent to harm, but there was a failure to exercise reasonable care (Wong, 2010); however, intentional torts are not uncommon if the **plaintiff** feels the injury was caused with an intent to harm (player vs. player) (Wolohan, 2008). Tort cases involving sports-related injuries generally seek to recover money to compensate the athlete for damages (medical expenses) that resulted from the defendant's alleged negligence.

Essential to proving a negligence tort is establishing that someone other than the athlete (injured party) acted in a negligent manner, and this behavior resulted in an injury. Wong (2010) identifies the four elements that must be present to prove negligence. They are listed in **Time Out 3.2**. Negligence involves either an act of **commission** (acting in an improper way) or an act of **omission** (failure to act or nonfeasance). An act of commission can be further divided into **misfeasance** or **malfeasance**. The essence of negligence is proving the proximate cause or causal connection between the resultant damage, duty of care, and breach of duty.

An example of negligence by an act of commission (misfeasance) is the high school football player (plaintiff) who claims that a significant knee injury resulted from the head coach throwing a tackling dummy at his legs to simulate illegal blocking and the techniques needed to avoid these tackles. In such a case, the athlete might claim the coach's actions caused the knee injury unnecessarily. The athlete would argue that the coach's actions constituted negligence because the coach acted in a way that he had the legal right to do (teach tackling techniques), but he did it with reckless behavior and incorrect techniques. The question that will be asked is, "Was the throwing of the tackling dummy at the legs of players a reasonable action by the coach in an attempt to teach a football technique?" This is known as the determination of reasonable care or the general desire to avoid creating risks that might result in an injury (Wong, 2010). An example of negligence by an act of omission (nonfeasance) is when the local high school failed to provide a certified lifeguard at the pool during a PE swimming class and a student drowns. The defendant (local school) would then be judged, in part, on the basis of what other school districts routinely do at their aquatic facilities. Physical education teachers, coaching staffs, and school districts are held to a predetermined standard of care for all those under their supervision. The question that will be asked is, "Should the school district have anticipated the risk of death by drowning to a participant in the swimming class?" This is known as the "foreseeability" of the injury and, in essence, determines if the school district and physical education teacher provided the appropriate standard of care to the members of the swimming class. If not, then the defendants may be found to have been negligent.

In school sports cases, tort claims often name as many defendants as possible. For example, in the scenarios given, the list of defendants might include the physical education teacher, head coach, assistant coach, school principal, athletic director, and school district administration, and perhaps even the state high school athletic association. Tort claims generally ask for monetary rewards; therefore, it is only logical that defendants are selected, in part, based on their ability to pay such awards. This is commonly referred to as "going for the deepest pocket."

According to Wong (2010), showing proof of one of the following legal doctrines is the best way to defeat a negligence suit. However, it should be noted that each state has laws that may or may not allow one of these defenses, especially in the cases of minors.

- *No negligence.* The defendant disputes the claim of negligence by attacking one of the four elements of negligence as outlined in Time Out 3.2. In this case, the defendant did not have a duty or did not breach the applicable duty of care. An act of God (act of nature) is also used in a no negligence defense as it concedes that the injury occurred as a result of factors beyond the control of

---

TIME OUT 3.2

Four Elements of Negligence

1. **Duty of care:** An obligation recognized by the law requiring a person to conform to a certain standard of conduct for the protection of others against unreasonable risks. There is a duty to act in a reasonable manner and a duty not to act in an unreasonable manner.
2. **Breach of duty:** Violation of the established duty (direct evidence), a failure to conform to the standard required, or inference from circumstantial evidence.
3. **Actual or proximate causation:** A reasonably close causal connection between the conduct (breach of duty) and the resulting injury.
4. **Damage:** Actual losses that are considered compensatory (e.g., medical expenses, future income, mental stress).

the defendant and could not have been prevented by the exercise of prudence, care, or diligence. For example, being injured or killed by an earthquake that occurs during a cross-country running event would, in all probability, be considered an act of God.

- *Contributory negligence.* The plaintiff is found to be in part or totally responsible for the injury. Therefore, the defendant must prove that the plaintiff failed to exercise due care for his or her own safety.

- *Comparative negligence.* This provides a basis of recovery for the injured plaintiff while assigning fault to both parties. It allows for the plaintiff to receive partial compensation on a prorated basis, dependent on a judgment regarding the extent of *contributory negligence.* In other words, if a monetary reward is given, it is based only on the percentage of negligence assigned to the plaintiff.

- *Assumption of risk.* This means that the plaintiff has voluntarily consented to assume responsibility for injury. There are two types, including *expressed* and *implied* assumption of risk. Expressed risk is when a plaintiff gives advanced notice (signs a waiver) to take the chances of known risks. Implied is an inference that by participating in a risky event where negligence is possible, the plaintiff is releasing the defendant from a duty of care. Assumption of risk defenses can only be used in states that do not have comparative negligence laws. Also, it is important to note that signing an assumption of risk form does not always remove the defendant from responsibility, as there are many legal issues that surround these forms.

- *Statute of limitations.* There are specific time periods (statutes) in which plaintiffs can file lawsuits. Most are based on a time period relative to the time of discovery of the harm.

- *Immunity.* Immunity is a condition that protects defendants from tort actions because of their position related to their capacity or their relationship with the plaintiff. Each state determines types of conditions for establishing immunity. Sovereign immunity is where local government entities have immunity from many tort cases. However, coaches or teachers employed by local governments (e.g., state universities) cannot assume sovereign immunity because of their position as each state's laws may vary.

- *Good Samaritan laws.* This is type of immunity specific to those who attempt to aid another person that was put into a dangerous situation by a third party. Most states have Good Samaritan laws in place, which serve to protect citizens (even medical personnel) who voluntarily provide first aid to an injured person. Such laws were developed, in part, to encourage the average citizen or medical personnel to render first aid in an emergency, even though these individuals do not have a duty to provide such care. These laws protect most caregivers if the care was not reckless or did not worsen the condition of the injured person. Good Samaritan laws vary greatly from state to state in regard to the categories of people the statutes protect and as to the circumstances in which they apply (Quandt, 2009). However, coaches and other school personnel do have a duty to provide appropriate emergency care, and, as a result, they typically do not enjoy immunity from tort claims under the tenets of Good Samaritan laws.

What Is the Physical Educator's or Coach's Liability?

Anyone serving in a coaching capacity, whether voluntarily or paid, bears considerable responsibility for the health and safety of athletes. Historically, a coach employed by government institutions such as school districts or universities has enjoyed a certain degree of immunity from tort litigation under the doctrine of sovereign immunity. This in essence protects government institutions and their personnel from liability claims. However, some states have determined through legislative action that tort litigation against such agencies may be possible, depending on the specific circumstances (Wong, 2010). Consequently, more injury liability cases are now being contested successfully against coaching

plaintiff The individual who was injured and brings the lawsuit.

commission A legal liability arising when a person commits an act that is not legally his or hers to perform.

omission A legal liability arising when a person does not perform an action that ought to be taken.

misfeasance An act of commission where lawful conduct is performed but done improperly.

malfeasance An act of commission where conduct is performed that is wholly unlawful.

TIME OUT 3.3

Potentially Negligent Actions by Coaches

- **Failure to provide adequate supervision.** The coach is required to supervise activities to an extent that is determined, in part, by the age, skill, and experience of the participants. Thus, inexperienced children involved in a high-risk sport such as football require a higher level of supervision than do senior varsity athletes in the same sport. Anytime children are involved, regardless of the activity, the coach is responsible for providing proper supervision. Proper supervision may not be required only during practices and games, but also when athletes are in other settings like locker rooms or buses. Coaches should also be aware that encouraging violent conduct, unsafe conduct outside of the scope of the sport, or belligerent acts by players or other personnel can be considered as a failure to supervise.

- **Failure to provide competent personnel.** When a head coach hires an assistant or an administrator hires a physical education teacher, he or she assumes some responsibility for the competence, or lack thereof, of that assistant or teacher. If the assistant coach or teacher fails to give proper instruction or supervision to the athlete, the head coach or administrator could be found to be negligent.

- **Failure to provide appropriate training and instruction.** Coaches and physical education teachers should be qualified to teach the particular activity they are supervising. This involves providing proper instruction on the fundamental and advanced skills required for participation, as well as injury prevention techniques. The coach must make sure that the participants receive adequate conditioning exercises geared toward sports performance. The coach must also instruct athletes on the rules and regulations regarding participation. Using established guidelines provided by governing bodies and keeping a log of all practice activities is the best way to prevent negligence.

- **Failure to provide proper use of safe equipment.** Because the coach may be responsible for the selection and purchase of protective equipment, he or she must make sure that any such equipment does not place an athlete in jeopardy. The coach or physical education teacher may also be held responsible for failure to maintain and/or replace damaged sport equipment. Procedures need to be established for the regular inspection of personal protective gear and sport equipment.

- **Failure to warn of latent dangers.** The coach has the obligation to warn participants of any dangers that may not be obvious. Coaches and physical education teachers have a duty to warn about the nature of the activity and the techniques involved, the condition of the playing surface, and the use of equipment. For example, a coach has a duty to warn about adverse field conditions and is responsible to prevent those under his supervision from competing on a dangerous field. When dealing with minors, any warnings should also be given to the parent(s) or guardian.

- **Failure to provide prompt and competent medical care.** The coach should know what medical personnel are present and should determine accessibility in advance. If there is no medical personnel available, the coach is required to provide medical care to an injured athlete. Given this mandate, the prudent coach should have basic training in proper first aid procedures for common athletic injuries. Coaches have been found liable for failing to provide appropriate first aid, moving an injured athlete incorrectly, or not providing reasonable care in sending an athlete for advance medical treatment, and applying correct procedures but doing so inappropriately. It is critical that a coach remove an athlete from participation if there is any question about his or her immediate health status. Note: Many states have now passed laws mandating that all athletic events have qualified medical personnel present (see the discussion of athletic trainers later in this chapter).

- **Failure to prevent injured athletes from competing.** Although the decision for return to play needs to be made by qualified medical personnel, under no circumstances should injured players be allowed to play if there is a risk of further injury. The coach is ultimately responsible for ensuring that an athlete is ready to resume participation at their previous level or with their previous group.

- **Failure to match athletes of similar competitive levels.** Coaches and physical educators have a duty not to mismatch players by matching players of unequal skill, size, weight, or strength against one another in practices or games. Reducing the risk of serious injury should always be at the forefront of decisions regarding match-ups. Also, coaches must be careful that they do not injure players during practices because of their higher skill levels.

Source: McCaskey & Biedzynski, 1996; Quandt, 2009; Wong, 2010.

personnel. Therefore, it appears that protection under the doctrine of sovereign immunity is no longer guaranteed (Wong, 2010).

The coach must always use reasonable care to avoid creating a foreseeable risk of harm to others (Wong, 2010). The legal mechanisms by which coaches and physical educators can protect themselves have evolved over time. Whether they are staff members or volunteers, coaches and others should familiarize themselves with the duties they owe to their participants (McCaskey & Biedzynski, 1996). They also need to understand any written job duties or contractual agreements afforded by their employer or local entity. The best way for coaches to prevent exposure to liability is to know the attendant risks of the sport and to be knowledgeable and prepared so foreseeable consequences can be anticipated (McCaskey & Biedzynski, 1996). However, coaches and physical educators are not insurers of a participant's safety and will not be held liable for injuries resulting from the inherent dangers of the sport or activity provided they satisfied their duties as coaches or educators (McCaskey & Biedzynski, 1996). Wong (2010), Quandt (2009), and McCaskey and Biedzynski (1996) present several specific duties for coaches and/or physical educators to use to minimize risk of injury for participants. These are explained in **Time Out 3.3**.

Are Coaches and Physical Educators Protected?

The best protection a coach or physical educator can have against the risk of litigation is to avoid the problems listed in Time Out 3.3. Today's coaches and teachers must be constantly aware of potential risks to participants and must take appropriate action to reduce or eliminate those risks. This ongoing process of risk management involves being ever vigilant for potential risks to participants and will help reduce the chances of successful litigation because it indicates the staff has met the standard of care by eliminating all foreseeable risks for injury. Remember there are some limits to immunity and the Good Samaritan laws, because coaches and other school personnel have a duty to provide appropriate emergency care.

Because most tort claims seek monetary rewards, it is obvious that a coach's personal assets may be in jeopardy in the event of an unfavorable court decision. Therefore, it is imperative that the coach chooses to be protected by some form of liability insurance (McCaskey & Biedzynski, 1996). A coach in an interscholastic or intercollegiate setting is generally covered by insurance provided by the employer. However, it is wise to

ascertain the specific type of coverage provided. Coaches must not assume they are protected. A volunteer coach may not have any liability coverage, in which case the purchase of personal liability or catastrophic accident insurance is advisable.

A good rule of thumb is for coaches never to assume that they are covered. Before beginning the playing season, coaches should contact their employer, sponsoring organization, or an insurance company representative to determine which type of coverage they have and whether it offers the best protection (McCaskey & Biedzynski, 1996).

How to Reduce the Chances of Going to Court

The following is a list of several important preventive steps a coach can implement to reduce the chances of being sued:

1. **Written contract.** This document should state in detail the expectations and limitations of the coach's service. (It is advisable to have an attorney examine any contract to determine what liabilities may be included.)

2. **Certification in basic or advanced first aid, cardiopulmonary resuscitation (CPR), and the use of an automated external defibrillator (AED).** Coaches should ensure that their certification is current and that they periodically practice their skills. Such training is available through a variety of agencies such as the American Heart Association, the American Red Cross, and the National Safety Council. Several youth or high school sports associations also offer training designed to help coaches review techniques.

3. **Emergency action plan.** It is essential that a formal emergency action plan be developed for both home and out-of-town contests. These plans should be in written form and posted publicly. All parties involved with their implementation should also have copies. Furthermore, the emergency plan should be periodically rehearsed to ensure that it will function effectively during a real crisis (Almquist et al., 2004; Casa et al., 2013).

4. **Parental consent form (for athletes younger than 18 years of age).** These forms provide an excellent opportunity to inform the athletes and their parents/guardians about the potential risk for injury that is inherent in participation. However, these

Athletic Trainers SPEAK Out

Courtesy of A. Louise Fincher, EdD, ATC, LAT, Department Chair-Kinesiology, The University of Texas at Arlington.

How has athletic training education kept up with the ever-changing healthcare needs of the physically active?

The 5th edition of the Athletic Training Education Competencies (Competencies) serves as the current guide for the professional education of athletic training students. Published by the National Athletic Trainers' Association (NATA), the Competencies identify the knowledge, skills and clinical abilities that students are expected to master when enrolled in professional athletic training education programs. The Competencies are purposely updated and revised every five years to ensure that they reflect the latest evidence and best practice in athletic training patient care.

Notable additions to the 5th edition of the Competencies include expanded knowledge and skills for the acute care of medical emergencies involving athletes and other physically active individuals. For example, athletic training students must now be able to demonstrate the ability to assess oxygen saturation, and blood glucose levels, as well as to use a nebulizer, supplemental oxygen and glucometer. The incorporation of these new skills related to the management of conditions like asthma and diabetes is just one example of how the Competencies continue to ensure that entry-level athletic trainers are prepared to provide quality health care to their athletes, patients and clients.

—A. Louise Fincher, EdD, ATC, LAT

A. Louise Fincher is the Chair of the Department of Kinesiology at The University of Texas at Arlington.

Courtesy of A. Louise Fincher, EdD, ATC, LAT, Department Chair-Kinesiology, The University of Texas at Arlington.

---

do not typically release sports personnel from legal liability in cases where negligence may have occurred (Wong, 2010).

5. **Mandatory comprehensive preparticipation physical evaluation.** A preparticipation physical evaluation (PPE) must be a requirement for all participants. A medial doctor (MD or DO) should administer the evaluation and all pertinent information should be recorded on an appropriate form. Athletes should not be allowed to participate in sports activities until they have undergone the physical. Most school districts, colleges, and universities have standard forms for these physical exams. The National Athletic Trainers' Association (NATA) has a support statement titled "Appropriate Medical Care for Secondary School-Age Athletes," which includes a listing of specific elements that should be included in a comprehensive PPE form (Almquist et al., 2004). Information collected should be on file with the athletic administrator and handled confidentially. Whenever possible,

the PPE should include some sort of neuropsychological or postural stability testing to establish a baseline for comparative purposes later if the athlete sustains a head injury at some point in the future (Osborne, 2001).

Comprehensive guidelines for the PPE have been published by a consortium of medical groups, including the American Academy of Family Physicians (AAFP), the American Academy of Pediatrics, the American Medical Society for Sports Medicine, the American Orthopaedic Society for Sports Medicine, the National Athletic Trainers' Association, and the American Osteopathic Academy of Sports Medicine. The AAFP's *Preparticipation Physical Evaluation, Monograph 4th Edition*, is a valuable resource and is recommended reading because requiring a PPE that follows these guidelines will likely be interpreted by the courts as reasonable care toward athletes.

6. **Documentation of all injuries.** Regardless of severity, a detailed description of the initial care and treatment—as well as the cause(s)—of all

injuries must be recorded on a standard form. The school personnel should make sure that all pertinent information regarding an injury is collected and placed on file with the athletic administrator. If an athletic trainer is not on staff and keeping medical records, it is advisable for the administration to maintain an athlete's history of injuries. In this way, coaching and medical personnel are aware of all recent injuries a given athlete may have sustained.

Federal regulations known as the Health Insurance Portability and Accountability Act (HIPAA) and Family Educational Rights and Privacy Act (FERPA) have had a dramatic impact on the health care of adolescents, including the sports medicine field (Quandt, 2009). Although a comprehensive discussion of HIPAA or FERPA is beyond the scope of this text, coaches, physical education teachers, and other members of the athletic healthcare team should be familiar with those aspects of these regulations that can affect their place of employment or professional practice. For example, these regulations place strict limitations on the release of personal health information to third parties, such as family, teammates, and the media. Because sports are of great interest to the general public and because sports injuries are often somewhat public by their very nature, school personnel must carefully monitor how information regarding an athlete's injury is distributed, if at all.

7. **Completion of seminars and/or postgraduate classes.** Owing in large part to the increased concern regarding sports-injury litigation, many states now require specific safety training for all personnel associated with youth athletes. These often include specific training on topics like heat illness and concussions. School districts often meet this requirement by conducting training on the topic of the care and prevention of athletic injuries or requiring school personnel to complete online training offered by various groups. The National Federation of State High School Associations (NFHS) offers one of the more comprehensive groupings of educational modules (which can be found at http://www.nfhs-learn.com/). For volunteer coaches, the National Alliance for Youth Sports (NAYS) offers online training videos that include injury prevention, first aid, and concussion management modules. These modules can be found at http://www.nays.org. In addition, coaches are often encouraged by school administrators to enroll in postgraduate

classes pertaining to the care and prevention of sports injuries. Completion of voluntary training or courses demonstrates a willingness on the part of coaching personnel to remain informed regarding current standards of care and prevention of sports injury.

8. **Inspections of facilities and/or equipment.** Foresee accidents before they happen by conducting routine inspections to ensure that any potential hazards are corrected. All equipment should be inspected before every use. Athletes are generally responsible for their own personal protective equipment; however, coaches and physical educators are responsible for facility and general equipment inspections. In addition, it is advisable for coaches to notify the athletic administrator, in writing, of any hazards that remain uncorrected.

9. **Development and maintenance of effective lines of communication.** Communication with athletes, parents, athletic administrators, and medical personnel is essential to providing safe activity for sports participants.

10. **Enforce rules and regulations, especially those that are designed to safeguard student athletes.** Inform participants of the inherent risks associated with specific sports. Use teachable moments on the practice field to prevent the risk of injury in game situations.

11. **Be aware of laws that govern sports participation.** It is in the best interest of any person involved in coaching, teaching, or refereeing sports to review state law in regard to regulations governing participation and potential liability. For example, 44 states including the District of Columbia passed laws on concussions in sports for youth and/or high school athletes. These concussion laws typically provide guidelines for the removal of an athlete from play, the requirement of return-to-play permission from medical professionals, and the education of coaches, parents, and athletes.

WHAT IF?

You are asked to take a part-time position coaching girls' volleyball at a local junior high school. What specific steps can you take to protect yourself from a potential lawsuit if an injury occurs to one of your athletes?

What Coaches or Physical Educators Can Do If They Get Sued

If a coach is about to be sued in a tort case, it is critical that the coach take the appropriate steps to protect him- or herself. It is recommended that coaches or physical educators first contact their lawyer and call their insurance company (Appenzeller, 2000). This allows the coaches or physical educators to obtain proper advice about how to further protect themselves. Furthermore, this allows all pertinent facts related to the case to be recorded while events are still recent.

It is important for the coach to write a detailed description of all events leading up to and immediately following the injury. This should include signed statements by eyewitnesses if possible. It is also advised that the coach not make statements to the media or to other parties without the advice of an attorney (Appenzeller, 2000). In this way, coaches can avoid compromising their position during a subsequent trial or appeal.

Role of the Athletic Trainer

The National Athletic Trainers' Association (NATA) defines certified athletic trainers as "health care professionals who specialize in preventing, recognizing, managing, and rehabilitating injuries that result from physical activity" (Quandt, 2009). Ideally, coaches and physical educators will have direct access to athletic trainers within their school or district. Athletic trainers can assist school personnel in maintaining safe environments for athletes and students and are likely to help prevent acts of negligence. A few states have already mandated athletic trainers at the secondary school level, but now that there are 44 states along with the District of Columbia that have passed laws in regard to concussion management, more attention is being focused on the need for youth safety at all levels of athletic participation. Legislation encouraging schools to develop and adopt best practices and standards to prevent and address student athlete injury are being moved forward by organizations including the NATA and the National Alliance for Youth Sports.

Several types of state regulation of athletic trainers are presently in place in 48 of the 50 states. Licensure is considered the "gold standard" for professional regulation of athletic trainers, and the majority of those states (41 of 48) with regulations in place have incorporated some form of licensing. The intent of state regulation is to protect the public from incompetent practitioners. Other forms of state regulation include registration and certification. In general, state regulation defines the scope and practice of athletic training in a particular state. Anyone certified by the Board of Certification, Inc. (BOC), planning to practice in a state with regulations must contact the state regulatory body to determine the steps necessary for eligibility to practice in that state. Most often an application process is required and will be strictly enforced. It is in the best interest of the coach or school personnel to have an athletic trainer on staff and to ensure he or she is certified nationally and has the appropriate state regulation paperwork. For more information about athletic training visit the website of the National Athletic Trainers' Association (http://www.nata.org/) or Board of Certification (http://www.bocatc.org).

REVIEW QUESTIONS

1. Define the terms *tort* and *negligence* as discussed in the text.
2. Briefly describe the two types of negligence—acts of commission and acts of omission—discussed in the chapter.
3. What are the four elements that must be present to prove negligence?
4. Describe briefly the ways that a negligence suit may be defeated.
5. Does liability differ for a paid coach versus a volunteer?
6. Do Good Samaritan laws protect school personnel, such as coaches, from litigation?
7. List and describe the reasons a coach or physical educator may be found negligent.
8. Outline the steps that can reduce a coach's chances of being sued.
9. What are the first two things a coach should do when notified of an impending lawsuit?
10. Elaborate on the sociologic pressures exerted on today's coach that may challenge his or her sense of professional ethics.
11. True or false: The courts have found that a coach is responsible for giving instruction to athletes regarding the rules and regulations of participation in sports.

12. What do the acronyms HIPPA and FERPA stand for?
13. What do athletic trainers provide to the secondary school setting?

14. What is the purpose of state regulation of athletic trainers, and how many states presently regulate the profession?

RECOMMENDED READING

Bernhardt DT, Roberts WO (eds). (2010). *American Academy of Family Physicians' Preparticipation Physical Evaluation* (4th ed.). Leawood, Kan: American Academy of

Family Physicians. Available: https://nf.aafp.org/Shop/forms-downloads/preparticipation-physican-evaluation-monograph.

REFERENCES

Almquist JL, Valvovich McLeod T, Cavanna A, et al. (2004). Appropriate medical care for the secondary school-age athlete: Communication. Available: http://www.nata.org/sites/default/files/AppropriateMedCare4SecondarySchoolAgeAthlete.pdf.

Appenzeller T. (2000). *Youth Sport and the Law*. Durham, NC: Carolina Academic Press.

Beahm J. (2010). Max Gilpin school football death suit settles. Available: http://blogs.findlaw.com/injured/2010/09/max-gilpin-school-football-death-suit-settles.html.

Braun MJ, Powell JW, Ewing ME, Nogle SE, Branta CF. (2009). First aid and injury prevention knowledge of youth basketball, football, and soccer coaches. *Int J Coach Sci*. 3(1):55–67.

Casa DJ, Almquist JL, Anderson SA, Baker L, et al. (2013). The inter-association task force for preventing sudden death in secondary school athletics programs: Best practices recommendations. *J Athl Train*. 48(4):546–553.

Cohen A. (2009). High school to pay $15 million settlement to paralyzed wrestler. *Athletic Business*. 33(6):24.

Dunn LR, Ransone JW. (1999). Assessment of first aid knowledge and decision-making of high school coaches. *J Athl Train*. 34(3):267–271.

McCaskey AS, Biedzynski KW. (1996). A guide to the legal liability of coaches for a sports participant's injuries. *Seton Hall J. Sport L*. 6(1):8–97.

McLeod TCV, McGaugh JW, Boquiren ML, Bay RC. (2008). Youth sports coaches do not have adequate knowledge

regarding first-aid and injury prevention. *Applied Research in Coaching and Athletics Annual*. 23:130–146.

National Federation of State High School Associations. (n.d.). NFHS Learning Center (State Requirements). Available: http://www.nfhslearn.com/StatePricingRegs.aspx.

Osborne B. (2001). Principles of liability for athletic trainers: Managing sport-related concussion. *J Athl Train*. 36(3):316–321.

Podgers J. (2011). State of the Union: The nation's lawyer population continues to grow, but barely. *ABA Journal*. June issue. Available: http://www.abajournal.com/magazine/article/state_of_the_union_the_nations_lawyer_population_continues_to_grow_but_bare/.

Popke M. (2013). Supervision Quest. *Athletic Business*. 37(2):40–44.

Quandt EF, Mitton MJ, Black JS. (2009). Legal liability in covering athletic events. *Sports Health*. 1(1):84–90.

Ray R, Konin J. (2011). *Management Strategies in Athletic Training* (4th ed.). Champaign, Ill: Human Kinetics.

Wolohan JT. (2008). By the boards. *Athletic Business*. 32(10):28–32.

Wolohan JT. (2010). Settling scores. *Athletic Business*. 34(12):20–22.

Wong G. (2010). *Essentials of Sports Law* (2nd ed.). Santa Barbara, Calif: Praeger.

Sports-Injury Prevention

MAJOR CONCEPTS

Prevention of sports-related injuries must be a priority for everyone involved in organized sports, particularly coaches, physical educators, officials, administrators, sports medicine personnel, and athletes and their parents. This chapter describes the critical steps that must be taken to reduce the likelihood of injury. First, it differentiates between two major categories of injury risk factors—intrinsic (age, gender, skill) and extrinsic (equipment, environment, sport). It then distinguishes between two essential prevention strategies related to intrinsic factors: preparticipation physical examination (PPE) and physical conditioning with an emphasis on periodization of the training year. As is outlined in this chapter, periodization of the training program optimizes the performance objectives of the conditioning program while avoiding training-induced injuries. Finally, the chapter concludes with a description of the major factors to be considered to modify the common extrinsic risk factors related to sports injuries.

go.jblearning.com/PfeifferCWS

For a full suite of assignments and additional learning activities (indicated by the icons throughout the text), use the access code found in the front of your text. If you do not have an access code, you can obtain one at go.jblearning.com/PfeifferCWS.

There are more than 7.6 million students participating in organized secondary school athletics in the United States alone (Courson et al., 2013). Athletics add to the overall growth of an adolescent, and those involved in athletics with proper coaching learn lifelong lessons for success and demonstrate better academic achievements (National Federation of State High School Associations [NFHS], 2013). Therefore, it is in everyone's best interest to reduce the number of injuries and continue an athlete's ability to participate in athletics through a well planned, coordinated program of injury prevention. However, before such an endeavor can be effective, causative factors must be identified that contribute to injuries. Because of the risk and scope of sports injuries and the legal implications of catastrophic injuries, all parties involved including the athletic healthcare team, coaches, physical educators, officials, parents, and athletes should take steps to eliminate or at least reduce the risk and/or the severity of injury. At first, this may seem to be a simple process with regard to common sports injuries. For example, when a football running back collides with a linebacker and sustains a sprained knee ligament, the cause of the injury would seem to be related to the force of the collision or playing field conditions. (See **Figure 4.1**.) However, other factors may

FIGURE 4.1 In some sports, the cause of an injury might seem obvious, but other factors may also contribute.

have played a role in creating the injury, including the player's skill, age, strength-to-weight ratio, shoe type, fatigue, and/or previous injuries.

Causative Factors in Injury

Sports scientists have collected considerable information regarding injuries, and some have conducted research to identify causative factors. They propose two general categories of risk factors: extrinsic factors and intrinsic factors. Extrinsic factors include sports equipment, environment, type of activity, and playing field conditions. Intrinsic factors include age, gender, body size, history of injury, fitness, muscle strength (especially imbalances), ligamentous laxity, skill, psychological status, and perhaps even overall intelligence (Taimela, Kujala, & Osterman, 1990). For example, the type of injury has been linked with sex in collegiate athletes. Males had a higher acute injury rate compared to females, whereas female athletes had a higher rate of overuse injury than male athletes (Yang et al., 2012).

In an effort to delineate between extrinsic and intrinsic factors, several studies have sought to investigate risk factors for particular sports (Badgeley et al., 2013; Steinberg et al., 2012) and body area (Murphy et al., 2003). For example, Badgeley and colleagues (2013) identified two extrinsic factors including player–player contact and player–surface contact as the leading mechanisms of injury for high school football players. Conversely, young dancers' mechanisms of injury were more often related to intrinsic factors, including joint hypermobility, anatomical anomalies, and technique (Steinberg et al., 2012). Both investigations also found that "sport" position played a significant role in the type of injury, because dancers who spent more time *en pointe* had more injuries (Steinberg et al., 2012) and offensive football players suffered more heat strokes (Badgeley et al., 2013). In relation to body area, Murphy and colleagues (2003) identified five extrinsic and more than 18 intrinsic risk factors that typically lead to injury in the lower extremities. The extrinsic factors included playing surface, protective equipment, and level of competition and the intrinsic factors included tight or weak muscles, limb dominance, joint malalignments, poor muscle conditioning, and ineffective rehabilitation post injury. The upper extremities also had similar intrinsic risk factors associated with injury, including range of motion and strength differences between nondominant and dominant limbs, age, gender, and injury mechanism (fall, contact, no contact) (Hjelm et al., 2012; Sytema et al., 2010).

It is clear that not all of these factors can be eliminated or changed. However, it is certainly possible to reduce or eliminate problems such as poor or faulty equipment, inadequate muscle strength, poor skills, and training errors.

Intervention Strategies

It is the responsibility of all members of the athletic healthcare team to remain vigilant in an effort to identify causative factors before an injury occurs. Many of the extrinsic factors are more recognizable than intrinsic factors; however, there are techniques and methods that can be employed in an effort to prevent injury. For example, regular inspections of protective equipment and athletic facilities to alert personnel to potential problems and requiring physical exams before athletic participation are convenient ways to minimize risk. Regular inspection of equipment and facilities takes on different meaning depending on the type of personal or sports equipment and facilities. In regard to personal protective equipment, regular inspection often involves daily assessment of safety, whereas athletic facilities may only require regular inspection prior to competitions or monthly to semiannual inspection by maintenance staff.

Extrinsic Factors

Extrinsic risk factors for sports injuries include the practice/competition environment, facilities, protective equipment, and officiating and coaching. It is critical that coaching personnel, physical educators, athletic program administrators, and, if on staff, Board of Certification, Inc. (BOC)–certified athletic trainers monitor all of these factors in an effort to identify and eliminate any potential risks to the athletes.

Practice/Competition Environment

Whether outdoors or indoors, the environment must be assessed to determine whether it represents a potential health risk. This is particularly true when athletes exercise in conditions of high relative heat and humidity. It is important to remember that indoor activity can also pose a significant risk of thermal injury, particularly if the participant is not properly hydrated or if the indoor temperature and humidity are high.

Facilities

All sports facilities must be designed, maintained, and frequently inspected for the safety of the participants. Budgets and local building codes must be considered; however, these factors should never be allowed to supersede safety. Shared facilities are common; for example, football fields are often surrounded by an outdoor running track with field event equipment (landing pits for high jump and pole-vault, shot-put ring, etc.) either on the playing field or on the ends of the field. Baseball fields may be located next to a soccer field or perhaps even share some of the same ground. Regardless of the specific situation, it is critical that care be taken that all facilities meet the minimum requirements for safe participation. These include such things as integrity of safety fences, batting cages, location of dugouts in baseball and softball, type of bases used (breakaway or fixed), soccer goals that are correctly constructed and anchored, location of water and sanitation facilities, and emergency medical services (EMS) access routes. It is important for coaches, physical educators, and administrators to remember that several deaths have been attributed to faulty integrity of sports equipment, including soccer goals and batting cages.

With respect to indoor facilities, primary concerns center on lighting, playing surfaces, and room dimensions. Poor lighting may contribute to accidents resulting from poor visibility. A floor that is not cleaned regularly or that is improperly finished may become slippery and thus contribute to collisions. Budgetary constraints may mean that some gymnasiums are built that do not provide adequate space between the basketball baskets and the adjacent wall. This is especially common at the junior high and elementary school levels. In such situations, it is critical that protective padding be placed on the walls behind the basketball backboards to reduce players' collisions with the walls.

Locker rooms and shower facilities should be designed to enable participants to move around safely, with adequate ventilation, lighting, and nonskid floors. It is imperative that medical equipment such as whirlpool baths and other therapeutic modalities such as ultrasound or diathermy machines not be available for use in the locker room. Such equipment represents a significant safety risk and greatly increases the legal liability of the school.

Protective Equipment

Protective equipment plays a vital role in the prevention of injuries. This is especially true in sports such as tackle football, ice hockey, baseball, and softball. However, virtually all sports can benefit from the use of some form of safety equipment—even something as simple as shin guards in soccer or mouth guards in basketball or wrestling. Most equipment companies provide instructions for the fitting and maintenance of protective equipment, including helmets. National associations also govern the regular inspection and recertification of sport helmets and other protective equipment.

Intrinsic Factors

Many of the intrinsic factors are not as easily recognized, therefore athletes in high-risk sports must be informed of the potential hazards and prevention strategies. For example, in tackle football, players should be taught proper blocking and tackling techniques in an effort to avoid using the helmeted head as a weapon. It has been found that the incidence of serious head and neck injuries can be greatly reduced in this way (Cantu & Mueller, 2000). Athletes must also undergo a preparticipation physical exam (PPE) designed to identify risk factors associated with sports participation.

Historically, PPEs all too often consisted of a simple quick check of the major physiologic systems. As a result, in an effort to improve the overall quality of PPEs nationally, a consortium of professional medical organizations (the American Academy of Family Physicians [AAFP] in association with the American Academy of Pediatrics, the American College of Sports Medicine, the American Medical Society for Sports Medicine, the American Orthopaedic Society for Sports Medicine, and the American Osteopathic Academy of Sports Medicine) developed and published a comprehensive set of guidelines in 1992 titled "Preparticipation Physical Evaluation (PPE)." The guidelines have since been updated several times, and the latest monograph is the fourth edition, with the most recent version published in 2010 (AAFP et al., 2010).

Two factors have contributed to the development of these comprehensive guidelines regarding PPE. First, since the late 1970s there has been explosive growth in the number of sports participants. It has become ever more difficult for school officials to monitor the health of all of their incoming student athletes on an annual basis. Second, U.S. society has become more litigious in recent years and, as a result, coaches, educational institutions, and sports associations have a greater fear of being sued if and when an athlete is injured as a result of inadequate health screening. Therefore, the PPE is an important tool for all concerned. The primary purposes of the PPE are to identify preexisting risk factors for injury and to ascertain any injuries or diseases that may create problems for the student athlete as a result of sports participation.

Both the National Collegiate Athletic Association (NCAA) and the National Federation of State High School Associations (NFHS) have developed and implemented guidelines regarding medical evaluations of student athletes. The NCAA guideline requires that all student athletes receive a preparticipation physical examination (medical evaluation) at the initial entrance into the institution's athletic program. The initial PPE should include a comprehensive medical history, an immunization history (defined by the Centers for Disease Control and Prevention [CDC]), and a physical exam that includes an emphasis on musculoskeletal, neurological, and cardiovascular evaluation (NCAA, 2012). Division I and Division II schools also require new student athletes to complete a sickle cell solubility test prior to participation. Thereafter, an annual updated medical history is required unless an additional medical examination is warranted based on the updated history or a new medical condition (NCAA, 2012). The NFHS continues to recommend a yearly medical evaluation prior to participation in interscholastic sports. The medical evaluation needs to include a physical exam plus medical history questions about a personal and family history of cardiovascular disease and questions that focus on any history of neurologic or musculoskeletal problems (Kurowski & Chandran, 2000). The cardiac history is very important because 12–36 sudden cardiac deaths occur annually in youths under 18 years of age (Small, 2010). **Time Out 4.1** includes common questions used for cardiac medical history.

TIME OUT 4.1

Most Important Questions for Cardiac Medical History

1. Have you fainted/passed out (or nearly fainted) during or after exercise?
2. Have you ever had discomfort, pain, tightness, or pressure in your chest during exercise?
3. Does your heart ever race or skip beats during exercise?
4. Do you get lightheaded, feel more short of breath, or feel more fatigued than expected during exercise?
5. Has a doctor ever told you that you have any heart problems?
6. Has any family member or relative died of heart problems or had an unexpected or unexplained sudden death before age 50?
7. Does anyone in your family have a heart condition, such as hypertrophic cardiomyopathy or dilated cardiomyopathy, Marfan syndrome, arrhythmias, or long QT syndrome?

Source: Data from Small E. (2010). Sports participation. In: *Performing preventative services: A bright futures handbook.* Elk Grove Village, Ill.: American Academy of Pediatrics; Bernhardt DT, Roberts WO (eds.). (2010). *American Academy of Family Physicians' Preparticipation Physical Evaluation* (4th ed.). Leawood, Kan: American Academy of Family Physicians.

Considerable debate exists about the appropriate frequency of the PPE. Many school districts require a PPE on an annual basis. However, as costs for such procedures increase, there is pressure to amend this requirement to a format that would require an updated physical evaluation whenever an athlete reaches a new level of competition. It is also advised that whenever an athlete has sustained a more serious injury, such as head or spinal trauma, he or she should receive a complete physical evaluation by a physician prior to being allowed to return to participation. The AAFP, along with five other consensus groups, recommends that younger secondary-school-level athletes receive a comprehensive PPE biannually and at 2- to 3-year intervals for older athletes. In addition, it is recommended that a comprehensive PPE be administered for athletes entering either middle or high school or those transferring to a new school. Further, all athletes should receive annual updates that consist of a comprehensive medical history, along with assessment of height, weight, and blood pressure. Follow-up examination for any problem(s) detected in the history is also recommended (Bernhardt & Roberts, 2010).

A well administered PPE provides a great deal of information about the athlete's readiness for participation by evaluating cardiac, neurological, and musculoskeletal systems using history questions and physical examination techniques. Commonly identified conditions include congenital disorders such as spina bifida occulta (incomplete closure of the vertebral neural arch), absence of one of a paired set of organs (eye, kidney, testicle), postural problems such as abnormal spinal curvatures, or abnormalities of the upper and lower extremities, muscle imbalances, obesity, high blood pressure, cardiac defects or disorders of cardiac rhythm, respiratory conditions such as asthma, drug allergies, skin infections, and vision problems. Typical physical exams involve an assessment of general appearance, eyes, cardiac auscultation and blood pressure measurement, respiratory assessment, abdominal palpation, skin assessment, hernia check (males), and musculoskeletal assessment including range of motion, general strength, and joint laxity (Kurowski & Chandran, 2000). The results of the PPE will fall into one of three categories in relation to sports participation: An athlete will be cleared, not cleared, or in need of further evaluation for clearance. The most confusing area is when further evaluation is needed because this usually occurs from orthopedic injury, concussion, or systemic illness (mononucleosis). All athletes who receive an "in need of further evaluation" status must then be referred via a coordinated approach with the family and associated sports medicine team (Bernhardt & Roberts, 2010; Small, 2010).

Two basic PPE formats are currently recommended. One option is for the athlete's personal physician to perform the PPE in the physician's office; this is considered the ideal option. However, with the increased numbers of sports participants since the 1990s, the demand on the medical community for these services has increased. Obviously, as the costs of health care in general have escalated, so have the costs of undergoing a PPE. As a result, many young athletes simply cannot afford to visit a personal physician (assuming they have one) each year for such an evaluation. It has even been reported that the PPE is often the only time healthy children come into contact with a physician during the year (Koester, 1995). The other option accommodates groups of athletes in one session and is called the "coordinated medical team" approach (Bernhardt & Roberts, 2010).

Both formats can be highly effective tools for the delivery of the PPE. The advantages of the individual PPE performed by the athlete's personal physician include familiarity of the physician with the athlete's medical history and immediate access to medical records that include such information as immunization history. In addition, the athlete's personal physician in all likelihood has established a relationship of trust with the athlete that will allow for some discussion regarding health risk behaviors such as drug use and sexual behavior. In some situations, however, the office visit with a personal physician may not be possible. For example, when a group of athletes such as a basketball or volleyball team all need PPEs, the team physician may prefer to arrange for the team to be evaluated by a team of clinicians that include primary care physicians, as well as athletic trainers, physical therapists, exercise physiologists, and nutritionists. According to the AAFP, this approach to the administration of the PPE does have some advantages over the office visit format. These include possible cost savings to the athletes, as well as provision of PPEs to athletes who do not have a personal physician. To expedite the PPE process, it is recommended that the athlete complete a PPE medical history in advance of the actual evaluation. Whenever possible, the medical history should be done with the athlete and parent(s) or guardian(s) together.

Regardless of which type of PPE is employed, the procedure can provide valuable information relative to an athlete's readiness for participation. Coaches, as well as sports medicine personnel, must be aware of any pre-existing conditions that may make the athlete vulnerable to specific medical problems. A thorough medical history, including previous injuries, represents information essential to the welfare of the athlete.

Athletes with medical conditions such as asthma, diabetes, epilepsy, and drug allergies should be identified in case of subsequent injury or other problems related to their condition. Special populations need to be evaluated on the basis of injury risk factors that may not be present in the general population. It is recommended that special populations be evaluated by physicians who are familiar with the medical implications of each specific disorder. Obviously, all information obtained during a physical examination should be handled confidentially according to the Family Educational Rights and Privacy Act (FERPA) and Health Insurance Portability and Accountability Act (HIPPA).

Concern has been raised in the sports medicine community regarding the safety of participation for athletes who are missing one of a paired set of organs—for example, those who have only one eye, kidney, or testicle. This issue is addressed by the American Academy of Pediatrics (AAP), which has updated its policy statement that presents guidelines to physicians when considering an array of medical conditions that could affect sports participation (Rice, 2008). It is recognized that this is a complex issue and a number of variables must be considered, including the relative risk associated with a particular sport, for example, collision versus limited-contact sports. This may be an important factor when considering an athlete who is missing one of a paired set of organs. As such, the AAP policy statement gives a "qualified yes" to athletes who are missing one of paired organs such as kidneys or testicles based on the premise that with proper protection, participation even in collision and limited-contact sports may be acceptable assuming appropriate protective equipment remains in place (Rice, 2008). The AAP policy statement also recommends that if the physician advises against participation for medical reasons and the family chooses to allow the child to participate, a signed informed consent document, preferably in the parent's (or guardian's) own handwriting, be obtained that verifies they have been advised of the risks. Further, it is advised that the athlete also sign that he or she understands these risks (Rice, 2008).

WHAT IF?

A group of parents asks you, the soccer coach at the local high school, your recommendation for the best way to provide preseason physical evaluations that are required by the state high school association. What would you recommend?

Injury Prevention and Conditioning

An essential aspect of any injury prevention program is the optimal development of physical fitness in the athlete, because many of the intrinsic risk factors can be significantly modified as a result of effective conditioning programs. The old saying "You don't play sports to get fit, you get fit to play sports" is certainly valid today. The role of a coach cannot be underestimated when it comes to injury prevention via appropriate conditioning programs, because recent estimates indicate that young athletes can spend an average of 326 hours of practice time under the supervision of a coach, which is far more than the time spent with individual teachers, physicians, or other allied healthcare professionals (Koester, 2000).

School-age youth are encouraged to participate in 60 minutes or more of moderate to vigorous physical activity each day (Carter & Micheli, 2011; Faigenbaum, 2013). These activities should be developmentally appropriate, enjoyable, and safe. Children can safely participate in aerobic activities such as swimming, running, and bicycling, and increasing evidence indicates that strength training can also be a safe and effective activity for children. A significant body of evidence also exists supporting the premise that injury prevention strategies should focus on preseason conditioning and training throughout the season that includes strength, balance, and functional sport-specific skills (Abernathy & Bleakley, 2007). It has also been demonstrated that supervised training programs that focus on developing neuromuscular control of the lower extremities via plyometric, strengthening, and proprioception exercises can prevent anterior cruciate ligament (ACL) injuries.

The components of fitness include cardiorespiratory (aerobic) fitness, muscular strength and endurance, flexibility, and body composition (Fulton et al., 2004). Athletes in any sport are well advised to develop a total conditioning program that addresses all of these components and also nutrition. By so doing, the athlete benefits in two ways—improved performance and reduction in injuries. It is important to remember that a conditioning program consists of two primary components, general conditioning and sport-specific conditioning. The general conditioning program focuses on the major fitness components as listed earlier, whereas the sport-specific conditioning focuses on any aspect of a particular sport or activity that is unique to it. For example, the shoulder girdle and glenohumeral joint muscles in a tennis player need to receive special attention to avoid overuse injuries related to repetitive overhand strokes, which are inherent to the sport. To be effective, the conditioning program should allow for general conditioning and strength training on a year-round basis. This is best accomplished by incorporating the concept of **periodization** in the total conditioning program, which is the process of arranging training around specific goals and objectives with predetermined amounts of time spent training and resting. The purpose of periodization is to tailor the training program to meet the specific needs of the individual athlete to maximize performance at the time of competition(s) and at the same time to avoid training-related injury. The process of periodization is discussed later in this chapter.

Aerobic Fitness

Aerobic fitness, also commonly termed *aerobic power*, is defined as the amount of work that can be accomplished using the oxidative system of converting nutrients into energy. Aerobic power (VO_2 max) can be tested in the laboratory and is normally expressed in a formula that states the volume of oxygen consumed per unit of body weight per unit of time. The most common expression is in milliliters of oxygen per kilogram of body weight per minute ($mL/kg/min^{-1}$). A high VO_2 max is important for successful aerobic performance; however, other factors like good exercise economy, fuel substrate use (fat use vs. glucose use), muscle fiber type (Type I), and high lactate threshold can also contribute to successful performance in aerobic events (Reuter & Hagerman, 2008). Continuous activities with durations in excess of a minute or longer rely on aerobic power for muscle energy. However, athletes involved in short-duration anaerobic (energy production in the absence of oxygen) activities can benefit indirectly from having a high level of aerobic fitness. Poor physical fitness is a risk factor for sports-related injury in addition to having negative health consequences (Carter & Micheli, 2011). It has been shown that aerobic fitness can assist in injury avoidance by preventing general fatigue, which decreases muscle strength, reaction time, and neuromuscular coordination (Carter & Micheli, 2011).

In short, regardless of the sport, athletes who enter the season with a high level of aerobic fitness are less prone to injury. Aerobic fitness can be enhanced by regular participation in activities such as running, bicycling, swimming, cross-country skiing, inline skating, stair-stepping, and aerobic dance. However, any aerobic program needs to be tailored to the strengths, weaknesses, and needs of the individual youth athlete. As a general rule, training programs designed to improve aerobic fitness must overload the physiological system beyond what it is used to at rest or low levels of activity. Besides the mode or type of aerobic activity, four primary program design variables including training intensity, training frequency, exercise duration, and exercise progression are essential for success (Reuter & Hagerman, 2008). Training intensity is most commonly assessed by heart rate or perceived exertion. Percentages greater than 60% of maximal heart rate are most often used to elicit training adaptations (Reuter & Hagerman, 2008). Training intensity, frequency, and duration have unique interactions and vary in relation to one another. In training periods where intensity is high, the frequency and duration are typically lower. Typically, athletes who are not participating in an aerobic sport should include some sort of aerobic training at least 3 days per week. All training programs should be regularly progressed relative to the athlete's goals. A general rule is that frequency, intensity, and duration should not increase by more than 10% in one week (Reuter & Hagerman, 2008).

Anaerobic Fitness

Anaerobic fitness is defined as the amount of work that can be accomplished using the creatine-phosphate or glycogen systems (nonoxidative) to produce energy. Anaerobic training typically consists of resistance training, plyometrics, speed, agility, and speed-endurance training (Baechle, Earle, & Wathen, 2008). Our focus in this chapter is on resistance training programs. It is widely accepted that muscle and connective tissues (fascia, tendons, ligaments) undergo physiological and morphological changes, and tissue becomes stronger as a result of resistive exercise (Ratamess, 2008). Furthermore, bone density increases and bone becomes less susceptible to both trauma and fractures related to overuse. Improved muscle strength has also been found to be helpful in reducing the chances of musculoskeletal injury, because strengthening the muscles that surround a joint helps the athlete protect the joint from injury. Improving the strength ratio between opposing muscle groups, such as hamstrings and quadriceps, continues to be a generally well accepted technique for preventing injury.

periodization The organization of training into a cyclical structure to attain the optimal development of an athlete's performance capacities.

aerobic fitness The amount of work that can be accomplished using the oxidative system of converting nutrients into energy. Also commonly termed *aerobic power*.

anaerobic fitness The amount of work that can be accomplished using the creatine-phosphate or glycogen systems (nonoxidative) to produce energy.

Coaches and physical educators are encouraged to use the Youth Resistance Training position statement developed by the National Strength and Conditioning Association (NSCA) (Faigenbaum et al., 2009) when designing strength training programs for young athletes. Faigenbaum and colleagues (2009) reported that a properly designed and supervised resistance training program is relatively safe for youth and can enhance the muscular strength and power of youth, improve the cardiovascular risk profile of youth, improve motor skill performance and may contribute to enhanced sports performance of youth, increase a young athlete's resistance to sports-related injuries, help improve the psychosocial well-being of youth, and help promote and develop exercise habits during childhood and adolescence. Recent scientific evidence has also dispelled the following myths: 1) strength training will stunt the growth of children, 2) children will experience bone growth plate damage as a result of strength training, and 3) children cannot increase strength because they do not have enough testosterone (Faigenbaum, 2013).

A PPE prior to beginning resistance training programs is also recommended. Minimally, any youth with signs or symptoms suggestive of injury or disease or with known injury or disease should have a medical examination performed by their personal physician (Faigenbaum et al., 2009). Understanding the unique physical and psychosocial needs of children and adolescents is important in the instruction and supervision of resistance training programs. Coaches are encouraged to obtain this training through various resources offered by local and national youth sports coaching associations.

Muscle Strength, Power, and Endurance

Strength (resistance) training refers to a systematic program of exercises designed to increase an individual's ability to exert or resist force (Faigenbaum et al., 2013). *Muscle strength* is defined as the maximum amount of force that can be produced in one repetition, often referred to as a repetition maximum (1 RM). *Muscle power* can be defined as "the time rate of performing work" and can be expressed in the following equation:

$$\text{Power} = \text{Force} \times \text{Velocity}$$

In essence, for most athletic applications, muscle power is much more important to performance than is pure strength, because performance is most often time dependent. That is, to be effective, athletes need to be quicker and more explosive in their performance. *Muscle endurance*, in contrast to strength, is defined as the ability to sustain a muscle activity. Muscle strength, power, and endurance are typically improved with some form of resistance training, commonly called weight-training exercises. Each requires distinctly different types of training and must be based on a needs analysis (individual assessment; Baechle et al., 2008). Effective training is achieved by manipulation of the training volume, training intensity, training frequency, frequency and duration of rest (recovery) periods, exercise selection, and exercise order (Baechle et al., 2008).

Training volume represents the number of repetitions the weight is lifted, and it is simply calculated by multiplying the number of sets by the number of repetitions to calculate the total number of repetitions. However, another volume term may be more important: load-volume. *Load-volume* is defined as the total amount of weight lifted in a given workout session. The calculation includes the amount of weight lifted in addition to the repetitions and the sets (Baechle et al., 2008). The load-volume for an exercise where 3 sets of 10 repetitions (reps) using a progressively increasing weight value of 175, 185, and 195 pounds would be calculated by multiplying the total number of sets and repetitions by the amount of weight lifted in each set. Therefore, the first set would have 175 lbs × 10 reps = 1750 units, the second set 185 lbs × 10 reps = 1850 units, and the third 195 lbs × 10 reps = 1950 units, for a total training volume of 1750 + 1850 + 1950 = 5550 units. To calculate the average weight lifted per repetition per workout session, divide the load-volume by the training volume. As a general rule, the average weight will represent quality of work performed in the training session. The higher the average weight in a given workout is, the higher the true intensity for the total workout is (Baechle et al., 2008).

Training intensity for an exercise in a resistance training session is most often defined as the amount of weight lifted per repetition, thus a lift of 50 pounds for 10 repetitions (5 intensity units) would be one-half the intensity of a lift of 100 pounds for 10 repetitions (10 intensity units). Typically, intensity is represented as a percentage of the maximum amount of weight an athlete can lift only one time (1-repetition maximum, or 1-RM). The number of times (training volume) an exercise can be performed is inversely related to the load lifted. Sets completed with heavy loads will have fewer repetitions and sets completed with lighter loads will have more repetitions (Baechle et al., 2008). It is the training goal that dictates the training intensity. When the goal is primarily strength, the training intensity is usually ≥ 85% 1-RM, and when the goal is primarily endurance, the training intensity is usually ≤ 65% 1-RM (Baechle et al., 2008). Therefore, athletes training for more muscle strength will use heavier loads and fewer repetitions (~6–12 reps), whereas athletes training for more muscular endurance will use lighter loads and more repetitions (≥ 12 reps). Another way to define training intensity is in terms of velocity of movement; that is, the faster the repetition is performed, the higher the intensity (Baechle et al., 2008). Exercises performed at high speeds are commonly known as muscular power exercises. Explosive power training should be performed only under the guidance of someone with expertise in program design because inappropriate forms of explosive power training can result in injury.

Training frequency is the number of training sessions completed in a given period of time (Baechle et al., 2008). The most common way to express frequency is by recording the number of workouts per week or, in some cases, number of workouts per day. A number of factors must be considered when determining the training frequency. These include the training goal and current fitness status of the athlete, the training volume and intensity, and the specific type(s) of exercises planned (Baechle et al., 2008). As a general rule, most strength-training programs incorporate between three and five workouts per week. As programs become more sophisticated and complex, frequency can be increased; however, such programs usually divide the training into segments such as legs, trunk, or arms, so that each area is developed in separate workouts throughout the week. It is critical to remember that physiologically there are limits on how quickly muscle tissue can adapt to a given workout. In general, moderate- to high-intensity training requires 24 to 48 hours for full recovery to occur. The amount of time allowed for the body or specific muscle group to recover between training sessions is as important as the frequency of training sessions used in an athlete's program. Failure to consider these physiologic adaptations may result in overuse injuries related to the training program.

Rest periods are usually specific to the amount of time allowed between sets in a given training session. However, rest can be used in a broader sense to describe the recovery between training days. The rest period allowed between sets of lifts in a given training session can, to a great extent, determine the specific effects of that session. For example, when the goal of the training session is absolute strength or muscle power, the training intensity will be high; therefore, the recovery period between sets should be relatively long, for example, 2 to 5 minutes (Baechle et al., 2008). Conversely, when training for muscle endurance, the rest periods between sets can be shorter, sometimes as short as 15 to 30 seconds. Another way is to use a work-to-rest ratio to help calculate rest periods between sets. Because strength exercises are usually done for fewer repetitions and less time but need longer rest for muscle regeneration, the work-to-rest ratio is usually 1:5–1:12. For muscle endurance exercises the work-to-rest ratio is usually 1:1–1:3.

Exercise selection is choosing a resistance training exercise based on the movement and the muscular requirements for the sport. It is also based on athlete experience, available equipment, and amount of time available for training (Baechle et al., 2008). Exercises typically fall into two categories including core/structural and assistance. Core exercises are focused on the larger muscle group areas (hip, back, chest, and shoulder) and assistance exercises (upper arm, calves/shins, abdominals) are focused on smaller muscle groups. Core exercises are usually multi-joint exercises and assistance exercises are usually single-joint exercises that isolate a specific muscle or muscle group. When planning a training session, core exercises receive priority status and should be done when the young athlete is not fatigued (Baechle et al., 2008). Muscle balance must also be maintained within a program and both agonists and antagonists should be trained in relative proportion based on sport demand.

Exercise order refers to the sequence of the resistance training exercises within one training session (Baechle et al., 2008). Adaptation of muscles requires overload; however, fatigue of muscle groups too early in a resistance training session can hamper an athletes' ability to produce maximal force throughout the workout. There are several common methods for ordering resistance exercises in a training session, including alternating upper and lower body exercises, performing multi-joint exercises before single-joint exercise, alternating push and pull exercises, or performing pairs of exercises among agonists or agonist/antagonist groups (Baechle et al., 2008).

Flexibility

Flexibility is a measure of range of motion (ROM) of a joint or combination of joints (Baechle et al., 2008). Flexibility has both static and dynamic components. Static flexibility is the ROM of a joint and its surrounding muscles as a result of passive (nonvoluntary) movement; it is achieved by the passive manipulation of a joint by another person while the muscles are relaxed. Dynamic flexibility requires voluntary muscle activity and refers to the ROM during active motions; it is

flexibility The range of motion (ROM) in a given joint or combination of joints.

typically greater than static flexibility (Baechle et al., 2008). Baechle and colleagues (2008) note that several factors determine the ROM of a given joint, including age; sex; bone structure; tissue mass surrounding the joint; and extensibility of tendons, ligaments, muscles, and skin surrounding the joint. In general, flexibility decreases with age, although maintaining an active lifestyle may greatly reduce such changes. In addition, females have been found to be more flexible than their male counterparts. The temperature of the tissue, which is mediated by metabolism, local blood flow, and external (ambient) temperature, can also significantly affect joint ROM. Warmup exercises that increase heart rate above resting levels have been found to be effective in increasing tissue temperatures temporarily.

Static and dynamic stretching have been demonstrated to improve ROM at targeted joints; however, it takes significant amounts of time to create permanent or plastic changes in muscle and surrounding connective tissue (McHugh & Cosgrave, 2010). Elastic or nonpermanent changes in ROM are evident after both static and dynamic stretching protocols but these changes are time limited and the tissue will return to its normal resting length soon after the activity is discontinued (McHugh & Cosgrave, 2010). Therefore, stretching protocols can be valuable in improving ROM right after their application, but there is limited evidence that the application of brief stretching bouts prior to activity can actually improve ROM over the long term. Therefore, controversy exists among coaches, physical educators, and fitness professionals in regard to the effectiveness of stretching in reducing injury. However, a recent scientific review of research on the effectiveness of stretching on injury prevention has demonstrated that stretching before and after physical activity does not appreciably reduce all-injury risk but seems to reduce the risk of some injuries to muscles, ligaments, and tendons (Jamtvedt et al., 2010). The evidence suggests that long duration (12-week) stretching programs were more likely to reduce the chance of injury than any other application. Stretching activities were also determined to reduce the risk of bothersome soreness (Jamtvedt et al., 2010) when compared to exercisers who did not stretch as a part of their activity plan. Therefore, stretching activities before and after sports participation should be continued; however, its limitations in preventing all sports injury must be understood.

Stretching exercises can be grouped into four different categories based on the method employed. **Ballistic stretching** involves powerful contractions of muscles to force a joint to a greater ROM. A typical example is what is commonly called a standing toe touch where the athlete bends over and makes an effort to force the hands down to touch his or her toes. The athlete typically repeatedly extends the trunk back up and then forcefully bends downward again in an effort to get the hands closer to the feet. The muscles presumably being targeted in this stretch are the hamstrings as well as the trunk extensors (erector spinae). Ballistic stretching is not recommended because it triggers a muscle spasm that defeats the purpose of stretching (Baechle et al., 2008). **Static stretching**, as the name implies, involves moving a joint to a position where tension can be felt in the target muscles being stretched, with the position being sustained (held) for a time period ranging from 30 seconds up to a minute or longer (Baechle et al., 2008). The length of time to hold a static stretch has often been debated; however, static stretches need to be held at least 30 seconds for tissue length to appreciably change (McHugh & Cosgrave, 2010). **Dynamic stretching** involves mobility drills and places an emphasis on the sport activity that will be performed. Drills are used to mimic sport movements that an athlete may experience during participation and include taking joints through controlled full ROM activities designed to prepare the body for the activity to come (Baechle et al., 2008). Examples include knee lifts, marching drills, arms swings, and torso twists. The key difference between dynamic stretching and ballistic stretching is that there is no bouncing and full ROM of joints is used. **Proprioceptive neuromuscular facilitation (PNF)** involves a technique originally developed for use with patients suffering from paralysis. Essentially, PNF uses the body's proprioceptive system to stimulate muscles to relax. A variety of manual techniques have been developed, all using PNF principles. To use PNF techniques effectively, specialized training is required. However, basic PNF techniques for muscles that commonly benefit from stretching, such as the hamstrings, can be taught to nonmedical professionals and can be executed effectively by teammates during warmup prior to practice or competitions.

Research comparing these techniques continues to produce varied results in regard to the effectiveness of the different stretching techniques on improving ROM. Static stretching is probably the most effective, with effects lasting up to 90 minutes (Safran, Seaber, & Garrett, 1989). Evidence suggests that the best time to use static stretching is at the end of a workout when the tissues are warmer as a result of increased blood flow (Weaver, Moore, & Howe, 1996). Ballistic stretching is considered the least effective method and may even result in injury.

Body Composition

The dietary habits and body composition of any athlete, regardless of the sport, have a profound influence on overall performance and recovery from injury. Maintaining a healthy composition between lean mass (bones, muscles, organs) and fat mass is essential for optimal performance. Nutrition plays a very important role in maintaining appropriate body compositions for age, sex, and sport. The body responds to a conditioning program in a more positive manner when adequate amounts of essential nutrients are consumed in the daily diet. Two conditions on opposite spectrums of the body composition scales are affecting young sports participants in today's society. Many boys and girls are reporting to school-sponsored sports with body compositions over the recommended level for healthy maturation. There are also groups of young athletes who are exposed to an overemphasis on leanness, especially in performance sports like gymnastics, diving, and weight lifting. General statistics indicate that the rate of childhood obesity has more than doubled in children and tripled in adolescents since the early 1980s (CDC, 2013), and the occurrence of disordered eating in an attempt to control body size has also increased in both boys and girls since the early 2000s (National Institute of Mental Health, n.d.).

Periodization

As mentioned earlier in this chapter, a conditioning program should be designed to develop all fitness components to an optimal level, while at the same time allowing adequate intervals for rest and recovery. The periodization model includes several components that represent increasingly smaller units of training time. The largest unit is known as a macrocycle and typically encompasses 1 calendar year. The macrocycle can then be divided into smaller units known as mesocycles, which last from several weeks to a month or more, depending on the number of competitive seasons in the macrocycle. The smallest component is called a microcycle and consists of 2 to 4 weeks of training with fluctuations in intensity, duration, and frequency (Wathen, Baechle, & Earle, 2008). A mesocycle consists of several successive microcycles leading to a specific conditioning goal—for example, **hypertrophy** of leg muscles. A transition phase is a period of 2 to 4 weeks that occurs between training seasons or between successive mesocycles. During a transition phase, training is adjusted gradually, either to bring an athlete to peak fitness or to allow the athlete to rest and recover after the competitive season. In short, the function of the transition phase is to give the body time to recover from the previous cycle to be ready for the next segment of the training season.

The components of a macrocycle are determined by the number of competitive seasons contained in a given calendar year. For an athlete who competes in one sport per year with one competitive season, the macrocycle typically includes postseason, off-season, preseason, and in-season components. Conversely, for an athlete with more than one competition season in the same calendar year, there may be two or more groups of training cycles composed of an off season, preseason, and in season. This would be a model for the college-level football player who has two seasons each year, "spring ball" and the "regular season."

Periodized programs that include a goal of the development of muscle power have a preparatory period, normally placed in the off-season portion of the training year, which progresses the athlete through three distinct phases. These are hypertrophy/endurance, strength, and, finally, power. The rationale for this progression is based on sound science of muscle physiology. The purpose of the hypertrophy/endurance phase is to strengthen the connective tissue surrounding the muscle fibers and the tendons attaching the muscles to bones. This development of connective tissue enables the athlete to progress safely to the higher intensity training that follows without risking training-related injury. The intensity levels in the hypertrophy/endurance phase are generally low with higher volumes, which equates to more repetitions completed per session with a smaller percentage of the 1-RM weight for each exercise. The strength phase is next and represents a significant change in both the objectives and the protocol. The objective of this phase is obviously to increase the strength of the involved muscle groups. The exercise intensity levels are increased progressively to as high as 80% of 1-RM for

ballistic stretching Stretching technique that uses repetitive bouncing motions.

static stretching Passively stretching an antagonistic muscle by placing it in a maximal stretch and holding it there.

dynamic stretching A voluntary stretching technique that uses full-range, sport-like motions to warm up.

proprioceptive neuromuscular facilitation (PNF) Stretching techniques that involve combinations of alternating contractions and stretches.

passive stretching Movement of a joint through its ROM by someone other than the athlete.

hypertrophy Enlargement of a part caused by an increase in the size of its cells.

WHAT IF?

One of your cross-country runners, who suffers from chronic hamstring tightness, comes to you for advice on how to improve flexibility. What would you advise?

each exercise. Conversely, volume is decreased to several sets of 5-RM to 8-RM levels (five to eight repetitions per set; Wathen, Baechle, & Earle, 2008). The final phase, known as the power phase, focuses on the development of higher velocity movements. By definition, the intensity during the power phase is very high—often as high as 90% of 1-RM for each exercise, with lower training volumes.

A typical application of periodization for a two-season-per-year athlete can be illustrated with a collegiate-level football lineman preparing for the spring football season. During the preseason phase, he may spend the first 3 weeks working on muscle strength and hypertrophy (microcycle), followed by 3 weeks of high-intensity, low-volume strength training to develop muscle power (microcycle). These two microcycles constitute a mesocycle with the goal of improving lower extremity power. A transition phase is then inserted just prior to the onset of the competitive season. During the spring season, the player reduces his weekly frequency of weight training to maintain the gains achieved during the preseason phase. This player would have a similar program established for his preparation for the regular season as well, and it would build on the gains made in the program just described.

Athletic Trainers SPEAK Out

Courtesy of Skylar Richards, ATC, LAT, Head Athletic Trainer and Director of Sport Science, FC Dallas Football Club (Major League Soccer).

How do athletic trainers and strength and conditioning specialists work together to prepare athletes for the rigors of competition?

The three major tenants of athletic training are injury evaluation, injury rehabilitation, and injury prevention. Of these, injury prevention is often the most neglected but arguably the most important. Success in all areas in the continuum of care can be measured by comparison to previously measured parameters. Strength and conditioning (S&C) specialists can work with athletic trainers by collecting baseline performance measures, which provide starting and ending points for our continuum of care. These measures give AT the ability to use quantitative data to make better clinical decisions. Baseline biomechanical, cardiovascular, and neuromuscular/power measures also provide sport specific goals to quantifiably show what percentage of an athlete's ability has returned. Using data collected when the athlete was performing optimally allows us to decrease the likelihood of re-injuries (an injury to the same muscle fibers) or secondary injuries (injury caused by the deconditioning or compensation from the previous injury), which would lengthen time away from the field.

Although the AT and S&C can combine throughout the continuum of care, I believe the best two places for complete interaction are within the injury prevention and the injury rehabilitation phases. **Injury Prevention:** Typically prevention is left solely with S&C specialist. And although developing strength and power is important to prevention, it is an AT's knowledge of injury history, mechanisms of injury, and biology that can help elevate any prevention program. Adding unbalanced surfaces to typical strength exercises, altering joint positions to avoid overuse injury, or using individual injury history to customize the prevention approach are just some of the ways the AT can enhance a strength coach's prevention program. **Injury Rehabilitation:** I have seen this integration by two different systems. In one the S&C specialist oversees only the final phase of rehabilitation. This system is fairly common and easily integrated. However, the second, and preferable in my opinion, is to have the S&C involved in each phase in a planned fashion. **Phase 1:** AT—swelling control and table-based exercises, S&C—basic strength maintenance and pure aerobic energy system development. **Phase 2:** AT—joint range of motion, soft tissue mobility, and proprioception. S&C—progression of power development, stability, force absorption, and muscular endurance with glycolytic energy system development. **Phase 3:** AT—eccentric movement control, tissue monitoring with volume progression, and data comparison to baseline. S&C—sport-specific movements, advanced gait analysis, and energy system integration.

In the end, if we understand the health continuum as: prevention → healthy athlete → excess load → injury → rehabilitation → healthy athlete, then we realize that ATs and S&Cs are a team and cooperation will result in the best outcomes for return to play and the rigors of competition.

—Skylar Richards, MS, ATC, LAT

Skylar Richards is the Head Athletic Trainer and Director of Sport Science Football Club Dallas (Major League Soccer)

REVIEW QUESTIONS

1. Differentiate between intrinsic and extrinsic types of causative factors leading to sports injury. Provide several examples of both types.

2. List four types of intrinsic factors related to sports injury that a medical doctor might identify during a preparticipation physical evaluation.

3. What are two disadvantages to using an individual format for a preparticipation physical evaluation?

4. List the components of fitness as described in the chapter.

5. Briefly describe the relationship between volume, intensity, and frequency of training as they relate to periodization.

6. Describe how exercise order and exercise selection can influence the outcomes of resistance training programs.

7. Define the terms *macrocycle, mesocycle,* and *microcycle* as they relate to a sports training program.

8. True or false: According to the chapter, athletes, regardless of sport, can benefit from possessing a relatively high level of aerobic fitness.

9. What is the meaning of the acronym ROM?

10. Discuss the advantages and disadvantages of the four categories of stretching exercises.

REFERENCES

Abernethy L, Bleakley C. (2007). Strategies to prevent injury in adolescent sport: a systematic review. *Br J Sports Med.* 41:627–638.

American Academy of Family Physicians in association with the American Academy of Pediatrics, the American College of Sports Medicine, the American Medical Society for Sports Medicine, the American Orthopaedic Society for Sports Medicine, and the American Osteopathic Academy of Sports Medicine. (2010). Preparticipation physical evaluation: History form. Available: http://www.aap.org/en-us/professional-resources/practice-support/Documents/Preparticipation-Physical-Exam-Form.pdf.

Badgeley MA, McIlvain NM, Yard EE, Fields SK, Comstock RD. (2013). Epidemiology of 10,000 high school football injuries: Patterns of injury by position played. *J Phys Act Health.*10(2):160–169.

Baechle TR, Earle RW, Wathen D. (2008). Load assignment. In Baechle TR, Earle RW (eds.), *Essentials of Strength Training and Conditioning* (3rd ed.). Champaign, Ill: Human Kinetics. pp. 381–411.

Bernhardt DT, Roberts WO (eds.). (2010). *Preparticipation Physical Evaluation* (4th ed.). Leawood, Kan: American Academy of Family Physicians.

Cantu RC, Mueller FO. (2000). Catastrophic football injuries: 1977–1998. *Neurosurgery.* 47(3):673–677.

Carter CW, Micheli LJ. (2011). Training the child athlete: physical fitness, health and injury. *Br J Sports Med.* 45:880–885.

Centers for Disease Control and Prevention. (2013). Childhood obesity facts. Available: http://www.cdc.gov/healthyyouth/obesity/facts.htm.

Courson R, Goldenberg M, Adams K. (2013). Inter-association consensus statement on best practices for sports medicine management for secondary schools and colleges.

Available: http://www.nata.org/sites/default/files/SportsMedicineManagement.pdf.

Faigenbaum AD, Kraemer WJ, Blimkie CJ, Jeffreys I, Micheli LJ, Nitka M, Rowland TW. (2009). Youth resistance training: Updated position statement paper from the National Strength and Conditioning Association. *J Strength Cond Res.* 23(5 Suppl):S60–79.

Faigenbaum AD. (2013). Youth strength training: Facts and fallacies. American College of Sports Medicine. Available: http://www.acsm.org/access-public-information/articles/2012/01/13/youth-strength-training-facts-and-fallacies.

Fulton JE, Garg M, Galuska DA, Rattay KT, Caspersen CJ. (2004). Public health and clinical recommendations for physical activity and physical fitness: Special focus on overweight youth. *Sports Med.* 34(9):581–599.

Hjelm N, Werner S, Renstrom P. (2012). Injury risk factors in junior tennis players: a prospective 2-year study. *Scand J Med Sci Sports.* 22:40–48.

Jamtvedt G, Herbert RD, Flottorp S, Odgaard-Jensen J, Håvelsrud H, Barratt A, Mathieu E, Burls A, Oxman AD. (2010). A pragmatic randomised trial of stretching before and after physical activity to prevent injury and soreness. *Br J Sports Med.* 44:1002–1009.

Koester MC. (1995). Refocusing the adolescent preparticipation physical evaluation toward preventative health care. *J Athl Train.* 30(4):352–360.

Koester MC. (2000). Youth sports: A pediatrician's perspective on coaching and injury prevention. *J Athl Train.* 35(4):466–470.

Kurowski K, Chandran S. (2000). The preparticipation athletic evaluation. *Am Fam Physician.* 61(9):2683–2690.

McHugh MP, Cosgrave CH. (2010). To stretch or not to stretch: the role of stretching in injury prevention and performance. *Scand J Med Sci Sports.* 20:169–181.

Murphy DF, Connolly DAJ, Beynnon BD. (2003). Risk factors for lower extremity injury: A review of the literature. *Br J Sports Med.* 37:13–29.

National Collegiate Athletic Association. (2012). *2012–13 NCAA Sports Medicine Handbook.* Indianapolis, Ind: Author.

National Federation of State High School Associations. (2013). The case for high school activities. Available: https://www.nchsaa.org/intranet/downloadManagerControl.php?mode=getFile&elementID=7680&type=5&atomID=9981.

National Institute of Mental Health. (n.d.). Eating disorders among children. Available: http://www.nimh.nih.gov/statistics/1eat_child.shtml.

Ratamess NA. (2008). Adaptations to anaerobic training programs. In: Baechle TR, Earle RW (eds.), *Essentials of Strength Training and Conditioning* (3rd ed.). Champaign, Ill: Human Kinetics. pp. 93–118.

Reuter BH, Hagerman PS. (2008). Aerobic endurance and exercise training. In: Baechle TR, Earle RW (eds.), *Essentials of Strength Training and Conditioning* (3rd ed.). Champaign, Ill: Human Kinetics. pp. 490–504.

Rice SG. (2008). Medical conditions affecting sports participation. *Pediatrics.* 121:841–848.

Safran MR, Seaber AV, Garrett WE. (1989). Warm-up and muscular injury prevention: An update. *Sports Med.* 8(4):239–249.

Small E. (2010) *Performing preventative services: A bright futures handbook.* Elk Grove Village, Ill.: American Academy of Pediatrics.

Steinberg N, Siev-Ner I, Pelegi S, Dar G, Masharas Y, Zeev A, Hershkovitz, I. (2012). Extrinsic and intrinsic risk factors associated with injuries in young dancers aged 8–16 years. *J Sports Sci.* 30(5):485–495.

Sytema R et al. (2010). Upper extremity sports injury: Risk factors in comparison to lower extremity injury in more than 25,000 cases. *Clin J Sport Med.* 20:256–263.

Taimela S, Kujala UM, Osterman K. (1990). Intrinsic risk factors and athletic injuries. *Sports Med.* 9(4):205–215.

Wathen D, Baechle TR, Earle RW. (2008). Periodization. In: Baechle TR, Earle RW (eds.), *Essentials of Strength Training and Conditioning* (3rd ed.). Champaign, Ill: Human Kinetics. pp. 507–522.

Weaver J, Moore CK, Howe WB. (1996). Injury prevention. In: Caine DJ, Caine CG, Lindner KJ (eds.), *Epidemiology of Sports Injuries* (Chapter 26). Champaign, Ill: Human Kinetics.

Yang J, Tibbetts AS, Covassin T, Cheng G, Nayar S, Heiden E. (2012). Epidemiology of overuse and acute injuries among competitive collegiate athletes. *J Athl Train.* 47(2):198–204.

The Psychology of Athletes and Sports Injury

MAJOR CONCEPTS

Sports injuries can be caused by more than physical trauma and often involve more than damaged ligaments, tendons, and muscles. An athlete's mental health prior to injury and his or her perception of and reaction to an injury will play a major role in the recovery process. This chapter introduces the reader to seminal research on the psychology of athletes and presents the psychological effects of injury and rehabilitation on athletes. It begins with an examination of primary personality variables: trait anxiety, general personality, and locus of control. The relationship between athletes and their social environment is examined, with a focus on how participation in athletics along with normal life stressors can predispose athletes to physical or mental exhaustion and sports injury. The chapter also gives special attention to the effects of competitive stress on the adolescent athlete and the role of coaches and parents in reducing the negative effects of sport participation. Research into depression and the disorder known as seasonal affective disorder (SAD) is also presented, along with their implications for the athletic community. The chapter concludes with an in-depth discussion of eating disorders as they affect today's athletes. It discusses anorexia nervosa, bulimia nervosa, and muscle dysmorphia in terms of early warning signs and recommended treatments.

go.jblearning.com/PfeifferCWS

For a full suite of assignments and additional learning activities (indicated by the icons throughout the text), use the access code found in the front of your text. If you do not have an access code, you can obtain one at go.jblearning.com/PfeifferCWS.

Phenomena such as environmental conditions, type of playing surface, quality of protective equipment, player skill, years of experience, relative muscle strength, and type of sport are all identified as being possible contributors to, or risk factors for, injury. Implementation of strategies designed to reduce or eliminate the impact of these risk factors represents a major responsibility of all those involved in the administration of organized sports programs. However, despite significant improvements in coaching and physical conditioning techniques, rule changes, better officiating, advances in protective equipment technology, and enhanced facilities, injuries still occur. Although this phenomenon may be partly a result of increased numbers of participants and improved systems for reporting injuries, acute and chronic injuries continue to be a significant threat to a large percentage of adolescent and collegiate athletes.

A wide variety of psychological factors might affect the mental and physical health of an individual, and early research investigating the relationship between psychological stress and disease in the general population indicated that individuals experiencing high levels of stress were more prone to illness (Holmes & Rahe, 1967). In an effort to relate these findings to athletes, sports scientists have been investigating the possible relationship between psychological variables and sports injuries (**Figure 5.1**). For example, there is evidence that high levels of stress in athletes can result in physical fatigue and reduced peripheral vision, either of which could conceivably increase the chances of becoming injured (Hanson, McCullugh, & Tonymon, 1992; Perna & McDowell, 1995). Vetter and Symonds (2010) have also reported correlations between injury and physical exhaustion in collegiate athletes. In a survey of 149 college athletes, females had a higher percentage of acute and chronic injuries when compared to their male counterparts, and females reported exhaustion occurring frequently (30%) or sometimes (66%) while males reported exhaustion occurring frequently (23%) or sometimes (59%) during the competitive season. The researchers concluded that the higher percentage of injuries in females was likely due to the increased occurrence of fatigue and exhaustion. A recent report (Malinauskas, 2010) also indicated differences in the psychosocial variables between collegiate athletes suffering major athletic injuries (time loss greater than 1 week) and those suffering minor athletic injuries (time loss less than 1 week). Major injuries were associated with greater perceived stress and less perceived social support and life satisfaction. Therefore, perceived stress, levels of social support, and fatigue may all be connected to sports injury and need to be addressed because they present problems for athletes in their sport and life.

However, it is important to understand there are very complex interactions between life situations, personality, and current situations so research typically seeks to define relationships between variables in an effort to improve treatment and recognition. To help better understand these relationships, the psychological attributes of athletes are divided into two general categories—personality variables and psychosocial variables.

Personality Variables

According to Matthews, Deary, and Whiteman (2003), the idea of personality traits may be as old as human language. Trait theory assumes that individual personalities are composed of broad dispositions that are stable over time and influence behavior (Matthews et al., 2003). Traits are permanent personality characteristics, whereas personality states are temporary changes in personal characteristics. The types of trait personalities have been debated in the scientific literature for years; however, five personality traits are consistently used to capture the general dimensions of trait personality. These five general traits are extraversion, agreeableness, conscientiousness

FIGURE 5.1 Competition can create a great deal of psychological stress.

(dependability), neuroticism (emotional stability), and openness (Goldberg, 1990). In relation to sports participation, it is widely accepted there is no one perfect definition of which personality traits lead to sport choice (Fleming, 2009). There are conflicting reports in regard to personality and sport choice. The most common belief is that extroverted athletes typically choose team sports whereas introverted athletes often choose individual sports. Eagleton, McKelvie, and deMan (2007) provided evidence for these observations; however, Dobersek and Bartling (2008) found the contrary. Therefore, personality traits are very complex and might only be part of what determines sports disposition.

In relation to sports injury, both state and trait aspects of personality become important for the athlete. It is the complex interaction of these personality aspects that is likely to cause injury. For example, athletes who tend to be anxious and feel they do not have strong resources for success participating in a sporting event with high demands and big consequences may be more likely to suffer injury (Kleinert, 2002). Williams and Andersen (1998) developed the stress-injury model which integrates state and *trait variables* into the occurrence of injury. According to the model, when a potentially stressful situation is recognized, there will be a stress response that is influenced by a cognitive appraisal (e.g., it is it serious) and physiological/attentional changes (e.g., heart rate and focus). When the stress response results in an appraisal of harm and there are physiological changes that cause performance decrements, then an injury is likely. Williams and Anderson (1998) proposed that an athlete's personality trait, history of stressors, and coping resources determined whether their response to the stressful situation would result in injury. Three areas of personality including trait anxiety, locus of control, and self-concept are often explored in their relation to the stress response. **Trait anxiety** is associated with the personality trait of neuroticism (emotional stability) and is connected with a person's general disposition or tendency to perceive certain situations as threatening and to react with an anxiety response (physiological and emotional; Matthews et al., 2003). Sports injury trait anxiety is the widely indefinite concern or worry about sustaining an injury in sport (Kleinert, 2002). **Locus of control** has to do with people's belief, or lack thereof, that they are in control of events occurring in their lives. Two general types of individuals have been identified—those with an external locus of control and those with an internal locus of control. The former feel they have very little control over events in their lives. These people believe factors such as destiny, luck, or fate determine life events. Individuals with an internal

locus of control feel they are responsible for what happens to them—they are in charge. Research to date that has attempted to link incidence and/or severity of injury to locus of control has yielded inconclusive results. There is evidence that such connections, if they do exist, may be sport specific—that is, locus of control and trait anxiety may play a role in injury in only certain types of sports. For example, Petrie (1993) found a positive correlation between trait anxiety and days missed because of injury for intercollegiate football players. Conversely, track and field athletes demonstrated no evidence of a relationship between injury and locus of control (Hanson et al., 1992). **Self-concept** may also be a risk factor with regard to injury. Athletes with low self-concept have been found to demonstrate a statistically significant relationship with sports injuries (Lamb, 1986). For example, Lamb established a strong negative correlation (–0.917) between self-concept and frequency of injury among a group of female collegiate field hockey players. Although these findings support the theory that low self-concept functions as a significant risk factor for athletic injury, researchers are still trying to adequately define a true relationship (Kleinert, 2002). Apparently, athletes with a low self-concept are less able to deal effectively with the high stress of competition, especially where there is pressure to succeed. This inability to cope may even result in behavior that leads to injury. In extreme cases, being injured may become an attractive alternative to participation, because it gives the athlete a legitimate excuse to avoid playing. The prudent coach should consider the administration of a screening test such as the Tennessee Self-Concept Scale (TSCS) to identify athletes with low self-concept. Coaches lacking experience in the administration of these tests should seek the services of a trained professional, such as a sports psychologist, school psychologist, or guidance counselor. Athletes identified as having a low self-concept may be aided by a variety of intervention strategies. There is evidence that self-concept can be raised through a program of individualized counseling and exercise. Obviously, a coach should attempt any sort of counseling with extreme caution to avoid making a

trait anxiety A general disposition or tendency to perceive certain situations as threatening and to react with an anxiety response.
locus of control People's belief, or lack thereof, of being in control of events occurring in their lives.
self-concept The image of the self that is constructed from the beliefs one holds about oneself.

WHAT IF?

You are coaching wrestling in a northern Michigan high school. It is early December, and one of your athletes comes to you complaining of chronic fatigue, a craving for sweets, and a loss of interest in the sport. Could these complaints be symptoms of a psychological disorder, and if so, what would you do to help this athlete?

bad situation worse. Once identified, athletes with low self-concept should be advised to consult a professional sports psychologist, a guidance counselor, or even a clinical psychiatrist for help. The coach must exercise good judgment and tact to avoid labeling an athlete in a negative manner.

Psychosocial Variables

Although overall correlations between general personality traits and injuries have been weak, more convincing findings have been produced from research examining the relationship between psychosocial factors (e.g., social environment, life stress, and mood) and injury rates (Wiese-Bjornstal, 2010). We live in a time of changing social environments as a result of increased economic and family stresses; therefore, it is important to consider these ever-changing psychosocial variables in the injury equation. Specifically, attention has been given to studying the effects of stressful life events on athletes. Stressful life events have been defined as positive or negative episodes that usually evoke some adaptive or coping behavior or significant change in the ongoing life pattern of the individual (Holmes & Rahe, 1967). This theory holds that life events can be very stressful—even those most people would consider positive, such as getting married, taking a vacation, or winning the lottery. Researchers have endeavored to study the effects of life events on different populations, including athletes. A variety of questionnaires has been developed, including the Social Readjustment Rating Scale (SRRS), the Social and Athletic Readjustment Rating Scale (SARRS), the Life Event Scale for Adolescents (LESA), the Life Event Questionnaire (LEQ), the Life Event Survey for Collegiate Athletes (LESCA), and the Athletic Life Experience Survey (ALES).

The stress-injury model proposed by Williams and Andersen (1998) indicated that two psychosocial variables, a history of stressors and coping resources, play a significant role in the cognitive appraisal and the

physiological responses to stressful situations and that they may both influence the occurrence of injuries. A number of studies have revealed relationships (correlations) between stressful life events and sports injuries (Andersen & Williams, 1988; Hanson et al., 1992; Ivarsson & Johnson, 2010; Lamb, 1986; Malinauskas, 2010; Petrie, 1993; Williams & Andersen, 1998). For example, recent research on elite soccer players in Sweden revealed that injured players had higher levels of self-blame, susceptibility to stress, "feeling other's pain," somatic anxiety symptoms, and trait irritability (Ivarsson & Johnson, 2010). Malinauskas (2010) has also demonstrated an association between the severity of injury and psychosocial factors. Athletes with major injuries (time loss greater than 21 days) had greater perceived stress and lower life satisfaction when compared to those with a minor injury (time loss less than 1 week; Malinauskas, 2010). Evidence suggests that when an athlete is experiencing significant personal changes, especially those seen as negative, the chances of injury increase. As was the case with determination of self-concept status, the coaching staff may find it helpful to assess the life-stress status of athletes prior to the beginning of the season and on a follow-up basis. In this way, athletes who are at high risk—that is, those with high life-stress scores—can be identified and referred to a counselor in an effort to improve coping skills. There is evidence that athletes with a higher degree of such skills are less likely to be injured (Hanson et al., 1992). The administration and interpretation of psychometric tests are most effectively conducted by sports psychologists and other trained professionals. Coaching personnel should avoid the temptation to play amateur psychologist with athletes because they may only make a bad situation worse.

In addition to stressful life events, depression and seasonal affective disorder (SAD) may be causes of injury. In the student population, women are twice as likely to experience depression as men, and 1 in 10 students will suffer from depressive symptoms in a 1-year timeframe (National Collegiate Athletic Association [NCAA], 2012). Data also indicate that student athletes experience depressive symptoms and illness at similar or increased rates than do nonathlete students (NCAA, 2012). Even though athletes typically have higher levels of self-esteem and social connectedness when compared to nonathletes, it is interesting to note that these positive psychosocial attributes were not significant deterrents to depressive symptoms; therefore, coaches, parents, and athletic trainers need to be aware of depressive symptoms and provide athletes with referrals for help as necessary (Armstrong & Oomen-Early, 2009). Athletes may experience events that possibly trigger or even worsen their emotional health, including concussions, poor sports performance, lack of playing time, being cut from the team, and/or injuries

TABLE 5.1

DEPRESSIVE SIGNS AND SYMPTOMS

- Decreased performance in school or sports
- Noticeable restlessness
- Significant weight loss or weight gain
- Changes in appetite nearly every day

Individuals might express:
- Depressed, sad, or "empty" mood for most of the day and nearly every day
- Indecisiveness and difficulty concentrating
- Feeling sad or unusually crying
- Lack of or loss of interest or pleasure in activities that were once enjoyable (hanging out with friends, practice, school, or sex)
- Frequent feelings of worthlessness, low self-esteem, hopelessness, helplessness, or inappropriate guilt
- Recurrent thoughts of death or thoughts about suicide

Source: Data from National Collegiate Athletic Association. (2012). *Sports Medicine Handbook (2012–2013).* Indianapolis, Ind: Author. pp. 80.

with time loss (NCAA, 2012). Regarding injuries with time loss greater than 1 week, Appaneal and collagues (2009) reported that male and female athletes who were tested 1 week post-injury had higher depressive symptom scores than healthy athletes; however, these differences were no longer present after 1 month or 3 months. Therefore, athletic trainers treating athletes during the acute and subacute phases of an injury may play a valuable role in the recognition of depressive symptoms.

Depression

Identification, referral, and treatment for depression or other mental illnesses are extremely important, yet may be inhibited within athletic culture, because physical injury is easier to detect, history and tradition prevent change, athletic departments may not have adequate resources, and the high-profile status of athletes may prevent them from reporting symptoms. Team dynamics also may be a factor in the recognition of depression, because seeking help is often seen as a sign of weakness or failure rather than a sign of strength (NCAA, 2012).

Depressive illnesses come in different forms and the number, severity, and duration of symptoms vary. Depression is more than the "blues" or other letdowns related to daily hassles (NCAA, 2012). Major depression, dysthymia, and bipolar disorder are the most common forms of depression. **Major depression** is more severe but is often short term, **dysthymia** is less severe and more chronic, and **bipolar disorder** is characterized by manic episodes. **Table 5.1** lists common signs and symptoms of depression. Athletics departments are encouraged to stay in tune with student athletes' mental well-being

by including mental health checkups, especially around high-risk times such as the loss of a coach or teammate, significant injury, being cut from the team, or other catastrophic events. Mental health checkups can be as simple as providing empathetic listening and encouraging student athletes to talk about situations that may trigger depressive episodes. Several self-help strategies can also be provided to student athletes in an attempt to improve mild depressive symptoms. **Time Out 5.1** lists several recommended self-help strategies.

Developing a mental health action plan is important, especially for collegiate athletic departments, because many athletes experience **adjustment disorders**. Otherwise, fostering relationships with mental health resources on campus or within the school district or local community enables coaches, physical educators, and athletic trainers to develop an effective referral plan for student

major depression Characterized by a combination of five or more symptoms and noticeable changes in usual functioning like sleep, eating, work, or school.

dysthymia Characterized by nondisabling depressive symptoms that are chronic but do not cause changes in usual functioning.

bipolar disorder A manic-depressive illness that involves cycling mood swings from major depression to mania where individuals feel full of energy.

adjustment disorders A disorder in which mild depressive or anxiety symptoms occur in response to specific events.

TIME OUT 5.1

Self-Help Strategies to Improve Mild Depressive Symptoms

- Increase positive thinking
- Let family, friends, coaches, and athletic trainers help you
- Break large tasks into smaller ones; set realistic goals
- Eat regular and nutritious meals
- Engage in regular and adequate sleep habits
- Reduce consumption of alcohol
- Participate in activities that make you feel better

Source: Data from National Collegiate Athletic Association. (2012). *Sports Medicine Handbook (2012–2013).* Indianapolis, Ind: Author. pp. 79–80.

---

athletes (NCAA, 2012). For more advanced screening, it is recommended that sports medicine teams use the Center for Epidemiological Studies Depression Scale Revised (CESD-R) published by the National Institute for Mental Health (NIMH). The CESD-R is free to use and available at http://cesd-r.com. However, caution must be used when interpreting any screening tools; it is essential that a licensed professional (physician, psychiatrist, counselor) be consulted if there is any concern that an athlete may be suffering from depression.

Seasonal Affective Disorder

Seasonal affective disorder (SAD) is a psychiatric disorder that affects the general population, including athletes, primarily in the fall and winter seasons. Previously, SAD was classified as a mood disorder. However, SAD is a distinct category within major depressive disorder and is linked to the colder months of fall and winter, when there is less sunlight. SAD has been linked to a wide array of symptoms, including a loss of physical capacity and energy, increased appetite (especially carbohydrate craving), decreased libido, hypersomnia (excessive sleep or drowsiness), anhedonia (lack of interest in normally pleasurable activities), and impaired social activity (Rosen et al., 1996).

Rosen and colleagues (1996) studied 68 NCAA Division I ice hockey players to ascertain the frequency of SAD. Specifically, these players were all located in northern latitudes, where there is decreased daylight in the fall and winter months. The players were studied for one complete season, during which time they were given a set of questionnaires designed to identify players exhibiting either symptomatic or subsyndromal SAD (a mildly dysfunctional state, which is insufficient in intensity to meet criteria for a major depressive disorder; Kasper et al., 1989). The findings of this research were alarming: 22 of the 68 players in the study were found to be suffering from either symptomatic SAD (n = 56 [9%]) or subsyndromal SAD (n = 16 [25%]).

Considering the fact that many of the symptoms of this disorder may negatively affect performance or, worse, predispose some to injury, it seems prudent for parents, coaches, and athletic trainers to become familiar with the specific signs and symptoms of SAD. Although subsyndromal SAD represents a less severe form of the affliction, the potential for problems is high given that athletes may fail to seek medical attention. Accurate diagnostic tests are available for SAD, and anyone exhibiting such symptoms as described herein should be referred to a specialist for evaluation. Regarding treatment, Rosen and colleagues (1996) report promising results using light therapy (phototherapy).

Competitive Stress and the Child/Adolescent

Sports are one of the most popular achievement domains for children and adolescents (Treasure, 2001). It is probable that the majority of children, even today, get involved in sports for recreational and social reasons. However, it is also true that the intensity of competition is being increased drastically in some sports at exceedingly early ages. Sports such as women's gymnastics, tennis, figure skating, bicycle motocross (BMX), and professional skateboarding routinely produce regional and national champions under the age of 16 years. Because many young athletes perceive losing as failure and winning as success, many professionals in psychology and sociology have raised serious concerns regarding the psychological impact of competition on youth (Nash, 1987).

The pressure to win can come from parents, coaches, peers, sponsors, and even the media. Recent research by Jowett and Cramer (2010) has demonstrated that athletes' physical self-concept (skill set and appearance) is more influenced by their relationship quality with their coaches rather than their relationship quality with their parents. However, parents are highly involved and visible in youth sports, and parents can influence their children positively and negatively because they can also provide immediate and specific feedback (Frederick & Eccles, 2004). Overall, an athlete's physical self-concept was more markedly reduced if conflict occurred between the athlete-coach and the athlete-parent (Jowett & Cramer, 2010). In addition to physical self-concept, athletes' fear

Athletic Trainers SPEAK Out

Courtesy of John Erwin, MS, ATC, LAT, Assistant AD for Sports Medicine, Southeastern Louisiana University.

Why is addressing the psychology of injury important in the rehabilitation and recovery process? How can an AT best do this?

As an athletic trainer, I recognize the importance of not only addressing the injury for my student-athletes but also addressing their mentality towards the injury and how it may affect them. This is a vital piece of the recovery process. Many times, in my setting, it may be the first time the athletes have ever been injured. Many questions can come to mind such as: How long will I be hurt? Can I play? Can I practice? Etc. Many times, this will be the fear of the unknown. As their athletic trainer, I do my best to install a sense of confidence within them. Not only confidence in themselves but also confidence in me and my staff's ability to return them to play and assist them through the injury. This can be done in a variety of ways. More than anything exuding a confident and energetic tone when speaking with them and rehabbing them helps. Constant positive feedback can go miles when dealing with the psyche of an athlete. Maintaining their focus on small goals, small victories and showing them that they are in fact making progress towards being "normal" again goes a long way. Along with this, many times I will ask about class work, family, friends, current events, sports, or any other subject they may be able to relate to in order to keep their mind diverted from their condition. We do not just rehab musculoskeletal injury, we also rehabilitate the mind itself.

—John Erwin, MS, ATC, LAT

John Erwin is the Assistant Athletic Director for Sports Medicine at Southeastern Louisiana University.

Courtesy of John Erwin, MS, ATC, LAT, Assistant AD for Sports Medicine, Southeastern Louisiana University.

---

of failure is also governed by parental practices and socialization, including punitive behavior, controlling behavior, and high expectations for achievement (Sagar & Lavellee, 2010). According to Sagar and Lavelle (2010), these behaviors are rooted in the parents' own fear of their child losing and the effects losing will have on the child's future participation and success in sports.

Although the immediate effects of such pressure on children may be difficult to gauge, it is safe to assume that children and adolescents do not possess the psychological coping skills of adults. Consequently, the stress of competition may result in significant problems for some youths. Young athletes may be more prone to injury, psychosomatic illnesses, emotional burnout, and other stress-related afflictions. Parents and coaches must take care not to force children beyond their ability to cope with an activity. It is a sad commentary on the values of today's society to think that some children may be driven from a sport that they love simply because they were pushed too hard, too early.

It is important for coaches to recognize their own behavior toward children and adolescents, but parents also need to be aware of their own behavior. A number of resources are available for coaches and parents in regard to minimizing competitive stress in the adolescent. According to the Association for Applied Sport Psychology, the following are some warning signs that an athlete may be having trouble at home and experiencing stress related to their participation in athletics: Concern should be raised if conversations at home are dominated by sport discussions, the child is allowed little time to spend with friends, the child's education becomes a distant second priority to competition and talent development, and the child is overly nervous about competing, especially when parents are watching (Lauer, n.d.). In an attempt to help coaches and parents, several dos and don'ts related to youth sports participation are listed here.

The Dos:

1. Do allow children to be interested in and play whatever sport they choose.

2. Do teach children to respect their coach(es) and parent(s).

3. Do be willing to let children make their own mistakes and learn from them.

4. Do be interested and supportive, light and playful, understanding and openhearted, and accepting and tolerant of children's learning process and their physical abilities.

5. Do model flexibility of your own opinions.

The Don'ts:

1. Don't try to relive your youth through children and adolescents.

2. Don't blame the equipment, team members, referees, or even the weather if the team does not do well or win.

3. Don't "push, push, push." Children and adolescents who are pushed beyond their capabilities may lose their self-confidence, become resistant and resentful toward their parent(s), become unsure of themselves and their abilities, and may stop trying.

4. Don't expect perfection or tie your ego or image to the young person's performance.

Source: Adapted from: Porter, n.d.

Psychology of the Injured Athlete

An injury represents a potent form of psychological stress for the athlete. For most, the possibility of being sidelined by a traumatic episode is an ever-present fear (**Figure 5.2**). Research on this topic supports the premise that, for most athletes, an injury produces a predictable psychological response (Wiese-Bjornstal, 2010). Groundbreaking research by Weiss and Troxel (1986) reported that an injury could cause a psychophysiologic reaction in the athlete that follows the classic stress-response model originally formulated by Selye (**Figure 5.3**).

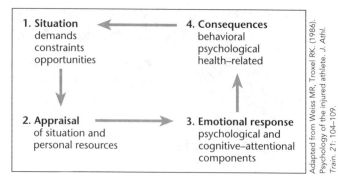

Adapted from Weiss MR, Troxel RK. (1986). Psychology of the injured athlete. *J. Athl. Train.* 21: 104–109.

FIGURE 5.3 The stress process.

As depicted in Figure 5.3, in phase 1 the injury serves as a potent **stressor** and requires the athlete to adapt to a restriction of normal activity. Phase 2 involves an appraisal of the significance of the injury, both in a short- and long-term sense. Weiss and Troxel (1986) reported that this phase is when an athlete may engage in negative self-doubt ("What if I can't recover by the next game?"). Phase 3 of the stress model involves an emotional response that can precipitate a host of physical and psychological reactions, ranging from severe anxiety, depression, and anger to increased muscle tension, blood pressure, and heart rate. Ermler and Thomas (1990) and Pedersen (1986) have developed models of injury response that fit well into this phase of the stress-response model. Ermler and Thomas theorized that an injury causes an athlete to experience feelings of alienation. Pedersen compared the effects of an injury with the grief response experienced following the death of a loved one. The fourth stage involves the long-term consequences of the emotional response in phase 3. If an athlete fails to respond to an injury in a positive manner, he or she may suffer from a wide variety of problems, including sleep disorders, loss of appetite, and perhaps decreased motivation (Weiss & Troxel, 1986). As a result of the development of these injury-response models, recommendations have been made regarding how best to assist the injured athlete in coping with an injury. Weiss and Troxel (1986) developed a list of guidelines for personnel to follow when working with an injured athlete. These are enumerated in **Time Out 5.2**.

Several themes have emerged from interviews with injured collegiate athletes, including fluctuations in emotions characterized by feelings of loss, decreased self-esteem, frustration, and anger (Tracey, 2003). Psychological symptoms even persist after athletes are cleared to play. Even though they may

FIGURE 5.2 The potential for injury is an ever present fear for most athletes.

be ready physically, they are not prepared mentally to return. Podlog and Eklund (2006) identified decreased confidence, increased fear of reinjury or further injury, and increased anxiety and stress in athletes who had experienced an injury and subsequent rehabilitation.

Research examining the effects of severe sports injuries on adolescents has also yielded some disturbing results. Boys and girls (average age 16.7 years) who played football, girls' soccer, basketball, and volleyball were studied to determine whether an injury classified as severe by the National Collegiate Athletic Association Injury Surveillance System (NCAA-ISS) resulted in posttraumatic distress. The study found avoidance behaviors and intrusive thoughts were pervasive in the injury group. The researchers also noted that these effects "may persist even after physical recovery has occurred" (Newcomer & Perna, 2003). Therefore, coaches, parents, and athletic trainers must be aware that in addition to treating the physical aspects of injury, they need to protect athletes' physical and mental health and address the psychological aspects of injury recovery (Wiese-Bjornstal, 2010).

Recommendations

Several suggestions have come from applied sports psychologists in regard to addressing the psychological needs of athletes after injury and during rehabilitation. Rehabilitation adherence is complex and multidimensional; therefore, providing multiple treatment options is important (Fischer, 1999). Social support has been identified as a key component of psychological recovery from injury. When Ievleva and Orlick (1991) compared slow and fast healers, they found that athletes who recovered quickly reported more positive comments and that the learning during the process enhanced

insight into sport. Fast healers were found to take personal responsibility for healing, had desire and determination, maintained a positive attitude, used creative visualization, and had more social support. Therefore, applied sports psychologists suggest helping athletes by providing a connection to their team during rehabilitation, comfort during the hard work of returning to play, an understanding of the injury and what to expect from the rehabilitation process, and support for completing day-to-day rehabilitation tasks (Shelley, Trowbridge, & Detling, 2003). Social support should be emotional, educational, and tangible (Hedstrom, n.d.). Although more research is needed in this area, these results do indicate that sports injuries may well be responsible for lingering psychological effects in young athletes.

Eating Disorders

With few exceptions, all sports impose an extremely narrow set of parameters for the appropriate body type required for success. It is difficult to imagine, for example, a world-class gymnast who is 6 feet tall and weighs 240 pounds or a successful long-distance runner or figure skater who is obese.

Reality dictates that specific sports require specific body types for athletes to be competitive. Some sports, such as those mentioned, demand leanness for at least two reasons. First, the **biomechanics** of the sport may require a lean and muscular body for the athlete to perform highly complex skills effectively. Second, the sports community and society as a whole have come to expect that successful athletes look lean and muscular. In recent years, media exposure of many top athletes has focused as much on physical appearance as on performance. This has created the need for many aspiring athletes to conform to a certain very narrowly defined body type (**Figure 5.4**). This is especially true for female athletes, but male athletes also suffer from distorted body images.

Psychologists are beginning to discover that this emphasis on the ideal body has resulted in serious negative effects on the athletic community. An increasing number of athletes demonstrate abnormal eating behaviors (disordered eating) or even **pathogenic**

stressor Anything that affects the body's physiological or psychological condition and upsets the homeostatic balance.

biomechanics Branch of study that applies the laws of mechanics, internal or external, to the living body.

pathogenic Causing disease.

© John Lumb/ShutterStock, Inc.

FIGURE 5.4 Many athletes feel compelled to conform to a certain body type.

eating behaviors that may have deeper psychological origins. These pathogenic eating behaviors are on the increase within the athletic community and include **bulimia nervosa** and **anorexia nervosa**, with the former being more prevalent. Overall, abnormal eating behaviors are higher in adolescent elite athletes than matched controls and higher in female athletes than male athletes (Marinsen & Sundgot-Borgen, 2013). Even though the majority of athletes with eating disorders are female, recent studies demonstrate that males are also affected and should not be excluded from continuing discussions (Chatterton & Petrie, 2013). To better understand eating disorders and their ramifications, readers are encouraged to learn more at the website of the National Eating Disorders Association (http://www.nationaleatingdisorders.org/) or the website of the National Association of Anorexia Nervosa and Associated Disorders (http://www.anad.org/). Additionally, readers can access the National Athletic Trainers' Association "Position Statement: Preventing, Detecting, and Managing Disordered Eating in Athletes" (Bonci et al., 2008; this document is available at http://www.nata.org/sites/default/files/PreventingDetecting AndManagingDisorderedEating.pdf). Four factors have

been identified as having the greatest effect on the risk of athletes developing disordered eating: 1) features of the *sport task* such as revealing uniforms or being physically evaluated; 2) the *sport environment*, which can include comments from teammates, coaches, parents, or judges, as well as the audience; 3) *biological characteristics* such as metabolism and physical size; and 4) *psychological characteristics* of the individual, which can include self-esteem, body image, and anxiety about being evaluated by others (also known as social physique anxiety; Monsma, 2006). Stirling and Kerr (2012) have also described personal qualities of perfectionism, achievement-motivation, self-absorption, competitiveness, and self-control as vulnerabilities to disordered eating behaviors. Interestingly, the ability to tolerate pain and to enjoy hunger pains were shown to increase vulnerability to disordered eating (Stirling & Kerr, 2012).

Anorexia Nervosa and Bulimia Nervosa

It is important to note that disordered eating behaviors are not always represented by a clinical diagnosis of anorexia nervosa or bulimia nervosa. Many subclinical eating disorders (eating disorders otherwise nonspecified) are associated with a variety of warning signs. These warning signs are presented in **Table 5.2**.

Anorexia nervosa is the third most common illness for adolescents and is characterized by a pattern of self-starvation motivated by an obsession with being thin and an overwhelming fear of being fat (National

TABLE 5.2
WARNING SIGNS OF NONSPECIFIC DISORDERED EATING
• Dieting obsessively when not overweight
• Claiming to feel "fat" when overweight is not a reality
• Preoccupation with food, calories, nutrition, and cooking
• Being overly active
• Frequent weighing
• Strange food-related behaviors
• Rapid weight loss
• Depression
• Slowness of thought/memory difficulties
• Hair loss
• Fatigue and irritability
• Loss of menstrual period (females)

Source: Data from Monsma E. (2006). Disordered eating and the controlling aspect of synchronized skating. *Synchronized Skating Magazine.* 3(2).

Association of Anorexia Nervosa and Associated Disorders [ANAD], 2013). An intake of only a few hundred calories a day is not uncommon. It is very common for those with this illness to have a grossly distorted body image in which they think of themselves as being fat when they are, in fact, abnormally lean. Several warning signs, including deliberate self-starvation with weight loss, persistent fear of gaining weight, refusal to eat or highly restrictive eating, sensitivity to cold, and absent or irregular menstruation are characteristic of anorexic individuals (Bonci et al., 2008). In regard to weight, anorexic individuals typically refuse to maintain weight at 85% of their ideal body weight (Bonci et al., 2008). Bulimia nervosa is characterized by repeated bouts of binge eating followed by some form of purging—for example, vomiting, taking laxatives, fasting, or undertaking vigorous, excessive exercise (Bonci et al., 2008). The bingeing and purging must occur more than twice a week for at least 3 months in order to be considered bulimia nervosa. Because those persons suffering from bulimia nervosa often have normal weight, it is important to pay attention to several specific warning signs, including preoccupation with food, secret eating and purging, gastrointestinal problems, laxative addiction, tooth decay, swollen salivary glands, and broken blood vessels in the eyes (ANAD, 2013). Both anorexia and bulimia are considered to be serious psychological problems and are classified as psychological disorders by the American Psychological Association.

Research

Research indicates that more than one-third of athletes have reported to use at least one extreme dieting method, 51% have tried to lose weight in the past month, and 77% want to lose weight (Montenegro, 2006). When questioned, athletes reported they engage in abnormal eating behaviors in an effort to improve either performance or appearance, or both. Perhaps more alarming, one study found that 70% of those reporting pathogenic eating behaviors felt such practices were harmless (Rosen et al., 1986).

Rosen and colleagues (1986) surveyed the eating habits of 182 female collegiate athletes and determined that 32% regularly practiced pathogenic eating—where binges were followed by self-induced vomiting (more than two times weekly) or they demonstrated regular use of laxatives, diet pills, and/or diuretics. In a more recent study (n = 204), 25% of females were classified as having symptoms and patterns of clinical disordered eating, and 2% were classified as needing a clinical diagnosis of an eating disorder (Greenleaf et al., 2009). Aesthetic and power sports, including gymnastics, diving,

cheerleading, crew, power lifting, and downhill skiing, had the most symptomatic athletes (33–40%) and cross country, swimming, track, and ball sports had 21–27% (Greenleaf et al., 2009).

Other recent studies have had mixed results when compared with earlier studies; however, Sanford-Martens and colleagues (2005) reported increases in male subclinical disorders (21%) and decreases in female subclinical eating disorders (14%) over the years. Despite these population changes, females still exhibit more clinical eating disorders than males do (5% females and 2% males).

Even though the prevalence is increasing, little is known about pathogenic eating behaviors and disordered eating among male athletes. However, Chatterton and Petrie (2013) identified that most eating disturbances in males occur at the subclinical level and that athletes who participate in weight class sports are more likely to be classified as symptomatic and engage in pathogenic eating, weight control, or excessive exercise behaviors when compared to endurance sport or ball game male athletes. Research also indicates that in aesthetic sports (diving, dance, or gymnastics), sports where low body fat is advantageous (e.g., distance running), or sports where athletes need to "make weight" (such as wrestling and horse racing), there is a danger of pathogenic eating behaviors in males (Baum, 2006). Historically, the sport of wrestling has received the most attention with regard to this problem. It is common knowledge that many wrestlers routinely practice a variety of strange eating and training behaviors, especially just prior to competition. These include fasting, restriction of fluids, the use of laxatives, vomiting, and sweating off weight by wearing a rubber suit in the sauna. Obviously, all of these practices are to be discouraged. At best, they result in a short-term water loss; at worst, they can cause severe illness and even death. More research is needed to determine whether male athletes are vulnerable to the same pressures as their female counterparts when it comes to maintaining body build and leanness. Additionally, it needs to be determined whether the reported low incidence of clinical eating disorders in male athletes is an accurate reflection of the true incidence in this population.

bulimia nervosa A disorder characterized by repeated bouts of binge eating followed by some form of purging, such as vomiting, use of laxatives, fasting, and vigorous and excessive exercise.

anorexia nervosa A disorder characterized by a pattern of self-starvation with a concomitant obsession with being thin and an overwhelming fear of being fat.

Sport Specificity and Eating Disorders

It has been well documented that certain sports carry a high risk that participants will develop eating disorders. These include aesthetic sports such as gymnastics, ballet, swimming, diving, and figure skating. All of these activities place a heavy emphasis on lean, muscular body builds. In a survey of young (9 to 18 years old) competitive swimmers, Dummer and colleagues (1987) found that of 289 postmenarcheal females, 25% reported practicing some form of pathogenic eating behavior. A meta-analysis of 92 published studies on eating disorders concluded that female athletes involved in sports that place a premium on physical appearance (aesthetic sports) demonstrate a significantly higher prevalence of eating disorder symptoms than do female nonathletes (Hausenblas & Carron, 1999). Greenleaf and colleagues (2009) surveyed female athletes from a variety of different university sports and found that power and aesthetic sports did have the highest percentages (40% and 33%, respectively), but there were no statistical differences between the sports.

Not surprisingly, there is growing evidence that eating disorders may be gaining a foothold in sports historically immune to such problems. Rosen and colleagues (1986) found that significant percentages of female athletes participating in field hockey, softball, volleyball, track, and tennis reported pathogenic eating behaviors. Greenleaf and colleagues (2009) reported a 28% incidence of disordered eating in ball sports and a 22% incidence in endurance sports (including swimming); therefore, recent research confirms these findings.

A variety of physical and psychological problems are associated with anorexia and bulimia. Thornton (1990) reports that anorexic and bulimic athletes run the risk of esophageal inflammation, erosion of tooth enamel, and hormone imbalances. These physiological changes can lead to osteoporosis, **amenorrhea**, and electrolyte imbalances that can cause kidney and heart problems. The female athlete triad that links disordered eating (low energy availability) to the occurrence of osteoporosis and amenorrhea has been prevalent in the medical literature in the early 2000s (Nattiv et. al, 2007). Females should be educated on the health and performance consequences of menstrual irregularities and the importance of seeking timely medical intervention at the first sign of any abnormalities (Marinsen & Sundgot-Borgen, 2013). Likewise, males should be educated about the connection between health and performance. Recently, the concept of a male athlete triad that includes a connection between energy

---

TABLE 5.3

SAMPLE DISORDERED EATING QUESTIONNAIRE

Part 1: How often do eating behaviors interfere with your:

	Never	Rarely	Sometimes	Often	Always
Daily interactions with peers and coaches	1	2	3	4	5
Daily thoughts or feelings about yourself	1	2	3	4	5
Daily participation in athletics	1	2	3	4	5

Part 2: How often do you weigh or measure your body size?

_____ 5 times a day	_____ once a week	_____ once every 2 months
_____ 3–5 times a day	_____ 3 times/week	_____ once every 3 months
_____ 1–3 times a day	_____ once every 2 weeks	_____ once a year
_____ once a day	_____ once a month	_____ never

Part 3: Please respond to the following using the scale below in regard to your sport:

	Never	Rarely	Sometimes	Often	Always
Weight loss is required for increased performance.	1	2	3	4	5
Weight loss was required to meet a lower weight category.	1	2	3	4	5
Weight loss was required to reach an aesthetic ideal.	1	2	3	4	5
Coaching staff makes remarks concerning my weight.	1	2	3	4	5
I am weighed in front of my teammates.	1	2	3	4	5
Team members' weights are made public.	1	2	3	4	5
Mandated decrease in body fat percentage.	1	2	3	4	5
Fear of losing a position on team if weight is not controlled.	1	2	3	4	5

Source: Reproduced from Koszewski W, Chopak JS, Buxton BP. (1997). Risk factors for disordered eating in athletes. *Athl Ther Today.* 2(2):7–11. Reprinted with permission from Human Kinetics (Champaign, Ill.).

deficits, bone loss, and low sperm counts has been linked to possible hormonal changes associated with low testosterone, low estradiol, and high glucocorticoids (Chatterton & Petrie, 2013).

Prevention

Prevention of eating disorders, including bulimia and anorexia nervosa, must be the goal of all those involved with organized sports. Coaches need to place less emphasis on body weight and fat when working with athletes. Referring to weight in a negative manner, requiring mandatory weigh-ins, or publicly ostracizing an athlete for being overweight are all practices to be condemned. Negative body image has also been identified as a precursor to disordered eating. Body image refers to the thoughts, feelings, and perceptions an individual has about his or her body appearance and shape (Greenleaf et al., 2009). Negative self-perceptions should be of concern because they are detrimental to the health and wellness of athletes. Athletes suffering from poor body image are encouraged to engage in positive body talk, focus on what their body can do, and accept the idea that healthy and happy bodies come in all shapes and sizes.

Coaches and parents need to be alert to the early warning signs of eating disorders (Table 5.2). Screening for athletes who may be at risk for an eating disorder can commence at the time of the preparticipation physical examination (PPE). The athlete can complete a simple questionnaire (**Table 5.3**) during the PPE. If an athlete achieves a score indicative of someone who may be at risk, he or she can be referred for psychological counseling (Koszewski, Chopak, & Buxton, 1997). However, two research projects have suggested physiological screening and clinical interviews are superior to self-report measures. Marinsen and Sundgot-Borgen (2013) indicated that the clinical interview might be better than other screening tools, especially in an athletic population. Black and colleagues (2003) reported that a physiological screening including skinfold body fat assessment, waist-to-hip ratio, standing diastolic blood pressure, and parotid (salivary) gland size was better,

WHAT IF?

You are coaching high school track and field and one of your players demonstrates strange eating behaviors and excessive workout patterns. Other members of the team tell you that she also weighs herself all the time. What could such behavior imply? What would be your best course of action?

TIME OUT 5.3

Advice for Coaches

1. Be aware that you are a role model for your athletes. Your influence goes a long way in their lives.
2. If an athlete has signs of an eating disorder, do not become the "food police." Refer the individual for help.
3. Be sensitive in making comments about your athlete and/or team expectations and how you address body image.
4. Avoid discriminating against athletes because of their weight. Refrain from weigh-ins and asking athletes to lose weight or diet.
5. Provide educational resources concerning nutrition, growth and development, exercise, and disordered eating.
6. Be positive and empathetic.

Courtesy of Eva Monsma, PhD, Associate Professor, Developmental Sport Psychology, University of South Carolina.

because it was designed for females and bias was less because the purpose of the assessments are less obvious. They encourage further research on existing screening tools, especially with different sports populations.

Tips for coaches are provided in **Time Out 5.3**. However, coaches should encourage the adoption of peer-led programs such as Athletes Targeting Healthy Exercise and Nutrition Alternatives (ATHENA). This program has been very successful in encouraging lifelong skills directed toward sustainable dietary habits. Overall, researchers conclude that education about health, performance-related nutrition, and body composition should be administered prior to high school (Marinsen & Sundgot-Borgen, 2013).

Treatment

Treatment of eating disorders ranges from simple counseling and education (when diagnosed in early stages) to hospitalization in severe cases. It must be remembered that in many cases an eating disorder may be a symptom of a psychological problem such as depression or anxiety. Despite improved treatment programs, experts report that at least one-third of these cases do not respond to therapy. It is hoped that continued research will improve the prognosis for these individuals.

amenorrhea Absence or suppression of menstruation.

REVIEW QUESTIONS

1. Briefly define several of the personality variables described in the chapter.

2. Discuss the relationship between an athlete's self-concept and the risk of sports injury.

3. Describe briefly the relationship between psycho-social variables and the risk of sports injury.

4. Discuss the possible relationship between high levels of competitive stress and the psychology of the adolescent athlete.

5. How can parents and coaches increase the psychological stress an adolescent athlete experiences?

6. Discuss the psychological impact of a sports injury on an athlete in terms of the stress model shown in the chapter.

7. List five common signs or behaviors that may indicate the development of a depressive disorder.

8. Define the acronym SAD and discuss its implications for competitive athletes.

9. List the recommended guidelines for dealing with an injured athlete.

10. Define anorexia nervosa and bulimia nervosa.

11. True or false: Nonathletes show a greater percentage of disordered eating behaviors than do athletes.

12. True or false: Male athletes do not show significant patterns of disordered eating.

13. List several common forms of disordered eating behaviors practiced by athletes.

14. What are the female athlete triad and the male athlete triad?

15. List three ways a coach can help prevent eating disorders.

REFERENCES

Andersen MB, Williams JM. (1988). A model of stress and athletic injury: Prediction and prevention. *J Sport Exercise Psychol.* 10:294–306.

Appaneal RN, Levine BR, Perna FM, Roh JL. (2009). Measuring postinjury depression among male and female competitive athletes. *J Sport Exerc Psychol.* 31:60–76.

Armstrong S, Oomen-Early J. (2009). Social connectedness, self-esteem, and depression symptomatology among collegiate athletes versus nonathletes. *J Am Coll Health.* 57(5):521–526.

Baum A. (2006). Eating disorders in the male athlete. *Sports Med.* 36(1):1–6.

Black DR, Larkin LJS, Coster DC, Leverenz LJ, Abood DA. (2003). Physiologic screening test for eating disorders/disordered eating among female collegiate athletes. *J Athl Train.* 38(4):286–297.

Bonci CM, Bonci LJ, Granger LR, Johnson CL, Malina RM, Milne LW, Ryan RR, Vanderbunt EM. (2008). National Athletic Trainers' Association position statement: Preventing, detecting, and managing disordered eating in athletes. *J Athl Train.* 43(1):80–108.

Chatterton JM, Petrie TA. (2013). Prevalence of disordered eating and pathogenic weight control behaviors among male collegiate athletes. *Eat Disord.* 21(4):328–341.

Dobersek U, Bartling C. (2008). Connection between personality type and sport. *Am J Psychol Res.* 4(1):21–28.

Dummer GM, Rosen LW, Heusner WW. (1987). Pathogenic weight-control behaviors in young competitive swimmers. *Phys Sportsmed.* 15(5):75–84.

Eagleton JR, McKelvie SJ, deMan A. (2007). Extraversion and neuroticism in team sport participants, individual sport participants, and nonparticipants. *Percept Mot Skills.* 105(1):265–275.

Ermler KL, Thomas CE. (1990). Interventions for the alienating effect of injury. *J Athl Train.* 25(3):269–271.

Fischer AC. (1999). Counseling for improved rehabilitation adherence. In: Ray RA, Wiese-Bjornstal DM (eds.), *Counseling in Sports Medicine.* Champaign, Ill: Human Kinetics.

Fleming S. (2009). The riddle of personality and sport. Psychology in the News. Available: http://intro2psych.wordpress.com/2009/05/15/the-riddle-of-personality-and-sport/.

Fredricks JA, Eccles JS. (2004). Parental influences on youth involvement in sports. In: Weiss MR (ed.), *Developmental Sport and Exercise Psychology: A Lifespan Perspective.* Morgantown, WV: Fitness Information Technology. pp. 145–164.

Goldberg LR. (1990). An alternative "description of personality": The big-five factor structure. *J Pers Soc Psychol.* 59(6):1216–1229.

Greenleaf C, Petrie TA, Carter J, Reel J. (2009). Female collegiate athletes: Prevalence of eating disorders and disordered eating behaviors. *J Am College Health.* 57(5):489–495.

Hanson SJ, McCullugh P, Tonymon P. (1992). The relationship of personality characteristics, life stress, and coping resources to athletic injury. *J Sport Exercise Psychol.* 14:262–272.

Hausenblas HA, Carron AV. (1999). Eating disorder indices and athletes: An integration. *J Sport Exercise Psychol.* 21:230–258.

Hedstrom R. (n.d.). With a little help from my friends: Using your social support network when dealing with injury. Association for Applied Sport Psychology. Available: http://www.appliedsportpsych.org/resource-center/injury-rehabilitation/with-a-little-help-from-my-friends/.

Holmes H, Rahe RH. (1967). The Social Readjustment Rating Scale. *J Psychol Res.* 11:213–218.

Ievleva L, Orlick T. (1991). Mental links to enhanced healing: An exploratory study. *Sport Psychologist.* 5(1):25–40.

Ivarsson A, Johnson U. (2010) Psychological factors as predictors of injuries among senior soccer players. A prospective study. *J Sports Sci Med.* 9:347–352.

Jowett S, Cramer D. (2010). The prediction of young athletes' physical self from perceptions of relationships with parents and coaches. *Psychol Sport Exerc.* 11:140–147.

Kasper S, Wehr TA, Bartko JJ, Gaist PA, Rosenthal NE. (1989). Epidemiological findings of seasonal changes in mood and behavior. *Arch Gen Psychiatr.* 40:823–833.

Kleinert J. (2002). An approach to sport injury trait anxiety: Scale construction and structure analysis. *Eur J Sport Sci.* 2(3):1–12.

Koszewski W, Chopak JS, Buxton BP. (1997). Risk factors for disordered eating in athletes. *Athletic Therapy Today.* 2(2):7–11.

Lamb M. (1986). Self-concept and injury frequency among female college field-hockey players. *J Athl Train.* 21(3):220–224.

Lauer L. (n.d.). Keeping perspective in youth sport. Association for Applied Sport Psychology. Available: http://www.appliedsportpsych.org/resource-center/resources-for-parents/keeping-perspective-in-youth-sport/.

Malinauskas R. (2010). The associations among social support, stress, and life satisfaction as perceived by injured college athletes. *Soc Behav Pers.* 38(6):741–752.

Marinsen M, Sundgot-Borgen J. (2013). Higher prevalence of eating disorders among adolescent elite athletes than controls. *Med. Sci. Sports Exerc.* 45(6):1188–1197.

Matthews G, Deary I, Whiteman M. (2003). *Personality Traits.* (2nd ed.). Cambridge, United Kingdom: Cambridge University Press.

Monsma, E. (2006). Disordered eating and the controlling aspect of synchronized skating. *Synchronized Skating Magazine.* 3(2).

Montenegro SO. (2006). Disordered eating in athletes. *Athletic Therapy Today.* 11(1):60–62.

Nash HL. (1987). Elite child-athletes: How much does victory cost? *Phys Sportsmed.* 15(8):129–133.

National Association of Anorexia Nervosa and Associated Disorders. (2013). Eating disorders statistics. Available: http://www.anad.org/get-information/about-eating-disorders/eating-disorders-statistics/.

National Collegiate Athletic Association. (2012). *Sports Medicine Handbook* (2012–2013). Indianapolis, Ind: Author.

Nattiv A, Loucks AB, Manore MM, Sanborn CF, Sundgot-Borgen J, Warren MP. (2007). The female athlete triad. *Med Sci Sports Exer.* 39(10):1867–1882.

Newcomer RR, Perna FM. (2003). Features of posttraumatic distress among adolescent athletes. *J Athl Train.* 38(2):163–166.

Pedersen P. (1986). The grief response and injury: A special challenge for athletes and athletic trainers. *J Athl Train.* 21(4):312–314.

Perna FM, McDowell SL. (1995). Role of psychological stress in cortisol recovery from exhaustive exercise among elite athletes. *Int J Behav Med.* 2(1):13–26.

Petrie TA. (1993). Coping skills, competitive trait anxiety, and playing status: Moderating effects on the life stress-injury relationship. *J Sports Exercise Psychol.* 15:261–274.

Podlog L, Eklund RC. (2006). A longitudinal investigation of competitive athletes' return to sport following serious injury. *J Appl Sport Psychol.* 18:44–68.

Porter K. (n.d.). Do's and don'ts for parents of young athletes. Association for Applied Sport Psychology. Available: http://www.appliedsportpsych.org/resource-center/resources-for-parents/dos-and-donts-for-parents-of-young-athletes/.

Rosen LW, et al. (1986). Pathogenic weight-control behavior in female athletes. *Phys Sportsmed.* 14(1):79–86.

Rosen LW, Shafer CL, Smokler C, Carrier D, McKeag DB. (1996). Seasonal mood disturbances in collegiate hockey players. *J Athl Train.* 31(3):225–228.

Sagar SS, Lavallee D. (2010). The developmental origins of fear of failure in adolescent athletes: Examining parental practices. *Psychol Sport Exerc.* 11:177–187.

Sanford-Martens TC, Davidson MM, Yakushko OF, Martens MP, Hinton P. (2005). Clinical and subclinical eating disorders: An examination of collegiate athletes. *J Appl Sport Psychol.* 17:79–86.

Shelley GA, Trowbridge CA, Detling N. (2003). Practical counseling skills for the athletic therapist. *Athletic Therapy Today.* 8(2):57–63.

Stirling A, Kerr G. (2012). Development of disordered eating behaviours. *European J Sport Science.* 12(3):262–273.

Thornton JS. (1990). Feast or famine: Eating disorders in athletes. *J Athl Train.* 18(4):116–122.

Tracey J. (2003). The emotional response to the injury and rehabilitation process. *J Appl Sport Psychol.* 15:279–293.

Treasure DC. (2001). Enhancing young people's motivation in youth sport: An achievement goal approach. In: Roberts GC (ed.), *Advances in Motivation in Sport and Exercise.* Champaign, Ill: Human Kinetics. pp. 177–198.

Vetter RE, Symonds ML. (2010). Correlations between injury, training intensity, and physical and mental exhaustion among college athletes. *J Strength Cond Res.* 24(3):587–596.

Weiss MR, Troxel RK. (1986). Psychology of the injured athlete. *J Athl Train.* 21(2):104–105.

Wiese-Bjornstal DM. (2010). Psychology and socioculture affect injury risk, response, and recovery in high-intensity athletes: a consensus statement. *Scand J Med Sci Sports.* 20(Suppl. 2):103–111.

Williams JM, Andersen MB. (1998). Psychological antecedents of sport injury: Review and critique of the stress and injury model. *J Appl Sport Psychol.* 10:5–25.

Nutritional Considerations

MAJOR CONCEPTS

Research shows that, regardless of the sport, an athlete's diet plays a critical, if not essential, role in performance. Yet misinformation and misconceptions persist among coaches and athletes regarding what constitutes an adequate diet. This chapter first examines available evidence concerning the dietary knowledge and practices of coaches and athletes. It next outlines dietary recommendations for healthy eating, including the roles of carbohydrates, proteins, fats, vitamins, and minerals. Precompetition, competition, and postcompetition nutrition are also explored. The nutritional requirements during injury rehabilitation are also reviewed. Special attention is given to females and to the sport of wrestling. Wrestling has been plagued with the problem of athletes attempting to lose body weight rapidly by dehydration, so a simple method is provided to assess an athlete's ability to maintain a healthy weight and rehydrate adequately. This chapter concludes with a brief discussion regarding ergogenic aids and nutritional supplements commonly used in sports.

go.jblearning.com/PfeifferCWS

For a full suite of assignments and additional learning activities (indicated by the icons throughout the text), use the access code found in the front of your text. If you do not have an access code, you can obtain one at go.jblearning.com/PfeifferCWS.

Proper nutritional knowledge is imperative for all individuals, but especially for those involved in athletic competitions (Jacobson, Sobonya, & Ransone, 2001). An athlete's diet has a direct impact on performance, recovery from training and competition, resistance to environmental extremes, recovery from injury, and, to some extent, likelihood of injury. In essence, diet influences virtually all aspects of sports participation.

Yet research over time has demonstrated that both coaches and athletes are largely uneducated regarding proper nutrition (Corley, Demarest-Litchford, & Bazzarre, 1990; Parr, Porter, & Hodgson, 1984; Sossin et al., 1997; Torres-McGehee et al., 2012). Parr and colleagues (1984) reported that 61% of the coaches they surveyed had no formal training in nutrition and 78% reported they lacked adequate nutritional knowledge. Corley and colleagues (1990) reported that 82% of college athletic coaches never had a college-level nutrition class, and when given a true/false test on basic nutritional knowledge including food groups, diet composition for weight loss, gain, or maintenance, caloric distribution (fat, carbohydrate, and protein) for meals, and hydration techniques they scored around 70%. When high school wrestling coaches were tested on nutritional knowledge, including dehydration and body composition, they scored below 60% on these topics (Sossin et al., 1997). More recently, Torres-McGehee and colleagues (2012) reported that only 39.5% of Division I coaches scored above a 75% on a nutritional knowledge test that included questions about macronutrients, micronutrients, hydration, supplements and performance, and weight control and eating disorders. These data support the premise that many coaches are ill prepared to provide good nutritional counsel to their athletes.

Most athletes (68%) were familiar with the food groups and 71% reported incorporating them into their diet, but Parr and colleagues (1984) also demonstrated that athletes largely relied on parents for information about nutrition—followed by television commercials and magazines. Although the knowledge of most parents concerning nutrition cannot be measured, it is probably safe to assume that both parents and the media represent, at best, marginal sources of current nutritional information. Torres-McGehee and colleagues (2012) further substantiate these reports and opinions by demonstrating that in a sample of 185 Division I, II, and III athletes only 9% scored above the correct answer benchmark (75% of questions correct) on a nutritional knowledge test. The good news is that there are knowledgeable individuals within athletic departments. Board of Certification, Inc. (BOC)–certified athletic trainers (ATs) and certified strength and conditioning specialists (SCSs) were the

most knowledgeable regarding nutrition (Torres-McGehee et al., 2012). Other studies (Froiland et al., 2004; Jacobson et al., 2001) have demonstrated that athletes are probably receiving better nutritional education from more reliable sources. But, there is still education to be done: Jacobson and colleagues (2001) reported that only 55% of college athletes received nutritional advice always or often during their college careers, and Torres-McGehee and colleagues (2012) reported that 71.4% of ATs and 83.1% of SCSs demonstrated better then adequate knowledge on their comprehensive nutrition test (ATs scored 78% $\pm$ 10% and SCSs scored 82% $\pm$ 10%).

Nutrients: An Overview

The following section provides an overview of the fundamental concepts of nutrition and is presented as a basis for the chapter content that follows. According to the Academy of Nutrition and Dietetics (2009), eating correctly for sports performance will: 1) help the athlete train longer and at a higher intensity, 2) delay the onset of fatigue, 3) promote recovery, 4) help the athlete's body adapt to workouts, 5) improve body composition and strength, 6) enhance concentration, 7) help maintain healthy immune function, 8) reduce the chance of injury, and 9) reduce the risk of heat cramps and stomachaches.

Although a comprehensive investigation of all topics related to nutrition is beyond the scope of this text, we provide an overview of caloric intake and the cost of activity plus a review of both macronutrients (required in large amounts) and micronutrients (required in small, or trace, amounts). The six classes of nutrients are presented. Carbohydrates, fats, and proteins are the macronutrients, and each is important in the diet. The mix of these may change based on fitness levels, exercise goals, and personal food preferences. Vitamins and minerals are the micronutrients that contribute to metabolic reactions and tissue structure. And, finally, water, which is essential for substrate transport, waste removal, and joint health, is also discussed (McArdle, Katch, & Katch, 2009).

Caloric Intake (Rest + Activity)

A proper nutrition plan begins with an individual assessment of the athlete's caloric intake needs based on his or her age, height, and weight and should include the extra calories needed to sustain physical activity. The recent National Athletic Trainers' Association (NATA) position statement regarding safe weight loss and management for those involved in sport or exercise indicates the following in regard to caloric and nutrient intake (Sammarone Turocy et al., 2011):

- Caloric intake should be based on the body weight goal.
- Total caloric intake should be determined by calculating the basal metabolic rate (BMR) and the energy needs for activity.
- The metabolic qualities of the activity should be considered when calculating the need for each energy-producing nutrient (carbohydrates, fats, proteins).

A safe and healthy dietary plan that supplies sufficient energy and nutrients should be maintained throughout the year, so a body weight goal must be established based on ideal body fat percentages. Healthy body fat ranges are 10%–22% for males and 20%–32% for females. However, lower body fat can be maintained in athletes. The lowest reference body fat for males is 5% and in females it is 12% (Sammarone Turocy et al., 2011). To calculate goal weight, athletes should be encouraged to use the following formulas from the NATA position statement:

Current % body fat – Desired % body fat
= Nonessential body fat %

Current body weight × Nonessential body fat (decimal format) % = Nonessential fat (lbs)

Current body weight – Nonessential fat (lbs)
= Ideal body weight (lbs)

Then based on their ideal body weight, athletes can use one of the following formulas to calculate their daily energy needs at rest, also called the **basal metabolic rate (BMR)**. According to Sammarone Turocy and colleagues (2011), the Harris Benedict formulas are most commonly used to establish the BMR in kilocalories (kcals), which are also known as Calories:

Female BMR = 655.1 + (9.6 × weight [kg])
+ (1.9 × height [cm]) – (4.7 × age [years])

Male BMR = 66.5 + (13.8 × weight [kg])
+ (5 × height [cm]) – (6.8 × age [years])

Once the BMR is calculated, the amount of energy expended in daily activity must be added to the total (Sammarone Turocy et al., 2011). A very simple way to do this is to add the following percentages of the BMR to the total received using the gender-specific BMR equation:

- Sedentary (mostly sitting): 20%–40% of BMR
- Light activity (sitting, standing, some walking): 55%–65% of BMR
- Moderate activity (standing and some exercise): 70%–75% of BMR
- Heavy activity (exercise): 80%–100% of BMR
- Sport participation is likely to be up to or greater than 200% of BMR (depending on duration and intensity).

It should be noted that these are only estimates. However, they provide a place to begin. A registered dietician should perform all detailed nutritional counseling.

Carbohydrates

Carbohydrates (CHO) are molecules that, by way of their metabolic breakdown, provide energy for high-intensity exercise. The specific forms of CHO used within the body are glucose and glycogen (the storage form of glucose) found in the blood, liver, and skeletal muscle. Carbohydrates consist of carbon, hydrogen, and oxygen atoms, with the number of carbon atoms ranging from three to seven. They fall into three general categories, based on the complexity of the molecule. The simplest forms of CHO are the monosaccharides (a single molecule), which include sugars such as fructose, glucose (blood sugar), and galactose. The next group is the disaccharides (two monosaccharide molecules combined), which include commonly known sugars such as lactose (milk sugar), sucrose (the most common form of sugar in the diet), and maltose. The complex carbohydrates are known as polysaccharides (10 to thousands of monosaccharides linked together) and include compounds such as glycogen, starch, and cellulose (dietary fiber).

The majority of dietary CHO is derived from plant sources, primarily grains, seeds, fruits, and vegetables (**Figure 6.1**). In a practical context, carbohydrates are classified as either simple (monosaccharides) or complex. In general, complex CHO contain more nutrients and fiber than simple CHO do. The most common form of dietary CHO intake is from simple sugars, primarily from foods high in sucrose such as soft drinks, candies, and cereals (high in sugar). Although high in caloric content, these foods stimulate insulin release, cause fluctuations in blood glucose levels, and provide little in the way of other nutrients; therefore, they are often referred to as "empty calorie" foods.

basal metabolic rate (BMR) The amount of energy needed to sustain functioning at rest.

© Hurst Photo/ShutterStock, Inc.

FIGURE 6.1 Carbohydrates come from a variety of sources including breads, cereals, and grains.

A superior form of dietary CHO is derived from eating more complex CHO from sources such as whole-grain cereals and breads, vegetables, and fruits. The CHO in these foods are in the form of starch found in the cereals and breads or cellulose found in leaves, stems, roots, seeds, and coverings of plants. An added benefit of consuming complex CHO is that they typically contain dietary fiber (indigestible CHO), which may lower cholesterol absorption and is also beneficial to the digestive tract. Daily fiber intake should be between 21 and 38 grams (g) depending on gender and age (McArdle et al., 2009).

Another excellent source of CHO is fruits, which can provide a significant amount of CHO in the form of fructose. Fructose, a monosaccharide, is much sweeter than sucrose; however, the benefit of fructose is that it "does not stimulate pancreatic insulin secretion" and, as a result, "helps to stabilize blood-glucose and insulin levels" (McArdle et al., 2009). An added benefit of whole-grain breads, cereals, fruits, and vegetables is that they typically contain a wide variety of other nutrients and, as such, help to provide a balanced diet.

Although the classifications of simple and complex CHO often are suitable to describe foods containing CHO, these classifications do not represent the ways simple and complex CHO are hydrolyzed and absorbed by the body (Manore, Meyer, & Thompson, 2009). Foods are now also classified as producing either high, moderate, or low glycemic responses and are often classified in regard to how fast they are oxidized. Foods classified as having a high glycemic response are quickly oxidized (~60 g/hour) and typically result in a large and rapid rise in blood glucose and insulin, followed by a rapid decrease in blood glucose. Foods with a slower oxidation rate (~30 g/hour) and a lower glycemic response

cause a steadier rise and decline in blood glucose and insulin. Low glycemic index CHO improve diabetes management, reduce the risk of heart disease, reduce hunger, reduce gastrointestinal distress during exercise, and prolong physical endurance, whereas high glycemic CHO help refuel carbohydrate stores after exercise but may cause gastrointestinal distress during exercise. **Table 6.1** provides a small list of foods sorted according to glycemic index (rating based on white bread = 100) and types of sugars based on oxidation rate. For more information, go to http://www.glycemicindex.com or http://www.diabetes.org/food-and-fitness/food/planning-meals/the-glycemic-index-of-foods.html.

Muscles require CHO as a fuel source during exercise. The recommended percentage proportion of CHO in the diet should range between 60% and 70% of the total calories consumed daily, depending on the exercise frequency and intensity (McArdle et al., 2009). Regardless of the type of CHO consumed, they all provide approximately 4 kcal/g CHO. (A kilocalorie, or kcal, sometimes called a nutritional calorie, is the energy equivalent required to raise the temperature of 1 kg of water 1°C.) The average person stores approximately 1500 to 2000 kcal of CHO, the majority of which is in the form of muscle and liver glycogen, with a small portion available as blood glucose (McArdle et al., 2009). All individuals need to consume carbohydrates to maintain body functions or support exercise; however, athletes engaging in intense activities need to consume carbohydrates at greater levels than sedentary individuals do. See recommendations for intake based on body weight in **Table 6.2**.

Carbohydrate (Glycogen) Loading

As stated earlier, the majority of CHO in the body is stored in the skeletal muscles and liver in the form of glycogen. Physiologically, it is to the athlete's advantage if the total amount of stored glycogen can be increased prior to a competition. Athletes involved in aerobic sports, especially those with durations in excess of 60 minutes, benefit the most from an increased level of stored glycogen.

Essentially, the process of CHO loading involves the systematic decrease of dietary CHO intake in conjunction with a significant increase in exercise intensity. Early procedures for CHO loading were particularly Spartan in nature, requiring multiple days of intense exercise (depletion phase) combined with dietary restriction of CHO intake. Ironically, although such protocols often did result in an increase in stored glycogen, the negative impacts often outweighed the benefits to performance. These included severe physical fatigue associated with the depletion phase, along with negative emotional changes such as hyperirritability. In addition, another problem

TABLE 6.1

GLYCEMIC INDEX (GI) FOR FOODS

High Glycemic Index Foods (GI > 70)
White bread
Rice cakes, English muffin, or bagel
Grape Nuts™, Corn Flakes™, Cheerios™

Muesli
Pretzels
Sport drinks

Baked or mashed potatoes
Watermelons
Hard candy

Moderate Glycemic Index Foods (GI = 56–69)
100% whole-wheat bread, pita bread
Sweet potato
Mini Wheats™, Raisin Bran™, Froot Loops™

Brown or wild rice
Oatmeal (quick oats)
Raisins

Bananas (ripe)
Sweet corn
Popcorn

Low Glycemic Index Foods (GI = < 55)
Oatmeal (rolled or steel-cut)
Most fruits including apples, grapes, oranges, and pears
Yam

Barley and bulgur
Peas, legumes, and lentils
All Bran™ cereal

Carrots
Milk (all types)
Yogurt (most types)

Oxidation Rates of Different Types of Sugars
Rapidly oxidized ~60 g/hr
Glucose (a sugar formed by the breakdown of starch)
Sucrose (table sugar—glucose plus fructose)
Maltose (two glucose molecules)
Maltodextrin (from starch breakdown)
Amylopectin (from starch breakdown)

Slowly oxidized ~30 g/hr
Fructose (a sugar found in honey, fruits, etc.)
Galactose (a sugar found in sugar beets)
Isomaltulose (a sugar found in honey and sugarcane)
Trehalose (a sugar found in microorganisms)
Amylose (from starch breakdown)

Source: Glycemic index data from: http://www.glycemicindex.com and American Diabetes Association. Oxidation rates adapted from: Jeukendrup A. (2007). Carbohydrate supplementation during exercise: Does it help? How much is too much? *GSSI: Sport Science Exchange.* 20(3):1–6.

related to CHO loading is that for every gram of CHO stored, an additional 2.7 g of water is also stored. As such, the process of CHO loading results in an overall increase in body weight that, in sports such as distance running, may represent a performance detriment.

Modified, less draconian versions of CHO loading have been developed and have been found to be highly effective in elevating stored glycogen levels well above what can be achieved by consuming a high-CHO diet. Research verifies that a properly executed regimen of CHO loading can boost the level of stored glycogen from the normal of 1.7 g of glycogen/100 g of muscle tissue to 4 to 5 g of glycogen/100 g of muscle tissue. A typical modified regimen begins approximately 1 week prior to the competition and includes a gradual tapering of physical activity accompanied with a slight increase in CHO ingestion. Exercise (75% maximal oxygen consumption [VO$_2$ max]) over the first 3 days follows a steady decline in total time (1.5 hours/day to 40 minutes) while CHO consumption is maintained at 50% of total caloric intake. Over the next 3 days, exercise time is decreased to about 10–15 minutes while CHO consumption is increased to 75% of total caloric intake. A normal protein and fat intake is maintained. A high-CHO meal is then consumed on the day of the competition (McArdle et al., 2009).

Fats (Lipids)

Fats serve a variety of functions in the body, including providing energy for muscle contraction; insulation,

TABLE 6.2

RECOMMENDED CARBOHYDRATE (CHO) INTAKE BASED ON INTENSE TRAINING

Type of Training	Daily CHO Needs
Light to moderate training	5–7 g/kg OR 2.3–3.2 g/lb
Heavy training load or high intensity	7–10 g/kg OR 3.2–4.5 g/lb
Extreme training and high-intensity races (> 4–5 hours)	10–12 g/kg OR > 4.5–5.5 g/lb

Source: Adapted from: Academy of Nutrition and Dietetics. http://www.eatright.org.

primarily in the form of subcutaneous fat; and protection of vital organs such as the kidneys and heart. Dietary fats are either simple or complex, depending on their specific molecular structure. Fats, like CHO, consist of carbon, hydrogen, and oxygen atoms; however, the ratio of hydrogen to oxygen is far greater in fats than in carbohydrates. Depending on their molecular structure, fats can exist either in liquid (oils) or solid form. Simple fats consist of two components, glycerol and a fatty acid, and can be either saturated or unsaturated. The term *saturated* describes the fact that in this form of fat all of the available bonding sites on the fatty acid molecule are occupied by a hydrogen atom. Most dietary sources of saturated fats are derived from animal sources (e.g., beef, pork, poultry, and dairy products) and are generally solid at room temperature. Unsaturated fats, as the term implies, are structured in such a way as to prevent all of the available bonding sites from being occupied by a hydrogen atom. The majority of unsaturated fats exist as liquids at room temperature. Unsaturated fats exist in two forms, monounsaturated and polyunsaturated. Mono-unsaturated fat molecules include a single site on the carbon chain where a double bond exists, thus preventing hydrogen atoms from bonding at that site. Polyunsaturated fats have two or more double bonds and, as such, have at least two sites that cannot be occupied by hydrogen atoms.

The recommended percentage proportion of fats in the diet should be 30% or less of the total calories consumed daily (McArdle et al., 2009). It is recommended that saturated fats make up only 10% of total fats (20–25 g based on a diet of 2000–2500 kcal/day); therefore, the majority of fats consumed should be unsaturated. This helps avoid the problems attributed to excessive consumption of saturated fats, including high cholesterol and cardiovascular disease. Dietary sources of fats, as stated earlier, are animal products such as beef, poultry, and pork. Other sources include dairy products, such as milk, butter, and cheese. In addition, plant sources of fats include nuts and plant oils such as corn oil, olive oil, and soybean oil. See **Table 6.3** for common foods and their fat and caloric content.

Like CHO, fat is an important source of energy during rest and exercise. CHO and fats are oxidized for energy at the same time. The proportion of energy that comes from CHO and fats is dependent on the duration, intensity, and type of exercise as well as the athlete's fitness level and the meal eaten prior to exercise (Manore et al., 2009). Regardless of the type of fat consumed, all forms provide approximately 9 kcal/g; therefore, fats are calorie dense. One tablespoon of butter has the same kilocalories as 4 cups of chopped broccoli (100 kcal). The available amount of energy in the form of stored body fat is significantly greater than what is available from CHO. For example, the available energy in a 70-kilogram (kg) person who has 18% body fat is calculated to be around 113,400 kcal (70 kg × 0.18 = 12.6 kg of fat; 12.6 × 1000 = 12,600 g of fat; 12,600 × 9 kcal = 113,400 kcal).

TABLE 6.3

ENERGY AND COMPOSITION OF FAT-CONTAINING FOOD

Food	Serving Size	Energy (kcal)	Fat (g)
Milk, whole	8 oz	150	8.2
Milk, 1%	8 oz	102	2.6
Cheese, cheddar	1 oz	111	9.1
Peanut butter	1 tbsp	95	8.2
Cookies, Oreos	3 cookies	160	7.0
Mayonnaise, reg	1 tbsp	100	1.0
Apple	1 medium	81	.5
Avocado	1 medium	324	29.0
Egg	1 large	80	5.5
Strawberries	1 cup	45	1.0
Ground beef	3 oz	231	15.5
Flounder	3 oz	80	1.0
Chicken breast	3 oz	140	3.1

Source: Data from Manore MM, Meyer NL, Thompson J. (2009). *Sport Nutrition for Health and Performance* (2nd ed.). Champaign, Ill: Human Kinetics; and NaturoDoc. (n.d.). Fat calories in foods. Available: http://www.naturodoc.com/library/nutrition/fatcontent.htm.

Proteins

As with carbohydrates and fats, proteins also contain carbon, hydrogen, and oxygen atoms in their molecules. However, proteins also include nitrogen and, as such, they are unique molecules compared to the other nutrients. Protein molecules are assembled by combining amino acids using peptide bonds to form large, complex molecules. There are 20 specific amino acids required by the body to produce the thousands of proteins necessary for life. The majority of the body's protein is found in muscle and connective tissues. Proteins are also found in the body fluids and in the blood from thousands of different enzymes and structures related to blood clotting such as fibrin and fibrinogen. In addition, muscle protein is used as an energy source during prolonged exercise, producing as much as 10% to 15% of the energy requirements for long-duration activity. Research suggests that a regimen of regular aerobic exercise enhances the body's ability to generate energy from the metabolism of proteins (Sumida & Donovan, 1995).

The body builds proteins from the amino acids that are available from the protein that is consumed in the diet. Of the 20 amino acids required to construct the body's proteins, 8 cannot be synthesized by the body and must, therefore, be ingested in the diet. These eight amino acids are known as "essential," implying that they must be present in the diet. They are isoleucine, leucine, lysine, methionine, phenylalanine, threonine, tryptophan, and valine. The best dietary sources of the essential amino acids are eggs, meats, and dairy products, all known as complete proteins (**Figure 6.2**). Incomplete proteins are those that lack one or more or contain insufficient amounts of one or more of the essential amino acids. They include foods found in the legume and grain categories. Athletes who are on vegetarian diets must take care to eat foods in the correct combination to provide all of the essential amino acids. A solution to the problem is for such athletes to include either eggs (ovo vegetarian), milk products (lacto vegetarian), or both (ovo-lacto vegetarian) to ensure adequate supplies of essential amino acids.

FIGURE 6.2 Proteins come from both animal and plant sources.

Protein Supplementation

Because dietary protein is associated with building muscle mass, many athletes are curious about the benefits of extra protein consumption beyond that found in their regular diets. A study of 61 high school football players reported that 64% are ingesting protein supplements in an attempt to gain strength or improve performance (Duellman et al., 2008). Unfortunately, the researchers also found that more than 60% of these athletes believe there are no risks to excessive protein intake. However, at least two problems are associated with the practice of consuming additional protein. The first is that many sources of dietary protein also contain a large amount of saturated fat, such as beef and pork products. The second problem is that in certain cases the body may be unable to eliminate the byproducts of excess protein breakdown efficiently, and, as such, organs such as the liver and kidney are stressed.

Today there is a huge commercial market for what are commonly known as protein supplements, often sold at health-food stores, grocery chains, and sporting good stores and through mail order and the Internet. Most of these products consist of meat byproducts that are processed into a powder form that is then mixed with water or some other liquid and consumed orally. Unfortunately, because these products are marketed as food supplements, their purity is not monitored by the U.S. Food and Drug Administration (FDA). In addition, many of them are extremely expensive on a per-pound basis, often exceeding the cost of more common sources of protein such as meat and dairy products.

Unfortunately, there is virtually no scientific research that supports the premise of protein supplementation enhancing muscle development. Muscle mass does not increase simply by eating high-protein foods or special preparations of amino acids (McArdle et al., 2009). At present, available research indicates athletes involved in intense training, particularly strength training, need to consume between 1.2 g and 1.8 g of protein for each kilogram of body weight (McArdle et al., 2009), whereas the sedentary person or light exerciser needs to consume only 0.83–1.2 g/kg. A more complete listing is provided in **Table 6.4**. To put this into a practical context, the calculated protein requirement for a 60-kg (132-lb) athlete involved in moderate to heavy training would range from 72 g to 108 g per day. Eight ounces of broiled salmon provide approximately 62 g of protein, 8 ounces of lean sirloin steak provide approximately 65 g of protein, and an 8-ounce skinless chicken breast yields a little over 70 g of protein. It can be seen that adequate protein to meet the daily requirements of an athlete in heavy training can easily be achieved through meals

TABLE 6.4	
RECOMMENDED PROTEIN INTAKE	
Type Person	**Protein Intake**
Vegetarians	0.9–1 g/kg of body mass (0.41–0.45 g/lb of body weight)
General population	0.8–1 g/kg of body mass (0.36–0.45 g/lb of body weight)
Endurance athletes	1.2–1.4 g/kg of body mass (0.55–0.64 g/lb of body weight)
Strength athletes	1.7–1.8 g/kg of body mass (0.77–0.82 g/lb of body weight) (2 g/kg is maximum)

Source: Data from Torres-McGehee T, Pritchett K, Zippel D, Minton D, Cellamare A, and Sibilia M. (2012). Sports nutrition knowledge among collegiate athletes, coaches, athletic trainers, and strength and conditioning specialists. *J Athl Train.* 47(2): 205–211. Available: http://www.natajournals.org/doi/pdf/10.4085/1062-6050-47.2.205.

without the need of additional supplements. Only growing infants and children, pregnant or nursing women, or adults suffering from certain disease or injury states should consume more than the recommended amount (McArdle et al., 2009).

Vitamins

Vitamins are chemicals that are needed by the body in relatively small amounts and, therefore, are classified as micronutrients. This should not be interpreted, however, to mean that vitamins have little importance nutritionally. On the contrary, adequate amounts of vitamins are essential to health and performance. Vitamins serve a multitude of functions in the body, essentially helping to regulate biochemical reactions such as energy metabolism and cell and tissue generation, as well as serving as antioxidants (antioxidants protect structures such as cell membranes from the damaging effects of free radicals that are released during vigorous exercise). Vitamins contain no caloric value and, as such, do not directly provide energy for muscle contraction (**Figure 6.3**).

So far, 13 specific vitamins have been identified and are divided into two groups, water-soluble and fat soluble. The water-soluble group includes vitamins C (ascorbic acid) and the B vitamins (B_1, B_2, B_6, B_{12}, niacin, folic acid, biotin, and pantothenic acid). Water-soluble vitamins, with the exception of B_{12}, are not stored in the body, and excess amounts are excreted via the kidneys and urine. Fat-soluble vitamins are vitamins A, D, E, and K, and because of their solubility, they are stored in the fat tissues of the body. In fact, excess consumption of fat-soluble vitamins beyond what is recommended (in the U.S. Department of Agriculture's Recommended Daily Allowance [RDA]) can result in

buildup of and eventual toxic reaction to the stored vitamin (McArdle et al., 2009).

There is no evidence that taking any vitamin in an amount greater than the recommended level provides any sort of performance enhancement. Athletes who

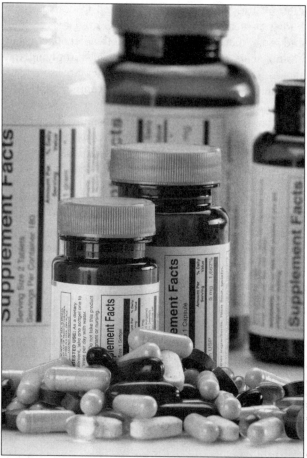

FIGURE 6.3 Various vitamin and mineral resources.

© monticello/ShutterStock, Inc.

consume balanced diets most likely are getting adequate amounts of vitamins through their food and beverage consumption. For athletes who are eating less than an ideal diet, a daily multivitamin supplement that meets the RDAs for all necessary vitamins is advised. There is no evidence that vitamins marketed as organic or natural provide any benefit over those that are manufactured synthetically and often sold at a lower cost. To be effective, vitamins should be taken after meals to optimize absorption because they work best in the presence of other nutrients (Clark, 1997).

Minerals

Minerals are elements that must be consumed regularly to ensure normal body functions. They provide structure, help maintain normal heart rhythm, assist muscle contractility, promote neural conductivity, and regulate metabolism (McArdle et al., 2009). A typical over-the-counter daily vitamin and mineral supplement usually includes all of the minerals listed in **Table 6.5**. As is the case with vitamins, there is no scientific evidence that consuming minerals in excess of the RDA provides any advantage in performance. In addition, a well balanced diet can provide all the necessary dietary minerals.

TABLE 6.5

MAJOR MINERALS AND TRACE MINERALS

Major Minerals (100 mg daily minimum)

Calcium
Chloride
Magnesium
Phosphorus
Potassium
Sodium
Sulfur

Trace Minerals (less than 15 mg daily)

Boron
Chromium
Copper
Fluorine
Iodine
Iron
Manganese
Molybdenum
Nickel
Tin
Selenium
Silicon
Vanadium
Zinc

The best known minerals are iron and calcium. Perron and Endres (1985) investigated the nutritional habits of 31 female high school volleyball players. Seventy percent of them did not meet the RDAs for energy (total calories), calcium, and iron. Iron is associated with red blood cell formation, oxygen storage and transport, and enzymatic reactions related to protein and carbohydrate metabolism (Manore et al., 2009). Iron is available from plant (nonheme) and animal (heme) sources. It is best absorbed from animal sources. RDA for iron is 10 milligrams (mg) for males and 18 mg for females. Females require more iron than males, especially during their menstrual cycles (RDA increases to 20 mg). Inadequate intake of iron or limited rates of iron absorption can cause anemia, resulting in lethargy and shortness of breath. Physically active individuals need only include the RDA levels of iron in their daily diet; they should steer clear of supplements unless a deficiency exists because excess iron can be very toxic to the body (McArdle et al., 2009). However, endurance, vegetarian, and female athletes may want to consult a physician for assessment and maintenance of proper iron balances. Current thought among sports scientists is that iron deficiency is common in athletes involved in endurance sports (Pattini & Schena, 1990). In fact, Deuster and colleagues (1986) report that even though female runners were taking some sort of iron supplement, 43% were found to be consuming less than the adult RDA for iron (18 mg for females). It is speculated that iron may be lost through sweating, gastrointestinal bleeding, menstrual bleeding, and excessive red blood cell destruction (hemolysis) in the blood vessels. During menstruation, female athletes may lose as much as 2 mg of iron daily. This loss may be offset by a dietary adjustment of iron-rich foods, such as organ meats or enriched whole-grain products. A convenient method of supplementation is a daily multivitamin and mineral tablet. Numerous products are available over the counter that provide the adult RDA of iron.

Calcium is metabolically associated with normal bone and dental health. It is the most prevalent mineral in the body and is easily obtained in the diet by consuming dairy products or other foods/beverages that have been artificially fortified with calcium. Scientific evidence suggests that some groups of athletes may be at an increased risk of calcium deficiency (Deuster et al., 1986; Moffatt, 1984). Female athletes involved in aerobic running sports, as well as gymnasts, have been found to be consuming too little calcium. This places these people at risk for inadequate bone development and can contribute to osteopenia or osteoporosis in later life. In these high-risk groups, calcium supplementation is most certainly warranted. Again, it is important to note that a supplement that provides the RDA is appropriate because consuming calcium in excess of this level may lead to other problems. The recommended daily dosage for adolescent females is 1500 mg.

Evidence suggests that some athletes do not eat well balanced diets and, therefore, should be advised to include a daily vitamin and mineral supplement in their diet. It must be emphasized that this supplement should be of the type that provides only the RDA of each nutrient and not a product that contains megadoses of the nutrients. Vitamin and mineral supplementation beyond the RDA values usually proves physiologically and economically wasteful and could adversely affect health (McArdle et al., 2009).

Water

There is virtually no debate in the sports medicine community regarding the importance of water, not only to human performance but to survival as well! Water serves myriad functions in the body because the molecule is necessary for cellular function, heat regulation, and elimination of waste products. Water is housed in the body in two general locations—extracellular fluids (those fluids outside of the cells, commonly called interstitial fluid) and intracellular fluids (those fluids contained in the cell). Water is constantly being lost through normal body functions such as breathing, elimination of wastes, and sweating.

At rest the adult requirement for water is approximately 2.5 liters (L) of water daily. Under conditions of heavy exercise, especially in conditions of high ambient temperature, water requirements can escalate to 5 L to 10 L daily (McArdle et al., 2009). During exercise, a significant amount of body water is lost to eliminate metabolic heat. The circulatory system transports this excess heat via the blood to the skin, where, in harmony with the body's sweat glands, heat is carried from the surface by way of evaporation. The process of sweat evaporation from the skin surface can easily result in an hourly water loss from the body of 2 L or more for each hour of exercise. The most serious consequence of profuse sweating is the loss of body water. A reduction in body weight of 2%–5% can result in reduced performance and stress on internal organs. To calculate the reduction in body weight due to fluid loss, weigh the athlete before and after practice. Take the number of pounds lost in activity and divide that number by the prepractice weight. This fluid must be replaced, or serious, even life-threatening, consequences can result. Current recommendations suggest that for every pound of water weight lost, an athlete should consume 20–24 ounces (oz) of fluid (McArdle et al., 2009). The process of

WHAT IF?

A female high school gymnast (17 years old, 110 lbs, 5 feet 1 inch, and 14% body fat) asks you for recommendations for her training diet. How many kilocalories would you suggest she consume on a daily basis to remain competitive, and what is the breakdown for carbohydrates, protein, and fats?

controlling the body's core temperature during exercise is known as thermoregulation.

Nutritional Knowledge of Athletes and Coaches: What the Research Shows

As presented previously, athletes are largely uneducated regarding proper nutrition, even though they understand the importance of adhering to a quality diet (Torres-McGehee et al., 2012). Therefore, this might result in damaging nutritional practices, because they often fail to incorporate sound principles of nutrition into their training diets. For example, Division I college athletes still use a variety of sources for nutritional and supplement information, like family members (32%), fellow athletes (32%), athletic trainers (ATs; 30%), dietitians (30%), coaches (28%), and TV, radio, or the Internet (10%) to obtain their information (Froiland et al., 2004). The good news is they are relying on trained professionals more often, and ATs and SCSs demonstrate solid understanding of the importance of athletes adhering to quality diets and they also understand the athletes' nutritional needs (Torres-McGehee et al., 2012).

Only 3%, 12%, and 29% of collegiate athletes ($n = 330$) correctly identified recommended percentages of total calorie intake for protein, fat, and carbohydrates, respectively (Jacobson et al., 2001). These athletes underestimated their carbohydrate needs and overestimated their fat and protein needs. In fact, 21% believed that protein provides immediate energy. In further support of athletes' lack of nutrition knowledge, Hilton (2005) reported that 70% of university athletes ($n = 345$) are falling short of their daily caloric needs and 81% of females and 90% of males were not eating the recommended amounts of CHO. These reported percentages definitely conflict with recommendations by experts who advise a distribution of 60% to 70% carbohydrates, 12% to 15% protein, and less than 30% fat (McArdle et al., 2009). In addition to macronutrient

Athletic Trainers SPEAK Out

Courtesy of Paula Sammarone Turocy, EdD, LAT, ATC, Associate Professor, Rangos School of Health Sciences, Duquesne University.

A 15-year-old athlete, who had recently gone through puberty, and his parents approached me after church, because they heard that I might be able to help their son gain weight (primarily muscle) for football season. The athlete informed me that he had purchased and was using a creatine muscle-building supplement and was following the older kids' strength workouts to get bigger and stronger, but he still was unable to get any bigger or add any muscle weight. My first concern was about the safety of the supplements. So, I inspected the packaging for the National Sanitation Foundation (NSF; http://www.nsf.org) seal and then went online to see if a complaint or concern was filed about the product. I also checked the World Anti-Doping Agency site (http://www.wada-ama.org), Drug Free Sport (http://www.drugfreesport.com), and examined recent literature, including systematic reviews, to validate the claims made about the ingredients. To help the young man and his parents understand muscle building and strength development, I discussed that not only does the body produce its own creatine, but that creatine is available naturally in foods that are generally high in protein. We discussed that he had only recently gone through puberty, and that no matter how hard he worked on strength and muscle development, his ability to add muscle/size was limited by his developmental stage. To maximize his ability to gain muscle mass, I assisted him in restructuring his workouts to better build strength and power. I also assessed his current body composition, and then calculated his total caloric need for a weight that included an additional 15 lbs of muscle and approximately 5 lbs of fat. Finally, I suggested that, before he spent a lot of money buying individual supplements, he consider modifying his diet to ensure that he was eating from all food groups, taking in enough calories to meet his body's energy demands, and maximizing his protein (maximum of 2.0 g/kg body weight) and fluid intake. The good news is that following this simple plan the athlete was able to put on the additional muscle and extra body fat in approximately 3 months.

—Paula Sammarone Turocy EdD, LAT, ATC

Paula Sammarone Turocy is an Associate Professor, Rangos School of Health Sciences, Duquesne University.

Courtesy of Paula Sammarone Turocy, EdD, LAT, ATC, Associate Professor, Rangos School of Health Sciences, Duquesne University.

---

confusion, only 35% to 40% correctly identified the role of vitamins, and many (30%) thought that vitamins provide immediate energy (Jacobson et al., 2001).

Coaches are also not informed about the composition of a proper diet and nutrition plan. Corley et al. (1990) reported that only 20% of college coaches ($n = 105$) had the correct distribution of CHO, fats, and proteins, and 15% still felt that the best way to increase body mass was to take protein supplements. Sossin and colleagues (1997) reported that 91% of wrestling coaches ($n = 311$) believe that wrestlers should restrict CHO and not fat in their diets. The elevated levels of fat consumed by athletes in these studies may indicate that they were consuming a high percentage of red meats and other protein sources high in fat (Jacobson et al., 2001). Such dietary practices might create several cardiovascular problems, including arteriosclerosis and heart disease.

It may be more than a curious coincidence that the life expectancy of an NFL football player is 52 to 55 years (Nelson, 1989). The findings of these studies indicate that collegiate athletes and coaches persist in the myths that surround nutrition and athletic success. However, there may be hope: Jacobson and colleagues (2001) reported that compared to a similar study in the previous decade, there was improvement in the athletes' knowledge base and their sources of nutritional knowledge. More recent research (Torres-McGehee et al., 2012) reported that 55% ± 13% of athletes scored above a benchmark of adequate knowledge on a comprehensive test on macronutrients, micronutrients, supplements, weight control, and hydration. In general, the lowest area of knowledge was on weight control and eating disorders, where only 47% ± 22% of athletes scored above the benchmark.

Special Considerations
Female Athletes

Recent research on a sample of high school students ($n = 5740$) reported that 15% of girls versus 4% of boys scored higher than the threshold for concern on an Eating Attitude Test (EAT-26) (Austin et al., 2008). As more women become involved in organized sports, concerns have been raised regarding special nutritional considerations for female athletes, especially those involved in aesthetic sports that place an emphasis on being lean, such as gymnastics, diving, and dancing. A survey of adolescent female gymnasts (n = 76) indicated that these young athletes were consuming less than the RDA in a number of vitamins and minerals and were consuming too few total calories, especially in the form of carbohydrates (Loosli & Benson, 1990). Moffatt (1984) surveyed the dietary habits of 13 female high school gymnasts who competed at advanced levels and determined they also had diets low (below the RDA) in vitamin B_6, folic acid, iron, calcium, zinc, and magnesium. Because gymnastics place great emphasis on being lean, it is not surprising that the majority of these girls demonstrated a deficient caloric intake and altered micronutrient consumption.

However, gymnastics is not alone. Greenleaf and colleagues (2009) surveyed 204 female college athletes from 17 sports and determined that 54% were dissatisfied with their current weight. Torstveit, Rosenvinge, and Sundgot-Borgen (2008) also reported that 47% of athletes in "lean" sports (i.e., cross country, swimming/diving, crew/rowing, and cheerleading), in contrast to 20% in "non-lean" sports (i.e., basketball, softball, and lacrosse), had clinical disordered eating, which includes calorie restriction.

Endurance Sports

Upgrove and Achterberg (1990) investigated the nutritional habits of male and female high school cross-country runners. Ironically, in a sport in which a diet high in carbohydrates is a prerequisite to success, these young runners were poorly versed in the role of this essential nutrient. In addition, they reported that coaches were their preferred source of information on nutrition. This is particularly alarming considering that many coaches are ill prepared to give sound advice on nutrition.

Deuster and colleagues (1986) examined the dietary habits of a group of 51 top-level female distance runners. The runners' reported intake of protein, fat, and carbohydrates was 13%, 32%, and 55%, respectively. These percentages indicate a diet somewhat high in fat and low in carbohydrates. Even with the high fat content, their diets were still too low in caloric content. In effect, these women were training and racing while adhering to diets that failed to provide adequate calories for such activity.

The scenario in which athletes, both males and females, are not consuming enough calories presents a new concern that is emerging in athletics called **athletic energy deficit**. Athletic energy deficit occurs when an athlete is not matching his or her caloric output by consuming enough calories to properly sustain body function. Typically, athletic energy deficit develops when there is a pressure to change eating habits in an effort to accomplish a sporting goal (American Bone Health, 2010). Beyond not having enough energy to properly fuel the activity, athletes with athletic energy deficit will be unable to support vital body functions including bone growth. In many cases of athletic energy deficit, athletes are at a deficit of 1000 kcal/day (Deutz et al., 2000). When there is insufficient energy for the natural repair that occurs after exercise, hormones can be negatively affected. In females, estrogen can be significantly lowered, causing amenorrhea and slower bone growth. In males and females, athletic energy deficit may cause shortages of vitamin D and calcium, both essential to bone growth. As a result, poor bone growth may occur, which can lead to stress fractures and early onset osteoporosis in males and females. Athletic energy deficit can also lead to a series of other adverse health-related consequences including depression, lethargy, attention deficits, sleep disorders, and increases in body fat.

Wrestling

Despite improved efforts by sanctioning bodies, officials, parents, and even many athletes, the sport of wrestling continues to be plagued with the problem of athletes practicing rapid, often unhealthy weight-loss procedures. Wrestling is one of only a few sports that match participants on the basis of weight. Yet, in an effort to gain an advantage, many wrestlers attempt to shed pounds rapidly to compete in a lighter weight category. Unfortunately, the only form of rapid weight loss, short of surgical removal of tissue, is through dehydration. Water weighs approximately 7 pounds per gallon; therefore, an athlete can significantly reduce weight by reducing the body's water content. Wrestlers have been known to use a variety of methods to rapidly lose weight, including fluid restriction, the use of laxatives and diuretics, artificially induced sweating, and even starvation. There is no definitive proof that such tactics actually present an advantage, and there are plenty of reasons not to engage in such behavior. The short-term effects of repeated bouts of extreme, rapid weight loss include strength depletion, increased blood viscosity (blood thickening), blood clots, kidney and liver problems, swelling of the pancreas (which produces insulin), and ulcers (Nelson, 1989; Williams, 1992). The long-term effects are not known at this time; however, there is speculation in the scientific community that these techniques may interfere with normal growth and development in the adolescent athlete.

In an effort to reduce the likelihood of unhealthy weight-loss practices ("weight cutting") in high school wrestlers, the state of Wisconsin instituted the Wrestling Minimum Weight Project (WMWP) in 1989 (Oppliger et al., 1995). This project involved the establishment of minimum weight-loss and body-composition criteria that limit all participants to a body fat minimum of 7% and a maximum of 3 pounds of weight loss per week. A trained network of volunteers tested the athletes and provided an extensive offering of nutrition education for coaches around the state. Feedback regarding the program has been positive from 95% of the coaches, and wrestling participation has increased in Wisconsin as well. As a result of the WMWP, starting with the 1996–1997 season, the National Federation of State High School Associations (NFHS) modified wrestling rule 1-3-1 to include the following statement: "An ideal program would be one where a medical professional would assist in establishing a minimum weight through the use of checking body fat and hydration. The recommended minimum body fat should not be lower than 7%" (NFHS, 2011).

In addition, the American College of Sports Medicine (ACSM; Oppliger et al., 1996, updated in 2010) has published a position statement regarding weight loss in competitive wrestling. The ACSM notes that "weight cutting" can have several physiological effects on performance including reduction in muscle strength, reduction in anaerobic capacity, reduced endurance capacity, impaired thermoregulatory processes, and lower oxygen consumption. "Weight cutting" can also deplete fluids, electrolytes, and glycogen causing increased protein breakdown, impaired coordination, and cardiac arrhythmias. Based on the variety of health risks associated with the practice of "weight cutting," the following recommendations are given by the ACSM in regard to the sport of wrestling:

- Education about the adverse consequences of prolonged fasting and dehydration on physical performance and physical health should be provided to coaches and wrestlers.
- Rubber suits, steam rooms, hot boxes, saunas, laxatives, and diuretics should not be used for making weight.

WHAT IF?

You are asked to make a presentation to parents of high school wrestlers on the topic of effective weight-loss techniques. What specific recommendations would you make to parents regarding their children's dietary habits?

- State or national governing body legislation that schedules weigh-ins immediately prior to competition should be adopted.
- Daily weigh-ins need to be scheduled before and after practice to monitor weight loss and dehydration. Any weight lost during practice should be regained through adequate food and fluid intake.
- The body composition of each wrestler needs to be assessed prior to the season using valid methods for this population. Medical clearances will be needed for males younger than 16 years of age with body fat below 7% or those older than 16 years with body fat below 5% and for female wrestlers below 12%–14%.
- Caloric intake needs to support the normal developmental needs of the young wrestler. Emphasize the standard percentages of macronutrients along with a minimal caloric intake of 1700 to 2500 kcal/day. Remind wrestlers that rigorous training will increase the requirement up to an additional 1000 calories per day.

Wrestling is a time-honored sport, but techniques used in the past to "make weight" are not only out of date, but can cause life-threatening consequences. Therefore, these recommendations need to be carefully implemented at all levels of participation and competition. In the end, many of these recommendations can apply to any sport but are significantly important for male and female wrestlers.

Conclusions

Based on the results of research pertaining to the nutritional behavior of athletes, it appears that some important conclusions can be made regarding the dietary practices of athletes (ACSM, 2009):

athletic energy deficit When sustained activity is not balanced with a proportional increase in nutrition, the calories out balances with the calories in.

1. Many athletes do not consume the proper proportions of protein, carbohydrates, and fat. Athletes should consume diets that provide at least the RDA for all micronutrients.

2. Carbohydrate consumption should be approximately 6–10 g/kg body mass (2.7–4.5 g/lb body weight). Carbohydrates maintain blood glucose levels during exercise and replace muscle glycogen. The amount required depends on the athlete's total daily energy expenditure, type of sport, sex, and environmental conditions (see Table 6.2).

3. Protein recommendations for endurance and strength-trained athletes range from 1.2 to 1.8 g/kg body mass (0.5–0.9 g/lb body weight). These recommended protein intakes can generally be met through diet alone, without the use of protein or amino acid supplements. For example, to compute the recommended 1-day protein intake for an 85-lb female gymnast, make the following calculations:

   Body weight in kilograms = 38.6
   (85 lbs ÷ 2.2 = lbs per kg)
   38.6 kg × 1.2 g of protein = 46.4 g daily protein requirement
   A chicken breast (8 oz) will provide the protein requirement.

4. Because of convenience, athletes tend to consume too many calories in the form of junk food, which is laden with fat and extra protein (**Figure 6.4**). Fat intake should range from 20% to 30% of total energy intake. Consuming less than or equal to 20% of energy from fat does not benefit performance because fat is a source of energy, fat-soluble vitamins, and essential fatty acids.

5. Athletes participating in sports that stress lean builds and low body fat tend to follow diets too low in total calories. Athletes who restrict energy intake, use severe weight-loss practices, or eliminate one or more food groups from their diet are at greatest risk of macronutrient and micronutrient deficiencies. Severe restriction over time can lead to athletic energy deficit.

6. Many athletes' diets are deficient in at least some important minerals, such as calcium, iron, and zinc. However, the best sources are natural foods and not supplements unless specifically guided by a physician. Short- and long-term supplementation above recommended doses does not improve exercise performance or training responses (McArdle et al., 2009).

© Jones & Bartlett Learning. Photographed by Kimberly Potvin.

FIGURE 6.4 Fast foods contain many nutrients but are typically high in fat content.

Educating Athletes: What Can the Coach Do?

Research indicates that many athletes consider the coach to be responsible for providing guidelines on proper diet. As reported earlier in the chapter, Froiland and colleagues (2004) noted that 28% of athletes typically use coaches to obtain their nutrition information. Unfortunately, most coaches lack any sort of formal training in basic nutrition (Corley et al., 1990). The good news is that students entering the coaching profession and earning either a major or minor in physical education or a related field will probably be required to take at least one class in nutrition. The same is often true for those earning a coaching endorsement or minor.

If those planning to coach did not major in a health-related field, they should incorporate at least one nutrition course into their continuing education. Coaches can attend in-service meetings, professional conferences, and community education programs on nutrition-related topics. An excellent source of current nutritional information can be obtained via a subscription to a professional journal in the field of coaching or sports science. Furthermore, many excellent books on sports nutrition are now on the market and hospitals often employ registered dietitians who are highly trained and may be more than happy to provide information on nutrition for a coach's athletes. For assistance in locating an expert in their area, coaches can contact the Academy of Nutrition and Dietetics (formerly the American Dietetic Association; http://www.eatright.org/public/fard.aspx).

Another option for coaches who live near a university is to contact a member of the institution's sports medicine or strength and conditioning staff. Typically, this is a BOC-certified athletic trainer or certified strength coach (by the National Strength and Conditioning Association [NSCA]). In addition, universities often employ faculty with graduate degrees in nutrition science, and they may be willing to serve as a resource as well.

Coaches should encourage, perhaps even require, that athletes keep a record of what they eat and drink. This information can be combined with a training diary. Coaches or other professionals (certified athletic trainer, exercise science professor, or registered dietitian) should periodically review what athletes are eating and make recommendations based on sound nutritional principles. Such a record need not be a complex, detailed document. Athletes need only record the content and approximate amount of foods and beverages consumed during each meal. Most food packages provide information regarding the nutritional content of the product. With practice, it is relatively simple to determine whether an athlete is consuming the correct amount of nutrients.

Recently, programs designed to teach athletes nutrition and life skills have been developed. The National Collegiate Athletic Association (NCAA) works in cooperation with the ACSM and Academy of Nutrition and Dietetics to provide athletes with up-to-date information in regard to nutrition and performance. The Oregon Health and Science University has developed a program for females titled Athletes Targeting Healthy Exercise and Nutrition Alternatives (ATHENA). This program is peer-led and addresses the connection between young women in sports, disordered eating behaviors, and body-shaping drug use (Elliot et al., 2008). Students learn attitudes and skills that will help them make healthy choices in sports and throughout their lives. Coaches and student team leaders are trained to teach goal setting and self-monitoring of nutritional behaviors. Long-term follow-up studies indicate that females who go through ATHENA training report better nutrition habits and reduced use of diet pills and supplements. The program's website is http://www .ohsu.edu/xd/education/schools/school-of-medicine/ departments/clinical-departments/medicine/divisions/ hpsm/research/athena.cfm.

When working with children, coaches should discuss the nutritional needs of athletes with parents. A significant amount of nutritional information is available online from the Sports, Cardiovascular, and Wellness Nutrition practice group, a division of the Academy of Nutrition and Dietetics (http://www.scandpg.org/); STOP Sports Injuries (http://www.stopsportsinjuries .org/sports-nutrition.aspx); and the U.S. Department of Agriculture's (USDA) Nutrient Data Laboratory website (http://www.ars.usda.gov/). The USDA site provides an extensive, searchable listing of the nutrient contents of hundreds of different foods. This information

can be useful when making decisions about food choices. Another useful site is maintained by the USDA Center for Nutrition Policy and Promotion (http:// www.cnpp.usda.gov/), which provides online dietary analyses. After registering and entering all necessary dietary information, a detailed nutritional assessment is generated. Because this analysis is completed online, athletes should be encouraged to complete it at home; minors will ideally have parental involvement.

General Dietary Guidelines for Athletes

Daily Diet: Nutritional Maintenance

Although each sport and each athlete have specific nutritional requirements and preferences, some general recommendations can be made based on current knowledge. The basic differences between a nonathlete's and an athlete's diet are that athletes require additional energy to support physical activity and additional fluid to cover sweat losses. It should be noted, however, that (like a conditioning program) the athlete's diet should be tailored to meet individual needs. A gymnast may need to control her body composition within a very narrow set of parameters; a football lineman may wish to gain additional lean body mass. Thus, the nutrition program must be based on the physical characteristics of the athlete and the individual demands of the sport.

All sports nutrition programs should prepare athletes for practice and competition, encourage athletes to consume food and beverages during competition to maintain energy sources, and ensure adequate recovery between training sessions and after competitions (Brotherhood, 1984).

Athletes need to be educated about proper food selections to maintain the correct proportions of carbohydrates, fats, and protein. Sport scientists recommend the following breakdown of total daily calories: 60% to 70% carbohydrates, 12% to 15% protein, and less than 30% fat (McArdle et al., 2009). It may be best to keep dietary recommendations in regard to carbohydrates as simple as possible because most foods contain significant amounts of carbohydrates. It is important that athletes understand that many protein sources contain significant amounts of fat; therefore, these foods should be consumed less frequently than lean sources of protein (beans, eggs, and dairy). Most experts agree that even highly active athletes need only 1.2 g to 1.8 g of protein per day for each kilogram of body mass (ACSM, 2009). This means that a football player who weighs 195 lbs (88.6 kg) needs to consume a maximum of 177 g of protein per day. This amount could be supplied in one big meal (typical of many football players). For example, see the protein provided by this simple meal:

4 cups of milk	32 g
9 ounces of lean beef	72 g
4 cups of macaroni and cheese	72 g
Total =	176 g

Not surprisingly, research shows that professional and collegiate football players and international rugby players often consume more than 2 g of protein per day for each kilogram of body mass (Holway & Spriet, 2011). Although, many football coaches recommend a diet high in carbohydrates and low in fat for optimal performance, they also primarily recommend beef, chicken, fish, beans, dairy products, and protein supplements to football players who want to gain lean body mass (Bair, Dean, & Lambrinides, 1994). Unfortunately, these recommendations are contrary to each other as diets high in meat products along with protein supplementation are likely to contain more overall calories and fat. Not only are such diets expensive, but they may be unhealthy as well. As described earlier in this chapter, excess protein produces metabolic waste products, especially nitrogen, that can put stress on the kidneys and the liver. Dehydration may also occur as the kidneys increase urine output.

Assuming athletes are sticking to a balanced diet, there is no need to be concerned about them getting enough vitamins and minerals. These compounds are needed in small amounts, and there is little evidence that athletes need to consume extra vitamins and minerals to perform (McArdle et al., 2009). However, dietary supplementation may be warranted in cases of identified deficiencies. As discussed previously, two minerals that may prove to be exceptions are iron and calcium. Athletes who complain of chronic fatigue, repeated stress fractures, loss of fitness, or inability to perform—despite adequate diet and rest—should be referred to a physician for evaluation. A simple blood test can determine whether a true iron or calcium deficiency is the problem. Researchers recommend that high-risk groups be tested periodically for iron deficiency, with subsequent supplementation of iron when deemed appropriate by a physician (Magazanik et al., 1988).

Coaches should be conservative when making dietary recommendations, especially to younger athletes. Offering a few well proven, simple guidelines probably represents the most effective approach. An excellent resource is the interactive website http://choosemyplate.gov/ that is made available to the public by the U.S. Department

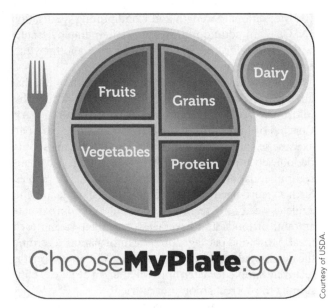

FIGURE 6.5 ChooseMyPlate.gov.

of Agriculture (**Figure 6.5**). This site enables the user to develop a personalized dietary plan based on factors such as age, gender, and physical activity level; it has replaced the Food Guide Pyramid. However, athletes interested in developing a more sophisticated dietary regimen should consider performing a dietary analysis with a sports dietitian.

Precompetition Diets

Precompetition diets should be determined based on the sport or activity. As a general rule, it is advised that athletes, regardless of sport, not consume a meal immediately prior to an event. The process of digestion takes 2 to 3 hours or longer; thus, foods eaten just before a contest will contribute virtually nothing to performance. It should also be noted that gastrointestinal distress is common if a meal is eaten too close to practice or competition, because the body reallocates blood flow to muscles away from the gastrointestinal system once exercise begins (McArdle et al., 2009). A precompetition meal should provide sufficient fluid to maintain hydration and be relatively high in carbohydrates (low glycemic index), moderate in protein, low in fat, low in fiber, and easy to digest. This facilitates gastric emptying and minimizes gastrointestinal distress while maintaining blood glucose (ACSM, 2009). Experts recommend that the typical pregame meal should be eaten between 1 and 4 hours prior to the contest (ACSM, 2009). However, a very light snack (easy to digest food) and fluid can be consumed within 20 to 30 minutes of any exercise situation.

If acceptable to the athlete, liquid diets offer some distinct advantages over the more traditional precompetition meal. Commercially manufactured liquid meals typically contain a high percentage of CHO in a form that facilitates rapid digestion and absorption. In addition, they contain water, which helps the athlete with respect to achieving adequate precompetition hydration. It is recommended that the precompetition diet contain between 150 g and 300 g of CHO (3–5 g/kg body weight; McArdle et al., 2009). These guidelines are especially important for athletes participating in endurance sports. However, athletes involved in power sports such as football would also benefit from such a regimen. The traditional meal of steak and potatoes just prior to the game provides only a psychological effect; it may cause bloating and a feeling of heaviness in some athletes. Remember, athletes need to choose foods and beverages that work best for them and should experiment before competitions (ACSM, 2009).

Nutrition During Competition

Research has shown that consumption of CHO during activity, both aerobic and anaerobic, can be beneficial. It is known that the body has a limited capacity for storing glycogen and that athletes may deplete glycogen supplies in the muscles and liver before completing an event. One hour of highly intense exercise can reduce liver glycogen by 55% and 2 hours can almost completely deplete both liver and muscle glycogen (McArdle et al., 2009). This is commonly referred to as "hitting the wall."

Research supports the premise that consuming carbohydrates during long-duration exercise (1 to 3 hours at 70% to 80% maximum aerobic capacity) allows active muscle tissue to rely on blood glucose for energy and not deplete important liver and muscle stores (Coyle, 1988). Many commercially made carbohydrate products are now available. Coaches and athletes can also prepare their own preferred beverages. Sports drinks typically provide a 6%–8% carbohydrate solution by volume, and approximately 8 ounces should be consumed about every 15 to 20 minutes (between 30 and 60 g/hour). This is especially important in athletes who exercise in the morning after an overnight fast when liver glycogen levels are decreased.

Although the intake of carbohydrates is essential for optimal performance, a relatively high intake of carbohydrates during exercise will likely increase the incidence of upper (nausea, heartburn, or belching) and lower (bloating, diarrhea, and abdominal cramps) gastrointestinal symptoms. Two theories are used to explain such gastrointestinal distress, including malabsorption of contents due to limited blood flow to gut or the attraction of excessive fluid from the blood into the intestines to balance out the excess electrolytes (Jeukendrup, 2007). It is hypothesized that too many carbohydrates or carbohydrates that oxidize too fast (Table 6.1) can be ingested at rates in excess of 60 g/hour, and this will likely result in **hyperosmolality** of the stomach contents, which then leads to the gastrointestinal discomfort (Jeukendrup, 2007).

Nutrition for Post Exercise

After exercise, dietary goals are to replace muscle glycogen and ensure quick recovery. Composition and timing of the recovery meal or snack depend on the length and intensity of the exercise session (ACSM, 2009). Glycogen depletion can occur after 2–3 hours of exercise at 60%–80% VO_2 max (Manore et al., 2009). Post-exercise meals need to provide adequate fluids, electrolytes, carbohydrates, and protein. A carbohydrate intake of approximately 1.0–1.5 g/kg body mass (0.5–0.7 g/lb) during the first 30 minutes and again every 2 hours for 4–6 hours is adequate to replace glycogen stores (ACSM, 2009). The timing of CHO ingestion is important because glycogen levels replenish faster if the food is consumed within 30 minutes to 1 hour. The type of food is also significant because consumption of high glycemic index CHO results in higher muscle glycogen levels 24 hours after a glycogen-depleting exercise as compared with the same amount of low glycemic index carbohydrates. Also, there was no difference in glycogen replacement when CHO was eaten alone or paired with protein and fat. Protein consumed after exercise provides amino acids for building and repair of muscle tissue (ACSM, 2009). It is recommended to consume foods that will provide a ratio of 4 grams of carbohydrates to 1 gram of protein (e.g., low-fat chocolate milk, sports nutrition bars).

Pamphlets of nutritional information about eating before, during, and after exercise are available online at the Sports, Cardiovascular, and Wellness Nutrition practice group (http://www.scandpg.org).

Nutrition and Injury Recovery

Obviously, proper nutrition is vital to tissue healing and recovery. Although there is no evidence that supplementing vitamins and minerals shortens recovery time, it is essential that their consumption be adequate (Wilmore & Costill, 1988).

hyperosmolality   Increased concentration of a solution.

A major concern for many injured athletes is weight gain during periods of forced inactivity. Some athletes find it difficult to adjust eating habits to reduce caloric intake when they are not exercising. During injury rehabilitation, activity may have ceased but metabolism has often increased as the body is repairing itself; therefore, athletes should be advised against significantly reducing total caloric intake during rehabilitation out of fear of weight gain (daily caloric recommendation is 35 kcal/kg/day; Harrison, n.d.). It is important that the coach advise an injured athlete about these dietary changes during recovery. It may be possible for some injured athletes to continue exercising with some form of alternate activity. Runners can often ride a stationary bicycle or run in a swimming pool, thereby maintaining aerobic fitness and burning off excess calories. Players who are suffering from infectious illnesses may be unable to exercise and should take care to establish a caloric intake based on their BMR until they are healthy.

Unfortunately, there have been few publications in the area of nutrition and sports injury recovery; however, there are extensive publications regarding the role of nutrition in recovery from disease. Therefore, many of the following recommendations are pulled from research on tissue healing and nutrition through the lifespan and during disease (Bucci, 1995). Simple recommendations in regard to the macronutrients include maintaining carbohydrate consumption based on healing processes and rehabilitation activity levels, maintaining protein levels as long as they are greater than 1 g/kg/day, and consuming fats with a concentration on "good" fats (olive oil, avocados, nuts and seeds, ground flax or flax oil). Of course, adequate hydration should also be maintained throughout rehabilitation and increases should occur with fluid loss through sweating.

Carbohydrates are a direct form of energy for cell metabolism that also stimulate insulin and insulin growth factor, which help in tissue building. Proteins contain the building blocks for connective tissue and muscle. Amino acids in proteins are essential. Several amino acids, including arginine and ornithine $-\alpha-$ ketoglutarate (OKG), glutamine, and leucine, have all been recommended (Harrison, n.d.); however, caution must be applied when supplementing amino acids (discussed in more detail later in this chapter). Foods with anti-inflammatory properties are also recommended, but inflammation is a necessary process in healing and it should not be stopped. Garlic, cocoa, tea, blueberries, and pineapple are known for their anti-inflammatory effect (Bucci, 1995). Pineapples along with papaya, cheese, sourdough, and rye also all provide proteolytic enzymes (Harrison, n.d.). These enzymes are known to inactivate bradykinins, reduce viscosity of extracellular fluid (swelling), and help molecular debridement (Bucci, 1995). Finally, free fatty acids, especially omega-3 (anti-inflammatory) and omega-6 (proinflammatory), are known to contain eicosanoids, which can reduce pain but also cause vasodilation and enhance the immune system. Omega-3 fatty acids can be found in fish oil and cold water fish (salmon, herring), and omega-6 fatty acids (linoleic acid) can be found in seeds, nuts, and a variety of vegetable oils. It is important to keep omega-3 and omega-6 fatty acids in balance rather than over-consume one or the other. It is currently recommended to consume 3–9 g/day of each when rehabilitating from an injury (Harrison, n.d.).

Managing Body Weight

Athletes wishing to gain or lose weight must be educated about the various ways that body weight can be changed. To maintain weight an athlete's caloric intake must equal caloric expenditure (basic metabolic needs plus exercise demands). Unsafe weight management practices can negatively affect an athlete's overall health in addition to compromising his or her athletic performance. Encouraging weight management by limiting calories or specific nutrients, engaging in deadly weight control methods, or simply not eating or drinking much at all are very dangerous practices for anyone, but especially for athletes (Sammarone Turocy et al., 2011). Safe weight loss and management can be accomplished using scientific evidence and credible resources. First and foremost, athletes, coaches, and parents are encouraged to visit with a registered dietician when weight management is an issue; however, athletic trainers and strength and conditioning specialists can also be valuable resources. The National Athletic Trainers' Association position statement on "Safe weight loss and maintenance practices in sport and exercise" (Sammarone Turocy et al., 2011) is an excellent resource and can be downloaded at: http://www.nata.org/position-statements.

Body weight can be categorized as three basic forms: water, fat tissue, and lean tissue. Water makes up a substantial portion of nearly all the tissues in the body. From a practical standpoint, skeletal muscles make up the majority of lean-tissue weight. The majority of body fat is found just under the skin and is known as subcutaneous fat. The human body has devised a highly efficient method of storing excess dietary calories. When an athlete consumes more calories per day than the body requires for a given activity level, the excess calories are converted to fat. Conversely, if an athlete fails to consume enough calories to meet the daily requirement, stored fat is metabolized to form energy. Curiously, when an athlete severely restricts caloric intake, such as in fasting, the body consumes muscle tissue to generate energy (Williams, 1992). Therefore, an athlete will reduce lean-tissue mass, which in most cases results in loss of performance.

If athletes are striving to maintain a desirable body weight, they should weigh themselves weekly, at about the same time of day, after going to the bathroom. Their body weight should not fluctuate too much from week to week but can fluctuate daily because of sweating from physical activity. It is also important to remember that female athletes may experience weight gains immediately preceding their menstrual period. However, determining body weight by standing on a scale may be of limited value, because a given volume of muscle tissue weighs more than the same volume of fat. The ratio of fat to lean body weight is a better measurement; this is commonly referred to as body composition. It is represented as a percentage of body fat; the percentage of essential fat is 2%–5% in men, 10%–13% in women, 7% for adolescent boys, and 14% for adolescent girls. The range for most active young females is 14%–24% and active young males is 7%–17%; however, obesity is increasing in epidemic proportions across society, and average females' body fat is 25%–31% and average males' is 18%–24% (Muth, 2009).

There are athletes who, for a variety of reasons, desire to change their body weight. Those involved in sports that require a specific body weight, such as wrestling, boxing, or light-weight crew, may attempt to lose pounds rapidly to compete in a lighter weight category. These competitors need to understand that rapid weight fluctuations typically involve dehydration, and significant water loss can cause a number of undesirable consequences resulting in an overall loss of performance. The sport of wrestling has been very been proactive in guarding against this and developed minimum body fat standards for male and female athletes. In the high school setting, male wrestlers cannot be lower than 7% body fat and females cannot be lower than 12%. Currently, all official body fat and body weight measures must be obtained when an athlete is properly hydrated. To determine appropriate hydration, a refractometer and/or urine dipstick assessment can be used to measure urine specific gravity or protein content, respectively. The urine dipstick method is more sensitive to acute dehydration (Sammarone Turocy et al., 2011). Appropriate hydration is achieved if the urine's specific gravity is less than 1.025 (NFHS, 2011). A minimal competitive weight should be established for all weight class athletes using the required minimal body fats for the sport or using the essential fat guidelines. Wrestlers and other weight class athletes should determine their healthy body weight and body composition during the off-season, and then concentrate on preparing for that weight category in the upcoming season. It is important

to remember that the current recommendation is to limit weight loss to 1.5% of current body weight per week (NFHS, 2011).

Minimal Competitive Weight

The minimal competitive weight can then be calculated by dividing the athlete's lean body weight by one minus the percentage of (1 – %) fat desired (Wilmore & Costill, 1988). Fat desired is governed by rules of sport, minimal essential fat, or personal choice. The minimum percentage of fat for male wrestlers is 7%. To use this formula, the body weight and percentage of fat of the athlete must be determined. Although there are many ways of estimating body fat, the most practical method employs skin-fold measurements. However, the technique is only as good as the person administering the test. Hence, testing of body composition should be conducted by a person who has been properly trained, such as an exercise physiologist or BOC-certified athletic trainer. After the body fat percentage has been determined, lean body weight (**LBW**) can be calculated with the following formula:

Fat weight = Body weight × Body fat %

LBW = Total body weight – Fat weight

If an athlete weighs 135 lbs and has 14% body fat, fat weight can be determined by multiplying percentage of fat by body weight: 0.14 × 135 = 18.9 lbs. Thus, fat weight is approximately 20 lbs. Determining this athlete's LBW is calculated by subtracting fat weight from total body weight: 135 – 20 = 115 lbs. To determine the minimal competitive weight for this athlete, make the following calculation:

Minimal competitive weight (MCW) =
Lean body weight ÷ (1 – % fat desired)
MCW = 115 ÷ 0.93 (1 – 0.7) = 124 lbs

Thus, this athlete should not compete if weight drops below 124 lbs. Using the same equation, a 115-lb female wrestler who has 17% body fat should not be allowed to compete if her weight drops below 108 lbs:

115 × 0.17 (% body fat) = 19.5 lbs of fat

115 – 19.5 lbs of fat = 95.5 lbs LBW

MCW = 95.5 ÷ 0.88 (1 – 0.12) = 108 lbs

Athletes involved in other sports that have aesthetic components, such as gymnastics, dancing, or diving, may

LBW Lean body weight.

TABLE 6.6

EXAMPLES OF VARIOUS ERGOGENIC SUBSTANCES USED BY ATHLETES

Prescription and Over-the-Counter Substances

Generic Names (Brand Names Vary)	Perceived Benefits	Potential Adverse Effects
Androstenedione	Development of muscle mass	Reduction of testosterone production
		Banned by the U.S. government (2005), International Olympic Committee (IOC), and National Football League (NFL)
		Available by prescription in the United States
Dehydroepiandrosterone (DHEA complex)	Development of muscle mass Reduction of body fat and "antiaging"	Banned by the IOC and National Collegiate Athletic Association (NCAA)
		Stomach upset, high blood pressure, changes in menstrual cycle, facial hair in women, deepening of the voice in women, unfavorable cholesterol changes, aggressive behavior
Hydroxymethylbutyrate (HMB, derivative of leucine)	Muscle repair	Undetermined at this point
Amino acids (branch chain amino acids [BCAA])	Development of muscle mass and repair after exhaustive exercise	Fatigue and loss of coordination. Various risks associated with liver and kidney
Creatine	Production of energy at the muscle cell by converting ADP to ATP	Kidney damage, fluid retention, muscle cramps, upset stomach, and diarrhea
Dietary nitrate	Reduces resting blood pressure, lowers the oxygen cost of submaximal exercise (i.e., enhances muscle efficiency), and may enhance overall exercise performance	Health risks associated with the consumption of nitrate salts may lead to cardiovascular collapse, coma, and/or death
Estrogen inhibitors	Inhibits estrogen activity to enhance muscle development (typically used in conjunction with androstenedione)	Reduction of estrogen activity in males and females
Gamma-hydroxybutyrate (GHB)	Promotes deep sleep—argued to enhance GH release	ILLEGAL SUBSTANCE: Can result in death
	Also known as a "date rape drug"	Available by prescription in the United States

Herbs

Herb (Common Name)	Perceived Benefits	Potential Adverse Effects
Ephedra (Chinese ephedra, ma huang)	Powerfully stimulates the nervous system and heart	Banned by FDA
	Used for weight loss, increased energy, and enhanced athletic performance	Seizures, anxiety, heart arrhythmias, stroke, heart attack, and death
Arnica (mountain tobacco)	Muscle pain, stiffness, osteoarthritis	May increase effects of anticoagulants

(Continued)

TABLE 6.6

EXAMPLES OF VARIOUS ERGOGENIC SUBSTANCES USED BY ATHLETES (*Continued*)

Echinacea (purple coneflower or Indian head)	Weak immune system, colds, infections	May interfere with immunosuppressants
Zingiberis rhizoma (ginger)	Nausea, vomiting, motion sickness, osteoarthritis	May interact with anticoagulants and antidiabetes drugs
Rhodiola (golden root)	Lethargy, fatigue, poor endurance	May interact with other herbs
Ginseng (Russian root)	Poor endurance performance, low energy, weak immune system	May interfere with anticoagulants
Guarana (Zoom cocoa, Brazilian cocoa)	Excess body fat, lethargy	Contains caffeine

Key: ADP, adenosine diphosphate; ATP, adenosine triphosphate; GH, growth hormone.

also be faced with a dilemma when attempting to alter their appearance. These athletes should never go below a body fat percentage that is essential for maturation (see earlier in chapter). It is important for these athletes to remember that the cost of starvation and other deadly methods of weight control are likely to attack their muscle mass. Because these activities are considered to be anaerobic, deriving the required energy from glycogen supplies in working muscles, they may experience more decrements in performance and potential sport injury. Any athlete who demonstrates abnormal eating behaviors or exhibits unusual or unwarranted concerns about excess body fat should be referred to an expert for evaluation and dietary counseling.

Supplements and Ergogenic Aids

Sport nutritional supplements have become very popular with athletes of all calibers. Supplements can also be called **ergogenic aids**. For something to be ergogenic, it must have the potential to increase work output. When work output is increased, the person is able to perform at higher intensities and work longer and is capable of putting greater stresses on the body. Based on the overload principle of training, an athlete who is using ergogenic aids may be able to increase his capacity to train, thereby increasing his athletic potential (size, speed, etc.). Typically, the supplement manufacturers claim that these substances are either not available in a normal diet or are needed by athletes in greater amounts than the body can acquire through normal dietary habits and that these substances are necessary for improved performance.

The use of supplements, once basically confined to professional or Olympic athletes, has now become a popular technique for gaining an edge for athletes of all ages and categories. Many coaches or parents tell their athletes that by using nutritional supplements they can become bigger, stronger, and faster. This is exactly what the athlete wants to hear, and he or she will often spend significant amounts of money buying a variety of supplements to help reach the goal of becoming the best athlete. For many high school athletes, being a top-tier athlete can mean a college scholarship. The collegiate athlete may want to become better so that he or she can obtain a professional contract. Many supplements are marketed to make athletes think that by taking a pill or powder or drinking an ergogenic beverage they will improve their personal performance and reach their goals faster. These are just a few of the many reasons athletes will take nutritional supplements. Athletes must remember that not all marketed supplements create bigger, stronger, or faster athletes, and many supplements pose adverse health risks or are illegal and their use will result in disqualification or other penalties. Nutritional supplementation by athletes can be individual studies in toxicity, resulting in few benefits and many possible consequences.

Ergogenic aids and supplements (**Table 6.6**) include both illegal and legal substances. In general, the legality

ergogenic aids Foods or beverages that have the potential to increase the work output of the person using them.

of a supplement within a sport is not determined by whether the supplement is considered natural or an athlete can buy it over the counter (via retail outlets, catalogs, magazines, and the Internet) or have it provided via a physician prescription. It is important to note that supplements sold in a retail store or online are not guaranteed to be legal in a particular league or sport. A supplement usually includes a variety of ingredients. If a supplement contains ingredients that are banned by the U.S. Food and Drug Administration (FDA), World Anti-Doping Agency (WADA), or U.S. Anti-Doping Agency (USADA), then it should be considered illegal by the athlete or coach. Supplements that contain one or more of the following ingredients typically fall into an illegal category. These ingredients include but are not limited to anabolic steroids, hormones or metabolic modulators, diuretics, and stimulants. For a complete list of illegal (prohibited) ingredients, WADA (http://www.wada-ama.org) and USADA (http://www.usada.org) provide updated lists. It is up to the coach, athlete, and/or parent to be aware of the substances that can be legally purchased but will result in suspensions from teams and events. To determine the overall safety of nutritional supplements, a fairly new tool developed by USADA is now available to the public called Supplement 411 (http://www.usada.org/supplement411). It contains testimonials from athletes who were banned from sports because of the use of a variety of nutritional supplements, and it has accurate and official information regarding the safety and efficacy of commonly available supplements. In the end, it investigates the athlete's primary dilemma, the risk versus the reward of using various nutritional supplements in light of the fact that their use may result in a positive doping test or serious health consequences including death.

The popularity of nutritional supplements has increased tremendously since the 1990s and so has number of ingredients deemed to be beneficial for athletic performance. As a result, several national organizations have developed position stands in regard to supplements in sports. Most recently, NATA released two comprehensive position stands evaluating dietary supplements (Buell et al., 2013) and anabolic-androgenic steroids (Kersey et al., 2012).

Buell and colleagues (2013) emphasize the philosophy of food first to meet nutritional and performance needs, because dietary supplement labels do not require third-party verification; purity (truth in labeling) and noncontamination cannot be assumed. A food-first philosophy indicates that essential nutrients can be obtained naturally from a healthy diet. The authors go on to explain the Dietary Supplement Health and Education Act (DSHEA) of 1994 that allowed the nutritional supplement market to explode. The DSHEA does require manufacturers and distributors of dietary supplements to ensure their products are safe before they are marketed, but once the product is marketed, no third-party screening is required to ensure its effectiveness or safety. In order to get a product removed from the market, the FDA must show that the supplement is actually unsafe (results in serious health consequences or deaths) before it can be removed from the marketplace (Buell et al., 2013). The use and abuse of anabolic-androgenic steroids goes well beyond nutritional supplements and borders on illicit drug use, so an extensive discussion of these is not warranted. The most notable supplements in this category are anabolic steroids, growth hormone, and erythropoietin (EPO). These products cannot be purchased in a retail store, thus they are typically purchased through an underground source. Athletes will go to extreme measures to obtain and use these supplements. They will also go to extreme lengths to hide the use of these illegal supplements. Unfortunately, many can be legal substances when prescribed by a medical professional for the proper reasons. Kersey and colleagues (2012) indicate that anabolic-androgenic products can be used safely in therapeutic doses; however, it is the nontherapeutic and unregulated use by athletes that can pose serious health risks.

Nutritional Supplements

Stimulants are often the most popular legal supplements for ergogenic purposes. In many cases, a variety of stimulants are combined in products. Three common products include caffeine, guarana, and ephedra. They all affect the way the brain recognizes exhaustion during exercise. These supplements, in separate ways, override the brain's recognition of exhaustion during exercise and permit the athlete to continue training when the brain is telling the body to stop. Caffeine is typically touted to be a safe aid and can provide a boost of energy for the athlete. It is purported to aid endurance activities by assisting substrate metabolism and delaying fatigue. However, there have been large ranges of reported performance increases across research studies and further research should identify the individual factors that make caffeine an ergogenic aid (Ganio et al., 2009). Currently, caffeine is still regulated by the NCAA, but the dose required for disqualification is well beyond that provided in typical beverages. On the other hand, guarana and ephedra are very controversial ergogenic aids. Ephedra has recently been banned because it was linked with more than 155 deaths (Hampton, 2005). In early 2004, the FDA banned the use of ephedra as a supplement. The FDA ban in 2004 was challenged in court and the substance was again sold over the counter (OTC) in 2005, but OTC sale of products containing ephedra was again suspended by the government in 2006. However, ephedra continues to be available in foreign countries and can be purchased over the Internet or by other illegal means. It is important for the coach or athletic trainer to discourage the use of guarana or ephedra during exercise situations. The use of these mixtures is most prevalent during two-a-day practices to boost energy levels and has been suspected in the deaths of several athletes. Their use is dangerous and even deadly when environmental factors such as excessive heat and humidity plus excessive training regimens are coupled with the athlete's unwillingness to stop exercising at the appropriate time.

Other commonly known supplements the athlete may be tempted to use are testosterone precursors. Androstenedione is a testosterone precursor taken by athletes with the intent to build muscle tissue. Androstenedione (andro) was made famous by professional baseball player Mark McGwire. Over-the-counter sales of andro were banned by the U.S. government in January 2005; however, an athlete may be able to purchase this drug over the Internet, and it is also available by prescription, and thus an athlete may be able to obtain it legally. Another testosterone precursor currently popular with athletes is dehydroepiandrosterone (DHEA), a hormone found in the blood that is converted to androstenedione and then to testosterone (Brown et al., 1999; Wallace et al., 1999). Testosterone increases protein synthesis and slows protein breakdown, which can generate increased muscle bulk with proper training. The adverse effect of using testosterone or testosterone precursors is the reduction of natural androgen hormone production by the body. Andro is banned by the International Olympic Committee (IOC), the National Football League (NFL), and Major League Baseball (MLB); DHEA is banned by the IOC, NFL, National Basketball Association (NBA), MLB, and NCAA. Many of the athletes using testosterone precursors also use estrogen inhibitors, which increase the effectiveness of the andro. Using an estrogen inhibitor reduces the estrogen in the body. In female athletes, this reduction of estrogen combined with the increase in overall testosterone over a long period of time leads to an increase in male characteristics.

Creatine is the ergogenic aid that is currently the most widely used supplement to enhance recovery and increase muscle mass (ACSM, 2009). Most coaches and athletes are familiar with it because it produces an increase in energy, allowing the athlete to train for longer periods of time. In a survey of 167 male college athletes, creatine use was three times that of any other nutritional supplement. Creatine is a component in the cell that converts adenosine diphosphate (ADP) to adenosine triphosphate (ATP) and thus produces energy for the cell. By putting more creatine in the system, the cell can produce more energy and the athlete can train longer. Thus, the athlete can overload the body and produce greater muscle mass. The scientific evidence regarding the effectiveness of creatine in generating muscle mass is equivocal. Many published studies on creatine report conflicting results. Therefore, many athletes follow the advice of fellow athletes when it comes to deciding whether they will use creatine. It has been demonstrated that creatine is more helpful to the athlete who uses short bursts of energy (sprinters, weight lifters, etc.) than to endurance athletes (soccer players, swimmers, etc.) (Bemben & Lamont, 2005). Now creatine is being combined with β-alanine so that the athlete can experience a higher quality workout, which may result in greater strength gains. The addition of β-alanine as a supplement appears to have a positive effect on lean-tissue accruement and body fat composition (Hoffman et al., 2006). The adverse effects associated with creatine are kidney damage, fluid retention, muscle cramps, upset stomach, and diarrhea. Creatine is available in many different forms, but most athletes use the powdered form combined with some type of fruit juice. It is an expensive supplement and can be purchased over the counter without a physician's prescription. Athletes considering the use of creatine should be encouraged to carefully weigh the purpose of using this or any supplement before they begin its use because the long-term effects of creatine supplementation have not been determined (Rawson & Clarkson, 2003).

Amino acids (including whey protein) along with beta-hydroxy beta-methylbutyrate (HMB) are marketed for muscle building and repair. In rigorous research studies, isolated amino acids used for the purpose of muscle building have not been shown to be effective (McArdle et al., 2009). A well balanced diet provides the essential amino acids for most people. Athletes needing extra amino acids are encouraged to eat increased amounts of food during training and conditioning periods to obtain them. Amino acids are water soluble, and when excess amounts are taken they are cleared through the kidneys and eliminated through the urine. These processes can apply extra stress to the urinary system and result in permanent damage.

Nitric oxide (NO) is a newer supplement now readily available to athletes in a variety of products. It is purported to reduce resting blood pressure, lower the oxygen cost of submaximal exercise (i.e., enhance muscle efficiency), and enhance overall exercise performance (Jones, 2013). Nitric oxide is readily available in green leafy vegetables and beets; however, recent evidence indicates that NO availability can be enhanced by dietary supplementation with inorganic nitrate (Jones, 2013). Currently, the amount of nitrate necessary to produce beneficial changes for the athlete is undetermined; therefore, there are a variety of regimens that are being recommended. Although NO does seem to have a benefit, its unregulated dosing concerns the medical community. Consumption of excessive nitrate salts can have health risks including gastric cancer. At this time, a food-first philosophy (leafy greens and beet root juice) is the best way to get extra amounts of NO into an athlete's diet (Jones, 2013).

Athletes can also readily purchase and take herbal supplements as ergogenic aids. The standardization of herbs is not required and there is little consistency among different batches of herbs from different manufacturers (Buell et al., 2013). Some herbs produce a stimulatory effect (ginseng, guarana, ephedra, etc.), and others produce relaxation to reduce musculoskeletal stress in the athlete (chamomile, arnica, etc.). Some athletes don't understand that using herbs in combination with OTC or prescription drugs can result in either reduced effectiveness of both the drug and the herb or increased action of both the herb and the drug in the body, which can have detrimental health effects.

Anabolic-Androgenic Products

Anabolic steroids are legal products, used by many medical doctors and veterinarians in therapeutic dosages to help heal muscle damage, but they are used illegally by athletes in much higher dosages to build muscles. Athletes can use oral or injectable steroids, and many times they use both types in a "stacking" routine (Kersey et al., 2012). Because the athlete is obtaining these supplements through an illegal source, the dosages used are sometimes as high as 100 times or more than the therapeutic dose. Steroids injected directly into the muscle are more effective than those taken by mouth because a higher percentage is delivered directly to the muscle after injection. Oral intake allows the drug to metabolize and degrade in the digestive and hepatic (liver) systems. Unfortunately, many times the athlete injecting steroids does not have the proper equipment for injections and must share needles and syringes, which is very dangerous. By using anabolic steroids in large amounts, athletes can contract blood-borne diseases, damage internal organs, increase risk of heart attack, develop unwanted aggression and secondary sex

characteristics, and cause changes to their body composition that may not help them in their preferred sport. The National Strength and Conditioning Association (NSCA) rejects the use of anabolic steroids on the basis of fair play and concerns for the athlete's health. It also encourages that research and funding be dedicated to educational programs and documentation of both short- and long-term effects of anabolic steroid abuse (Hoffman et al., 2009).

EPO is a natural substance produced by the kidneys that stimulates red blood cell proliferation. EPO can now be synthesized in the laboratory and is used for cancer patients on chemotherapy and other individuals with chronic illnesses who need to augment their red blood cell levels. Athletes who compete in endurance activities can benefit from an increase in the number of circulating red blood cells (Hoffman & Stout, 2008). The red blood cells carry oxygen; the more oxygen the blood stream can carry to the cells, the longer the cells can function. The longer the cells function, the longer the athlete can compete at a higher level. Endurance athletes such as swimmers, marathon runners, cyclists, and others have been known to use this drug. The adverse effect of using EPO is that the athlete may take too much and get too many red blood cells circulating. This situation increases the viscosity of the blood and makes the heart work much harder to pump this thick blood through the body. If the heart has to work too hard for too long, the athlete can experience heart failure and die.

Stimulants including amphetamines can also be obtained by athletes and are used to give them some energy when they are tired. Athletes can legally and illegally obtain prescription stimulants such as Dexedrine (dextroamphetamine), Adderall (amphetamine and dextroamphetamine), and Ritalin (methylphenidate) in an effort to boost energy and focus. In general, amphetamines are commonly used during two-a-day practices or prior to intense competitions. These prescription stimulants affect the brain and body much the same way as the OTC stimulants (caffeine, guarana) do because they block the fatigue messages to the brain and increase focus so athletes can exercise beyond their usual capability. However, like other stimulants, these drugs can make the body more sensitive to heat or cardiac problems. Major league baseball is taking an aggressive approach to the overuse of attention deficit hyperactivity disorder (ADHD) stimulants (Ritalin and Adderall) and are now requiring players who request exemptions in order to take prescription medications for ADHD diagnoses to get the approval of a three-expert panel (Thurm, 2012).

Gamma-hydroxybutyrate (GHB) is an illegal substance (it is also known as a date rape drug) but can be obtained by some athletes. Those who sell GHB to athletes claim it helps the athlete get into the deepest phase of sleep and stay in that sleep phase longer. Deep sleep is suggested to be the cycle during which human growth hormone is released, making longer deep sleep potentially valuable for increased muscle growth (Van Cauter et al., 1997). The use of GHB can be lethal to the athlete. It is an illegal substance, and all athletes should be discouraged from its use.

Coaches, athletes, and parents should be reminded that there is very poor regulatory control over nutritional and ergogenic supplements despite attempts by government agencies to improve regulation. Therefore, it is important for the consumer to evaluate the marketing claims, research studies, and safety issues associated with ergogenic aids (Buell et al., 2013; Kersey et al., 2012; Manore et al., 2009). Several studies have identified unrecognized risks of supplementation, so consumers should be aware of deceptive marketing techniques including outstanding claims, patents, testimonials, and media campaigns. Research studies that are presented outside of peer-reviewed journals should not be trusted. If presented with research, evaluate whether the authors report subject demographics, methods, and study limitations. Finally, always be aware of safety issues associated with supplement use. Do not attempt to compensate for poor nutrient or energy intake by taking supplements and be very careful about toxicity effects. Whole food products provide the essential macro- and micronutrients needed by physically active individuals, and using illegal substances or doses of single supplements in higher quantities than recommended levels may have detrimental effects on healthy tissue and normal absorption of nutrients (Buell et al., 2013). Athletes and coaches should remember that the most promising area of positive health outcomes related to nutrition is with dietary patterns and not nutrient supplementation (Lichtenstein & Russell, 2005).

REVIEW QUESTIONS

1. Describe the similarities and differences between the basic molecular structure of carbohydrates, fats, and proteins.

2. Describe the major problems associated with excessive consumption of dietary protein.

3. According to the chapter, a survey of coaches, athletes, and BOC-certified athletic trainers revealed that athletes depended on which sources for their information about nutrition?

4. What is the recommended level of dietary protein for adolescent athletes?

5. How much water do you need under conditions of heavy exercise in high ambient temperatures?

6. Calculate the BMR for an 18-year-old male athlete who weighs 200 lbs, is 6 feet tall, and has 18% body fat.

7. Calculate the MCW for the athlete from question 6 if he would like to have 16% body fat.

8. Discuss briefly the short-term effects of repeated episodes of extreme, rapid weight loss.

9. What should be the three goals of any sports nutrition program?

10. What are the recommended percentages of protein, fat, and carbohydrates in an ideal training diet?

11. Using the equation provided in the chapter, compute the protein requirement (in grams) for a football player who weighs 94 kilograms.

12. Briefly list the general guidelines regarding the composition of a precompetition meal.

13. True or false: During times of heavy exertion, it is not possible to lose more than 0.5 to 1 liter of water for each hour of exercise.

14. Compute the fluid deficiency (% dehydration and amount of fluid [ounces] necessary for proper replacement) of an athlete (175 lbs) who weighs 5.5 lbs less after practice than he did prior to practice.

15. What are the effects of dietary fasting on muscle tissue?

16. True or false: Sports scientists recommend a training diet in which 30% to 40% of daily calories consumed are in the form of protein.

17. What are the nutritional concerns of an injured athlete who is recovering from an injury?

18. Name the risks associated with nutritional supplementation.

19. What drugs are typically used illegally in sports to obtain an advantage?

20. What resources should an athlete use to obtain credible information about ergogenic aids?

REFERENCES

Academy of Nutrition and Dietetics. (2009). *Eat Right for Sports and Performance.* Available: http://www.eatright.org/Public/content.aspx?id=7056&terms=Sports%20performance.

American Bone Health. (2010). Athletic energy deficit. Available: http://www.americanbonehealth.org/young-adults/about-aed.

American College of Sports Medicine. (1996). Position statement on weight loss in wrestlers. *Med Sci Sports Exerc.* 28(6):ix–xii.

American College of Sports Medicine. (2009). Position statement on nutrition and athletic performance. *Med Sci Sports Exerc.* 41(3):709–731.

American Diabetes Association. (2013). The glycemic index of foods. Available: http://www.diabetes.org/food-and-fitness/food/planning-meals/the-glycemic-index-of-foods.html.

Austin S, Ziyadeh N, Forman S, Prokop L, Keliher A, Jacobs D. (2008). Screening high school students for eating disorders: Results of a national initiative. *Prev Chronic Dis.* 5(4). http://www.cdc.gov/pcd/issues/2008/oct/07_0164.htm.

Baer JT, Dean DJ, Lambrinides T. (1994). How high school football coaches recommend their players gain lean body mass. *J Strength and Cond Res.* 8(2):72–75.

Bemben MG, Lamont HS. (2005). Creatine supplementation and exercise performance: Recent findings. *Sports Medicine.* 35(2):107–125.

Brotherhood JR. (1984). Nutrition and sports performance. *Sports Med.* 1:350–389.

Brown GA, Vukovich MD, Sharp RL, Reifenrath TA, Parsons KA, King DS. (1999). Effect of oral DHEA on serum testosterone and adaptations to resistance training in young men. *J Appl Physiol.* 87(6):2274–2283.

Bucci L. (1995). *Nutrition Applied to Injury Rehabilitation and Sports Medicine.* Boca Raton, Fla: CRC Press.

Buell J, Franks R, Ransone J, Powers ME, Laquale KM, Carlson-Phillips A. (2013). National Athletic Trainers' Association position statement: Evaluation of dietary supplements for performance nutrition. *J Athl Train.* 48(1):124–136.

Clark N. (1997). Eating for vitamins: Do you need supplements? *Phys Sportsmed.* 25(7):103.

Corley G, Demarest-Litchford M, Bazzarre TL. (1990). Nutrition knowledge and dietary practices of college coaches. *J Am Diet Association.* 90(5):705–709.

Coyle EF. (1988). Carbohydrates and athletic performance. *Sports Science Exchange.* 1(7).

Deuster PA, Kyle SB, Moser PB, Vigersky RA, Singh A, Schoomaker EB. (1986). Nutritional survey of highly trained women runners. *Am J Clin Nutr.* 44:954–962.

Deutz R, Benardot D, Martin D, Cody M. (2000). Relationship between energy deficits and body composition in elite female gymnasts and runners. *Med Sci Sports Exerc.* 32(3):659–668.

Duellman MC, Lukaszuk JM, Prawitz AD, Brandenburg JP. (2008). Protein supplement users among high school athletes have misconceptions about effectiveness. *J Strength Cond Res.* 22(4):1124–1129.

Elliot DL, Goldberg L, Moe EL, DeFrancesco CA, Durham MB, McGinnis W, Lockwood C. (2008). Long-term outcomes of the ATHENA (Athletes Targeting Healthy Exercise and Nutrition Alternatives) program for female high school athletes. *J Alcohol Drug Educ.* 52(2):73–92.

Froiland K, Koszewski W, Hingst J, Kopecky L. (2004). Nutritional supplement use among college athletes and their sources of information. *Int J Sport Exerc Meta.* 14(1):104–120.

Ganio MS, Klau JF, Casa DJ, Armstrong LE, Maresh CM. (2009). Effect of caffeine on sport-specific endurance performance: A systematic review. *J Strength Cond Res.* 23(1):315–324.

Glycemic Index. (2013). Available: http://www.glycemicindex.com/index.php.

Greenleaf C, Petrie TA, Carter J, Reel JJ. (2009). Female collegiate athletes: Prevalence of eating disorders and disordered eating behaviors. *J Am College Health.* 57(5):489–496.

Hampton T. (2005). More scrutiny for dietary supplements? *JAMA.* 293(1):27–28.

Harrison B. (n.d.). Nutritional considerations in athletic injury rehabilitation. Available: https://www.signup4.net/Upload/MIDA11A/MAAT12E/Nutritional_considerations_in_athletic_injury_rehabilitation.pdf.

Hilton P. (2005). Running on empty. *Training Conditioning.* 15(6):11–18.

Hoffman J, Ratamess N, Kang J, Mangine G, Faigenbaum A, Stout J. (2006). Effect of creatine and beta-alanine supplementation on performance and endocrine response in strength/power athletes. *Int J Sport Nutr Exercise Metabol.* 16:430–446.

Hoffman J, Stout J. (2008). Performance-enhancing substances. In: Baechle T, Earle R (eds.), *NSCA Essentials of Strength Training and Conditioning* (3rd ed., pp. 189–190). Champaign, Ill: Human Kinetics.

Hoffman JR, Kraemer WJ, Bhasin S, Storer T, Ratamess NA, Haff GG, Willoughby DS, Rogol AD. (2009). Position stand on androgen and human growth hormone use. *J Strength Cond Res.* 23(5):S1–S59.

Holway FE, Spriet LL. (2011). Sport-specific nutrition: Practical strategies for team sports. *J Sports Sciences.* 29(supl):S115–S125.

Jacobson BH, Sobonya C, Ransone J. (2001). Nutrition practices and knowledge of college varsity athletes: A follow-up. *J Strength Cond Res.* 15(1):63–68.

Jeukendrup A. (2007) Carbohydrate supplementation during exercise: Does it help? How much is too much? *GSSI: Sport Science Exchange.* 20(3):1–6.

Jones A. (2013). Dietary nitrate: The new magic bullet? *GSSI: Sport Science Exchange.* 26(110):1–5.

Kersey R, Elliot DL, Goldberg L, Kanayama G, Leone JE, Pavlovich M, Pope HG Jr. (2012). National Athletic Trainers' Association position statement: Anabolic-androgenic steroids. *J Athl Train.* 47(5):567–588.

Lichtenstein AH, Russell RM. (2005). Essential nutrients: Food or supplements? Where should the emphasis be? *JAMA.* 294(3):351–358.

Loosli AR, Benson J. (1990). Nutritional intakes in adolescent athletes. *Pediatr Clin North Am.* 37(5):1143–1152.

Magazanik A, Weinstein Y, Dlin RA, Derin M, Schwartzman S, Allalouf D. (1988). Iron deficiency caused by 7 weeks of intensive physical exercise. *Eur J App Phys.* 57:198–202.

Manore MM, Meyer NL, Thompson J. (2009) *Sport Nutrition for Health and Performance* (2nd ed.). Champaign, Ill: Human Kinetics.

McArdle WD, Katch FI, Katch VL. (2009). *Sports and Exercise Nutrition* (3rd ed.). Philadelphia, Pa: Lippincott Williams & Wilkins.

Moffatt RJ. (1984). Dietary status of elite female high-school gymnasts: Inadequacy of vitamin and mineral intake. *J Am Diet Assoc.* 84(11):1361–1363.

Muth N. (2009). What are the guidelines for percentage of body fat loss? *American Council on Exercise (ACE).* Available: http://www.acefitness.org/acefit/healthy-living-article/60/112/what-are-the-guidelines-for-percentage-of/.

National Federation of State High School Associations. (2011). Weight management in wrestling. *Sports Medicine Handbook* (4th ed.). Indianapolis, Ind.

Nelson RA. (1989). Nutrition for the athlete. In: Ryan AJ, Allman FL (eds.), *Sports Medicine* (pp. 165–181). San Diego, Calif: Academic Press.

Oppliger RA, Harms RD, Herrmann DE, Streich CM, Clark RR. (1995). The Wisconsin Wrestling Minimum Weight Project: A model for weight control among high school wrestlers. *Med Sci Sports.* 27(8):1220–1224.

Oppliger R, Case S, Horswill C, Landry G, Shetler A. (1996). American College of Sports Medicine position stand: Weight loss in wrestlers. Med Sci Sports Exerc. 28(6):ix–xii.

Parr RB, Porter MA, Hodgson SC. (1984). Nutrition knowledge and practice of coaches, trainers, and athletes. *Phys Sportsmed.* 12(3):127–138.

Pattini A, Schena F. (1990). Effects of training and iron supplementation on iron status of cross-country skiers. *J Sportsmed Phys Fit.* 30:347–353.

Perron M, Endres J. (1985). Knowledge, attitudes, and dietary practices of female athletes. *J Am Diet Assoc.* 85(5):573–576.

Rawson E, Clarkson P. (2003). Scientifically debatable: Is creatine worth its weight? *GSSI: Sport Science Exchange.* 16(4):1–8.

Sammarone Turocy P, DePalma BF, Horswill CA, Laquale KM, Martin TJ, Perry AC, Somova MJ, Utter AC. (2011). National Athletic Trainers' Association position statement: Safe weight loss and maintenance practices in sport and exercise. *J Athl Train.* 46(3):322–336.

Slavin JL, Lanners G, Engstrom MA. (1988). Amino-acid supplements: Beneficial or risky? *Phys Sportsmed.* 16(3):221–224.

Sossin K, Gizis F, Marquart LF, Sobal J. (1997). Nutrition beliefs, attitudes, and resources use of high school wrestling coaches. *Int J Sport Nutr.* 7(3):219–228.

Sumida KD, Donovan CM. (1995). Enhanced hepatic gluconeogenic capacity for selected precursors after endurance training. *J Appl Physiol.* 79:1883–1888.

Thurm W. (2012). Is there an ADHD epidemic in major league baseball? *Baseball Nation.* Available: http://www.baseballnation.com/2012/6/29/3104332/is-there-an-adhd-epidemic-in-major-league-baseball.

Torres-McGehee T, Pritchett K, Zippel D, Minton D, Cellamare A, Sibilia M. (2012). Sports nutrition knowledge among collegiate athletes, coaches, athletic trainers, and strength and conditioning specialists. *J Athl Train.* 47(2):205–211.

Torstveit MK, Rosenvinge JH, Sundgot-Borgen J. (2008). Prevalence of eating disorders and the predictive power of risk models in female elite athletes: A controlled study. *Scand J Med Sci Sports.* 18:108–118.

Upgrove NA, Achterberg CL. (1990). The conceptual relationship between training and eating in high-school distance runners. *J Nutr Educ.* 23(1):18–24.

Van Cauter E, Plat L, Scharf MB, Leproult R, Cespedes S, L'Hermite-Balériaux M, Copinschi G. (1997). Simultaneous stimulation of slow-wave sleep and growth hormone secretion by gamma-hydroxybutyrate in normal young men. *J Clin Invest.* 100:745–749.

Wallace MB, Lim J, Cutler A, Bucci L. (1999). Effects of dehydroepiandrosterone vs androstenedione supplementation in men. *Med Sci Sports Exerc.* 31(12):1788–1792.

Williams MH. (1992). *Nutrition for Fitness and Sport.* Dubuque, Ia: William C. Brown.

Wilmore JH, Costill DL. (1988). *Training for Sport and Activity: The Physiological Basis of the Conditioning Process.* Dubuque, Ia: William C. Brown.

Emergency Plan and Initial Injury Evaluation

MAJOR CONCEPTS

Coaching and other athletic personnel have a legal duty to develop and implement an emergency action plan to be followed if an athlete is injured while participating in sports. To be effective, the emergency plan must be carefully planned by all the principal parties involved, including all members of the athletic healthcare team in conjunction with emergency medical services (EMS) providers in the community. In the primary/secondary school setting, the appropriate institutional representatives, such as the athletic director and/or school principal, should be involved as well. Whereas in the collegiate/university setting, it is the athletic director, police department, vice presidents, and the board of regents that are often involved in emergency planning. The plan must be flexible to allow for changes in personnel or in facilities and venues. In addition, it must incorporate an education component that includes periodic rehearsal to ensure that it will work effectively if and when an emergency arises. Skills of available personnel must be recognized, and roles and responsibilities should be carefully documented. Details such as emergency equipment inventory, communications, and transportation must all be carefully considered. In addition, the emergency plan must extend beyond the traditional game day and practice paradigm to include off-season components such as summer conditioning camps and, if it is a separate facility, the strength and conditioning room. The plan must also address the potential issue of an injured or ill fan, sideline participant, or official. This chapter provides a step-by-step outline of the vital components in the development of an effective emergency plan. It discusses the process of injury evaluation in the unique situations presented in the sports environment.

go.jblearning.com/PfeifferCWS

For a full suite of assignments and additional learning activities (indicated by the icons throughout the text), use the access code found in the front of your text. If you do not have an access code, you can obtain one at go.jblearning.com/PfeifferCWS.

Sports injuries are an inevitable outcome of participation for millions of high school athletes and hundreds of thousands of collegiate athletes each year. A few of the major health and safety concerns for secondary school athletes includes lack of emergency planning and policies, lack of medical staff, and lack of proper emergency equipment (Casa et al., 2013). Proper planning is essential to ensure appropriate initial first aid management of limb and life-threatening injuries, because many of these injuries occur without warning (Andersen et al., 2002). There are primarily two good reasons for developing a formal emergency action plan for sports injuries. First, anything that can be done ahead of time to improve the health care of injured athletes, coaches, officials, or fans should be a priority. Second, from a legal standpoint, failure to have an emergency plan in place has been found to constitute negligence in litigation resulting from a sports injury (Quandt, Mitton, & Black, 2009). According to McCaskey and Biedzynski (1996) a major source of liability for coaches is causing unnecessary aggravation or complications by failing to identify and properly deal with injuries.

Emergency action plans (EAPs) are written blueprints for handling emergencies that should be easily understood and clearly establish accountability for the management of emergencies (Andersen et al., 2002). Several key elements identified by the National Athletic Trainers' Association (Andersen et al., 2002) for the development of EAPs are as follows:

1. An emergency plan for athletics identifies the personnel (emergency team) involved in carrying out the emergency plan and outlines the qualifications of those executing the plan. Sports medicine professionals, officials, physical educators, and coaches should be trained in automatic external defibrillator (AED) use, cardiopulmonary resuscitation (CPR), first aid, and prevention of disease transmission.

2. The emergency plan should specify the equipment needed to carry out the tasks required in the event of an emergency. In addition, the emergency plan should outline the location of the emergency equipment. Further, the equipment available should be appropriate to the level of training of the personnel involved.

3. With respect to emergency medical services, it is important that arrangements be made to have EMS personnel present at all athletic events whenever possible (**Figure 7.1**). However, if EMS personnel are not present at the event, then all staff members should know the mechanisms for

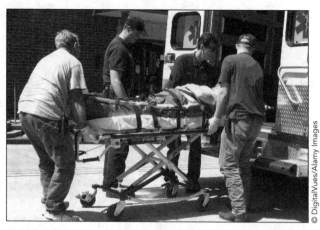

FIGURE 7.1 It is important that arrangements be made to have EMS personnel present at athletic events whenever possible.

© DigitalVues/Alamy Images

communication to appropriate emergency care service providers. Situations are different from community to community so all key members of the staff must know the emergency number and have access to either a cellular phone or a land line. In many cases, an emergency call box may be available to summon EMS directly. In addition to notifying EMS, emergency plans must identify the mode of transportation for the injured participant to the emergency vehicle if the EMS cannot directly access the field or court of play.

4. The emergency plan should be specific to the activity venue. That is, each activity site should have a defined emergency plan that is derived from the overall institutional or organizational policies on emergency planning. In particular, specific addresses to each venue, access routes to playing areas from roads, and the location of keys to any gates or doors that may present barriers to emergency personnel should be delineated in the emergency plan.

5. Emergency plans should incorporate the emergency care facilities to which the injured individual will be taken. Emergency receiving facilities should be notified in advance of scheduled events and contests. If possible, personnel from the emergency receiving facilities should be included in the development of the emergency plan for the institution or organization.

6. The emergency plan specifies the necessary documentation supporting the implementation and evaluation of the emergency plan. This documentation should identify responsibility for documenting

actions taken during the emergency, evaluation of the emergency response, and institutional personnel training.

7. The emergency plan should be reviewed and rehearsed annually, although more frequent review and rehearsal may be necessary if there are staff changes. Changes in staff, facilities, playing schedules, EMS personnel, and playing seasons can all impact the effectiveness of any emergency plan. The results of these reviews and rehearsals should be documented and should indicate whether the emergency plan was modified, with further documentation reflecting how the plan was changed.

8. The emergency plan should be reviewed by the administration and legal counsel of the sponsoring organization or institution.

Emergency Team

In any school setting, it is recommended that all personnel directly involved with the interscholastic sports program take part in the development and implementation of the emergency plan. This should include coaches, directors/administrators, the team physician and athletic trainer (if available), school nurses, local EMS personnel, student athletic trainers (if present), and other staff members (managers and administrative assistants) involved with the program. Typically, the athletic trainers and student trainers (if present), team physician, coaches, and managers associated directly with the interscholastic sports program are the personnel that make up what is known as the emergency team at an event. They provide four functions with respect to the emergency plan: 1) immediate care of the athlete, 2) equipment retrieval (emergency equipment), 3) activation of EMS (when the situation is deemed of sufficient magnitude), and 4) signaling the EMS to the field if they are already present or directing EMS to the scene of the injury if they were not originally present. A decision should be made ahead of time as to who will remain with the injured athlete, who will call or signal emergency personnel, and who will retrieve equipment and/or unlock/open access points for arriving emergency services. The emergency team should stipulate ahead of time what type of signals will be used 1) to alert on-site EMS personnel to come onto the field and render care if necessary, 2) to alert the team physician to come to the field, and 3) to indicate the specific equipment that is needed on site (Andersen et al., 2002).

Best Practices for Emergency Planning for Athletics

Several best practices related to the construction and implementation of emergency action plans within athletic settings have been developed to guide secondary schools, colleges, and communities in the removal of barriers that jeopardize the delivery of optimal safety and preventive measures to the athletic community (Casa et al., 2013; Courson et al., 2013):

1. No scheduled athletic activity, including conditioning sessions, should occur until the appropriate administrator(s) has confirmed that coaches and all support staff are fully familiar with the EAP.

2. Post the specific EAP at each venue.

3. Establish an efficient communication system to activate on-site emergency team members.

4. Establish an efficient communication system to activate and assist off-site EMS.

5. Post the specific location of all emergency equipment and assign team members responsibility for specific equipment retrieval and readiness checks prior to event.

6. Place automated external defibrillators (AEDs) and other CPR equipment to allow for immediate retrieval (no more than 1–3 minutes is ideal) after recognizing an emergency.

7. Train members of emergency team in proper use and maintenance of all equipment including battery replacement and documentation of maintenance records.

8. Determine the role of each emergency team member in regard to evaluation and care of the injured party.

Emergency Care Training

It should be obvious that all personnel involved with organized sports programs must be trained in basic first aid and CPR. Recent developments in AEDs have made it possible for these devices to be made available to schools and recreational facilities. As such, members of the athletic healthcare team should be trained in the use of AEDs. First aid, CPR, and AED training is available through several different agencies nationwide, including the National Safety Council, the American Heart Association, the Red Cross, and the Emergency Care and Safety Institute. It is strongly recommended that all personnel upgrade their training according to recommendations

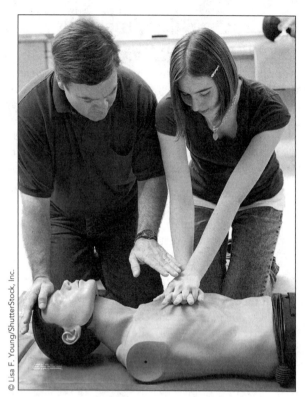

FIGURE 7.2 CPR training.

by each agency; however, annual practice and periodic mock emergency drills should be done to verify the effectiveness of the emergency plan. Emergency care skills deteriorate quickly and should be reviewed regularly (**Figure 7.2**). In addition to completing emergency skills training, coaches should be trained to recognize life-threatening situations and should be educated about factors contributing to sudden death (Casa et al., 2013).

Injury Evaluation Procedures

The Coach's Responsibility

Immediate management of an acute sports injury presents the coach with a challenge unlike any other related to the profession. The primary objective of immediate management by coaching personnel is for them to provide appropriate initial care, including sustaining the injured athlete's life, if necessary, until an athletic trainer or EMS personnel arrives at the scene. Immediate care is critical in determining the severity of the injury. Because sports injuries generally occur amid the confusion of a contest or practice, it is imperative that the coach maintains a clear head and remains objective in the initial assessment of any injury. By law, the coach is the person most often held accountable for proper injury management when no athletic trainer or physician is present. Therefore, even though every situation is unique, the coach must make it clear to everyone in the immediate vicinity of the injured athlete that he or she is in charge, and the athlete should not be moved unless there is imminent danger.

Coaches will typically be seen as "first responders" to an injured athlete and should focus on providing emergency care to the extent of their training and expertise, so coaches must avoid going beyond their level of training when assessing an injured athlete. For example, performing clinical tests for the integrity of the ligaments of a joint goes beyond the training of most coaches and should be performed only by those personnel who have advanced training such as physicians and Board of Certification (BOC)–certified athletic trainers or state-licensed athletic trainers. However, coaches can be trained in the recognition of life-threatening conditions such as exertional heat stroke, head and neck injuries, exertional sickling, sudden cardiac arrest, or airway obstructions and respiratory arrest. If left unattended, any of these conditions can result in sudden death. First, cervical spine injury should be assumed in unconscious patients and should be ruled out for all injured but conscious patients before moving them. Second, in cases where athletes may be suffering from exertional heat stress, immediate cooling should be implemented before transport by EMS. Cold-water immersion is preferred, but any cooling modality can be used until immersion is ready. Third, all coaches need to be aware of which athletes have the sickle cell trait and recognize that lower extremity or low back pain, weakness, difficulty recovering, or shortness of breath may indicate exertional sickling. This requires the athlete stop participating immediately and is attended to using advanced care including oxygen supplementation. Finally, coaches must be trained to deal effectively with cardiac arrest or respiratory problems, so CPR and the use of an AED or removing obstructions and performing rescue breathing must be practiced periodically.

The Evaluation Process

To be effective in the initial process of injury management, the person rendering first aid must have a prepared protocol to follow. The emergency treatment protocol must be generic enough to be effective regardless of the type of injury. By following a preplanned format, the coach is assured of first evaluating all vital life functions and following up with a step-by-step examination to determine any serious injuries that the athlete may have sustained. In this way, tragedy can be avoided. For example, not recognizing exertional sickling and treating it as heat illness or treating an unconscious athlete's head wound without first assessing the airway and determining if the athlete is breathing could result in sudden death.

WHAT IF?

You are a football coach in Tucson, Arizona. You are trained in CPR, first aid, and AED use, and all of your athletes have passed their preparticipation physical examination. What equipment and student-athlete information would you request from your athletic director in order to prevent sudden death from occurring at practices that often occur when the temperature is above 100°F?

As stated earlier, each injury presents the coach with a unique set of circumstances; however, the coach's responsibilities remain the same. Coaches must have a basic knowledge of sports injuries and, more important, the ability to differentiate between life-threatening, major, and minor injuries. A central theme in the remainder of this text is the development of initial assessment skills necessary to determine which injuries should be referred to medical personnel and which can be treated with simple first aid. Such determinations represent a major dilemma for many in the coaching profession. This is especially true when no athletic trainer or physician is immediately available, which more often than not is the case. The coach must be familiar with the preexisting emergency plan and be able to function effectively as a "first responder" on the athletic healthcare team in the absence of more qualified personnel.

Assessment of the Injured Athlete: Initial Check

The assessment of the injured athlete consists of two phases known as the initial check (primary survey) and the physical exam (secondary survey). The purpose of the initial check is to determine if the athlete's life is in immediate jeopardy. According to the American Academy of Orthopaedic Surgeons (AAOS, 2006), the initial check must include assessments of the following (in order of importance):

- Responsiveness
- Airway
- Breathing
- Severe bleeding

Generally, it is best not to move an athlete unless there is a good reason like further risk of injury. Therefore, during the initial check, the coach should make every effort to perform the assessment without moving the athlete or allowing others to move the athlete. In some cases, this may not be possible; for example, it may be necessary to roll an athlete onto his or her back to deliver life-saving CPR. Remember, it is important to follow appropriate first aid procedures whenever moving an athlete and often it is not necessary to move an athlete until advance care has arrived, especially if the athlete is breathing. If the athlete needs no life-saving measures, then the secondary survey that includes a physical exam can be conducted. Again, coaches are reminded to not diagnose injuries and only perform essential stabilization of bones or joints, stop severe bleeding, or provide appropriate first aid for obvious closed (sprains or strains) or open (cuts, abrasions) wounds.

Determining Responsiveness

Before making any decisions about rendering care to an injured athlete, it is essential that his or her level of responsiveness be determined. Assessment of the neurologic status of an injured person can be a daunting task, even for the experienced medical professional. The complexity of the central nervous system (CNS) cannot be disputed; however, from an assessment standpoint, dividing the CNS into the brain and spinal cord is helpful. As recommended by the National Safety Council (2001), this can be accomplished quickly and consistently by using the AVPU scale: A = *a*lert and *a*ware, V = responds to *v*erbal stimulus, P = responds to *p*ainful stimulus, U = *u*nresponsive to any stimulus.

When assessing "alertness," the coach should note whether the athlete's eyes are open and, further, if he or she can accurately state the date, time, and/or location, as well as his or her name. If the athlete can successfully accomplish these simple tasks, he or she is said to be alert. If the athlete does not appear to be alert, then the coach must attempt to verify the athlete's ability to respond to verbal stimulus. If verbal communication can be established, regardless of the accuracy of the communication, the athlete is said to be "responsive to verbal stimulus." In the event the athlete does not appear to be able to communicate verbally at any level, the coach must attempt to verify a response to painful stimuli by pinching the skin overlying a bone such as the clavicle or skin on the inside of the upper arm or thigh. If the coach observes a response to these stimuli, either verbally, through facial gestures, or by attempts to move a limb to avoid being pinched, the athlete is said to be "responsive only to painful stimuli." If the athlete fails to show any form of response, that is, opening of the eyes, verbal communication, or response to painful stimuli, the athlete is said to be "unresponsive to any stimulus." If spinal or head injury is suspected, steps must be taken immediately to immobilize the head and neck to prevent aggravation of the injury.

Respiratory System

Assessment of the respiratory system is the first priority when rendering first aid to an injured athlete. This portion of the initial check should require only a few seconds (no more than 5–10 seconds) and can be initiated en route to the injured athlete if he or she is within visual proximity. If the athlete is obviously responsive, then it can be assumed that the airway is open and respiration is occurring. When level of responsiveness is in question or the athlete is unresponsive, other means of airway and respiration assessment may be necessary.

Airway Assessment

Initial assessment can be facilitated by asking the athlete a simple question. If the athlete responds verbally, this implies the airway is open and the level of responsiveness is high, which indicates that circulation is adequate (Hargarten, 1993). If the victim is unresponsive, the coach should assess for breathing first by looking at the victim's chest in the position in which he or she was found. If the victim is on his or her stomach or side and appears not to be breathing, then life takes priority over the spine. The coach must carefully roll the athlete as a unit onto his or her back to continue the assessment.

If there appear to be no indications of serious head or spinal injury, the head-tilt/chin-lift technique (**Figure 7.3**) should be used. The procedure is as follows: Place one hand on the athlete's forehead while gently lifting the chin with the other hand. In the case of a helmeted athlete, such as a football player, do not remove the helmet or face mask to open the airway. Opening an airway and checking for breathing can be accomplished with the helmet in place. Attempts to remove the helmet can easily aggravate an existing spinal injury.

When there is reason to believe a spinal injury may have occurred, the preferred method of opening the airway is the jaw-thrust technique (**Figure 7.4**). The procedure is as follows: While at the athlete's side, place fingers below the ear lobes and gently push the jaw upward while not moving the head; this should open the airway.

The coach should remember to check for any foreign objects in the airway, such as gum, a mouthpiece, chewing tobacco, a dental appliance, or other material. If an object is seen, then remove any objects using the finger-sweep method (**Figure 7.5**).

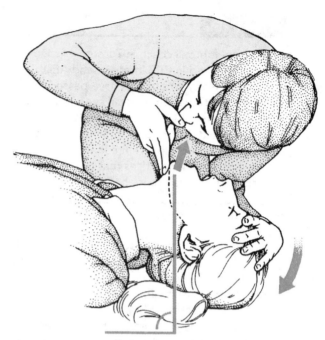

FIGURE 7.3 Head-tilt/chin-lift method.

Breathing Assessment

The responsive athlete is obviously breathing; however, the coach should continue to observe for difficulty in breathing and listen for abnormal sounds, like gasping, that may indicate a problem. It is easiest to look for the chest to rise and fall and feel the chest for movement due to airflow. The unresponsive athlete may not be breathing; however, circulation must be prioritized and if there are signs of no circulation then CPR chest compressions need to be started.

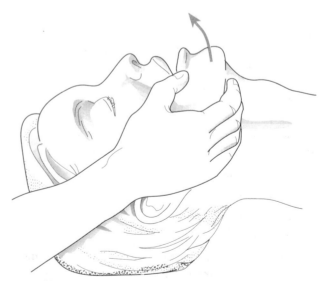

FIGURE 7.4 Jaw-thrust maneuver.

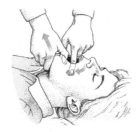

Finger-sweep method
- With index finger of your hand, slide finger down along the inside of one cheek deeply into mouth and use a hooking action across to other cheek to dislodge foreign object.
- If foreign body comes within reach, grab and remove it. Do not force object deeper.

FIGURE 7.5 Finger-sweep method.

Circulatory System

Determination of the status of the circulatory system is a critical component of the initial survey and is intended to verify the integrity of the heart and blood vessels. The two major concerns are the presence or absence of the signs of circulation (breathing and heart rate) and presence or absence of loss of blood (hemorrhage), either internally or externally. Circulation assessment should be executed quickly by looking at skin color and feeling for a pulse at the carotid artery on the neck. Identification of external hemorrhage is also executed quickly by looking for blood; however, identification of internal hemorrhage may present the coach with a greater challenge. Signs of internal bleeding can be noted by discoloration or rigidity on the skin surface and are also associated with shock related to blood loss.

Circulation Assessment

A responsive athlete who is breathing will have the signs of circulation, including pulse and blood flow. The coach should determine if the signs of circulation are present in an unresponsive victim after opening the airway and quickly checking for breathing. If the coach sees no signs of circulation, he or she can begin chest compressions associated with CPR. Recent American Heart Association guidelines (Fields et al., 2010) emphasize a change in the order of emergency treatment of unresponsiveness. The initials AB-CABS are used to prime first aid providers with memory of task order. As described earlier, the airway should be carefully opened, breathing should be quickly assessed (5–10 seconds), and then chest compressions should be started prior to providing ventilation to the unresponsive athlete. The sequence of C-A-B, where airway opening and breaths follow compressions, is continued until advanced care arrives, the athlete is revived, or the rescuer tires. In

an unresponsive athlete situation, the coach's primary responsibility is to keep the athlete alive and to ensure that help is summoned. There is no reason to move the athlete from the playing field or practice area. The possibility of delaying a game or practice does not justify moving someone in this situation.

Hemorrhage Assessment

Extensive external bleeding is extremely rare in athletics. Most external bleeding is obvious and can be controlled by the appropriate first aid procedures—use of direct pressure, elevation, pressure points, pressure bandage, or tourniquet. In major injuries to extremities where bleeding cannot be stopped with pressure and elevation, the application of tourniquets is recommended (Kragh et al., 2008) in an effort to save limbs and lives. It is understandable that a coach may not feel comfortable applying a tourniquet, but new first aid training includes instruction in application techniques. Anytime blood or other bodily fluids are exposed, the coach should, whenever possible, take precautions to protect against the transmission of bloodborne pathogens. Coaches are encouraged to wear medical exam gloves and eye protection to help prevent exposure.

Internal hemorrhaging is difficult if not impossible to detect during the initial survey. One of the earliest signs of severe internal bleeding is **hypovolemic shock**, which is caused by too little blood in the vascular system. Two important signs of this condition are rapid, weak pulse and rapid, shallow breathing. Changes in the condition of the skin surface may also provide clues to this condition. Moist, clammy-feeling skin, associated with blue color inside the lips and under the nail beds, indicates shock. Such cases represent true medical emergencies, and the primary objective must be to treat for shock and arrange for transport to a medical facility.

Summary

Remember that the purpose of the initial check is to determine whether there is a life-threatening injury. If an airway exists, breathing and pulse appear normal, and no bleeding is detected, the next step in the evaluation process is the physical exam. The purpose of the physical exam is to give the injured athlete a complete evaluation for any other injuries not found during the

hypovolemic shock Inability of the cardiovascular system to maintain adequate circulation to all parts of the body.

initial check. To be effective, the physical exam must be conducted in a preplanned, sequential fashion. In cases in which injuries are obvious, it may be possible to skip certain portions of the physical exam to render appropriate first aid sooner. However, even after attending to the obvious injury, the coach should complete the remaining portions of the survey in an effort to rule out other conditions. A good example is a basketball player who falls to the floor immediately after having attempted to get a rebound. If the coach sees the incident—and notices that the athlete grabbed her ankle and was in obvious pain—the coach would be correct in performing a quick initial check followed by a visual assessment of the ankle to determine if there are obvious fractures or open wounds. Then, assuming there were no serious injuries, the application of ice and compression as well as elevation of the injured ankle would be appropriate. This entire process should take no more than a few minutes, after which the coach should perform a more thorough physical exam if other medical personnel have not arrived.

Assessment of the Injured Athlete: Physical Exam

The **physical exam** should include specific components that enable the coach to collect as much information about the injury as possible under the circumstances. The essential parts of the survey are as follows:

- *History.* Have a discussion about the mechanism of injury with the athlete and/or onlookers. Ask the athlete about his or her current signs and symptoms.
- *Observation.* Observe for obvious signs and/or symptoms related to the injury.
- *Palpation.* Feel the injured area to collect more information.

Overall, the purpose of the physical exam is for the coach to note signs and symptoms related to the injury. It is important that while administering the physical exam the coach continually monitors the injured athlete's signs of breathing and circulation. Although the purpose of the initial check is to verify circulation and respiration, both of these vital functions may change quickly related to the body's response to the injury. For example, an athlete who has sustained a significant head injury may initially have normal circulation and respiration that rather quickly decline as bleeding in the skull continues. As such, the coach must remain ever vigilant during the physical exam for changes in the condition of

the athlete that may be life threatening. The coach must also be observant for signs and symptoms of shock, which can also escalate into a life-threatening phenomenon. Critical to this is a basic understanding that a **sign** involves objective findings such as bleeding, swelling, discoloration, and deformity. **Symptoms** are subjective in nature and may not be as reliable in determining the nature of the injury. Symptoms include findings such as headache, nausea, pain, and **point tenderness**. The coach begins observing for signs and symptoms related to the athlete even before he or she is near enough to render any aid. As the coach approaches the injured athlete, he or she must note the body position and look for signs of possible significance such as odd behavior or actions. If he or she saw the injury occur, the forces involved and the mechanism of injury will be clearer. This information can be related to possible type(s) of injury (fracture vs. sprain).

Medical History

Whether the athlete is responsive or unresponsive, collecting a history is considered the third part of victim assessment. Obviously, if the athlete is unresponsive, the coach needs to collect information from bystanders, typically teammates or other coaching personnel. Regardless of the circumstances, when rendering care to an unresponsive athlete, the coach must always assume that there are serious head and spinal injuries that require the stabilization of the athlete's head and neck. The priorities must be basic life support—cardiac function, airway, and breathing—followed by contacting EMS. In the case of the conscious athlete, the history process begins as soon as the coach arrives on the scene (**Figure 7.6**). Its purpose is to collect information critical to identifying the body areas involved as well as the severity and mechanism(s) of injury (Booher &

FIGURE 7.6 A coach obtains a history of injury from an injured athlete while athletic trainer stabilizes head and neck.

Thibodeau, 1989). Traumatic injuries usually present a more obvious set of complaints and possible causes than do chronic injuries.

Although each injury is unique, the coach's questions to the athlete should be phrased in simple, easy-to-understand terms that can elicit the desired information without leading the athlete to giving a preferred answer. The coach should avoid using terminology too advanced for the athlete and always take care not to increase the anxiety level by losing his or her composure. Questions should require only brief responses—preferably a yes or a no. Initially, the coach can attempt to gain the confidence of the athlete by letting him or her know what she is doing and that she is there to ensure the athlete's welfare. In the case of rendering care to someone the coach does not know, it is always best for the coach to identify herself and indicate that she is there to render first aid care. Ask the athlete to explain what happened and to describe perceptions of the injury. Inquire if there is pain—and if so, where. Also ask whether the athlete heard any strange sounds during the injury or feels anything abnormal. With respect to injuries of the extremities, the coach should ask if the athlete felt a pop or snap, as if something "let go" within the joint or elsewhere within the extremity. If possible, compare the injured side with the uninjured area on the opposite side of the body. The athlete's answers provide essential information to assist the coach in the evaluation of both the location and magnitude of the injury. Do not forget to inquire about the injury history (both long and short term) of the involved area. A good example of how such information could be useful is the case of a suspected shoulder subluxation (partial dislocation). Such an injury may be very difficult to evaluate. However, if during the history taking, the athlete admits that the shoulder has been dislocated several times in the past year, the coach may then focus efforts on determining the integrity of that specific joint because that injury tends to have a high rate of recurrence. Information regarding the injury history of the athlete should always be passed on to the medical personnel who evaluate the athlete later.

In some cases, the medical emergency may be difficult to ascertain, as is the case with certain conditions such as diabetes, **exercise-induced asthma (EIA)**, and head injury. Clues to the problem may be given during the history process, if done correctly. In the case of metabolic emergencies, the questions are obvious. ("Do you have diabetes—and if so, did you take your insulin today?" "Do you have epilepsy—and if so, are you on any sort of medication?") In the case of the conscious athlete with a possible head injury, behavior may be incongruent with the circumstances. The coach's questions should assist in determining the level of consciousness, as well as the integrity of higher thought processes.

Observation and Palpation

Essentially, the goal of the physical exam is to identify all injuries, regardless of severity, treat them appropriately, and refer the athlete for medical care if it is deemed necessary. With a responsive athlete, the coach can ask him or her to point out the site(s) of injury. The coach can then look and feel for the signs of injury, including deformity, open wounds, tenderness, and swelling. With an unresponsive athlete, as long as breathing and circulation are maintained, the physical exam should be thought of as a head-to-toe assessment of the athlete. The coach should look and feel (palpate) for abnormalities or open wounds by starting at the head and progressing through the neck, chest, abdomen, pelvis, and extremities. The National Safety Council (2001) defines **palpation** as "the act of feeling with the hands for the purpose of determining the consistency of the part beneath." With good palpation skills, any noticeable irregularities could indicate fractures, dislocations, or other types of tissue damage. With practice, palpation skills can be refined to the point where identification of injury-related problems such as swelling, muscle spasm, localized fever, abdominal rigidity (sign of internal bleeding in abdominal cavity), deformity, crepitus (grating feeling beneath the skin surface), and skin tension can be easily detected.

Palpation is a learned skill and does involve some amount of contact with the injured athlete (**Figure 7.7**). Consequently, it is important that great care is taken to

physical exam Checking a victim of an emergency for signs and symptoms associated with injury and/or illness.

sign Objective evidence of an abnormal situation within the body.

symptom Subjective evidence of an abnormal situation within the body.

point tenderness Pain produced when an injury site is palpated.

exercise-induced asthma (EIA) Acute, reversible, self-limiting bronchospasm occurring during or after exercise.

palpation The act of feeling with the hands for the purpose of determining the consistency of the part beneath.

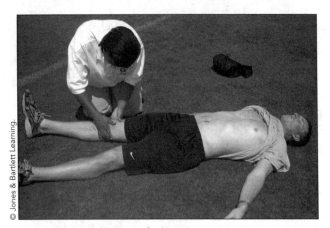

FIGURE 7.7 Palpation of a knee injury.

avoid aggravation of existing injuries. Also, when evaluating a conscious athlete, an explanation of the purposes of the evaluation can be helpful in relieving anxiety. It is recommended that whenever possible the palpation process should begin in a body area away from where there are obvious injuries (Booher & Thibodeau, 1989). This allows the athlete to develop confidence in the coach's palpation skill prior to actual evaluation of the injury (or injuries). In the case of injury to an extremity, evaluation of the uninjured limb first is recommended as well. This provides an immediate basis for comparison when the actual injury is evaluated.

In cases of possible significant injury in which much of the body is covered with equipment and clothing, it is best to remove garments from the suspected area of injury by cutting away clothing with scissors rather than removing it in a normal fashion. In this way, unnecessary movement of the athlete can be avoided. Obviously, care must be taken not to cause embarrassment to the athlete. However, in the case of a potential life-or-death situation, saving the athlete's life must always take priority over modesty.

Shock

Shock is an acute, life-threatening condition that involves the body's failure to maintain adequate circulation to the vital organs. As previously described, shock may result from severe hemorrhage; however, shock can be caused by a number of other conditions, including cardiogenic (heart failure), neurogenic (dilated blood vessels), and simple psychogenic (fainting) conditions. The signs and symptoms of shock can include any combination of the following: profuse sweating; cool, clammy-feeling skin; dilated pupils; elevated pulse and respiration rate; irritable behavior; complaints of extreme thirst; and nausea and/or vomiting. Treatment

for shock includes having the athlete in a supine position with the legs elevated approximately 8 to 12 inches. The coach should also try to calm the athlete with reassuring comments. To avoid further loss of body heat, the coach can cover the athlete with a blanket. In the case of a suspected spinal injury, do not move the athlete from the position he or she is in. Rather, monitor vital signs and cover with a blanket if environmental conditions are such that loss of body heat is possible.

Removal from Field/Court

It is important that during all phases of the athlete examination process, significant findings are noted and recalled for later use. Normally, the entire evaluation process should be completed in a matter of minutes, after which the appropriate first aid treatment should be initiated. If further evaluation is deemed necessary, the decision must be made to move the athlete from the playing field or practice area. Athletes who are conscious, responsive, and have no obvious lower extremity injuries that preclude walking may be able to leave the area under their own power (with assistance). If a lower extremity injury exists, it is best to use some form of transport device, such as a stretcher, spine board, or even a two-person carry, to remove the athlete from the site of injury. In the case of an unconscious athlete, or one who may have sustained a head or neck injury, the best policy is to stay with the athlete, monitor vital signs, treat for shock, and summon EMS personnel. Unless the athlete is in immediate danger of being injured further, there is no justification for movement prior to the arrival of EMS personnel.

Return to Play?

In the absence of a trained medical professional such as a physician or BOC-certified or state-licensed athletic trainer, the coach must answer the question, "Should this athlete be allowed to return to play?" In some cases, this decision is quite easy, as in the case of a suspected head or neck injury or a fractured bone. In other cases, coaches are often presented with ethical dilemmas that arise whenever an athlete's best medical interests conflict with the performance expectations of the athlete, team, or parents, but it is important that a coach understands his or her legal liability in relationship to negligent treatment of a suspected injury. For example, any athlete who must leave a practice or game because of a neurologic injury (concussion) should not be allowed to return until evaluated by a trained medical professional. This is true even in the case of what is commonly known as "getting one's bell rung." Such an episode can lead to serious, even life-threatening, complications if the athlete is allowed to return to participation without medical evaluation. Likewise, an athlete who appears to be suffering from heat-related problems, should be removed from participation and cleared for return only by a medical professional.

Without question, the most difficult decisions involve injuries to the musculoskeletal system such as joint injuries, muscle strains, and contusions. In general, if the injury results in any degree of functional loss, the athlete should not be allowed to return to participation. Functional loss in the lower extremities can be verified by asking the athlete to perform simple drills such as hopping up and down on one leg or running a figure eight. In the case of upper extremity injury in the shoulder region, for example, asking the athlete to place his hand on the center of his upper back as if to scratch his back will verify normal range of motion. To test muscle strength and joint integrity, ask the athlete to perform a push-up. Failure to execute any simple functional test should result in removal from participation that day and medical referral. Such an athlete should be allowed to return to participation only after receiving medical clearance from a physician.

It is important to always remember that signs such as swelling, discoloration, limping, and facial expressions

 **WHAT IF?**

You are coaching junior varsity football, specifically the linebackers, when suddenly someone yells that an athlete has been hurt on the other end of the practice field. When you arrive on the scene, the athlete is lying face down on the field and not moving. What should your initial actions be in this situation?

related to pain and symptoms such as pain, popping, clicking in a joint, or uncontrolled muscle spasm all potentially indicate a more serious injury. When in doubt, the coach should always err on the conservative side and remove the athlete from participation until a medical professional can perform a more complete evaluation.

The Coach's Limitations

In the absence of a BOC-certified or state-licensed athletic trainer, medical doctor, or other designated healthcare provider, the coach is responsible for the initial management of injuries sustained by an athlete.

Athletic Trainers SPEAK Out

Courtesy of Michael Carroll, MEd, ATC, LAT, Head Athletic Trainer/Assistant Athletic Director, Stephenville, Texas.

How important is an emergency action plan and is there a situation you can describe where it worked really well?

Having a site-specific emergency action plan and practicing that plan is critical for athletic trainers. When the inevitable emergency happens the athletic trainer must decisively put a preexisting EAP into motion. This can and will help to minimize any confusion that the involved individuals, which may include health care providers, coaches, students, or other staff, may have. Without an emergency action plan a potentially life-threatening event could have catastrophic consequences.

At my school we had a young man who suffered a fracture dislocation of his ankle during an off-season workout. We immediately put the emergency action plan into motion and everything went very smoothly from the beginning of the treatment to the transport to the hospital. The parent of the young man (who is a nurse) complimented the district on how professionally everything was handled and how it made her feel good as a parent that her son was taken care of so well.

—Michael Carroll, MEd, ATC, LAT

Michael Carroll is the Head Athletic Trainer/Assistant Athletic Director at Stephenville High School.
Courtesy of Michael Carroll, MEd, ATC, LAT, Head Athletic Trainer/Assistant Athletic Director, Stephenville, Texas.

Yet coaches must take special care not to overstep the bounds of their training, experience, and expertise. In short, coaches should avoid the urge to attempt to provide care beyond their first aid training. All of the procedures described so far can be classified as appropriate first aid care that should be rendered by coaching personnel at the time of an injury. The critical point to remember, however, is that the coach should not perform procedures that are clearly in the domain of medical doctors or allied health personnel such as a athletic trainers. For example, performing special tests on joints to determine injury to ligaments, attempting to reduce (put back into place) a dislocated joint, and removing stitches, a splint, or a cast are clearly procedures that fall in the domain of trained medical professionals and not coaching staff members.

REVIEW QUESTIONS

1. What are the key elements to an emergency action plan (EAP)?

2. List several best practices for an emergency action plan that help eliminate barriers to optimal health and safety.

3. In regard to emergency planning, what are the four (4) items the emergency team should stipulate before a game or other competition?

4. What is the order of assessment and performance of life-saving skills when a participant appears not to be breathing or not to have a pulse?

5. Briefly describe the initial check and the physical exam as they relate to the initial assessment of an injured athlete.

6. When performing an initial check of an injured athlete, what is the recommended procedure for opening an airway when a neck injury is suspected?

7. True or false: It is imperative that the helmet be removed from an injured, unresponsive football player as soon as possible to establish an open airway.

8. What is one of the earliest clues that internal bleeding may be occurring?

9. List the essential components of the physical exam.

10. Differentiate between a sign and a symptom.

11. True or false: When collecting a history from an injured athlete, questions should be kept brief and use minimal complicated terminology.

12. True or false: A coach should put the team's priorities over the health of an athlete.

REFERENCES

American Academy of Orthopaedic Surgeons. (2006). *First Aid, CPR, and AED* (5th ed.). Sudbury, Mass: Jones and Bartlett Publishers.

Andersen J, Courson RW, Kleiner DM, McLoda TA (2002). National Athletic Trainers' Association position statement: Emergency planning in athletics. *J Athl Train.* 37(1):99–104. Adapted with permission.

Booher JM, Thibodeau GA. (1989). *Athletic Injury Assessment.* St. Louis, Mo: Times Mirror/Mosby.

Casa DJ, Almquist J, Anderson SA, Baker L, Bergeron MF, Biagioli B, Boden B, Brenner JS, Carroll M, Colgate B, Cooper L, Courson R, Csillan D, Demartini JK, Drezner JA, Erickson T, Ferrara MS, Fleck SJ, Franks R, Guskiewicz KM, Holcomb WR, Huggins RA, Lopez RM, Mayer T, McHenry P, Mihalik JP, O'Connor FG, Pagnotta KD, Pryor RR, Reynolds J, Stearns RL, Valentine V. (2013). The inter-association task force for preventing sudden death in secondary school athletics programs: Best-practices recommendations. *J Athl Train.* 48(4):546–553.

Courson RC, Goldenberg M, Adams KG, Scott A, Anderson SA, Colgate B, Cooper L, Dewald L, Floyd RT, Gregory DB, Indelicato PA, Klossner D, O'Leary R, Ray T, Selgo T, Thompson C, Turbak G. (2013). Inter-association consensus statement on best practices for sports medicine management for secondary schools and colleges. Available: http://www.nata.org/sites/default/files/Sports MedicineManagement.pdf.

Fields JM, Hazinski MF, Sayre MR, Chameides L, Schexnayder SM, Hemphill R, Samson RA, Kattwinkel J, Berg RA, Bhanji F, Cave DM, Jauch EC, Kudenchuk PJ, Neumar RW, Peberdy MA, Perlman JM, Sinz E, Travers AH, Berg MD, Billi JE, Eigel B, Hickey RW, Kleinman ME, Link MS, Morrison LJ, O'Connor RE, Shuster M, Callaway CW, Cucchiara B, Ferguson JD, Rea TD, Vanden Hoek TL. (2010). Part 1: Executive summary: 2010 American Heart Association guidelines for cardiopulmonary resuscitation and emergency cardiovascular care: *Circulation.* 122(Suppl 3):S640–S656.

Hargarten KM. (1993). Rapid injury assessment. *Phys Sportsmed*. 21(2):33–40.

Kragh JF, Walters TJ, Baer DG, Fox CJ, Wade CE, Salinas J, Holcomb JB. (2008). Practical use of emergency tourniquets to stop bleeding in major limb trauma. *J Trauma*. 64(Suppl 2):S38–S50.

McCaskey AS, Biedzynski KW. (1996). A guide to the legal liability of coaches for a sports participant's injuries. *Seton Hall J Sport L*. 6(1):8–97.

National Safety Council. (2001). *First Aid and CPR* (4th ed.). Sudbury, Mass: Jones and Bartlett Publishers.

Quandt EF, Mitton MJ, Black JS. (2009). Legal liability in covering athletic events. *Sports Health*. 1(1):84–90.

The Injury Process

MAJOR CONCEPTS

This chapter examines the complex topic of the tissue healing process in reaction to trauma. It begins with an overview of the types of tissues and the forces involved in sports injuries, followed by a detailed, phase-by-phase description of the healing process, which includes the inflammatory response, fibroblastic repair, and maturation/remodeling phases. The inflammatory response phase is often the most limiting phase to physical activity or exercise; therefore, it is critical that coaches and physical educators grasp the basic physiology of this process to better understand the recommended procedures for treating inflammation. Successful management depends on whether the inflammatory response phase is acute or chronic, so correctly recognizing the signs and symptoms associated with these phases can guide management. Depending on the signs and symptoms, treatment can include application of therapeutic cold (e.g., crushed ice or commercial cold packs), compression, and elevation or the administration of therapeutic heat (e.g., hot packs or warm whirlpool). Pharmacologic agents, such as anti-inflammatories or pain relievers, should be recommended by a physician or another allied health care provider. Even though many pharmacological agents are available over the counter, recent evidence suggests that dosage mistakes are common and can result in serious side effects, including death. This chapter concludes with a discussion of the role of exercise in the rehabilitation process.

go.jblearning.com/PfeifferCWS

For a full suite of assignments and additional learning activities (indicated by the icons throughout the text), use the access code found in the front of your text. If you do not have an access code, you can obtain one at go.jblearning.com/PfeifferCWS.

The Physics of Sports Injury

The human body consists of many different types of tissue, each serving a specific purpose. Some are highly specialized (e.g., the retina of the eye contains tissue that is sensitive to light and is not found anywhere else in the body), whereas other types of tissue are distributed throughout the body. **Connective tissue**, for example, is the most common type in the body (Cailliet, 1977). Areolar (loosely woven and irregularly arranged) and dense (tightly packed and organized) connective tissues help form ligaments, retinaculum, joint capsules, bone, cartilage, fascia, and tendons (Houglum, 2010). Cailliet (1977) classifies other general categories of tissue as epithelial (for protection, secretion, and absorption), muscular (for contraction), and nervous (for sensation and conductivity). Connective tissues are the primary components that create the musculoskeletal system, so it is no surprise that they are commonly involved in acute and chronic sports injuries. Collegiate athletes experience a variety of acute and chronic injuries, and recent research establishes that the musculoskeletal system is involved in a significant portion of those injuries (Yang et al., 2012). For example, the most common acute injuries are sprains and strains (62% of total), and tendonitis (15% of total) is the one of most common chronic injuries.

Three basic types of forces can affect connective tissues: tensile, compressive, and shear (**Figure 8.1**). Tendons are designed to resist tensile forces, but are less effective when subjected to shear forces and are poorly designed to deal with compressive forces. Conversely, bone tissue is designed to absorb compressive forces, but it is less effective against tensile and shear forces (Curwin & Stanish, 1984). Ligament tissue, like that of tendons, is best suited to resist tensile forces while being more vulnerable to shear and compressive mechanisms.

Tendons are extremely strong structures able to withstand stresses ranging from 8700 to 18,000 pounds per square inch. Yet, activities such as running and jumping may generate forces in excess of these physiologic limits because tissue stress can be as high as nine times body weight (Curwin & Stanish, 1984). Muscle tissue and its surrounding connective tissue (fascia) are most commonly injured when excess tension is applied while contraction (shortening) is occurring. Furthermore, it is commonly held that more injuries to muscles and fascia occur during eccentric contractions, which are described as "the simultaneous processes of muscle contraction and stretch of the muscle–tendon unit by an extrinsic force" (Safran, Seaber, & Garrett, 1989). When strains occur, the damage is typically found at the proximal musculotendinous junction (MTJ; Ingersoll & Mistry, 2006). However, each tissue type has a limit to

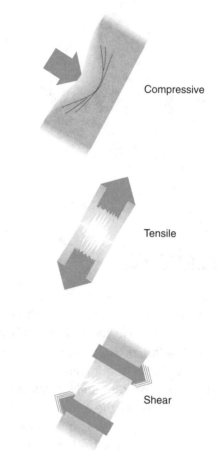

FIGURE 8.1 Mechanical forces of injury. Compression (application of inward pushing force), tensile (application of outward pulling force), and shear (application of forces to displace layers parallel to one another).

how much force it can withstand. This limit has been referred to as the critical force (Nigg & Bobbert, 1990). The critical force value varies for each type of tissue in the body. Even within the same type of tissue, the critical force value may vary owing to changes in the tissue structure. For example, factors such as age, temperature, skeletal maturity, gender, and body weight can affect the mechanical properties of ligaments (Akeson, Amiel, & Woo, 1986). More research into the specific causes of musculoskeletal injuries is warranted, because it has been well documented that soft-tissue injuries are very common in sports (Yang et al., 2012).

The Physiology of Sports Injury

Whenever tissues are damaged as a result of **trauma**, the body reacts quickly with a predictable sequence of physiologic actions designed to lead ultimately to the resolution, regeneration, or repair of the involved tissues.

Resolution is complete healing in which dead cells and cellular debris are removed and the tissue is left functionally the same. **Regeneration** occurs when damaged tissue is replaced by some cells of the same type along with scar tissue and it retains most of its original structure. **Repair** occurs when the original tissue is replaced by scar tissue and the original structure and function are lost.

Regardless of what tissue has been injured, the body's initial response to trauma is inflammation. This process begins immediately following the injury. The normal signs and symptoms of inflammation include swelling, pain, reddening of the skin (known as **erythema**), increases in the temperature of the area involved, and loss of function (Ingersoll & Mistry, 2006). (See **Figure 8.2**.) However, the healing process consists of several specific phases. It begins with the inflammatory response phase followed by the fibroblastic repair phase, and ends with the maturation/remodeling phase (Ingersoll & Mistry, 2006). Each serves a specific purpose, and all are essential to proper repair of the structures involved.

Inflammatory Response Phase

When tissues are damaged as a result of trauma, millions of cells are destroyed. However, the destruction is what triggers the body's healing response. Several steps characterize this phase and are designed to minimize the initial (primary) injury and begin the development of new tissue. These steps include vascular, cellular, and metabolic changes that are mediated by a variety of chemicals, including **histamine**, **bradykinin**, and **prostaglandins** (Figure 8.2). A good analogy to better understand this process is the construction of a new building. The first step is the implosion (injury) of the old structure, so a new building can be started. After the implosion (injury), the site is fenced in and crews begin to clean up the debris. The new foundation can only be laid when the debris has been cleaned. Basically, the inflammatory response phase is meant to destroy injured tissue, contain the area, localize the actual site of injury, protect the injured tissue, and defend against infection (Houglum, 2010). In essence, the entire acute inflammatory phase results in a walling off of the damaged area from the rest of the body—along with the formation of a mass of cellular debris, enzymes, and chemicals that serves to clean up the destroyed structures while also providing the necessary components for tissue repair. The acute inflammatory phase of injury lasts until new tissue material can arrive (approximately 3 to 4 days; Arnheim, 1989). However, if an athlete returns to participation too soon and the area is disturbed by additional trauma, the inflammatory response phase will last much longer. Therefore, protection

(splinting or crutches) and rest are often the prescribed treatment. For example, with the majority of fractures, some type of immobilization is required, usually in the form of a splint or a plaster or synthetic cast. In severely displaced fractures, surgical placement of appliances such as plates and screws may be necessary to stabilize the bony fragments to facilitate healing.

The mechanical force of the injury usually results in damage to a variety of soft tissues, including the blood vessels. As a result, the sudden increase in blood flow into the interstitial (between the cells) spaces results in the formation of a hematoma. Blood pooling within tissue is known clinically as a hematoma and is defined as a "localized collection of blood in the damaged area" (Delforge, 2002), and it represents an important step in the inflammatory process. A hematoma can develop quickly, so **vasoconstriction** is initiated to reduce blood flow and promote clotting in the damaged vessels. However, after only a few minutes, this is followed by **vasodilation** of blood vessels. The increased diameter of

connective tissue The most common tissue in the body; includes ligaments, bones, retinaculum, joint capsules, cartilage, fascia, and tendons.

trauma Wound or injury.

resolution Complete healing where dead cells and cellular debris are removed and the tissue is left functionally the same.

regeneration Damaged tissue is replaced by some cells of the same type along with scar tissue, and it retains most of its original structure.

repair Original tissue is replaced by scar tissue and the structure and function are lost.

erythema Red discoloration of the skin.

histamine Powerful inflammatory chemical that causes an increase in vascular permeability and vasodilation.

bradykinin Inflammatory chemical released when tissues are damaged; it results in increased pain in the area and may play a role in the production of other inflammatory chemicals such as prostaglandins.

prostaglandins Perhaps some of the most powerful chemicals produced in the body; related to the inflammatory process, they cause a variety of effects including vasodilation, increased vascular permeability, pain, fever, and clotting.

vasoconstriction Decrease in the diameter of a blood vessel resulting in a decreased blood flow.

vasodilation Increase in the diameter of a blood vessel resulting in an increased blood flow.

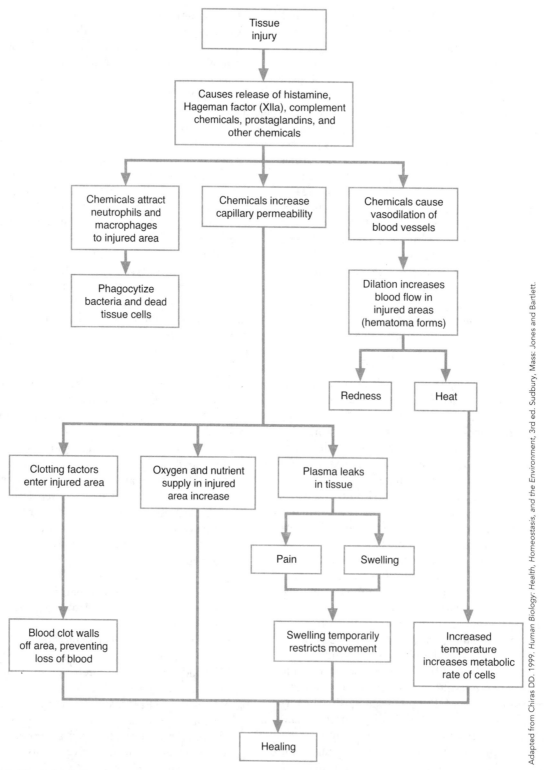

FIGURE 8.2 The inflammatory process.

the blood vessels also increases vessel permeability, thereby bringing essential cells and chemicals to the site of injury to assist in repair.

Three specific groups of chemicals have been identified as being active during the acute phase of the inflammatory response. They are vasoactive substances that cause vasodilation, chemotactic factors that mediate function and attract other types of cells, and degenerative enzymes that cause cellular breakdown (Fick & Johnson, 1993).

As mentioned before, several chemical mediators are responsible for the vascular, cellular, and metabolic changes that precede all the other cellular changes initiated in the inflammatory response phase. Histamine is a powerful inflammatory chemical and is released from a number of different types of cells, resulting in short-term vasodilation and increased vascular permeability. Histamine is also known for causing redness around the site of trauma and sometimes an itching sensation, especially when the trauma is an insect bite or sting. In addition to histamine, when tissue damage occurs an enzyme known as Hageman factor (XIIa) becomes active within the bloodstream. The Hageman factor induces a number of localized changes in the region of damage including activation of the **complement system**. A complete discussion of the complement system is beyond the scope of this text. However, it includes a variety of chemically similar structures (i.e., cytokines) that play major roles in the inflammatory response, including activation of **leukocytes**, **lysosomes**, and the attraction of cellular building material into the area. The leukocytes are the primary response team to injury; they are essential to healing and are transported via blood vessels to the injury site. Through a complex process including vasodilation these leukocytes (e.g., neutrophils, macrophages, and monocytes) adhere to blood vessel walls and then fall out into the tissue space due to the gaps created by vasodilation and permeability (Wilkerson, 1985). Lysosomes contain powerful enzymes that, when released, hasten the breakdown of cellular structure (degradation effect). The process of attracting lysosomes, leukocytes, and other cellular building material is known as chemotaxis and is essential to the process of inflammation. The Hageman factor is also responsible for the manufacture of another powerful inflammatory chemical called bradykinin. It affects the vasculature by increasing vascular permeability, and it also causes a pain response. In addition, bradykinin triggers the release of prostaglandins, which are among the most powerful chemicals in the human body (Wilkerson, 1985). Prostaglandins have a number of effects in the damaged area, including vasodilation, increased vascular permeability, increased pain, and stimulation of the clotting mechanism (Lachmann & Jenner, 1994). Another important chemical mediator of the acute inflammatory process is **arachidonic acid**, which is the product of the interaction between enzymes supplied by leukocytes and phospholipids derived from the membranes of destroyed cells (American Academy of Orthopaedic Surgeons [AAOS], 1991). Arachidonic acid serves as the catalyst for a series of reactions that yield a variety of substances, including leukotrienes, which play a role in the inflammatory phase by attracting leukocytes to the damaged area. In the end, it is the combination of these chemical mediators, hemodynamic changes (vasoconstriction and vasodilation), and metabolic changes that allow for the necessary cleanup of damaged tissue and the initiation of cellular building.

The hemodynamic changes initiated by the chemical mediators are essential because the tissue cleanup process is made possible due to an increase in vascular permeability. This allows large structures, such as plasma proteins, platelets, and leukocytes (primarily neutrophils), to pass out of capillaries and into the damaged tissue (Wilkerson, 1985). By way of **phagocytosis** (cell eating), leukocytes and lysosomes dispose of damaged cells and tissue debris. The number of neutrophils in the damaged area can increase greatly in the first few hours of acute inflammation—to as high as four to five times the normal levels (Guyton, 1986). Neutrophils arrive quickly at the site of injury; however, they live for only a short time period (approximately 7 hours) and have no means of reproduction. When neutrophils expire, they release chemicals that attract a second type of leukocyte known as a macrophage. Macrophages also consume cellular debris via the process of phagocytosis. However, unlike neutrophils, macrophages can live for months and do have the ability to reproduce (Knight, 1995).

complement system Part of the immune system. It is innate and complements the antibodies and cleaning cells to clear pathogens from damaged tissue.

leukocytes White blood cells.

lysosomes Cellular organelles that contain enzymes that break down waste materials and cellular debris.

arachidonic acid Chemical released when cells are damaged that serves as a precursor to the formation of other inflammatory chemicals including leukotrienes and prostaglandins.

phagocytosis Destruction of injurious cells or particles by phagocytes (white blood cells).

Unfortunately, the inflammatory response phase can last longer or be of a larger magnitude than optimally needed for all types of trauma. As a result, previously healthy tissue can be damaged as part of the repair process; this is called secondary injury. Secondary injury adds to the total trauma area. An example of secondary injury is after a lateral ankle sprain, the hemorrhage (swelling) and subsequent **edema** can often affect the lower leg and toes. When edema (fluid accumulation) and associated chemicals, lysosomes, and leukocytes start to invade areas of healthy tissue, they cause tissue destruction. The fluid accumulation along with the previously damaged blood vessels may cause further obstruction of blood flow to the area surrounding the tissue damage. The lack of blood flow prevents the arrival of oxygen and other energy sources to not only the injured tissue but also the surrounding undamaged tissue. This may result in a specific type of secondary injury called **secondary metabolic injury**. This type of secondary injury results from the energy needs of tissue being greater than the energy available, and as a result healthy tissue "dies" because of a lack of appropriate metabolic provisions (Knight, 1967; Merrick, 2002). Furthermore, during extended phagocytosis, the neutrophils and some macrophages cause another type of secondary injury called **secondary enzymatic injury**. Basically, the cell membranes of healthy cells are compromised due to the chemical waste products produced by the required phagocytosis of real tissue debris (Merrick, 2002). When a cell membrane is compromised it can no longer maintain homeostasis and will likely experience **apoptosis** (programmed cell death). In addition to apoptosis, some healthy cells are even consumed by overly aggressive neutrophils and macrophages because they are unable to distinguish between the tissue debris and surrounding healthy tissue.

As previously stated, in the absence of further irritation or trauma, the inflammatory phase usually ends 3 to 4 days after the initial injury. At this time, the earliest steps in tissue repair begin to occur, with the migration into the area of specialized cells, including polymorphs and monocytes (both specialized forms of leukocytes) and histiocytes (a type of macrophage). These cells continue the process of breaking down the cellular debris, preparing for generation of new tissue. Building of new tissue is always a two-step process of tissue breakdown (lysis) and tissue buildup (synthesis). The balance between these two allows for the appropriate growth of new tissue. The stage is then set for the fibroblastic repair phase.

Fibroblastic Repair Phase

With the exception of bones, connective tissues of the body heal themselves by replacing damaged cells with like cells (resolution and regeneration) or forming scar tissue (regeneration and repair). New connective tissue begins to form as soon as the inflammatory response phase nears its end. If we continue with the analogy of building a new structure, this phase is where the scaffolding (walls) is secured to the foundation to form the overall structure of the "new" building. At this point, the tissue now has some form and can withstand some pressure; therefore, early mobilization of joints and muscles is often favored at this time. The fibroblastic repair phase begins with the damaged capillaries repairing themselves in just a few days after the initial injury. This process, known technically as **angiogenesis**, involves the actual formation of new capillaries, which interconnect to form new vessels. With the formation of a new vascular supply, the new tissue is able to receive valuable nutrients and proteins to assist in the rebuilding process. Then, the process continues with the migration of fibroblasts into the area. **Fibroblasts** are immature, fiber-producing cells located in healthy connective tissue, and they are responsible for producing collagen and other structures as part of tissue healing (Ingersoll & Mistry, 2006). Due to chemical mediation (complement system), fibroblasts become active at this time, producing collagen fibers and proteoglycans (protein macromolecules), which help retain water in the tissues. This is particularly important in tissues such as articular cartilage, which act much like a sponge when exposed to fluids in joints. Bone injuries heal in a similar fashion to soft tissues; however, specialized cells known as **osteoclasts** migrate to the region of injury and remove destroyed cells and other debris, and then specialized fibroblasts known as **osteoblasts** migrate to the injured area from adjacent periosteum and bone. New osteoblasts are also manufactured on a large scale in the same region (Guyton, 1986). The function of the osteoblasts is to develop a zone of collagen and cartilage that is vascularized; this is known as a callus. A callus fills the space between the fractured bone ends and can be seen quite clearly on a standard X-ray photograph (**Figure 8.3**). As in the building analogy, the callus is only the scaffolding and is not of sufficient strength to substitute for the original bone, it is just the beginning phase, which through a process of maturation will becomes fully functional bone.

Maturation and Remodeling Phase

Using the analogy of building a new structure, this phase is when the finishing touches are put on the structure. For example, with a building walls are fortified (matured) and landscaping (remodeling) is done so the property is functional. Maturation and remodeling is the final phase of healing and may last up to 12 months depending on

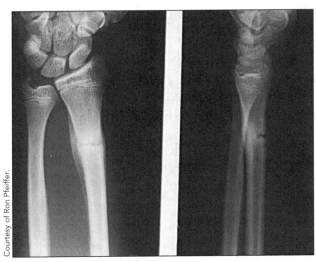

FIGURE 8.3 Callus forming around a fracture of the distal radius.

the type of tissue injured (Houglum, 2010). Tendons and ligaments often take the longest, because they are required to be strong and elastic and their blood supply can be limited. On the other hand, muscle tissue can heal relatively quickly because it has a very extensive network of capillaries and specialized cells that trigger muscle growth. In cases where scar tissue (collagen) is necessary to heal the injured area, it also undergoes maturation and remodeling. Under ideal conditions, scar tissue can be 95% as strong as the original tissue; it may, however, achieve considerably less strength, perhaps up to 30% less (AAOS, 1991).

Stress is essential in this phase; the new tissue will adapt its new collagen and tissue-specific fibers along the stress lines to form a much stronger configuration. Appropriate rehabilitative exercises are critical to this process. Two principles guide the rehabilitation exercises: the overload principle and the specific adaptations to imposed demands (SAID) principle. Tissue must be overloaded above normal demands to adapt and grow. Also, tissue will adapt according to the type of stresses placed on it (SAID principle). For example, rehabilitation exercises must be prescribed to challenge the individual and they must be done in directions or modes (strength, endurance, power) that are specific to the required needs (Houglum, 2010).

Pain and Acute Injury

Although swelling or edema is often the most visible aspect of an acute injury, from the athlete's perspective, pain is often the biggest immediate problem. It is important to remember that although everyone has

experienced pain associated with injury, everyone copes with pain differently, and further, pain is as much psychological (cognitive and emotional) as it is physiologic (tissue damage; Thomas, 1997). As a physiologic phenomenon, pain is essentially the result of sensory input received through the nervous system that indicates the location of the damage.

Pain has been defined as "the perception of an uncomfortable stimulus or the presentation or response to that stimulus by the individual" (Thomas, 1997). As such, it must be remembered that each individual responds to pain differently. It is essential to the process of the initial evaluation of an injury for the coach to be familiar with the athlete's typical response to pain. An athlete with an extremely high pain tolerance may underestimate the severity of an injury; conversely, an athlete with low pain tolerance may grossly exaggerate the severity of an injury. An injured athlete may also downplay the level of pain out of fear of losing a starting position on the team. Pain is typically measured subjectively using different scales to rank the severity and quality of pain. One common scale is the numeric rating scale, where no pain receives a 0 and the most severe

edema Abnormal accumulation of fluid in the interstitial tissue between the skin and body cavities. Homeostasis of fluid mechanics is disturbed.

secondary metabolic injury Indirect result of tissue trauma. Healthy tissues surrounding primary injury die due to lack of blood flow and lack of metabolic supplies. The energy needed exceeds that of the energy available.

secondary enzymatic injury Indirect result of tissue trauma. Healthy tissues surrounding primary injury die due to aggressive eating of healthy tissue within area of original injury. Waste products also damage cell membranes of healthy cells causing cell death.

apoptosis Process of programmed cell death. Biochemical events can lead to changes in cell characteristics thereby causing cell death.

angiogenesis Formation of capillaries, which interconnect, resulting in the formation of new vessels.

fibroblast Immature, fiber-producing cells of connective tissue that can mature into one of several different cell types.

osteoclasts Bone cells that remove bone tissue by breaking up the organic bone.

osteoblasts Cells that synthesize bone. Function in groups of connected cells.

Athletic Trainers SPEAK Out

Courtesy of Troyce Solley, MS, ATC, LAT, Assistant Athletic Trainer, Campbell University.

Why is prevention of injury such an important task for the athletic trainer?

Prevention is the athletic trainer's first responsibility when helping athletes achieve their goal of performing at their highest level. Preventing injury and minimizing time loss during training and practice allows the athlete optimal performance.

What are ways to prevent injuries in your setting at the college level?

At Campbell University (Buies Creek, NC) we take a three-tiered approach to injury prevention with our men's basketball team. When a new player arrives on campus, an orthopedic screening (portion of a preparticipation exam [PPE]) is performed looking for any history of previous orthopedic injuries, muscle imbalances or deficiencies, and anatomical or structural abnormalities. We also assess for biomechanical patterns associated with common sport motions, so we can determine if there are issues that might predispose the athlete to a new injury. A preparticipation balance assessment using functional motions also provides us with information about the athlete's neuromuscular control, including his proprioceptive abilities and kinesthetic awareness. We use the information gathered from the preparticipation evaluation to develop individualized therapeutic exercises specifically designed to help prevent injuries for each athlete. For example, an athlete with a history of Achilles tendinopathy might be assigned stretching and strengthening exercises for his gastrocnemius/soleus complex. I also work closely with our strength and conditioning specialist to incorporate specific exercises into their strength training program that are designed to address muscle imbalances created by the unique demands of basketball. Our last step in preventing injuries is mandatory taping or bracing of any at-risk joints for sport participation. However, the athletes are encouraged to participate in strength training sessions, skill development drills, and other conditioning without tape or bracing to allow for strengthening and proprioceptive development of the joints and surrounding musculature.

—Troyce Solley, MS, ATC, LAT

Troyce Solley is an Assistant Athletic Trainer, Campbell University, Buies Creek, NC.
Courtesy of Troyce Solley MS, ATC, LAT, Assistant Athletic Trainer, Campbell University.

pain receives a 10 (Houglum, 2010). However, recent evidence is providing scientists with an objective way to measure pain using functional magnetic resonance imaging of the brain (Wager et al., 2013). But this technology is a long way from being used clinically. In short, because pain is largely subjective, it may not be a useful indicator of the severity of an injury. When a coach must make a decision about the significance of an injury, it is best to err on the conservative side and, when in doubt, refer the athlete to medical personnel. Pain may also be thought of as the athlete's friend in that it serves as a mechanism to reduce the athlete's activity level until adequate tissue healing has occurred. It is critical to remember that the treatment of pain should be the domain of sports medicine personnel. Even though the

main goal is for a return to play, coaches, athletes, and parents should not attempt to treat the pain associated with an injury by using medications or unproven techniques. Sports medicine personnel can use a variety of **modalities** to treat pain associated with injury. **Table 8.1** shows the commonly used modalities to help control pain associated with an injury.

Intervention Procedures

Although it is clear that the acute inflammatory process is a necessary component of healing, athletes, coaches, and even many sports medicine personnel typically think of inflammation as something to be avoided at all

TABLE 8.1

COMMON MODALITIES USED TO TREAT PAIN

Modality	Afferent Nerve Stimulated
Ice	Temperature receptors
Heat	Temperature receptors
Electrical stimulation	Touch receptors
Massage	Touch receptors
Prophylactic wrapping	Touch and proprioceptive receptors

costs. This sentiment is so common in the sports community that the variety of suggested first aid treatments for acute injuries can be overwhelming. Suggested treatments of inflammation include the application of **cryotherapy** (therapeutic use of cold), such as crushed ice packs, ice cups applied via massage, ice-water baths, commercially available chemical cold-packs, intermittent compression and cold, and aerosol coolants (ethyl chloride). After the acute inflammatory phase has passed (there is no redness or heat) and ice is no longer bringing significant change (Starkey, 2013), **thermotherapy** (therapeutic use of heat)—including commercially available hydrocollator packs, warm and moist towels, and ultrasound diathermy—may be appropriate. It should be noted, however, that use of modalities such as ultrasound and diathermy should always be done under the direct supervision of trained allied health personnel such as a Board of Certification, Inc. (BOC)–certified athletic trainer, physical therapist, or physician.

In addition to cold and heat therapy, pharmacologic agents—drugs designed to prevent swelling (**anti-inflammatories**) or drugs designed to prevent pain (**analgesics**)—are often used to treat the inflammatory response. The majority of these drugs must be prescribed by a medical doctor and represent treatment beyond the training of coaching personnel. However, some anti-inflammatory drugs, such as aspirin, ibuprofen, and naproxen, are available over the counter (OTC) and are often effective for minor acute injuries. Caution should be exercised, however, particularly when the coach is dealing with athletes under the age of 18 years; he or she should always consult with parents prior to recommending any sort of pharmacologic agent, including OTC medications.

Experts agree that some sort of treatment, beyond simple rest, be applied during both the inflammatory response phase as well as in the later stages of healing. Available research supports the use of modalities such as

ice, compression, and elevation in addition to some pharmacologic agents during the inflammatory response phase. Likewise, clinical evidence strongly supports the use of modalities such as ice and therapeutic heat (moist hot packs, whirlpool, paraffin) and more sophisticated modalities such as ultrasound, diathermy (radio-frequency energy), and electrotherapies such as transcutaneous electrical nerve stimulation (TENS), neuromuscular electrical stimulation (NMES), and interferential stimulation (IFS) during the fibroblastic repair and maturation/remodeling phases. Application of any of these modalities is typically regulated by medical practice acts in each state; therefore, they should be applied only by qualified allied health personnel under the direct supervision of a physician and in the parameters stipulated by the practice act.

Cryotherapy and Thermotherapy

It has been found that changing the temperature of injured tissues can have dramatic effects on the physiologic activities of healing. Inflammation is a fundamental part of the healing process and should not be considered as a negative entity; however, excessive vasodilation and vessel permeability can cause the swelling and edema to be too much or too long in duration. Therefore, during the first few minutes of the inflammatory phase, direct application of cold (generally in the form of crushed ice) may reduce vasodilation, thereby reducing the amount of initial swelling or edema. Additionally, in the case of an injury to an extremity, protection, rest, ice, compression, and elevation (PRICE) are all extremely helpful and effective. The application of PRICE is a standard first aid procedure for injuries such as sprains, strains, dislocations, contusions, and fractures. However, recent evidence demonstrates that rest should not be complete and early mobilization of the joint or muscle will assist in the healing process (Bleakley, 2009).

Though many variations on application of cryotherapy exist, experts recommend that the most effective

modalities Physical agents that help create an optimal healing environment.
cryotherapy Therapeutic use of cold.
thermotherapy Therapeutic use of heat.
anti-inflammatories Drugs designed to prevent swelling. Two basic categories are currently in use: steroidal and nonsteroidal.
analgesic Agent that relieves pain without causing a complete loss of sensation.

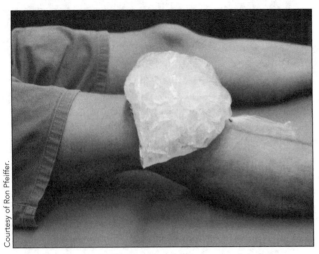

FIGURE 8.4 Bags filled with crushed ice are the most convenient way of applying cold to an injury.

way of applying cold to the body is a plastic bag filled with crushed ice (**Figure 8.4**). Nothing exotic need be used—a plastic sandwich bag with some type of closure is most effective. Crushed ice is made relatively inexpensively by ice machines, which are a good investment for a school athletic department. Crushed ice can even be purchased prior to a game or practice session and be stored in a cooler for later use. Commercially available chemical cold-packs and aerosol sprays (ethyl chloride) are less effective than crushed ice is and can even be dangerous in some situations (Starkey, 2013). Research has shown that the risk of frostbite during the application of a bag of crushed ice is minimal. Human tissues freeze at around 25°F; a bag of crushed ice reaches a low temperature of only 32°F. It has traditionally been recommended that an ice bag be left in place for 20–30 minutes, and then be removed. However, the only studies that have shown significant reductions in metabolism and protection against secondary injury were done on animals, and the ice was applied continuously for 5–6 hours (Bleakley, 2009); therefore, we do not really have a defined duration or type of application that is best for cryotherapy. Recent research comparing an intermittent application of ice (10 minutes on, 10 minutes off, 10 minutes on) to 20 minutes of continuous application of ice on acute ankle injuries demonstrated a greater reduction in pain during the first week of treatments for athletes who used the intermittent technique (Bleakley et al., 2006). Therefore, the current recommendations for pain relief are to cool the skin enough to provide for analgesia and to promote early mobilization (5–15 minutes). However, more controlled research needs to be performed regarding the use of cryotherapy during the inflammatory response phase and the amount of time required to achieve

decreases in tissue temperature necessary for slowing the onset of secondary injury (Bleakley & Hopkins, 2010).

Compression is best achieved by using a commercially available elastic wrap (Tomchuk, 2010; **Figure 8.5A**). Wraps come in a variety of sizes, ranging in widths that can accommodate almost any anatomic site and body size. It is best to place the ice bag directly against the skin with the elastic wrap secured over the bag. Wrap in a closed spiral fashion, starting distally and finishing proximally. Care must be taken not to make the wrap excessively tight because this could compromise circulation. Always check the pulse distal to the wrap after it is in place. One should be able to slip two fingers easily under the elastic after it is secured. Leave the wrap in place until the injury is seen by medical personnel. Newer forms of compression are also available. Systems that deliver intermittent pneumatic compression and cold via sleeves are gaining popularity in the sports medicine setting (**Figure 8.5B**). In essence, compression enhances the cooling capabilities of the cold modality because it increases skin surface contact.

Elevation of the injury is self-explanatory; however, some precautions are necessary. When elevating an injury to the lower extremity, make sure adjacent joints are supported with padding. Elevation during sleep can be accomplished simply by raising the foot end of the bed a few inches off the floor.

Generally, there is some sort of delay in transporting the participant from the playing field to the sideline or perhaps to a treatment area a considerable distance from the site of injury. The period immediately after the injury has occurred is generally considered to be the best time to evaluate the extent of injury. Coaching personnel should avoid the temptation, however, to perform

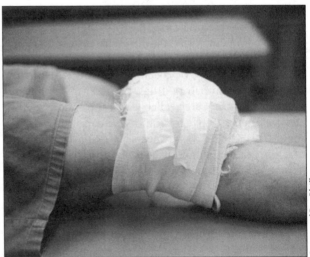

FIGURE 8.5A Elastic wrap provides a convenient method of compression.

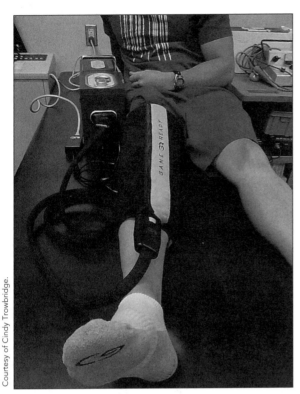

Courtesy of Cindy Trowbridge.

FIGURE 8.5B A common continuous cooling and intermittent compression device.

medical tests, such as ligament laxity assessments. Such testing should be performed only by properly trained medical personnel such as physicians, BOC-certified athletic trainers, or physical therapists with additional training in acute injury evaluation. When such tests are performed improperly, the injury may be aggravated.

Knight (1985) reports that the application of ice to an injury during the inflammatory response phase helps decrease the recovery time. This occurs for two reasons. First, the tissue cooling slows aggressive neutrophils and macrophages and helps prevent excessive waste products and unnecessary destruction of healthy cells. Second, the tissue cooling reduces the metabolic activity of the healthy cells in the injured area, thereby reducing their need for oxygen (Merrick, 2002). Consequently, the healthy cells are better able to survive the initial period of inflammation when oxygen is in short supply. This sparing of cells contributes to a smaller collection of debris in the region of the injury, thereby promoting an earlier repair phase. In essence, the immediate application of ice helps reduce the signs and symptoms of acute inflammation and the overall severity of the secondary injury, as described earlier in this chapter. While it might not be possible to achieve temperatures that can significantly reduce metabolism, coaches are correct to apply ice to acute injuries as this treatment most likely mitigates the metabolic changes associated with

inflammation thereby preventing an over-response and subsequent secondary injury (Bleakely & Hopkins, 2010). Finally, coaches can use cold to provide an analgesic effect that can reduce muscle spasm and promote early mobilization. In the end, these two effects allow the athlete to engage in therapeutic activities more effectively.

Thermotherapeutic agents such as moist heat packs, diathermy, or ultrasound may also have a beneficial effect on soft-tissue injury. However, available research is unanimous that such treatments should never be applied during the acute inflammatory phase when redness and heat are present. By heating the tissue during the early phases of the injury, the metabolic activity of the inflammatory agents is increased, thereby resulting in an increase in inflammation (Wilkerson, 1985). However, thermotherapies may be useful during the final phases of injury repair by increasing available oxygen and stimulating vasodilation in the region of the injured tissues. In addition, heat increases local metabolic activities, including those resulting in regeneration of tissues. Therefore, coaches can recommend thermotherapies to their athletes if they are confident the acute signs of inflammation (redness, heat, active edema) are not present.

Pharmacologic Agents

A wide variety of pharmacologic agents are currently available for the treatment of inflammation. Based on fundamental chemical configuration, they can be classified into two groups: steroidal and nonsteroidal anti-inflammatory drugs (NSAIDs). Both groups seem to interfere with some aspect of the inflammatory process, thereby reducing either the amount of swelling (anti-inflammatory) or pain (analgesic).

Steroidal Anti-Inflammatory Drugs

Steroidal drugs are manufactured in such a way as to resemble a group of naturally occurring chemicals in the body known collectively as glucocorticoids, which are active in the body relative to the metabolism of carbohydrates, fats, and proteins. Curiously, the exact mechanism of action of steroidal drugs on the inflammatory process is not clearly understood. There is evidence that steroids lower the amount of chemicals released from intracellular lysosomes, decrease the permeability of capillaries, diminish the ability of white blood cells to phagocytize tissues, and reduce local fever (Guyton, 1986). Probably the best known of the steroidal preparations is cortisone; however, others commonly used include hydrocortisone, prednisone, prednisolone, triamcinolone, and dexamethasone.

Steroidal preparations are generally either orally ingested or injected. They may even be introduced through the skin via **phonophoresis** (using ultrasound energy) or **iontophoresis** (using electrical current; Fick & Johnson, 1993). Problems with steroidal chemicals involve the negative effects they have on the process of collagen formation. In essence, steroids can decrease the overall strength of the connective tissue structures in an injured region. Great care must be taken when using these powerful drugs. The medications should be prescribed only by a physician and the risks and benefits should be discussed with the athlete and parents (if athlete is a minor) before treatment.

Nonsteroidal Anti-Inflammatory Drugs

NSAIDs block specific reactions in the inflammatory process; however, they do not seem to significantly delay collagen formation. These drugs have become extremely popular in the medical community. The commonly used NSAIDs are listed in **Table 8.2**. As a group, these drugs appear to block the breakdown of arachidonic acid to prostaglandin, which in turn decreases the inflammatory response to injury (AAOS, 1991). Aspirin, known chemically as acetylsalicylic acid, produces several effects—anti-inflammatory, analgesic, and **antipyretic** (reducing fever). Acetaminophen (Tylenol) is not an NSAID and is strictly an analgesic/antipyretic. However, there are increasing concerns over the safety of Tylenol and the current recommended dosages and new warnings by the U.S. Food and Drug Administration (FDA) have been posted in regard to liver damage and death (Gerth & Miller, 2013).

Though the physiologic effects of NSAIDs on inflammation are quite clear, what remains to be clarified is their effect, if any, on the rate and completeness of the healing process. There are concerns among scientists and physicians that the consumption of NSAIDs during the acute stages of injury may slow or even stop the very important inflammatory response phase. Recall that in order for new tissue to rebuild, the damaged tissue must first go through a complete inflammatory response phase. When healing tissue does not complete the early inflammatory phases, the tissue strength of the regenerated tissue is in question (Hertel, 1997). Even though NSAIDs are widely used to treat acute soft tissue injury, their efficacy is not in the scientific literature. In fact, their side effects often garner more attention. Gastrointestinal, kidney, and liver damage as well as connective tissue malformations can all be a result of over-consumption of NSAIDs (Hertel, 1997). There is also little evidence to support the claim that NSAIDs hasten the return of injured athletes to competition (Hertel, 1997).

TABLE 8.2

SAMPLE NONSTEROIDAL ANTI-INFLAMMATORY DRUGS

Generic name	Brand name(s)
Salicylic acids	
Aspirin (acetylsalicylic acid)	Ascriptin, Bayer, Ecotrin
Propionic acids	
Ibuprofen	Advil, Motrin, Nuprin
Naproxen	Aleve, Anaprox, Naprelan, Naprosyn
Oxaprozin	Daypro
Ketoprofen	Actron, Orudis, Oruvail
Acetic acids	
Diclofenac	Cataflam, Voltaren
Indomethacin	Indocin
Enolic acids	
Meloxicam	Mobic
Piroxicam	Feldene, Fexicam
Fenamic acids	
Meclofenamate	Meclomen
Mefenamic acid	Ponstel
Napthylalkanones	
Nabumetone	Relafen
Pyrenecarboxylic acids	
Etodolac	Lodine
Pyrroles	
Ketorolac	Toradol
COX-2 inhibitors	
Celecoxib	Celebrex

Source: Data from Ullrich P. Types of NSAIDs. Available: http://www.spine-health.com/treatment/pain-medication/types-nsaids. Accessed: September 28, 2013.

WHAT IF?

A parent asks you for advice on what over-the-counter drug would be best to give his daughter to help her recover from a second-degree ankle sprain. What would you suggest?

Until more conclusive research is available, it would appear that the best approach to treating the majority of soft-tissue injuries involves the application of PRICE during the acute inflammatory phase, followed by a combination of PRICE, prescribed and properly supervised rehabilitative exercises, and prescribed pharmacologic agent(s). From a legal and ethical standpoint, the coach or other nonmedical personnel should provide only initial first aid to any soft-tissue injury and then refer the athlete to the appropriate medical authority. Nonmedical personnel should avoid prescribing any type of medication, even an OTC drug such as aspirin or acetaminophen. It is always best to have any injury seen by medical personnel before further treatment (in any form) is given.

The Role of Exercise Rehabilitation

It may seem paradoxical, but the most effective treatment for many sports injuries, especially those involving soft tissues, is physical activity. Obviously, asking an athlete to run on a sprained ankle is incorrect, but a properly constructed and supervised exercise regimen can have a dramatic impact on the healing process when the overload and SAID principles are followed (**Figure 8.6**). Research indicates that rehabilitative exercise can exert a variety of positive effects on collagen formation (AAOS, 1991). Because **collagen** is a major constituent of tendon and ligament tissues, exercise is a logical form of treatment. According to Knight (1995), exercise is essential during the healing process for two reasons.

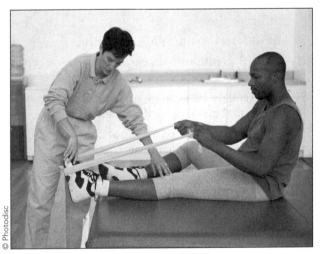

FIGURE 8.6 Exercise can be the most effective treatment for many athletes who have sustained sports injuries.

First, exercise results in increased circulation with a concomitant increase in oxygen supply to the healing tissue. Second, exercise stresses the healing tissue and in essence "guides" the proper structuring of collagen. It is important to remember, however, that although exercise is essential to proper tissue healing, the old saying "too much too soon" is worth remembering during the rehabilitation process. At the very least, the process of collagen formation and tissue regeneration requires 2 to 3 weeks (Page, 1995). Further, after the final phase of healing the athlete should, when appropriate, have the area properly protected with adhesive taping, wrapping, or bracing. Decisions concerning any return to participation should be made by a medical professional with experience in sports injuries. Coaches should avoid returning an athlete to participation too early just because he or she may be critical to the team's success.

Any injury severe enough to warrant a medical diagnosis should be treated with a comprehensive program of exercise rehabilitation. Such a program must consist of essential components and must be planned by professionals with the appropriate training—either a BOC-certified athletic trainer or a physical therapist who has sports medicine training. Responsibility for implementation and supervision of the exercise program usually falls on the coach or physical educator. Thus, communication among the athlete, coach, and medical personnel is essential for any program to be effective.

Rehabilitative exercise, often called therapeutic exercise, is a four-phase process consisting of categories of exercise based on a continuum of severity and recovery. If the athlete's injury is severe, the initial exercise protocol may make the athlete a passive participant; a therapist actually moves the injured extremity through a series of passive exercises. The benefits are the reestablishment of a normal range of motion (ROM) and reduction of swelling and muscle spasm. As the injury improves, the next phase of exercise is active assisted. During this phase, the athlete becomes a working partner in the exercise process, making a voluntary effort to move the injured joint while being assisted by a therapist. The benefits of this phase are

phonophoresis Introduction of ions of soluble salt into the body through ultrasound.

iontophoresis Using an electrical current to drive a chemical directly through the skin.

NSAID Nonsteroidal anti-inflammatory drug.

antipyretic Agent that relieves or reduces fever.

collagen The major protein of connective tissue.

improved ROM and increased muscle strength. The next phase in the rehabilitation process is active exercise. At this point, the athlete continues moving the joint through a full ROM, using gravity as resistance to stimulate development of muscle strength. The important aspect of this phase is that the therapist merely supervises the activity; no physical assistance is given to the athlete. The final phase of the recovery program is known as resistive: External resistance is applied to the joint movements. This can be done via manual resistance provided by the therapist, through the use of resistive exercise machines, or even with free weights. The primary objective of this phase is to improve the strength of the muscles surrounding the injured area to protect the injured area from future injury. This last phase must incorporate exercises known as "functional" activities that include movements identical to those typically exhibited in the athlete's sport, for example, running and cutting drills for those athletes in sports such as basketball, football, and soccer. Published experts within the sports medicine community concur that such a protocol is necessary for adequate healing of damaged soft-tissue structures, especially in the lower extremities (Delforge, 2002).

Injury rehabilitation should be considered an ongoing process: Injury-specific exercise should be a permanent component in the total training and conditioning program of the athlete. Without such an approach, the likelihood of reinjury is high in many cases. The coach must communicate with the appropriate members of the athletic healthcare team—athletic trainer, physical therapist, and/or physician—to plan and implement an effective program of therapeutic exercise.

REVIEW QUESTIONS

1. During which type of muscular contraction does the majority of muscle and/or fascia injuries occur?

2. True or false: The proximal musculotendinous junction has been found to be the most common site for injuries.

3. List the three types of mechanical forces that can cause soft-tissue injury.

4. Define critical force.

5. Describe the major steps that occur during the healing process of an injury—with particular emphasis on vasoconstriction, vasodilation, and subsequent hematoma formation.

6. Define chemotaxis.

7. Describe briefly two of the chemical mediators and their physiologic effects during the acute phase of an injury.

8. Briefly describe the overall purpose of the inflammatory phase of an injury.

9. List the types of cells that migrate to the injured area during the early part of the resolution phase.

10. What type of tissue does not heal itself with scar tissue?

11. What are fibroblasts?

12. What is angiogenesis?

13. What is the relationship between a bony formation known as a callus and the healing of a fracture?

14. Describe the mechanism for the secondary injury as described by Knight (1967) and Merrick (2002).

15. What is the effect of ice application on the secondary injury?

16. Explain briefly the physiologic effects of the application of ice, compression, and elevation on acute inflammation.

17. What is an easy and effective way of applying cold and compression simultaneously to an injury?

18. What is the recommended duration of ice application for the treatment of pain during acute inflammation?

19. At what temperature do human tissues freeze?

20. At what point during the process of injury repair can thermotherapies be useful?

21. Differentiate between steroidal and nonsteroidal anti-inflammatory pharmacologic agents.

22. What is the mode of action of NSAIDs with respect to the acute inflammatory phase of an injury?

23. Define the acronym OTC.

24. What are the concerns about the administration of NSAIDs over a period of time?

25. Give a brief explanation of the four types of therapeutic exercise outlined in the chapter—passive, active assisted, active, and resistive.

REFERENCES

Akeson WH, Amiel D, Woo SL-Y. (1986). Cartilage and ligament: Physiology and repair processes. In: Nicholas JA, Hershman EB (eds.), *The Lower Extremity and Spine in Sports Medicine* (pp. 3–41). St. Louis, Mo: Mosby.

American Academy of Orthopaedic Surgeons. (1991). *Athletic Training and Sports Medicine* (2nd ed.). Park Ridge, Ill: American Academy of Orthopaedic Surgeons.

Arnheim DD. (1989). *Modern Principles of Athletic Training* (7th ed.). St. Louis, Mo: Times Mirror/Mosby; pp. 198–231.

Bleakley C, McDonough S, MacAuley D. (2006). Cryotherapy for acute ankle sprains: A randomized controlled study of two different icing protocols. *Br J Sports Med.* 40: 700–705.

Bleakley C. (2009). Current concepts in the use of PRICE for soft tissue injury management. *Physiotherapy Ireland.* 30(2):19–20.

Bleakley C, Hopkins J. (2010). Is it possible to achieve optimal levels of tissue cooling in cryotherapy? *Phys Ther Rev.* 15(4):344–350.

Cailliet R. (1977). *Soft-Tissue Pain and Disability.* Philadelphia, Pa: F. A. Davis.

Curwin S, Stanish WD. (1984). *Tendinitis: Its Etiology and Treatment.* Lexington, Mass: D. C. Heath and Company.

Delforge G. (2002). *Musculoskeletal Trauma: Implications for Sports Injury Management.* Champaign, Ill: Human Kinetics; p. 110.

Fick DS, Johnson JS. (1993). Resolving inflammation in active patients. *Phys Sportsmed.* 21:55–63.

Gerth J, Miller TC. (2013). Use only as directed. *ProPublica.* Available: http://www.propublica.org/article/tylenol-mcneil-fda-use-only-as-directed/.

Guyton AC. (1986). *Textbook of Medical Physiology.* Philadelphia, Pa: W. B. Saunders.

Hertel J. (1997). The role of nonsteroidal anti-inflammatory drugs in the treatment of acute soft tissue injuries. *J Athl Train.* 32(4):350–358.

Houglum P. (2010). *Therapeutic Exercise for Musculoskeletal Injuries* (3rd ed., pp. 122–127). Champaign, Ill: Human Kinetics.

Ingersoll CD, Mistry DJ. (2006). Soft tissue injury management. In: Starkey C, Johnson G (eds.), *Athletic Training and Sports Medicine* (p. 24). Sudbury, Mass: Jones and Bartlett Publishers.

Knight KL. (1976). Effects of hypothermia on inflammation and swelling. *Athl Train.* 11:7–10.

Knight KL. (1985). *Cryotherapy: Theory, Technique, and Physiology.* Chattanooga, Tenn: Chattanooga Corp.

Knight KL. (1995). *Cryotherapy in Sport Injury Management.* Champaign, Ill: Human Kinetics.

Lachmann S, Jenner JR. (1994). *Soft Tissue Injury in Sport.* Oxford, England: Blackwell Scientific.

Merrick MA. (2002). Secondary injury after musculoskeletal trauma: a review and update. *J Athl Train.* 37(2):209–217.

Nigg BM, Bobbert M. (1990). On the potential of various approaches in load analysis to reduce the frequency of sports injuries. *J Biomech.* 23:3–12.

Page P. (1995). Pathophysiology of acute exercise-induced muscular injury: Clinical implications. *J Athl Train.* 30: 29–34.

Safran MR, Seaber AV, Garrett WE. (1989). Warm-up and muscular injury prevention—an update. *Sports Med.* 8: 239–249.

Starkey C. (2013). *Therapeutic Modalities* (4th ed). Philadelphia, Pa: F.A. Davis; pp. 125–127.

Thomas CL (ed.). (1997). *Taber's Cyclopedic Medical Dictionary* (18th ed.). Philadelphia, Pa: F. A. Davis.

Tomchuk D. (2010). The magnitude of tissue cooling during cryotherapy with varied types of compression. *J Athl Train.* 45(3):230–237.

Wager T, Atlas L, Lindquist M, Roy M, Woo C, Kross E. (2013). An fMRI-based neurologic signature of physical pain. *N Engl J Med.* 368:1388–1397.

Wilkerson GB. (1985). Inflammation in connective tissue: Etiology and management. *Athl Train.* 20:298–301.

Yang J, Tibbetts AS, Covassin T, Cheng G, Nayar S, Heiden E. (2012). Epidemiology of overuse and acute injuries among competitive collegiate athletes. *J Athl Train.* 47(2):198–204.

Injuries to the Head, Neck, and Face

MAJOR CONCEPTS

Injuries to the head, neck, and face present some of the most perplexing problems associated with sports injury. The current state of knowledge regarding these injuries is constantly being updated and the reader is encouraged to always seek the most current peer-reviewed research regarding recognition, treatment, and disposition of these injuries. This chapter begins with a review of the gross anatomy of the head, neck, and face. It goes on to describe the central nervous system, giving special attention to the structures often involved in head and neck injuries, along with data on the incidence and severity of such injuries in a variety of sports. It provides new evidence-based material regarding detection, treatment, and return to play progression after a concussion. Severe forms of head injury, including intracranial injuries and second impact syndrome are presented, along with recommendations on how best to avoid these potentially lethal problems. In addition, this chapter contains a special section on the helmeted tackle football player that includes guidelines on the initial treatment of suspected head injuries.

Next, the chapter outlines major mechanisms of cervical spine injuries, followed by a discussion of the various types of injuries that can occur, including simple sprains and strains, as well as more severe forms such as disk herniations and vertebral dislocations and fractures. In addition, it presents information regarding the mechanisms and signs and symptoms of brachial plexus injuries. As with head injuries, it features guidelines for the initial treatment of suspected injuries to the cervical spine.

The remainder of the chapter deals with recognition and care of injuries to the maxillofacial region (face, teeth, eyes, nose, and ears).

go.jblearning.com/PfeifferCWS

For a full suite of assignments and additional learning activities (indicated by the icons throughout the text), use the access code found in the front of your text. If you do not have an access code, you can obtain one at go.jblearning.com/PfeifferCWS.

ANATOMY REVIEW

In a practical sense, the head may be considered as a single structure with a variety of functions. These include housing the brain; providing sockets for the eyes and openings for the ears, nose, and mouth; and providing a site of attachment for the vertebral column. The neck serves as the mechanism for attachment of the head to the body. Though this arrangement works well for the day-to-day functions of our species, in the context of sports such an anatomic arrangement provides significant potential for a multitude of injuries. The brain, consisting of neural tissues that are easily damaged, must be protected, especially when one considers the potential forces involved in many different sports and activities.

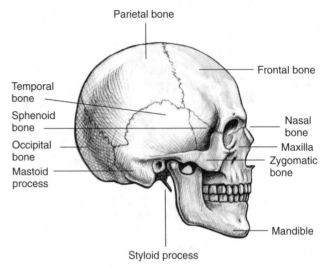

FIGURE 9.1 The bones of the human cranium.

Skull

The skull, which consists of 8 cranial bones and 14 facial bones, is a complex structure. The brain (encephalon) is housed in the cranium and is afforded considerable protection via an ingenious system of bony and soft-tissue structures.

The bones of the cranium (**Figure 9.1**) form a rigid housing for the brain and are held together by specialized articulations known as suture joints. Curiously, the suture joints of the cranium are not rigid at birth; in fact, they do not complete their ossification process until

human beings are between 20 and 30 years old (Gray, 1985). However, the anatomic arrangement of the cranial bones and their respective joints provides a protective outer structure for the brain.

The soft-tissue structures that serve a protective function include the five layers of tissues of the scalp. These are illustrated in **Figure 9.2**; they include the skin, a layer of dense connective tissue, the galea aponeurotica (essentially a broad, flat tendon), loose connective tissue, and the periosteum of the cranial bone.

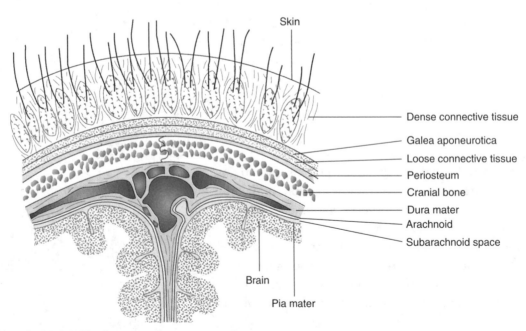

FIGURE 9.2 The human scalp: a cross section.

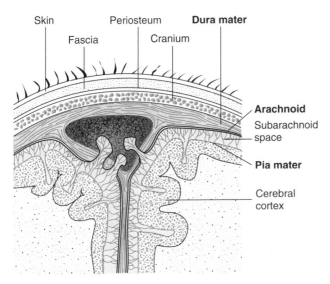

Skin   Fascia   Periosteum   Cranium   **Dura mater**

Arachnoid
Subarachnoid space
Pia mater
Cerebral cortex

FIGURE 9.3 The cerebral meninges.

The Meninges

Below the cranial bones another group of soft-tissue structures can be found that protect the brain as well. These are collectively referred to as the cerebral meninges (**Figure 9.3**). They consist of three distinct layers of tissues located between the underside of the cranium and the surface of the brain. The outermost layer is known as the dura mater. It consists of tough, fibrous connective tissue that functions as periosteum to the inside surfaces of the cranial bones and as a protective membrane to the brain (Gray, 1985). The dura mater is highly vascular, containing arteries and veins that transport blood to and from the cranial bones. The middle meningeal layer is the arachnoid; compared with the dura mater, it has significantly less strength and contains no blood supply. The arachnoid is separated from the dura mater by a small amount of fluid. Below the arachnoid is the subarachnoid space containing cerebrospinal fluid (**CSF**). The purposes of CSF are to protect the brain from acute blood pressure changes, transport chemicals, and cushion the brain and spinal cord from external forces such as those encountered in collision and contact sports. CSF gives the brain natural buoyancy, so its density of neurons does not impair its own blood supply because of the weight of the brain. The CSF suspends the mass of the brain so that even though a brain can weight as much as 1400 grams it feels like 25 grams (Saladin, 2007). Children's brains typically have less CSF during certain stages of development, which might create extra weight of brain. Therefore, any blow to the head might result in more impairment of blood supply because the brain was not able to absorb the impact (Chatelin et al., 2012). The innermost meningeal layer is the pia mater, which is physically attached to the brain tissue and serves to provide a framework for an extensive vasculature that supplies the brain. The pia mater is a very thin, delicate membrane; like the arachnoid, it is more susceptible to trauma than the dura mater is.

The Central Nervous System

The brain (encephalon), along with the spinal cord, composes the central nervous system (**CNS**). Both the brain and spinal cord are protected by the meninges and the bony structure of the cranium and vertebrae. The CNS receives an extensive blood supply that must remain constant for it to function. Even brief interruptions of blood flow lasting only seconds may result in loss of consciousness. As a result, neural tissue may be destroyed when deprived of blood for only a few minutes. The CNS tissue consists of gray and white matter that represent two distinct types of neural tissues. The brain of an adult weighs 3 to 3.5 pounds and contains approximately 100 billion neurons (Van De Graaff, 1998). The brain consists of three basic parts: cerebrum, cerebellum, and brain stem. The cerebrum is the largest of the three and is involved in complex functions such as cognition, reasoning, and intellectual functioning. The cerebellum, located in the lower posterior portion of the cranial area, performs functions related to complex motor skills. The brain stem is located at the base of the brain and serves to connect the brain to the spinal cord.

The young child brain appears to be three to four times less stiff than adult brain; therefore, children's brains are far more plastic or impressionable than the adult brain (Chatelin et al., 2012). This clearly has positive effects during maturation, but can have negative effects associated with brain injury, as the child's brain is less resistant to trauma. The child's brain may also have a slower recovery due to lower quantities of **myelin** (fatty cells that cover nerves) and metabolic sensitivities (Field et al., 2003). Because myelin is much more highly concentrated in the adult brain, it allows for quicker repair to nerves after injury and more controlled metabolic responses.

CSF   Cerebrospinal fluid.
CNS   Central nervous system.
myelin   Performs an insulating function to the axon of a nerve. Composed of fats and proteins.

The Peripheral Nervous System

Neural impulses travel to and from the CNS via the peripheral nerves located within the peripheral nervous system (**PNS**). The cranial, spinal, and autonomic nerves compose the portion of the nervous system known as the peripheral nervous system. Cranial nerves travel directly from the brain and spinal nerves exit the spinal cord. Autonomic nerves include the sympathetic and parasympathetic nerves. This system helps govern our involuntary reactions to stress and relaxation. Sympathetic nerves are associated with "fight-or-flight" response (increased heart rate and blood pressure), and parasympathetic nerves are associated with decreases in heart and respiration rate. There are 12 pairs of cranial nerves that are directly attached to the base of the brain and exit the CNS through openings (foramina) in the base of the skull. The spinal nerves are attached to either side of the spinal cord and exit the CNS at precise intervals through the intervertebral foramina of the spinal column. There are 31 pairs of spinal nerves: 8 cervical, 12 thoracic, 5 lumbar, 5 sacral, and 1 coccygeal.

The Face

The human face is composed of an outer layer of skin placed loosely over underlying bones. There are some subcutaneous muscles, cartilage, and fat deposits offering minimal protection from trauma. The facial bones consist of the maxilla (upper jaw), the right and left palatine, the right and left zygomatic, the right and left lacrimal, the right and left nasal, the right and left inferior nasal concha, the vomer, the mandible (lower jaw), and the hyoid.

Several areas around the face are especially prominent and thus prone to injury. The orbits for the eyes, particularly the supraorbital regions, are vulnerable to contusions. The nasal bones are located centrally on the face and can also receive direct blows, often resulting in fractures. The lower jaw (mandible) is subject to excessive external forces as well.

The Neck (Cervical Spine)

The bones of the neck are the seven cervical vertebrae (**Figure 9.4**) that provide support for the head and protection for the upper portion of the spinal cord. The first cervical (C-1) vertebra (atlas) articulates directly with the occipital bone to form the right and left atlanto-occipital joints. The skull and C-1 articulate as a unit with the second cervical (C-2) vertebra (axis) to form the atlantoaxial joint, which allows for rotation of the head on the neck. The remaining five cervical vertebrae become progressively larger as they approach the thoracic spine.

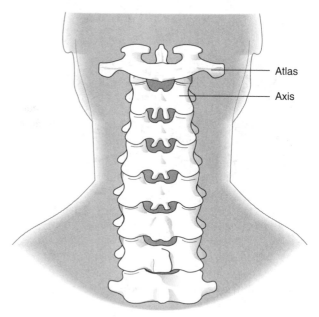

Atlas

Axis

FIGURE 9.4 The cervical spine (posterior view).

Head Injuries in Sports
Background Information

Although the majority of contusions to most parts of the body result in injuries that are self-correcting and without serious consequence, even relatively minor trauma to the head can result in severe, sometimes life-threatening injury. Because of the inability of brain tissue to repair itself, any loss of tissue results in some level of temporary or permanent disability. If the injury is severe enough, death can result. The possible mechanisms, types, and severity of head injuries in sports are nearly infinite. However, significant advances in our understanding regarding head injuries in sports have been made in recent years. As a result, with appropriate education coaches and physical educators can learn to recognize head injuries and render effective first aid when necessary.

Head injuries can occur in almost any sport or activity and scientific surveys have provided additional insight into which sports appear to carry a higher risk. Epidemiologic research on the incidence of head, brain, and neck injuries is ongoing, with accurate data available from relatively recent playing seasons. However, there is wide variability in the literature regarding the occurrence of concussions since the 1990s, because reporting standards and awareness have changed. For high school sports, Marar and colleagues (2012) reported that there were approximately 300,000 concussions over a 2-year period (2008–2010). Recent data from the

TABLE 9.1

CONCUSSION STATISTICS*

High School Sport (2011–2012)	% Concussions of Total Injuries	Rank (Top 10 Injuries)	Most Common Sport Situation
Boys' Football	22.6%	1	Tackled/being tackled
Boys' Soccer	29%	1	Heading ball
Girls' Soccer	31%	1	Mostly heading ball/general play
Boys' Volleyball	18%	2	General play
Girls' Volleyball	15%	2	Digging/general play
Boys' Basketball	15%	2	Defending
Girls' Basketball	22%	1 (tied)	Rebounding/general play
Wrestling	23%	1	Takedown
Baseball	12%	1	Running bases/batted ball
Softball	18%	1	Thrown and batted ball
Girls' Gymnastics	5%	6	Tumbling
Boys' Ice Hockey	40%	1	Checking
Cheerleading	37%	1	Stunts
Boys' Swimming/Diving	17%	2	Swimming/platform
Girls' Swimming/Diving	11%	3	Starting/platform
Boys' Track/Field	<2%	10	Jumping/landing
Girls' Track/Field	<2%	10,	Jumping/landing
Girls' Field Hockey	19%	2	General play
Boys' Lacrosse	34%	1	General play

*Statistics of concussions in a convenience sample of high school sports during the 2011–2012 school year (n = 174 high schools; n = 4126 [males]; n = 1857 [females]).

Source: Data from Comstock R, Collins C, Fletcher E. (2013). Convenience sample summary report: National high school sports-related injury surveillance study (2011–2012 school year). Available at: http://www.nationwidechildrens.org/cirp-rio-study-reports.

High School Sports-Related Injury Surveillance Study that catalogued injuries during the 2011–2012 boys' and girls' high school sport seasons (174 high schools surveyed) show that head/face concussions were ranked most frequent of 10 injuries because they accounted for 21% of the 6203 injuries recorded (Comstock, Collins, & Fletcher, 2013). Ankle strains/sprains were second most common (14%), hip or thigh strains/sprains were third (8%), and knee strains/sprains were fourth (7%; Comstock et al., 2013). See **Table 9.1** for the percentage of concussions in each sport surveyed. For collegiate sports, including Division I, II, and III institutions (1988–1989 season to 2003–2004 season), the highest number of concussions occurred in women's ice hockey (18%) and the lowest number was in men's baseball (2.5%; Daneshvar et al., 2011). Men's football, women's lacrosse, and women's soccer reported concussions were between 5% and 6% of the total injuries (Daneshvar et al., 2011). Data from a 1-year period (2005–2006) in 180 National Collegiate Athletic Association (NCAA) schools indicated that 482 concussions (0.43 per 1000 athlete exposures) were reported and more occurred in competition than in practice (Gessel et al., 2007).

Clearly, concussions are a high-volume injury in high school and collegiate sports. More importantly, coaches and physical educators need to understand that players sustaining one concussion had a threefold increased risk of sustaining an additional concussion when compared with their nonconcussed teammates (Guskiewicz et al., 2000). Thus, this is where immediate recognition and referral for treatment can make the biggest difference.

The most recent research available from the National Center for Catastrophic Sport Injury Research (http://www.unc.edu/depts/nccsi/) indicates that fatal and nonfatal (incomplete recovery) and serious head and neck injuries continue to occur in many sports. Unfortunately, cheerleading alone accounts for 65% to 66% of all deaths in female high school and collegiate sports, and most of these deaths are attributed to neck and brain injuries (Mueller & Cantu, 2011). From 1983 to 2011, cheerleading led to 3 fatalities, 45 nonfatal

PNS Peripheral nervous system.

injuries, and 71 serious injuries among high school and collegiate participants (Mueller & Cantu, 2011). In 2010 alone head and neck injuries accounted for 19.3% of the total cheerleading injuries and 1579 were concussions; however, there was only one fatality. But each year has seen a steady increase in the number of emergency room visits related to cheerleading incidents; in 2010 there were 36,288 (Mueller & Cantu, 2011). The good news is that 98% of these were treated and released. The deaths and injuries associated with cheerleading have been attributed to the escalation in the degree of difficulty in cheerleading routines, as it has become a competitive sport. In addition, the number of participants in cheerleading has dramatically increased since the 1980s.

When examining high school and collegiate sports separately, Mueller and Cantu (2011) provide data in regard to direct catastrophic injuries by dividing sports into seasons (Fall, Winter, and Spring). The statistics are easy to access via their website and provide detailed assessment of the different injuries reported by sport and season, plus they provide a historical perspective that connects the number of injuries to possible causes. Data related directly to brain injury in football (professional, semiprofessional, high school, and college) have provided some interesting numbers. As a whole, the number of fatalities in football that can be attributed to brain injuries has decreased since 1961; however, the number of disabilities associated with brain injury has gone up (Mueller & Cantu, 2012). For example, in the decade from 1961–1970, there were 128 fatalities in football associated with brain injuries and that has decreased to 37 in 1991–2000 and to 32 during 2001–2010. In contrast, there were 52 permanent disability brain injuries in football from 1991–2000 but there were 66 for the decade from 2001–2010. Fewer fatalities demonstrate significant strides in rules, tackling techniques, and injury management; however, the fact that there are more injuries that result in disability is still very disturbing (Mueller & Cantu, 2012). As a result, the community of healthcare providers, coaches, physical educators, and parents needs to better understand brain injury and the importance of proper management.

Type and Mechanism of Injury

There is a multitude of descriptive classifications for head injuries. However, all head injuries can be placed into three general categories: mild head injury or concussion, intercranial hemorrhage, and skull fracture (Shultz, Houglum, & Perrin, 2000). Head injuries associated with sports involve either direct or indirect injury mechanisms. Direct mechanisms involve a blow to the head resulting in brain injury at the site of impact,

known as a coup type of injury. When injury also happens on the opposite side of the skull from the site of impact, the injury is known as a contrecoup type. The contrecoup-associated injury occurs when the head is moving and stops abruptly. For example, when a tackle is made in football, the brain keeps moving in the skull and it is subsequently compressed on the side opposite from the initial impact. Indirect mechanisms of injury involve damaging forces traveling from other areas of the body, such as blows to the face or jaw. Rapid and violent movement of the cervical spine, such as seen in whiplash injuries related to automobile accidents, may also result in indirect injuries to the brain. An understanding of these mechanisms of injury highlights the validity of the often used cliché in sports medicine circles, "Treat every head injury as if there is a neck injury, and every neck injury as if there is also a head injury."

Concussion (Mild Traumatic Brain Injury)

Concussion, sometimes called mild traumatic brain injury, has been defined as a complex pathophysiological process affecting the brain, induced by biomechanical forces (McCory et al., 2013). Concussions usually result in immediate and often short-lived impairment of neurological functions (**Time Out 9.1**), but many time signs and symptoms can evolve over a number of minutes to even hours (McCory et al., 2013). In essence, any sort of external blow of sufficient magnitude or indirect force that causes the brain to move inside the skull can cause temporary disruption of normal neurologic function. Recent evidence suggests that in most concussions the injury occurs due to a complex metabolic crisis in the brain often related to restrictions in blood flow; however, in some there may be a level of structural damage (Harmon et al., 2013). Nerve cells (axons) suffer from a metabolic and ionic disruption causing energy deficits and neural transmission problems; as a result the axons cannot transmit necessary signals with the efficiency or effectiveness they had prior to injury (Harmon et al., 2013). Researchers now understand that brain tissue not destroyed remains extremely vulnerable to subsequent trauma or other stresses (physical, cognitive, or emotional), which may result in phenomena such as minor changes in blood flow, intracranial pressure, or anoxia (Cantu, 2001; Harmon et al., 2013).

Current science has moved away from classification systems for cerebral concussion. Any trauma that causes one or more signs and symptoms (Time Out 9.1) is considered a concussion. No one concussion is like another concussion, so grading systems have been abandoned and serial monitoring of signs and symptoms including intensity and duration are currently the best way to determine the severity and the required treatment (Guskiewicz et al., 2004). Recent evidence has indicated that loss of consciousness (LOC) and post-traumatic amnesia (PTA) were not appropriate designates of concussion severity because LOC occurs in only 9% of concussions and PTA in 27% concussions (Guskiewicz et al., 2000). However, it is important to note that any loss of consciousness or extended post-traumatic amnesia are significant signs and symptoms and should be respected, even though their presence does not indicate severity. The intent of moving away from a grading system was to simplify the decision-making process by members of the athletic healthcare team when evaluating the status of an athlete suspected of having sustained a head injury. Given the potential implications of a bad decision in such situations, *the current recommendation states that any athlete who exhibits signs and symptoms of a concussion should be removed from play or practice and not return that day* (Harmon et al., 2013; McCory et al., 2013). Future return decisions should also be made by a qualified healthcare provider, thereby helping the coaching staff avoid errors in judgment (Harmon et al., 2013; McCory et al., 2013).

The majority of concussions (80%–90%) will resolve in less than 10 days in most people; however, adolescents and children may take longer (McCory et al., 2013). However, post-concussive syndrome (discussed in more detail in the section that follows) can occur; post-concussive syndrome typically involves long-lasting signs and symptoms such as headaches and balance disturbance remain, memory problems (PTA), poor concentration, fatigue and sleep problems, and emotional changes. Two types of PTA have been identified as resulting from head injury: anterograde and retrograde. **Anterograde amnesia** involves an inability to recall events that have transpired since the time of the injury. **Retrograde amnesia** is present when the athlete is unable to recall events that occurred just prior to the injury. However, it is now generally thought that retrograde amnesia is hard to measure and is poorly reflective of the severity of head injury. Recent evidence suggests that it is the duration of all post-concussive symptoms rather than the presence, type, or duration of amnesia that suggests neurological problems (McCory et al., 2013). All cases of concussions that have symptoms that last for more than 10 days should be managed in a multidisciplinary way (involving physicians, neuropsychologists, psychiatrists, and counselors; McCory et al., 2013).

Post-Concussive Syndrome

Post-concussive syndrome (PCS) involves cases in which the signs and symptoms of a concussion last weeks, months, and even years beyond the initial injury

anterograde amnesia Inability to recall events that have occurred since an injury.

retrograde amnesia Inability to recall events that occurred just prior to an injury.

(Harmon et al., 2013). Unfortunately, PCS is ill defined and poorly understood because signs and symptoms are both subjective and objective and are often vague (Harmon et al., 2013). Several common signs and symptoms include headaches, anxiety, depression, sensitivity to light and noise, memory loss, poor concentration and problem solving, and insomnia (Harmon et al., 2013; Mueller & Cantu, 2012). Two recent studies have emphasized that post-concussion symptoms can last for years. In investigations of retired NFL football players, those who experienced concussions were more likely to demonstrate cognitive deficits and depression (Guskiewicz et al., 2005; Hart et al., 2013) and also demonstrated changes in cerebral blood flow and some white matter abnormalities when compared to age, IQ, and education matched controls (Hart et al., 2013). Although there has been significant research in regard to PCS, there have been no proven or accepted correlations between the severity of the concussion(s) and initial symptoms and the likelihood of developing physical, cognitive, or emotional PCS (Harmon et al., 2013). However, there are some risk factors that are gaining attention but need more scientific investigation. These risk factors include: being female, being younger, having a history of learning disabilities, having a history of migraines, having a history of depression, and having a dangerous style of athletic play (Harmon et al., 2013; Scorza, Raleigh, & O'Connor, 2012).

As mentioned in the previous section, a healthcare team should manage the treatment of persistent symptoms of head injury. There is poor evidence for use of medications for PCS, because some medications can mask any worsening effects (Scorza et al., 2012). Recovery can be very frustrating because it is a long, slow process that may remove athletes from their normal activities like work and school. However, there has been some recent evidence suggesting that cognitive therapies, supervised low-level exercise programs, and vestibular therapy might have a role in future treatment protocols but evidence remains to be gathered (Harmon et al., 2013).

Because of recent media coverage and the outcome of a major lawsuit filed by former players against the NFL, the condition of **chronic traumatic encephalopathy** (CTE) should be discussed. CTE is only diagnosed postmortem and was long associated with boxers. Its recent discovery in the brains of several deceased football players alerted the medical community to investigate it further. Qualified scientists are engaging in seminal research in an effort to better understand CTE and its relationship to concussions and contact sports. First and foremost it must be understood that research science has yet to establish a cause-and-effect relationship between CTE and concussions or exposure to contact sports (McCory et al., 2013). Therefore, any fears caused by media pressure should be mitigated with rational behaviors until a time comes when we have clear evidence of the exact relationship.

Second Impact Syndrome

Second impact syndrome (SIS) is an area in which we do have significant cause-and-effect evidence; therefore, the sports medicine community needs to be concerned about and develop a more cautious approach to the care and management of athletes who sustain concussions. SIS, according to medical experts, "occurs when an athlete who has sustained an initial head injury, most often a concussion, then sustains a second head injury before symptoms associated with the first have fully cleared" (Cantu & Voy, 1995). Essentially, SIS involves the loss of autoregulation of the brain's blood supply that can cause the rapid development of catastrophic swelling of the brain, specifically to a region known as the uncus of the temporal lobes, which puts pressure directly against the brain stem (**Figure 9.5**). Ultimately, SIS can cause coma or death. A limited number of cases of SIS have been reported in the research literature; however, it is more common in adolescents under the age of 18 (Harmon et al., 2013).

A typical scenario involves an athlete receiving a concussion with associated symptoms that include headache, nausea, poor concentration, and excessive drowsiness. The athlete returns to play prior to the clearance of symptoms like the headache and poor concentration. Upon return to the sport, the same athlete, while engaging in the same activity, receives another relatively minor blow to the head. Shortly thereafter, the athlete collapses, becomes unresponsive, and is taken to a healthcare facility. While there, the athlete lies in a deep coma. If death results, on autopsy, the cause of death is confirmed as massive cerebral edema resulting from uncontrolled vascular engorgement of brain tissue (or SIS). It is crucial to realize that any athlete who sustains what appears to be even a minor concussion should be examined carefully by a healthcare provider and cleared by a physician before being allowed to return to participation. This concern is especially acute in the case of an athlete with a history of concussions. It is important to remember that symptoms related to a concussion may take days or even weeks to be resolved. As such, medical personnel, athletes, coaches, and parents should apply extreme caution when making decisions regarding return to play for an athlete with a history of head injuries.

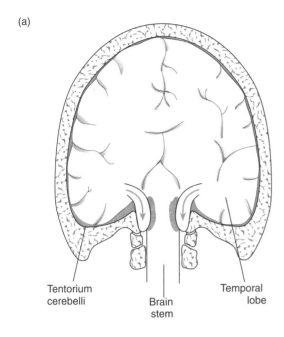

(a)

Tentorium cerebelli
Brain stem
Temporal lobe

(b)

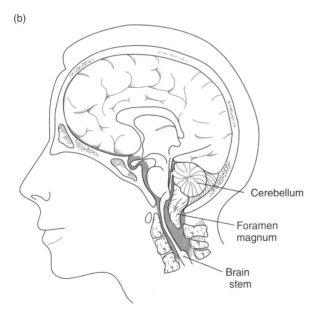

Cerebellum

Foramen magnum

Brain stem

FIGURE 9.5 In second impact syndrome, vascular engorgement in the cranium increases intracranial pressure, leading to herniation of the uncus of the temporal lobes (arrows) below the tentorium in this frontal section (a), or to herniation of the cerebellar tonsils (arrows) through the foramen magnum in this midsagittal section (b). These changes compromise the brain stem, and coma and respiratory failure rapidly develop. The shaded areas of the brain stem represent the areas of compression. (*Source:* Robert Cantu, MD, FACSM, Neurological Surgery, Inc., Concord, Mass. Reprinted with permission.)

Intracranial Injury

There is also strong evidence that intracranial injury in sports represents a potentially life-threatening situation. These injuries can be the result of a variety of mechanisms, including direct blows, rapid deceleration, and even rapid rotational motions of the head. By far, the majority of intracranial injuries result from blunt trauma to the head. The injury is characterized by disruption of blood vessels, either veins or arteries, resulting in the development of a hematoma or swelling in the confines of the cranium. Such a condition places the brain tissues in jeopardy because these structures are extremely sensitive to pressure.

Jordan (1989) identifies the major forms of **intracranial injury** as **epidural hematoma** (bleeding between the dura and the cranial bones), **subdural hematoma** (bleeding below the dura mater), **intracerebral hematoma** (bleeding within the brain tissues), and **cerebral contusion** (bruising of the brain tissue). It is important to note that an epidural hematoma involves arterial bleeding; therefore, the signs and symptoms of injury will usually develop rather quickly. Because of the vascular anatomy of the dura mater, a subdural hematoma can involve rapid arterial bleeding with symptoms developing in minutes, or bleeding may be venous, with pooling and clotting developing over many hours. In some cases, symptoms don't appear for hours or even days after the initial injury. Although there are not particular signs and symptoms that may worsen, any changes in visual functioning and pupil reaction or increases in disorientation or equilibrium are of extreme concern. If these changes are not recognized

chronic traumatic encephalopathy A condition that can only be identified after death with a brain autopsy. It is a degenerative disease characterized by a distinct collection of tau proteins in several areas of the brain that affect function.

intracranial injury Head injury characterized by disruption of blood vessels, either veins or arteries, resulting in the development of a hematoma or swelling within the confines of the cranium.

epidural hematoma Bleeding between the dura and the cranial bones.

subdural hematoma Bleeding below the dura mater.

intracerebral hematoma Bleeding within the brain tissues.

cerebral contusion Bruising of the brain tissue.

WHAT IF?

You are coaching soccer practice when suddenly a wing player collides with the goalie while attempting to kick a goal. On your arrival at the scene, the goalie appears to be okay; however, the other player is conscious but confused and unable to remember the current score or the team she is playing against. What type of injury has probably occurred given this history and these symptoms?

immediately and the injured athlete is not transported immediately to the hospital, any of these conditions can result in some degree of permanent neurologic damage and even death. Therefore, it is extremely important to serially monitor the signs and symptoms (Table 9.1) of a concussed athlete. Any worsening of signs and symptoms indicates the need for immediate follow-up with a physician, possibly including an emergency room visit. If an athlete is taken to the emergency room and advanced scanning techniques (magnetic resonance imaging [MRI], computed tomography [CT] scan) are performed, coaches and parents need to be aware that negative findings of bleeding or structural damage to the brain *do not* clear them from complications of a concussion and extended recovery. Imaging is often overused and contributes little to management of concussion, other than ruling out more serious traumatic brain injuries or skull fractures (Scorza et al., 2012). These negative findings only indicate that the damage was not structural and likely is metabolic.

Cranial Injury

Cranial injuries involve the bones of the skull. In the majority of cases, the force injuring the bones is of sufficient magnitude to also cause damage to the tissues of the scalp. Thus, along with cranial injury there may also be some bleeding and soft-tissue damage. Skull fractures can be simple, linear fractures with no damage to underlying tissue. In many cases, these injuries produce few neurologic problems. The more severe forms of cranial injuries involve what are known as depressed skull fractures. These are potentially much more serious because bone fragments have been pushed into the cranial region. Obviously, this type of injury is more likely to produce serious, possibly life-threatening, neurologic damage. A variety of signs and symptoms of cranial injuries may be present. These are discussed in some detail later in this chapter.

Initial Treatment of a Suspected Head Injury: Guidelines

As mentioned previously, as a general rule, any athlete who sustains an apparent head injury should be treated as if a neck injury is also present; conversely, any athlete sustaining a neck injury should be treated as if there is also a head injury. The mechanism of injury for both is similar; consequently, it is possible that both could occur simultaneously.

The following guidelines for the emergency care of an athlete suspected of having sustained a head injury are divided into procedures while the athlete is at the site of injury, followed by guidelines for the injured athlete after he or she has been removed to a secondary site (sideline, courtside, etc.). It is critical to understand that if any significant signs and/or symptoms of head or neck injury (numbness, tingling, loss of consciousness) are present when evaluating the athlete at the site of initial injury, he or she should not be moved until emergency medical services (EMS) personnel have arrived on the scene. By default, any athlete who, based on the initial evaluation, has sustained any level of concussion should be removed from play and not allowed to return until examined by a physician (Harmon et al., 2013; McCory et al., 2013; Scorza et al., 2012).

Despite the urge, often encouraged by overzealous athletes, teammates, parents, and even coaches, to return a player to participation, it is important that this not be allowed in cases when an athlete sustained any form of head trauma, including a concussion. The best policy is to remove any athlete who sustains what appears to be a head injury, regardless of how minor it seems initially, from further participation, administer the appropriate sideline assessment, and refer to an allied healthcare provider or physician for further evaluation to obtain follow-up care and direction regarding return to play. Although strict enforcement of such a policy may not be popular with all athletes, fans, and even some coaches, the reality is that to do otherwise may result in more serious, and in some cases irreversible, injury. It is worth noting that management of athletes suspected of having suffered a head injury is becoming a major legal issue at the state level. In 2009, the state of Washington was the first to pass legislation considered by some to be the toughest law on the books to date. Among other things, the law requires that any youth sports athlete who is suspected of having sustained a concussion must be removed from participation and cannot return until he or she is evaluated by a licensed healthcare professional and receives written permission to return to participation. (This legislation can be reviewed at the Washington State Legislature website: http://apps.leg.wa.gov/rcw/

default.aspx?cite=28A.600.190). As of June 2013, 49 states and the District of Columbia have passed legislation to reduce overall impact of concussions among youth athletes (Sun, 2013). Many of the laws (82%) require parents to sign an information sheet about concussions (Tomei et al., 2012), but state legislation varies in what policies are applied to different school settings (public versus private) and different age groups of children (Harvey, 2013; Tomei et al., 2012). Most state policies also leave out club and recreational sports, and the type of information given is usually left up to schools or state high school federations (Harvey, 2013).

Initial Check

After the coach reaches the athlete, the first step in the management of an athlete with a suspected head injury incorporates basic first aid procedures. This is accomplished by executing the initial check. The first few seconds of the initial check should provide important information about the injured player. On reaching the athlete, the coach should note body position, movement or lack thereof, unusual limb positions, and (if present) the position of helmet, facemask, and/or mouth guard. It is critical that the coaching staff be trained and well rehearsed in dealing with such situations, because immobilization of the head and neck should also take place at this time. The coach should stabilize the head and neck (**Figure 9.6**) prior to attempting to arouse the injured athlete by placing hands on the shoulders, chest, or upper back and speaking loudly directly toward the athlete's head. If the athlete is conscious, the airway in all probability is open. If the athlete appears to be unconscious, the coach should make a mental note of the time; this will be of great value when the athlete arrives later at an emergency healthcare facility. Now,

the coach needs to determine if the athlete is in either respiratory or cardiac arrest. Any problems, such as an obstructed airway or cardiac arrest, must be attended to before continuing with any further evaluation of injuries.

Breathing Assessment

In the case of a helmeted football player, it is not necessary to remove the helmet to determine if the athlete is breathing. (Refer to the guidelines later in this section regarding removal of a facemask from a football player with a head and/or neck injury.) Breathing can usually be detected by looking at the chest cavity or abdomen for the rise and fall associated with breathing or by placing an ear near the athlete's face and listening for the typical sounds of respiration. By doing this, the coach may also detect sounds indicating airway obstruction, such as gagging, wheezing, or choking.

Circulation Assessment

A responsive athlete who is breathing will have the signs of circulation—breathing, coughing, and movement. The coach must determine if the signs of circulation are present in an unresponsive victim after initial breaths by looking for other movement of extremities and skin color changes or feeling for a pulse. If no signs of circulation are present, coaching personnel can begin cardiopulmonary resuscitation (CPR) and activate the emergency plan, which must include contacting the emergency medical services (EMS) provider. If the athlete is prone, carefully logroll the athlete to a supine position following accepted first aid guidelines that include vital steps such as stabilizing the head and maintaining an airway while performing the logroll. In such a situation, the coach's primary responsibility is to keep the athlete alive and to ensure that help is summoned. There is no reason to move the athlete from the playing field or practice area. The possibility of delaying a game or practice does not justify moving someone in this situation.

Physical Examination

At no time should the coaching staff attempt to revive an unconscious athlete by using a commercially made inhalant such as ammonia capsules. An athlete may attempt to jerk his head away from the inhalant, resulting in aggravation of an existing neck injury. Obviously, an athlete who is conscious and alert represents a less complicated case than does a player who appears to be unconscious and not breathing. Once the initial check has been completed, which can be accomplished with practice in around 10–30 seconds, and the athlete's vital

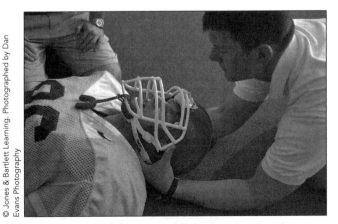

FIGURE 9.6 Stabilizing an athlete's head and neck.

signs have been ascertained, the coach can proceed to the physical exam, in which the coach collects as much information about the suspected head injury as possible. At this point it is prudent for the coach to retain stabilization of the head and neck until specific signs and symptoms have been cleared. The physical exam must include assessments of the following (see detailed descriptions later in this chapter):

C—Consciousness (is it changing?)

E—Extremity sensation and strength ("Squeeze my hand." "Pull your foot up." Test without moving neck.)

M—Mental function ("Do you know where you are?" "Who are we playing?" "Can you tell me what half/quarter it is?")

E—Eye signs and movements

P—Pain specific to the neck or on palpation to neck structures

S—Spasm of neck musculature (palpation reveals)

It is important for the coaching staff to remember the following statements when evaluating a helmeted athlete with a suspected head injury:

- Don't remove the helmet of a football player. Remove other helmets only if they are impeding stabilization and evaluation efforts.
- Don't move the athlete.
- Don't rush through the physical exam.

If the athlete is conscious, coaching staff can conduct a series of quick, simple tests to determine if any significant neurologic damage has occurred. To help determine if consciousness is diminishing, the coach should note whether the athlete is no longer opening eyes or following verbal commands with answers or movements. For extremity sensation and strength, a staff member can place two fingers in one of the athlete's hands and ask him or her to squeeze as hard as possible. Then, the staff member performs the test on the opposite hand and compares grip strength. The assessor can also place her hands on the tops of the athlete's feet and ask the player to dorsiflex (move the toes/top of foot toward the leg) to compare bilateral strength. The coaching personnel should check sensation on both sides of the body by pinching the skin on the insides of the arms, thorax, and legs. To determine orientation, a coach can ask a number of quick, easy-to-answer questions that help to establish an athlete's mental awareness of self and location. The eyes are often the great revealers of neurological damage, so to determine possible brain injury a coach

should monitor the athlete's eyes by noting the size of the pupils. The assessor places her hand over one of the athlete's eyes and removes it quickly to determine if the pupil reacts to light. Perform the same test on the other eye. Pupils are generally the same size; however, in rare cases, some people normally have pupils of unequal size, known technically as **anisocoria**. The assessor can hold a finger or pen directly in front of the athlete's face and move it from side to side slowly while asking the player to indicate when it is no longer visible. Note any difference in peripheral vision, comparing right and left, and also any jerking movements of the eyeballs, especially when the athlete is following a finger or object without moving their head. Loss of peripheral vision or jerking of the eyes is indicative of possible brain injury. Finally, the coach should ask about neck pain and spasm and gently palpate the athlete's neck, beginning at the base of the skull and then working slowly down to the bottom of the neck. Note any deformity, such as cervical protrusions or muscle spasms. Ask the athlete if pain occurs at any specific area during the evaluation.

Based on the results of this portion of the injury evaluation, the coach should be able to determine if an athlete needs immediate transportation to a hospital. Any concussion represents a potentially serious medical emergency. Continued loss of consciousness or deterioration of physical condition during the on-field evaluation also indicates that the injury is a medical emergency. If the athlete experiences signs and symptoms of a concussion (Time Out 9.1), regardless of whether he or she was rendered unconscious (even if only for a few seconds), they are not to return to the game. A coach should not move an athlete from the site of initial injury if he or she continues to suffer severe symptoms or altered consciousness. Rather, the coach should continue to monitor the vital signs of the athlete and summon EMS. Prior to the arrival of EMS, even if the athlete's condition improves, no attempt should be made to move the athlete away from the site of initial injury because this may aggravate the injury.

In all probability, an athlete who suffers a concussion will be able, with assistance, to walk to the sideline or courtside. At that point, he or she should be monitored and a complete medical evaluation by an allied health-care provider or physician should be performed. Of course, the process of referral and medical evaluation should be predetermined by way of the emergency plan. Removal from the site of injury should be done with great care and without haste. Assuming the athlete is in a laying-down position, the first step in moving the athlete is to raise him or her to a sitting position. With assistance on both sides of the athlete by two members of the emergency team, assist the athlete to a sitting position by applying some force under his or her armpits while providing support in the event he or she loses balance. After the athlete is in a sitting position, monitor vital signs and overall behavior for 1 to 2 minutes. If they appear to be normal, the next step is to assist the athlete to a standing position, again with support on both the right and left sides by members of the emergency team. After the athlete is in a standing position, again monitor his or her vital signs and sense of balance for 1 to 2 minutes. If they appear to be normal, ask the athlete to begin walking slowly toward the area where he or she can be examined more carefully away from the site of the initial injury. Again, it is critical that members of the emergency team provide continual physical support on each side of the athlete as he or she walks in the event that he or she loses balance and begins to fall. After the athlete arrives at the site for further evaluation, assist him or her to a seated position and begin the next phase of the examination.

Sideline Assessment

Once the athlete is seated away from the playing area and can be assessed without interference from fellow athletes, a more detailed assessment of his or her condition must be conducted. The objective of this phase of the evaluation is to determine the presence of any signs or symptoms of head injury that may have developed since the time of the initial injury. This information is of vital importance to making decisions regarding appropriate medical referral. It is no longer acceptable simply to sit an athlete out for a few minutes after having his or her "bell rung" and then return the player to participation based on an apparent return to preinjury status.

Research since 2000 examining the best practices in dealing with athletes who may have sustained a concussion indicates that even in the absence of trained medical professionals, follow-up assessments that include a standardized list of typical symptoms should be used to help determine the status of someone suspected of having sustained a concussion. Although the ideal situation would employ the skills and training of a medical professional such as a Board of Certification, Inc. (BOC)–certified athletic trainer or physician, there are options available to programs that do not have trained medical professionals directly on staff (McCory et al., 2013). With very little training, a tool called the Pocket Sports Concussion Recognition Tool (http://bjsm.bmj .com/content/47/5/267.full.pdf) can be used to identify a suspected concussion (McCory et al., 2013). It is a very simple tool that instructs the evaluator to look for visible signs of a concussion (dazed or stunned look), identify any signs and symptoms the athlete may be experiencing (Time Out 9.1), and briefly assess the

athlete's memory ("Where are we?" "What team did we play last week?"). It also identifies several red flags (e.g., seizures, deterioration of mental status) that indicate the athlete needs immediate medical attention and EMS should be called. This is a basic tool that is used for recognition only. The pocket guide clearly states "Any athlete with a suspected concussion should be *immediately removed from play*, and should not be returned to activity until they are assessed medically. Athletes with a suspected concussion should not be left alone and should not drive a motor vehicle" (McCory et al., 2013).

Currently, athletic trainers and other medical professionals are using the Sport Concussion Assessment Tool (SCAT). The SCAT is in its third edition and is called the SCAT3; it was developed as a part of the 4th International Conference on Concussion (McCory et al., 2013). The authors of the tool encourage distribution in printed form. The SCAT3 is intended for anyone age 13 or older and it can be downloaded for free at: http://bjsm.bmj.com/content/47/5/259.full.pdf. For children 12 years and younger, the Child SCAT3 can be downloaded for free at: http://bjsm.bmj.com/content/ 47/5/263.full.pdf. With proper training, coaches can utilize these two assessment tools to obtain critical information while at the site of injury (courtside or sideline). Then the information can be relayed to medical personnel. Even though coaches can be trained to administer the SCAT3, it is *not* designed to provide a diagnosis. Medical professionals make diagnoses because determination of a concussion is a clinical judgment (McCory et al., 2013). Therefore, it is important for coaches to note that an athlete may have a concussion even if their SCAT3 is "normal" (McCory et al., 2013). So, the rule of *no return to play* after a concussion or with any signs and symptoms of a concussion should be strictly followed.

The SCAT3 assessment tools include 10 basic areas of assessment. The differences between the Child SCAT3 and the SCAT3 are subtle, but allow the tool to involve parents and more relevant memory questions for those younger than 12 years of age. Each tool contains the Glasgow Coma Scale (GCS) for responsiveness; an interview for determining if consciousness was lost and assessing if the athlete has a blank stare or vacant look; a Maddocks Score for immediate orientation; history questions in regard to previous concussive injuries; a

anisocoria Rare but naturally occurring condition where the pupils are of unequal size, not related to any acute condition such as head injury.

graded symptom-scale checklist; a cognitive assessment for orientation, concentration, and short-term memory; a neck examination; a balance examination (balance error scoring system [BESS]), a coordination test (finger to nose); and a delayed-recall test. The symptom-scale checklist is a very useful tool and can be used by the athlete repeatedly after the concussion. It simply lists common symptoms and asks the athlete to grade them as none, mild, moderate, or severe. The cognitive section is accomplished by asking the injured athlete to answer a series of questions as well as perform some cognitive skills. These include knowing the correct month, date, year, and time of day. Memory tests include testing the ability to recall five words in the correct order plus reciting lists of numbers and months of the year in reverse order. The balance examination is done via the BESS, which is a reliable and valid measure used to assess two-foot, one-foot, and tandem stance balance on normal surface and foam surface. Continued errors, like opening eyes, lifting hands, or stumbling, are counted over a 20-second trial. Regardless of which specific sideline assessment is used, it is critical that in the absence of trained medical professionals, coaches receive proper training on the use of these assessment tools and, further, that coaches understand their main role is to protect the health and safety of athletes and that "if in doubt, sit them out."

Home Instructions

Because most young athletes will be released to the care of a parent or guardian and college-age athletes will be released to roommates or friends, it is important to provide instructions for care. If a medical provider has not seen the athlete, then an appointment should be encouraged. If the athlete has seen a medical provider, then a follow-up appointment should be set. In fact, most states now require a written physician's note in order for an athlete to return to practice or play. "Take-home" information should be in a written form and should be discussed with the athlete and appropriate caregiver (Harmon et al., 2013). Minimally, the instructions should have a list of red flags that warrant transportation to a hospital and advice to avoid cognitive and physical exertion until evaluated by a medical provider. Athletes should be allowed to sleep and not be awakened every 2 hours. If there are concerns about an athlete not regaining consciousness if he falls asleep, then he should be transported. Currently, there is no strong evidence that taking an aspirin or nonsteroidal anti-inflammatory drug (NSAID) will increase bleeding, but for safety these are generally avoided and acetaminophen is recommended (Harmon et al., 2013). College-age athletes should also be warned about the consumption of alcohol and how it can mask worsening symptoms.

Return to Play

A graduated return to play (RTP) is the current recommendation for athletes who have experienced a concussion (Harmon et al., 2013; McCory et al., 2013; Scorza et al., 2012). All RTP protocols should be individualized and progressive using a stepwise graduated physical exertion plan. The time to start an RTP protocol is the decision of the treating medical provider and will take into account the current signs and symptoms, concussion history and frequency, and the presence of any modifying conditions (Harmon et al., 2013). The steps are listed in **Table 9.2**. All RTP protocols begin with rest and a resolution of all signs and symptoms. After the no-activity period ends (sign and symptom free); each step should be performed in no less than a 24-hour time period. Successful completion of a step is performance of exercise tasks without a reoccurrence of any signs and symptoms that day or the following day. If any signs and symptoms are experienced during one of the exercise steps, then the athlete is to stop all activity and rest until the next day. Assuming the athlete is symptom-free the following day, they then drop back to the previously asymptomatic level (McCory et al., 2013) and

---

TABLE 9.2

RETURN TO PLAY PROGRESSION

Instructions:
Follow a stepwise progression with typically 24 hours between each step. Progression through steps is delayed if post-concussive signs or symptoms develop at any point. Before progression begins again, all signs and symptoms need to have cleared.

Activities:
1. No activity—limited cognitive and physical activity; general rest
2. Light aerobic exercise (< 70% maximum heart rate); no resistance training
3. Sport-specific exercise (no head impact activity)
4. Noncontact training drills and resistance training
5. Full contact practice
6. Return to play

Source: Data from McCory P, et al. (2013). Consensus statement on concussion in sport: The 4th international conference on concussion in sport held in Zurich, November 2012. *Br J Sports Med.* 47:250–258.

the progression begins again. The minimum time for a graduated return to play is typically 7 days; however, it can take months to successfully return an athlete to play depending on the individual responses and any modifying circumstances (Harmon et al., 2013).

Computerized Neurocognitive Assessment

Paper and pencil neuropsychological testing has been identified as the "cornerstone" of concussion management (McCory et al., 2013). Although professional sports can often afford and have access to trained neuropsychologists and advanced testing, the logistics of being able to assess youth and collegiate sports participants with concussions is far fetched at best. Therefore, since the early 2000s the use of computerized platforms for neuropsychological testing has emerged. Even though they are no substitute for formal evaluation, these brief cognitive evaluation tools have become the mainstay of many collegiate and high school sports programs. Currently, a variety of platforms is available for use under the guidance of an athletic trainer, team physician, or neuropsychologist. Each platform contains a variety of assessments that typically include verbal and visual memory, visual motor speed, reaction time, impulse control, and symptom scales. However, controversy still exists in regard to the overall benefits of baseline computerized testing and its role in the diagnosis of a concussion and its ability to measure readiness to return to physical conditioning (McCory et al., 2013). The question of baseline testing of all sports participants has been raised recently as there has been disagreement in the literature regarding the quality of the computerized norms provided in the software programs. Although several sports programs stand by their decisions to baseline test and a recent research paper demonstrated the added value of having a personal baseline test (Roebuck-Spencer et al., 2013), the neuroscience community believes there is insufficient evidence to recommend widespread baseline testing (McCory et al., 2013). In regard to using it for serial assessment in an attempt to assist with return to play, there have been some questions about the reliability of repeat performances within specific software platforms. The evidence of increased numbers of false-positives (software says athlete has a concussion and he or she does not) and false-negatives (software says athlete is fine but he or she does have a concussion) has been highlighted in recent research (Resch et al., 2013). However, previous research indicates that the ability to correctly and accurately diagnose a concussion goes up significantly when computerized testing is included as a part of a test battery that includes a thorough severity- and duration-graded symptom scale and a balance

WHAT IF?

You are confronted with a situation during a tackle football game in which a player is apparently knocked unconscious during a play. When you arrive at the scene, the player is lying facedown and is not moving. What would you do to ascertain the athlete's level of injury? What would you not do, and why?

assessment (Broglio, Macciocchi, & Ferrara, 2007). Therefore, computerized testing can be included with other tests, but should not be used as a stand-alone diagnosis tool. In the end, the clinician, not a computer, needs to make the return to physical training decision.

Concussion Education

Athletes, parents, and coaches need to seek out continuing education on concussions because our understanding and general treatment of these injuries has changed over the years. A variety of programs offer information to coaches and athletes, and some high school federations have made concussion training mandatory for all participants. The Sports Legacy Institute Concussion Education (SLICE) campaign for youth athletes (Bagley et al., 2012), the Centers for Disease Control and Prevention's *Heads Up* campaign for coaches and medical providers (Sarmiento et al., 2010), and the coach training program for coaches from brainline.org (Glang et al., 2010) have all been able to increase knowledge of concussions in these populations. (SLICE can be found at: http://www .sportslegacy.org/education/slice/. *Heads up* can be found at: http://www.cdc.gov/concussion/HeadsUp/ youth.html. The coach training program can be found at: http://brain101.orcasinc.com/4100/.)

Cervical Spine Injuries

Background Information

Injuries involving the cervical spine occur in a variety of sports, but most often in tackle football, lacrosse, rugby, ice hockey, soccer, diving, cheerleading, and gymnastics. Neck (cervical) injuries can involve a variety of tissues in the region, including bones, ligaments, intervertebral disks, spinal cord, spinal nerve roots, and/or the spinal nerves themselves (Torg, 1989). Any injury to this region of the body is potentially serious, therefore it is incumbent upon those personnel charged with providing emergency care to be as prepared as possible

Athletic Trainers SPEAK Out

Courtesy of Chris H. Hummel, MS, ATC, Clinical Associate Professor and Athletic Trainer, Ithaca College.

The world of concussion recognition, assessment, and management has gone through many changes in the last few years and continues to evolve every day. The evolution of assessment, especially highlighting the importance of multiple testing platforms (self-reported signs and symptoms, neuropsychological testing, and balance testing), has greatly helped our athletes and athletic training staff when trying to make return to play (RTP) decisions. The improved quality of assessment procedures and the advent of evidence-based concussion management tools have allowed us more confidence in our RTP decisions. In the end, we are providing for optimal health and safety of our athletes at Ithaca College. The following case of a football player gives an example of the benefit that multiple testing platforms can have on RTP confidence. At the end of one of our last football practices of preseason camp, one offensive lineman approached us complaining of concussion-like signs and symptoms. He had never been diagnosed with a concussion before but decided to come to us after listening to the concussion education talk given at the opening football meeting. He complained of the classic symptoms of headache and dizziness following a couple of blows to the helmet. He promptly met with our team physician to discuss management. As was expected, his symptoms lessened in severity over the next few days. Within 1 week post-injury, the athlete stated that he was feeling normal and ready to begin the RTP progression. Before we began the progression, he was given a modified BESS test to assess his balance and completed follow-up neuropsychological testing. The results of the tests indicated that his reaction time and balance were still impaired. The athlete's perception of his readiness for progression changed after the testing, when along with his poor balance during the BESS, he also saw the significant difference between his reaction time on baseline and post-injury neuropsychological tests. A few days later these tests were taken again with improved results. He then was able to successfully complete the stepwise RTP progression. By taking a more holistic approach to recognition, assessment, and management (e.g., self-reported signs and symptoms, neuropsychological testing, balance testing, physician clearance, RTP guidelines), we can ensure a safe progression and return following sports-related concussion.

—Chris H. Hummel, MS, ATC

Chris Hummel is a Clinical Associate Professor and Athletic Trainer at Ithaca College.

Courtesy of Chris H. Hummel, MS, ATC, Clinical Associate Professor and Athletic Trainer, Ithaca College.

for such injuries. Although a single catastrophic cervical spine injury is devastating, the overall incidence should be viewed in perspective, because 2 in 100,000 neck injuries meet the criteria for being categorized as catastrophic (Wiesenfarth & Briner, 1996). Comparatively, tackle football produces the highest number of spine injuries in the catastrophic category (Mueller & Cantu, 2011). Although this is certainly worthy of note, it is important to also note that football has a very large number of participants (approximately 1.8 million). As such, the relative incidence of catastrophic injuries in this sport is quite low on a per-participant basis. For example, in 2009, the rate of such injuries was 0.50/100,000 (Mueller & Cantu, 2012). This is not to suggest that these injuries are not serious; however, they do represent relatively rare events. The National Center for Catastrophic Sport Injury Research has been tracking catastrophic injuries in high school and collegiate football since 1977. Data presented in the 2012 annual report (Mueller & Cantu, 2012) are shown in

TABLE 9.3

ANNUAL SURVEY OF CATASTROPHIC CERVICAL CORD FOOTBALL INJURIES, 1977–2009

Year	Sandlot	Pro and Semipro	High School	College	Total
1977–1989	3	3	114	18	138
1990–1999	1	4	60	9	74
2000–2012	4	12	151	20	187

Source: Data from National Center for Catastrophic Sport Injury Research. (2011). Annual survey of catastrophic football injuries, 1977–2012. Available: http://www.unc.edu/depts/nccsi/FBAnnual2012.pdf.

Table 9.3. These data represent the incidence of cervical spine injuries that resulted in some level of disability at the time of the injury; however, in some cases, the athletes made a full recovery. These data have been reduced to represent groups of years together. To pull out very recent numbers, there were 14 catastrophic injuries in 2008, but by the 2012 football season there was a total of three cervical cord injuries with incomplete neurological recovery. One of the injuries occurred at the high school level and two at the college level. Therefore, the number of catastrophic neck injuries in football is decreasing over time, in part, because of the many of the rules that have been put into effect to reduce their number, through education of athletes on appropriate tackling and falling techniques, and the increasing accuracy of the medical response.

The extent and severity of neurologic damage that occur in a neck injury depend on the magnitude of the mechanism of injury, the resulting movement of the neck, and the extent of tissue damage. In the case of simple neck strains, neurologic involvement is extremely rare. Cervical injuries are expressly more serious when displacement of an intact vertebra occurs, when fragments of a vertebral fracture are displaced, or when an intervertebral disk ruptures, placing pressure directly on the spinal cord or nerve roots. In these situations, the potential for permanent neurologic damage is high. Curiously, significant neurologic symptoms may be totally absent even when considerable damage has occurred to tissues surrounding the spinal cord. Therefore, it is critical that the coach be objective and complete during the initial assessment process to avoid converting a treatable injury into a permanent one. Although it is not expected that the coach conduct a complete neurologic evaluation that would be expected of an athletic trainer or a physician, the simple field tests (CEMEPS) described earlier in this chapter often can yield sufficient information to make an informed decision regarding initial management of the athlete.

Mechanisms of Injury

Historically, the mechanism of injury considered to be potentially the most common and serious was excessive forced flexion (hyperflexion) of the cervical spine. However, extensive film analysis and objective research have disputed this long-held belief. Most experts now agree that the mechanism known technically as *axial load* produces the majority of serious cervical spine injuries. This is especially true in tackle football; prior to the mid-1970s, tackling with the crown of the helmet (spearing) was a common practice. Axial loading of the cervical spine occurs when the head is lowered (flexed slightly) just prior to impact—the net effect being a straightening of the normal vertebral curve (extension; Burstein, Otis, & Torg, 1982). In this position, forces applied to the top of the head are absorbed directly by the bones of the vertebral column without the protective assistance of surrounding ligaments and muscles. In 1976, the NCAA enacted a rule change that prohibited spearing or leading with the head for contact. The results were impressive; there was a significant drop in the number of cervical cord injuries the following year.

The data in Table 9.2 seem to show that despite ongoing efforts to reduce the incidence of these injuries, they are still a problem. The data for 2000–2012 show more than double the total number of injuries compared to the previous 9 years and significantly more than the 12 years directly after spearing rules were implemented (Mueller & Cantu, 2012). As a result, there is research that supports the premise that even changing the rules in football to penalize high-risk tackling techniques such as spearing may not be as effective as once thought. Heck (1996) examined game films from a New Jersey high school for two seasons, 1975 and 1990, to determine if the incidence of spearing, by position, had been reduced. Curiously, the overall rate of spearing differed very little; that is, the incidence was 1 in 2.5 plays in 1975 compared with 1 in 2.4 plays in

1990. Spearing by running backs actually increased in 1990 when compared with 1975, and it was noted that tacklers were more likely to spear if the running back was spearing. The only decrease in spearing was noted among defensive linemen and independent tacklers. Heck determined that the majority of spearing involved defensive backs and linebackers.

Assuming Heck's (1996) research is representative of high school football participants nationally, compliance or, rather, noncompliance with the no-spearing rule makes it seem that more emphasis needs to be given to teaching young athletes not to practice this extremely dangerous maneuver. Coaches, officials, parents, and sports medicine personnel all share some responsibility in monitoring young athletes during games and practice. In 2005, the NCAA updated its tackle football rules by eliminating the problem of determining whether the maneuver was performed intentionally by the athlete in an effort to discourage athletes from contacting an opponent with the top or crown of the helmet or the facemask (Boden et al., 2006). The National Athletic Trainers' Association (NATA), National Football League (NFL), and NCAA are actively working to educate football participants regarding the dangers of these high-risk maneuvers. Two videos (available online) produced by NATA emphasize the concept of athletes initiating tackles with their shoulders and keeping their head up throughout contact (to watch the videos go to: Part 1 of 2, http://www.youtube.com/watch?v=KkBAiK7WEFA), and Part 2 of 2, http://www.youtube.com/watch?v=l87K6PoLD60).

Although spearing (axial loading) has been identified as a continuing problem and an extremely hazardous practice among football players, it is also true that any forced movement of the cervical spine, including hyperflexion, hyperextension, rotation, and lateral flexion, can result in injury. The types and severity of injury to the cervical spine are extensive; however, they can be classified according to the tissues involved and the extent of the damage. In order of severity, these range from simple compression or stretch of the brachial plexus nerve complex, which is self-correcting within minutes of the injury, to more severe problems involving ruptures of the intervertebral disks and fractures of the vertebrae.

Brachial Plexus Injuries

Known commonly as "burners" or "stingers," brachial plexus injuries are a frequent occurrence in sports such as football where the athlete's body may be forced in one direction while an arm may be pulled in the opposite direction. An injury to the brachial plexus typically results in significant but transient symptoms ranging from an intense burning sensation in the shoulder, arm, and hand to loss of sensation in the same areas. As shown in Figure 9.7, injury to the brachial plexus involves an abnormal traction or compression of one or more of the large nerves that comprise the entire plexus (Sallis, Jones, & Knopp, 1992).

Signs and symptoms of brachial plexus injury include the following:

- Immediate neurologic symptoms radiate into the affected arm, often described as an intense burning or stinging sensation.
- There is significant decrease in voluntary use of the arm (often the arm appears limp).
- Symptoms should be self-correcting and the involved extremity should return to normal sensation in a few minutes.
- In repeat cases, symptoms as described may persist for days or even weeks. Muscle atrophy, especially of the deltoid muscle, may be apparent. In such cases, medical evaluation is essential before the athlete is allowed to return to participation.

First aid care of brachial plexus injury involves the following:

1. Because of the nature of brachial plexus injuries, little can be done with respect to first aid other than to remove the athlete from participation until the symptoms subside.
2. Once on the sideline, continue to monitor the athlete's recovery and do not allow him or her to return to participation until the symptoms have abated and grip strength in the affected extremity is normal compared to the opposite arm.
3. If symptoms as described do not abate after 10 minutes, refer the athlete for a medical evaluation and require medical clearance prior to return to participation.

Sprains

Sprains of the cervical spine are common in some sports and generally involve portions of the major ligaments that serve to stabilize the vertebrae. The common mechanisms for these injuries are hyperflexion, hyperextension, lateral flexion, and rotation. These injuries generally involve a significant amount of force, as is seen in contact/collision sports such as football, ice hockey, and wrestling. Such injuries are usually self-correcting and resolve themselves over a period of days. Occasionally, however, the mechanism of a sprain is severe enough to result in an actual displacement of vertebrae, which can result in more serious neurologic problems.

Signs and symptoms of sprains include the following:

- Localized pain in the region of the cervical spine
- Point tenderness over the site of the injury
- Limited range of motion in neck movements
- No obvious neurologic deficits (as verified by the neurologic test described in the section titled "Physical Examination" earlier in this chapter)

First aid care of sprains involves the following:

1. Remove the athlete from practice/competition that day.
2. Apply ice (best accomplished with a plastic bag filled with crushed ice).
3. If available, place a properly sized commercial cervical collar on the athlete.
4. Refer the athlete for a medical evaluation prior to being allowed to return to participation.

Strains

Strains involve the muscles and tendons of the neck region and are normally more painful than serious. Exceptions to this are injuries such as whiplash, which consists of a combination of joint sprain and musculotendinous strain to the region. In addition, in severe whiplash injuries, indirect head injury is also possible. The mechanism of injury for strains is virtually the same as described previously for sprains.

Signs and symptoms of strains include the following:

- Localized pain in the region of the cervical spine
- Muscle spasm
- Limited range of motion in neck movements
- No obvious neurologic deficits (as verified by the neurologic test described in the section titled "Physical Examination" earlier in this chapter)

First aid care of strains involves the following:

1. Remove the athlete from practice/competition that day.
2. Apply ice (best accomplished with a plastic bag filled with crushed ice).
3. If available, place a properly sized commercial cervical collar on the athlete.
4. Refer the athlete for a medical evaluation prior to being allowed to return to participation.

Fractures and Dislocations

The most extreme forms of cervical injury occur when the damage involves fractures or dislocations resulting in pressure being placed directly on the spinal cord. The spinal cord is extremely sensitive to such trauma, and permanent neurologic damage and even death can occur depending on the specific location of the injury. The spinal cord may also suffer damage secondary to the initial trauma as a result of circulatory problems related to blood supply. When the spinal cord is bruised, bleeding and swelling may ensue, resulting in neurologic problems (Bailes, 1990). Any of the mechanisms described earlier can result in either a fracture or dislocation; however, axial loading is associated with many of the more severe forms of injury. It is critical to remember that these injuries represent true medical emergencies and therefore require the best care possible.

Signs and symptoms are as follows (in the case of an unconscious athlete, the primary objectives are to provide basic life support, stabilize the head and neck, and summon EMS):

- Athlete reports having felt or heard something pop or snap in his or her neck at the time of injury
- Severe pain localized in the region of the cervical spine associated with muscle spasm
- Difficulty in swallowing
- Deformity in the vertebrae, as detected by palpation
- Burning, numbness, or tingling sensations in the extremities and/or trunk
- Weakness in grip strength and/or dorsiflexion, either bilaterally or unilaterally
- Complete absence of sensation in the extremities and/or trunk
- Complete absence of motor function in the extremities and/or trunk
- Loss of bowel/bladder control

First aid care involves:

1. Complete the initial check and ascertain status of vital signs.
2. After initial check is complete, proceed to the physical examination. If any of the previously listed signs/symptoms are present, proceed to the following steps.
3. Stabilize the head and neck immediately. The emergency plan should designate a team leader who will immediately apply manual spinal stabilization (**Figures 9.6** and **9.9**)—in the case of a

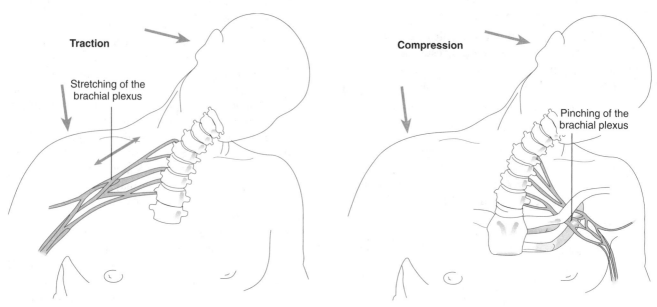

FIGURE 9.7 Common mechanisms of injury to the brachial plexus.

helmeted football player, do not remove the helmet; rather, use the helmet to assist in stabilization of the head and neck.

4. If CPR is necessary, the front of the shoulder pads can be opened to allow access. This is recommended prior to the decision to remove any other equipment (Kleiner, 1998). If the decision is made to remove the shoulder pads, the helmet should be removed as well to maintain proper spinal alignment.

5. Summon EMS.

6. Do not attempt to move the athlete—rather, when EMS personnel arrive, assist them in placing the athlete onto the spine board or other spinal immobilization device.

7. Continue to monitor vital signs until arrival of EMS.

Initial Treatment of a Suspected Neck Injury: Guidelines

When considering specific actions in treating an athlete with a suspected neck injury, an immediate distinction must be made. Is the athlete conscious or unconscious? The answer to this question determines the initial treatment approach. With the unconscious athlete, it must be assumed that both head and neck injuries are present. The primary objective is to determine if the athlete's life is in immediate jeopardy. Does the athlete have an open

airway? Is the athlete breathing? Does the athlete have a pulse? These questions are answered during the initial check discussed earlier. If the answer to any of these questions is no, then basic life support must be initiated and continued until the arrival of EMS personnel.

The coaching staff should have a preplanned emergency protocol for handling athletes with head and neck injuries. One staff member must be designated as the emergency team leader, whose primary responsibility is the supervision of the entire management process. In addition, the team leader must monitor the position of the athlete's head and neck, making sure that the injured player is not moved unnecessarily. Although sports medicine literature is replete with explanations of how to effectively and safely transport athletes with head and neck injuries, there does not seem to be much practice of these measures when actual cases are examined in retrospect. In the vast majority of school sports situations, which are normally located in population centers, emergency medical services should be readily available. Even in rural settings, EMS are typically only minutes away. Although it is important that coaching personnel be trained in proper transportation techniques, it should be remembered that training does not mandate implementation. This is especially true when considering the potential for catastrophic injury if a head or neck injury is improperly handled. Special consideration must be given to the care and handling of the helmeted football player (discussed in more detail in the section that follows).

In general, when dealing with an unconscious athlete, the most important criterion should be prevention of further injury (Vegso, Bryant, & Torg, 1982).

The team leader or designate should immediately stabilize the head and neck manually and continue doing so throughout the evaluation (Swartz et al., 2009). The next step involves checking the airway, breathing, and pulse. If the athlete is breathing and has a pulse, the next step is to summon EMS while maintaining support of the athlete's head and neck while continuously monitoring the airway, breathing, and circulation (known as the ABCs).

If any delay of EMS is anticipated in excess of 30 minutes, it is prudent to place the athlete on a spine board to ensure adequate immobilization. This procedure requires a properly constructed spine board (**Figure 9.8**) and a trained staff of a minimum of five people, including the team leader. The team leader is charged with maintaining the head and neck in a neutral position and directing the actions of the other team members. As shown in **Figures 9.9** through **9.12**, team members should be positioned at the athlete's shoulders, hips, and legs to roll the athlete properly onto the spine board. A fifth team member is required to slide the spine board under the athlete after he or she has been rolled onto the side by the other team members. The athlete should then be secured to the board and the head and neck supported by sandbags or towels, with straps properly placed to immobilize not only the head and neck, but also the entire body. The head should always be secured after all other parts of the body are immobilized (Swartz et al., 2009). Adhesive tape works well to provide additional immobilization to the head; place a strip across the athlete's forehead and chin. It is important to remember that placing an injured athlete on a spine board should be done only if absolutely necessary and, further, that the procedures for placing an athlete on this device be rehearsed frequently according to the recommendations of the emergency plan.

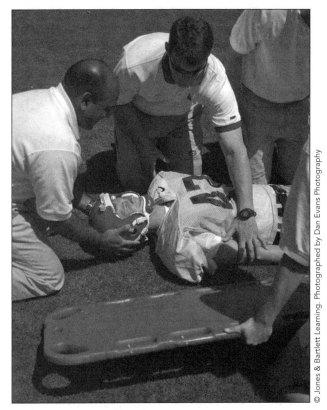

FIGURE 9.9 Members of the rescue team are stationed at the legs, hips, and shoulders, with the team leader providing stabilization to the head and neck.

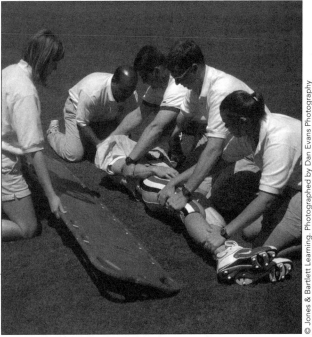

FIGURE 9.10 At the command of the team leader, the team rotates the athlete, as a unit, to enable movement of the spine board.

FIGURE 9.8 Examples of spine boards used to immobilize injured athletes.

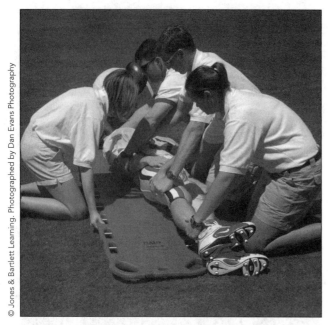

FIGURE 9.11 A fifth team member slides the spine board under the athlete. Note how the straps are placed to facilitate ease of securing the athlete to the board.

With the conscious athlete, the initial treatment procedures differ from those employed with the unconscious athlete. With the conscious athlete, the coach can obtain immediate feedback regarding the player's condition. The athlete should be questioned regarding numbness of extremities, **dysesthesia** (impairment of the sense of touch), weakness, or neck pain (Bailes, 1990). In addition, if the athlete reports a loss of ability to move a limb or limbs or significant strength deficit (involving grip strength, or plantar or dorsiflexion), arrangements must be made to stabilize the head and neck, and EMS must be summoned.

Emergency Procedures for the Treatment of Head and Neck Injuries in Football

Though head and neck injuries carry the potential of catastrophic results regardless of the sport, football players who sustain such injuries present special problems because of their equipment. The standard equipment protecting the player's head and neck is a helmet with an attached facemask, chin strap, and some type of mouth guard (**Figure 9.13**). This apparatus can make dealing with airway problems very difficult. Management procedures for the helmeted athlete have become a major issue in the sports medicine community—with strong opinions on how best

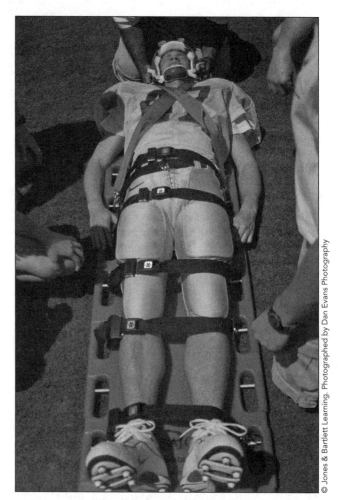

FIGURE 9.12 The athlete is firmly secured to the board with straps holding the ankles/feet, thigh/pelvis/arms, shoulders, and head and neck.

FIGURE 9.13 Plastic straps and screws secure the facemask to most football helmets.

TIME OUT 9.2

Guidelines for Appropriate Care of the Cervical Spine–Injured Athlete

General Guidelines

- Any athlete suspected of having a cervical spinal injury should not be moved and should be managed as though a spinal injury exists.
- The athlete's airway, breathing, circulation, neurological status, and level of consciousness should be assessed.
- The athlete should not be moved unless absolutely essential to maintain airway, breathing, and circulation.
- If the athlete must be moved to maintain airway, breathing, and circulation, the athlete should be placed in a supine position while maintaining spinal immobilization.
- When moving a suspected spine-injured athlete, the head and trunk should be moved as a unit. One accepted technique is to manually splint the head to the trunk.

Facemask Removal

- The facemask should be removed prior to transportation, regardless of current respiratory status.
- Those involved in the acute management of a cervical spine injury in injured football players should have the tools for facemask removal readily available, including cordless screwdriver and alternative cutting tool (anvil pruners, FM extractor).

Football Helmet Removal

The athletic helmet and chin strap should only be removed in the following circumstance:

- If the helmet and chin strap do not hold the head securely, such that immobilization of the helmet does not also immobilize the head.
- If the design of the helmet and chin strap is such that, even after removal of the facemask, the airway cannot be controlled nor ventilation provided.

- If the facemask cannot be removed after a reasonable period of time.
- If the helmet prevents immobilization for transportation in an appropriate position.

Helmet Removal

Spinal immobilization must be maintained while removing the helmet.

- Helmet removal should be frequently practiced under proper supervision.
- Specific guidelines for helmet removal need to be developed by emergency response team members.
- In most circumstances, it may be helpful to remove cheek padding and/or deflate air padding prior to helmet removal.

Equipment

- There needs to be a realization that the helmet and shoulder pads elevate an athlete's trunk when in the supine position.
- Should either the helmet or shoulder pads be removed—or if only one of these is present—appropriate spinal alignment must be maintained.
- The front of the shoulder pads can be opened to allow access for CPR and defibrillation.

Additional Guidelines

- A local emergency care plan should include communication with the institution's administration and those directly involved with the assessment and transportation of the injured athlete.
- All providers of acute cervical spine injury care should practice and be competent in all of the skills identified in these guidelines before they are needed in an emergency situation.

Source: Adapted from Swartz E, Boden BP, Courson RW, et al. (2009). National Athletic Trainers' Association position statement: Acute management of the cervical spine–injured athlete. *J Athl Train.* 44(3):306–331; and Kleiner DM, Almquist JL, Bailes J, et al. (2001). Prehospital care of the spine-injured athlete: A document from the Inter-Association Task Force for Appropriate Care of the Spine-Injured Athlete. Available: http://www.nata.org/sites/default/files/PreHospitalCare4SpineInjuredAthlete.pdf.

---

to handle such an athlete (Feld, 1993; Putman, 1992; Ray et al., 2002; Segan, Cassidy, & Bentkowski, 1993; Swartz et al., 2009).

NATA convened an interagency task force in 1998 to develop standardized medical guidelines for the proper care of the spine-injured athlete. The intent was to eliminate the confusion that existed at that time between different medical providers as to what constituted the

proper care for athletes suspected to have this type of injury. The task force published a position statement titled "Pre-hospital Care of the Spine-Injured Athlete"

dysesthesia Impairment of the sense of touch.

that was subsequently updated in 2009 with a position statement (Swartz et al., 2009; the entire document is available on the NATA website: http://www.nata.org/position-statements). Specific guidelines are presented in the document for the management of a helmeted athlete suspected of a cervical spine injury (see **Time Out 9.2**). The updated position statement provides the most current information regarding the acute management of a suspected of a cervical spine injury (Swartz et al., 2009).

Coaching personnel are advised to exercise extreme caution when making decisions about immediate care of a helmeted athlete with possible head and/or neck injury. Removal of the helmet, unless executed by a physician or other emergency care provider such as an athletic trainer or paramedic, should be avoided unless absolutely necessary.

In situations in which an airway must be established, careful and properly executed removal of the facemask is the most prudent approach. Depending on the age and design of the helmet, removal of the facemask can be accomplished in a variety of ways. Research on the most effective method of facemask removal has produced varying results, depending on the type of facemask clip system and whether it had been altered from manufacturer's specifications. However, the recommended technique is to use a cordless screwdriver (assuming the facemask is attached to the helmet and is secured with screws). It is further recommended that if this fails for some reason, the first responder should have an appropriate cutting tool on hand to simply cut the straps (Swartz et al., 2009; Swartz et al., 2010). It is critical to remember that the head and neck must be stabilized at all times, including during removal of the facemask (**Figure 9.14A** and **14B**). The majority of current designs secure the facemask to the helmet with small plastic clips (loop straps) attached to the helmet with screws (Figure 9.13), but newer designs now involve quick-release systems that come with a special device to spring-release the clip.

Removal of the plastic straps on the top and each side of the facemask—using devices such as a cordless screwdriver, anvil pruner, wire cutters, or tin snips (**Figure 9.15**)—while the head and neck are stabilized will allow the mask to be removed completely (**Figure 9.14B**). It is important to lift the facemask from the helmet as opposed to rotating it because this causes more motion. It is imperative that coaching personnel be aware of the specific types of equipment their athletes are wearing in the event that such an emergency arises.

Remember, in most instances, there is no reason to move an injured player from the field before EMS personnel arrive. No game or practice is so important that it cannot be delayed to ensure proper first aid for an injured player.

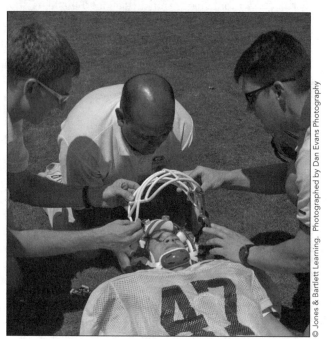

FIGURE 9.14 Top: In the event of a neck injury, the helmet provides an excellent means of cervical immobilization. Bottom: Once the facemask has been released, it can be lifted up and away from the player's face and then completely removed from area.

Injuries to the Maxillofacial Region

A variety of injuries can occur to the maxillofacial region of the body, which includes the jaw and teeth, eyes, ears, nose, throat, facial bones, and facial skin. Fortunately, with the advent of modern technology, protective equipment has been developed for use in high-risk sports (Matthews, 1990). These devices have significantly reduced the overall numbers of injuries to this region.

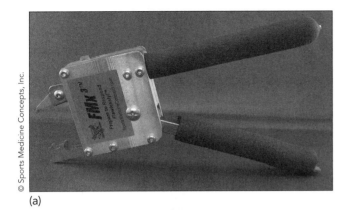

(a)

(b)

FIGURE 9.15 In the event of an injury, qualified personnel can use cutting tools such as the FM Extractor (FME) (a) to cut the straps on each side of the player's facemask or a cordless screwdriver to unscrew the attachments for the face clips (b).

Dental Injuries

There are 32 teeth in the adult human jaws, the majority of which are located just inside the front and sides of the mouth, where they are vulnerable to external blows common in collision and contact sports. Teeth are firmly secured into either the maxilla (upper jaw) or mandible (lower jaw) by way of the root, which is cemented into the sockets of the jaws with a specialized form of bone known as cementum. In addition, the sockets are lined with periosteum that aids in securing the teeth to the jaw.

Specific Injuries

The majority of dental injuries in sports are from direct blows resulting in tooth displacement, a fracture or avulsion, and, in extreme cases, fracture of the jaw or other facial bones. Signs and symptoms of dental injury are listed in **Time Out 9.3** along with the most likely injury.

Initial Check and Treatment: Guidelines

Whenever rendering first aid to someone suffering a dental injury, it is important to avoid exposure to any injury-related blood. As such, bloodborne pathogen prevention steps should be taken, which include protective gloves (latex) and, if possible, eye protection, such as goggles. Collect the history of the accident; this is an important component of the physical exam. Check to

TIME OUT 9.3

Dental Injuries

Type of Injury	Signs and Symptoms
Tooth displacement	A single tooth or several displaced teeth pushed either forward or backward, with bleeding along the gum line.
Tooth fracture	There are obvious defects (missing fragments) along the crown of the tooth or a visible fracture line vertically placed in the tooth. Less severe fractures are not painful when breathing through the mouth, whereas more severe fractures (at or below gum line) are extremely painful and the tooth is often loose.
Fracture of the jaw or other bones	Fractures of the jaw (mandible or maxilla), result in loosening of adjacent teeth, along with bleeding gums and numbness. In the case of fracture of the mandible, obvious deformity and an inability to open or close the mouth are apparent.
Tooth avulsion	Missing tooth with bleeding from the exposed socket

see if the athlete can open and close the mouth without pain or difficulty. Assess the general symmetry of the teeth; that is, look for irregularities visible in adjacent teeth. Examine the upper and lower teeth separately and carefully note any bleeding around the gum line or teeth or obvious chips or fractures.

Treatment for dental injuries includes direct finger pressure with sterile gauze over the area of bleeding, if any. For loose teeth, gently push them back into their normal position. In the case of avulsions, make every effort to locate the tooth and protect it by placing it into either a commercially prepared solution or sterile saline (Matthews, 1990). Send the athlete to a dentist or physician immediately to have the tooth put back in place. Time is of the essence in these situations, and the prognosis for the tooth is poor if more than 2 hours elapse between the time of the injury and time of replantation (Godwin, 1996).

Protection Against Injury

The most common method of dental protection in sports is the mouth guard, and many varieties are currently available. Properly fitted, a mouth guard can significantly reduce or even prevent many dental injuries and dislocations of the temporomandibular joint, as well as jaw fractures. All mouth guards fall into one of three groups: stock, mouth formed (boil and bite), and custom (Godwin, 1996). Stock versions are the least expensive; however, they are generally thought to be the least effective. The most commonly used are the mouth-formed type and, short of visiting the dentist to get a custom fit, they are probably the most cost effective for junior and senior high school athletes. The custom mouth guard provides the best possible fit and protection; however, the costs can be prohibitive for many athletes. Regardless of what type of mouth guard is used, it should be fitted to cover the upper and lower teeth and the gums. In addition, it should be cleaned regularly with an appropriate cleaning agent.

Obviously, in high-risk sports such as tackle football, a well fitted mouth guard should be utilized to protect the athlete from such injuries. In the United States, the use of mouth guards has been required in high school football since 1966. In 1974, the NCAA mandated their use in tackle football as well. Since then, ice hockey, field hockey, and men's and women's lacrosse have been added to the list of sports that require a mouth guard at the high school and collegiate levels. The use of either stock or custom-made mouth guards is strongly recommended—by the American Association of Oral and Maxillofacial Surgeons and the U.S. Olympic Committee—for protection in a variety of sports, including ice hockey, soccer, gymnastics, field hockey, rugby, wrestling, boxing, basketball, lacrosse, skiing, weight lifting, shot-putting, discus throwing, and even horseback riding (American Association of Oral and Maxillofacial Surgeons [AAOMS], 2010; Kerr, 1986).

Eye Injuries

The human eye is an incredibly complex structure located in the orbit of the skull (**Figure 9.16**). The front of the eye consists of clear tissue known as the cornea, behind which the iris (pupil) and lens are situated. Located in the eyeball is the vitreous body, consisting of transparent, semi-gelatinous material that essentially fills the globe of the eye. The posterior surface of the inside of the eye is covered by the retina, which contains the specialized neural cells of vision known as rods and cones. With the exception of the clear tissue on the anterior surface of the eye, the majority of the eyeball is encased in a tough tissue known as the sclera.

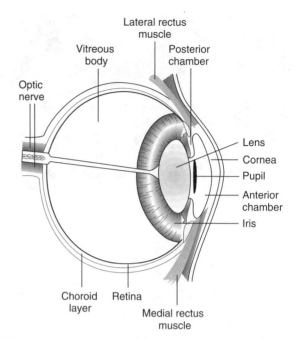

FIGURE 9.16 Anatomy of the eye.

It has been reported that approximately 42,000 sports-related eye injuries occur annually in the United States, costing more than $175 million. One-third of the victims are under the age of 16 years, and many of these injuries lead to vision loss and permanent blindness (Hamill, 2005). The average cost of an eye injury to a child can be around $3000. The sports with the highest associated risks are basketball, baseball, hockey, racquet sports, lacrosse, fencing, paintball, boxing, water polo, soccer, football, and downhill skiing. Perhaps most distressing is the conclusion by medical experts that the majority of these injuries (90%) are preventable with properly fitting eye protection (Rodriguez et al., 2003). With their increasing popularity, sports such as racquetball, squash, and badminton have produced an increase in eye trauma as well. Problems related to these sports include the small size of the striking objects (balls and shuttlecocks), their velocity (**Table 9.4**), and the confined areas in which the games are played. Together, these factors greatly increase the probability of injury.

Specific Injuries

Jones (1989) groups eye injuries into two different categories: contusional and penetrating. A contusional injury is the result of a blow from a blunt object such as a squash or tennis ball. Contusional injuries vary greatly in severity, ranging from simple corneal abrasions to major distortions of the eyeball resulting in rupture of the eye, fracture of the inner orbit, or a combination of

TABLE 9.4

POTENTIAL SPEED OF OBJECTS IN RACKET

Potential Speed of Objects in Racket Sports*

Squash ball	62 [140]
Badminton shuttlecock	57 [130]
Racquetball	48 [110]
Tennis ball	48 [110]

*Velocity is measured in meters per second [miles per hour].

Source: Data from Jones NP. (1989). Eye injury in sport. Sports Med. 7(3):168. Reprinted with permission.

the two. Additionally, the retina may be torn away from the inside of the eye, resulting in an injury commonly known as a detached retina. Penetrating injuries of the eye are less common, but can occur in shooting sports or even as the result of protective eye equipment that is defective. Signs and symptoms of eye injury are listed in **Time Out 9.4**.

Initial Check and Treatment: Guidelines

Before administering treatment for any eye injury, consider whether or not an ophthalmologic referral is needed (Pujalte, 2010). Referral is needed if there is visual field obstruction or physical damage to the anatomy of the eye. A simple penlight can be used to investigate and compare the injured eye with the uninjured eye. The majority of sports-related eye problems involve either simple corneal abrasions or a small foreign object in the eye, which will likely not need referral if there are no visual changes. The symptoms for each are often nearly identical: pain, irritation, and excessive tearing. A quick examination of the eye can be conducted by gently holding the upper eyelid up and away from the eye while checking the anterior of the eyeball for any problems (**Figure 9.17**). Small foreign bodies are usually washed away from the center of the eye by tears. Therefore, the particle may be located below the lower eyelid or on the side of the eyeball at a site known as the medial canthus. If the foreign object can be seen, it can usually be carefully removed with a moist cotton swab or piece of gauze. If no object can be seen in the eye, the injury is most likely a corneal abrasion. Do not allow the athlete to continue participation until the symptoms abate. If they persist or vision is severely disturbed, the athlete should be referred to the appropriate medical specialist for further evaluation. If the small object appears to

TIME OUT 9.4

Eye Injuries

Type of Injury	Signs and Symptoms
Corneal abrasion/ small foreign object	Pain, irritation, reddening, and excessive tearing. In the case of a small foreign object, the object may be visible when the eyelid is pulled away from the eye.
Orbital hematoma (contusion or black eye)	Vision distorted (blurred); pain, discoloration around eyelid and surrounding soft tissue.
Fractured orbit	Similar to contusions, but orbit bones are fractured. In addition to contusion signs and symptoms, difficulty in moving the eyeball (eye might appear trapped), diplopia, rapid swelling above the eye, ecchymosis.
Hyphema	Happens after severe contusion. Blood pools in the anterior portion of eye. It appears as if the pupil area is filling with blood. Blurred vision or blocked vision.
Retinal detachment	Often an insidious onset after severe contusion or "whipping of head." Abrupt changes in the amount of light or visual field seen; flashing light; blurred vision; floating particles in the field of vision.

be imbedded in the eye tissue, cover both eyes carefully with clean gauze and immediately arrange for transport of the athlete to a medical facility. It is important to cover the uninjured eye to avoid movement of the damaged eye, because the eyes normally move together to produce a visual image. This is known as "sympathetic eye movement."

When the eye receives a significant blow or contusion—from being hit by an elbow in a game of basketball or by a racquetball, for example—vision is usually at least temporarily disturbed. In most cases, this causes a black eye

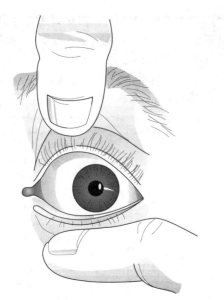

FIGURE 9.17 Proper positioning of fingers when initially examining the eye.

resulting from hemorrhaging of tissue surrounding the eye. The immediate care of this injury is periodic application of cold until the acute signs of inflammation resolve. In the case of severe contusions, bleeding into the anterior portion of the eye (hyphema) may occur quickly and typically results in the visual field being completely or partially blocked. This is a potentially serious sign because it may indicate vascular damage in the eyeball. An athlete with a hyphema should have both eyes patched and be referred immediately for appropriate medical evaluation.

Additionally, contusions to the eye area can cause the eyeball itself to rupture (globe rupture), the socket (orbit) to fracture (orbital blowout), or the retina to detach. An athlete with any of these injuries should be immediately referred for further medical evaluation. Patching of the eyes is warranted with a ruptured globe. Symptoms of a ruptured globe include pain (especially when attempting to move the eye), double vision (**diplopia**), poor visual acuity, and possibly irregular pupils (Pujalte, 2010). An orbital blowout happens when pressure inside the eye increases and causes the floor of the orbit to fracture. Diplopia, pain, swelling, and discoloration around the eye structure are evident, along with restricted movement of eye (Pujalte, 2010). Because it is the floor of the orbit that often fractures, the inferior tissue structure may also become trapped and the athlete will be unable to move the eye upward. Injuries resulting in a detached retina can be caused by the mechanisms previously described; however, the symptoms may not be immediately apparent. An **insidious** aspect of this injury is that the retina may slowly fall away from the posterior section of the eye over a period

of days, weeks, or even months in some cases. Early symptoms include seeing particles floating inside the eye, distorted vision, and abrupt changes in the amount of light or visual field seen. Any athlete with a history of blunt trauma to the eye who later complains of any of these symptoms may have a retinal detachment and should be referred to a medical specialist.

Contact Lens Problems

Many athletes are fitted with contact lenses (both hard and soft). Few difficulties occur with these appliances; however, as a rule, more problems arise with hard lenses. Most result from the lens slipping out of place or dust that gets trapped between the lens and the eye. Soft lenses cover the entire anterior portion of the eye and are less able to migrate around on the eye surface. The coach should have the necessary materials handy in the first aid kit—including commercially prepared wetting solution, a small mirror, and perhaps even a contact-lens case—to deal with problems involving contact lenses.

Protection Against Injury

Although presently not required by the NCAA or high school sports regulatory bodies, protective eyewear is strongly recommended and is growing in popularity. The primary forms of protective eyewear are goggles, used in sports such as basketball and racket sports, and face shields (usually attached to a safety helmet), used in sports such as football, ice hockey, and baseball/softball. Although many of these products are made of plastic, the best material is polycarbonate, which is extremely strong and protects well against impacts (Hamill, 2005). It is recommended when purchasing protective eye devices that the device be approved by the American Society for Testing and Materials (ASTM; http://www.astm.org/) or the Canadian Standards Association (CSA group; http://www.csagroup.org/).

Nose Injuries

The human nose is, by nature of its location, often subjected to trauma in sports. The classic nosebleed (**epistaxis**) may well be one of the most common facial injuries in sports. Anatomically, the nose consists of a combination bone–cartilage framework over which the skin is attached. The nose consists mostly of soft tissue (cartilage and skin) and can absorb significant amounts of force. The bones of the nose include the right and left nasal bones and the frontal processes of the maxilla (Gray, 1985). The superior portions of the nasal bones meet with the frontal bone between the orbits. The nose has two openings, commonly called nostrils (nares), which are separated in the middle by the cartilaginous septum. The areas immediately inside the nares contain hairs that trap large particles during respiration. Farther up, the nares tissue is covered with mucous membrane.

Initial Check and Treatment: Guidelines

When an athlete receives a blow to the nose that results in bleeding, the nose should immediately be examined for the possibility of fracture. The signs of such a fracture include an obvious deformity of the bridge of the nose, which usually swells quickly. Fractures of the nasal bones constitute the most frequent fractures of the facial region (Booher & Thibodeau, 1989). If one is suspected, first control the nosebleed and then immediately refer the athlete for medical evaluation. Generally, a physician can easily correct uncomplicated nasal fractures, and any complicated fractures will be addressed after swelling goes down. It is recommended that an athlete only take acetaminophen if they have pain because aspirin or other NSAIDs are blood thinners.

Care of a simple nosebleed should include application of finger pressure directly against the nostril that is bleeding. The person rendering first aid should wear a latex glove for protection against exposure to blood. If the bleeding persists, application of a cold compress against the nasal region is usually effective in causing immediate vasoconstriction of the affected vessels. In addition, the athlete should be instructed to lean forward or lie on the same side as the bleeding nostril. If the athlete needs to continue participation, the nose can be packed with gauze, which should be allowed to protrude slightly from the nose to aid with extraction later.

Septal injuries present unique problems and the possibility of later complications. As a result of external blows, the septum can be bruised; bleeding can occur between the septum and the mucous membrane covering it. This injury is referred to as a septal hematoma and can lead to serious septal erosion if not corrected. The signs of a septal hematoma are swelling that is usually visible both inside and outside the nose. In addition, the nose may appear red and infected externally, and the athlete will complain of pain, especially when the nose is gently palpated. This injury should be referred to the appropriate medical specialist for diagnosis and correction. The coach or athlete should not attempt to drain a septal hematoma because the likelihood of infection and permanent damage is high.

Ear Injuries

Anatomically, the human ear shares some common characteristics with the nose. Externally it appears as a cartilaginous framework covered with a layer of skin, but it has an extensive internal structure as well.

Specifically, the ear can be divided into several anatomic components. The external ear consists of the large expanded portion, called the auricula, and the opening into the ear canal, known as the external acoustic meatus. The middle ear, which is a small space within the temporal bone, contains a small group of bones that transmit vibrations to the tympanic membrane (eardrum). The inner ear comprises the complex structure known as the labyrinth or specialized bones (vestibule, semicircular canals, and cochlea) that are directly attached with the vestibulocochlear nerve (Gray, 1985). The structures of the inner ear also play a major role in the maintenance of equilibrium (Van De Graaff, 1998). Thus, injuries to this area often affect not only hearing but also balance.

With the exception of aquatic sports, the majority of sports-related medical problems of the ear affect its external parts. Sports such as wrestling, which involves a great deal of body contact between opponents and the playing surface, result in a large number of abrasions and contusions to the auricula. Although the use of protective equipment has reduced the overall numbers of such injuries, they do still occur. Because the tissues of the auricula have a fairly high degree of vascularity, trauma can lead to the development of a hematoma between the skin and underlying cartilage, known technically as an auricular hematoma (Matthews, 1990). If this condition is not treated properly or is repeatedly irritated prior to treatment, a serious cosmetic problem known as cauliflower ear can occur. In extreme cases, the cartilage of the auricula may even begin to break down, thereby complicating the problem. Signs and symptoms of auricular hematoma include skin redness, local increase in tissue temperature, pain, and/or a burning sensation. This condition should be treated immediately with a cold pack. If swelling in the auricula occurs, the athlete should be referred to a physician so that the fluid can be removed via aspiration. The ear will then be packed with a special material to prevent swelling from returning. Athletes with a history of this injury or those involved in high-risk sports such as wrestling should be required to wear properly fitted protection.

Any athlete who receives a blow to the ear region that is immediately followed by a sudden reduction in hearing and/or occurrence of dizziness requires

diplopia Double vision.
insidious Slow onset or signs and symptoms occur with no obvious mechanism.
epistaxis Nosebleed.

immediate referral to a physician. Blows to the outer ear can produce dramatic increases in pressure in the ear, resulting in ruptures of either the eardrum or a specialized structure known as the oval window. When such an injury occurs, the immediate effects are significant reduction in hearing and transient loss of equilibrium. Other signs and symptoms may include bleeding from the ear and persistent and intense ringing in the ear. Damage to the oval window may require surgical intervention to correct the problem (Matthews, 1990). Athletes with external or middle ear infections should see a physician so the proper medication can be prescribed or recommended over the counter. Those with ear infections are advised not to participate in aquatic sports until the problem has resolved itself. This is particularly true in diving because the infection and subsequent inflammation in the ear may make it impossible for the athlete to clear the pressure that develops in ears while underwater, which often results in injury to the eardrum.

Fractures of the Face (Non-Nasal)

Though fractures can occur almost anywhere on the face, certain sites are more often involved in sports-related injuries. A relatively common form of facial fracture involves the mandible (lower jaw) and occurs in boxing and other collision sports. The signs and symptoms of such an injury include obvious pain and swelling at the site of the fracture, observable deformity, and malocclusion (misalignment of the maxillary and mandibular teeth). Treatment entails gentle application of a cold pack and immediate referral to a physician. If a fracture has occurred, the jaw will be treated by wiring the mouth closed; in severe cases, surgical fixation may be required until the fracture is healed (Matthews, 1990).

A related injury is dislocation of the jaw, which can result from the same type of mechanism. Here, the joint involved is the temporomandibular joint (**TMJ**), which is classified as ellipsoid and is formed by the union of the mandibular condyle and the mandibular fossa of the temporal bone (**Figure 9.18**). The TMJ is held together by numerous ligaments and joint capsules. Because of its bony configuration, this joint tends to dislocate relatively easily. The signs and symptoms of this injury include extreme pain and deformity in the region of the TMJ and inability to move the lower jaw; in some cases, the mouth may be locked in an open position. Treatment for this injury is essentially the same as for a fracture. It is important that on-site reductions (putting the joint back in place) not be attempted.

Other bones of the face may be fractured, including the zygomatic (cheek) bone. Generally, the signs

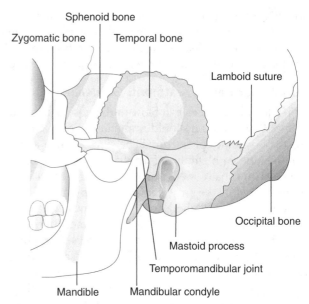

FIGURE 9.18 The temporomandibular joint.

and symptoms include pain and swelling at the site of injury. In the case of the zygomatic bone, swelling and discoloration may also spread to the orbit of the eye, and the athlete may experience diplopia and numbness. Any athlete with a history of a blow to the face who has some or all of the previous signs and symptoms should be referred immediately to a physician for diagnosis and treatment.

Wounds of the Facial Region

Wounds to the face may take many forms; in general, their treatment should be based on basic first aid guidelines. Carefully clean the wound with mild soap and warm water; apply a sterile, commercially prepared dressing (not loose cotton) like an adhesive bandage. For minor injuries, referral to a physician is only

WHAT IF?

You are asked to provide first aid care to a high school basketball player who just received a blow to his mouth from an opponent's elbow. She notes that two teeth have been completely knocked out of their sockets. The teeth were recovered by the athlete and are in her hand. What would you do for this athlete? What would change if the teeth were avulsed but still in the sockets?

required if there are signs of an infection. Facial wounds take on greater significance than injuries to other parts of the body primarily because of cosmetic reasons. Thus, any wound to the face, whether it is a simple **abrasion** (scraped skin), a more serious incision (smooth edged, bleeds freely), or a laceration (skin cut with jagged, irregular edges), should be evaluated relative to the potential long-term cosmetic effects. As a general rule, any incision or laceration resulting in an observable space between the margins of the skin should be seen by a physician for suturing (Matthews, 1990). Usually, athletes can return to participation after the wound has been treated and (when necessary) sutured. The decision to release such an athlete to return to activity is best determined by the attending physician (Crow, 1993).

TMJ Temporomandibular joint.
abrasion Rubbing or scraping off of skin.

REVIEW QUESTIONS

1. List the names of the cranial bones and give a description of their anatomic relationship.

2. What are the correct names of specialized tissues known collectively as the cerebral meninges?

3. What is located in the subarachnoid space?

4. What is the approximate weight in pounds of an adult human's brain?

5. What are the three basic components of the human brain?

6. What are some of the differences between a child and an adult brain?

7. List the correct number of cervical, thoracic, lumbar, sacral, and coccygeal nerves.

8. According to the chapter, what is a cerebral concussion?

9. What are the four categories of signs and symptoms for a concussion? Name one in each category.

10. What percentage of concussions result in a loss of consciousness?

11. What percentage of concussions result in post-traumatic amnesia?

12. How many days does it take for the typical concussion to resolve?

13. How long can athletes experience signs and symptoms if they are diagnosed with post-concussive syndrome?

14. True or false: An athlete can return to play the same day after receiving a concussion.

15. True or false: More than three-quarters of the states in the United States have laws that dictate the care and treatment of concussed athletes.

16. Describe the condition known as anisocoria.

17. What is anterograde amnesia as it relates to a head injury?

18. Define subdural, epidural, and intracerebral hematomas; also define cerebral contusion.

19. When rendering first aid to an athlete with a suspected head injury, what are the top three objectives?

20. True or false: The single most important indicator of the severity of head injury is the level of consciousness.

21. True or false: Baseline computerized neuropsychological testing is recommended for all high school athletes.

22. What are the general areas of neurocognitive function that are assessed by the SCAT3?

23. What is the most likely mechanism of a sports-related injury to the cervical spine?

24. What conditions must be assumed present whenever treating an unconscious athlete?

25. What types of information should be obtained when treating a conscious athlete with a suspected head and/or neck injury?

26. True or false: Experts agree that 90% of eye injuries could be prevented if athletes wore adequate eye protection.

27. What is the cause of the majority of dental injuries?

28. What is a simple, practical form of dental protection in sports?

29. True or false: The majority of sports-related eye injuries occur in basketball.

30. What is the recommended method of removing a small, nonimbedded object from an athlete's eye?

31. What is an orbital blowout?

32. What materials should the coach have available in a first aid kit for treating problems related to athletes wearing contact lenses?

33. Define the term *epistaxis*.

34. Describe the appropriate method for controlling a nosebleed.

35. True or false: With the exception of aquatic sports, the majority of sports-related medical problems with the ear involve the auricula.

36. Briefly describe the process leading to the condition known as cauliflower ear.

37. Why are facial wounds of greater significance than wounds on other areas of the body?

REFERENCES

American Association of Oral and Maxillofacial Surgeons. (2010). Treating and Preventing Facial Injury. Available: http://www.aaoms.org/facial_injury.php.

Bagley A, Daneshvar DH, Schanker BD, Zurakowski D, d'Hemecourt CA, Nowinski CJ, Cantu RC, Goulet K. (2012). Effectiveness of the SLICE Program for Youth Concussion Education. *Clin J Sport Med*. 22(5):385–389.

Bailes JE. (1990). Management of cervical spine sports injuries. *Athl Train*. 25:156–159.

Boden BP, Tacchetti RL, Cantu RC, Knowles SB, Mueller FO. (2006). Catastrophic cervical spine injuries in high school and college football players. *Am J Sports Med*. 34(8):1223–1232.

Booher JM, Thibodeau GA. (1989). *Athletic Injury Assessment*. St. Louis, Mo: Times Mirror/Mosby.

Broglio S, Macciocchi S, Ferrara M. (2007). Sensitivity of the concussion assessment battery. *Neurosurgery*. 60(6):1050–1058.

Burstein AH, Otis JC, Torg JS. (1982). Mechanisms and pathomechanics of athletic injuries to the cervical spine. In: Torg JS (ed.), *Athletic Injuries to the Head, Neck, and Face* (pp. 139–145). Philadelphia, Pa: Lea & Febiger.

Cantu RC. (2001). Posttraumatic retrograde and anterograde amnesia: Pathophysiology and implications in grading and safe return to play. *J Athl Train*. 36(3):244–248.

Cantu RC, Voy R. (1995). Second impact syndrome—a risk in any contact sport. *Phys Sportsmed*. 23(6):27–34.

Chatelin S, Vappou J, Roth S, Raul J, Willinger R. (2012). Towards child versus adult brain mechanical properties. *J Mech Behav Biomed Mater*. 6:166–173.

Child SCAT3. (2013). *Br J Sports Med*. 47:263–268. Available: http://bjsm.bmj.com/content/47/5/263.full.pdf.

Comstock R, Collins C, Fletcher E. (2013). Convenience sample summary report: National high school sports-related injury surveillance study (2011–2012 school year). Available: http://www.nationwidechildrens.org/cirp-rio-study-reports.

Crow RW. (1993). Sports-related lacerations—promoting healing and limiting scarring. *Phys Sportsmed*. 21: 143–147.

Daneshvar D, Nowinski J, McKee A, Cantu R. (2011). The epidemiology of sport-related concussion. *Clin Sports Med*. 30:1–17.

Feld F. (1993). Management of the critically injured football player. *J Athl Train*. 28(3):206–212.

Field M, Collins M, Lovell M, Maroon J. (2003). Does age play a role in recovery from sports-related concussion? A comparison of high school and collegiate athletes. *J Pediatr*. 142:546–553.

Gessel L, Fields S, Collins C, Dick RW, Comstock RD. (2007). Concussions among United States high school and collegiate athletes. *J Athl Train*. 42(4):495–503.

Glang A, Koester M, Beaver S, Clan J, McLaughlin K. (2010). Online training in sports concussion for youth sports coaches. *Int J Sports Sci Coach*. 5(1):1–11.

Godwin WC. (1996). A tale of two teeth. *Training Conditioning*. IV(3):39–42.

Gray H. (1985). *Anatomy of the Human Body*. Philadelphia, Pa: Lea & Febiger.

Guskiewicz KM, Weaver NL, Padua DA, Garrett WE Jr. (2000). Epidemiology of concussion in collegiate and high school football players. *Am J Sports Med*. 28(5):643–650.

Guskiewicz K, Bruce SL, Cantu RC, Ferrara MS, Kelly JP, McCrea M, Putukian M, Valovich McLeod TC. (2004). National Athletic Trainers' Association position statement: Management of sports-related concussion. *J Athl Train*. 39(3):280–297.

Guskiewicz K, Marshall SW, Bailes J, McCrea M, Cantu RC, Randolph C, Jordan BD. (2005). Association between recurrent concussion and late-life cognitive impairment in retired professional football players. *Neurosurgery*. 57(4):719–726.

Hamill M. (2005). Think "protective eyewear" when playing sports. *American Academy of Ophthalmology*. Available: http://www.sportseyeinjuries.com/docs/Think_Protective.pdf.

Harmon K, Drezner JA, Gammons M, Guskiewicz KM, Halstead M, Herring SA, Kutcher JS, Pana A, Putukian M, Roberts WO. (2013). American Medical Society for Sports Medicine position statement: Concussion in sport. *Br J Sports Med*. 47:15–26.

Hart J Jr, Kraut MA, Womack KB, Strain J, Didehbani N, Bartz E, Conover H, Mansinghani S, Lu H, Cullum CM. (2013). Neuroimaging of cognitive dysfunction and depression in aging retired national football league players. *JAMA Neurol*. 70(3):326–335.

Harvey H. (2013). Reducing traumatic brain injuries in youth sports: Youth sports traumatic brain injury state laws, January 2009–December 2012. *Am J Public Health*, 103(7), 1249–1254.

Heck JF. (1996). The incidence of spearing during a high school's 1975 and 1990 football seasons. *J Athl Train.* 31:31–37.

Jones NP. (1989). Eye injury in sport. *Sports Med.* 7(3):163–181.

Jordan BD. (1989). Head injury in sports. In: Jordan BD, Tsairis P, Warren RR (eds.), *Sports Neurology* (pp. 75–83). New York, NY: Aspen Publishers.

Kerr IL. (1986). Mouth guards for the prevention of injuries in contact sports. *Sports Med.* 3:415–427.

Kleiner DM. (1998). New guidelines for the appropriate care of a suspected spine injury. *Athl Ther Today.* 3(5):50–51.

Kleiner DM, Almquist JL, Bailes J, et al. (2001). Prehospital care of the spine-injured athlete: A document from the Inter-Association Task Force for Appropriate Care of the Spine-Injured Athlete. Available: http://www.nata.org/sites/default/files/PreHospitalCare4SpineInjuredAthlete.pdf.

Marar M, McIlvain H, Field S, Comstock R. (2012). Epidemiology of concussions among United States high school athletes in 20 sports. *Am J Sports Med.* 40(4):747–755.

Matthews B. (1990). Maxillofacial trauma from athletic endeavors. *Athl Train.* 25:132–137.

McCory P, Meeuwisse WH, Aubry M, Cantu B, Dvorák J, Echemendia RJ, Engebretsen L, Johnston K, Kutcher JS, Raftery M, Sills A, Benson BW, Davis GA, Ellenbogen RG, Guskiewicz K, Herring SA, Iverson GL, Jordan BD, Kissick J, McCrea M, McIntosh AS, Maddocks D, Makdissi M, Purcell L, Putukian M, Schneider K, Tator CH, Turner M. (2013). Consensus statement on concussion in sport: The 4th international conference on concussion in sport held in Zurich, November 2012. *Br J Sports Med.* 47:250–258.

Mueller F, Cantu R. (2011). Catastrophic sports injury research—29th annual report Fall 1982-Spring 2011. Available: http://www.unc.edu/depts/nccsi/2011Allsport.pdf.

Mueller F, Cantu R. (2012). Annual survey of catastrophic football injuries (1977–2012). Available: http://www.unc.edu/depts/nccsi/FBAnnual2012.pdf.

Pujalte G. (2010). Eye injuries in sports. *Athletic Therapy Today.* 15(5):14–18.

Putman LA. (1992). Alternative methods for football helmet face-mask removal. *J Athl Train.* 27(2):170–172.

Ray R, Luchies C, Abfall Frens M, Hughes W, Sturmfels R. (2002). Cervical spine motion in football players during three airway-exposure techniques. *J Athl Train.* 37(2):172–177.

Resch J, Driscoll A, McCaffrey N, Brown C, Ferrara MS, Macciocchi S, Baumgartner T, Walpert K. (2013). ImPact test-retest reliability: reliably unreliable? *J Ahtl Train.* 48(4):506–511.

Rodriguez JO, Lavina AM, Agarwal A (2003). Prevention and treatment of common eye injuries in sports. *Am Fam Physician.* 67(7):1481–1488.

Roebuck-Spencer T, Vincent AS, Schlegel RE, Gilliland K. (2013). Evidence for added value of baseline testing in computer-based cognitive assessment. *J Ahtl Train.* 48(4):499–505.

Saladin K. (2007). *Anatomy and Physiology: The Unity of Form and Function.* Columbus, Ohio: McGraw-Hill. pp. 520–522.

Sallis RE, Jones K, Knopp W. (1992). Burners—offensive strategy for an underreported injury. *Phys Sportsmed.* 20:47–55.

Sarmiento K, Mitchko J, Klien C, Wong S. (2010). Evaluation of the Centers for Disease Control and Prevention's concussion intuitive for high school coaches: "Head Up: Concussion in High School Sports." *J School Health.* 80(3):112–118.

SCAT3. (2013). *Br J Sports Med.* 47:259–262. Available: http://bjsm.bmj.com/content/47/5/259.full.pdf.

Scorza K, Raleigh M, O'Connor F. (2012). Current concepts in concussion: Evaluation and management. *Am Fam Physician.* 85(2):123–132.

Segan R, Cassidy D, Bentkowski J. (1993). A discussion of the issue of football helmet removal in suspected cervical spine injuries. *J Athl Train.* 28(4):294–305.

Shultz SJ, Houglum PA, Perrin DH. (2000). *Assessment of Athletic Injuries.* Champaign, Ill: Human Kinetics.

Sun JF. (2013). See where your state stands on concussion law. Available: http://usafootball.com/news/featured-articles/see-where-your-state-stands-concussion-law.

Swartz EE, Boden, BP, Courson, RW, Decoster LC, Horodyski M, Norkus SA, Rehberg RS, Waninger KN. (2009). National Athletic Trainers' Association position statement: Acute management of the cervical spine-injured athlete. *J Athl Train.* 44(3):306–331.

Swartz E, Belmore K, Decoster L, Armstrong C. (2010). Emergency face-mask removal effectiveness: A comparison of traditional and nontraditional football helmet face-mask attachment systems. *J Athl Train.* 45(6):560–569.

Tomei K, Doe C, Prestigiacomo C, Gandhi C. (2012). Comparative analysis of state-level concussion legislation and review of current practices in concussion. *Neurosurgeon Focus.* 33(6):1–9.

Torg JS. (1989). Athletic injuries to the cervical spine. In: Jordan BD, Tsairis P, Warren RR (eds.), *Sports Neurology* (pp. 133–158). New York, NY: Aspen Publishers.

Van De Graaff KM. (1998). *Human Anatomy* (5th ed.). Dubuque, Ia: William. C. Brown.

Vegso JJ, Bryant MH, Torg JS. (1982). Field evaluation of head and neck injuries. In: Torg JS (ed.), *Athletic Injuries to the Head, Neck, and Face* (pp. 39–52). Philadelphia, Pa: Lea & Febiger.

Wiesenfarth J, Briner W. (1996). Neck injuries—urgent decisions and actions. *Phys Sportsmed.* 24:35–41.

Injuries to the Thoracic Through Coccygeal Spine

MAJOR CONCEPTS

This chapter presents a brief review of the gross anatomy of the thoracic spine and thoracic cage along with a discussion of possible injuries to the region. Although relatively uncommon in sports, injuries to the thoracic spine do occasionally occur. These injuries are usually sprains; much less frequently they involve fractures. The chapter covers typical mechanisms of injury as well as common signs and symptoms and recommended initial treatment for both sprains and fractures. Injuries to the lumbar spine in sports are quite common: The vast majority are related to an anatomic defect known as spondylolysis. This chapter provides descriptions of the common problems associated with this part of the spinal column along with information regarding the signs and symptoms of related lumbar spinal disorders. It also discusses traumatic sprains, strains, and intervertebral disk injuries, with a focus on recognition and initial management.

go.jblearning.com/PfeifferCWS

For a full suite of assignments and additional learning activities (indicated by the icons throughout the text), use the access code found in the front of your text. If you do not have an access code, you can obtain one at go.jblearning.com/PfeifferCWS.

ANATOMY REVIEW OF THE THORACIC SPINE

The portion of the human vertebral column known as the thoracic spine consists of 12 vertebrae that articulate at the top with the cervical spine and at the bottom with the lumbar spine. Viewed from the side, the human vertebral column includes several curvatures that correspond with specific regions of the spine. Both the cervical and lumbar portions of the spine represent concave curves, whereas the thoracic portion of the vertebral column is convex, curving in the opposite direction to both the cervical and lumbar components. The curves of the spine, along with the ligaments and intervertebral discs, are important to the overall strength of the spinal column (**Figure 10.1**). The thoracic vertebrae are commonly numbered 1 through 12, beginning with the uppermost vertebra and ending with the 12th at the junction with the lumbar spine. An intervertebral disk is located between each thoracic vertebra. A unique aspect of the thoracic vertebrae is their relationship with the 12 pairs of ribs in the human skeleton. The thoracic vertebrae, their

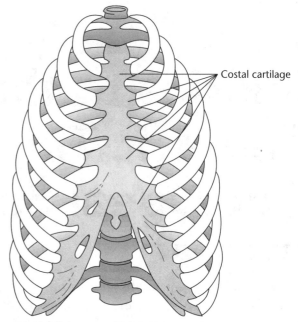

FIGURE 10.2 The thoracic cage (anterior view).

corresponding ribs, and the sternum form a strong **thoracic cage (Figure 10.2)**, which among other things serves to protect the internal organs of the region, including the heart and lungs (Gray, 1985).

Because of the bony union of the ribs and adjacent vertebrae, the thoracic spine is much less mobile than either the cervical or lumbar sections of the spine. The majority of movements in the thoracic region of the spine result from the process of respiration (Rasch, 1989). The limited movements of the thoracic vertebrae help to make injuries to this part of the body uncommon.

Common Sports Injuries

As stated, sports injuries to the thoracic spine are rare. Those sports-related injuries that do occur can be divided into two groups: skeletal and soft tissue (ligaments, muscles and tendons, and intervertebral disks). Available data demonstrate that bone-related injuries in this region are more common than those involving soft tissues (American Academy of Orthopaedic Surgeons [AAOS], 1991).

Skeletal Injuries

The most common injury to the thoracic spine involves a compression type of fracture to the vertebral body (O'Leary & Boiardo, 1986). This injury occurs near the junction of the thoracic and lumbar spines and is usually related to violent, ballistic movements that are unique to sports involving high velocities. An athlete with a history of recent trauma to the thoracic spine who complains of severe pain in the region or

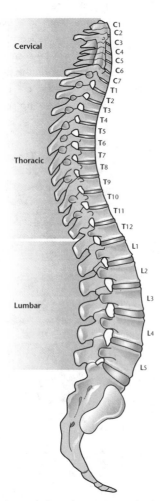

FIGURE 10.1 Lateral view, human vertebral column.

perhaps even neurologic signs (pain or numbness of the extremities) should be referred to a medical doctor immediately for evaluation.

Another problem related to the vertebrae of the thoracic spine is Scheuermann's disease, which is sometimes seen in adolescents and is characterized by **kyphosis** (an abnormal amount of convexity of the spine). Children involved in activities that subject the spine to severe bending, such as gymnastics, may develop this condition. A child who complains of recurrent pain in the region of the thoracic spine that is associated with activity should be evaluated. A quick visual examination may confirm an abnormal amount of spinal curvature, which is made worse when the child bends forward as if to touch the toes. In some cases, related spinal problems such as **scoliosis** (lateral curvature) and lumbar **lordosis** (swayback) may also be present. Children with either of these disorders need to be referred to a doctor for extensive evaluation. If a diagnosis of Scheuermann's disease is made, treatment will involve both prescribed exercises and spinal bracing.

Vertebral Fractures

Fractures involving the thoracic spine are extremely rare; however, they can result from either a direct blow to the posterior thorax or extreme flexion of the thoracic spine, resulting in a compression of the vertebral body. In spite of the fact that neurologic complications related to vertebral fractures in this region are rare, significant soft-tissue damage can occur to the skin and underlying muscles. The mechanism of injury described earlier can occur in a tackle in football, a collision in soccer, or while landing on the opponent's knee during a takedown move in wrestling.

Signs and symptoms include the following:

1. Pain in the area of the injury.
2. Although the athlete may be able to stand and even move about, any motion specific to the trunk such as extension, flexion, or rotation will be extremely painful.
3. Swelling and discoloration in the area of injury may be apparent.
4. Muscle spasm over the injured area.

First aid care:

1. Immediately apply rest, ice, compression, and elevation (RICE) (generally best accomplished with a 6- or 8-inch-wide elastic wrap and a bag of crushed ice).
2. Remove the athlete from participation for 24 hours, with a follow-up evaluation.

3. If symptoms persist, referral to a physician is warranted.
4. If neurologic symptoms are present during the initial evaluation, refer immediately to a physician.

Rib Fractures

Another type of fracture that may occur in this region involves the ribs and is known as a posterior rib fracture (AAOS, 1991). The mechanism for this injury is typically a direct blow to the lateral or posterior thorax. Fractures may occur anywhere along the rib; however, most commonly they occur near an angle of the rib, which is anatomically the weakest point (Booher & Thibodeau, 1989).

Signs and symptoms include the following:

1. Painful respiration.
2. Deformity in the region of the injury, including a protruding rib or a depression where the normal contour of the rib should be.
3. Swelling and discoloration.
4. Pain when the rib cage is compressed gently by the examiner.
5. In severe cases, lung damage may result in symptoms associated with pneumothorax (see Chapter 13).

First aid care:

1. Immediately apply RICE (generally best accomplished with a 6- or 8-inch-wide elastic wrap and a bag of crushed ice).
2. Treat for shock.
3. Refer for medical evaluation by a physician.

Complications of these injuries are rare; however, when they do occur they can be quite dangerous. Displaced rib fractures may damage internal thoracic structures, particularly the lungs, resulting in either a traumatic **pneumothorax** (**Figure 10.3**) or **hemothorax**

thoracic cage Thoracic vertebrae, their corresponding ribs, and the sternum.

kyphosis Exaggeration of the normal curve of the thoracic spine.

scoliosis Lateral and/or rotary curvature of the spine.

lordosis Abnormal curvature of the lumbar vertebrae.

pneumothorax Collapse of a lung as a result of air in the pleural cavity.

hemothorax Bloody fluid in the pleural cavity.

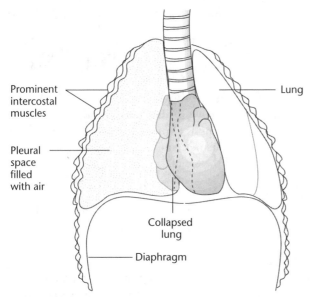

FIGURE 10.3 Pneumothorax.

(blood and air in the thorax). Such injuries will result in significant changes in breathing and may also induce shock. For more detailed information on the care and management of these injuries, refer to Chapter 13.

Sprains

Sprains occur whenever a joint is forced through an abnormal range of motion (ROM) that results in damage to supporting structures such as ligaments and joint capsules. Because the thoracic spine is well supported, limited movement is allowed, thereby reducing the incidence of sprains. Evaluation of a sprain to the thoracic spine is difficult and must be based on a detailed history of the injury. An athlete with such an injury will usually report having sustained an unusual movement of the thoracic spine that is associated with localized pain, a

feeling of popping or snapping, and in some cases swelling. A consistent symptom of injury to the thoracic area is painful respiration, which is associated with many different injuries to the region, including rib fractures and contusions. First aid for sprains to the thoracic spine includes the application of RICE. If significant symptoms such as **dyspnea** (difficulty breathing) persist for more than 24 hours, the athlete should be referred to a medical doctor.

Strains

Strains involve primarily contractile tissues and their support structures—muscles, fascia, and tendons. The muscles of the thoracic spine region include the erector spinae and the intercostals. Strains may occur related to maximum exertion in sports requiring large amounts of force, such as tackle football, wrestling, or ice hockey. Signs and symptoms of strains may be very difficult to differentiate from sprains. Often the injury mechanism will be identical to that of a sprain. Muscle spasms of erector spinae in the region may be noticeable. These muscles may also be sensitive to touch (palpation) and should be inspected for this symptom. First aid for suspected strains of this region is the same as for sprains: application of RICE.

Intervertebral Disk Injuries

Although extremely rare in the thoracic region of the spine, injuries can occur to the intervertebral disks located between each of the vertebrae. Disk problems may be secondary to a compression fracture of thoracic vertebrae. Any athlete who complains of persistent neurologic symptoms, such as numbness or pain radiating around the thoracic region or into one or more of the extremities, should be referred immediately to a medical doctor for a more detailed evaluation.

Athletic Trainers SPEAK Out

Courtesy of Doris Flores, California State University, Sacramento.

To be in this field [one] definitely has to be a people person. Good communication skills are a necessity for [being effective] because you deal with so many individuals and groups as part of your responsibilities. Organizing the care of the athlete, from prevention to total rehabilitation, involves a number of people with [you] at the core.

—Doris E. Flores, ATC

Doris Flores is the Coordinator for the Athletic Training Program and the Director of the Athletic Training Laboratory at California State University at Sacramento.

Courtesy of Doris Flores, California State University, Sacramento.

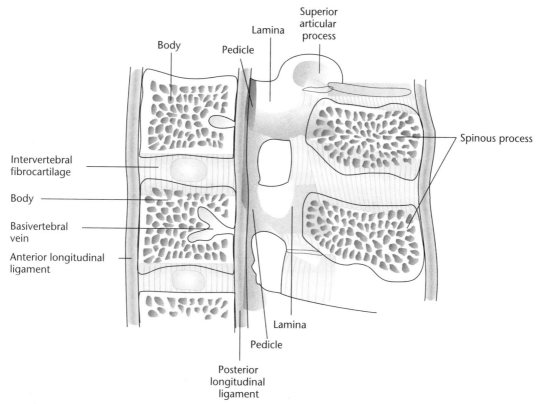

FIGURE 10.4 The lumbar vertebrae (sagittal view).

ANATOMY REVIEW OF THE LUMBAR SPINE DISTALLY TO THE COCCYX

The lumbar spine consists of five vertebrae that articulate superiorly with the thoracic vertebral column and inferiorly with the sacrum. The lumbar vertebrae are the largest vertebrae of all those that move—that is, cervical, thoracic, and lumbar (Gray, 1985). The lumbar vertebrae are numbered L-1 to L-5, from proximal to distal. As is the case with the thoracic and cervical sections of the spine, intervertebral disks are located between each of the lumbar vertebrae, as well as between T-12 and L-1 and between L-5 and S-1 (the first sacral vertebra). Additionally, large, strong ligaments assist in stabilization of the lumbar vertebrae (**Figure 10.4**), along with the thoracic spine and the sacrum. The anterior and posterior longitudinal ligaments are located on the anterior and posterior surfaces of the vertebral bodies (within the spinal cord canal), respectively. Both of these important ligaments span the vertebral column from the level of C-2 (axis) distal to the sacrum.

The sacrum, consisting of five fused vertebrae, is located between the two pelvic bones posteriorly. In essence, the sacrum serves to connect the spinal column to the pelvis (**Figure 10.5**). Two articulations, the right and left

sacroiliac joints, are formed by the union of the sacrum and the pelvis.

The most distal portion of the vertebral column is a small, arrowhead-shaped structure called the coccyx.

Common Sports Injuries

Injuries are more common to the lumbar spine than to the thoracic. Of all the injuries that can affect the bony portion of the lumbar spine, the most common is spondylolysis.

Spondylolysis and Spondylolisthesis

Spondylolysis (**Figure 10.6**) is a defect in the part of a vertebra that forms the bony ring around the spinal cord known as the neural arch (**Figure 10.7**). Spondylolysis involves the portion of the neural arch known as the pars interarticularis (there are two on each vertebra,

dyspnea Difficult or painful breathing.

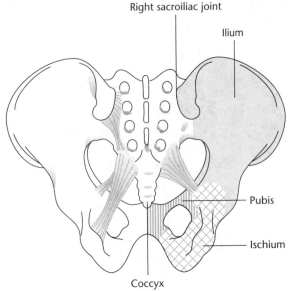

FIGURE 10.5 The pelvis (posterior view).

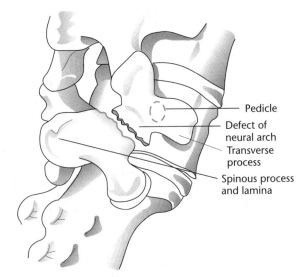

FIGURE 10.6 Defect of the neural arch that causes spondylolysis.

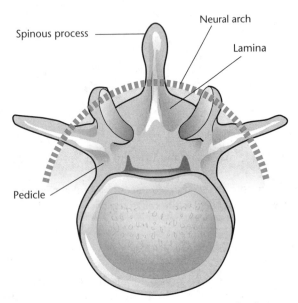

FIGURE 10.7 Overhead view of the neural arch of a typical lumbar vertebra.

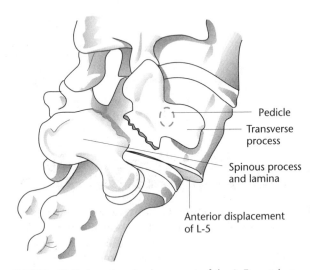

FIGURE 10.8 Anterior displacement of the L-5 vertebra that induces spondylolisthesis.

one on the right side and one on the left). The significance of bony defects in this region relates to superior articulations with adjacent vertebrae. Thus, any defect of the neural arch in this area can compromise the integrity of the articulation between any two vertebrae.

In cases in which both the right and left neural arches are affected, the involved vertebra has the potential to slide forward, thus producing a condition known as **spondylolisthesis**. As can be seen in **Figure 10.8**, the most common site for this condition is between L-5 and the sacrum (O'Leary & Boiardo, 1986). Given the normal slope of the sacrum, bony instability of the last lumbar vertebra makes anterior displacement possible,

especially when the lumbar region is subjected to abnormal amounts of stress, such as occurs in gymnastics, tackle football, or competitive weight lifting.

The exact **etiology** of spondylolysis is not clear; however, evidence suggests that the bony defects may be either congenital (present at birth) or related to excessive stress to the bones during childhood. The symptoms of spondylolysis include lower back pain, which becomes particularly acute when the lumbar spine is placed into **hyperextension**. When the defect is unilateral (one side only), standing on one leg in conjunction with lumbar hyperextension will elicit pain only on the side of the defect (Halpern & Smith, 1991). If spondylolysis progresses to spondylolisthesis, symptoms may become more severe. Pain in the lumbar region may increase during activity, and in some cases radiating pain may occur in the buttocks and upper thighs (Booher & Thibodeau, 1989).

Any athlete complaining of symptoms of this type, particularly those involved in high-risk sports for lumbar injuries (gymnastics, tackle football, and weight lifting), should be referred to a medical doctor for further evaluation. Treatment for spondylolysis and spondylolisthesis may include rest, drug therapy, lumbar bracing, exclusion from certain sports, and in severe cases surgical spinal fusion.

Traumatic Fractures

Traumatic fractures of the lumbar vertebrae are infrequent in sports. Such injuries will normally be associated with a history of a severe blow to the lumbar region. Depending on the specific location and type of fracture, neurologic symptoms, such as radiating pain into the buttocks or legs, may be present. Such injuries need to be treated initially with great care via immobilization on a spine board and transport to a medical facility, where complete evaluation by a physician can take place. It must be remembered that an external blow to the lumbar region may also cause injury to internal organs, specifically the kidneys. Thus, it is important that the athlete be evaluated for such an injury. Special attention should be given to the signs and symptoms of internal injury, such as deep abdominal pain, **hematuria**, or shock.

Injuries to the sacrum or coccyx are generally limited to those caused by direct blows. Such injuries are normally self-limited and require only protection from future trauma. One notable exception is a severe blow to the coccyx, which may result in a fracture or severe bruise. Such an injury can occur when an athlete falls backward, landing hard on the buttocks and impacting the coccygeal region. The signs and symptoms of this injury involve an observable bruise in the coccygeal region, severe point tenderness, and swelling. This injury needs to be evaluated by a medical doctor because a fracture may be present.

Sprains and Strains

By far the most common soft-tissue injuries to the lumbar region are strains and sprains (O'Leary & Boiardo, 1986). Strains involve the contractile tissues of the region, or the erector spinae muscles (**Figure 10.9**).

Sprains involve the many ligaments and joint capsules of the region. As previously mentioned, there are large ligaments (the anterior and posterior longitudinal ligaments) that bind the vertebral bodies together. In addition, there are ligaments and capsules binding the joints

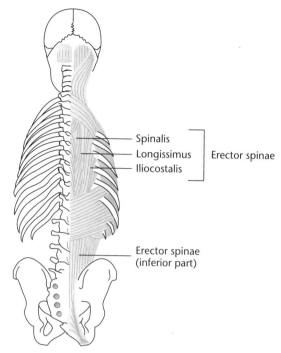

FIGURE 10.9 The erector spinae muscles of the upper and lower back.

between adjacent neural arches (facet joints). Major joints in the region include the lumbosacral, sacroiliac, and the sacrococcygeal. Generally, injuries to the joints are rare in this region. However, muscle strains occur frequently, particularly in sports that place significant stress on the lumbar spine. Activities such as gymnastics, tackle football, and weight lifting can place the athlete in situations in which abnormal loads are exerted on the lumbar region of the spine.

Signs and symptoms include the following:

1. Localized muscle spasm.
2. Pain that is increased with trunk movements.
3. Postural abnormality of the trunk, which often involves a lateral tilting of the trunk away from the affected side.
4. The athlete can link a specific incident with the onset of symptoms.

spondylolysis A defect in the neural arch (pars interarticularis) of the vertebrae.

spondylolisthesis Forward slippage of vertebra, usually between the fifth lumbar and the sacrum.

etiology Science dealing with causes of disease.

hyperextension Extreme stretching of a body part.

hematuria Blood in the urine.

5. In simple strains or sprains, pain will *not* radiate into the buttock or lower extremities.

First aid care:

1. Remove the athlete from participation with assistance, as any voluntary attempts to move will usually increase the pain.

2. Place the athlete in a position of lying supine, with the legs parallel and both knees drawn up so the knees and hips are flexed (**Figure 10.10**).

3. Place a rolled towel or some other soft material into the lumbar region for support.

4. Place a bag of crushed ice into the lumbar region.

5. Athlete should be instructed to sleep in this position and to continue ice application over the next 24 hours.

6. If symptoms are not significantly reduced during the first 24 hours after the injury, medical referral is warranted.

It is important to remember that an injury mechanism of sufficient magnitude to cause a strain may have also caused more severe injury. It is always best to refer such athletes for further evaluation by a medical doctor (Shankman, 1991). This is especially important in cases in which the athlete complains of pain radiating into one or both legs. Such symptoms can indicate a significant injury, such as a herniated disk (O'Leary & Boiardo, 1986).

Lumbar Disk Injuries

A more serious form of soft-tissue injury to the lumbar region involves damage within an intervertebral disk, commonly known as a **herniated disk**. Though such injuries can occur to any of the disks of the spine,

those most commonly injured in the lumbar region are L-4 and L-5 (Anderson, Hall, & Martin, 2000). Most often these injuries occur when an athlete is subjected to a great deal of force while in an awkward position. The anatomy of a typical intervertebral disk consists of an outer ring called the annulus fibrosus and a softer, inner portion known as the nucleus pulposus (Gray, 1985). In the case of a herniation, a weakness develops in the annulus, which then allows the nucleus pulposus to cause a protrusion through the wall of the annulus. Depending on the exact location of the herniation, pressure may be placed directly on the large spinal nerves passing through the region (**Figure 10.11**).

Signs and symptoms include the following:

1. Intense local pain that is aggravated with any attempts to sit up, walk, or stand.

2. Pain radiating into the buttock and lower extremity—radiating pain follows the distribution of the sciatic nerve.

3. Sensory loss or tingling/burning sensation radiating into the lower extremity.

4. Pain will be greatly increased by attempting maneuvers such as a straight-leg raise or a sit-up.

5. Muscle spasm and postural abnormalities.

6. In severe cases, disk herniation may interfere with normal bladder and/or bowel function.

First aid care:

1. Remove the athlete from participation with assistance because any voluntary attempts to move will usually increase the pain.

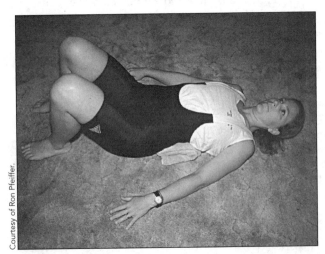

FIGURE 10.10 Recommended position for an athlete with acute lower back pain.

Courtesy of Ron Pfeiffer.

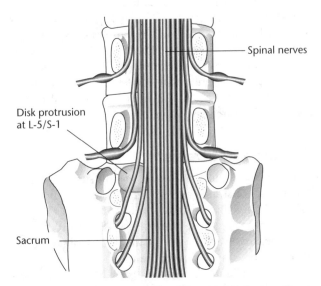

FIGURE 10.11 Disk protrusion at level L-5/S-1 may affect sacral nerves.

Spinal nerves

Disk protrusion at L-5/S-1

Sacrum

WHAT IF?

You are coaching gymnastics. One of your athletes just overrotated on a "double-back" on floor. As soon as she hit the mat, she collapsed to the floor, complaining of severe pain in her lumbar region. In addition, she complains of a burning sensation in the back of her thigh and lower leg. What type of injury might she have? What type of first aid care would you provide?

2. Place the athlete in a position of lying supine, with the legs parallel and both knees drawn up so the knees and hips are flexed (Figure 10.10); if this position is uncomfortable, allow the athlete to assume a position that is the least painful.

3. Place a rolled towel or some other soft material into the lumbar region for support.

4. Place a bag of crushed ice into the lumbar region.

5. Arrange for transport to a medical facility for evaluation.

6. Although little can be done in the field for such injuries, much can be done to alleviate long-term symptoms with a combination of physical therapy and drug therapy. The major goal of such a strategy is to return the athlete to participation and avoid the need for surgery.

herniated disk Rupture or protrusion of the nucleus pulposus through the annulus fibrosus of an intervertebral disk.

REVIEW QUESTIONS

1. True or false: Because of the bony relationship between the ribs and adjacent vertebrae, the thoracic spine is much less mobile than either the cervical or lumbar region of the spine is.

2. True or false: Available data indicate that soft-tissue injuries of the thoracic spine are more frequent than bone-related injuries are.

3. Describe briefly the condition known as Scheuermann's disease along with its signs and symptoms.

4. Define scoliosis, kyphosis, and lordosis.

5. What is a posterior rib fracture, and what are its common signs and symptoms?

6. What is a consistent symptom related to sprains in the thoracic spine?

7. True or false: Intervertebral disk injuries are extremely common to the thoracic spine.

8. Anatomically, the sacrum consists of how many fused vertebrae?

9. Describe the condition known as spondylolysis.

10. Describe briefly the condition known as spondylolisthesis, including both the signs and symptoms and recommended treatment.

11. What is the recommended immediate treatment for a suspected strain or sprain of the lumbar spine?

12. Describe briefly the normal anatomy of a typical lumbar intervertebral disk as well as the process of disk herniation.

13. What are the signs and symptoms of lumbar disk herniation?

REFERENCES

American Academy of Orthopaedic Surgeons (AAOS). (1991). *Athletic Training and Sports Medicine* (2d ed.). Park Ridge, Ill: American Academy of Orthopaedic Surgeons.

Anderson MK, Hall SJ, Martin M. (2000). *Sports Injury Management* (2d ed.). Philadelphia, Pa: Lippincott Williams & Wilkins.

Booher JM, Thibodeau GA. (1989). *Athletic Injury Assessment.* St. Louis, Mo: Times Mirror/Mosby.

Gray H. (1985). *Anatomy of the Human Body.* Philadelphia, Pa: Lea & Febiger.

Halpern BC, Smith AD. (1991). Catching the cause of low-back pain. *Phys Sportsmed.* 19:71–79.

O'Leary P, Boiardo R. (1986). The diagnosis and treatment of injuries of the spine in athletes. In Nicholas JA, Hershman EB (eds.). *The Lower Extremity and Spine in Sports Medicine* (pp. 1171–1229). St. Louis, Mo: Mosby.

Rasch PJ. (1989). *Kinesiology and Applied Anatomy.* Philadelphia, Pa: Lea & Febiger.

Shankman G. (1991). *Athletic Injury Care and Sports Conditioning.* Woodstock, Ga: Sports Health Education.

Injuries to the Shoulder Region

go.jblearning.com/PfeifferCWS

For a full suite of assignments and additional learning activities (indicated by the icons throughout the text), use the access code found in the front of your text. If you do not have an access code, you can obtain one at go.jblearning.com/PfeifferCWS.

The shoulder allows for a great deal of movement while at the same time providing a point of attachment for the arm to the thorax. The skeleton of the shoulder (**Figure 11.1**) consists of the bones of the shoulder girdle and the upper arm bone (humerus). The clavicle and the scapula make up the shoulder girdle, so named because these two bones surround (girdle) the upper thorax. The head of the humerus combines with the shallow glenoid fossa of the scapula to form the highly mobile **glenohumeral (GH) joint**, commonly known as the shoulder joint (**Figure 11.2**). The GH joint is provided with additional stability by a fibrocartilaginous cuplike structure known as the glenoid labrum, which is directly attached to the glenoid fossa (Gray, 1985). The labrum extends out into the GH joint, making the glenoid fossa a deeper receptacle for the head of the humerus (Snyder, Rames, & Wolber, 1991). In addition, the long-head tendon of the biceps brachii muscle is attached to the superior labrum and to the supraglenoid tubercle at the top of the GH joint. The shoulder region also includes the **acromioclavicular (AC) joint**, located between the distal end of the clavicle and the acromion of the scapula (Figure 11.2), and the **sternoclavicular (SC) joint**, located between the proximal end of the clavicle and the manubrium of the sternum (**Figure 11.3**). Each of these joints is held together with ligaments and joint capsules that provide stability while also allowing for necessary movement, which is quite limited.

Many muscles move both the shoulder girdle and the GH joint in a multitude of directions. In nearly all motions the

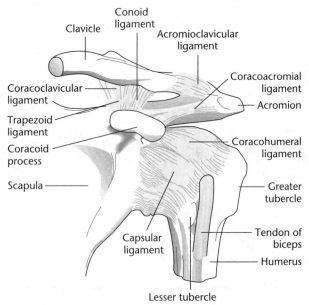

FIGURE 11.2 Ligaments of the acromioclavicular and glenohumeral joints.

shoulder girdle and the GH joint work together to move the arm. Consequently, any limitation from injury to the shoulder girdle will indirectly affect the GH joint. The muscles in the region of the shoulder can be divided into two groups—those that act on the shoulder girdle and those that act on the GH joint (**Figures 11.4** and **11.5**). The muscles of the shoulder girdle are the levator scapulae, trapezius, rhomboids, subclavius, pectoralis minor, and serratus anterior. These muscles collectively contribute to the movements of the shoulder girdle, which include scapular retraction and protraction, upward and downward scapular rotation, elevation, and depression. The muscles are listed with their specific actions and innervations in **Time Out 11.1**.

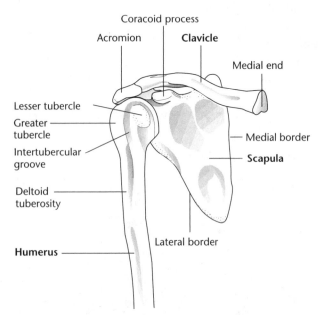

FIGURE 11.1 Skeleton of the shoulder region.

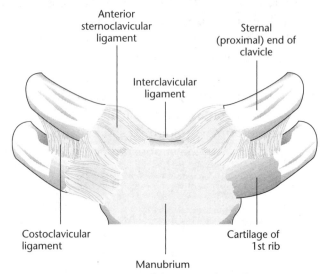

FIGURE 11.3 Ligaments of the sternoclavicular joint.

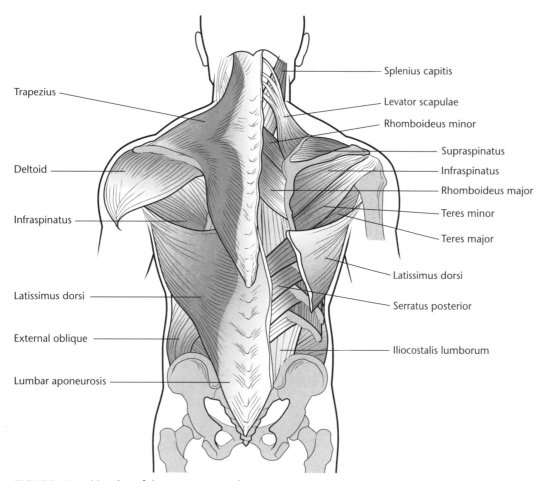

Trapezius

Deltoid

Infraspinatus

Latissimus dorsi

External oblique

Lumbar aponeurosis

Splenius capitis

Levator scapulae

Rhomboideus minor

Supraspinatus

Infraspinatus

Rhomboideus major

Teres minor

Teres major

Latissimus dorsi

Serratus posterior

Iliocostalis lumborum

FIGURE 11.4 Muscles of the posterior trunk region.

The muscles that act on the GH joint include the pectoralis major, latissimus dorsi, deltoid, teres major, rotator cuff muscles (supraspinatus, infraspinatus, teres minor, subscapularis), and coracobrachialis. The GH joint enjoys an astounding amount of movement, virtually in any direction; however, the following are the movements normally attributed to the joint: flexion, extension, horizontal flexion and extension, internal and external rotation, abduction, and adduction. The muscles are listed with their specific actions and innervations in **Time Out 11.2**.

In athletes a large amount of soft tissue covers both the shoulder girdle and the GH joint; as a result, they are somewhat protected from external blows. However, even in extremely muscular athletes both the AC and SC joints lie just under the skin and are therefore more exposed to external blows and subsequent injury. The blood supply to the entire upper extremity, including the shoulder, originates from branches of the subclavian artery. As this artery passes into the axillary region it becomes the axillary artery; it continues into the upper arm, becoming the brachial artery, and splits just distal to the elbow into the radial and ulnar arteries that extend into the forearm and hand (**Figure 11.6**).

The major nerves of the shoulder and upper extremity originate from the group known collectively as the brachial plexus (**Figure 11.7**). The brachial plexus originates from the ventral primary divisions of the fifth through the eighth cervical nerves and the first thoracic

glenohumeral (GH) joint Articulation (spheroid) formed by the head of the humerus and the glenoid fossa of the scapula.

acromioclavicular (AC) joint Articulation (arthrodial) formed by the distal end of the clavicle and the acromion process.

sternoclavicular (SC) joint Articulation (arthrodial) formed by the union of the proximal clavicle and the manubrium of the sternum.

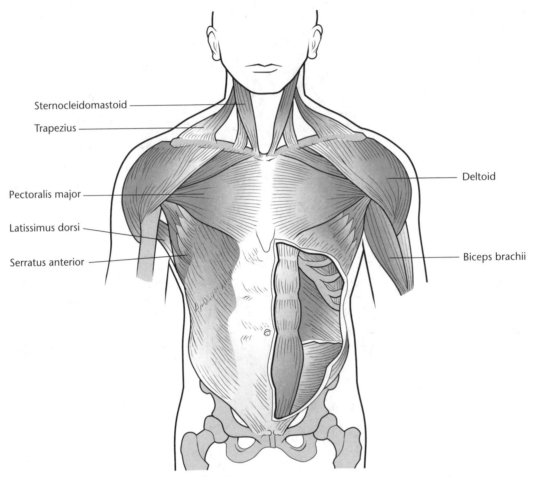

Sternocleidomastoid

Trapezius

Pectoralis major

Latissimus dorsi

Serratus anterior

Deltoid

Biceps brachii

FIGURE 11.5 Muscles of the pectoral region.

TIME OUT 11.1

Muscles, Actions, and Innervations of the Shoulder Girdle

Muscle	Action(s)	Innervation
Levator scapulae	Scapular elevation	Dorsal scapular
Rhomboids	Scapular retraction Downward rotation	Dorsal scapular
Trapezius	Elevation Retraction Upward rotation Depression	Spinal accessory
Pectoralis minor	Depression	Medial pectoral
Serratus anterior	Protraction Upward rotation	Long thoracic
Subclavius	Depression Stabilization of the SC joint	Nerve to the subclavius

Muscles, Actions, and Innervations of the Glenohumeral Joint

Muscle	Action(s)	Innervation
Pectoralis major	Adduction Internal rotation Flexion Extension	Medial and lateral pectoral
Latissimus dorsi	Extension Adduction Internal rotation	Thoracodorsal
Deltoid	Adduction Internal rotation Extension and lateral rotation Flexion and internal rotation	Axillary
Teres major	Adduction Internal rotation	Lower subscapular
Coracobrachialis	Flexion Adduction	Musculocutaneous
Rotator Cuff		
Supraspinatus	Adduction	Suprascapular
Infraspinatus	External rotation	Suprascapular
Teres minor	External rotation	Axillary
Subscapularis	Internal rotation Adduction	Upper and lower subscapular

nerve (Gray, 1985). Through a complex series of divisions, the brachial plexus provides all the major nerves to the entire upper extremity.

Common Sports Injuries

Injuries to the shoulder region are common in many sports and in some cases are highly sport specific. For example, injuries to the GH and AC joints are quite common in wrestling. Sports that emphasize a throwing or swinging action often produce injuries caused by overuse to the muscles of the rotator cuff (infraspinatus, supraspinatus, teres minor, subscapularis), which act on the GH joint. The rotator cuff muscles are extremely important to the stability of the GH joint because this large ball-and-socket structure lacks inherent strength due to the combination of the geometry of the glenoid fossa and the extensive joint capsule. Sports such as cycling and ice and in-line skating produce a large number of fractures of the clavicle brought about by falls. Injuries of the shoulder region can be classified as either acute (of sudden onset) or chronic (resulting from

overuse). Sports involving heavy contact or collisions yield more acute injuries; those necessitating repeated movements tend to produce more chronic injuries.

Skeletal Injuries
Fractured Clavicle

The most common fracture of the shoulder region is a fracture of the clavicle. Such fractures can result from direct blows to the bone; however, the majority occur as a result of falls that transmit the force to the clavicle either through the arm or shoulder. The majority of clavicular fractures occur about midshaft (**Figure 11.8**); the remainder involve either the proximal or distal end of the bone (American Academy of Orthopaedic Surgeons [AAOS], 1991). In the adolescent athlete another type of clavicular fracture, commonly known as a "greenstick fracture," can occur. This fracture occurs in immature bone and involves a cracking, splintering type of injury. Although a fractured clavicle is potentially dangerous given the close proximity of the bone to major blood vessels and nerves, the vast majority of these injuries cause few complications. It is critical that

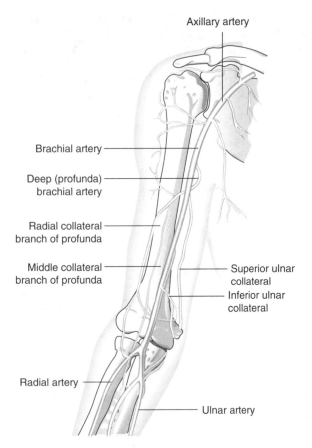

FIGURE 11.6 Major arteries of the arm.

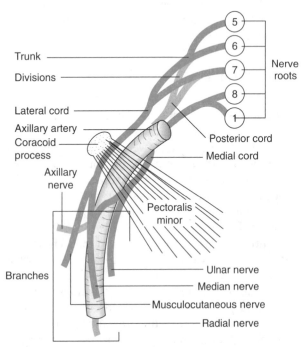

FIGURE 11.7 The nerves of the brachial plexus.

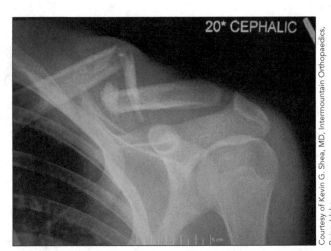

FIGURE 11.8 Fracture of the left clavicle (left shoulder).

Courtesy of Kevin G. Shea, MD, Intermountain Orthopaedics, Boise, Idaho.

appropriate first aid be applied to prevent unnecessary movement of the fracture that can result in additional soft-tissue damage.

Signs and symptoms of a fractured clavicle include the following:

- Swelling and/or deformity of the clavicle
- Discoloration at the site of the fracture
- Possible broken bone end projecting through the skin
- Athlete reporting that a snap or pop was felt or heard
- Athlete holding the arm on the affected side to relieve pressure on the shoulder girdle

To provide first aid care for a fractured clavicle:

1. Treat for possible shock.
2. Carefully apply a sling-and-swathe bandage as shown in **Figure 11.9** (National Safety Council, 1991).

Courtesy of Ron Pfeiffer.

FIGURE 11.9 A sling-and-swathe bandage is effective for a variety of injuries to the upper extremity.

3. Apply sterile dressings to any related wounds.

4. Arrange for transport to a medical facility.

Fractured Scapula

A much less common type of fracture in the shoulder region involves the scapula. A unique group of scapular fractures among professional football players was described by Cain and Hamilton (1992) in the *American Journal of Sports Medicine*. In all cases these fractures resulted from direct blows to the shoulder region. The symptoms of this type of fracture are less clear than those related to fractures of the clavicle. An athlete with a history of a severe blow to the shoulder region followed immediately by considerable pain and loss of function should be referred to a physician for further evaluation. This injury can be identified only by X-ray analysis. Treatment is determined by the specific location and extent of the fracture(s). Typically the athlete's arm will be placed in a sling, and the player will be removed from sports participation for a period of 6 weeks.

Soft-Tissue Injuries

A variety of sprains and strains involving any number of specific ligaments and tendons occurs in this region of the body. Although any joint can sustain a sprain, the GH and AC joints are the most commonly injured in the shoulder region in sports.

Acromioclavicular Joint Injuries

Located just under the skin on the lateral superior surface of the shoulder is the AC joint. This synoviated articulation is supported by the superior and inferior AC ligaments and contains an intra-articular cartilaginous disk (Dias & Gregg, 1991). Additional support to the AC joint is provided by the coracoclavicular (CC) ligament (see Figure 11.2), which comprises the trapezoid and conoid ligaments. The CC ligament is attached between the superior coracoid process and the inferior lateral surface of the clavicle.

The typical mechanism of injury for the AC joint is a downward blow, caused by falling or by some external blow other than a fall to the distal end of the clavicle, which results in the acromion process being driven inferiorly while the distal clavicle remains in place. Another mechanism, resulting in what has been described as an "indirect" injury, is a fall forward on an outstretched arm, which then transmits the force up the extremity and results in the humeral head being driven up into the acromion, again, resulting in disruption of the supporting ligaments (Mazzocca, Arciero, & Bicos, 2007).

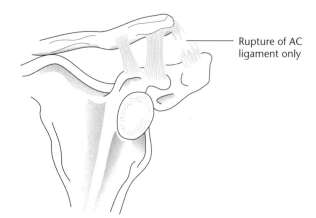

FIGURE 11.10 Type II injury—complete rupture of the acromioclavicular ligament with an intact coracoclavicular ligament.

Either of these two mechanisms can result in varying degrees of ligament damage. According to Rockwood, Williams, and Young (1998), AC injuries can be classified into one of six types, with the least severe being Type I with no AC ligament damage (sprain); Type II involves a tear of the AC ligament with the CC ligaments intact (**Figure 11.10**); Type III involves tearing of the AC and CC ligaments along with a dislocation of the AC joint (**Figure 11.11**); Type IV is characterized by ligament disruption along with a gross displacement of the clavicle posteriorly, piercing the trapezius muscle; Type V is characterized by a significant dislocation of the distal clavicle 100% to 300% from normal along with additional damage to the deltotrapezial fascia; Type VI involves a complete dislocation of the distal

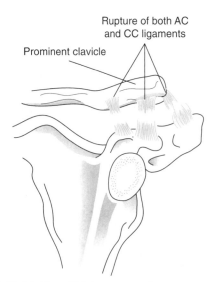

FIGURE 11.11 Type III injury—complete rupture of both the acromioclavicular and coracoclavicular ligaments.

clavicle to an inferior position (subacromial or subcoracoid) (Rockwood et al., 1998). The severity of the injury is graded based on the amount of damage to specific ligaments; however, any injury can be placed into one of the three following categories:

Signs and symptoms of AC joint sprains include the following:

- With Type I and II sprains, there will be mild swelling with point tenderness and discoloration around the AC joint. In the case of Type II, there will normally be more swelling and pain.
- Any movement of the shoulder region will elicit pain.
- With Type III and higher, there will be significant deformity in the region of the AC joint. Since these injuries involve complete ruptures of the AC and CC ligaments, there will be significant deformity present. Superior displacement of the clavicle results from the weight of the arm pulling down on the shoulder while the clavicle tends to move superiorly, creating the displacement that can be seen easily upon visual examination.
- The athlete may report having felt a snap or heard a pop.

To provide first aid care for AC joint sprains:

1. Immediately apply ice and compression. This is best accomplished by placing a bag of crushed ice over the AC joint and securing it with an elastic wrap tied in a figure-eight configuration.
2. Once the ice and compression are in place, apply a standard sling-and-swathe bandage as described by the National Safety Council (1991). This is a critical step because the sling helps to remove the stress to the injured AC joint by supporting the weight of the arm in the sling.
3. Immediately refer the athlete to a medical facility for further evaluation. In the event of severe injury, arrange for transport and treat for shock.

Long-term treatment for AC separations is dependent on the level of severity of the injury. Treatment for Types I and II is typically nonsurgical and includes rest and nonsteroidal anti-inflammatory drugs (NSAIDs), and in some cases the athlete will be asked to wear a special sling that uses straps to support the AC joint while healing. Once healed, depending on the sport, the athlete may be fitted with a sling/strap device that secures a protective pad over the AC joint.

There is ongoing debate within the medical community regarding the best treatment approach for Type III AC joint injuries. However, recent research supports a nonsurgical approach, even for athletes (Mazzocca et al., 2007). Given the extensive soft-tissue damage and clavicular displacement in more severe AC joint injuries (Types IV–VI), surgery is indicated.

Glenohumeral (GH) Joint Injuries

This articulation consists of the relatively large humeral head opposing the rather shallow glenoid fossa of the scapula. This bony arrangement is effective in giving the joint a great deal of mobility. As stated in the Anatomy Review section of this chapter, the stability of the joint is increased by the glenoid labrum. The GH joint is classified as a spheroidal articulation that moves within all three planes of motion: frontal, sagittal, and transverse. However, this mobility makes the GH joint very unstable (Grabiner, 1989). The major soft-tissue structures of the GH joint (Figure 11.2) include the capsular ligaments and the coracohumeral ligament (Gray, 1985).

The typical mechanism for a traumatic injury for the GH joint involves having the arm abducted and externally rotated. In this position the anterior portion of the joint capsule, specifically the GH ligament, can be stressed beyond its capacity. If the ligament fails, the head of the humerus can move forward and out of place, resulting in the most common type of GH joint dislocation, an anterior dislocation (**Figure 11.12**). Depending on the severity, this injury may be either a subluxation or a complete dislocation.

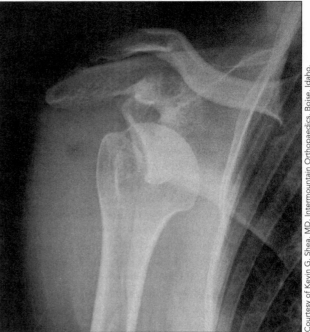

FIGURE 11.12 Anterior dislocation of the glenohumeral joint (right shoulder). Note the position of the humeral head relative to the glenoid fossa.

Courtesy of Kevin G. Shea, MD, Intermountain Orthopaedics, Boise, Idaho.

Signs and symptoms of an anterior GH joint dislocation include the following:

- Deformity of the shoulder joint: The normal contour of the shoulder is lost, and it appears to slope down abnormally.
- The arm of the affected side will appear longer than normal.
- The head of the humerus will be palpable with the axilla.
- The athlete will be supporting the arm on the affected side with the opposite arm; the affected arm will be slightly abducted at the shoulder and flexed at the elbow.
- The athlete will resist all efforts passively or actively to move the GH joint.
- Special note: In cases of subluxations of the GH joint, the shoulder may appear normal. However, it will be extremely painful for the athlete to attempt any movement. In addition, the joint may be point tender.

To provide first aid care for an anterior GH joint dislocation:

1. Immediately apply ice and compression. Put a rolled towel in the axilla. Place a bag of crushed ice on the front and back of the shoulder joint and secure with an elastic wrap tied in a figure-eight configuration.
2. After the ice and compression are in place, apply a standard sling-and-swathe bandage as described by the National Safety Council (1991).
3. Immediately refer the athlete to a medical facility for further evaluation.
4. Because soft-tissue injury may be extensive, treat for shock.

A common complication of GH joint sprains is chronic GH joint subluxation. It has been reported that, once sustained, up to 85% to 90% of all traumatic anterior GH joint dislocations recur (Arnheim, 1987). The joint capsule, ligaments, and supporting musculature are often stretched; therefore, as the athlete continues to participate in stressful activity the joint becomes progressively less stable. The athlete typically will report that during certain movements, often those placing the GH joint in abduction and external rotation, the joint will pop out and then return to its normal position.

Such cases are usually treated conservatively with rest and exercises that specifically focus on the muscles surrounding the joint, including those of the rotator cuff. In severe cases surgical reconstructive procedures may be prescribed.

As described earlier in this chapter, the glenoid labrum serves to help make the GH joint more stable. In addition, the long head of the biceps brachii provides stability to the GH joint by passing across the top of the humeral head en route to its attachment on the superior labrum and supraglenoid tubercle. An injury that is unique to this specific area of the GH joint is known as a superior labrum, anterior and posterior (SLAP) lesion (Snyder et al., 1990). The injury involves some level of damage to the superior labrum and in more severe cases it also involves damage to the attachment of the long head of the biceps brachii. The mechanisms of injury most recognized are either traction, such as in overhead throwing, or compression of the head of the humerus into the glenoid, which could occur when falling forward and reaching out to break the fall (Nam & Snyder, 2003). According to Snyder and colleagues (1990), there are four types of SLAP lesions, each distinguished from the others based either on the level of damage or the specific structures involved. Type I lesions are the least severe and are essentially limited to degenerative changes to the superior labrum without any associated disruption of either the labrum or the biceps tendon. Type II lesions involve the same degenerative types of changes to the otherwise intact labrum, however in this injury the biceps tendon is torn away from the supraglenoid tubercle. Type III lesions involve a tear of the superior labrum with an intact biceps tendon, and Type IV lesions have labral damage like Type III, but also have damage into the biceps tendon.

Signs and symptoms of a SLAP include the following:

- While this injury likely results from a single incident, the symptoms are highly variable and may persist, demonstrating a pattern of periodic remissions followed by recurrence of symptoms.
- With Types I and II, pain in and around the GH joint is sometimes associated with certain movements, including overhead movements such as throwing or reaching up.
- In more severe cases, the athlete may complain of a snapping or popping sensation within the GH joint (Nam & Snyder, 2003).
- The athlete may exhibit symptoms of a rotator cuff injury—weakness and nocturnal pain in the GH joint (Nam & Snyder, 2003).

To provide first aid care for SLAP:

1. Immediately apply ice and compression. This is best accomplished by placing a bag of crushed ice over the GH joint and securing it with an elastic wrap tied in a figure-eight configuration.

2. Once the ice and compression are in place, apply a standard sling-and-swathe bandage as described by the National Safety Council (1991). This is a critical step because the sling helps to remove the stress to the injured GH joint by supporting the weight of the arm in the sling.

3. Immediately refer the athlete to a medical facility for further evaluation. In the event of severe injury, arrange for transport and treat for shock.

Sternoclavicular Joint Injuries

The SC joint is formed by the union of the proximal end of the clavicle and the manubrium of the sternum. This synoviated articulation is strengthened by several ligaments (Figure 11.3). These include the joint capsule, the anterior and posterior SC ligaments, the interclavicular and costoclavicular ligaments, and an articular disk located within the joint (Gray, 1985).

Although there are fewer injuries to the SC joint than to either the AC or GH joints, the coach should be prepared to recognize and treat them correctly. The mechanism of injury for the SC joint involves an external blow to the shoulder region that results in a dislocation of the proximal clavicle, most commonly with the bone moving anteriorly and superiorly. A sprain to the SC joint can range in severity from minor stretching, with no actual tearing of tissues, to a complete rupture of ligaments and extensive soft-tissue damage. Fortunately, anterior/superior dislocations cause few additional problems and are easily treated. Occurring much less frequently, but potentially more dangerous, is a posterior SC dislocation. In this instance the proximal end of the clavicle is displaced posteriorly, with the possibility of placing direct pressure on soft-tissue structures in the region, such as blood vessels or even the esophagus and trachea (AAOS, 1991).

Signs and symptoms of SC joint injuries include the following:

* In most cases (second- and third-degree sprains), there will be gross deformity present at the SC joint.
* In all but the least severe cases, swelling will be immediate.
* Movement of the entire shoulder girdle will be limited owing to pain within the SC joint.
* The athlete will typically report having heard a snapping sound or may have experienced a tearing sensation at the SC joint.
* Note the body position of the athlete, because in this injury the arm may be held close to the body and the head/neck may be tilted/flexed toward the injured shoulder (Wroble, 1995).

To provide first aid care for SC joint injuries:

1. Apply ice and compression, which is best accomplished using a plastic bag filled with crushed ice that is secured with an elastic wrap tied in a figure-eight configuration. Take care not to put pressure over the airway when wrapping the shoulder for compression of the SC joint.

2. Place the arm of the affected shoulder in a standard sling-and-swathe bandage as described by the National Safety Council (1991).

3. In cases of severe soft-tissue damage, treat the athlete for shock.

Medical treatment for the majority of SC joint sprains is conservative, that is, reduction of the dislocation if present followed by 2 to 3 weeks of support with a sling-and-swathe bandage. It is very rare that any sort of surgical correction is attempted, especially in the case of anterior dislocations. Obviously, a sound program of rehabilitation exercises prescribed by a competent sports medicine professional will be helpful in getting the athlete back into action.

Strains of the Shoulder Region

A large number of muscles attach to the bones of the shoulder girdle, any one of which can suffer a strain. As mentioned earlier, certain sports produce very specific injuries to the shoulder. Perhaps the most common strain involves the muscles of the rotator cuff.

Rotator Cuff

The muscles of the **rotator cuff** (**Figures 11.13** and **11.14**) serve a variety of purposes, including stabilization of the humeral head in the glenoid fossa as well as abduction and internal and external rotation of the GH joint.

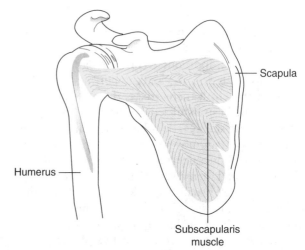

FIGURE 11.13 The rotator cuff (anterior view).

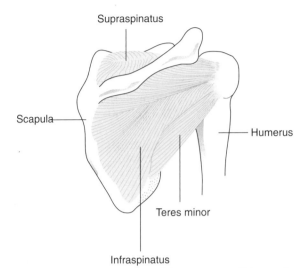

FIGURE 11.14 The muscles of the rotator cuff (posterior view).

To better understand the mechanism of injuries involving the rotator cuff, it is necessary to review the kinesiology of the overhand throw and/or swing. Throwing has been described as a five-phase process involving windup, cocking, acceleration, release, and follow-through (AAOS, 1991). Essentially, the windup phase requires putting the entire body into the best position to generate throwing forces. The cocking stage involves pulling the throwing arm into an abducted and externally rotated position at the GH joint; this incorporates a **concentric contraction** of several of the rotator cuff muscles, as well as other muscles of the shoulder region. The acceleration phase involves a sudden reversal of cocking: The arm is moved rapidly into internal rotation, horizontal flexion, and adduction of the GH joint via concentric contractions of muscles such as the pectoralis major, anterior deltoid, teres major, latissimus dorsi, and triceps. Depending on the skill and strength of the athlete, the forces generated during the acceleration phase can be substantial and must be dealt with effectively during follow-through. The release phase is the shortest in the throwing cycle and involves timing the release at the point of maximum velocity. The follow-through phase requires that the entire upper extremity be decelerated immediately after the release. It is critical to note that several muscles of the rotator cuff are actively contracting eccentrically in an effort to slow the arm down.

The vast majority of strains to the rotator cuff occur during the follow-through phase, specifically during the eccentric phase of the contraction. This problem is made worse when the muscles of the rotator cuff are significantly weaker than those muscles involved in the acceleration phase. This problem can best be addressed with a properly designed conditioning program aimed at strengthening the muscles of the rotator cuff.

Strains to the rotator cuff are normally the result of overuse: They develop slowly over many weeks or months. Athletes who are involved in sports that require throwing and swinging are at risk for this type of injury, especially athletes with weak rotator cuffs or those who are older. Proper warm-up of the throwing and/or swinging arm can help reduce the stress on the musculature of the shoulder girdle. Often errors in execution of the throw or swing can contribute to overuse injury. Therefore, it is critical that athletes learn correct techniques to reduce the chances of developing an injury.

Signs and symptoms of rotator cuff injuries include the following:

- Pain within the shoulder, especially during the follow-through phase of a throw or swing
- Difficulty in bringing the arm up and back during the cocking phase of a throw or swing
- Pain and stiffness within the shoulder region 12 to 24 hours after a practice or competition that involved throwing or swinging
- Point tenderness around the region of the humeral head that appears to be deep within the deltoid muscle (It should be noted that rotator cuff injuries can mimic many others common to the shoulder region, including **bursitis** and **tendinitis**.)

First aid care of rotator cuff strains must take the following into consideration:

1. Overuse injuries are difficult to treat effectively without a thorough medical evaluation. When symptoms occur, the application of ice and compression may prove helpful in reducing the pain and loss of function associated with the injury.

2. In the majority of cases, the athlete will report repeated episodes of symptoms spanning many weeks or even months. Therefore, medical referral for a complete evaluation is essential.

rotator cuff Group of four muscles of the glenohumeral joint: subscapularis, supraspinatus, infraspinatus, and teres minor.
concentric contraction Occurs when a muscle shortens and there is movement at the joint accompanied by contraction against resistance.
bursitis Inflammation of a bursa.
tendinitis Inflammation of a tendon.

Glenohumeral Joint–Related Impingement Syndrome

To *impinge* means to be forced "upon or against something" (Guralnik & Friend, 1966). A **syndrome** is defined as "a number of symptoms occurring together and characterizing a specific disease" (Guralnik & Friend, 1966). Hence, an impingement syndrome of the shoulder occurs when a soft-tissue structure such as a bursa or tendon is squeezed between moving joint structures, resulting in irritation and pain. In the case of the GH joint, the most common impingement occurs to the tendon of the supraspinatus muscle as it passes across the top of the joint en route to its insertion (Lo, Hsu, & Chan, 1990). The normal anatomy of the GH joint is a tight fit relative to the amount of available space for structures above the joint capsule. This region, located directly beneath the acromion process, is known as the subacromial space. The floor of the subacromial space is the GH joint capsule. The ceiling comprises the acromion process and the coracoacromial ligament, which form an arch across the top of the GH joint known as the coracoacromial arch (**Figure 11.15**).

Any condition, whether related to sports or congenital, that decreases the size of the subacromial space may result in the development of an impingement syndrome. Various experts in the sports medicine community have reported that the most common causes of GH joint–related impingement syndromes are "anatomic variations in the coracoacromial arch" that cause damage to the structures found in the subacromial space (Burns & Turba, 1992).

Athletes who participate in sports placing an emphasis on arm movements above the shoulder level demonstrate a higher rate of impingement problems when compared with athletes who take part in sports not emphasizing such movements. A survey of athletes in sports requiring repetitive arm motions found the high-risk sports to include volleyball, badminton, basketball, gymnastics, squash, swimming, table tennis, tennis, and track and field events (Lo, Hsu, & Chan, 1990).

Signs and symptoms of impingement syndromes include the following:

- Pain when the GH joint is abducted and externally rotated in conjunction with loss of strength
- Pain whenever the arm is abducted beyond 80 to 90 degrees
- Nocturnal pain (AAOS, 1991)
- Pain felt deep within the shoulder (AAOS, 1991)

First aid care of impingement syndromes involving the GH joint is not required because they tend to develop over many days, weeks, or even months. Rather, any athlete complaining of the signs and symptoms listed should be referred for a complete medical evaluation. Treatment will consist of rest, anti-inflammatory drugs, and physical therapy. If these fail, surgery to correct the problem may be prescribed. In many cases this can be done via arthroscopy; typically, it involves procedures such as removal of bone spurs from beneath the acromion process, release of the coracoacromial ligament, or a resectioning of a

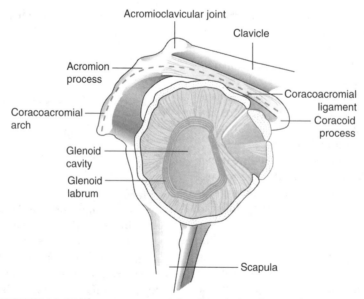

FIGURE 11.15 The coracoacromial arch and glenohumeral joint (lateral view).

portion of the undersurface of the acromion process (partial acromionectomy; AAOS, 1991).

Biceps Tendon Problems

The anatomy of the GH joint (**Figure 11.16**) includes the tendon of the long head of the biceps brachii muscle. The tendon passes into the joint capsule and is surrounded by a specialized portion of the synovium of the joint. As the tendon continues through the joint, it runs across the superior surface of the humeral head; in this position the tendon helps to stabilize the humeral head when the joint is abducted. The tendon of the long head of the biceps brachii originates from the supraglenoid tubercle (Gray, 1985). The short head of the biceps brachii derives from the nearby coracoid process. This tendon, however, remains anatomically separate from the GH joint.

The tendon of the long head of the biceps brachii is located directly beneath the acromion process; therefore, it can suffer a type of impingement similar to that seen in the supraspinatus tendon. As the joint is abducted the tendon may be compressed within the subacromial space. Consequently, symptoms similar to those of impingement of the supraspinatus will develop. Athletes at risk for this injury include those involved in sports that place an emphasis on repetitive overhead movements with the arms.

Another problem related to the long-head tendon of the biceps brachii is tendinitis, which may lead to a subluxation of the tendon from the bicipital groove. In most cases, tendinitis will develop slowly over a period of weeks or months. As the tendon enlarges as a result of the inflammation, it becomes less stable in the groove, where it is held by way of the transverse humeral ligament.

In chronic cases, a sudden violent force such as is commonly generated in throwing may cause the tendon to subluxate out of the groove, thereby stretching and tearing the ligament. The athlete will notice significant symptoms if the tendon subluxates from the bicipital groove.

Signs and symptoms of biceps tendon problems include the following:

- Painful abduction of the shoulder joint similar to that seen in impingement problems
- Pain in the shoulder joint when the athlete supinates the forearm against any resistance
- When actively flexing and supinating the forearm against resistance, the athlete may note a popping or snapping sensation as the tendon of the long head of the biceps brachii subluxates.

First aid care of biceps tendon problems is not a practical concern because they generally develop over time and fall into the category of a chronic injury. However, if the athlete should subluxate the biceps tendon from the bicipital groove, the initial episode of this injury can require first aid. In such cases, the immediate application of ice and compression is recommended. Long-term care for this injury includes rest, anti-inflammatories, and gradually progressive exercise rehabilitation. If symptoms persist and the tendon continues to subluxate from the bicipital groove, then surgery may be required to stabilize the tendon.

Contusions of the Shoulder Region

External blows around the shoulder region are a common occurrence in a variety of sports. The GH joint is well protected by muscles crossing over the joint, such as the deltoid. The nearby AC joint, however, is exposed and quite vulnerable to external blows. If the athlete sustains a contusion to this joint, the result can be an extremely painful condition known as a **shoulder pointer**.

Signs and symptoms of shoulder contusions include the following:

- History of a recent blow to the shoulder, with resulting pain and decreased range of motion

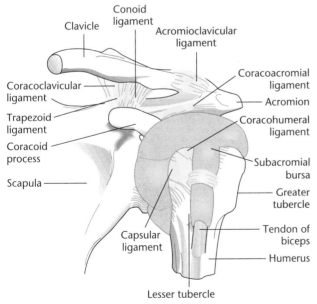

FIGURE 11.16 The glenohumeral joint (anterior view).

Labels: Clavicle; Conoid ligament; Acromioclavicular ligament; Coracoacromial ligament; Acromion; Coracohumeral ligament; Subacromial bursa; Greater tubercle; Tendon of biceps; Humerus; Lesser tubercle; Capsular ligament; Scapula; Coracoid process; Trapezoid ligament; Coracoclavicular ligament

syndrome Group of typical symptoms or conditions that characterize a deficiency or disease.

shoulder pointer Contusion and subsequent hematoma in the region of the acromioclavicular joint.

Athletic Trainers SPEAK Out

When there is an emergency in athletics, everyone looks to the certified athletic trainer for leadership and confidence in handling the situation. Practicing a simple task can help make sure you are always prepared: Every day when walking out to your venue, consider the worst-case scenario that could transpire, and mentally review each step you need to do to successfully manage it. Because each day and every practice is different, training your mental skills for emergency situations is an excellent preparation for unexpected events. It is the single most important exercise I do daily to prepare me for any situation in athletics. I highly recommend you incorporate it in your daily walk to practice.

—Katie Walsh, EdD, ATC, LAT

Katie Walsh is Director of the Sports Medicine/Athletic Training Program at East Carolina University.

Courtesy of Katie Walsh, East Carolina University.

Courtesy of Katie Walsh, East Carolina University.

- Spasm if muscle tissue is involved
- Discoloration and swelling, especially over bony regions such as the AC joint

First aid care of shoulder contusions includes the following:

1. Immediately apply ice and compression directly over the area(s) involved. This is best accomplished with a bag of crushed ice and an elastic wrap.
2. In cases of severe pain, apply an arm sling to relieve stress on the shoulder region.
3. If significant swelling persists for more than 72 hours in the region of the AC joint, refer the athlete to a physician. In some cases the AC ligament may have sustained a sprain.

WHAT IF?

You are at a high school wrestling tournament examining an athlete who just sustained a shoulder injury. You notice a large mass in the armpit area as well as a definite sloping of the shoulder's contour. The athlete is holding his arm in slight abduction and states that he felt his shoulder "pop out." What would you conclude based upon all of this information? How would you manage this injury?

WHAT IF?

You are examining a baseball player (center fielder) who is complaining of chronic pain in the back of his shoulder. He notices the pain especially after he throws a ball, and he is point tender in the region of the posterior scapula. What structure could be involved in this case?

REVIEW QUESTIONS

1. Which two bones make up the shoulder girdle?
2. To what structure is the glenoid labrum attached?
3. Which one of the following arteries provides the blood supply to the shoulder region and upper extremity?
   a. Common iliac
   b. Ulnar
   c. Internal carotid
   d. Subclavian
   e. Axillary
4. Which one of the following is the correct derivation of the brachial plexus?
   a. C-5/T-2
   b. C-3/T-1
   c. C-1/T-5
   d. C-1/T-1
   e. C-5/T-1
5. List the four muscles of the rotator cuff group and identify one action common to each muscle.

6. List four signs and/or symptoms of a fractured clavicle.

7. Describe and/or demonstrate the appropriate first aid procedures for a fractured clavicle.

8. Describe the major ligaments that form the AC joint.

9. Describe briefly the two mechanisms of injury for the AC joint as discussed in the chapter.

10. Describe the common signs and symptoms of AC joint injuries.

11. Explain and/or demonstrate the appropriate first aid care for AC joint injuries.

12. List the major ligaments of the GH joint.

13. True or false: The most common type of GH joint dislocation is posterior.

14. Describe the common signs and symptoms of a GH joint dislocation.

15. Explain and/or demonstrate the appropriate first aid treatment of an athlete with a suspected GH joint dislocation.

16. Define the condition known as chronic GH joint subluxation.

17. Describe the primary ligaments of the SC joint.

18. Describe the common signs and symptoms of injury to this articulation.

19. Explain and/or demonstrate the appropriate first aid treatment of an athlete with a suspected SC joint injury.

20. Explain the five phases of an overhand throw and/or swing and give a brief description of the types of muscle contractions involved in each.

21. True or false: The vast majority of strains of the rotator cuff occur during the windup and cocking phases of the throw and/or swing.

22. List several of the signs and symptoms of rotator cuff strain as described in the chapter.

23. What anatomic structure forms a ceiling for the subacromial space?

24. True or false: Athletes involved in sports placing a heavy emphasis on arm movements below the shoulder level demonstrate a higher incidence of impingement syndromes.

25. List four signs and/or symptoms of impingement syndrome of the GH joint.

26. Which one of the following structures (ligaments) holds the biceps (long head) tendon in the bicipital groove?
    a. Annular ligament
    b. Medial collateral ligament
    c. Capsular ligament
    d. Transverse humeral ligament

REFERENCES

American Academy of Orthopaedic Surgeons (AAOS). (1991). *Athletic Training and Sports Medicine* (2nd ed.). Park Ridge, Ill: American Academy of Orthopaedic Surgeons.

Arnheim DD. (1987). *Essentials of Athletic Training* (1st ed.). St. Louis, Mo: Times Mirror/Mosby.

Bach BR, VanFleet TA, Novak PJ. (1992). Acromioclavicular injuries—controversies in treatment. *Phys Sportsmed.* 20:87–101.

Burns TP, Turba JE. (1992). Arthroscopic treatment of shoulder impingement in athletes. *Am J Sports Med.* 20:13–16.

Cain TE, Hamilton WP. (1992). Scapular fractures in professional football players. *Am J Sports Med.* 20:363–365.

Dias JJ, Gregg PJ. (1991). Acromioclavicular joint injuries in sport—recommendations for treatment. *Sports Med.* 11:125–132.

Grabiner MD. (1989). The shoulder complex. In: Rasch PJ (ed.), *Kinesiology and Applied Anatomy.* Philadelphia, Pa: Lea & Febiger.

Gray H. (1985). *Anatomy of the Human Body.* Philadelphia, Pa: Lea & Febiger.

Guralnik DB, Friend JH (eds.). (1966). *Webster's New World Dictionary of the American Language.* Cleveland, Oh: The World Publishing Company.

Lo YPC, Hsu YCS, Chan KM. (1990). Epidemiology of shoulder impingement in upper-arm sports events. *Br J Sports Med.* 24:173–177.

Mazzocca AD, Arciero RA, Bicos, J. (2007). Evaluation and treatment of acromioclavicular joint injuries. *Am J Sports Med.* 35(2):316–329.

Nam EK, Snyder SJ. (2003). The diagnosis and treatment of superior labrum, anterior and posterior (SLAP) lesions. *Am J Sports Med.* 31(5):798–810.

National Safety Council. (1991). *First Aid and CPR.* Boston, Mass: Jones and Bartlett.

Rockwood CJ, Williams G, Young D. (1998). Disorders of the acromioclavicular joint. In: Rockwood CJ, Matsen FA, III (eds.), *The Shoulder.* Philadelphia, PA: WB Saunders.

Snyder SJ, Karzel RP, Del Pizzo W, Ferkel RD, Friedman MJ. (1990). SLAP lesions of the shoulder. *Arthroscopy.* 6:274–279.

Snyder SJ, Rames RD, Wolber E. (1991). Labral lesions. In: McGinty JB (ed.), *Operative Arthroscopy.* New York: Raven Press.

Wroble RR. (1995). Sternoclavicular injuries—managing damage to an overlooked joint. *Phys Sportsmed.* 23:19–26.

Injuries to the Arm, Wrist, and Hand

MAJOR CONCEPTS

This chapter begins with a brief review of the gross anatomy of the entire arm region with special emphasis on arthrology. It goes on to discuss upper arm (brachial region) injuries, focusing especially on contusions and fractures. Given the potentially serious consequences of fractures of the humerus, the chapter provides detailed instructions for proper first aid care of these injuries. Next, the chapter reviews elbow injuries, outlining current information regarding the typical mechanisms, signs and symptoms, and critical first aid procedures. Again, because there are potential catastrophic consequences of a mismanaged elbow injury, this section provides specific first aid instructions. It also discusses problems related to the muscle attachments surrounding the elbow, clinically known as epicondylitis, along with special attention paid to the possible causes, signs and symptoms, and care.

Although quite rare, forearm injuries do occasionally occur, and the chapter reviews the more frequent varieties, along with guidelines on signs and symptoms and first aid care. Next it discusses injuries to the wrist, emphasizing relatively common injuries such as fractures of the scaphoid bone and dislocations of the lunate bone. Nerve injuries of the wrist region are common; carpal tunnel syndrome is perhaps the most well known. Therefore, the chapter outlines specific signs and symptoms for nerve problems involving the median and ulnar nerves.

Finally, the chapter discusses hand and finger injuries, which are both extremely common in sports.

go.jblearning.com/PfeifferCWS

For a full suite of assignments and additional learning activities (indicated by the icons throughout the text), use the access code found in the front of your text. If you do not have an access code, you can obtain one at go.jblearning.com/PfeifferCWS.

ANATOMY REVIEW

The bones of the arm are the humerus (upper arm), the radius, and the ulna (forearm). The proximal end of the humerus (head) articulates with the glenoid fossa of the scapula to form the shoulder (glenohumeral) joint. The distal end of the humerus articulates with both of the forearm bones to form the elbow joint, which actually comprises three specific articulations—the **humeroulnar**, **humeroradial**, and proximal **radioulnar** joints. The distal end of the forearm articulates with the wrist (carpal) bones, forming the **radiocarpal** (wrist) and distal radioulnar joints. The joints of the arm allow for a great variety of motions, including flexion/extension and pronation/supination at the elbow as well as flexion/extension and radial and ulnar deviation at the wrist. The elbow (**Figure 12.1**) and wrist joints are held together with several ligaments that may be subject to trauma related to sports participation. Certainly one of the more distinctive ligament structures in the human body is the annular ligament of the elbow (**Figure 12.2**). This ligament holds the head of the radius in the proximal radioulnar joint; in so doing it allows that articulation to pronate and supinate while simultaneously allowing the radial head to articulate with the capitellum of the humerus.

As can be seen in **Figure 12.3**, the musculature of the arm is extensive. It is dominated by the elbow extensor and flexors that include the biceps brachii, brachialis, triceps brachii, and anconeus. The muscles of the arm collectively contribute to several of the movements of the elbow; they are extension, flexion, and supination. The muscles

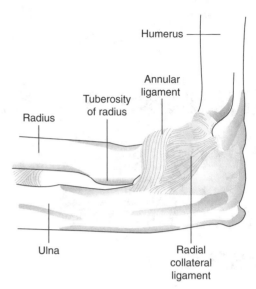
FIGURE 12.2 The elbow joint (lateral view).

are listed along with their specific actions and innervations in **Time Out 12.1**.

The forearm includes a large number of muscles for the movements of the forearm, wrist, hand, and fingers. The majority of the forearm muscles originate from the regions of the humeral epicondyles, either lateral or medial, that are located immediately proximal to the elbow joint. The muscles of the forearm can be divided into the extensor/supinator and flexor/pronator groups (**Figures 12.4 and 12.5**). These muscles collectively contribute to the pronation and supination of the elbow, flexion and extension of the wrist and fingers, flexion and extension of the thumb, and radial and ulnar deviation of the wrist. The muscles are listed with their specific actions and innervations in **Time Out 12.2**.

Soft-Tissue Injuries to the Upper Arm

The majority of injuries to the upper arm are either contusions or fractures. Though strains do occur to this region, they are exceedingly uncommon. Because of the nature of contact sports, blows to the arm region are a common occurrence. A typical scenario involves a football lineman blocking with arms flexed at the elbows and receiving blows to the lateral surfaces of the upper arms. The underlying muscle tissue is compressed between the overlying skin and the bone of the humerus. Depending on the magnitude of the blow(s), damage to the muscle tissue may be significant. If such episodes are repeated, the athlete may develop a condition known as myositis ossificans traumatica.

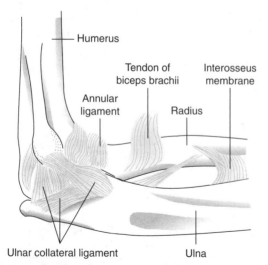
FIGURE 12.1 The elbow joint (medial view).

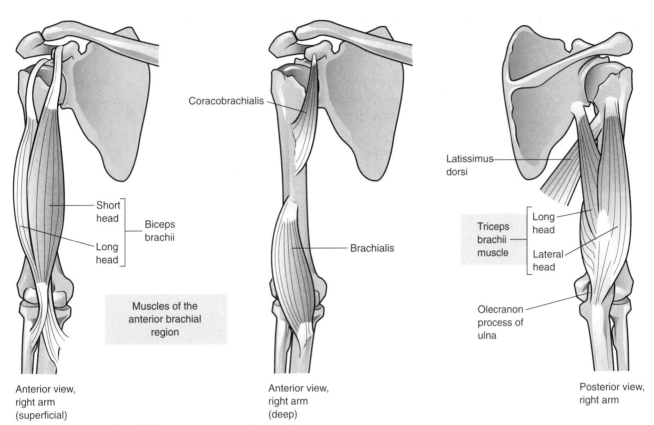

Anterior view, right arm (superficial)

Short head ⎤
Long head ⎦ Biceps brachii

Muscles of the anterior brachial region

Anterior view, right arm (deep)

Coracobrachialis

Brachialis

Posterior view, right arm

Latissimus dorsi

Triceps brachii muscle ⎱ Long head / Lateral head

Olecranon process of ulna

FIGURE 12.3 Muscles of the arm, anterior and posterior.

Myositis Ossificans Traumatica

Myositis ossificans traumatica involves chronic inflammation of muscle, leading to the development of bonelike tissue in the muscle. It is quite common in football—so much so that the condition has become known as **tackler's exostosis** (American Academy of Orthopaedic Surgeons [AAOS], 1991). An **exostosis** is defined as "a benign growth projecting from a bone surface characteristically capped by cartilage" (Friel, 1977). Myositis ossificans traumatica develops over a period of weeks or even months and therefore tends to be ignored in early stages of development, when it is typically dismissed as a simple bruise. It is important that the coach recognize that such an injury can develop into a more serious one and evaluate it accordingly.

Signs and symptoms of upper arm contusions include the following:

* Recent history of contusion to the region
* Pain, discoloration, and swelling in the region of the injury
* Muscle spasm and subsequent loss of strength in the affected muscle

humeroulnar joint Articulation (ginglymus) formed by the proximal end of the ulna, specifically the trochlear notch, with the distal end of the humerus, specifically the trochlea.

humeroradial joint Articulation (arthrodial) formed by the proximal end of the radius and the distal end of the humerus, specifically the capitellum.

radioulnar joints Two articulations (pivot) formed by the proximal and distal radius and ulna, known commonly as the proximal and distal radioulnar joints.

radiocarpal joint Articulation (ellipsoidal) formed by the distal end of the radius and three bones of the wrist: navicular, lunate, and triquetral.

myositis Inflammation of muscle.

tackler's exostosis Formation of a benign growth projecting from the humerus that is caused by repeated blows to the upper arm region; common in tackle football.

exostosis Bony outgrowths that protrude from the surface of a bone where there is not a typical bony formation.

- Possible neurologic symptoms, including loss of sensation or muscle function distal to the site of injury

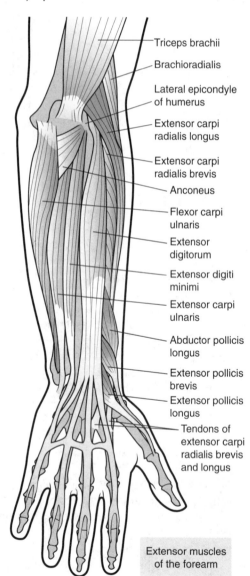

- Triceps brachii
- Brachioradialis
- Lateral epicondyle of humerus
- Extensor carpi radialis longus
- Extensor carpi radialis brevis
- Anconeus
- Flexor carpi ulnaris
- Extensor digitorum
- Extensor digiti minimi
- Extensor carpi ulnaris
- Abductor pollicis longus
- Extensor pollicis brevis
- Extensor pollicis longus
- Tendons of extensor carpi radialis brevis and longus

Extensor muscles of the forearm

FIGURE 12.4 Extensor muscles of the forearm.

First aid care of upper arm contusions involves the following:

1. Immediately apply ice and compression. This is best accomplished by using a bag of crushed ice that is secured with a wide elastic wrap tied around the arm.

2. Place the arm in a sling to immobilize the limb for a period of 24 hours.

In cases of severe acute pain or symptoms that persist beyond 72 hours, refer the athlete for a complete medical evaluation.

Triceps Injuries

A less common group of injuries to the upper arm involves the triceps muscle. The mechanism of injury may be either a direct blow to the posterior elbow or a fall on an outstretched hand. Either mechanism can result in a partial or complete rupture in the muscle or its tendon. The majority of these injuries involve an avulsion fracture of the triceps insertion on the olecranon process of the ulna (Anderson, Hall, & Martin, 2005). While these injuries are relatively rare, they can be extremely disabling and may be associated with either a fracture of the radial head or the olecranon process. Anderson and colleagues (2005) found that they occurred among a wide range of athletes, including a competitive weight lifter, a body builder, an alpine skier, and a volleyball player. By definition, all these injuries fall into the general category of muscle strains and/or avulsion fractures; depending on their relative severity and precise location, they may require immediate medical attention. In cases that involve partial or complete ruptures or avulsion fractures of the olecranon process, surgical intervention is necessary (Anderson, Hall, & Martin, 2005). Even in less severe cases involving only partial tears, the injury requires an extensive period of immobilization (1 month) in a splint with the elbow positioned at 30 degrees of flexion (Holleb & Bach, 1990).

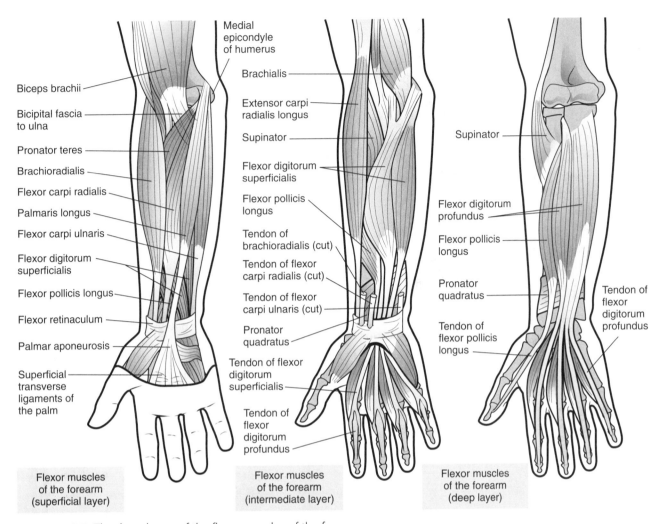

Biceps brachii

Bicipital fascia to ulna

Pronator teres

Brachioradialis

Flexor carpi radialis

Palmaris longus

Flexor carpi ulnaris

Flexor digitorum superficialis

Flexor pollicis longus

Flexor retinaculum

Palmar aponeurosis

Superficial transverse ligaments of the palm

Medial epicondyle of humerus

Brachialis

Extensor carpi radialis longus

Supinator

Flexor digitorum superficialis

Flexor pollicis longus

Tendon of brachioradialis (cut)

Tendon of flexor carpi radialis (cut)

Tendon of flexor carpi ulnaris (cut)

Pronator quadratus

Tendon of flexor digitorum superficialis

Tendon of flexor digitorum profundus

Supinator

Flexor digitorum profundus

Flexor pollicis longus

Pronator quadratus

Tendon of flexor pollicis longus

Tendon of flexor digitorum profundus

Flexor muscles of the forearm (superficial layer)

Flexor muscles of the forearm (intermediate layer)

Flexor muscles of the forearm (deep layer)

FIGURE 12.5 The three layers of the flexor muscles of the forearm.

Signs and symptoms of injuries to the triceps muscle include the following:

- The athlete may report having experienced a sudden popping in the region of the posterior humerus or elbow.
- Significant pain in the elbow region or just proximal in the area of the triceps tendon.
- Visible defect in the triceps muscle or in the tendon near the olecranon process.
- Discoloration and possible swelling, although both may be delayed for a period of hours after the injury.

First aid care of injuries to the triceps muscle involves the following:

1. Immediately apply ice and compression. This is best accomplished with a bag of crushed ice that is secured with a wide elastic wrap tied around the arm.

2. Place the arm in a sling with the elbow positioned at approximately 90 degrees of flexion if pain can be tolerated.

3. If pain is severe or there is a visible defect in the triceps muscle or its tendon, immediate medical referral is necessary.

Fractures of the Upper Arm

Little information is available about the frequency of proximal and mid-shaft humeral fractures related to sports. It would seem that activities involving collisions between participants, such as tackle football and ice hockey, or sports with a potential for high-speed falls, such as cycling or inline skating, would carry a higher risk for such injuries (**Figure 12.6**). Although considered to be quite rare, humeral stress fractures have been reported related to high-intensity weight training (Bartsokas, Palin, & Collier, 1992).

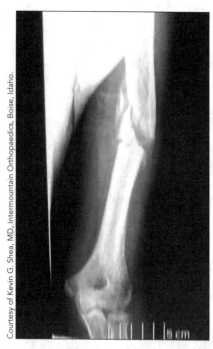

Courtesy of Kevin G. Shea, MD, Intermountain Orthopaedics, Boise, Idaho.

FIGURE 12.6 Mid-shaft fracture of the humerus (left arm).

Signs and symptoms of humeral fractures include the following:

- Severe pain in the region of the upper arm with a recent history of trauma to the area.
- Deformity may be present and visible, especially when compared with the opposite extremity.
- Loss of function or an unwillingness to use the extremity.
- Muscle spasm in the musculature surrounding the extremity.
- The athlete may report having felt a snap or heard a pop at the time of injury.
- If the radial nerve is involved there may be loss of sensation into the dorsum of the forearm and wrist. This may also result in loss of strength in the wrist extensors (AAOS, 1991).
- In cases of stress fracture, pain may not be associated with a specific traumatic incident. Instead, the athlete may report a change in a training program—for example, a sudden increase in the intensity or volume of a strength-training program.

TIME OUT 12.2

Muscles, Actions, and Innervations of the Forearm

Muscle	Action(s)	Innervation
Flexor digitorum profundus	Flexion of the distal interphalangeal joints of the fingers, and PIP and MP joints	Median and ulnar
Flexor digitorum superficialis	Flexion of the proximal interphalangeal joints of the finger, and MP joints	Median
Flexor pollicis longus	Flexion of the thumb	Median
Pronator quadratus	Pronation of the forearm	Median
Brachioradialis	Flexion of the forearm at the elbow Supination of the forearm	Radial
Extensor carpi radialis longus	Extension of the hand at the wrist Radial deviation of the hand at the wrist	Radial
Extensor carpi radialis brevis	Extension of the hand at the wrist Radial deviation of the hand at the wrist	Radial
Extensor digitorum	Extension of the fingers Extension of the hand at the wrist	Radial
Extensor digiti minimi	Extension of the little finger	Radial
Extensor indicis	Extension of the index finger	Radial
Extensor carpi ulnaris	Extension of the hand at the wrist Ulnar deviation of the hand at the wrist	Radial
Supinator	Supination of the forearm	Radial
Abductor pollicis longus	Abduction of the thumb	Radial
Extensor pollicis longus	Extension of the thumb	Radial
Extensor pollicis brevis	Extension of the thumb	Radial

First aid care of humeral fractures involves the following:

1. Immediately apply ice and compression in conjunction with a properly constructed splint. Many commercial splints are available and will work well when used according to the manufacturer's specifications. The application of ice and compression is best accomplished with a bag of crushed ice that is secured with a wide elastic wrap tied around the arm. Discontinue ice application if radial nerve involvement or circulatory deficiency is observed.

2. Apply a standard sling-and-swathe bandage as described by the National Safety Council (1991).

3. As with any injury requiring the application of a splint, periodic evaluation of circulation distal to the site of the splint is essential to guarantee that blood flow has not been impaired. This can be accomplished simply by squeezing the nail bed of a finger and observing the return of blood to the fingertip.

4. Humeral fractures are serious injuries often associated with significant soft-tissue damage. In such instances, the athlete should be treated for shock and immediately transported to a healthcare facility.

Elbow Injuries

Elbow injuries are common in sports and range from simple abrasions or contusions to complete dislocations or fractures. In sports involving repeated throwing or swinging actions, the elbow may develop an overuse injury related to muscular attachments on the humeral epicondyles, sometimes resulting in a condition known as **epicondylitis**. The epicondyles in the pediatric aged athlete are anatomically immature and are therefore classified as growth plates because they are sites for muscle attachments. As such, when these structures are damaged resulting in inflammation, typically as in an

WHAT IF?

You are asked to examine the elbow of a young softball pitcher. She has been suffering from elbow pain and reports that her elbow "locks" occasionally. When this happens she experiences sharp pain and swelling. What might be the cause of the problem, and what course of action would you recommend?

epicondylitis Inflammatory response at the epicondyle.

overuse injury, the injury is technically called apophysitis. The joint can also sustain sprains; the most common involve hyperextensions in which the joint is forced beyond its normal locked position in extension. Dislocations and fractures are probably the most severe types of injuries to this complex joint; if not cared for properly, either can lead to permanent complications.

Sprains and Dislocations

The three articulations of the elbow are bound together by several ligaments that combine to give support to the joint throughout its wide range of motion. The joint capsule of the elbow is extensive and is reinforced both medially and laterally by the ulnar and radial collateral ligaments, respectively. These two ligaments serve to protect the elbow from **valgus** and **varus** forces acting across the joint. In addition, the radial head is held in position by the annular ligament described previously.

The elbow may be sprained through a variety of mechanisms, including falls, particularly when an athlete falls backward with the elbow locked in extension. This mechanism results in a stretching and/or tearing of the anterior joint capsule as well as other soft-tissue structures in the anterior portion of the joint. Two other mechanisms for elbow sprains are valgus and varus forces that can occur suddenly in situations in which the arm is trapped in a vulnerable position, such as can happen in tackle football or wrestling.

Dislocations of the elbow are sprains in the extreme sense and involve damage to significant soft-tissue structures around the joint. The mechanism of injury is typically a fall in which the elbow is in either an extended or flexed position. The force of the impact causes the forearm bones to be driven posteriorly out of their normal position, with the olecranon process of the ulna coming to rest well behind the distal end of the humerus. The deformity is obvious, which makes the initial evaluation relatively straightforward. This injury may be associated with a fracture of either the radius or the ulna, or both.

Signs and symptoms of elbow sprains and dislocations include the following:

- In cases of minor sprains, mild swelling and localized pain.
- Difficulty in gripping objects or in making a fist.
- In cases of dislocations, gross deformity of the elbow with abnormal positioning of the forearm bones behind the distal end of the humerus (**Figure 12.7**).
- Severe pain and total dysfunction of the elbow joint.

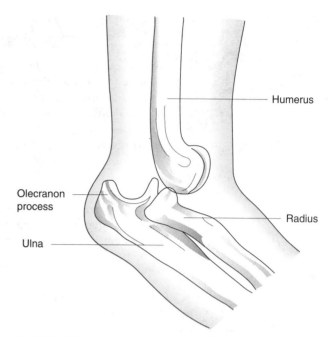

FIGURE 12.7 Posterior dislocation of the elbow.

- Possible neurologic symptoms distal to the elbow characterized by numbness along the distribution of major nerves. The ulnar nerve appears to be the most vulnerable to this specific injury (AAOS, 1991).

First aid care of elbow sprains and dislocations involves the following:

1. In cases of minor sprains the immediate application of ice and compression, using a bag of crushed ice held in place with an elastic wrap, is effective.

2. Once ice and compression are properly situated, the arm should be placed in a sling-and-swathe bandage as recommended by the National Safety Council (1991).

3. In cases of obvious dislocations, the primary concern is to prevent complications, which can be extremely serious and include compression on the neurovascular structures in the elbow region. Immediately apply ice and compression in combination with a properly applied splint.

4. Splinting of this injury requires special attention to avoid moving the displaced forearm bones. It is recommended by the National Safety Council (1991) that the splint be applied on either or both sides of the elbow as illustrated in **Figure 12.8**.

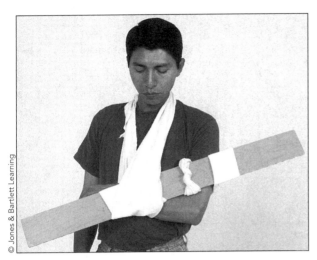

FIGURE 12.8 Splinting of an elbow injury.

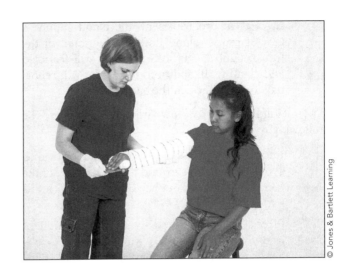

5. Elbow dislocations are serious injuries. The athlete should be treated for shock, and arrangements must be made for transportation to a medical facility.

Fractures

Elbow fractures generally involve the distal humerus, just above the epicondyles, known as supracondylar fractures, or the proximal ulna or radius. Supracondylar fractures are reported to be common in young (pediatric and adolescent) athletes (Pfeiffer, Shea, & Apel, 2006). Because of the complexity of the joint, any fracture represents potential problems for the athlete. As is the case with dislocations, neurovascular structures are in jeopardy when fractures result in displacement of bones. This is especially true if broken bones are moved inadvertently by the athlete or by someone else attempting to render first aid. A simple elbow fracture can easily be converted into an irreversible injury in such a situation. If the radial artery is compressed by broken bone ends, circulation to the forearm can be significantly reduced or stopped, resulting in a condition known as **Volkmann's contracture** (**Figure 12.9**). This condition involves the reaction of the forearm musculature to a lack of blood supply. If left uncorrected, it becomes a permanent deformity; therefore, it is imperative that elbow fractures be handled very carefully during the application of first aid procedures. Furthermore, it is important that the blood supply distal to the elbow be monitored until the athlete is transported to a medical facility.

The mechanisms of injury are similar to those of sprains and dislocations. Fractures of the olecranon process of the ulna are often associated with falls in which the elbow is in a flexed position and the impact

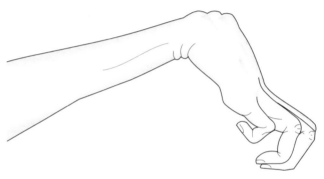

FIGURE 12.9 Volkmann's ischemic contracture.

occurs on the tip of the joint. When elbow fractures occur in adolescents, they require special attention to ensure that the injury will not adversely affect the growth centers of the bones involved.

Signs and symptoms of elbow fractures include the following:

- Recent history of significant trauma to the elbow in association with significant pain and dysfunction.
- Immediate swelling in the region of the injury.
- In the case of displaced fractures an obvious deformity will be noted.

valgus Position of a body part that is bent outward.

varus Position of a body part that is bend inward.

Volkmann's contracture Contracture of muscles of the forearm related to a loss of blood supply caused by a fracture and/or dislocation of either of the bones in the forearm or the humerus.

- In cases of problems with the blood supply, a lack of proper blood flow will be noted in the forearm and hand, both of which will feel cold and clammy. In addition, the victim will report pain or numbness in the hand.

First aid care of elbow fractures involves the following:

1. Immediately apply ice; however, it is critical to avoid compression around the joint owing to the increased risk for vascular compromise with this particular injury.

2. Place a bag of crushed ice over the region of injury and hold it in place with a nonelastic cloth bandage such as a commercially prepared triangular one.

3. The National Safety Council (1991) recommends applying some type of splint, taking great care to avoid moving the bones of the elbow, as shown in Figure 12.8.

4. Treat the athlete for shock and arrange for transport to a medical facility.

Epicondylitis of the Elbow

The epicondyles of the humerus are located immediately proximal to the distal articular surfaces of that bone—the capitellum and the trochlea. The more prominent medial epicondyle serves as the common site of attachment for flexor muscles of the forearm as well as for the ulnar collateral ligament. The smaller lateral epicondyle serves as the common site of attachment for the extensor muscles of the forearm as well as for the radial collateral ligament. As mentioned earlier in this chapter, in the pediatric aged athlete, the epicondyles are anatomically immature and represent growth plates. Thus, when these become inflamed, the condition is known as apophysitis. Regardless of age, these bony prominences are easily located near the elbow joint (**Figure 12.10**).

Activities that require continuous gripping of an object along with simultaneous wrist actions, such as is common in racket and throwing sports, place considerable stress on the tissues of the epicondylar regions. With respect to baseball (overhead) pitching, the stresses exerted at the elbow are profound. Biomechanical analysis indicates that the elbow moves through extension in the acceleration phase achieving velocities of 3000°/second. In addition, there is a compressive force on the lateral side of the elbow between the radial head and the humeral capitellum (Cain & Jugas, 2004). While the phrase "Little League elbow" was first coined in 1960 (Brogden & Crow, 1960), the first

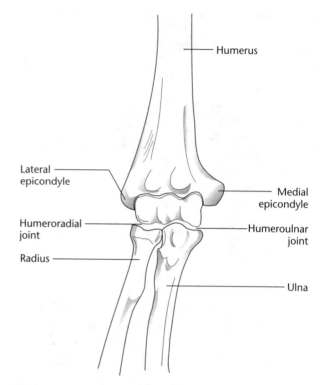

FIGURE 12.10 Epicondyles of the elbow joint.

major studies on the topic did not get published until more than a decade later. It was during the 1970s that two major papers on the topic were published, lending support to a national debate on the topic that included the medical community, sponsoring organizations, coaches, parents, and athletes (Gugenheim, Stanley, & Wood, 1976; Larson, Singer, & Bergstrom, 1976). During this time, considerable attention was given to identifying the contributors to these injuries, including type of pitch, appropriate technique, and total number of pitches thrown over the course of a game, a week, and an entire season. A major concern was that the throwing motion might cause degenerative changes and subsequent inflammation within the medial epicondyle of the elbows of young players, resulting in apophysitis on the medial side of the elbow. This condition results in significant pain around the region of the medial epicondyle and can severely limit the athlete's ability to flex or pronate the wrist and hand. In the adolescent, extreme cases can lead to actual fracturing of the epicondyle away from the humerus, known as an avulsion fracture. Subsequent studies did produce convincing evidence of a relationship between the throwing mechanism and apophyses around the elbow in children (Micheli & Fehlandt, 1992). As a result, rules that limited the maximum number of innings young pitchers could throw during a season were instituted. In spite of the increased awareness of this problem within the youth baseball community, it is estimated that Little League elbow continues to affect 10% to 25% of youth pitchers (Olsen, Fleisig, & Dun, 2006).

Another sport identified as a cause of medial epicondylitis in some athletes is golf. The condition, known as **golfer's elbow**, has been linked to players who have problems with their swing (Hutson, 1990). Available data support the premise that epicondylitis is less common on the medial side of the elbow when compared with the lateral side. Tennis has also been identified as a cause of epicondylitis. Tennis elbow involves the lateral humeral epicondyle and the extensor carpi radialis brevis tendon (Hannafin & Schelkun, 1996). It has been reported that 10% to 50% of all tennis players may suffer from this condition at some point in their career (Jobe & Ciccotti, 1994). Hutson (1990) reports that the problem is related to a variety of sports-related factors, including the following:

- Overload related to the sheer frequency of shots played
- Incorrect technique, particularly on the backhand
- Too small a racket handle
- Recent change of racket—for instance, from wood to graphite
- Too tight a grip between shots
- Muscle imbalance and/or loss of flexibility

Regardless of the type of epicondylitis, the first step in treating the problem is to identify the cause(s), including skill- and/or equipment-related problems. If the athlete treats only the symptoms without identifying the underlying problems, epicondylitis will most likely recur. After the cause(s) is identified, a program of aggressive treatment of symptoms with ice application (before and after practice) plus strengthening exercises, including wrist curls and extensions with pronation and supination against mild resistance, may prove helpful. During the early phase of treatment, exercises without weight may be advised, such as squeezing a tennis ball (finger flexors) and finger extension against the resistance of the opposite hand. Any rehabilitation program should be developed and supervised by a competent sports medicine practitioner such as an athletic trainer or a sports physical therapist.

Signs and symptoms of epicondylitis/apophysitis include the following:

- Pain in the region of either the medial or lateral epicondyle. Symptoms become worse during or immediately after participation.
- Pain radiating distally into either the flexor/pronator or extensor/supinator muscles, depending on which epicondyle is involved.
- Pain may be elicited in the region of the epicondyles during resisted wrist flexion or extension, depending on which epicondyle is involved.
- Swelling in the region of the painful epicondyle.
- In severe and chronic cases, crepitus (feeling hardened fragments through the skin) may be noted over the region of the affected epicondyle.

First aid care of epicondylitis/apophysitis involves the following:

1. Both medial and lateral epicondylitis tend to be chronic injuries resulting from overuse; therefore, first aid is not a practical solution. When symptoms worsen, however, the application of ice and compression can be helpful; this is best accomplished with a bag of crushed ice that is secured with an elastic wrap.

2. If symptoms persist, medical referral is necessary.

3. Long-term treatment includes rest, reduced participation in the activity, and sometimes use of anti-inflammatory drugs.

4. It is critical that the cause(s) of the injury be identified, which may include technique errors, overuse due to excessive participation in the absence of adequate rest, or equipment-related issues (tennis and golf).

Osteochondritis Dissecans of the Elbow

The mechanism of throwing can lead to a type of impingement syndrome in the elbow joint occurring between the radial head and the capitellum of the humerus. In young pitchers, the injury is associated with the late cocking and acceleration phases of the overhead throw. The action of high-velocity extension can cause the elbow to develop a valgus overload resulting in abnormal compression of the elbow on the lateral side of the joint (Hutson, 1990; Klingele & Kocher, 2002). Over time and with continued throwing, the cartilage on the proximal end of the radius can become inflamed and even begin to fracture, resulting in a condition known as

golfer's elbow Medial humeral epicondylitis related to incorrect golf technique.

osteochondritis dissecans (ODC). It has been reported that OCD involving the capitellum, rather than the radial head, in adolescent athletes, is the leading cause of elbow disability (Klingele & Kocher, 2002).

Another possible mechanism for this type of elbow injury is axial loading of the forearm. Such a mechanism is common in falls or in sports that place the forearms in a weight-bearing position, which typically occurs in gymnastics. In either case, the impact force is transmitted up the forearm and causes the head of the radius to be jammed against the humerus. Over time osteochondritis dissecans can result from such repeated insults to the joint.

Signs and symptoms of osteochondritis dissecans include the following:

- During the initial phases of development, the athlete will experience pain during participation.
- Joint inflammation and stiffness may be noted, particularly 12 to 24 hours after participation.
- In well established cases, cartilage fragments (loose bodies) may form in the joint; these are commonly known as joint mice.
- The athlete may experience a locking of the elbow, which occurs when a loose body is caught between the moving bone ends in the joint.
- In advanced cases the elbow may develop osteoarthritis.

First aid care of osteochondritis dissecans involves the following:

1. An athlete with a history of trauma to the elbow joint associated with the symptoms just described should be referred to the appropriate physician for a thorough diagnostic evaluation.
2. Immediate symptoms are best treated with a bag of crushed ice held in place with an elastic wrap.
3. If fragments are identified in the joint, the physician may recommend arthroscopic surgery to remove the loose bodies.
4. The conservative (nonsurgical) treatment for this condition involves rest followed by an extensive period of rehabilitative exercise designed to strengthen the muscles surrounding the elbow and the ligaments of the joint.

Contusions of the Elbow

External blows to the elbow region are common in sports. Little protective equipment is available for the joint, and its large range of motion and irregular shape make taping and wrapping impractical. Fortunately,

the vast majority of contusions result in only temporary discomfort that normally improves in a few days. An exception, however, is the olecranon bursa, which is a large sac located between the skin and the olecranon process of the ulna. Falling on a flexed elbow or sustaining repeated blows to the olecranon area can irritate this **bursa** and cause acute bursitis. Although bursitis does not directly affect the integrity of the elbow joint, persistent swelling, stiffness, and pain associated with this problem can reduce the quality of athletic performance.

Signs and symptoms of olecranon bursitis include the following:

- The most obvious sign of this injury is swelling located around the olecranon process of the ulna.
- Pain and stiffness, especially when the elbow is flexed.
- Skin temperature over the olecranon may be elevated.
- Skin over the olecranon process may appear taut, and the joint may show signs of internal hemorrhage.

First aid care of olecranon bursitis involves the following:

1. Immediate care of elbow contusions includes the application of a bag of crushed ice held in place with an elastic wrap.
2. If the signs and symptoms of olecranon bursitis appear, refer the athlete to the appropriate physician.

Wrist and Forearm Injuries

The anatomy of the human wrist is highly complex. Within this compact joint exists a large number of tendons (for the wrist, fingers, and thumb) that are tightly bound together underneath bands of connective tissue known as retinaculum (transverse carpal ligaments). Also passing through this region are the major nerves and blood vessels of the hand and fingers (**Figure 12.11**).

Aside from simple contusions, injuries to the forearm in sports are relatively uncommon. Usually, contusions can be easily treated with ice, compression, and elevation; this can be followed later with the application of protective padding. Probably the most serious forearm injuries involve fractures distal in the forearm, just proximal to the wrist joint. The most well known of these is a **Colles' fracture**, which involves a transverse fracture of the distal radius (**Figure 12.12**). Variations of this fracture include simultaneous fractures of both the radius and ulna as well as compound fractures of either bone;

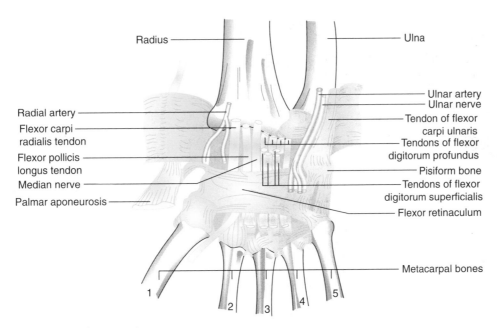

FIGURE 12.11 Right wrist (palmar view).

such injuries are serious and must be properly cared for to avoid complications. The mechanism of injury is highly variable; whatever the mechanism, a great deal of force will be required and many soft-tissue structures may be damaged in conjunction with the fracture.

Signs and symptoms of distal forearm fractures include the following:

- The athlete will have a recent history of significant trauma to the wrist region associated with having heard a popping sound and/or felt a snapping of the bones.

- A deformity, known as the silver fork deformity, between the arm and wrist is typical; in the case of a Colles' fracture the hand is driven backward and outward (radial deviation) (**Figure 12.13**).

- Swelling, often severe, develops quickly and may affect the hand and fingers.

- Pain is generally severe, and motion of the wrist, hand, or fingers will be significantly curtailed.

- In cases in which a broken bone(s) puts pressure on nerves, loss of sensation may be noted in either the hand or fingers, or both.

First aid care of distal forearm fractures include the following:

1. Immediately apply ice, compression, and elevation—abbreviated as **ICE**. This is best accomplished with a bag of crushed ice that is held in place with an elastic wrap. Do not apply ice if you suspect either vascular or nerve supply is compromised. In addition, some type of splint must be applied to protect the area from further injury (see **Figure 12.23**).

2. Make sure that the fingertips are exposed to monitor the blood supply to the hand. This is easily accomplished by squeezing a nail bed and noting the return (or lack thereof) of normal reddish color to the tissue.

3. Once ICE is in place, the forearm should be elevated carefully using a standard sling-and-swathe bandage as recommended by the National Safety Council (1991).

4. Because of the pain and damage associated with this type of injury, it is imperative that the athlete be treated for shock and transported to a medical facility immediately.

osteochondritis dissecans Condition in which a fragment of cartilage and underlying bone are detached from the articular surface.

bursa Small synovial sac typically located over bony prominences that assists in cushioning and reducing friction.

Colles' fracture Transverse fracture of the distal radius.

ICE Ice, compression, and elevation.

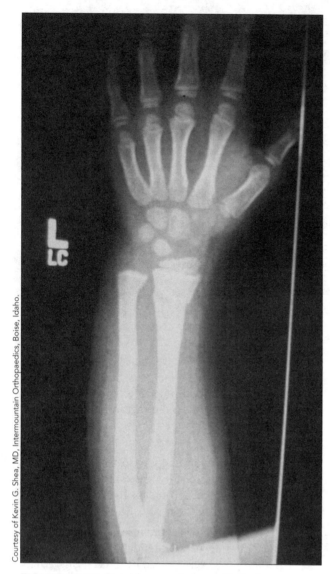

Courtesy of Kevin G. Shea, MD, Intermountain Orthopaedics, Boise, Idaho.

FIGURE 12.12 Distal forearm fracture (Colles').

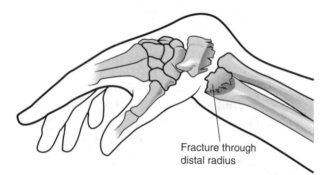

Fracture through distal radius

FIGURE 12.13 A Colles' fracture demonstrating the "silver fork" deformity.

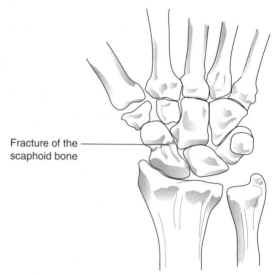

Fracture of the scaphoid bone

FIGURE 12.14 Fracture of the scaphoid bone is common in sports.

Wrist Fractures

Fractures of the carpal bones do occur in sports. According to multiple authors (Booher & Thibodeau, 2000; Saliba & McCue, 2006), the most common involve the scaphoid bone (**Figure 12.14**). This bone can receive considerable force when the wrist is placed into extension in sports such as tackle football (blocking) and gymnastics (vaulting and floor exercise). Simple falls can also cause fractures to this critical bone of the wrist. The fracture generally occurs in a specific site on the scaphoid bone known as the waist, which is the narrowest section of the bone.

Other bones of the wrist can also be fractured: Fractures of the lunate, pisiform, and hamate have been reported. Regardless of which specific bone is fractured, the signs and symptoms will be similar. Because the carpal bones are small, gross deformity is typically

 WHAT IF?

A young gymnast grabs her left wrist immediately after completing a vault. During your examination of her wrist you note that she has pain on movement. She reports that she felt a snap as soon as her hands hit the vaulting horse, and she is tender in the region known as the anatomic snuffbox. What would you conclude happened, and what would you do for initial care?

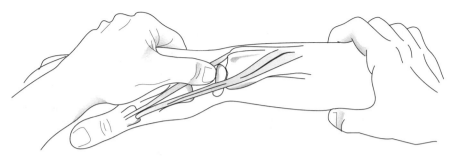

FIGURE 12.15 Palpation in the anatomic snuffbox.

not present, and evaluation of these injuries is difficult. When doubt exists about the extent or nature of the injury, the best policy is to refer the athlete to a physician for a more complete diagnostic evaluation.

Signs and symptoms of wrist fractures include the following:

- A recent history of trauma to the wrist, specifically forced extension associated with a snapping or popping sensation in the wrist.

- Pain in the wrist that is aggravated by movement. A simple test for the integrity of the scaphoid bone involves pressing lightly into the region at the base of the thumb known as the anatomic snuffbox (**Figure 12.15**), which is bordered by several tendons that attach within the thumb. The radial surface of the scaphoid bone is located within the anatomic snuffbox. Consequently, external pressure in this region may elicit a painful response from the athlete, which is a positive sign of a fracture of that bone.

- The athlete may be unable or unwilling to move the wrist, and doing so may result in considerable pain.

- The athlete may state that the wrist feels locked in a certain position; this can be an indication of a displaced fracture.

First aid care of wrist fractures involves the following:

1. Immediately apply ICE in conjunction with some type of splint that immobilizes the wrist (see Figure 12.23).

2. Once ICE is in place, the wrist should be elevated carefully by way of a standard sling-and-swathe bandage as described by the National Safety Council (1991).

3. Leave the fingertips exposed to facilitate monitoring blood flow to the hand beyond the level of the splint.

Wrist Sprains and Dislocations

The mechanism producing a fracture of the wrist may also produce a sprain or dislocation in that region when of lesser severity. Essentially, the wrist (radiocarpal) joint is bound together by a network of large, strong ligaments known as the palmar and dorsal radiocarpal ligaments (**Figures 12.16** and **12.17**). In addition, several smaller ligaments bind the remaining bones of the wrist to form a well supported series of joints known collectively as the intercarpal joints.

The most common sprain of the wrist is caused by forced hyperextension, which results in a stretching and possible tearing of the palmar radiocarpal ligament. Such an injury can, if severe enough, result in a dislocation of one or more of the carpal bones. In the case of a simple sprain, the carpal bones will remain in their normal position.

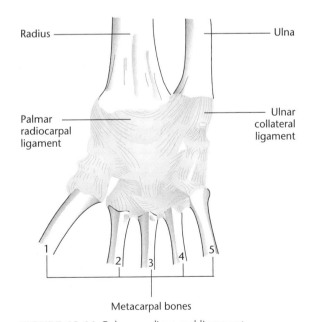

FIGURE 12.16 Palmar radiocarpal ligament.

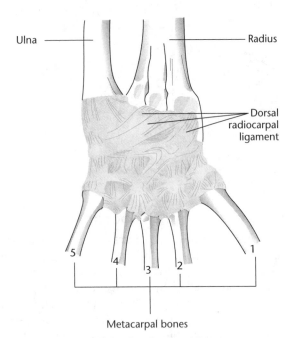

Ulna

Radius

Dorsal radiocarpal ligament

5 4 3 2 1

Metacarpal bones

FIGURE 12.17 Dorsal radiocarpal ligament.

The most common dislocation of the wrist involves the lunate bone, which is located between the distal end of the radius and the capitate bone (Booher & Thibodeau, 2000; Saliba & McCue, 2006). The mechanism of injury is forceful hyperextension; this causes the bone to shift out of its normal position and slide toward the palmar side of the wrist. In severe cases, the lunate will put pressure on the tendons and nerves of a region of the wrist known as the carpal tunnel, resulting in significant symptoms in the hand and fingers.

Signs and symptoms of wrist sprains and dislocations include the following:

- The athlete will report having sustained a forced hyperextension of the wrist in conjunction with a snapping or popping sensation in the bones of the joint.

- Movement, or attempted movements, of the wrist will be painful and meet with little success.

- In cases of dislocations, the wrist may be locked so that the athlete will be unable to voluntarily move the wrist.

- Numbness and/or pain may radiate from the wrist into the hand and fingers. In the case of lunate dislocations, these symptoms may involve the distribution of the median nerve, producing the symptoms known commonly as carpal tunnel syndrome.

- Swelling of the wrist may be limited owing to the nature of the ligaments of the region.

First aid care of wrist sprains and dislocations involves the following:

1. Immediately apply ICE and some type of splinting device designed to immobilize the wrist joint. A bag of crushed ice held in place by an elastic wrap is effective in most cases. Do not apply ice if you suspect either vascular or nerve supply is compromised. The splint may be secured with the wrap as well.

2. Elevation is best achieved using a standard sling-and-swathe bandage.

3. In cases of significant pain or a possible dislocation, it is important to refer the athlete to a healthcare facility for further evaluation and treatment.

Nerve Injuries to the Wrist

Three major nerves cross the wrist from the forearm into the hand to supply sensation and motor function to the hand and fingers. These nerves are the radial, the median, and the ulnar. Though any of these nerves may be damaged in a sports-related injury, the most commonly injured nerve is the median. This nerve passes through a region of the wrist known as the **carpal tunnel** (**Figure 12.18**), which also houses eight flexor tendons that pass into the hand. The tunnel is surrounded by dense, strong ligaments and bone.

The exact cause of **carpal tunnel syndrome** is unknown, but it probably involves swelling within the tunnel caused by tendinitis or sprains of the region. In any event, the pressure of the swelling has a negative effect on the median nerve. Although carpal tunnel syndrome can be caused by a single traumatic episode, such as a dislocated lunate bone, the majority of cases involving athletes tend to be the result of chronic overuse injuries. Sports with a high incidence include racket sports and those requiring the participant to grip an object tightly for extended periods of time. Unless treated properly, carpal tunnel syndrome can be extremely disabling and can often preclude an athlete from returning to the sport.

Another nerve-related injury in the wrist involves the ulnar nerve as it passes through the region on the ulnar side of the forearm. Specifically, the ulnar nerve is located in the vicinity of the pisiform bone and the hook of the hamate bone within the **tunnel of Guyon** (Hoppenfield, 1976). A blow to the wrist or tendinitis in the tendon of flexor carpi ulnaris can result in irritation to the nerve and a variety of symptoms. These include loss of sensation to a portion of the hand and fingers as well as loss of muscle strength in the fingers affected

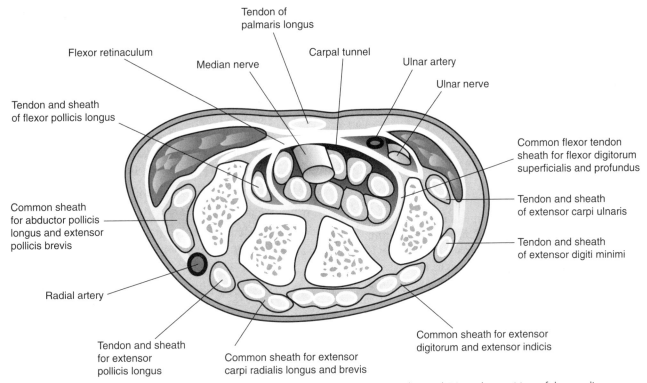

Flexor retinaculum

Tendon of palmaris longus

Median nerve

Carpal tunnel

Ulnar artery

Ulnar nerve

Tendon and sheath of flexor pollicis longus

Common sheath for abductor pollicis longus and extensor pollicis brevis

Radial artery

Common flexor tendon sheath for flexor digitorum superficialis and profundus

Tendon and sheath of extensor carpi ulnaris

Tendon and sheath of extensor digiti minimi

Tendon and sheath for extensor pollicis longus

Common sheath for extensor carpi radialis longus and brevis

Common sheath for extensor digitorum and extensor indicis

FIGURE 12.18 Cross-section view of the forearm at the wrist showing the carpal tunnel. Note the position of the median nerve.

by the ulnar nerve. The region of the hand that receives sensory impulses from the ulnar nerve is the medial portion of the palm, including the region known as the hypothenar eminence, as well as the medial half of the ring finger and the entire little finger.

Signs and symptoms of nerve injuries to the wrist include the following:

- Loss of sensation to a portion of the hand and/ or fingers that follows the distribution of a major nerve in the region. In some cases, pain may also radiate into the hand.
- Pain and tenderness around the region of the wrist on the palm side.
- Associated tendinitis of the wrist or recent history of trauma to the area, such as a contusion or sprain.
- Symptoms may become worse when the wrist is fully flexed or extended or an object is gripped tightly in the hand.

First aid care of nerve injuries to the wrist involves the following:

1. This type of injury tends to develop slowly over time. The exception is when a nerve of the wrist is aggravated by an acute injury such as a severe contusion or sprain.

2. When associated with an acute trauma, the best approach is the immediate application of ICE. Do not apply ice if you suspect either vascular or nerve supply is compromised. Splinting may be necessary depending on the specific injury.

3. Any athlete with a history of recurrent pain and stiffness in the wrist associated with the neurologic symptoms just described should be referred to a healthcare facility for a complete evaluation by a medical doctor.

4. If the medical diagnosis confirms a nerve-related problem, the initial care will generally involve

carpal tunnel Anatomic region of the wrist where the median nerve and the majority of the tendons of the forearm pass into the hand.

carpal tunnel syndrome A complex of symptoms resulting from pressure on the median nerve as it passes through the carpal tunnel of the wrist, causing soreness and numbness.

tunnel of Guyon Anatomic region formed by the hook of the hamate bone and the pisiform bone, whereby the ulnar nerve passes into the hand.

rest, anti-inflammatory drugs, and in some cases a splint. In severe cases surgical decompression of the nerve may be required.

Unique Tendon Problems of the Wrist

By definition, **tenosynovitis** is an "inflammation between tendon and surrounding tissues with consequent loss of smooth gliding motion" (American Medical Association [AMA], 1968). Perhaps the most common form of tenosynovitis in the wrist involves the tendons of the thumb (**Figure 12.19**) and is known as **de Quervain's disease**. In reality this is not a disease in the classic sense but rather a type of overuse injury specific to the wrist. De Quervain's disease most commonly involves the tendons of the extensor pollicis brevis and the abductor pollicis longus muscles as they pass across the radial styloid process. There is a third tendon in the region, the extensor pollicis longus; however, it is rarely involved in this condition.

The mechanism of injury for de Quervain's disease is vague, but it probably involves overuse of the wrist and/or thumb. Initially, the tendons and the synovial sheath around the tendons become inflamed, resulting in pain, swelling, and stiffness. As the injury progresses the tendons begin catching within the anatomic tunnel, at times with such force that the athlete will feel them as they break free. Using the thumb, particularly in flexion and extension, will be extremely painful, and even wrist movements will be impeded. Conservative treatment includes rest, heat and drug therapy, and splinting of the wrist to reduce movements of the thumb. In many cases this problem tends to recur and eventually may require surgical treatment to release (decompress) the tendons as they pass near the radial styloid process.

Signs and symptoms of de Quervain's disease include the following:

- Pain and tenderness within the region of the radial styloid process, specifically involving the tendons of the abductor pollicis longus and the extensor pollicis brevis.
- Swelling in the area of the radial styloid process and, in advanced cases, the development of a nodule on one or more of the tendons.
- The athlete may report that the tendons are catching within the wrist during activity.
- Thumb flexion in conjunction with ulnar deviation of the wrist will cause a significant increase in pain and related symptoms.

First aid care of de Quervain's disease involves the following:

1. If diagnosed early, the condition is treated with rest, immobilization with some type of splint, and drug therapy.

2. In advanced or recurring cases, surgical treatment has been found to be highly effective with this condition. The basic surgical objective is to create more room within the tunnel for the tendons.

Another unique tendon-related wrist problem is known as a ganglion cyst. Technically, a **ganglion** is a herniation of the synovium surrounding the tendons, often at the wrist. When this occurs, the herniated tissue will gradually begin to fill with synovial fluid, producing a protrusion often visible as a bump on the surface of the wrist (**Figure 12.20**). The most common site for wrist ganglions is on the extensor tendon (dorsal) side of the wrist, although cases have been reported on the flexor tendon side of the wrist as well. It appears that they are related to the chronic strain of wrist tendons but also can occur spontaneously

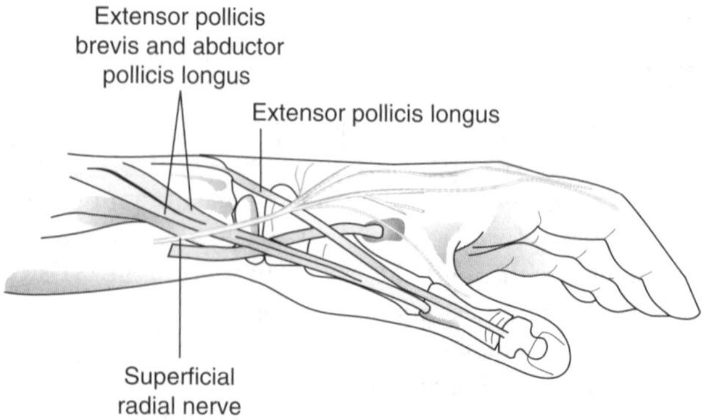

Extensor pollicis brevis and abductor pollicis longus

Extensor pollicis longus

Superficial radial nerve

FIGURE 12.19 Tendons of the thumb.

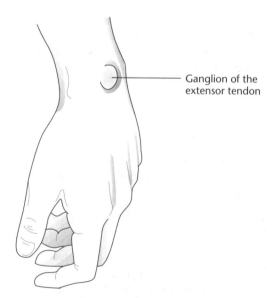

Ganglion of the extensor tendon

FIGURE 12.20 Ganglion of the wrist.

(Anderson, Hall, & Martin, 2005; O'Donoghue, 1976). Ganglions are highly variable in appearance. Some appear as soft, apparently fluid-filled masses just under the skin; others materialize as hard, painful masses over a tendon. Depending on their specific location, ganglions may interfere with an athlete's performance, but in most cases the problem is seen as primarily cosmetic.

Signs and symptoms of a ganglion include the following:

* The most obvious symptom is a visible swelling through the skin of the wrist in the region of the extensor or flexor tendons.
* In more advanced cases a painful, hardened nodule may be present directly over a tendon (see Figure 12.20).

First aid care of a ganglion involves the following:

1. In some cases ganglions regress on their own spontaneously.
2. In cases in which the ganglion does not interfere with performance, most physicians recommend leaving it alone.
3. In cases in which the ganglion does interfere with performance or is cosmetically unattractive, surgical removal in conjunction with repair of the synovial hernia is an option. It should be noted, however, that even after surgery ganglions may recur.

Hand Injuries

The hand, fingers, and thumb are often injured in sports, with some of the highest frequencies occurring in sports such as baseball, softball, basketball, and football. The variety of injuries seen is nearly infinite; however, those described in this section represent the most common injuries seen.

The hand contains 19 bones: the 5 metacarpals and the 14 separate **phalanges** of the fingers (**Figure 12.21**). The joints of the hand include the carpometacarpal joints at the base of the hand, the metacarpophalangeal joints (knuckles), and the interphalangeal joints of the fingers and thumb. All of these joints are freely movable and are supported by many ligaments and capsular tissues. Movements at each of these joints are affected by the many muscles originating from the forearm that pass tendons into the hand and fingers. Also within the hand there are small, intrinsic (originating within the hand) muscles that precisely move the thumb and fingers. The nerves and vessels of the hand are continuations of the

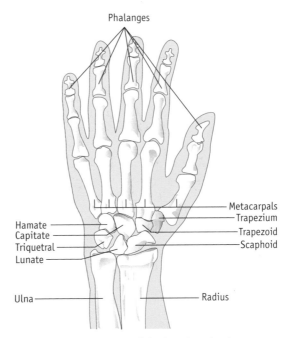

FIGURE 12.21 Bones of the hand and wrist.

major structures that cross the wrist: the radial, median, and ulnar nerves and the radial and ulnar arteries.

Hand Fractures

Fractures can occur to any of the 19 bones of the hand; however, certain types of fractures are seen more commonly in sports. An injury unique to the thumb is a **Bennett's fracture** (**Figure 12.22**). This injury often results from a blow to the hand while it is in a clenched-fist position; the force of the mechanism causes the proximal end of the first metacarpal bone to be driven into the wrist. The result is a **fracture-dislocation** of the

tenosynovitis Inflammation of the sheath of a tendon.

de Quervain's disease Inflammation of sheaths surrounding the extensor tendons of the thumb.

ganglion Herniation of the synovium surrounding a tendon and subsequent filling of the area with synovial fluid, resulting in a visible bump seen through the skin.

phalanges Anatomic name for the bones of both the fingers and/or toes.

Bennett's fracture Fracture and/or dislocation of the first metacarpal bone away from the greater multangular bone of the wrist.

fracture-dislocation An injury resulting in both the fracture of a bone and dislocation at the joint.

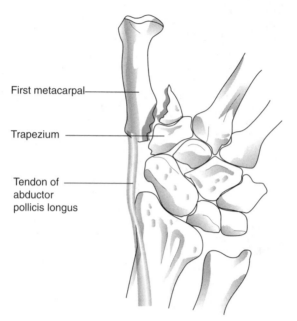

First metacarpal

Trapezium

Tendon of abductor pollicis longus

FIGURE 12.22 Bennett's fracture.

first metacarpal bone away from the greater multangular (trapezium) bone of the wrist. An obvious deformity appears with this injury, characterized by the thumb being shorter in appearance when compared with that of the opposite hand. Significant swelling will also be present near the base of the thumb over the carpometacarpal joint.

Fractures of the metacarpal bones of the fingers can also occur via a mechanism similar to that described for a Bennett's fracture, that is, a blow with a clenched fist. The most common injury involves the fourth and/or fifth metacarpal bone(s) near the proximal end(s) (base) and is known as a **boxer's fracture**. Because of the ligamentous structure of this area, displaced fractures are rare; consequently, deformity is usually not a common sign of injury. Another mechanism of injury for metacarpal fractures is a crushing force, such as having the hand stepped on by another athlete, which is common in sports such as tackle football.

Fractures of the phalanges also occur frequently in sports, particularly fractures of the proximal phalanges (O'Donoghue, 1976). Most of these fractures remain undisplaced (stable) and are relatively easily treated with splinting, requiring 2–8 weeks of recovery before returning to activity; few if any long-term complications ensue (Rettig, 2004). In cases in which the phalangeal fracture resists fixation and remains unstable, surgically implanted fixation is effective. This is critical because a serious complication of a finger fracture is rotational deformity, which results

when the broken bone ends fail to unite in the correct position (Hutson, 1990).

Signs and symptoms of hand fractures include the following:

- Recent history of significant trauma to the hand followed immediately by specific pain and dysfunction of the hand and/or finger(s).
- In cases of displaced fractures, deformity may be observable, either as a bump or protrusion in the hand or as an oddly shaped finger.
- In cases of compound fractures, the skin will be broken over the region of the fracture.
- There will be significant inflammation associated with any fracture in the hand or finger.

First aid care of hand fractures involves the following:

1. Immediately apply ICE and some type of splinting device. This is best accomplished using a small bag of crushed ice held in place with a narrow elastic wrap; take care to leave the fingernails exposed.

2. Elevation can be easily achieved by placing the arm in a standard sling-and-swathe bandage.

3. Depending on the specific site of the fracture, a variety of splinting techniques can be used. For example, for an isolated phalangeal fracture, a procedure known as buddy taping can be used, which simply involves taping the fractured finger to an adjacent one. Fractures of the metacarpal bones are best treated by immobilization of the entire hand (**Figure 12.23**).

4. The athlete should be transported to the appropriate healthcare facility for further medical evaluation and treatment. It is critical that fractures of the hand be treated as serious injuries.

Sprains and Dislocations of the Hand

Any of the many joints in the hand can be subject to sufficient trauma to cause a sprain of the supporting ligaments. If the force is severe enough, a dislocation of the joint may occur as well. Although virtually any of the joints of the hand may be injured, available information regarding sports-related injuries indicates that certain types are quite common. These include gamekeeper's thumb, mallet (baseball) finger, and boutonnière deformity.

Gamekeeper's Thumb

The metacarpophalangeal (MP) joint of the thumb is a large, condyloid joint allowing a considerable range of

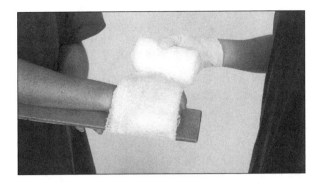

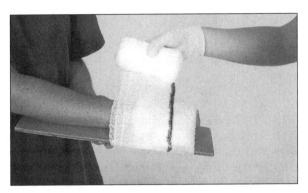

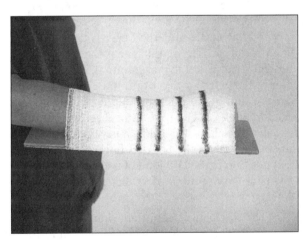

FIGURE 12.23 A splint provides immobilization for fractures of the forearm, wrist, and hand.

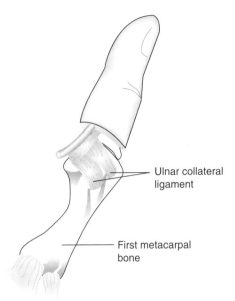

Ulnar collateral ligament

First metacarpal bone

FIGURE 12.24 Damage to the ulnar collateral ligament of the metacarpophalangeal joint can result in gamekeeper's thumb.

considerable damage to the ulnar collateral ligament of the thumb, causing chronic instability of the MP joint (Hutson, 1990). Although there are few gamekeepers today, the injury occurs with surprising frequency in sports such as alpine skiing. The mechanism of injury involves a valgus (force applied to the medial side of

 WHAT IF?

You are coaching a junior high basketball game. During the second half, your starting point guard injures her finger when receiving a passed ball. On examination you note obvious deformity with the distal phalanx pushed up so that the distal interphalangeal joint is dislocated. What is this injury, and how would you care for it initially?

motion in flexion and extension plus a slight amount of abduction and adduction. The joint is supported by both capsular and collateral ligaments. The latter are named according to their location relative to the radius and ulna: The collateral ligament on the lateral side of the joint is the radial collateral ligament, and the one on the medial side is the ulnar collateral ligament (**Figure 12.24**).

The term **gamekeeper's thumb** originated in the 1950s to describe an injury unique to gamekeepers, whose profession required them to break the necks of rabbits. Apparently this procedure resulted in

boxer's fracture Fracture of the proximal fourth and/or fifth metacarpal bones.

gamekeeper's thumb Sprain of the ulnar collateral ligament of the metacarpophalangeal joint of the thumb.

the joint) stress across the MP joint of the thumb; this results in stretching, partial tearing, or even complete rupture of the ulnar collateral ligament. (In skiing, certain types of pole grips place considerable stress on the MP joint of the thumb when planting a pole.)

Injury to the ulnar collateral ligament can produce a grossly unstable thumb, particularly when an athlete attempts to grasp or hold an object. Evidence suggests that 30% of the cases of ligament injuries occur in conjunction with an avulsion fracture of a bone fragment from the base of the proximal phalanx (Isani, 1990). Regardless of the specific type of injury, any significant sprain of the ulnar collateral ligament within the MP joint of the thumb must be carefully evaluated by a physician to determine the extent of joint laxity and bony integrity. It is important to note that if left uncorrected this injury can lead to a chronically unstable joint that can negatively affect use of the hand.

Signs and symptoms of gamekeeper's thumb include the following:

- Significant point tenderness over the region of the ulnar collateral ligament.
- The athlete may report having felt a snap during the initial injury.
- Significant swelling over the MP joint of the thumb.
- Inability and/or unwillingness by the athlete to move the thumb.

First aid care of gamekeeper's thumb involves the following:

1. Immediately apply ICE. This is best accomplished by placing a small bag of crushed ice around the injured joint and securing it with an elastic wrap.
2. The easiest method of achieving elevation is to place the arm in a simple sling.
3. Refer the athlete to a healthcare facility for further evaluation and treatment of the injury.

Mallet (Baseball) Finger

Mallet finger involves the distal phalanx of a finger, often the index or middle finger. The injury is so named because the resulting deformity gives the distal segment of the finger the appearance of a mallet. The term *baseball finger* arose because the injury is so common in that sport—getting hit on the fingertip by a ball is a frequent occurrence.

The anatomy of the distal finger includes the **distal interphalangeal (DIP) joint**, which functions as a hinge. The muscles acting at this joint are the flexor digitorum profundus and the extensor digitorum.

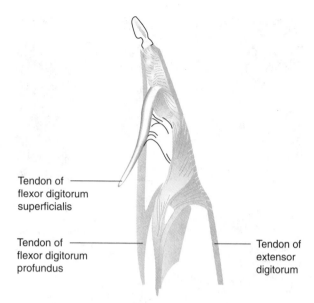

Tendon of flexor digitorum superficialis

Tendon of flexor digitorum profundus

Tendon of extensor digitorum

FIGURE 12.25 Tendons of the finger.

These two muscles are located in the forearm; however, their tendons pass through the hand, inserting into the bases of the distal phalanges of each of the four fingers (**Figure 12.25**). The mechanism of injury for mallet finger is quite precise: The tip of the finger must receive a blow at the time the finger is extending from a flexed position. The result is that the distal phalanx is suddenly and forcefully taken into flexion against the action of the extensor digitorum muscle. This can lead to an avulsion of the extensor tendon, with or without a small fragment of bone, from the insertion at the base of the distal phalanx. After this injury occurs the athlete is unable to extend the affected finger; it remains in a flexed position at the DIP joint (**Figure 12.26**).

Signs and symptoms of mallet finger include the following:

- The single most important sign is the deformity itself, which is associated with a recent history of trauma to the fingertip.

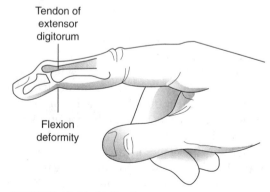

Tendon of extensor digitorum

Flexion deformity

FIGURE 12.26 Mallet finger.

- Point tenderness on the dorsal surface of the base of the distal phalanx, directly over the site of insertion of the extensor digitorum tendon.

First aid care of mallet finger involves the following:

1. Immediately apply ICE. This is best accomplished by placing a small bag of crushed ice around the involved finger and holding it in place with a small elastic wrap.
2. Immediately splint the finger with the DIP joint extended. Do not let the distal phalanx fall back into the flexed position.
3. The easiest method of achieving elevation is to place the arm in a simple sling.
4. Refer the athlete to a healthcare facility for further evaluation and treatment of the injury.

Jersey Finger

Jersey finger, much like mallet finger, involves a tearing away of a finger tendon from its attachment. In this case, however, the mechanism of injury involves catching a finger in an opponent's clothing, for example, a football jersey. In the attempt to grip the clothing, as the opponent pulls away, the tendon of the flexor digitorum profundus (FDP) is torn away from its attachment on the distal phalanx (**Figure 12.27**). Because the FDP is the only muscle that flexes the distal phalanx at the distal interphalangeal joint, this injury results in an inability to flex the DIP joint.

Signs and symptoms of jersey finger include the following:

- Inability to flex the DIP joint of the affected finger.
- Athlete reports having felt something snap, or tear away, at the area of the fingertip.

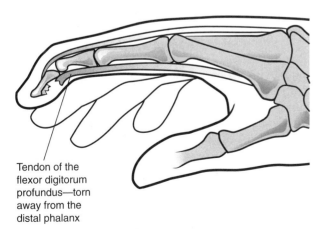

Tendon of the flexor digitorum profundus—torn away from the distal phalanx

FIGURE 12.27 Jersey finger.

- Point tenderness on the volar surface of the distal phalanx of the finger.

First aid care of jersey finger involves the following:

1. Immediately apply ICE. This is best accomplished by placing a small bag of crushed ice around the involved finger and holding it in place with a small elastic wrap.
2. Splint the finger in a position of extension at the DIP and proximal interphalangeal joints.
3. The easiest method of achieving elevation is to place the arm in a simple sling.
4. Refer the athlete to a healthcare facility for further evaluation and treatment of the injury.

Boutonnière Deformity

Boutonnière deformity (French for buttonhole) involves the **proximal interphalangeal (PIP) joint** of the fingers (Hutson, 1990). The structure of the extensor digitorum tendon is unique as it crosses the dorsal surface of the PIP joint. The tendon is divided into three distinct bands: one central and two lateral bands (**Figure 12.28**). This arrangement allows for full flexion of the PIP joint without interference from the extensor digitorum muscle.

The mechanism for this injury is characterized by severe forced finger flexion, such as having the hand contact a playing surface during a fall with the fingers in a flexed position while an attempt is made simultaneously to extend the fingers. This results in tearing the central portion of the extensor tendon. Initial symptoms are limited; the athlete will be able to extend the injured PIP joint, but with limited strength. If left uncorrected, the PIP joint will eventually pop through the opening in the central portion

mallet finger Deformity of the distal interphalangeal joint of the finger caused by an avulsion of the tendon of the extensor digitorum muscle from the distal phalanx.

distal interphalangeal (DIP) joint The joint formed by the articulation between the intermediate and distal phalanges of the digits (hinge type of joint).

boutonnière deformity Buttonhole deformity whereby the proximal interphalangeal joint of the finger is forced through the central band of the tendon of the extensor digitorum muscle.

proximal interphalangeal (PIP) joint The joint formed by the articulation between the proximal and intermediate phalanges of the digits (hinge type of joint).

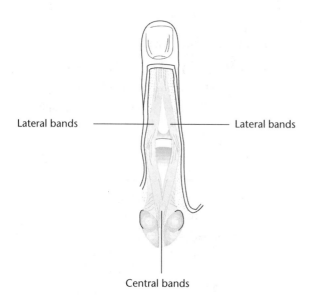

FIGURE 12.28 Bands of the extensor tendons.

of the tendon like a button popping up through a button-hole. This results in a deformity that places the finger in a position of flexion at the PIP joint in conjunction with hyperextension at both the MP and DIP joints (**Figure 12.29**). Treatment for the injury consists of splinting the finger in a position of extension of the PIP joint to allow the central portion of the extensor tendon to heal. Surgical correction is not recommended (Hutson, 1990).

Signs and symptoms of boutonnière deformity include the following:

- The athlete will report a violent flexion to the finger, perhaps associated with the sensation of tearing or popping over the PIP joint.

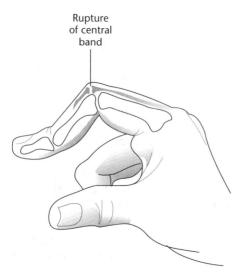

FIGURE 12.29 Boutonnière deformity.

- The injury will be followed immediately by significant weakness in extending the injured finger at the PIP joint.
- The PIP joint will become painful and swollen, then stiff.
- If left unattended, the injury may progress to the classic deformity, which is characterized by hyperextension of the MP and DIP joints, with flexion of the PIP joint.

First aid care of boutonnière deformity involves the following:

1. Initially, this injury should be treated as any soft-tissue and/or skeletal injury of the hand or finger: Apply ICE. This is best accomplished by using a small bag of crushed ice that is held in place with a small elastic wrap.

2. Elevation can be easily achieved using a simple sling.

3. If any of the previously stated signs and/or symptoms are present, the athlete should immediately be referred to a healthcare facility for medical evaluation.

4. In cases in which the initial injury has not been treated and has progressed to actual deformity, medical referral is mandatory.

Wrist and Thumb Taping

One of the taping procedures that can help prevent injuries in athletes involved in contact and collision sports is wrist and thumb taping. Taping the wrist and thumb before activity can help reduce excessive movement from contact, thus reducing the number of sprains to the area. It should be recognized that taping is both a science and an art that requires learning and practice. Once the coach or certified athletic trainer learns the basic concepts of a taping procedure, he or she needs to practice the application of the procedure. Books are available that demonstrate different taping procedures for many different joints. These books depict how the tape should be applied, but to really understand the reasons behind the procedures and to become a proficient applicator of the tape, an educational background is most helpful. The wrist and thumb taping pictures presented in **Figures 12.30** through **12.39** provide an overview of a preventive procedure that can be applied.

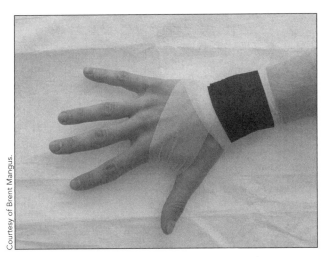

FIGURE 12.30 Start by applying pre-wrap as shown, followed by anchor strips around the wrist.

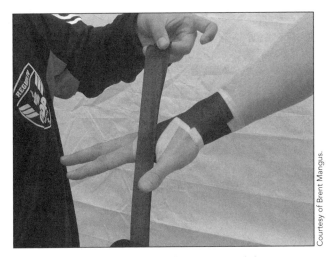

FIGURE 12.31 Apply figure-eight strips to stabilize wrist flexion and extension. A helpful hint in this step is to "pinch" the tape between the thumb and first finger to make the tape narrower and easier to follow the contours of the hand.

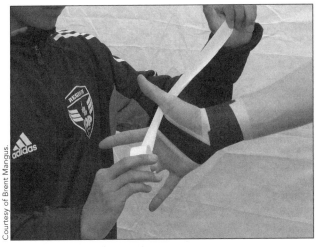

FIGURE 12.32 Apply thumb spica strips in an alternating pattern, moving from the base of the thumb to the nail.

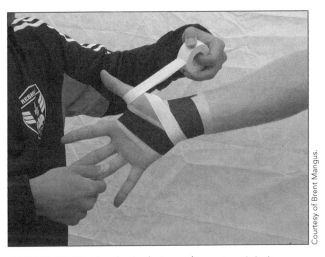

FIGURE 12.33 Use the technique shown to minimize any compromised blood flow.

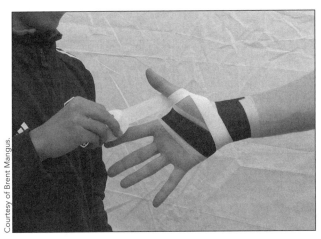

FIGURE 12.34 Thumb spica strips should be applied in opposite directions as they are placed in an alternating fashion.

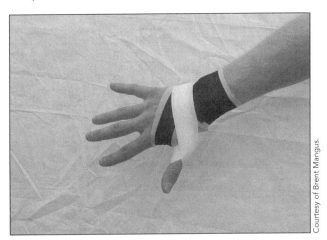

FIGURE 12.35 Wrist stabilization with thumb spicas applied.

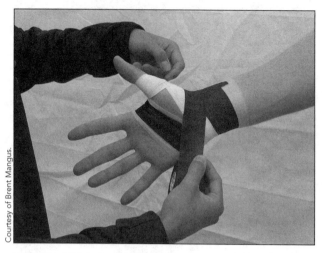

Courtesy of Brent Mangus.

FIGURE 12.36 Apply stabilizing strips to reduce thumb movement (extension).

Courtesy of Brent Mangus.

FIGURE 12.37 Alternate stabilizing strips from base of thumb, moving toward the nail.

Courtesy of Brent Mangus.

FIGURE 12.38 Apply finishing figure-eight strips to cover the thumb stabilizing strips.

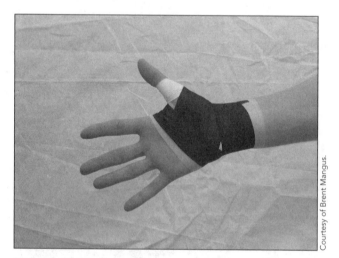

Courtesy of Brent Mangus.

FIGURE 12.39 Complete wrist and thumb taping procedure. Check the thumbnail for compromised blood flow. A blue thumbnail indicates that the tape is too tight.

REVIEW QUESTIONS

1. List the three articulations of the elbow.
2. Explain the term *myositis ossificans traumatica* as it relates to a condition of the upper arm known as tackler's exostosis.
3. List the signs and symptoms of a humeral fracture.
4. Explain and/or demonstrate the first aid procedures for an athlete with a suspected fracture of the humerus.
5. Describe briefly the mechanism of injury for a posterior dislocation of the elbow.
6. List the signs and symptoms of a dislocation of the elbow.
7. True or false: The ulnar nerve is the most commonly damaged nerve in a dislocation of the elbow.
8. Explain and/or demonstrate the appropriate first aid care for an athlete with a suspected dislocation of the elbow.
9. Define the term *Volkmann's contracture*.
10. Review the signs and symptoms of either medial or lateral epicondylitis of the elbow.
11. Define *osteochondritis dissecans*.
12. What are the signs and symptoms of osteochondritis dissecans of the elbow?

13. What is the location of the olecranon bursa of the elbow?

14. True or false: A Colles' fracture involves the carpal bones of the wrist.

15. Describe the signs and symptoms of a Colles' fracture.

16. Explain and/or demonstrate the appropriate first aid procedures for an athlete with a suspected Colles' fracture.

17. Which one of the following carpal bones can be located within a region at the base of the thumb known as the anatomic snuffbox?
    a. Lunate   d. Pisiform
    b. Hamate   e. Scaphoid
    c. Capitate

18. True or false: The most common form of wrist sprain is the result of forced hyperextension.

19. What anatomic structures in the wrist form the tunnel of Guyon?

20. Which major nerve passes through this tunnel?

21. What musculotendinous unit is most often involved in the condition known as de Quervain's disease?

22. Define the condition known as a ganglion.

23. Explain and demonstrate the appropriate first aid care for a suspected phalangeal fracture of the hand.

24. Which specific ligamentous structure is damaged in the condition known as gamekeeper's thumb?

25. Describe the signs and symptoms of gamekeeper's thumb; explain and demonstrate the appropriate first aid for an athlete suspected of having sustained such an injury.

26. Explain the mechanism of injury and the structures involved in the condition known as mallet finger.

27. Explain the mechanism of injury and the structures involved in the condition known as boutonnière deformity.

28. Explain the mechanism of injury and the structures involved in the condition known as jersey finger.

REFERENCES

American Academy of Orthopaedic Surgeons. (1991). *Athletic Training and Sports Medicine* (2nd ed.). Park Ridge, Ill: American Academy of Orthopaedic Surgeons.

American Medical Association. (1968). *Standard Nomenclature of Athletic Injuries* (1st ed.). Chicago, Ill: American Medical Association.

Anderson MK, Hall SJ, Martin M. (2005). *Foundations of Athletic Training: Prevention, Assessment, and Management* (3rd ed.). Philadelphia, Pa. Lippincott Williams & Wilkins.

Bartsokas TW, Palin DW, Collier DB. (1992). An unusual stress fracture site: midhumerus. *Phys Sportsmed.* 20:119–122.

Booher JM, Thibodeau GA. (2000). *Athletic Injury Assessment.* Boston, Mass: McGraw-Hill.

Brogden BS, Crow MD. (1960). Little Leaguer's elbow. *Am J Roentgenol.* 83:671–675.

Cain EL, Dugas JR. (2004). History and examination of the thrower's elbow. *Clin Sports Med.* 23:553–566.

Friel JP (ed.). (1977). *Dorland's Pocket Medical Dictionary.* Philadelphia, Pa: W. B. Saunders.

Gugenheim JJ, Stanley RF, Woods GW, Tullos HS. (1976). *Am. J Sports Med.* 4(5):189–200.

Hannafin JA, Schelkun PH. (1996). How I manage tennis and golfer's elbow. *Phys Sportsmed.* 24:63–68.

Holleb PD, Bach BR. (1990). Triceps brachii injuries. *Sports Med.* 10:273–276.

Hoppenfield S. (1976). *Physical Examination of the Spine and Extremities.* New York, NY: Appleton-Century-Crofts.

Hutson MA. (1990). *Sports Injuries—Recognition and Management.* New York, NY: Oxford University Press.

Isani A. (1990). Prevention and treatment of ligamentous sports injuries to the hand. *Sports Med.* 9:48–61.

Jobe FW, Ciccotti MG. (1994). Lateral and medial epicondylitis of the elbow. *J Am Acad Orthoped Surg.* 2:1–8.

Klingele KE, Kocher MS (2002). Little League elbow—valgus overload injury in the pediatric athlete. *Sports Med.* 32(15):1005–1015.

Larson RL, Singer KM, Bergstrom R, Thomas S. (1976). Little League survey: the Eugene study. *Am J Sports Med.* 4(5):201–209.

Micheli LJ, Fehlandt AF. (1992). Overuse injuries to tendons and apophyses in children and adolescents. *Clin Sports Med.* 11:713–726.

National Safety Council. (1991). *First Aid and CPR.* Boston, Mass: Jones and Bartlett Publishers.

O'Donoghue DH. (1976). *Treatment of Injuries to Athletes.* Philadelphia, Pa: W. B. Saunders.

Olsen S, Fleisig G, Dun R. (2006). Risk factors for shoulder and elbow injuries in adolescent baseball pitchers. *Am J Sports Med.* 34(6):905–912.

Pfeiffer RP, Shea KG, Apel PJ. (2006). Pediatric and Adolescent Athletes. In: Starkey C, Johnson G (eds.), *Athletic Training and Sports Medicine.* Sudbury, Mass: Jones and Bartlett Publishers.

Rettig AC. (2004). Athletic injuries of the wrist and hand—part II: overuse injuries of the wrist and traumatic injuries to the hand. *Am J Sports Med.* 32(1):262–273.

Saliba S, McCue FC (2006). Wrist, Hand, and Finger Pathologies. In: Starkey C, Johnson G (eds.), *Athletic Training and Sports Medicine.* Sudbury, Mass: Jones and Bartlett Publishers.

Injuries to the Thorax and Abdomen

MAJOR CONCEPTS

This chapter begins with an overview of the gross anatomy of the thorax and abdomen. Additionally, it discusses the internal organs associated with the thorax and abdomen that can be injured through sports participation. The internal organs and structures covered include the heart and lungs, liver, kidneys, spleen, stomach, and diaphragm.

The chapter also discusses external injuries such as fractures to the ribs, various joint-related problems, and breast injuries and contusions. It gives signs and symptoms of internal injuries to the heart, lungs, liver, kidneys, spleen, and bladder. At times, coaches overlook serious injuries to the internal organs; however, many injuries can have debilitating and even life-threatening effects if proper care is not applied.

go.jblearning.com/PfeifferCWS

For a full suite of assignments and additional learning activities (indicated by the icons throughout the text), use the access code found in the front of your text. If you do not have an access code, you can obtain one at go.jblearning.com/PfeifferCWS.

ANATOMY REVIEW

The thorax and abdominal cavities contain the majority of the vital organs of the body. This area is enclosed by the spinal column, the rib cage, and the clavicle, which provide bony protection for the area. The vertebrae in this area include the 12 thoracic vertebrae and the 5 lumbar vertebrae located posterior to the abdomen. There are 12 pairs of ribs in males and females. The first 7 (sometimes 8) pairs of ribs are connected to the spinal column posteriorly and to the sternum anteriorly; therefore, they are known as true ribs. The anterior connection of the true ribs is made via a costal cartilage for each rib (Moore, Daley, & Aqur, 2013). The remaining ribs, specifically ribs 8 through 10, connect via a common costal cartilage. Ribs 11 and 12 do not connect to the sternum anteriorly; thus, they are called floating ribs. The 8th to 12th pairs are sometimes referred to as false ribs. All of the joints between the ribs and the spinal column are reinforced with strong ligamentous support. This area is further strengthened by the anterior longitudinal ligament, which runs on the anterior surface of the spinal column from the occipital bone of the skull to the pelvic surface of the sacrum.

The main joints of the thorax include the intervertebral joints, the vertebral and rib joints, the sternocostal and costochondral joints, and the sternoclavicular joints. The intervertebral joints are those between each of the vertebral bodies. These joints are stabilized by ligaments and the intervertebral disks located between each vertebral body. The intervertebral disks are mostly fibrocartilaginous and play an important role in the weight-bearing ability of the spine. The ribs articulate with the vertebrae in an interesting manner. Each rib articulates with two adjacent vertebrae and the intervertebral disk. These joints are strengthened by ligaments that allow the gliding movements of the ribs at the vertebral column. Anteriorly, the 1st through the 7th ribs articulate with the sternum directly from their costal cartilage. Ribs 8 through 10 articulate with the sternum through a common cartilage. These joints are known as the sternocostal joints. The point at which the rib attaches to the costal cartilage is known as the costochondral joint. Typically, there is no movement at this joint (Gray, 1974).

One of the main joints of the thorax is the sternoclavicular joint. This is an articulation between the clavicle and the sternum. This is the only bony articulation between the thorax and the arm, and it is supported by strong ligaments. There is movement at this joint even though it is not viewed as a major site of movement, as are other joints within the region. Several muscles surround the thorax and abdomen. The main thoracic muscles include the intercostal muscles, both internal and external, which function primarily to lift the rib cage and assist with breathing. More superficially, the pectoralis major and minor are located in the upper chest area and mainly control arm movement. In the posterior thorax several muscles running the length of the spinal column are responsible for a variety of movements and stabilization of the spine. Most of the deep muscles running the length of the back, including the spinalis, longissimus, iliocostalis, and others, are responsible for keeping the spine erect. More superficially, muscles such as the latissimus dorsi, rhomboids,

TIME OUT 13.1

Main Muscles, Actions, and Innervations of the Thorax and Abdomen

Muscles	Action(s)	Innervation
Latissimus dorsi	Adducts, extends, and medially rotates the arm	Thoracodorsal
Rhomboids	Scapular adduction	Dorsal scapular
Trapezius	Elevates, rotates, and retracts scapula	Accessory and C3–4
Pectoralis major	Adduction and medial rotation of arm	Lateral and medial pectoral
Pectoralis minor	Draws shoulder anterior and inferior	Lateral and medial pectoral
External oblique	Tenses abdominal wall and flexes and rotates vertebral column	T6–12
Internal oblique	Tenses abdominal wall and rotates vertebral column	T6–12 and T1
Rectus abdominis	Tenses abdominal wall and flexes vertebral column	T7–12
Diaphragm	Inspiration	Phrenic
Transverse abdominis	Tenses abdominal wall	T6–12 and L1

trapezius, and deltoid are mainly responsible for movements of the upper extremity. See **Time Out 13.1** for specifics of muscle activity and innervation.

In the abdominal region there are also several important muscles. The main muscles of the anterior abdominal region are the external and internal obliques and the rectus abdominis. The oblique muscles help to flex and rotate the trunk; they also assist with support of the abdominal viscera. The rectus abdominis is the main muscle of the anterior abdominal wall. In the abdomen, the rectus abdominis acts to support the abdominal viscera and to flex the trunk. This muscle also assists in the lower extremity by helping to fixate the pelvis during movement, which allows the muscles of the lower extremity to function more effectively.

Internal Organs

The two main organs in the thorax (**Figure 13.1**) are the lungs and the heart. Each lung is encased in a separate and closed space called the pleural sac, which assists the lungs by helping to make respiration a smooth process. The lungs oxygenate blood as it circulates; they are normally light, soft, spongy, and pinkish in a healthy person. The right lung has three lobes, and the left lung has two, which makes the right one a little larger and heavier than the left. Located directly between the two lungs is the heart. The heart is situated in an area called the mediastinum, which also houses major blood vessels and parts of the respiratory and digestive systems (trachea and esophagus) along with nerve and lymphatic tissues. Inferior to the pleural cavities and the mediastinum is a muscle called the diaphragm. Essentially, the diaphragm separates the thoracic and abdominal cavities; it is considered the main muscle of respiration. The diaphragm is basically a circular muscle with a tendon in the middle that allows the muscle to contract and assist with breathing. There are several openings for blood vessels, nerves, and digestive structures to pass through the diaphragm.

For descriptive purposes, the abdominal region (**Figure 13.2**) is typically divided into four quadrants: the right upper and lower quadrants and the left upper and lower quadrants, with the umbilicus serving as the center point. The organs located within the right upper quadrant are the liver, gallbladder, and right kidney. In the right lower quadrant are the ascending colon and the appendix. In the left upper quadrant are the stomach, spleen, pancreas, and left kidney. In the left lower quadrant is the descending colon.

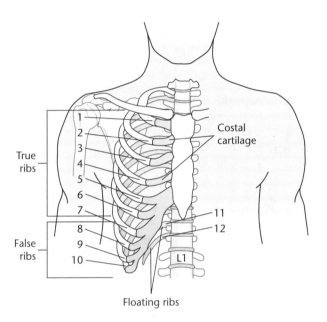

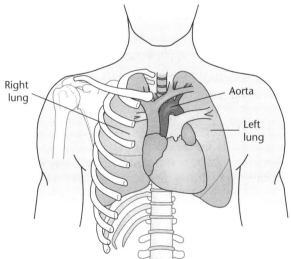

FIGURE 13.1 The internal organs of the thorax.

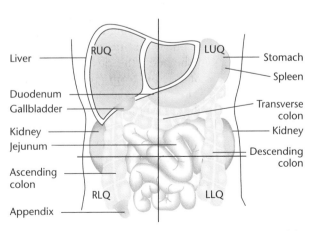

FIGURE 13.2 The four quadrants of the abdomen and the organs they house.

Common Sports Injuries

Sports injuries to the thorax and abdomen are relatively uncommon in children and adolescents. However, some injuries to the region require immediate attention to prevent long-term disability and possibly even death. The discussion first focuses on external injuries involving the skeletal, muscular, and other external components of the region. The discussion then reviews injuries to the internal organs of the thorax and abdomen.

External Injuries

Fractures

Fractures to the bones of the skeleton can occur as a result of direct trauma. An athlete may fracture a rib, the sternum, the clavicle, or possibly some part of a vertebra. Fractures to any of these structures should be cared for immediately. Without proper care, complications can occur; the athlete may develop a pneumothorax or hemothorax, both of which are life-threatening conditions. A pneumothorax is the presence of air in the pleural cavity; a hemothorax is the presence of blood in the pleural cavity. There is more detail on both of these pathologies in the lung injuries section to follow.

In the case of a sternal fracture, which is infrequent in sports, two complications may arise. First, if the manubrium is dislocated and moves posteriorly, the possibility of an airway obstruction exists. Second, if the sternum and ribs are separated completely, there is a likelihood of flail chest (loss of stability to the thoracic cage); the possible complications of this condition include a pneumothorax or hemothorax.

The other type of fracture to this region, which is more common in sports, is a rib fracture. Most often, ribs are fractured in contact sports when two players collide and the rib cage is violently compressed. The 5th through the 9th pairs of ribs are generally more susceptible to fracture. However, almost any one of the ribs can be fractured under specific circumstances. As with other bones in the body, the ribs can be broken in varying degrees of severity, from greenstick to displaced fractures. If a rib fracture is suspected, the athlete must be referred to the appropriate physician as soon as possible.

Signs and symptoms of a sternum or rib fracture include the following:

- Extreme localized pain at the site of injury that is typically aggravated by sneezing, coughing, forced inhalation, or sometimes movement.
- The athlete may grasp the chest wall at the point of injury.

- Mild swelling may occur at the site, and there may be bony deformity.
- The athlete may complain of breathing difficulties and take rapid, shallow breaths.

First aid care of a sternum or rib fracture involves the following:

1. Monitor the athlete's vital signs and watch for any respiratory distress.
2. Arrange for transport to a healthcare facility.

The athlete may also experience subluxations and dislocations at various joints in the skeleton of the thorax. The discussion here focuses on costochondral separations, which involve some type of disunion of the sternum and ribs. In a costochondral separation, the cartilage portion of the costosternal union is either separated from the sternum medially or from the rib laterally. Obviously, this requires a great deal of force, and this type of injury is usually associated with contact or collision sports. Typically, the athlete with a costochondral separation experiences a great deal of pain at the time of the injury and in many cases will complain of pain for weeks after the injury.

Signs and symptoms of a costochondral separation include the following:

- The athlete will report that a pop or snap occurred.
- A palpable defect may be felt because deformity may or may not be present; in addition, there may be swelling in the immediate area.
- Maximum or near maximum inhalation may be very difficult.
- The athlete experiences localized pain and tenderness over the area of the costochondral junction.

First aid care of a costochondral separation involves the following:

1. Immediately apply ice and light compression.
2. Treat for shock if necessary.
3. Arrange for transport to a medical facility.

Muscle Strains

The muscles in the area of the thorax and abdomen can be strained, which may result in significant pain and movement limitations. Strains of the pectoral muscles can occur when athletes are training in a strength and conditioning center with heavy weights. They can also result from the athlete putting the shoulder(s) into an extended position carrying excessive weight or being in this position when an opponent applies a high-velocity stretch through some type of mechanism. When the

Athletic Trainers SPEAK Out

Courtesy of Larry J. Leverenz, Purdue University.

During a routine high school varsity football practice on a Thursday afternoon, our players were running through the pass patterns when one of the receivers caught the ball and then tripped and fell on his stomach on the ball. Initially, he appeared to have had the wind knocked out of him but nothing more. I helped him off the field and sat him on a bench to let him recover. After getting his breath he still complained of pain in the upper abdominal region. It was different from the pain one might expect with a bruise. Although the possibility of an abdominal injury was considered, I felt that the mechanism did not seem to be violent enough to cause any serious injury. I decided, though, that because the athlete was not improving it might be wise to get him to the training room and contact our team physician. I escorted him to the training room; at this time he was complaining of pain moving to the shoulder. By the time the physician saw the athlete, all the signs and symptoms were present to indicate a spleen injury. Within 1 hour the athlete was in the operating room. Given the nonviolent nature of the drill and the lack of immediate signs, [the coaches admitted] they probably would have sent the athlete home to rest. This action would have delayed the treatment and certainly led to more serious consequences.

—Larry J. Leverenz, PhD, ATC

Larry J. Leverenz is the director of athletic training education and an athletic trainer at Purdue University.

Courtesy of Larry J. Leverenz, Purdue University.

intercostal muscles are strained, generally by a high-velocity stretching mechanism, the athlete may experience localized pain and breathing difficulty during exercise. Abdominal muscle strains can be a problem for athletes because the movements of the athlete during practice or competition can irritate the strained abdominal muscle, creating a chronic cycle of re-injury to the involved muscle(s). Even though the muscles in this area are not prime movers of any extremity, they do support the core and thus affect the overall movement capability of the athlete.

Breast Injuries

The breast is subject to injury depending on the type of sport and the gender of the athlete. Women do incur breast contusions as a result of contact in some sports. Sports bras typically do not provide protection from direct contact, but they do help to support the breast during activity. Women will have various preferences regarding the type and size of sports bra that will provide the required support. Conversely, some women will elect not to wear a bra during sports participation. This decision should be left up to the athlete, based on comfort and performance. However, if the athlete elects not to wear a sports bra, she should be aware of the possible long-term effects of not supplying proper breast

support during activity. Most often the major long-term effect is that the breast tissue stretches, resulting in loss of stability and natural breast contour.

Both men and women will at times experience nipple irritation. This problem is easily remedied by either changing tops or (if that is not possible) by placing a bandage over the nipple during competition so that irritation is reduced or eliminated.

Internal Injuries

Many organs and structures can be injured from direct trauma in collision during contact sports. It is not always easy to determine if an internal injury has occurred; therefore, the coach or athletic trainer must be educated and knowledgeable about the signs and symptoms of possible injury to an internal organ. Anatomically, the heart and lungs are separated from the abdominal viscera by the diaphragm, which is an important distinction to understand. The heart and lungs are encapsulated by their own separate membranes within the thorax. The membranes that surround these organs are important in maintaining the proper function of the heart and lungs (discussed in more detail later in this chapter). This discussion begins with the heart and lungs and continues with the internal viscera.

Heart Injuries

Although considered a rare occurrence, sudden death among athletes has become a more publicized event in recent years. In the National Collegiate Athletic Association (NCAA) athlete population, based on an analysis of reported deaths during 5 years inclusive of 2004–2008, it is estimated the death rate per year was 1:43,770 for all athletes (Harmon et al., 2011). Maron, Doerer, Haas, Tierney, and colleagues (2009) reported a steady increase in sudden death in athletes since 1993. Many times, sudden death in an athlete is the result of a cardiac problem (Asif et al., 2010). In a report by the U.S. National Registry of Sudden Death in Young Athletes (Minneapolis Heart Institute Foundation), from 1980 to 2006 there were 1866 reported sudden deaths in athletes (Maron, Doerer, Haas, Tierney, et al., 2009). During that 27-year reporting cycle, 56% (1049) of the reported sudden death events were "probably or definitely due to cardiac causes" (Maron, Doerer, Haas, Tierney, et al., 2009). A variety of cardiac events can and do result in the death of an athlete. However, some of those cardiac events can be helped through the quick and appropriate actions of a first responder. One of the cardiac events that may be most responsive to early and appropriate response is commotio cordis. Anytime the heart is compressed between the sternum and the spinal column by a violent external force, such as might be caused by being hit by the helmet of an opposing player or, a fast-moving baseball, lacrosse ball, or hockey puck, a cardiac contusion or other thoracic injures can result (Maron, Doerer, Haas, Estes, et al., 2009). When an athlete is hit in the chest and the impact is timed exactly with the repolarization phase of the contracting heart, it is possible for the athlete to experience ventricular fibrillation leading to death. This injury is known as commotio cordis and appears to be more prevalent in male youth playing lacrosse, hockey, football, basketball, and other sports (Maron, Doerer, Haas, Estes, et al., 2009; Maron, Doerer, Haas, Tierney, et al., 2009). Early intervention by trained professionals using an automated external defibrillator (AED; **Figure 13.3**) appears to be the most practical approach to saving lives threatened by commotio cordis (Casa et al., 2012; Marijon et al., 2011). Sudden cardiac arrest is an area that many medical organizations continue to emphasize as a situation that must have a well written and practiced plan of action to avoid serious complications or even death in the athlete. Specifically, the National Athletic Trainers' Association (NATA) published a statement regarding the best practices for preventing sudden death in secondary school athletics programs (Casa et al., 2013). The NATA statement primarily outlines a

The LIFEPAK® 1000 Defibrillator (AED) courtesy of Physio-Control. Used with permission of Physio-Control, Inc., and according to the Material Release form provided by Physio-Control.

FIGURE 13.3 Example of a commercially available AED for use by a trained individual.

need for a well defined emergency action plan (EAP) at all venues and training in cardiopulmonary resuscitation (CPR) and AED use for all likely early responders. Additionally, NATA issued a position statement relative to preventing sudden death in sports that points out the need for continual training for all members of the medical team in the prevention and care for athletes in the area of sudden death (Casa et al., 2012). A well-executed EAP in a time of need can save an athlete's life.

Watch any athlete with a chest injury for breathing problems, fainting, decreases in heart rate and blood pressure, and complaints of severe chest pains. Young and old athletes may experience numerous other cardiac pathologies. Athletes who have diagnosed cardiac pathology will have specific directives from their personal cardiologist regarding participation in activity. However, a condition known as hypertrophic cardiomyopathy (HCM) is a genetic disorder most often discovered after the death of an athlete. HCM is generally described as an excessive thickening of the left ventricular wall, resulting in a ventricle that is less efficient in pumping the necessary volume of blood (**Figure 13.4**). DeWeber and Beutler (2009) suggest nine questions that should be asked of each athlete during the preparticipation examination (see **Table 13.1**). The answers to these nine questions will assist the healthcare provider in determining whether the athlete may be at risk for HCM and need further testing by a cardiologist or other professional.

For many years, CPR has been the standard method of attempting resuscitation of a person when the heart has stopped beating. Many CPR curricula now include training in both cardiac compression techniques and the use of an AED. Again, it is important to remember

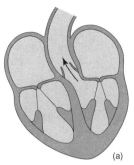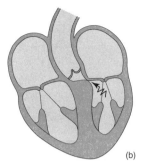

(a)   (b)

FIGURE 13.4 A comparison of normal cardiac function with malfunction characteristic of hypertrophic cardiomyopathy. (a) Normal heart, illustrating unobstructed flow of blood from left ventricle into aorta during ventricular systole. (b) Hypertrophic cardiomyopathy, illustrating obstruction to outflow of blood from left bentricle by hypertrophified septum, which impinges on anterior leaflet of mitral valve.

Courtesy of Schutt Sports.

FIGURE 13.5 Softball chest protector.

the early use of an AED has been shown to increase the success rates of life-saving measures in athletes and others experiencing specific cardiac problems.

The prevention of injuries to the heart, lungs, and chest is primarily a function of protective equipment as part of the sport or activity. In baseball and softball, the catcher is equipped with a chest protector (**Figure 13.5**). These days, chest protectors are made of materials that

TABLE 13.1
NINE QUESTIONS TO ASK ATHLETES TO DETERMINE IF FURTHER HCM TESTING MIGHT BE HELPFUL

1. Have you ever passed out or nearly passed out during exercise?
2. Have you ever passed out or nearly passed out after exercise?
3. Have you ever had discomfort, pain, or pressure in your chest during exercise?
4. Does your heart race or skip beats during exercise?
5. Has a doctor ever told you that you have a heart murmur?
6. Has a doctor ever ordered a test for your heart?
7. Has anyone in your family died for no apparent reason?
8. Does anyone in your family have a heart problem?
9. Has any family member or relative died of heart problems or of sudden death before age 50?

Source: Reprinted with permission from "Hypertrophic cardiomyopathy: Ask athletes these 9 questions," *The Journal of Family Practice*, November 2009, 579, Quadrant HealthComm.

are much better at attenuating the shock from a ball traveling at high speeds. In football, hockey, lacrosse, and some other contact sports, part of the uniform is protective equipment designed to reduce possible impact to the heart and chest area. Some sports, such as soccer and basketball, do not provide any preventative equipment protection from a blow to the chest area. In these sports, the athlete must be trained to protect the chest when specific situations arise. Certified athletic trainers and other likely early care providers must be current in their CPR training and prepared with either an AED or an emergency action plan that would provide immediate care for a player experiencing signs and symptoms of sudden cardiac arrest. An excellent source of detailed information on all aspects of HCM is a review article in *Heart Failure Clinics* (Ho, 2010).

Other Cardiac Defects

It is important that athletes are screened properly by the team physician or their personal physician, because a number of congenital defects need to be screened and ruled out before athletes should begin participation in sports. Nassar and colleagues (2011) suggest that athletes' hearts do goes through changes as they grow, develop, and continue their performance training. This group followed young World Cup soccer players for a year and documented that changes in the cardiac structure and function did occur in these young elite athletes. In addition to HCM, as noted earlier, some athletes are at a higher risk of sudden cardiac death for problems associated with Marfan syndrome, use of anabolic androgenic steroids (AAS), sickle cell trait, and other less common disorders (Casa et al., 2012; Far, Agren, & Thiblin, 2012; Harris et al., 2012; Hoffman et al., 2012). Marfan syndrome is a connective tissue disorder typically associated with the very tall athlete (male and female) that imposes a greater risk for sudden cardiac death in athletes due to a number of cardiac implications (Hoffman et al., 2012). Physicians doing the preparticipation physical exam should be well aware of this syndrome and its associated warning signs. If an athlete exhibits multiple warning signs during the PPE, the physician will refer the athlete to a cardiologist for further testing before participating in high-level athletic practices or competitions (Myerson, Sanchez-Ross, & Sherrid, 2012).

Athletes who abuse anabolic androgenic steroids must be made aware of the possibility of sudden cardiac death from the alterations in the heart after the use of these drugs in an illegal and abusive manner. By completing cardiac magnetic resonance (CMR) imaging on a control group, followed by a group of admitted AAS users all exercising regularly, it was demonstrated that the AAS users had structural abnormalities in the right ventricle, left ventricle, and left ventricular wall that were consistent with impaired ventricular flow (Luijkx et al., 2012). Even more conclusive were the findings after autopsy of 87 deceased males who tested positive for AAS use, which demonstrated abnormal cardiac hypertrophy after comparison to 173 age-adjusted controls (who were also deceased males; Far et al., 2012). Cardiac hypertrophy in this study was a leading factor in a direct cardiotropic effect.

Athletes, most commonly of African American descent, who have the sickle cell trait are susceptible to sudden cardiac death. Harris and colleagues (2012) report that sickle cell trait occurs in approximately 8% of African Americans and is generally a benign problem; however, in athletes working at high levels of physical capacity, most commonly college football players, there is a higher probability of sudden cardiac death. The report specifically points out the occurrence of sudden cardiac death during conditioning activities with this specific population. Be prepared for such an emergency with modified activity levels when needed (watch closely for muscle cramping, fatigue, excessive dyspnea), and ensure that proper hydration and cooling occur. An AED should be available at practices and competitions at all times.

Lung Injuries

In addition to a cardiac contusion, an athlete may experience a pulmonary contusion. This injury can be a complication of a rib fracture, contusion, or some other type of pulmonary injury and can go undetected.

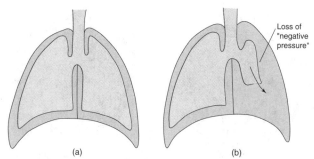

FIGURE 13.6 (a) Normal relation of lung to chest wall. Pleural space is exaggerated, and surfaces are normally in contact. "Negative pressure" is primarily a result of the tendency of the stretched lung to pull away from the chest wall. (b) Pneumothorax caused by a perforating injury of lung, allowing the air under atmospheric pressure to escape into the pleural cavity.

Pulmonary contusion can also occur in athletes experiencing blunt chest trauma. Ribs can fracture and puncture the pleural sac that surrounds the lung(s). If air gets into the pleural cavity, there is a possibility of a lung collapse (**Figure 13.6**). When a lung collapses, it is termed a pneumothorax. A more general description of a pneumothorax is the presence of air or a gas in the pleural cavity (space between the lungs and chest wall), which may cause a partial or complete collapse of the lung. As we all know, there is air inside the lungs; when outside air gets into the area of the chest cavity between the lungs and the ribs, it results in a loss of the appropriate pressure gradient between the inside and outside pressures affecting the lung and inhibits the lung's ability to expand for normal breathing to occur.

There is also the possibility of spontaneous pneumothorax among athletes. Spontaneous pneumothorax occurs without a preceding traumatic event. This injury is significant and must be attended to by a physician (**Figure 13.7**). When blood gets into the pleural cavity,

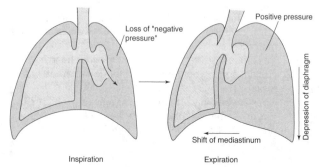

Inspiration   Expiration

FIGURE 13.7 X-ray illustrating pneumothorax secondary to multiple rib fractures in which broken ends of fractured ribs have torn through the pleura and torn underlying lung. The arrows indicate the surface of lung that is no longer in contact with chest wall.

it is commonly called hemothorax; again, this can occur without a preceding traumatic event. The coach or athletic trainer must be aware of the signs and symptoms of cardiac and pulmonary contusions and pneumothorax. The progress of the athlete should be monitored over a period of days by the athlete's healthcare provider, because some injuries have a tendency to exhibit complications later.

Signs and symptoms of a cardiac or pulmonary contusion and/or a pneumothorax include the following:

- The athlete will complain of severe pain in the chest area, sometimes radiating to the thoracic spine.
- The athlete will typically experience breathing problems—either shortness of breath or painful breathing exhibited by short, shallow breaths. Additionally, inspect for a loss of chest wall movement during breathing.
- The athlete may exhibit a nonproductive cough and may have a tachycardia heart rate.

First aid care of a cardiac or pulmonary contusion and/or a pneumothorax involves the following:

1. Treat the athlete for possible shock.
2. Monitor vital signs continuously.
3. Arrange for transport to a medical facility.

Respiratory problems can lead to or be a precursor to chest pain in the athlete. Whenever a coach or athletic trainer has an athlete who reports chest pain, that player should be seen immediately by the team physician. Chest pain and heart conditions in athletes must be reviewed by the proper medical personnel as soon as possible.

Liver

The liver aids in the production of plasma proteins and the detoxification of alcohol and other substances; it also has various digestive functions (Crowley, 2010). It is located in the upper right quadrant of the abdomen and can be susceptible to blunt trauma in collision sports such as football (Massie, Donnelly, & Ricker, 2009). The liver may be implicated if a rib fracture occurs in the upper right abdominal quadrant. Otherwise, the liver is fairly safe from injury associated with sports participation. The liver is, however, susceptible to various pathologies from the overuse of alcohol and drugs (especially massive amounts of steroids) as well as other insults from chemicals and diseases.

Kidneys

The kidneys serve to maintain the proper levels of waste, gas, salt, water, and other chemicals in the bloodstream (Crowley, 2010). The kidneys are located posteriorly and somewhat inferiorly on each side of the abdomen; they are susceptible to injury from blunt trauma or heat (via extreme exercise in the heat of the day, for example). The body can experience acute renal failure, and the kidneys will cease to function. An athlete who has hematuria (blood in the urine) after being hit by an opponent in the lower back or after having exercised strenuously in the heat should be seen by a physician. Both of these scenarios can indicate kidney problems or damage. The physician will determine how an athlete's exercise regimen will need to be modified until the urine is once again clear of any blood.

Spleen

The chief function of the spleen is to maintain a reserve of ready-to-use blood cells for the body (Crowley, 2010). It is located in the upper left quadrant of the abdomen and is somewhat protected by the ribs on the lower left side. Like most of the other internal organs, the spleen is susceptible to injury from blunt trauma and internal disorders. An athlete who gets hit quite hard in the abdomen over the spleen can suffer a lacerated spleen. Nevertheless, the spleen has the capacity to splint or patch itself at the site of the injury, because it is a reservoir of red blood cells. If the spleen does patch itself completely and the athlete is allowed to continue participating, there remains the possibility that the patch may be disrupted by even a small amount of trauma. This secondary trauma can allow internal bleeding to resume, and death can occur days after the original injury. If an athlete is hit hard in the upper left quadrant and later complains of pain in the abdomen and/or left shoulder and upper third of the left arm (sometimes the right shoulder), this is known as **Kehr's sign**. The athlete should be referred to a physician as soon as possible.

Additionally, if an athlete is suffering from mononucleosis, the spleen will probably be enlarged and susceptible to injury not only from blunt trauma but also from excessive movement during sports participation. The athlete with mononucleosis needs to be restricted in activity until the physician can discern whether the spleen has returned to normal size.

Bladder

The bladder acts as a reservoir for the urine produced by the kidneys. It is located under the midline of the

Kehr's sign Pain radiating into the left shoulder that is normally associated with an injury to the spleen.

abdominal quadrants; this is a well protected area, and the bladder is rarely injured by participation in sports and athletics. If the athlete receives a direct blow to the area of the bladder and injury does occur, the signs are pain in the localized area and possibly blood in the urine. Avoiding injury to the bladder is best accomplished by emptying it before practice or competition.

Abdominal Pain

Various types of abdominal pain occur in athletes before, during, and after competition. Some of the more common abdominal pain complaints can be linked to multiple sites in the abdomen. If an athlete is experiencing chronic pain in the same location, the athlete should see a physician as soon as possible. Another reason for abdominal pain is referred pain, as noted with the spleen or the diaphragm, either of which can be injured or irritated and result in shoulder tip pain. Esophageal problems are typically noted by the athlete as epigastric pain. Stomach problems such as duodenal ulcer are typically localized to the stomach area but have been known to produce low back pain complaints.

Exercise-related transient abdominal pain (ETAP) is a problem commonly called "side ache" or "stitch in the side" by athletes. This problem typically occurs during running early in an exercise regimen of an unconditioned athlete. The actual cause of this problem has not been exactly determined, but different hypotheses have been put forth to try to explain why this discomfort might occur in athletes. Some possible explanations are ischemia in the diaphragm, stress on the visceral connective tissues, or a cramping of the local musculature. Other theoretical explanations address the time of onset (early in the exercise program) and hypothesize that the acute increase in venous return from the lower extremities to the liver results in the extra blood flow stretching the vein near the liver. This acute stretching of the vein initiates a pain response to the brain, and the brain recognizes a pain in the right side. In response to the pain, the person typically slows his or her running pace or even stops. Following this decrease in exercise, blood flow equalizes and less stretch is placed on the vein, resulting in a decrease in the pain signal to the brain. When an athlete warms up appropriately, the incidence of this phenomenon reduces. Another theory for pain on the left side in the exercising athlete is that gas or fecal matter is being moved through the intestinal tract and that during exercise the timing is such that this movement is inhibited and could be stopped in one of the angles of the winding intestinal tract. Side aches do not appear to be a problem that eliminates athletes from participation in most sports, and most athletes learn how to deal with them on the rare occurrences when they take place.

It is also possible to have right side pain that is not a result of any of the previous causes but that can be an early sign of acute appendicitis. Initially, the athlete has a loss of appetite, followed by generalized abdominal pain. When the problem progresses, the chief complaint of the athlete with acute appendicitis is severe pain in the lower right quadrant. At times, this pain is excruciating and the athlete can be rendered immobile. Additionally, the athlete experiences nausea and possibly vomiting and has a fever that increases over time. The athlete will be point tender to palpation in the lower right quadrant (McBurney's point) and should be taken to the hospital immediately. Without medical attention, the athlete can die from the complications associated with a ruptured appendix.

Many parent groups now advocate that medical professionals be more diligent in determining methods to circumvent problems associated with injury or preexisting conditions of the heart, lungs, and abdominal contents. Although some athletes may have preexisting cardiac abnormalities, the uses of echocardiogram or echocardiography during the preparticipation screening are not deemed necessary by most medical organizations at the present time. There is a good deal of evidence on both sides of this debate relative to cost effectiveness and reliability of the testing (Baggish et al., 2010; Estes & Link, 2012). In Veneto, Italy, young competitive athletes were routinely screened during the preparticipation examination with a 12-lead ECG as part of the exam. Conversely, in the state of Minnesota, which has similar demographics to Veneto, Italy, the preparticipation examination for the cardiac portion focused on history and current symptoms. Over the 26-year period, the difference in the incidence of sudden death in athletes for each region was not significant (Maron, Haas, et al., 2009). Conversely, Wheeler and colleagues (2010) suggest that the inclusion of a 12-lead ECG in the athletic preparticipation exam is cost effective over the use of history and symptoms only. Support for the use of an

ECG in the preparticipation examination has been proposed in recent reports, arguing the added cost is minimal and can lead to a greater ability to identify athletes at risk. However, there is some question about the training of the physician providing the PPE and reading the ECG. If the physician is not well trained in reading the ECG, there can be errors made which can result in either unnecessary costs or missed opportunities to refer an athlete for further testing (Asif & Drezner, 2012). The advice and direction of the team or personal physician are critical for the final decision regarding what testing should be implemented to ensure the athlete's health. It is important to review each athlete's history very closely to determine whether a cardiac or respiratory problem may be exacerbated by an increased level of athletic participation. If an athlete has a family or personal history of cardiac or respiratory problems, the physician providing the preparticipation examination must make an informed decision as to the appropriateness of additional specific medical testing and of participation in a specific sport or activity for that athlete.

Preexisting conditions of the chest that may disqualify an athlete from participation can include but are not limited to problems such as HCM (abnormal left ventricle growth), heart murmurs and arrhythmias, significantly decreased lung function from disease or a disorder such as cystic fibrosis, or chronic obstructive pulmonary disease. Disqualification from sports participation based on these conditions is dependent on the type of sport being considered, the amount of stress the activity will place on the dependent structures or systems, and the ability to control potential problems during the activity. Athletes with what might be considered a severe cardiac or respiratory disorder may be able to participate in specific activities depending on the control of their disorder, the type of activity, and the willingness of the physician to help the athlete make the necessary adjustments for participation at some level.

1. True or false: Men and women have the same number of ribs.

2. Explain the difference between true ribs and floating ribs.

3. List the five main joints of the thorax.

4. With what necessary function do the intercostal muscles assist in the thorax?

5. True or false: Both lungs are the same size and configuration.

6. What is the name of the enclosed space where each lung is located?

7. True or false: The diaphragm separates the heart and lungs from the abdominal viscera.

8. Explain the difference between a pneumothorax and a hemothorax.

9. List the signs and symptoms of a costochondral separation.

10. What is the best indicator of kidney damage or disorder?

11. True or false: The spleen is able to splint itself if injured by blunt trauma.

12. Name the infection, prevalent among college-aged students, that causes the spleen to enlarge, requiring the athlete to reduce physical activity until the spleen is once again normal.

13. List four functions of the kidneys.

14. When pain occurs in the abdomen, what are some of the locations that the abdominal pain can be referred to?

15. Explain the best way to prevent bladder injury among athletes.

REFERENCES

Asif IM, Drezner JA. (2012). Sudden cardiac death and pre-participation screening: The debate continues—in support of electrocardiogram-inclusive preparticipation screening. *Prog Cardiovasc Dis*. 54:445–450.

Asif IM, Harmon KG, Drezner JA, Klossner D. (2010). Incidence and etiology of sudden death in National Collegiate Athletic Association (NCAA) athletes. *Clin J Sport Med*. 20(3):136.

Baggish AL, Hutter AM Jr, Wang F, Yared K, Weiner RB, Kupperman E, Picard MH, Wood MJ. (2010). Cardiovascular screening in collegiate athletes with and without electrocardiography: A cross sectional study. *Ann Int Med*. 152:269–275.

Casa DJ, Almquist J, Anderson SA, Baker L, Bergeron MF, Biagioli B, et al. (2013). The inter-association task force for preventing sudden death in secondary school athletics programs: Best-practices recommendations. *J Ath Train*, 48(4):548–553.

Casa DJ, Guskiewicz KM, Anderson SA, Courson RW, Heck JF, Jimenez CC, McDermott BP, Miller MG, Stearns RL, Swartz EE, Walsh KM. (2012). National Athletic Trainers' Association position statement: Preventing sudden death in sports. *J Ath Train*, 47(1):96–118.

Crowley LV. (2010). *An Introduction to Human Disease* (8th ed.). Sudbury, Mass: Jones & Bartlett Learning.

deWeber K, Beutler A. (2009). Hypertrophic cardiomyopathy: Ask athletes these 9 questions. *J Fam Practice*. 58(11): 576–584.

Estes NAM, Link MS. (2012). Preparticipation athletic screening including electrocardiogram: An unproven strategy for prevention of sudden cardiac death in the athlete. *Prog Cardiovasc Dis*. 54:451–454.

Far GRM, Agren G, Thiblin I. (2012). Cardiac hypertrophy in deceased users of anabolic androgenic steroids: An investigation of autopsy findings. *Cardiovascular Pathology*. 21:312–316.

Gray H. (1974). *Anatomy, Descriptive and Surgical*. Philadelphia, Pa: Running Press.

Harmon KG, Asif IM, Klossner D, Drezner JA. (2011). Incidence of sudden cardiac death in National Collegiate Athletic Association athletes. *Circulation*. 123:1594–1600.

Harris KM, Haas TS, Eichner ER, Maron BJ. (2012). Sickle cell trait associated with sudden death in competitive athletes. *Am J Cardiol*. 110:1185–1188.

Ho CY. (2010). Hypertrophic cardiomyopathy. *Heart Failure Clin*. 6:141–159.

Hoffman BA, Rybczynski M, Rostock T, Servatius H, Drewitz I, Steven D, Aydin A, Sheikhzadeh S, Darko V, von Kodolitsch Y, Willems S. (2012). Prospective risk stratification of sudden cardiac death in Marfan's syndrome. *Int J Cardiol*. 167(6):2539–2545.

Luijkx, T, Velthuis BK, Backx FJ, Buckens CF, Prakken NH, Rienks R, Mali WP, Cramer MJ. (2012). Anabolic androgenic steroid use is associated with ventricular dysfunction on cardiac MRI in strength trained athletes. *Int J Cardiol*. 167(3):664–668.

Marijon E, Tafflet M, Celermajer DS, Dumas F, Perier M-C, Mustafic H, Toussaint J-F, Desnos M, Rieu M, Benameur N, Le Heuzey J-Y, Empana J-P, Jouven X. (2011). Sports-related sudden death in the general population. *Circulation*, 124:672–681.

Maron BJ, Doerer JJ, Haas TS, Estes NA, Hodges JS, Link MS. (2009). Commotio cordis and the epidemiology of sudden death in competitive lacrosse. *Pediatrics*. 124(3):966–971.

Maron BJ, Doerer JJ, Haas TS, Tierney DM, Mueller FO. (2009). Sudden deaths in young competitive athletes. Analysis of 1866 deaths in the United States, 1980–2006. *Circulation*. 119:1085–1092.

Maron BJ, Haas TS, Doerer JJ, Thompson PD, Hodges JS. (2009). Comparison of U.S. and Italian experiences with sudden cardiac deaths in young competitive athletes and implications for preparticipation screening strategies. *Am J Cardiol*. 104:276–280.

Massie JB, Donnelly DV, Ricker KL. (2009). Liver laceration sustained by a college football player. *ATT*. 14(2):23–26.

Moore K, Dalley AF, Aqur AM. (2013). *Clinically Oriented Anatomy* (7th ed.). Philadelphia, Pa: Lippincott Williams & Wilkins.

Myerson M, Sanchez-Ross M, Sherrid MV. (2012). Preparticipation athletic screening for genetic heart disease. *Prog Cardiovasc Dis*. 54:543–552.

Nassar YS, Saber M, Farhan A, Moussa A, Elsherif A. (2011). One year cardiac follow up of young world cup football team compared to nonathletes. *Egypt Heart J*. 63:13–22.

Wheeler MT, Heidenreich PA, Froelicher VF, Hlatky MA, Ashley EA. (2010). Cost effectiveness of preparticipation screening for prevention of sudden cardiac death in young athletes. *Ann Int Med*. 152:276–286.

14

Injuries to the Hip and Pelvis

MAJOR CONCEPTS

This chapter includes a basic overview of the anatomy in the region of the hip and pelvis and a brief description of movements by the joints and actions of the musculature in the area. It discusses some of the more common hip and pelvis injuries incurred in sports and outlines emergency procedures. The chapter also includes a section about injuries to the area that are less common in athletes. Coaches need to be aware of these types of injuries because of the possibility of negative long-term consequences that can result from improper care. The chapter reviews injuries to the male genitalia, including testicular contusion and torsion. It also covers hernia and nerve problems and discusses proper referral.

go.jblearning.com/PfeifferCWS

For a full suite of assignments and additional learning activities (indicated by the icons throughout the text), use the access code found in the front of your text. If you do not have an access code, you can obtain one at go.jblearning.com/PfeifferCWS.

ANATOMY REVIEW

The hip and pelvis form a resemblance to a "square" in the way they are constructed. This area comprises the two large, irregularly shaped pelvic bones on the lateral sides, the sacrum and coccyx posteriorly, and the articulation of the pubic bones anteriorly. The pelvic bones are also known as the innominate bones and are made up of three distinct parts: the ilium, the ischium, and the pubis. In the adult, the three parts are fused and come together at a lateral point called the acetabulum, which is where the head of the femur articulates with the hip to form the hip joint (**Figure 14.1**).

The bony pelvis has several functions in the body: The lower extremities attach here, muscle attachments are prevalent, and it provides substantial protection for the entire pelvic region. In the female, the pelvis becomes important in the birth process (Moore, Dalley, & Aqur, 2013).

The major articulations of the bony pelvis include the hip joints, the sacroiliac joints, and the symphysis pubis. The hip joint is the articulation of the head of the femur and the acetabulum in the hip bone; it is a true ball-and-socket joint that is well supported by strong ligaments. The sacroiliac joints are formed by the sacral bones and the iliac portion of the hip bones. The symphysis pubis is formed by the two pubic bones meeting in the anterior portion of the bony pelvis. All of these joints have strong ligamentous support that assists in joint stability.

Several nerves and blood vessels course through the bony pelvis (**Figures 14.2** and **14.3**). Some of the more important nerves that course down the lower extremity are subdivisions that make up the cauda equina. The spinal cord ends at the L2 level, and the cauda equina

exits the spinal cord beginning at L2 and proceeding inferiorly (Gray, 1974). Nerves exiting the spinal cord below the L1 level typically pass through the bony pelvis. These nerves include the formation of the lumbar plexus, the sacral plexus, the coccygeal plexus, and other individual nerves. Probably the most well known of these is the sciatic nerve, which is the largest in the body and is made up of nerve roots L4 through S3. The sciatic nerve passes through the posterior portion of the bony pelvis and down the posterior aspect of the leg. The blood vessels of the area include both arteries and veins that supply the pelvis and lower extremities. The more well known of these vessels include the iliac artery and vein.

Many of the muscles that attach to the bony pelvis are ones that move the lower extremities. The smaller muscles consist of the medial and lateral rotators of the femur. Some of the medial rotators include the tensor fasciae latae and gluteus minimus. These muscles are quite active in many movements of the lower extremity. The lateral rotators of the hip are small muscles located deep within the hip area that are also quite active in many movements of the lower extremity. One of the muscles more commonly injured is the piriformis,

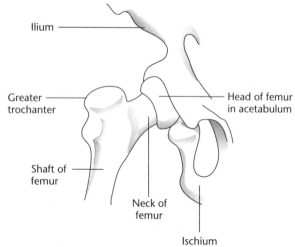
FIGURE 14.1 The ball-and-socket structure of the hip joint (anterior view).

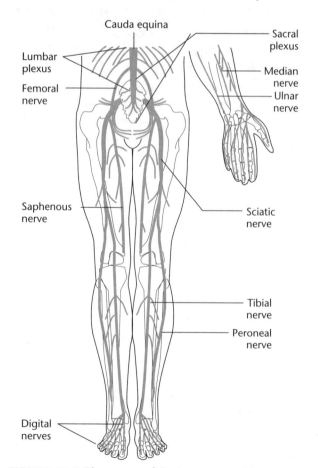
FIGURE 14.2 The nerves of the lower extremities.

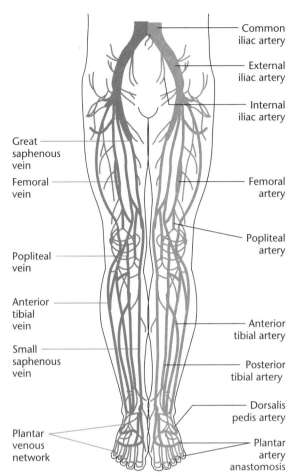

FIGURE 14.3 The blood vessels of the lower extremities.

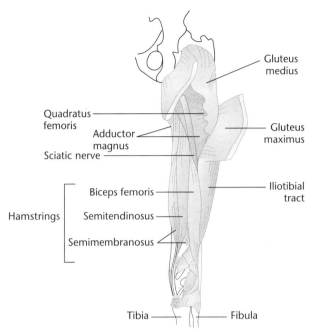

FIGURE 14.4 Hamstring and gluteal muscles (posterior view).

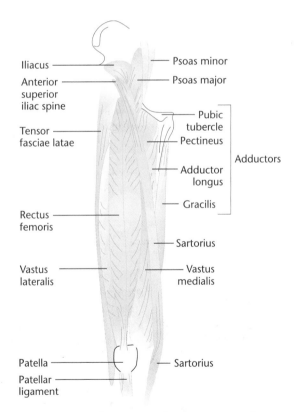

FIGURE 14.5 Quadriceps muscles (anterior view).

which attaches to the anterior surface of the sacrum and to the greater trochanter of the femur. The piriformis is a lateral rotator of the thigh; the sciatic nerve runs directly beneath the piriformis and can be irritated by the overuse of this muscle. Other external rotators of the thigh include the gemelli (superior and inferior), which attach on the ischium and run to the greater trochanter of the femur. All of these muscles (**Figure 14.4**) are small in comparison to the surrounding muscles, but they play an important part in the proper functioning of the hip and leg.

Many muscles attach on the pelvis and provide musculature for the leg, back, and abdomen. The muscles responsible for many of the large movements at the hip joint include flexors, extensors, adductors, and abductors. The main hip flexors include the rectus femoris, the iliopsoas group, the tensor fasciae latae, and the sartorius (**Figure 14.5**). The rectus femoris attaches at the anterior inferior iliac spine and runs down the front of the leg to the common attachment of the quadriceps group at the patellar tendon. The iliopsoas group is a combination of the iliacus and the psoas muscles, which attach on the anterior lumbar spine and iliac crest and come

together as they run down to the lesser trochanter of the femur. The tensor fasciae latae and sartorius attach on the anterior iliac spine. The tensor fasciae latae runs to the lateral condyle of the tibia, whereas the sartorius runs across the anterior thigh and attaches to the anterior medial aspect of the tibia. The sartorius becomes one of the muscles of the pes anserinus group.

The main muscles of hip extension are the gluteals and the hamstrings (Figure 14.4). The gluteus maximus is the main hip extensor of the gluteals. The gluteus maximus attaches on the posterior surface of the ilium and runs inferiorly to the femur. The hamstrings attach mainly on the ischial tuberosity; then, two of the muscles, the semitendinosus and semimembranosus, run more medially on the posterior leg and attach near the sartorius and on the posterior/medial condyle of the tibia, respectively. The biceps femoris runs more laterally on the posterior leg and attaches to the lateral aspect of the tibia and the head of the fibula.

The muscles that adduct the hip are located on the medial portion of the leg commonly called the groin area. The main muscles included in this group are the three adductors (brevis, longus, and magnus) and the pectineus and gracilis (Figure 14.5). The adductors attach on the pubis and run to the femur. The pectineus also attaches at the pubis and runs to the femur. The gracilis attaches on the inferior portion of the pubis and runs medially down the leg to the anterior medial portion of the tibia. The gracilis, sartorius, and semitendinosus compose the pes anserinus group.

Common Sports Injuries

The hip and pelvic regions are well designed anatomically: Sports-related injuries to the skeletal structures of the hip and pelvis are not common. Injuries to the soft tissues in the region are more common and can be quite debilitating to the athlete. Sports-related injuries to this area commonly involve collision sports or forceful movements pursuant to an activity that requires power and speed of the lower extremities. However, one must remember that overuse injuries can also be associated with the hip and pelvis.

Skeletal Injuries
Fractures of the Pelvis

One of the most devastating injuries to the pelvic region is the fracture of one of the pelvic bones. Typically, a great deal of force is necessary to cause a fracture of this type. This is not a common injury related to sports participation. Still, it can occur in sports such as hockey, pole-vaulting, or football, in which there is the possibility of direct compression from another athlete, a fall from a height, or being twisted and hit by another player. Skeletal injuries to the pelvis in the adolescent population can be extremely serious, especially if the injury involves an open epiphysis. Any suspected skeletal injury to this area should be referred to a physician as quickly as possible.

Signs and symptoms of a fractured pelvis include the following:

* Abnormal pain in the pelvic region after the injury.
* There might be swelling at the site, with the rare occurrence of a visual or palpable deformity at the injury.
* Pain is elicited when the iliac crests are pressed together by the examiner.
* Associated injuries to internal organs such as the bladder are possible and should be ruled out only by the proper medical personnel. Blood in the urine (hematuria) must be immediately reported.

Athletic Trainers SPEAK Out

Courtesy of Shawna Baker, MS, ATC.

A sports hernia or "Athletic Pubalgia" can be tricky and elusive to assess correctly. Athletes who do lots of kicking, twisting, and change in directions are most susceptible to this pathology. Athletes will present with chronic, vague, activity-related groin and/or lower abdominal pain that is unresponsive to conservative treatment. Oftentimes these symptoms are mistaken for other hip pathologies such as strains, sprains, bursitis, synovitis or bony involvement. Diagnostic imaging (X-ray, MRI, CT scans) can be helpful in excluding these differential diagnoses. If a regimen of conservative treatment that includes rest, ice, gentle stretching, and strengthening does not decrease the symptoms, surgical intervention may be needed to get the athlete back on the field or court.

—Shawna Baker, MS, ATC

Shawna Baker is the Head Athletic Trainer at Point Loma Nazarene University.
Courtesy of Shawna Baker, MS, ATC.

First aid care of a fractured pelvis involves the following:

1. Treat for possible shock and internal bleeding.
2. Monitor the athlete's vital signs regularly.
3. Transport the athlete to the hospital on a long spine board with the foot of the board elevated to eliminate pooling of blood in the lower extremities.

A fracture of the pelvis is a serious injury and should be evaluated by a physician as soon as possible. Treatment depends on the severity of the injury and should be complete before the athlete returns to practice or competition. Under no circumstances should an athlete with a suspected fracture of the pelvis return to competition before seeing a physician.

Other Adolescent Fractures

Femoral Neck Stress Fracture

This injury occurs more commonly in the thin amenorrheic athlete involved in running or an endurance sport. The femoral neck stress fracture is generally a result of a loss in shock-absorbing capacity of the fatigued muscles in the hip area. In the athlete, this problem can also result from improper or worn-out footwear, hard running surface(s), hip deformities, or other kinetic chain problems resulting in excess stresses in the leg(s). Athletes can complain of severe anterior thigh or groin pain when there is the possibility of a femoral neck stress fracture (Breugem, Hulscher, & Steller, 2009). The athlete will be able to walk but will experience significant pain during ambulation. Seeing a physician is necessary to get radiographs, which help to diagnose the problem. As with other stress fractures, initial conventional radiographs may be normal and the athlete will need to return to the physician at a later date if the symptoms persist (McSweeney et al., 2012).

Slipped Capital Femoral Epiphysis

This problem occurs most commonly in 10- to 15-year-old boys. Typically, it occurs in boys who are tall and have recently experienced a rapid growth period, or in boys who are overweight and in whom the secondary sex characteristics are late in appearing. The athlete experiencing this problem will exhibit a flexed hip, lack of hip motion, and pain in the anterior groin, hip, thigh, or knee. Children younger than the age of 12 experiencing significant chronic knee pain should definitely be referred to their physician to rule out the existence of a pathology that may exist.

Hip Pointer

Probably the most common injury to the region is a contusion to the superior/anterior portion of the iliac crest, which is commonly referred to as a **hip pointer**.

Typically, with this injury the athlete receives a direct blow to the area from an opponent's helmet or falls to the ground with great force. This can be an extremely painful and debilitating injury for the athlete, but it is not one that requires emergency attention or causes major complications if further activity is necessary.

Signs and symptoms of a hip pointer include the following:

- Swelling at the site of injury.
- Discoloration at the site of injury.
- Pain and discomfort at the site of injury.
- The athlete may walk with a slight limp on the affected side. Coughing, sneezing, and laughing may also produce pain at the site of injury.

First aid care of a hip pointer involves the following:

1. Immediately apply ice to the injured area.
2. Have the athlete rest and avoid activity that involves the lower extremities.
3. If the injury is severe, walking with crutches may be necessary for a few days.

Long-term care for this type of injury is rather simple. The contusion has in most cases caused minimal damage to an area where several muscles attach directly to bone tissue. The muscular attachments in the abdominal region are the cause of pain when the athlete coughs, sneezes, or laughs. The player will usually be able to participate on a limited basis within 1 to 2 weeks, depending on the severity of the injury. It is important to note that if an athlete wishes to continue participating in sports while recovering from a hip pointer, the area should be padded well so that further damage cannot occur if a similar incident happens before recovery is complete. This can be easily accomplished by securing a doughnut-shaped piece of foam padding over the area (**Figure 14.6**). Additionally, it is helpful to place hard plastic over the doughnut pad to provide even more protection to the area.

Other Hip Problems

Hip problems are becoming more common among all types and ages of athletes. This was verified in a study completed on elite soccer players, which demonstrated that 72% of male and 50% of female elite soccer players showed radiographic hip abnormalities (Gerhardt et al., 2012). Now that we are aware of the potential for hip injury in elite athletes, this information will assist the

hip pointer Contusion and associated hematoma to the superior/anterior portion of the iliac crest.

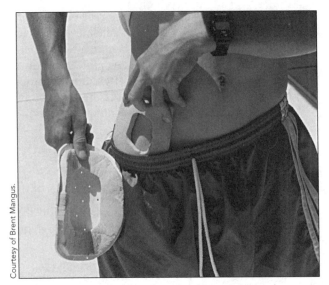

Courtesy of Brent Mangus.

FIGURE 14.6 An athlete inserts a hip-pointer pad.

medical community in becoming more progressive in the prevention and treatment of these injuries in all populations. Labral tears of the hip are also increasingly being recognized in the athletic population and the general population. In the athletic population, most labral tears result from trauma, repetitive excessive hip motions (soccer, hockey, dance), and/or femoroacetabular impingement (FAI; Hosalkar et al., 2012). Athletes experiencing this injury generally complain of anterior hip or groin pain, and some may indicate buttock or leg pain (Groh & Herrera, 2009). Hosalkar and colleagues (2012) suggest that a strain injury of the rectus femoris muscle may result in a concomitant tear of the acetabular labrum (particularly in highly active pediatric patients). If a tear of the labrum exists, the physician will want to follow the progress of the athlete closely to ensure a safe return to sports participation.

Femoroacetabular impingement (FAI) can be a major cause of hip pain in the athlete (McSweeney et al., 2012). The FAI injury is a result of the femoral head not being congruent with the acetabulum. When the hip is being heavily utilized in sports participation, the resulting trauma to the noncongruent bony structures results in hip pain and loss of movement. It is postulated that this problem not only causes immediate pain and loss of movement, but can result in osteoarthritis in populations such as ballet dancers and ice hockey goalies (Charbonnier et al., 2011; McSweeney et al., 2012). Signs and symptoms of FAI include generalized anterolateral hip pain either unilaterally or bilaterally (depending on the activity), sharp pain when turning (especially toward the affected side), pain from prolonged sitting or rising from a sitting position, and entering or exiting

a car. The athlete will need to be referred to the team physician or their personal physician who will start with a physical examination, radiographs, and other diagnostic testing (Kuhlman & Domb, 2009).

Athletes who participate in excessive running as a part of their sport can experience what is known as "snapping hip syndrome." Snapping hip is an abnormal sensation around the lateral hip area that occurs when the athlete moves the hip in a specific direction. Usually, there is little if any pain associated with snapping hip. This problem is attributed to one of the muscles in the lateral hip riding over the top of the greater trochanter of the femur. The structures that could be involved include the iliotibial band, tensor fascia lata, and gluteus medius. There could be subluxation of the hip or labral tears that induce extra movement of the femur during locomotion. The possibility of a problem occurring in the intra-articular area could produce a snapping hip sensation. Injuries such as labral tears, articular cartilage injury, intra-articular bodies, or other similar problems could be discovered via radiography (McSweeney et al., 2012). Typically, treatment consists of stretching tightened muscles that may contribute to the snapping sensation and correcting any biomechanical deviations of the area. The physician may also recommend anti-inflammatory medications to the athlete.

Some researchers have suggested a surgical release of some of the fibrous bands sliding over the greater trochanter, which can result in some relief for the athlete. This surgical intervention has been shown to have a low recurrence rate and a high rate of patient satisfaction (Yoon et al., 2009). However, most physicians do not view surgical intervention as the first line of treatment for snapping hip syndrome.

Trochanteric bursitis is another rare problem experienced by some athletes. It is a problem seen most often in middle-aged people, but athletes, especially runners, are becoming more prone to trochanteric bursitis. This bursitis is usually a result of either acute trauma to the specific area or repeated microtrauma to the tendon attachments with secondary inflammation of the bursae in the area. The iliotibial band can be a source of the problem if it is tight and the athlete continues to run when he or she is experiencing signs and symptoms of trochanteric bursitis. When an athlete is experiencing the onset of trochanteric bursitis, he or she will initially complain of pain over the greater trochanter followed by pain radiating down the anterior or lateral thigh and to the buttock region. Most athletes benefit from stretching the iliotibial band and the low back area in the proximity of the sacroiliac joints, and taking a nonsteroidal anti-inflammatory. For some athletes, it may be necessary to pad the area if there is a chance of external trauma such as falling or being hit by another athlete in the hip. On rare occurrences, athletes do not respond to conservative treatment and benefit from surgical management (Rowand, Chambliss, & Mackler, 2009). Few athletes will need surgery if proper treatment is initiated early in the injury cycle.

Osteitis Pubis

Another type of skeletal injury to the pelvic area is **osteitis pubis**, a condition resulting from continued stress and possibly some degeneration in the symphysis pubis joint. This injury is commonly a result of overuse and chronic strain on the joint. Sports in which the participant is required to kick, twist the upper body, or have frequent lateral movements during participation produce a greater number of these injuries. The largest numbers of osteitis pubis injuries are reported in soccer, rugby, football, and ice hockey players (Choi, McCartney, & Best, 2011). Osteitis pubis is a difficult injury to diagnose because of the many muscles and structures in the pelvic area, resulting in a delayed diagnosis or an undiagnosed problem (Beatty, 2012; Hill et al., 2011).

The athlete will complain of an insidious onset of pain that worsens progressively. The athlete may indicate that the pain is in the groin area (unilateral or bilateral) and complain of testicular or scrotal pain along with anterior pubic, suprapubic, or even hip pain when experiencing osteitis pubis (Beatty, 2012; Hill et al., 2011). An athlete complaining of these symptoms should be referred to the appropriate doctor for complete evaluation. Because this is a chronic problem, first aid is typically not necessary, but the athlete benefits from rest, ice, and antiinflammatory medications such as aspirin or ibuprofen. This disorder typically responds well to therapy, with very few if any long-term side effects. An athlete may take anywhere from 3 months to a year to return to preinjury functioning levels. If osteitis pubis is diagnosed by the physician at early onset, the timeframe for full return to activity may be reduced because treatment is initiated early. Athletes who do not respond to conservative therapy may be candidates for surgery.

Injury of the Sacroiliac Joint

The sacroiliac (SI) joint, which is the articulation between the sacrum and the pelvis (**Figure 14.7**), is a common site of pain in the posterior aspect of the pelvis. Movement at this joint is limited because of the configuration of the bones and numerous ligaments. This joint can present problems for the athlete if it becomes completely immobile or if it becomes inflamed from an injury or other problem. Injuries resulting in an immobile SI joint require specific movement techniques by a trained professional to restore the normal motion in the

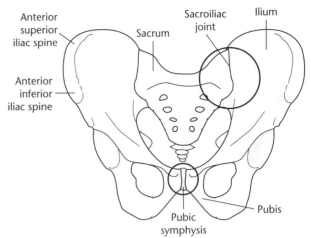

FIGURE 14.7 Common sites of hip injuries.

joint. Problems with inflammation in the SI joint can be treated by a certified athletic trainer or physical therapist under the direction of a physician.

Hip Dislocation

Infinitely more serious is a hip dislocation. This injury is actually quite rare in athletic events; however, it may occur to an athlete participating in contact sports. If a violent collision occurs between two players or between a player and another object (for example, the boards surrounding a hockey rink), this type of injury can happen. Typically, when this injury occurs the hip joint is in flexion, and the force is applied through the femur. Most often the hip dislocates posteriorly, and the athlete experiences extreme pain and loss of movement in the affected extremity.

Signs and symptoms of a dislocated hip include the following:

- Abnormal pain at the site of injury.
- Swelling at the site of injury, with a palpable defect.
- Knee of the involved extremity is angled toward the opposite leg.
- This injury is typically quite visible to the observer.

First aid care of a dislocated hip involves the following:

1. Treat for possible shock.
2. Immobilize the athlete and transport to the nearest medical center.
3. Care should be given to monitor blood flow to the leg at all times.

osteitis pubis Inflammation of the bones in the region of the symphysis pubis.

Soft-Tissue Injuries

Because of the size and functions of the musculature in the hip and pelvic region, soft-tissue injuries are not very common in sports. The ligamentous support of the hip, sacrum, and other structures in the area is very strong; as a result, sprains rarely occur here. However, several muscles attach in the area of the pelvis, including the musculature on both the anterior and posterior aspects of the thigh, and these are subject to avulsion.

Avulsion Fractures

The possibility of muscle avulsions during forceful activity always exists. Skeletally immature athletes are more prone to avulsion fractures around the hip because their tendons are stronger than their cartilaginous growth centers. The mechanism of this type of injury is a sudden near maximal muscle contraction. This results in the tendon pulling off a piece of bone at the attachment site. In a skeletally mature adult, this action usually results in a torn muscle or tendon because the bone is stronger than the tendon. In the adolescent, the tendon is stronger than the bone, so the result is an avulsion fracture. Avulsion fractures occur more commonly in adolescents who participate in sports requiring short bursts of maximal muscle contraction, such as soccer, tennis, sprinting, or jumping. The injured athlete will complain of severe localized pain and ecchymosis at the site of the injury. Common sites of injury in the adolescent are the anterior inferior iliac spine where the rectus femoris attaches, and the ischial tuberosities where the hamstrings attach.

Signs and symptoms of avulsion fractures in the pelvic region include the following:

- Pain and swelling at the site of injury.
- Inability to produce a specific movement that is usually accomplished easily.
- Point tenderness over the affected area.
- Movement of the muscle closer to its opposite attachment when contracted. This is not easily detected in many avulsion injuries.
- The athlete may report having felt or heard a snap or pop at the time of injury.

First aid care of avulsion fractures in the pelvic region involves the following:

1. Immediately apply ice and require the athlete to rest.
2. Limit motion as much as possible. Walking with crutches may be necessary.
3. Have the athlete evaluated by a physician as soon as possible to determine the extent of the injury if an avulsion fracture is suspected. Radiographs

done by the physician will document the avulsion fracture.

Avulsion fractures are debilitating and should be treated conservatively to reduce the amount of scar tissue that can result. It is very wise to allow an athletic trainer or physical therapist to rehabilitate the athlete according to the recommendations of a physician. Without proper treatment and rehabilitation, this type of injury can be a problem in an athlete's future career.

Injuries to the Male Genitalia

An injury that is experienced by male athletes and is typically transient in nature is testicular contusion. Most male athletes competing in contact sports considered high-risk activities for testicular trauma wear a cup protector. However, this device does not always provide complete protection, nor do athletes always wear one. When the athlete receives a contusion to the testicular region, there is extreme pain and usually a complete loss of mobility for a short period of time. Typically, this pain and the resulting partial loss of movement are transitory; however, severe damage such as a ruptured testicle can be caused by extreme trauma to the testicles.

Signs and symptoms of testicular or scrotal contusions include the following:

- Extreme pain and point tenderness.
- The athlete may get into the fetal position and grasp his testicles.
- The athlete will report a direct blow to the testicles.

 WHAT IF?

You are coaching a high school sophomore in the high hurdles on a cool, rainy afternoon in early spring. As the young man completes a start and five consecutive high hurdles, he grabs the back of his right leg, just below the buttock, and falls to the ground in obvious pain. You go to his aid immediately, and on examination you note that he is extremely tender in the region of the ischial tuberosity (origin of the hamstring muscles). He reports that he felt something tear and heard a pop while crossing the last hurdle, with immediate sharp pain. He has no history of a previous injury to this region. However, he has been complaining of tight hamstrings for the past several weeks. What type of injury may be present? What should be done for first aid? Should this athlete be referred to a physician?

First aid care of testicular or scrotal contusions involves the following:

1. Allow the athlete to rest on the sideline until he is ready to return to activity.
2. In severe cases, apply ice and allow the athlete to remain lying down in the locker room or athletic training facility when possible.
3. If there is swelling or lasting pain, refer the athlete to a physician as soon as possible.

The pain and debilitation associated with injuries to the testicles are transitory and should resolve without much intervention in a relatively short period of time (typically a few minutes). If the pain and debilitating effects last much longer than a few minutes, the athlete must see a physician to determine whether severe damage has been sustained by the testicles at the time of injury.

Testicular torsion, or twisting of the testicles, can occur and should be recognized quickly; if this happens the athlete should be referred to a physician immediately. One of the testicles may, for any number of reasons, get twisted within the scrotum; as a result, the blood supply is compromised to or from the area, causing swelling to occur in the scrotum. The swelling may become quite uncomfortable, and the athlete needs to be transported to a medical facility as quickly as possible for treatment. Swelling in the scrotum can have serious side effects if not cared for immediately.

Hernias

A **hernia** is the protrusion of abdominal viscera through the abdominal wall; this typically occurs in the groin area. In males, inguinal hernias are more common; femoral hernias are more prevalent among female athletes (Crowley, 2010). Most hernias are detected during a preparticipation physical evaluation. However, an athlete who is suffering from a hernia most likely has an abnormal protrusion in the groin area and experiences pain in the groin and/or testicles. The athlete should seek proper medical advice promptly to discern how soon the hernia will have to be repaired.

Athletes can experience "sports hernias" in which the posterior inguinal wall is weakened without any protrusion of abdominal contents through the abdominal wall. In this situation, no palpable hernia is discovered during a routine physical examination, yet the athlete complains of continuing pain in the groin and lower abdominal regions. The sports hernia is difficult to diagnose for the physician and usually exhibits diffuse, deep groin pain that does not have a specific onset and gradually gets worse as the days pass (**Figure 14.8**). The

athlete may complain of pain along the inguinal ligament and into the rectus muscles.

It has been suggested that sports hernias may be a common cause of chronic groin pain in athletes; however, there is now conflicting evidence relative to the exact cause of longstanding groin pain in athletes (Campanelli, 2010; Morales-Conde, Socas, & Barrnaco, 2010). Jansen and colleagues (2008) reviewed 45 published research findings that enumerated many causes of longstanding groin pain. These researchers list multiple pathologies including tendinopathies, osteitis pubis, nerve entrapment, sports hernia, and "undiagnosed chronic groin pain." Others indicate the sports hernia is one piece of a more complex syndrome sometimes referred to as groin disruption injury (Garvey, Read, & Turner, 2010). This clearly demonstrates the need for medical advice if, after a reasonable time period of conservative treatment, the groin pain is not resolved. A review of related literature indicates that the sports hernia rarely heals without surgical intervention (Caudill et al., 2008).

In any case, groin pain must be addressed with proper treatment and the course of action taken needs to follow a predetermined timeline. For example, conservative treatment of rest, ice, and stretching and a change in kicking biomechanics may be all that are needed to relieve groin pain in a soccer player. If the symptoms do not resolve over a 2-week period, it is time to have the team physician attend to the athlete. Athletes need to understand that many different techniques for surgical repair exist and new ideas are being reported in the literature every year (Muschaweck & Berger, 2010).

Nerve Problems

A common complaint among many athletes is a burning or tingling sensation radiating from the hip and buttocks area and going down the back of the leg. These symptoms are often the result of irritation of the sciatic nerve. There are many reasons why this nerve becomes inflamed or painful. Typically, if an athlete continues to pursue the activity that has caused the irritation, the pain will radiate farther down the leg to the foot and become more debilitating over time. The athlete must seek the advice of a physician and will need to rest and perform stretching and strengthening exercises depending on the cause of the problem.

hernia Protrusion of a part of an organ or tissue through an abnormal opening.

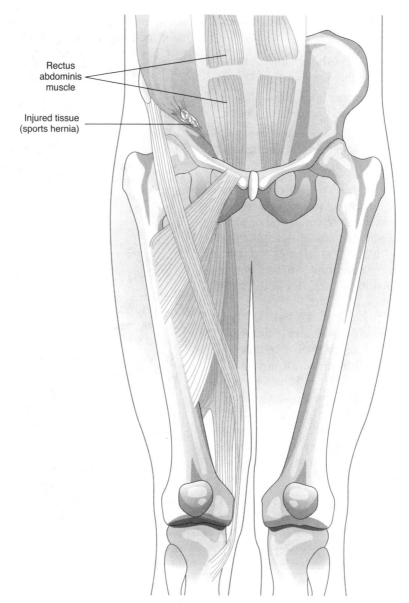

Rectus
abdominis
muscle

Injured tissue
(sports hernia)

FIGURE 14.8 Sports hernia is generally damage to the deep muscle tissue under the rectus abdominis.

Prevention

Many of the injuries to the hip and pelvis discussed in this chapter can be prevented by the use of proper conditioning and strengthening of the associated musculature. Adequate and appropriate conditioning of athletes decreases the amount of stress placed on specific muscle groups and results in fewer soft-tissue types of injury. Groin strains, osteitis pubis, and some of the stress types of fractures can be avoided by conditioning and strengthening techniques that follow a planned protocol that includes proper rest periods. Rest is important for the body to repair micro damages incurred by the stresses of training.

Prevention of the hip pointer injury is generally a function of protective equipment as part of the uniform. Specifically, football pants include a hip pad, but other uniforms do not typically provide protection for injury to the anterior hip region. Athletes may ask the certified athletic trainer to custom-make a protective device if they have a tendency to experience constant external trauma to the area of the hip pointer injury to reduce injury recurrence and long-term problems.

The use of proper shoes for each activity can be helpful in preventing slipping or sliding by the athlete that might result in overstretch or tearing of muscles. Soccer players or similar types of athletes slipping on a wet field can sustain severe groin injury. Baseball players typically elect to wear a protective cup in an attempt to reduce trauma to the testicles from a hit by a baseball, and catcher's masks now include a throat protector to deflect the shock of a foul-tipped ball away from the throat. Other sports also have equipment specific to that sport that has been developed for protection from potential injury.

Even though injuries to the hip and pelvis are relatively uncommon as a result of sports participation, it is important to realize that injuries to this area do occur and that they can be debilitating to the athlete. Always take into consideration the possibility of a severe injury when counseling an athlete about an injury to the hip and pelvis. First aid emergency care is important when treating these injuries. With most athletes, rehabilitation is also important if participants are to continue the enjoyment of specific sports.

REVIEW QUESTIONS

1. What type of joint is the hip joint?
2. Name the bones that make up the hip joint.
3. Explain the actions of the gluteal muscles.
4. Outline the location of the muscles that cause flexion, extension, adduction, and abduction of the hip.
5. List the bones in the hip area that are susceptible to fracture.
6. What structures are injured when an athlete suffers a hip pointer?
7. List the symptoms of osteitis pubis.
8. Explain the difference between testicular contusion and testicular torsion.
9. Define hernia and outline what a coach should do if one is suspected.
10. What should be done if an athlete is experiencing pain radiating down the back of the leg?

REFERENCES

Beatty T. (2012). Osteitis pubis in athletes. *Curr Sports Med Rep.* 11(2):96–98.

Breugem SJM, Hulscher JBF, Steller P. (2009). Stress fracture of the femoral neck in a young female athlete. *European J Trauma Emerg Surg.* 2:192–195.

Campanelli G. (2010). Pubic inguinal pain syndrome: The so called sports hernia. *Hernia.* 14:1–4.

Caudill P, Nyland J, Smith C, Yerasimides J, Lach J. (2008). Sports hernias: A systematic literature review. *Br J Sports Med.* 42(12):954–964.

Charbonnier C, Kolo FC, Duthon VB, Magnenat-Thalmann N, Becker CD, Hoffmeyer P, Menetrey J. (2011). Assessment of congruence and impingement of the hip joint in professional ballet dancers. *The Am J Spts Med.* 39(3): 557–566.

Choi H, McCartney M, Best TM. (2011). Treatment of osteitis pubis and osteomyelitis of the pubic symphysis in athletes: A systematic review. *Br J Sports Med.* 45:57–64.

Crowley LV. (2010). *An Introduction to Human Disease* (8th ed.). Sudbury, Mass: Jones & Bartlett Learning.

Garvey JFW, Read JW, Turner A. (2010). Sportsman hernia: What can we do? *Hernia.* 14:17–25.

Gerhardt MB, Romero AA, Silvers HJ, Harris DJ, Watanabe D, Mandelbaum BR. (2012). The prevalence of radiographic hip abnormalities in elite soccer players. *Am J Sports Med,* 40(3):584–588.

Gray H. (1974). *Anatomy, Descriptive and Surgical.* Philadelphia, Pa: Running Press.

Groh MM, Herrera J. (2009). A comprehensive review of hip labral tears. *Curr Rev Musculoskelet Med.* 2:105–117.

Hill CJ, Stevens KJ, Jamati MK, Garza D, Matheson GO. (2011). Athletic osteitis pubis. *Sports Med.* 41(5):361–376.

Hosalkar HS, Pennock AT, Zaps D, Schmitz MR, Bomar JD, Bittersohl B. (2012). The hip antero-superior labral tear with avulsion of rectus femoris (HALTAR) lesion: Does the SLAP equivalent in the hip exist? *Hip Int.* 22(4):391–398.

Jansen JACG, Mens JM, Backx FJ, Kolfschoten N, Stam HJ. (2008). Treatment of longstanding groin pain in athletes: A systematic review. *Scand J Med Sci Sports.* 18:263–274.

Kuhlman GS, Domb BG. (2009). Hip impingement: Identifying and treating a common cause of hip pain. *Am Fam Physician.* 80(12):1429–1434, 1439–1440.

McSweeney SE, Naraghi A, Salonen D, Theodoropoulos J, White LM. (2012). Hip and groin pain in the professional athlete. *Can Assoc Radiol J,* 63:87–99.

Moore K, Dalley AF, Aqur AM. (2013). *Clinically Oriented Anatomy* (7th ed.). Philadelphia, Pa: Lippincott Williams & Wilkins.

Morales-Conde S, Socas M, Barrnaco A. (2010). Sportsmen hernia: What do we know? *Hernia.* 14:5–15.

Muschaweck U, Berger L. (2010). Minimal repair technique of sportsmen's groin: An innovative open-suture repair to treat chronic inguinal pain. *Hernia.* 14:27–33.

Rowand M, Chambliss ML, Mackler L. (2009). How should you treat trochanteric bursitis? *J Fam Practice.* 58(9): 494, 500.

Yoon TR, Park KS, Diwanji SR, Seo CY, Seon JK. (2009). Clinical results of multiple fibrous band release for the external snapping hip. *J Orthopaed Sci.* 14:405–409.

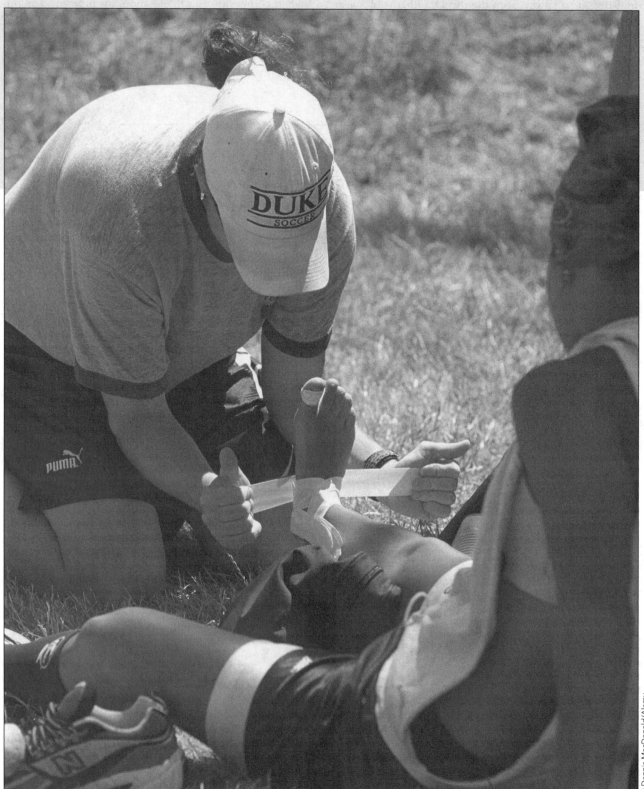

Injuries to the Thigh, Leg, and Knee

MAJOR CONCEPTS

Numerous injuries to the thighs and knees of male and female participants occur in a variety of sports. Because this area is difficult to protect and is a major location of body contact between opponents, it can experience repeated trauma in contact and collision sports, thereby compounding earlier injuries. Knowledge about potential injuries to the thigh and knee is important for people working with young athletes. Untreated or poorly treated injuries to the thigh and/or knee, like any other injury, can have long-term consequences on the health of the athlete.

This chapter begins with a brief anatomy overview that covers the bones, ligaments, tendons, muscles, nerves, and blood vessels of the region; it goes on to describe the kinesiology of movements created by the muscles through the major joints.

The chapter continues with a description of soft-tissue injuries to the thigh that can become debilitating if not cared for properly, including contusions, strains, and various joint-related injuries. The knee joint, much like the foot and ankle, is required to provide maximum stability and maximum mobility, thereby increasing the possibility of injury to this joint. The chapter covers problems such as osteochondritis dissecans, inflamed bursae, and patellar dislocation, along with injuries caused by chronic exercise. The knee joint is a complex configuration of bones, ligaments, and muscle tendons, any of which may be injured during sports participation. The chapter describes the four major ligaments of the knee and injuries to those ligaments; it also discusses the menisci (cartilage) within the knee joint that can be injured during sports participation. The chapter concludes with a discussion of prophylactic and functional knee bracing.

go.jblearning.com/PfeifferCWS

For a full suite of assignments and additional learning activities (indicated by the icons throughout the text), use the access code found in the front of your text. If you do not have an access code, you can obtain one at go.jblearning.com/PfeifferCWS.

ANATOMY REVIEW

The lower extremity is an area where many athletes experience some type of injury during their sports career. Injuries can occur to the thigh, knee, lower leg, ankle, or foot. The bones of this extremity include the femur, tibia, fibula, patella, and those of the foot (Gray, 1974). The femur, or thigh bone, is the longest, strongest, and heaviest bone in the body. It has a rounded, ball-like head that attaches to the hip bone with the help of a very strong network of ligaments. The head of the femur is attached to the shaft of the femur by a region known as the neck, which is susceptible to fractures. The femur becomes flatter and wider as it proceeds toward the knee joint, where it articulates with the tibia.

The thigh has a great deal of blood and nerve tissue going through it, both anteriorly and posteriorly. The anterior portion of the thigh contains the long saphenous vein and several branches of the femoral nerve. In the posterior section of the thigh are the deep femoral artery and the major nerve to the leg, the sciatic nerve. Most of the blood vessels and nerves are quite well protected by the musculature of the thigh.

The muscles of the thigh can be broken down into three basic regions. First, the anterior muscles of the thigh, commonly called the **quadriceps (Figure 15.1)**, have two functions. The vastus lateralis, vastus intermedius, vastus medialis, and rectus femoris work together to extend the leg at the knee joint. Three of these muscles (vastus medialis, intermedius, and lateralis) attach on the femur and run down the thigh to the quadriceps tendon. The rectus femoris is the main working muscle of this group; it helps the hip flexors to flex the thigh and assists in steadying the hip joint in this position. The rectus femoris attaches on the hip at the anterior inferior iliac spine and runs down the leg to the quadriceps tendon. The other muscle in the anterior portion of the thigh is the sartorius; it also attaches on the hip and runs somewhat diagonally down the thigh to the anterior medial portion of the tibial condyle. This muscle is responsible for flexing, abducting, and laterally rotating the thigh at the hip.

Next, the main muscles of the medial aspect of the thigh include the adductor longus, adductor brevis, adductor magnus, and the gracilis (Moore, Dalley, & Aqur, 2013). These muscles attach on the anterior aspect of the pelvis and run to the femur. The main function of these muscles is to adduct and help with flexion of the thigh. The third group of muscles in the thigh are in the posterior aspect of the thigh and are commonly known as the **hamstrings**. These include the semitendinosus, semimembranosus, and biceps femoris (Moore et al., 2013). All these muscles attach on the posterior aspect of the pelvis and run down the leg to the tibia. The main function of this group of muscles is to flex the leg at the knee. **Time Out 15.1** lists the thigh's muscle groups, actions, and innervations.

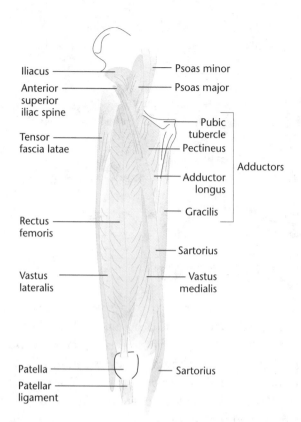

FIGURE 15.1 The quadriceps muscles of the anterior thigh serve two functions.

The knee is a very complex joint; it can be damaged through any number of accidents occurring during sports participation. The femur and the tibia articulate with each other here (**tibiofemoral joint**), and the patella and the femur also have an articulation (**patellofemoral joint**). The patella is a sesamoid bone, which means that it is totally enclosed within a tendon, in this case the quadriceps tendon. The patella does not articulate with the tibia. Many ligaments support the knee joint; however, four major ligaments serve as the primary stabilizers of this joint. They include the tibial or medial collateral ligament, the fibular or lateral collateral ligament, the anterior cruciate ligament, and the posterior cruciate ligament (**Figure 15.2**).

The tibial (medial) collateral ligament extends from the medial epicondyle of the femur down to the medial condyle of the tibia. The fibular (lateral) collateral ligament begins at the lateral epicondyle of the femur and extends to the head of the fibula. The fibular collateral ligament is the stronger of the two. Both ligaments help limit motion and/or disruption of the knee joint when movement at the joint is in a side-to-side direction, which is medically termed *valgus* (e.g., knock knees) and *varus* (e.g., bow legs).

The cruciate ligaments, unlike the collateral ligaments (which are located on the medial and lateral aspects of the knee joint proper), are situated on the inside of the joint.

TIME OUT 15.1

Main Muscle Groups, Actions, and Innervations of the Thigh

Muscle Group	Action(s)	Innervation
Quadriceps		
Rectus femoris	Knee extension	Femoral
	Hip flexion	
Vastus medialis	Knee extension	Femoral
Vastus lateralis	Knee extension	Femoral
Hamstrings	Knee flexion	
Semitendinosus	Knee extension	Tibial
Biceps femoris	Knee flexion	Long head—Tibial
		Short head—Common eroneal
Adductors	Thigh adduction	
Adductor longus	Adduction	Obturator
Adductor magnus	Adduction	Obturator
Adductor brevis	Adduction	Obturator
Abductors	Thigh abduction	
Gluteus medius	Abduction	Superior gluteal
Gluteus minimus	Abduction	Superior gluteal
Other		
Sartorius	Knee flexion	Femoral
	Hip abduction, external rotation, flexion	Superior gluteal
Tensor fasciae latae	Hip flexion	Gracilis
	Knee extension	

The anterior cruciate ligament attaches on the anterior portion of the intercondylar area of the tibia and runs superiorly and posteriorly to the internal aspect of the lateral femoral condyle. The posterior cruciate ligament attaches on the posterior aspect of the intercondylar area of the tibia and runs superiorly and anteriorly, passing the anterior cruciate ligament on the medial side and attaching to the internal aspect of the medial femoral condyle. The function of these two ligaments is primarily to reduce or prevent anterior and posterior displacement of the femur or the tibia.

Two semicircular fibrocartilaginous disks, commonly called cartilage and more scientifically termed the **menisci**, are located within the space between the tibia and femur. The menisci assist with the lubrication and nourishment of the knee joint, aid in the distribution of weight and stress applied to the joint surfaces, and help with the biomechanics of the joint (Levangie & Norkin, 2011). Serious injuries to

quadriceps Four muscles of the anterior thigh: rectus femoris, vastus medialis, vastus intermedius, and vastus lateralis.

hamstrings The three muscles that make up the posterior thigh: biceps femoris, semimembranosus, and semitendinosus.

tibiofemoral joint Articulation (bicondylar) formed by the medial and lateral femoral condyles and the medial and lateral tibial condyles.

patellofemoral joint Articulation (saddle) formed by the posterior surface of the patella and the anterior surface of the femoral condyles.

menisci Fibrocartilaginous structures that are between the hyaline cartilage surfaces in some synovial joints (e.g., the knee).

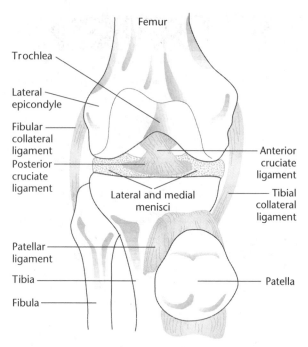

FIGURE 15.2 Major ligaments of the knee joint.

these disks, specifically the medial and lateral menisci, have caused the demise of many athletic careers. Orthopedic surgeons can repair some meniscus tears, and other tears they will carefully trim in order to maintain as much healthy tissue as possible. Thus, athletes can and do continue to participate in athletics after meniscus injury, surgery, and rehabilitation.

Tendons of the muscles mentioned earlier in the description of the thigh run across the knee. Between the tendons and bone are several bursae, which reduce the friction of muscle tendons rubbing over a prominent area of bone, thereby adding some padding for the exposed bony areas of the knee.

Common Sports Injuries

Injuries to the thigh and knee can occur in almost any sport. In addition, this area can sustain injuries that are a result of overuse, trauma caused by an opponent, or trauma produced by the power and explosive movements required in some sports. Due to the structure and function of the knee, it can be an often injured joint, and knee problems, not properly treated, have caused a great many athletes to shorten their athletic careers.

Because the knee is part of a complex mechanical system that includes the foot, ankle, lower leg, hip, and pelvis, there are times when another part of this system causes problems that can eventually be exhibited

in the knee. For this reason, it is wise to obtain competent medical advice when athletes are experiencing knee pain or chronic problems with the joint.

Skeletal Injuries

Femoral Fractures

The femur is the longest bone in the body and is therefore subject to being fractured; however, this requires a great deal of force and is not a common occurrence in sports. If a fracture does occur to the shaft of the femur as a result of sports participation, the injury is quite obvious; the athlete is in a great deal of pain, and ambulation will be difficult with the affected leg (see **Figure 15.3**). The athlete should not attempt to walk on a femoral fracture. In such instances, the athlete must be immediately transported to the nearest medical facility with the leg splinted and without bearing any weight on the affected limb. A femoral fracture requires urgent medical attention because the initial trauma can lead to multiple problems, including a lack of circulation, blocked nervous innervation, the potential of shock, and other urgent medical issues.

The neck of the femur can also be fractured. This can occur more often in sports than a fracture of the shaft, although neither happens frequently in healthy athletes. Older children and teenagers are at greater risk because a fracture in the area of the femoral neck can potentially affect a growth plate. Among younger athletes these

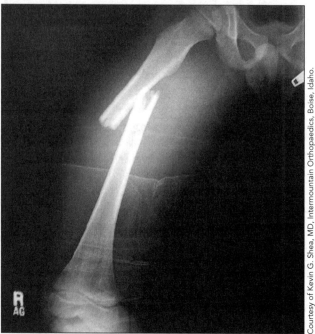

FIGURE 15.3 Femoral fracture of the right leg.

fractures can be the result of direct trauma or overuse. If direct trauma is the cause, the athlete typically had a foot planted and then got hit in the hip or upper thigh with a great deal of force. When this injury does occur, it needs to be evaluated by a physician as soon as possible. In any athlete, one complication of a fracture in the neck of the femur is **avascular necrosis** (tissue death) of the femoral head; this is caused by a decrease in the blood supply to the bony portion of the femoral head. (Bo Jackson experienced this injury playing professional football in 1991 and eventually had a hip replacement so that he could return to playing professional baseball.)

Signs and symptoms of a fracture of the femur include the following:

- Pain at the site of injury.
- Difficulty ambulating on the affected leg.
- Swelling and/or deformity may occur.
- The athlete may report a traumatic event as the cause.
- The athlete may report having heard or felt a severe pop or snap at the time of injury.

First aid care of a fracture of the femur involves the following:

1. Be prepared to treat the athlete for shock if necessary.
2. Splint the injured leg, preferably with a traction splint.
3. Apply sterile dressings to any related open wounds.
4. Monitor vital signs and circulation to the lower leg.
5. Arrange for transport to the nearest medical facility.

Patellar Fractures

Other skeletal problems that may arise include a fracture of the patella and dislocation of the knee or tibiofemoral joint. Although the patella can be fractured, this is not a common occurrence in sports participation. In most cases, a patellar fracture is caused by violent trauma, and the athlete is incapacitated for a short period of time following the trauma. There is a great deal of pain associated with this injury, and the athlete will need to see a physician as soon as possible. Because the patella is a sesamoid bone, the blood supply is limited, resulting in a longer healing time for such an injury.

Dislocation of Tibiofemoral Joint

Dislocation of the knee or tibiofemoral joint is possible and, in some instances, can compromise the blood flow to the lower leg. If there is a dislocation of the tibiofemoral joint, this is outwardly apparent, and the athlete will experience marked pain. This injury must be splinted, and the athlete must be referred to the nearest medical facility without delay. Circulation and nerve innervations to the knee and lower leg must not be compromised for even a brief period of time or significant tissue damage will ensue.

Soft-Tissue Injuries to the Thigh

Most of the soft-tissue injuries to the thigh are either the result of contact with an opponent or explosive movement by the athlete causing a self-inflicted muscle strain. Many sports, such as football and hockey, use some type of protective padding to prevent contact with an opponent to the thigh region. However, complete prevention is not always possible, and injuries do occur.

Myositis Ossificans

When an athlete receives a blow to the quadriceps muscle group from an opponent's knee, hip, or other body part, or there is a contusion to the musculature from some other violent force (internally or externally), bleeding and damage often occur within the muscle fibers. Depending on the force of impact and the muscles involved, the contusion may be of varying degrees of severity. In any case, the athlete must be counseled about the care of this injury and the long-term complications of improper care of a muscular contusion, which can result in a condition called myositis ossificans. The initial muscular contusion causes bleeding within the muscle; if not cared for properly, or if further damage occurs, there is an increase in the amount of blood lost in the same area. The body utilizes a natural process to remove the extra blood now loose in the muscle; however, continued insult and bleeding in the area can result in calcification within the muscle and abnormal bone growth, possibly leading to further disability.

Signs and symptoms of a muscular contusion include the following:

- The athlete will report a forceful impact to the area.
- Muscular tightness and swelling may be present.
- The athlete has decreased ability to forcefully contract the muscle.
- The athlete has difficulties in ambulating with the affected leg.

avascular necrosis Death of tissue caused by the lack of blood supply.

First aid care of a muscular contusion involves the following:

1. Apply ice and compression immediately.
2. If the injury is severe, place the athlete on crutches.
3. Have the athlete rest and avoid any contact with the area.

With this type of injury, the athlete must be allowed plenty of rest and time to permit the natural bodily processes to remove blood from the area so that healing will be complete. Early controlled movement of the contused muscle assists in regenerating the muscle when the athlete is ready to return to participation. The early mobilization in this case must be well controlled, and the athlete should not be allowed to participate in full-contact practice or competition until complete healing has occurred. Because further direct contact to the area may increase the risk of myositis ossificans, the area should be padded if the athlete continues to participate. Moreover, the player should be well aware of the long-term consequences of continued trauma to the area and should initiate treatment quickly if additional insult occurs.

Muscular Strains to the Thigh

Almost any of the muscles in the thigh region are susceptible to strains. Most of the strains to athletes, however, are to the hamstrings and adductor muscles. Strains to the adductor muscles are commonly known as groin pulls. Most strains occur to the muscle itself and not the tendon. Such strains are usually the result of muscles being stretched too far, which generally occurs in the adductor muscles. However, strains can be the result of miscommunication between **agonistic muscles** and **antagonistic muscles**, which is the case with many muscle strains involving the hamstrings.

If the muscle is stretched too far, the fibers of the muscle are damaged and bleeding occurs; the result is

WHAT IF?

You are coaching a junior high school basketball game. During the first half, your starting guard drives in for a layup, colliding with an opponent. The point of contact was her left thigh, which was struck severely by her opponent's knee. On further examination you note tightness and swelling in the quadriceps muscles and an unwillingness by the athlete to put weight on her leg. Based on this history and the signs and symptoms, what would you conclude? What would be the appropriate first aid in this situation?

loss of contractibility, stiffness, and impaired movement. In the case of the previously mentioned miscommunication between agonistic and antagonistic muscles, the quadriceps musculature is contracting while the hamstrings are also contracting, causing the weaker muscle to be torn and damaged. Typically, the hamstrings are the weaker of the two groups; therefore, this is the musculature that is usually strained, with subsequent bleeding and hematoma formation.

Many athletes experience chronic tightness and repetitive strains to the muscles of the thigh adductor (groin) region. Specifically, the adductor brevis, longus, and magnus muscles can exhibit problems, especially in athletes participating in activities requiring multiple changes in speed and/or direction. It is not uncommon for a track, soccer, football, or volleyball athlete to complain of tight, sore, or strained muscles in the groin region. The groin muscles are critical movers in speed and change-of-direction movements and can require extra time to warm up and prepare for competition. Special attention must be given to these muscles by the individual athletes as they prepare for practice or competition.

These groin injuries can be debilitating if not cared for properly and quickly (see **Time Out 15.2**). Typically, when a strain to one or more of the groin muscles occurs, the athlete feels a sharp pain in the medial side of the thigh, possibly associated with a "tearing" feeling. Not long after this incident, the athlete will complain of soreness, stiffness, and a lack of movement in the area. At times, even with continued use in even the most restricted situation, the muscle or muscles take a long time to heal completely. This is because the muscles affected are being used unconsciously for many daily activities in movements that cause small microtraumas that do not allow the damaged muscle to heal. To this end, constant adherence to the proper treatment regimen is necessary until a complete recovery is made.

During and after recovery, athletes need to implement a stretching program that specifically targets the adductor muscles. To reduce scarring of the affected muscles, stretching must be an integral part of the recovery from this and any other muscle strain injuries.

Signs and symptoms of muscle strains to the thigh include the following:

- A sharp pain in the affected muscle.
- Swelling and inflammation in the immediate area.
- Weakness and inability of the muscle to contract forcefully.
- After a few days, there may be discoloration of the area.
- In severe cases, a visible defect is noted in the muscle.

Case Study of a Ruptured Rectus Femoris Muscle

There is always a chance that a muscle injury can be more severe than first expected. The soccer player in this case study thought he had severely contused and strained his quadriceps muscle group during a soccer match when an opponent stepped on his thigh. There was abnormal swelling and a great deal of pain associated with the initial injury. Standard first aid procedures included ice, compression, and rest until the athlete attempted to play again on a wet field; at one point, when he planted his leg to start running, he felt something tear. At that point, he decided to take some time off to let the injury heal. Months later, when the athlete was still having problems with pain and a lack of contractile ability, it was discovered that the injury to the quadriceps muscle was much more severe than thought during the initial evaluation.

In this case, the rectus femoris muscle had torn from its attachment at the patellar tendon and had not been repaired in time to salvage the muscle attachment. As shown in **Figure 15.4**, the muscle belly of the rectus femoris muscle draws up the leg when the athlete forcefully extends the lower leg. This athlete now must deal with a weak quadriceps mechanism and a strange feeling in his thigh each time he contracts his quadriceps muscles in that leg. This injury has ended his participation in collegiate soccer.

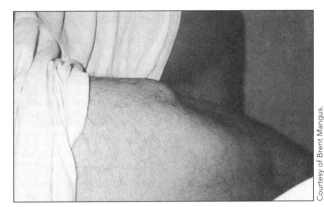

FIGURE 15.4 A soccer player with a ruptured rectus femoris muscle.

First aid care of muscle strains to the thigh involves the following:

1. Apply ice and compression immediately.
2. Have the athlete rest and use crutches if necessary.
3. Have the athlete evaluated by a member of the medical team.

Proper care for any injury to the thigh is important. Because a strain to the hamstrings or groin muscles is not considered serious, sometimes these injuries are not cared for properly. The result can be a shortened career for the athlete.

agonistic muscles Muscles in a state of contraction as related to opposing muscles.
antagonistic muscles Muscles that counteract the action of agonistic muscles.

Athletic Trainers SPEAK Out

When evaluating injuries, it is important to be aware of biological variations. For example, discoloration caused by a direct blow to the thigh may not be as readily seen in athletes with dark skin pigmentation as compared to athletes with light skin pigmentation. I once had an athlete sustain a severe hamstring injury that turned deep purple in color. It was through very careful inspection that I was able to detect the discoloration, as the athlete had very dark skin. If I had not noticed the discoloration, I may not have realized the severity of the injury. In this case, careful inspection led to appropriate first aid care.

—Rene Revis Shingles, PhD, ATC

Rene Revis Shingles is an assistant professor in the Athletic Training Education Program at Central Michigan University.

Courtesy of Rene Revis Shingles, Central Michigan University.

Patellofemoral Joint Injuries

Several injuries to the patellofemoral joint, both chronic and acute, can become debilitating if appropriate treatment is not instituted early. Early treatment and intervention are required if the athlete is to return to participation at peak level. Some of the problems causing injury are the result of faulty mechanics or growth in adolescents and are not caused by anything that could be prevented initially. Many of the injuries to the patellofemoral joint, however, can be helped via intervention by the athletic trainer or physician, and the athlete can participate at peak level when recovery is complete.

Osteochondritis Dissecans

Osteochondritis dissecans (OCD) has also been called "joint mice" because small pieces of bone that have been dislodged or chipped from the joint are floating within the joint capsule. In adolescents, OCD is a common cause of a loose body in the joint space. Damage to the joint surfaces caused by these osteochondral fragments can be a serious problem. When the joint surfaces are damaged and no longer make smooth contact with each other, further pain and joint damage are almost always inevitable. The piece of bone does not always have to be freely floating within the joint space: It may be partially dislodged yet still attached to the original bone and causing painful movement. If in fact the piece of bone is freely floating within the joint space, it can cause a blocking or locking action that limits the movement at the knee joint. The causes of OCD are not fully understood, although most experts believe it is a direct result of some type of trauma. When OCD occurs in juvenile athletes, the athlete should be referred to the physician for diagnosis and determination of the course of treatment. Many juvenile athletes respond to conservative treatment, whereas others may require surgical intervention.

Signs and symptoms of osteochondritis dissecans include the following:

- Chronic knee pain with exertion that is generalized, not specific.
- There may be chronic swelling present.
- The knee may lock if there is a loose body within the joint. The athlete may be unable to fully extend the extremity.
- The quadriceps group may atrophy.
- One or both femoral condyles may be tender to palpation when the knee is flexed.

First aid care of osteochondritis dissecans involves the following:

1. Apply ice and compression.

2. If the athlete has difficulty walking or the knee is locking, have the player use crutches.

3. Have the athlete see a physician for proper treatment.

Inflamed Bursae

A bursa is a small fluid-filled sac located at a strategic point in the body that assists in the prevention of friction between bony surfaces, tendons, muscles, or skin. There are numerous bursae in the knee joint; however, only a few are commonly irritated (**Figure 15.5**). A bursa can become inflamed as a result of trauma or infection. The inflammation can also be the result of chronic overuse and irritation of the bursa. The prepatellar bursa is located just under the skin and above the patella and can be susceptible to direct trauma. In the case of trauma, a football player may hit a knee quite hard on another player's helmet or on the playing surface, thereby causing the prepatellar bursa to become swollen and enlarged (**Figure 15.6**).

Most of the other bursae located throughout the knee complex are also susceptible to chronic insult. The constant use of the legs and knees in some exercises creates excessive friction in the area, and the bursae respond by becoming inflamed. It is also possible for these bursae to become inflamed from direct trauma, although this is not as common.

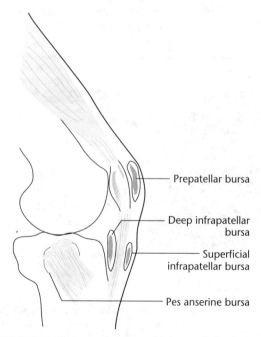

FIGURE 15.5 Commonly irritated bursae of the knee.

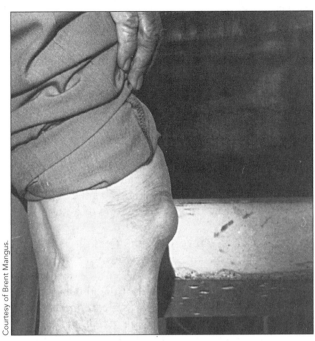

FIGURE 15.6 Prepatellar bursitis.

Signs and symptoms of an inflamed bursa include the following:

- Swelling and tenderness at the site.
- Increased pressure externally typically causes pain.
- The athlete may report direct trauma or a chronic buildup of swelling.

First aid care of an inflamed bursa involves the following:

1. Apply ice and compression.
2. Reduce activity for a short period of time.
3. In chronic cases, anti-inflammatory agents may be helpful.

Patellar Dislocation/Subluxation

When an athlete makes a quick, cutting motion to one side or another, a great deal of force is generated within the knee. If the sudden force is abnormal in nature, the patella can move laterally outside of the femoral groove, which can result in a dislocation (subluxation). Whether the patella remains dislocated or returns to its normal position spontaneously tends to be related to the distance it travels outside of its normal groove and the number of times this type of incident has occurred in the past. In some cases, if the athlete is a chronic subluxor, the patella will reduce (i.e., return to a normal position) without intervention. If it is the first time the patella has dislocated, it may or may not reduce spontaneously. In most instances of patellar dislocation, the athlete knows

that the patella has moved out of the normal position, the knee will be flexed, and the athlete will experience pain and anxiety and will not want to move the leg or foot.

Signs and symptoms of a dislocation/subluxation of the patella include the following:

- Athlete will report a great deal of pain and an abnormal movement of the patella when the injury occurred.
- There will be associated swelling.
- The knee and patella will be extremely tender, and upon visual inspection, the patella will appear to be moved laterally to the normal position.

First aid care of a dislocation/subluxation of the patella involves the following:

1. Apply ice immediately.
2. Compression and elevation will also be helpful.
3. Splint the entire leg.
4. Arrange for transport to the nearest medical facility.

When a patellar dislocation occurs, the patella most often moves laterally. In addition, when an athlete experiences a patellar dislocation, soft-tissue damage to the medial aspect of the knee will most likely accompany it. If not cared for properly, this injury can become a chronic problem.

Osgood-Schlatter Disease and Jumper's Knee

The attachment of the patellar tendon at the tibial tubercle can be the site of two similar problems associated with athletes who do a great deal of jumping, although jumping is not a prerequisite to experiencing either Osgood-Schlatter disease or jumper's knee. These two injuries can be confused with one another if the certified athletic trainer does not look carefully at the age of the athlete and the signs and symptoms the athlete is experiencing. The main difference in these two conditions is the exact location of the injury. Osgood-Schlatter disease is typically a problem at the junction of the patellar tendon and the tibial tuberosity in the adolescent athlete. On the other hand, jumper's knee can exhibit itself at multiple sites within the patellar tendon along the entire tendon down to the tibial tuberosity attachment.

Osgood-Schlatter disease is technically defined as an osteochondritis of the epiphysis of the tibial

Osgood-Schlatter disease Epiphyseal inflammation of the tibial tubercle.

tuberosity. For this to occur, there must be a growth plate at the site of the tibial tubercle; consequently, this condition is unique to children and adolescents. Constant jumping creates a pull on the patellar tendon and its attachment at the tibial tuberosity. During the growth phase, there is an epiphyseal plate that is being pulled on simultaneously by the attachment of the patellar tendon at the tibia. This irritation causes inflammation and swelling to occur just below the patella.

Signs and symptoms of Osgood-Schlatter disease include the following:

- Pain and tenderness about the patellar tendon complex.
- Swelling in the associated area. This swelling may be more localized to the tibial tuberosity.
- Decreased ability to use the quadriceps for running or jumping.
- If the inflammation continues, the area over the tibial tuberosity may become more solid when palpated.
- Symptoms seem to be exacerbated by activity.

First aid care of Osgood-Schlatter disease involves the following:

1. Apply ice and compression to the area.
2. Have the athlete see a physician as soon as possible.
3. Rest is important until the inflammation subsides.

Jumper's knee is also an irritation of the patellar tendon complex between its attachments on the tibia and the patella. This problem is common to the athlete who must jump a great deal as part of sports participation. Typically, the athlete experiences pain at one of three sites within this complex. The pain may be localized over the superior or inferior pole of the patella or at the tibial tuberosity. Regardless of the exact location of this condition, the athlete complains greatly of pain associated with jumping.

Signs and symptoms of jumper's knee include the following:

- Pain and tenderness about the patellar tendon complex.
- Swelling in the associated area. This swelling may spread from the patella to the tibial tuberosity.
- Decreased ability to use the quadriceps for running or jumping.
- Symptoms seem to be exacerbated by activity.

First aid care of jumper's knee involves the following:

1. Apply ice and compression to the area.
2. Have the athlete see a physician, who might prescribe anti-inflammatory medications.
3. Rest is helpful to the ailing athlete.

Patellofemoral Conditions

At times, athletes complain of nonspecific pain behind the patella. Sometimes this pain is caused by an increased quadriceps angle as known as the "Q angle," or the pain can be caused by any one of a number of other problems.

As shown in **Figure 15.7**, the **Q angle** is the difference between a straight line drawn from the anterior superior iliac spine and the center of the patella and one drawn from the center of the patella through the center of the tibia. This angle represents the vector of action between the quadriceps muscles and the patellar tendon. The larger this angle, the greater the chance of the patella being pulled too far laterally during extension of the knee; consequently, the patella rubs on the condyle of the femur, causing pain and irritation. It is generally accepted that this angle is larger in females because of the width of the pelvis (Cooney et al., 2012). Most authorities report that a Q angle of 15° to 20° is acceptable. However, this is highly individual, because there are often associated problems with patellar tracking, such as weak musculature or an abnormal patellofemoral skeletal configuration.

If there is abnormal patellofemoral configuration as a result of some skeletal, muscular, or mechanical dysfunction, this too can create retropatellar (behind the patella) pain of an **idiopathic** nature. A mechanical dysfunction may result in an abnormal amount of friction

 WHAT IF?

You are teaching a junior high school weight-training class. One of the young boys in your class comes to you complaining of a chronic aching he has had for several days in the anterior knee, inferior to the patella, at the insertion of the patellar tendon. The boy reports the pain is worse in the mornings, especially when walking up and down stairs. Based on this history, what is the likely cause of this pain? What do you recommend for this child?

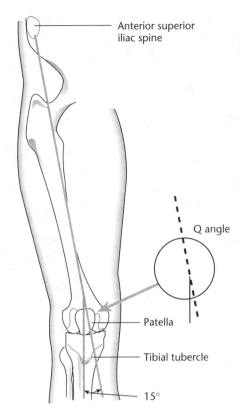

Anterior superior iliac spine

Q angle

Patella

Tibial tubercle

15°

FIGURE 15.7 Measuring the Q angle at the knee.

between the patella and the femur. This typically occurs in athletes such as runners or gymnasts who perform a great deal of repetitive movements in their sports activities. If this problem is allowed to continue, the possibility of chondromalacia exists. **Chondromalacia** is a softening and wearing out of the posterior cartilage surface of the patella. This is detrimental to the athlete's ability to perform in the future, because there is associated pain and tenderness with this disorder that inhibit movement.

In the case of retropatellar pain and discomfort, the athlete complains of chronic pain and disability. There is no immediate first aid care to be administered; however, the athlete may gain some comfort from rest, ice, compression, elevation, and the use of nonsteroidal anti-inflammatories. If the athlete has an abnormally large Q angle, muscular imbalances, or other predisposing conditions, he or she should seek the advice of a physician to assist in the care of retropatellar pain disorder.

Menisci Injuries

Injury to the meniscus in the active population is a fairly common episode, and as people age this appears to be more common. A large study (Jones et al., 2012)

of meniscus injuries was conducted by the U.S. military in all active-duty service members between 1998 and 2006. The records of all active military service people were accessed and the final report listed 100,201 acute meniscus injuries during the reporting period. Military men were more likely to experience a meniscus injury by almost 20%, and those over 40 years of age were 4 times more susceptible to this specific injury (Jones et al., 2012). As mentioned earlier, the menisci have partial attachments to other structures about the knee joint such as the cruciate ligaments, the tibial tubercles, and others; this creates problems when either the menisci or various other structures are damaged. If a violent force injures the medial collateral ligament, there is also the possibility of damage to the medial meniscus because of a partial attachment between the two structures.

More commonly, a meniscus is damaged by being torn as a result of quick, sharp, cutting movements that occur when the foot is stabilized and does not turn with the body. This movement and others that cause excessive stress in abnormal planes can tear the meniscus at different points. A torn meniscus can affect the athlete in a variety of ways. Some athletes can function normally; others cannot completely extend the leg at the knee joint because of a tear in the meniscus that causes a blocking or locking effect.

Signs and symptoms of a suspected torn meniscus include the following:

- The athlete reports that a pop or snap was heard when the knee twisted.
- The athlete may not have any swelling, depending on the structures involved in the injury.
- The athlete may not complain of any pain.
- Depending on the severity of the injury, there may be a loss of range of motion and/or movement with a blocking or locking effect.
- The athlete may be able to continue participation with the injury.
- The athlete may report a feeling of the knee "giving out" at times.

Q angle Angle made by the rectus femoris and the patellar tendon as they attach to the tibial tubercle.
idiopathic Cause of a condition is unknown.
chondromalacia Abnormal softening of cartilage, typically noted between the patella and femur.

First aid care of a suspected torn meniscus involves the following:

1. Apply ice and compression.
2. If the athlete has a blocked or locked knee, crutches should be used to aid in walking.
3. Encourage the athlete to see a physician as soon as possible.

Meniscus injuries do not necessarily have to end an athlete's playing season or career. New methods of surgery enable many athletes to return to participation relatively quickly. However, athletes should not be encouraged to finish the season with a suspected meniscus injury without first seeking the advice of a physician.

Knee Ligament Injuries

Several ligaments can be damaged through trauma; however, only four of the main ligaments are discussed here. The four that are most commonly injured are the medial (tibial) collateral ligament (MCL), the lateral (fibular) collateral ligament (LCL), the anterior cruciate ligament (ACL), and the posterior cruciate ligament (PCL). These ligaments are important stabilizers of the knee joint and are subject to many stresses, both internal and external. These ligaments, like any others in the body, can be traumatized and suffer first-, second-, or third-degree sprains.

The mechanisms by which ligaments can be injured include a broad range of maneuvers, from the athlete making a quick, sharp, cutting step and twisting the knee excessively to having an opposing lineman hit the knee from one side. Athletes also may be kicked in the tibia or attempt to stop an opponent and have the tibia driven forcefully anteriorly or posteriorly, all of which can damage one or more of the major supporting knee ligaments. It is important to remember that the knee can be injured by all types of forces, both internal and external, even when it does not appear that the athlete is in danger during an activity such as running.

Collateral Ligament Injuries

One of the more common injuries to knee ligaments in athletics is a sprain to the MCL (**Figure 15.8**). This occurs when an opponent is blocked or hits the athlete's leg and knee from the outside. The opponent lands forcefully on the lateral side of the knee, resulting in the joint being pushed medially (valgus stress); this creates stress on the MCL beyond what it can withstand (**Figure 15.9**).

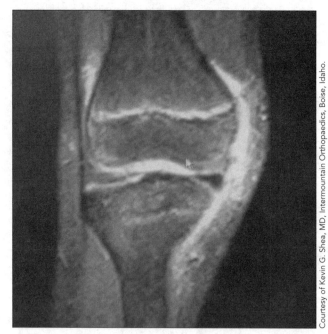

FIGURE 15.8 Coronal plane MRI image of a torn MCL. Note the brightly colored region along the medial side of the knee indicating damage to the MCL.

If just the opposite mechanism occurs and an opponent lands on the inside of a player's knee and pushes the joint laterally (varus stress), then the LCL is stressed beyond the normal level and sprained.

Both of these ligament injuries render the knee unstable in side-to-side movements. Because the knee is a hinge joint and little sideways movement occurs there, this would seem to create very few problems for the athlete. Although this may make logical sense, biomechanically, the collateral ligaments are important in assisting the knee with overall stability, and injury to either of these structures does result in significant instability in the knee (Levangie & Norkin, 2011). The more severe

FIGURE 15.9 Excessive stress on the MCL.

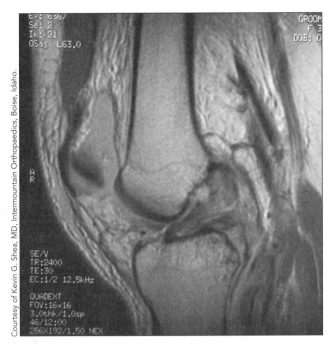

FIGURE 15.10 Sagittal plane MRI of a torn ACL in the right knee. Note the gap (lighter colored region) within the body of the ligament that is the area of the rupture.

the ligament injury, the more unstable the knee is during movement and activity.

Cruciate Ligament Injuries

The ACL can be injured by having the tibia moved forcefully in an anterior direction (**Figure 15.10**). This can occur when an athlete is making a very quick cutting motion on a hard surface, when an athlete gets hit from behind in the lower leg, or when the femur gets pushed backward while the tibia is held in place, as happens in contact sports. If the opposite occurs and the tibia is forced posteriorly, the PCL can be disrupted and injured. The main function of these two ligaments is to stabilize the knee in anterior and/or posterior directions. In addition, quick rotational forces can injure the ACL. A rotational injury can result from a noncontact mechanism. For example, a football player may make a very quick change in direction with a firmly planted foot, and if the upper body goes off balance, it causes the knee to absorb potentially abnormal forces built up by the upper body twisting. If the circumstances are such that the soft-tissue structures in the knee cannot withstand the extra forces, these structures can be damaged.

The cruciate ligaments work in conjunction with the collateral ligaments to create a stable knee; any time one or more of these ligaments is injured, the knee becomes unstable. A large majority of ACL injuries are from noncontact mechanisms. It is now

generally accepted that ACL injuries are multifactorial in nature. There are neuromuscular, biomechanical, anatomic, genetic, hormonal, environmental, and other factors that can be additive which result in an ACL injury. Over the years, there has been a great deal of research into the basis for these noncontact ACL injuries. Much of the research has focused on the sport of soccer and specifically the female athlete. It appears that female athletes are at a much higher risk for *noncontact* ACL injury when compared to males. However, football players have been reported to experience more *contact* ACL injuries and experience more knee injuries specifically in high school (Dragoo et al., 2012; Elliott, Goldberg, & Kuehl, 2012; Kobayashi et al., 2010; Shea et al., 2011). Each year the amount of sports injury data increases due to a number of organizations' efforts. High school sports injury data is collected by the National High School Sports-Related Injury Surveillance Study group (Comstock et al., 2012), college sports injury information is available through the National Collegiate Athletic Association (NCAA), and each professional sports organization maintains injury data specific for that professional sport. The NCAA maintains an injury database on their website to assist with an understanding of injury epidemiology of NCAA athletes. For the 2008–2009 years, the rates of ACL injury demonstrate the greatest number of injuries occurred in men's football, followed by gymnastics and then women's soccer (Dragoo et al., 2012). In the NCAA and the National Football League (NFL), injury rates to the ACL appear to increase when the athlete is participating on artificial surface (Dragoo, Braun, & Harris, 2012; Hershman et al., 2012). It should be noted that in almost every study being published, the authors are calling for more research on ACL injuries, because they do not feel there has been a large enough population studied to fully determine a common outcome.

Even though it appears female athletes experience more noncontact ACL injuries, researchers have been unable to discern the exact reason or reasons for this phenomenon. An article on the mechanisms of ACL injury and the underlying risk factors was written by Alentorn-Geli and colleagues (2009a) and is an excellent review of the literature regarding this question. In their review, the authors clearly list the main causes of most noncontact ACL injuries in athletes and outline the pertinent published research of each causal situation. One of the main causes of noncontact ACL injury is a change in direction or cutting movement combined with deceleration by the athlete. Other important mechanisms to be aware of are the anterior translation with forced rotation, landing in (or very near) knee full extension, pivoting with the knee in full extension, and hyperflexion/extension of the knee. The authors suggest that females are six times more prone to noncontact ACL injury. Alentorn-Geli and associates (2009a) provide detailed and research-based arguments for five different potential causes for noncontact ACL injury. There are **environmental** bases for these injuries, including the surface, weather, footwear, and shoe–surface interface research reports. The **anatomic** rationale that has been and is currently being studied includes mass, joint laxity, pelvis and trunk actions, Q angle, posterior tibial slope, notch width, and foot pronation studies. The effect of sex **hormones** during the monthly menstrual cycle is outlined and discussed in detail. The **neuromuscular** activity that continually occurs during movement, including strength and recruitment of muscle fibers, joint stiffness, and muscular fatigue are outlined. Finally, the **biomechanical** rationale for noncontact ACL injury with an analysis of the planes of movement is presented, again with an evaluation of the related literature. Looking at the overall picture of ACL injuries, a group of researchers and scholars gather regularly to review the results and direction of future research opportunities. At the ACL Research Retreat of 2012, there were updates of the known and researched factors of ACL injuries and a series of prevention discussions based on the most recent published research (Shultz et al., 2012). The attendees at this meeting divided into interest groups and provided updates relative to the most recent research findings. Some of the relevant findings from this meeting include:

1. Anatomical and structural risk factors are generally not alterable and prevention programs for ACL injuries need to address these factors in specific populations.

2. There appears to be a familial genetic risk factor in ACL injury; however, researchers are looking at such a wide variety of genetic factors along with environmental factors that an exact genetic link is difficult to ascertain.

3. In the female athlete, the ACL tissue characteristics based on sex hormones and the phase of the menstrual cycle appear to be important, yet not well understood. There appears to be a greater chance of ACL injury in the female athlete in the preovulatory phase as opposed to the postovulatory phase of the menstrual cycle.

4. ACL injury is related to a rapid internal rotation and tibial valgus stress movement. The more upright the athlete, the greater the chance of injury during this internal rotation and tibial valgus stress. Additionally, fatigue in the lower extremity appears to be an associated factor in an ACL injury.

5. Lower extremity biomechanics can be positively affected by improved hip, core, and upper body mechanics. Multidynamic, warm-up-style prevention programs appear to be effective in reducing ACL injury provided they are conducted 2–3 times per week for a minimum of 10–15 minutes. Compliance with these programs has been associated with a reduction in ACL injuries (Sugimoto et al., 2012).

Athletic trainers and coaches are interested in the prevention of the noncontact ACL injury, and there has been a great deal of progress made in this arena since the early 2000s. Many researchers are now proposing that players, parents, coaches, administrators, and others responsible for any and all of the parameters of sports programs be well versed in the types of and need for ACL injury-prevention programs (Finoff, 2012; Shultz et al., 2012; Sugimoto et al., 2012). Yoo and colleagues (2010) and Alentorn-Geli and associates (2009b) published excellent reviews of the literature on the prevention of the noncontact ACL injury. Most of the prevention programs target the female soccer player, but some programs encourage all players, male and female, to become involved in these prevention programs. It appears evident that the prevention programs targeted at enhancing the neuromuscular training are beneficial in reducing the number of noncontact ACL injuries in female soccer

WHAT IF?

You are coaching a high school basketball game. It is late in the game; your team is on the defense, with their opponent's guard driving to the basket. Suddenly, your post player, who was attempting to block the opponent's jump shot, falls to the floor, while simultaneously grabbing her left knee. On further examination she states that when she landed from jumping up to block the shot, her knee twisted and she felt something snap inside. You note that she also states that her knee feels very unstable. Given this information, what would you conclude? What would be the appropriate first aid for this injury?

players (Yoo et al., 2010) and in female and male soccer players (Alentorn-Geli et al., 2009b). Additionally, by implementing preseason conditioning and an in-season maintenance program, some noncontact ACL injuries can be avoided (Finoff, 2012; Shultz et al., 2012; Sugimoto et al., 2012).

Signs and symptoms of an injury to the knee ligaments include the following:

- Athlete reports that the knee was forced beyond its normal range.
- Athlete complains of pain at the site of injury.
- Swelling may occur in and around the knee.
- Athlete may complain of an unstable feeling in the knee.
- Athlete may report having felt a pop or tear or having heard a snapping sound.

First aid care of an injury to the knee ligaments involves the following:

1. Apply ice and compression immediately.
2. If the knee is unstable, have the athlete walk with crutches.
3. Have the athlete seek proper medical advice.

At times, an athlete will receive a blow from the lateral side that injures the MCL and ACL along with the medial meniscus. This has sometimes been called the terrible-triad injury. Obviously, injuring all of these structures creates a very unstable knee. Anytime an athlete has a suspected injury to knee ligaments, caution must be exercised, and care by the proper medical personnel is critical.

There are so many different types of knee injuries and each of those injuries can be significantly different in severity. It is important to always work with the physician of the team or encourage the athlete and his or her parents to ensure that proper care and level of activity are followed. **Table 15.1** provides a general outline of the type of care and possible activity level for athletes with knee injuries. This table is provided to assist the athletic trainer or coach in discussions with the physician caring for the injured athlete so that an activity level can be determined for the future participation of the athlete.

Prevention

The quest to prevent injuries to the leg and knee continues for athletes, coaches, and certified athletic trainers.

As discussed earlier, the increase in female ACL injuries has resulted in many research teams looking for an answer or model for prevention of such injuries. In the future, research will continue in an attempt to outline techniques that can prevent the various injuries to the thigh, leg, and knee.

The prevention of strain injuries to the musculature of the thigh and leg is very similar to the techniques used in other areas of the body that contain a great deal of muscle tissue. To many athletes, proper warmup and stretching of the muscles to be used are important in preparing for activity. Not all athletes require stretching before an activity, but some find it beneficial to their overall participation.

Preventing knee injuries has become much more of a focus of the medical and allied health professionals. For many years, and in the present day, a variety of bracing options purport to provide peripheral mechanical stabilization for the ligaments of the knee when forces are applied externally. Today, some football coaches require interior linemen and linebackers to wear bilateral prophylactic knee braces during practice and games. Much like stretching, knee bracing should be an individual choice for athletes. If athletes believe prophylactic knee bracing can benefit them, they should be provided the opportunity to use these devices. Knee braces continue to evolve and have been through many prototype tests and marketed units. Initially, the braces were designed to minimize medial and lateral stresses to the knee. As materials became available that were lighter and stronger than metal hinges taped to the athletes' legs, more options for knee protection became available.

The newest trend in prevention of ACL injuries is in using specific jumping and landing training techniques. Some authors suggest that specialized

environmental The aggregate of surrounding things, conditions, or influences.

anatomic Pertaining to anatomy.

hormones Various internally secreted compounds formed in endocrine glands that affect the functions of specifically receptive organs or tissues.

neuromuscular Pertaining to the nervous intervention of the muscles.

biomechanical The effect of external and internal forces on the anatomic tissues and the movements of the body.

TABLE 15.1

GENERAL SUGGESTIONS FOR PARTICIPATION OF ATHLETES WITH KNEE INJURIES

Common Locations		Severity	Possible Implications for Participation*
Ligament			
	MCL	1st	Limit movements of knee to flexion and extension with hinge brace (avoid valgus stresses)—avoid extremes of flexion and extension
		2nd	May need crutches—physician will determine length of time on crutches
		3rd	Physician to determine course of action
	LCL	1st	Hinge brace for protection and avoid extremes of flexion and extension
		2nd	Brace and immobilize—physician will determine further treatment(s)
		3rd	Brace and immobilize—surgery required for repair of ligament
	ACL	1st	Immobilize and brace required initially—physician will determine activity levels
		2nd	Immobilization followed by hinge brace to limit movement—surgery may be necessary
		3rd	Immobilization followed by hinge brace to limit movement—surgery required for repair of ligament
	PCL	1st	Limit movements of knee to flexion and extension
		2nd	Limit movement of knee totally
		3rd	Surgery required for repair of ligament
Cartilage			
	Meniscus		Early surgical intervention recommended—physician should explain the rationale for early or delayed treatment of meniscus injury
			Participation will depend on activity and pain tolerance; non-weight-bearing activities recommended
	Hyaline		Early surgical intervention recommended
			Participation will depend on activity and pain tolerance; non-weight-bearing activities recommended
	Osteochondritis		Participation limited to activities that have reduced impact on the knee
Tendon			
	Patellar/jumper's knee		Participation based on pain tolerance of the athlete and physician treatment options
	Osgood-Schlatter disease		Participation based on pain tolerance of the athlete and physician treatment options
	Tendinopathies		Limited participation depending on activity and level of pain experienced; repetitive activity should be avoided
Bursa Patella			
	Dislocation		All participation contraindicated until physician clearance
	Tracking		Participation allowed based on pain, inflammation, and treatment to correct problem
	Chondromalacia		Participation in repetitive activity movements limited—other activity based on pain tolerance—and weight lifting restricted
Fracture			
	Tibia		No participation
	Femur		No participation
	Patella		No participation

*Implications may vary greatly depending on the attending physician's diagnosis and standard of care philosophy.

proprioceptive training programs can decrease the number of ACL injuries in athletes (Yoo et al., 2010; Hubscher et al., 2010). Numerous jumping and landing training programs are being promoted by certified athletic trainers, strength and conditioning specialists, physical therapists, and other healthcare professionals. These programs are designed to enhance the dynamic function of the leg musculature. The concept of this type of training is to train the appropriate muscles in the leg to contract or relax at appropriate moments, with the idea that the muscles will assist the function of the ACL during activity. Many of the people promoting these programs claim that athletes (especially females) can benefit from this type of training and can reduce the chance of an ACL tear when they are participating in sports. It is worth looking into some of these proprioceptive training programs for athletes of any gender or sport because this area of research appears to be quite promising for reducing ACL injuries.

Knee Bracing

One of the biggest controversies in sports medicine literature and in many athletic departments across the country is the use of prophylactic knee bracing with athletes. A prophylactic knee brace has two attachments: one above the knee and one below the knee, with either unilateral or bilateral braces running medially and laterally. These braces are typically constructed of a lightweight material. The bracing is meant to augment the stabilizing effect on each side of the knee joint (**Figure 15.11**).

Reports of epidemiological and biomechanical studies on knee bracing have been published since the 1970s. Pietrosimone and colleagues (2008) performed a systematic review of the knee brace literature spanning the years 1970–2006. In that 36-year timeframe, they determined there were only seven published studies that met their criteria for scientific rigor. One part of their scientific rigor criteria was a direct comparison of braced to nonbraced collegiate football players. They concluded that there was insufficient evidence for or against the use of prophylactic knee bracing in college football. Many of the epidemiological studies have been criticized for lacking proper methods of study design. The biomechanical studies are criticized for not incorporating proper mechanisms and forces to study the effects of prophylactic braces.

Additionally, Rishiraj and colleagues (2009) conducted a review of knee-bracing studies on the prophylactic and functional roles of injury prevention. They reviewed more than 200 published studies and

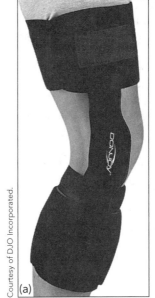
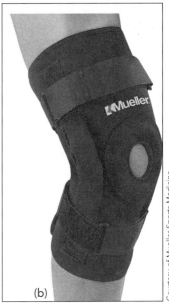

FIGURE 15.11 (a) An example of a prophylactic knee brace. (b) Neoprene knee sleeve with medial and lateral bracing. The neoprene is useful in keeping the joint warm during exercise.

came to a similar conclusion that there is a general lack of consistency in determining the effectiveness of either functional or prophylactic knee bracing. They do suggest that a functional knee brace is beneficial in providing stability to the ACL repaired knee (Rishiraj et al., 2009). One area of prophylactic knee brace research that has been ongoing concerns the movement of the brace on the leg while the athlete is participating. In early studies, it was demonstrated that prophylactic braces can move up or down the leg, some more than others, and this movement can lead to sometimes negative changes in the muscle activity, biomechanics, speed, and overall agility of the athlete (Greene et al., 2000; Osternig & Robertson, 1993). This has lead to poor compliance in wearing the braces by the athletes and thus a lack of well conducted and published research in documenting the effectiveness of prophylactic knee bracing in athletes. More recent studies indicate some prophylactic braces and knee sleeves are better fitting and do not have a negative effect on athletes' performance (Baltaci et al., 2011; Mortaza et al., 2012). Functional knee braces appear to have less detrimental effect on athletic performance after they have been worn by the athletes as they become more used to the brace through practice periods (Rishiraj et al., 2011).

The general consensus regarding prophylactic knee braces indicates that these braces are not completely successful in preventing knee ligament injury (Rishiraj et al.,

2009). More research in the area of ACL injuries resulting from contact and/or trauma needs to be completed before a definite recommendation can be made regarding the use of prophylactic knee braces.

Functional braces (i.e., braces specially constructed to assist an athlete who is returning to participation after a knee injury) appear to have a better record for assisting the athlete after surgical reconstruction. The functional brace (**Figure 15.12**) may initially slightly alter the biomechanics of the athlete's running, jumping, or landing, but the brace is constructed so that it provides some protection for the knee and minimizes future injury. After wearing the functional brace in practice for a week or more, the athlete will adapt to the feel of the functional brace and return to close to normal playing levels (Rishiraj et al., 2011). The athlete may be required by a physician to wear a functional knee brace after ACL reconstruction; therefore, the coach or athletic trainer will not be responsible for deciding whether the athlete should wear a knee brace. When the athlete is required to wear the brace during participation, the coach's or certified athletic trainer's role is to monitor compliance and make sure the athlete is wearing the brace until the physician releases the athlete to participate without the brace.

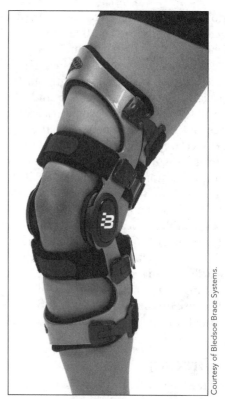

Courtesy of Bledsoe Brace Systems.

FIGURE 15.12 An example of a functional knee brace, used after ligament surgery or later in the healing/rehabilitation process.

REVIEW QUESTIONS

1. List the bones that comprise the knee joint.
2. Give the common name for the muscles located on the anterior portion of the thigh.
3. Give the common name for the muscles located on the posterior thigh region.
4. Give the common name for the muscles located on the medial aspect of the thigh.
5. Where do the quadriceps attach on the lower leg?
6. Define a sesamoid bone using the patella as an example.
7. Explain the articulation of the knee joint, including the involvement of the patella.
8. List and explain the attachments of the four main ligaments of the knee.
9. True or false: There are two menisci located in the knee joint.
10. Explain the first aid care for a severe contusion of the thigh.
11. Explain which muscles of the thigh can experience strains through athletic participation.
12. True or false: If the patella dislocates, it will not return to its proper position without surgical intervention.
13. Define joint mice.
14. What age group is most susceptible to Osgood-Schlatter disease?
15. Describe how to care for an athlete with jumper's knee.
16. What population is more susceptible to Q-angle alignment problems?
17. True or false: An athlete with a torn meniscus will always have a great deal of swelling in the knee joint after the injury.
18. Explain the mechanism by which the MCL and LCL are damaged.
19. Define and list the structures damaged if an athlete experiences a terrible-triad injury.
20. Explain why an athlete should or should not choose to use a prophylactic knee brace.

REFERENCES

Alentorn-Geli E, Myer GD, Silvers HJ, Samitier G, Romero D, Lázaro-Haro C, Cugat R. (2009a). Prevention of non-contact anterior cruciate ligament injuries in soccer players. Part I: Mechanisms of injury and underlying risk factors. *Knee Surg Sports Traumatol Arthrosc.* 17:705–729.

Alentorn-Geli E, Myer GD, Silvers HJ, Samitier G, Romero D, Lázaro-Haro C, Cugat R. (2009b). Prevention of non-contact anterior cruciate ligament injuries in soccer players. Part 2: A review of prevention programs aimed to modify risk factors and reduce injury rates. *Knee Surg Sports Traumatol Arthrosc.* 17:859–879.

Baltaci G, Aktas G, Camci E, Oksuz S, Yildiz S, Kalaycioglu T. (2011). The effect of prophylactic knee bracing on performance: Balance, proprioception, coordination, and muscular power. *Knee Surg Sports Traum Arthrosc.* 19:1722–1728.

Comstock RD, Collins CL, Corlette JD, Fletcher EN. (2012). National high school sports-related injury surveillance study, 2011–2012 school year. Available: http://www.nationwidechildrens.org/cirp-high-school-rio.

Cooney A, Kazi Z, Caplan N, Newby M, St Clair Gibson A, Kader DF. (2012). The relationship between quadriceps angle and tibial tuberosity-trochlear groove distance in patients with patellar instability. *Knee Surg Sports Traum Arthrosc.* 20(12):2399–2405.

Dragoo JL, Braun HJ, Durham JL, Chen MR, Harris AH. (2012). Incidence and risk factors for injuries to the anterior cruciate ligament in national collegiate athletic association football: Data from the 2004–2005 through 2008–2009 national collegiate athletic association injury surveillance system. *Am J Sports Med.* 40(5):990–995.

Dragoo JL, Braun HJ, Harris AH. (2012). The effect of playing surface on the incidence of ACL injuries in National Collegiate Athletic Association American football. *Knee.* 20(3):191–195.

Elliott DL, Goldberg L, Kuehl KS. (2012). Young women's anterior cruciate ligament injuries. *Sports Med.* 40(5):367–376.

Finoff JT. (2012). Preventive exercise in sports. *Physical Med & Rehab.* 4(Nov):862–866.

Gray H. (1974). *Anatomy, Descriptive and Surgical.* Philadelphia, Pa: Running Press.

Hershman EB, Anderson R, Bergfeld JA, Bradley JP, Coughlin MJ, Johnson RJ, Spindler KP, Wojtys E, Powell JW. (2012). An analysis of specific lower extremity injury rates on grass and FieldTurf playing surfaces in national football league games. *Am J Sports Med.* 40(10):2200–2205.

Hubscher M, Zech A, Pfeifer K, Hänsel F, Vogt L, Banzer W. (2010). Neuromuscular training for sports injury prevention: A systematic review. *MSSE.* 42(3):413–421.

Jones JC, Burks R, Owens BD, Sturdivant RX, Svoboda SJ, Cameron KL. (2012). Incidence and risk factors associated with meniscal injuries among active-duty US military service members. *J Athl Training.* 47(1):67–73.

Kobayashi H, Kanamura T, Koshida S, Miyashita K, Okado T, Shimizu T, Yokoe K. (2010). Mechanisms of the anterior cruciate ligament injury in sports activities: A twenty-year clinical research of 1,700 athletes. *J Sports Sci Med.* 9:669–675.

Levangie PK, Norkin CC. (2011). *Joint Structure and Function: A Comprehensive Analysis* (5th ed.). Philadelphia, Pa: F. A. Davis.

Moore K, Dalley AF, Aqur AM. (2013). *Clinically Oriented Anatomy* (7th ed.). Philadelphia, Pa: Lippincott, Williams and Wilkins.

Mortaza N, Ebrahimi I, Jamshidi AA, Abdollah V, Kamali M, Abas WA, Osman NA. (2012). The effects of a prophylactic knee brace and two neoprene knee sleeves on the performance of healthy athletes: A crossover randomized controlled trial. *Plos One.* 11(7):1–6.

Osternig LR, Robertson RN. (1993). Effects of prophylactic knee bracing on lower extremity joint position and muscle activation during running. *Am J Sports Med.* 21(5):733–738.

Pietrosimone BG, et al. (2008). A systematic review of prophylactic braces in the prevention of knee ligament injuries in collegiate football players. *J Athl Training.* 43(4):409–415.

Rishiraj N, Grindstaff TL, Linens SW, Uczekaj E, Hertel J. (2009). The potential role of prophylactic/functional knee bracing in preventing knee ligament injury. *Sports Med.* 39(11):937–960.

Rishiraj N, Taunton JE, Lloyd-Smith R, Regan W, Niven B, Woollard R. (2011). Effect of functional knee brace use on acceleration, agility, leg power and speed performance in healthy athletes. *Br J Sports Med.* 45:1230–1237.

Shea KG, Grimm NL, Ewing CK, Aoki SK. (2011). Youth sports anterior cruciate ligament and knee injury epidemiology: Who is getting injured? In what sports? When? *Clin Spts Med.* 30:691–706.

Shultz SJ, et al. (2012). ACL research retreat VI: An update on ACL injury risk and prevention. *J Athl Training.* 47(5):591–603.

Sugimoto D, Myer GD, Bush HM, Klugman MF, Medina McKeon JM, Hewett TE. (2012). Compliance with neuromuscular training and anterior cruciate ligament injury risk reduction in female athletes: A meta-analysis. *J Athl Training.* 47(6):714–723.

Yoo JH, Lim BO, Ha M, Lee SW, Oh SJ, Lee YS, Kim JG. (2010). A meta-analysis of the effect of neuromuscular training on the prevention of the anterior cruciate ligament injury in female athletes. *Knee Surg Sports Traumatol Arthrosc.* 18:824–830.

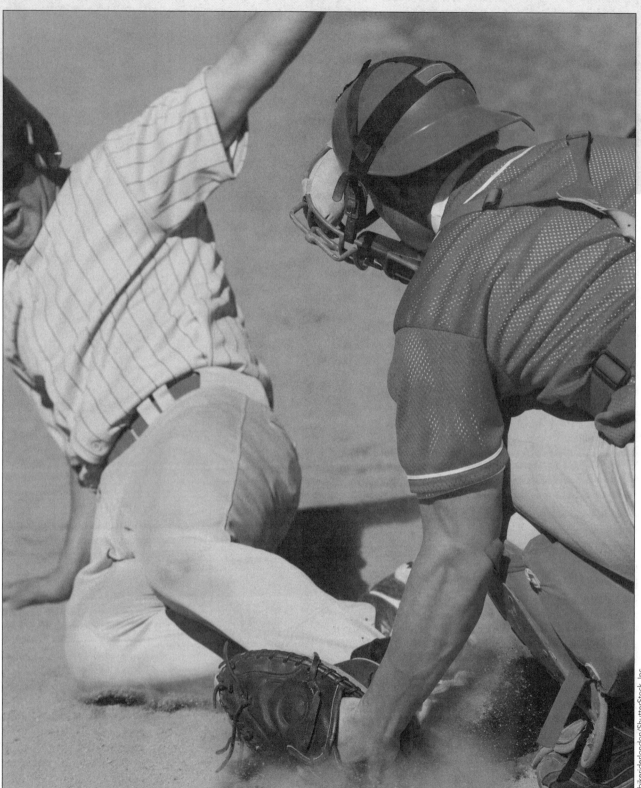

Injuries to the Lower Leg, Ankle, and Foot

MAJOR CONCEPTS

For an athlete to move well, there must be excellent functioning of the lower leg, ankle, and foot. The foot must provide a stable base of support and at the same time be flexible and extremely mobile. This chapter discusses the skeletal and muscular anatomy of the foot and lower leg, with emphasis on the ligaments of the ankle; it also covers the compartments of the lower leg, with an overview of the muscular actions of each compartment. Sports participation can cause fractures of the bones of the lower leg and foot as a result of acute trauma and chronic overuse. This chapter discusses such fractures and common sprains of ankle ligaments. Treatment of ankle sprains and control of possible future sprains are controversial issues and potential solutions should be studied, weighed, and considered carefully when determining if an athlete will be able to participate.

Injuries to the tendons that cross the ankle joint are also quite common among athletes. This chapter reports on the recognition, care, and treatment of tendon injuries along with compartment problems and considers the immediate and long-term effects of these disorders. It also focuses on the treatment and care of athletes with shin splints and considers ways to enhance the participation options of these athletes. Finally, the chapter discusses foot disorders such as plantar fasciitis, heel spurs, Morton's neuroma, arch problems, bunions, blisters, and calluses, providing guidelines for recognition, first aid treatment, and long-term care. It is critical to remember the importance of the lower leg, ankle, and foot when assisting the athlete to perform at peak levels; even small, seemingly insignificant injuries to these areas can affect an athlete's performance.

go.jblearning.com/PfeifferCWS

For a full suite of assignments and additional learning activities (indicated by the icons throughout the text), use the access code found in the front of your text. If you do not have an access code, you can obtain one at go.jblearning.com/PfeifferCWS.

The lower leg, ankle, and foot work together to provide a stable base of support and a dynamic system for movement. The skeleton of the lower leg consists of the tibia and fibula bones. The tibia is the larger and stronger of the two and is commonly called the shin bone; it typically supports about 98% of body weight. The fibula is a smaller bone that supports about 2% of body weight; in addition, it acts as an attachment for various muscles and helps to provide a mechanical advantage for some of them.

ANATOMY REVIEW

The normal foot contains 26 bones (**Figures 16.1** and **16.2**) that are interconnected and supported by numerous ligaments. Many joints within the foot (Figures 16.1 and 16.2) also assist with support and movement. The ankle or **talocrural joint**, where the tibia, fibula, and talus join, provides mainly plantar flexion and **dorsiflexion** of the foot. The **subtalar joint**, which is the articulation of the talus and the calcaneus, is primarily responsible for **inversion** and **eversion of the foot**. Both of these joints are synovial, which means they are surrounded by a capsule and supported by ligaments.

The ankle (talocrural) joint is supported on the medial side by the large and strong deltoid ligament (**Figure 16.3**). On the lateral side of the ankle, the joint is supported by the anterior talofibular, the posterior talofibular, and the calcaneofibular ligaments (**Figure 16.4**). These ligaments are not as large or as strong as the deltoid ligament. Additional lateral stability for the ankle joint is provided by the length of the fibula on the lateral side of the ankle. The ankle joint is strongest when it is placed in dorsiflexion because the talus fits much tighter between the tibia and fibula in this position. Conversely, the joint is weakest when placed in plantar flexion.

The joints, ligaments, and muscles help to create and maintain the two basic arches in the foot (Gray, 1974; Moore, Dalley, & Aqur, 2013). The longitudinal arch has medial and lateral divisions. There is one transverse arch running from side to side. These arches assist the foot as shock absorbers; they also provide propulsion assistance during movement.

As shown in **Time Out 16.1**, the muscles of the lower leg are divided into anterior, posterior, and lateral compartments. The muscles of the anterior compartment essentially produce dorsiflexion and extension of the toes. The muscles in this compartment include the tibialis anterior, extensor digitorum longus, extensor hallucis longus, and peroneus tertius. The anterior compartment is a very compact area with little room for any extra tissue or fluid.

The posterior compartment of the lower leg mainly functions to produce plantar flexion of the foot. This compartment is commonly referred to as the calf muscles.

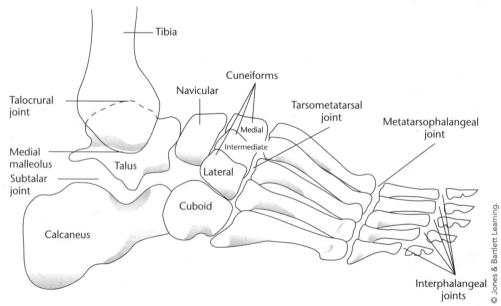

FIGURE 16.1 Major bones, joints, and arches of the foot (lateral view).

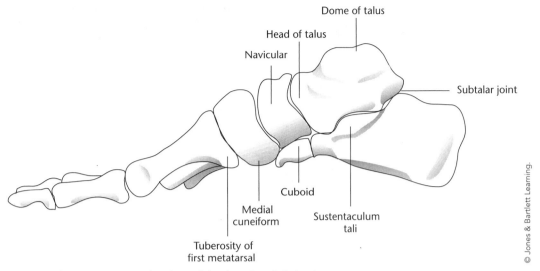

FIGURE 16.2 Major bones, joints, and arches of the foot (medial view).

Many anatomy books subdivide this compartment into superficial and deep sections. In the superficial section are the gastrocnemius, soleus, and plantaris muscles. The gastrocnemius and soleus muscles have a common attachment on the calcaneus via the Achilles tendon. The plantaris muscle is small and insignificant in action and may be absent in some individuals. The deep section of this compartment houses the tibialis posterior, flexor digitorum longus, flexor hallucis longus, and popliteus muscles. With the exception of the popliteus, these muscles course behind the medial malleolus of the tibia and along the bottom of the foot. They assist with plantar flexion as well as flexion of the toes. The popliteus muscle is important in knee flexion—it actually initiates knee flexion by unlocking the knee. The lateral compartment of the lower leg contains the peroneus longus and peroneus brevis muscles. These muscles are mainly evertors of the foot but do assist with some plantar flexion. Both of these muscles course

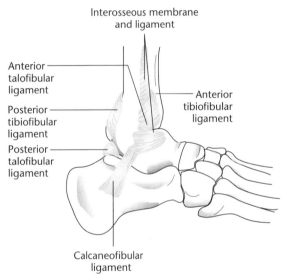

FIGURE 16.4 Major ligaments of the ankle joint (lateral view).

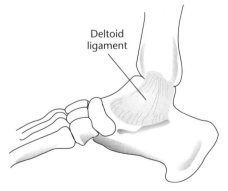

FIGURE 16.3 Major ligaments of the ankle joint (medial view).

talocrural joint Articulation (ginglymus) formed by the distal tibia and fibula with the superior surface (dome) of the talus.

dorsiflexion Bending toward the dorsum or rear; the opposite of plantar flexion.

subtalar joint Articulation (arthrodial) formed by the inferior surface of the talus and the superior surface of the calcaneus.

inversion of the foot To turn the foot inward; inner border of the foot lifts.

eversion of the foot To turn the foot outward.

TIME OUT 16.1

Main Muscle Groups, Actions, and Innervations of the Foot and Ankle

Muscle Group

Posterior Compartment	Action(s)	Innervation
Flexor digitorum longus	Flexion of 2–5 PIP and DIP Flexion of 2–5 MTP joints Assists in plantar flexion Assists in inversion	Tibial
Flexor hallucis longus	Flexion of 1st IP Assists in flexion of first MTP Assists with inversion Assists with plantar flexion	Tibial
Gastrocnemius	Ankle plantar flexion Assists with knee flexion	Tibial
Soleus	Ankle plantar flexion	Tibial
Plantaris	Assists with knee flexion	
Popliteus	Tibial rotation Assists with knee flexion	Tibial

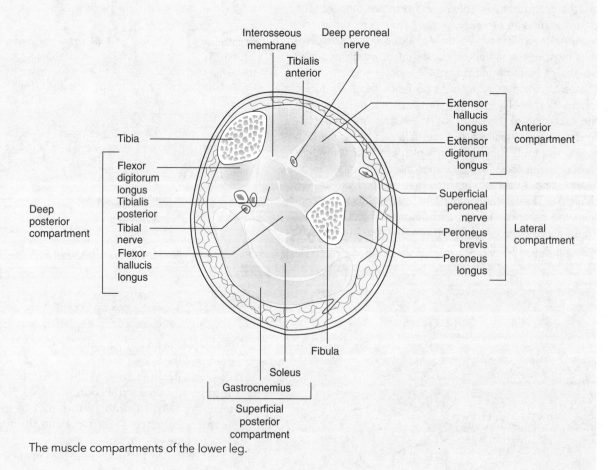

The muscle compartments of the lower leg.

(continues)

TIME OUT 16.1 (*continued*)

Main Muscles Groups, Actions, and Innervations of the Foot and Ankle

Muscle Group

Anterior Compartment	Action(s)	Innervation
Extensor digitorum longus	Extension of 2–5 MTP Assists with extension of 2–5 DIP and PIP Assists with eversion Assists with dorsiflexion	Deep peroneal
Extensor hallucis longus	Extension of first MP	Deep peroneal
Peroneus tertius	Extension Assist with eversion of foot Dorsiflexion of ankle	Deep peroneal
Tibialis anterior	Dorsiflexion of ankle deep peroneal inversion	Deep peroneal
Lateral Compartment		
Peroneus brevis	Eversion Assists with plantar flexion	Superficial peroneal
Peroneus longus	Eversion Assists with plantar flexion	Superficial peroneal

behind the lateral malleolus of the fibula, which provides a mechanical advantage for these muscles. The peroneus longus courses under the lateral side of the foot and runs across the bottom to the first metatarsal and cuneiform bones. The peroneus brevis attaches at the base of the fifth metatarsal and is subject to **avulsion**. Also in this compartment is the peroneal nerve, a superficial nerve that is susceptible to injury. The posterior tibial artery supplies blood to the peroneal muscles. The arteries of the leg can be compromised after trauma below the knee. It is important to always check the pulses of the foot to ensure there is blood flow to the area (discussed later in this chapter).

Common Sports Injuries

Many different sports-related injuries occur to the lower leg, ankle, and foot; some can be classified as traumatic, and others are chronic in nature. Traumatic injuries typically involve skeletal structures; chronic injuries usually involve damage to soft tissues in the area. However, there are definitely exceptions to this rule. There are times when overuse can be a factor in fractures, and there are occasions when trauma can be the cause of soft-tissue damage resulting in severe complications.

Skeletal Injuries
Fractures

Direct trauma through contact causes most fractures to the lower leg. The magnitude of contact necessary to fracture a bone such as the tibia or fibula can vary. (See **Figure 16.5**.) A fracture can be caused by being kicked by an opponent in a soccer match or by having a 300-pound lineman land on a leg in a professional football game. Fractures to the foot can also occur from trauma, for example, when an opponent lands forcefully on a player's foot. However, violent trauma is not always required in fractures of the bones of the leg and foot. Stress fractures can occur from overuse or **microtrauma**. In running, for example, each time the foot strikes the ground it produces a small amount of trauma to the bone. This trauma damages a few bone cells, which the body must repair as quickly as possible. When the body cannot maintain the repair process and keep up with repeated microtrauma to a specific bone, a stress fracture results (Shindle et al., 2012). Additionally,

avulsion Forcible tearing away or separation.
microtrauma Microscopic lesion or injury.

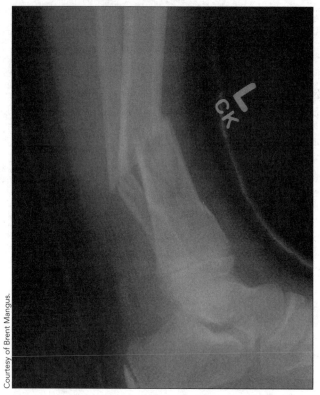

Courtesy of Brent Mangus.

FIGURE 16.5 Fracture of the tibia and fibula in the left leg.

an avulsion fracture of the fifth metatarsal can occur in association with a lateral ankle sprain; therefore, the possibility of such a fracture should be examined when an athlete sprains his or her ankle (Del Buono et al., 2012). Shindle and colleagues (2012) note that a fracture in the fifth metatarsal is considered high risk due to the poor blood supply to the bone and therefore these fractures have an increased incidence of nonunion. If there is any question about the viability of the bone after an injury to this area, have the athlete consult with a physician.

Signs and symptoms of a fracture in the lower leg or foot include the following:

- Swelling and/or deformity at the location of the trauma.
- Discoloration at the site of the trauma.
- Possible broken bone end projecting through the skin.
- The athlete reports that a snap or a pop was heard or felt.
- The athlete may not be able to bear weight on the affected extremity.
- In the case of a stress fracture or a growth plate fracture that did not result from a traumatic event, the athlete complains of extreme point tenderness and pain at the site of suspected injury.

First aid care of a fracture in the lower leg or foot involves the following:

1. Watch and treat for shock if necessary.
2. Apply sterile dressings to any related wounds (i.e., an open fracture).
3. Carefully immobilize the foot and leg using a splint.
4. Arrange for transport to a medical facility.

In the event that bones are fractured, the physician will either apply a cast to the foot and ankle or have the athlete immobilized in a walking boot for a specified time. When the fracture has healed properly, the physician will release the athlete for rehabilitation, practice, and competition, in that order. There are extreme cases of athletes participating in sporting events with a broken bone in the lower leg or foot. This may happen in professional sports in which athletes get paid for participation in the activity. Participation while a fracture is healing is not recommended, because it may slow the healing process. As noted earlier, it is also important to note that there is a possibility of nonunion of a fracture, especially in the fifth metatarsal of the foot, as a result of a diminished blood supply. Careful attention must be paid to the healing process of any broken bone.

Soft-Tissue Injuries

Ankle Injuries

One of the most common sports injuries to the lower leg and ankle is a sprained ankle (**Figure 16.6**). Sprains are abnormal stresses placed on ligamentous structures and cause various levels of damage. Sprains can occur to the lateral or medial ligaments of the ankle depending on which direction the foot moves when abnormal stress is placed on the ligaments as the foot rolls to one side.

By analyzing the anatomic relationships of the components of the ankle, it can be seen that the noncontractile structures on the lateral aspect of the ankle are most susceptible to injury. The formation of the bones of the ankle helps to stabilize it; the fibula extends inferiorly, approximating the lateral talus completely. Also, the ligaments on the lateral side—the anterior talofibular, the posterior talofibular, and the calcaneofibular ligaments—are not as large or strong as the deltoid ligament on the medial side of the ankle joint. With the wide anterior superior aspect of the talus being securely wedged in the mortise formed by the inferior surfaces of the tibia and fibula, the joint is most stable in a dorsiflexed position and weak in a position of plantar flexion. Therefore, when comparing the typical movements of

(a)

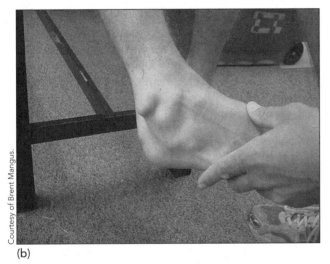

(b)

FIGURE 16.6 (a) Acute swelling after a second-degree ankle sprain. (b) The damage done to the lateral ligaments of the ankle from a sprain.

the foot with the anatomic structure of the ankle joint, it becomes clear that the lateral ligaments are more prone to damage via excessive movement than the deltoid ligament on the medial aspect of the ankle. It has been estimated that up to 85% of ankle sprains occur to the lateral ligaments (Ferrin & Maffulli, 2010). In a large study of emergency room visits from 2002–2004, more than 3 million ankle sprains were documented (Waterman et al., 2010). The study found that 49.3% of the ankle sprains occurred during athletic activity. In the 1.5 million athletic-related ankle sprains in this study, most occurred in basketball (41%), followed by football (9%) and soccer (7.9%). Males ages 15–24 had a higher rate of ankle sprains than females; however, after the age of 30, females incurred more ankle sprains overall (Waterman et al., 2010).

Ankle sprains can occur in virtually any sport and can limit the abilities of the athlete in performance until resolution of the injury is complete. As the severity of the ankle sprain increases, so does the instability of the ankle. It is generally accepted that an eversion ankle sprain is more severe, with greater instability, and should be cared for more conservatively. As mentioned earlier, the lateral sprain involves about 85% of the ankle sprains in athletes and the evaluation of the injury becomes a very important part of the treatment and rehabilitation processes. It is in the best interest of the athlete to have a competent healthcare provider evaluate this injury as concomitant injuries do occur and can be overlooked. There are times when an ankle sprain can also have associated injuries such as a fracture of the fifth metatarsal, navicular or talar dome injuries, and sometimes peroneal tendon injuries (Hall, Lundeen, & Shahin, 2012). It is wise to request a medical opinion on the sprained ankle to ensure the athlete will return to participation as soon as possible.

Signs and symptoms of a lateral ankle sprain include the following:

- First-degree sprain: Pain, mild disability, point tenderness, little laxity, little or no swelling
- Second-degree sprain: Pain, mild to moderate disability, point tenderness, loss of function, some laxity (abnormal movement), swelling (mild to moderate)
- Third-degree sprain: Pain and severe disability, point tenderness, loss of function, laxity (abnormal movement), swelling (moderate to severe)

First aid care of a lateral ankle sprain involves the following:

1. Immediately apply ice, compression, and elevation. A horseshoe- or doughnut-shaped pad kept in place by an elastic bandage aids at this stage in the compression and reduction of fluid (**Figure 16.7**).
2. Have the athlete rest and use crutches to ambulate with a three- or four-point gait if a second- or third-degree sprain has occurred.
3. If there is any question concerning the severity of the sprain, splint and transport the athlete to a medical facility for further evaluation by a physician.

It is important to recognize the possibility of a tibiofibular (tib/fib) syndesmosis sprain in conjunction with or masquerading as a lateral ankle sprain. At times, a tib/fib syndesmosis sprain can be treated as a lateral ankle

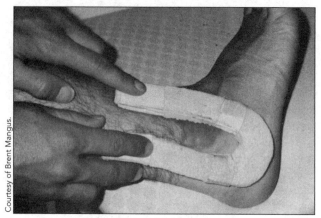

FIGURE 16.7 A horseshoe-shaped pad is used to ease inflammation after an ankle sprain.

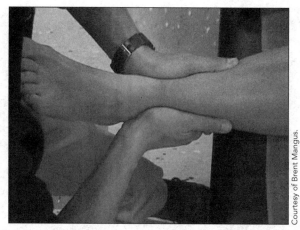

FIGURE 16.8 The "squeeze" test to determine if the tib/fib syndesmosis is involved in an injury.

sprain, which is inappropriate and will not allow the athlete to progress in the healing process as quickly as if the tib/fib syndesmosis sprain had been treated properly. To discern the difference in the two sprains, it is important to note that there is a significant difference in the etiology and specific location of the injury. With the lateral ankle sprain, there is an inversion mechanism, which includes supination. In the tib/fib syndesmosis sprain, the mechanism is dorsiflexion followed by axial loading of the lower leg, with external rotation of the foot and internal rotation of the lower leg (Mangus, Hoffman, & Parry, 1999). Typically, athletes have their foot planted firmly with the foot in external rotation, and the lower leg twists medially, forcing the talus into the ankle mortise; the axial load forces the tibia and fibula to separate slightly and sprain the syndesmosis. The syndesmosis sprain affects the interosseous membrane connecting the distal sections of the tibia and fibula (**Figure 16.8**). This area is immediately superior to

the joint mortise, which is why this is often referred to as a "high ankle sprain" in the media. The location of the lateral ankle sprain is generally distal with point tenderness and swelling occurring at or about the joint mortise area.

Signs and symptoms of a tib/fib syndesmosis sprain include the following:

- The mechanism of injury is different from a lateral ankle sprain; ankle dorsiflexion and foot external rotation are combined with internal rotation of the lower leg.
- The typical ankle sprain tests may be positive, but the athlete will complain of a great deal of pain and point tenderness in the area of the tib/fib syndesmosis.
- Performing the "squeeze" test (squeezing the tibia and fibula together superior to the syndesmosis; Figure 16.8) elicits pain in the syndesmosis area.

First aid care of a tib/fib syndesmosis sprain involves the following:

1. Immediately apply ice, compression, and elevation. A horseshoe- or doughnut-shaped pad kept in place by an elastic bandage aids at this stage in the compression and reduction of fluid accumulation in the local area. (See Figure 16.7.)

2. After the athlete has been diagnosed with a syndesmosis sprain by the physician, the athlete will be counseled to rest and use crutches to ambulate for the first 72 hours, followed by the use of a walking boot for a minimum of 3 days and preferably for 7 days following the initial injury (Mangus et al., 1999).

WHAT IF?

One of your high school soccer players has just injured his ankle, apparently while moving the ball downfield. He has fallen to the ground and is in obvious pain, holding his right ankle. During your examination, you note swelling and discoloration in the region of the lateral malleolus and point tenderness over the area of the lateral ankle ligaments. Based on this history and the signs and symptoms, what is the likely injury? What is the appropriate first aid for such injuries?

3. If there is any question concerning the severity of the sprain, splint and transport the athlete to a medical facility for further evaluation by a physician.

The control of subsequent ankle sprains is a source of a great deal of research and debate in sports medicine literature, although it is recognized that taping or bracing can reduce the number of ankle sprains (Verhagen & Bay, 2010). Some prefer to use the standard ankle-taping procedure as a prophylactic treatment for ankles with no history of previous injury; others choose to augment the taping procedure to prevent future ankle sprains if one has occurred before. In published research studies, ankle taping has been demonstrated to help with the neuromuscular response of the muscles (Lohrer, Alt, & Gollhofer, 1999) and to provide stability if done in a specific manner (Alt, Lohrer, & Gollhofer, 1999). Both of these factors can contribute to a reduction in ankle sprains.

Most researchers agree that the best known method of ankle support, the prophylactic adhesive-taping procedure, supports the ankle for only a short period of time after exercise begins (Lohkamp et al., 2009). It is suggested that the reason ankle taping loses its prophylactic effect over time is that the soft tissues of the ankle region become more mobile as the athlete utilizes them and they become more flexible as the practice or game progresses (Ricard, Schulthies, & Saret, 2000b).

Some researchers now maintain that bracing is better than taping for the prevention of ankle injuries, owing to the reduction in range of motion, either at excessive points or within normal ranges (Babins, 2012; Kaplan, 2011; McGuire, Brooks, & Hetzel, 2011; McGuire et al., 2012). Very good ankle braces are now on the market (**Figures 16.9** through **16.11**) that provide the necessary protection at a low overall cost. It has also been suggested that some high-top shoes may reduce the number of lateral ankle sprains (Ricard et al., 2000a). The combination of high-top shoes and taping or bracing can be helpful to athletes in reducing the number of ankle sprains they experience.

Recent research has been focusing on the prevention of lower extremity injury through proper warmup progressions or specific training techniques. Longo and colleagues (2012) demonstrated how a specific warmup program reduced injuries in basketball players over a 9-month season. Another area of research in injury prevention is through proprioception training. Proprioception training exercises can be helpful in reducing chronic ankle instability (Verhagen & Bay, 2010). Proprioception training can also be an important part of preventive and rehabilitative aspects of ankle

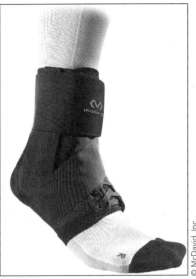

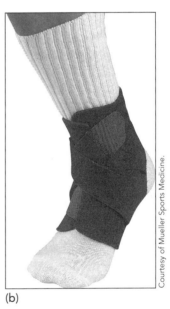

© McDavid, Inc.

Courtesy of Mueller Sports Medicine.

(a)

(b)

FIGURE 16.9 Companies have developed a wide variety of ankle braces. (a) Lace-up ankle braces are useful for prevention of ankle sprains. (b) This brace is neoprene (retains heat) and has supportive straps.

functioning (Hubscher et al., 2010). An interesting analysis of ankle sprain and fracture injuries was conducted by the U.S. Army on paratroopers, documenting that ankle injuries were the most common injury in these soldiers. The Army reported that up to 43% of all soldier injuries involved the ankle. The use of braces in paratroopers was implemented and the injury rate among these soldiers was significantly decreased. The Army medical staff calculated the use of ankle braces saved between $7 and $9 for every dollar spent on the purchase of the braces (Knapik et al., 2010).

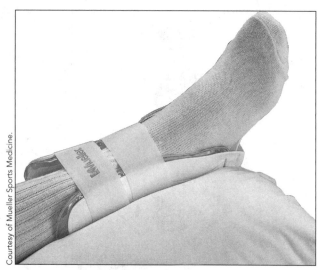

FIGURE 16.10 A rigid ankle brace is used for extra protection after an ankle has been sprained.

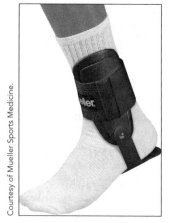 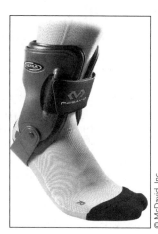

FIGURE 16.11 These rigid braces are also helpful in the prevention of ankle sprains.

Whatever the choice of the coach or athlete, many factors must be considered in preventing ankle sprains. These include the type of activity, the compliance of the athlete in wearing braces or prophylactic taping, the cost to the school or athlete, and the effectiveness of the brace as reported in research studies. Even though most coaches believe that adhesive taping is effective in reducing ankle-related injuries, there are some serious consequences of poorly applied adhesive tape, including blisters, tape cuts, and loss of circulation. If ankle taping is to be part of an athlete's protective equipment, then it must be applied properly to perform correctly (see the section titled "Preventive Ankle Taping" later in this chapter).

Tendon-Related Injuries

The Achilles tendon is commonly injured in long-distance runners, basketball players, and tennis players. The onset of tendinitis may be slow among runners but much more rapid among basketball or tennis players, who make a great many short-burst movements requiring jumping or rapid motion from side to side.

Some controversy exists about the actual injury that constitutes Achilles tendinitis. The Achilles tendon itself, which attaches the gastrocnemius and soleus muscles to the calcaneus, can become inflamed. However, either the tendon sheath or the subcutaneous bursa dorsal to the tendon can become inflamed, both of which can be part of Achilles tendinitis. Most agree that athletes who dramatically increase their running distance or workout times and who do so running on hard, uneven, or uphill surfaces are prone to Achilles

tendinitis (Omey & Micheli, 1999). It is estimated that 11% of runners and up to 52% of former elite runners experience an Achilles tendinopathy (Zafer, Mahmood, & Mafulli, 2009).

Superficially, Achilles tendinitis can produce an increased temperature in the immediate area; moreover, the tendon is painful on touch and movement and appears thickened. The pain associated with this condition is localized to a small area of the tendon and typically intensifies when movement is initiated after rest. These signs and symptoms can be seen over an extended period of time (days to weeks) or, in some athletes, over a shorter time period (days). Early detection of this problem usually enhances resolution of the symptoms and assists the athlete in returning earlier to practice and competition. Referring the athlete with an Achilles tendon problem to the team physician will put the athlete on the right track for treatment, rehabilitation, and avoiding this problem in the future. The physician will outline a treatment plan that will contain some or all of the components explained in the following paragraphs.

Treatment for chronic Achilles tendinitis is immediate rest until the swelling subsides. Usually the application of ice, nonsteroidal anti-inflammatories (e.g., aspirin or ibuprofen), and a small heel lift assist in the reduction of swelling and the return to practice and competition. Stretching can be beneficial to athletes with Achilles tendinitis. Controlled stretching on a slant board or against a wall each day will aid in a return to participation. Additionally, if an athlete must exercise or run, it is advised that this be done in a controlled environment, perhaps in a swimming pool. Controlled, gradual stretching exercises using the eccentric contraction of the Achilles, common to most activities, assist the athlete in returning to activity. An athlete's activity level and type of exercise must be closely monitored during the healing phase. Frequently, runners or other athletes do not accept complete rest as the route to healing. In such cases, decreasing the amount of work may be the only way that even a small amount of healing will occur. Without the proper amount of rest, the body has a hard time repairing injury, thereby increasing the amount of time the athlete experiences difficulty with the condition. Running in water is an option for those athletes who must maintain conditioning or want to work out even though they are injured. Other exercises may be completed by doing them at slower rates or in controlled situations, in which the stress placed on the Achilles tendon is limited.

Explosive jumping or direct trauma from some type of impact can cause traumatic injuries to the Achilles tendon by tearing or rupturing the tendon. These types of injuries have been known to occur in athletes participating in many different sports.

Signs and symptoms of a ruptured Achilles tendon include the following:

- Swelling and deformity at the site of injury.
- The athlete reports a pop or snap associated with the injury.
- Pain in the lower leg, which may range from mild to extreme.
- Loss of function, mainly in plantar flexion.

First aid care of a ruptured Achilles tendon involves the following:

1. Immediately apply ice and compression to the area.
2. Immobilize the foot by an air cast or splint.
3. Arrange for transportation to the nearest medical facility.

During the acute phase of the healing process, try to minimize active dorsiflexion and eliminate forced dorsiflexion because this movement can produce more damage and inflammation to the area.

The long-term effects of a ruptured Achilles tendon depend on the severity or completeness of the rupture. If surgery is necessary, the athlete will most likely be out of athletic participation for the rest of the season. In any case, the athlete will need to be careful and aware of the value of stretching and warming up in any future sports activity.

Other tendon problems typically occur with the tendons on the lateral side of the ankle, including those of the peroneus longus and peroneus brevis muscles. These muscles originate on the lateral aspect of the tibia and fibula; the tendons then run an inferior course behind the lateral malleolus in the peroneal groove and attach on the lateral and posterior aspects of the foot. There is a small retinaculum band attaching on the fibula and running posteriorly to the calcaneus, which assists in holding the tendons in place. As these tendons run their course behind the lateral malleolus, there is a possibility of their dislocating and/or subluxing as a result of trauma or extreme force and actually popping across the lateral malleolus. This can be very painful and is an unusual athletic injury.

The athlete with tendon problems should be seen by a member of the medical team, and a course of action should be outlined. Sometimes these problems can be controlled by taping or bracing and strengthening of the musculature in the area. Recurrent problems warrant further investigation by the physician; other modes of controlling recurrent subluxation are possible.

Compartment Syndrome

Another possible problem that can result from chronic or acute conditions is compartment syndrome. This syndrome is associated with the lower leg, which is divided into four very distinct compartments (see Time Out 16.1). The majority of compartment syndrome problems occur in the anterior compartment, which has very little room to expand if there is any extra swelling or effusion into this compact space.

Some athletes may chronically overuse the muscles in the anterior compartment, leading to an inflammatory process in the musculature and resulting in an overall increase in the pressure within the compartment. This may be followed by extreme pressure on the blood vessels and nerves in the compartment, thereby compromising their functions. Trauma to the anterior portion of the leg (by being kicked or hit with a ball, for example) can result in internal bleeding and swelling into the compartment. A similar scenario can cause the same results in the other compartments of the lower leg, which are so tightly packed with muscles, nerves, and blood vessels that there is little room for expansion when extra fluid is present. Any scenario that results in a pressure increase in the compartment requires immediate attention. Compartment injuries require early intervention and detection of any compromise in the dorsalis pedis and the posterior tibial arteries. Checking the pulses of both arteries is of critical importance in an athlete experiencing a lower leg problem (**Figure 16.12**). If either or both of the pulses are diminished or nonexistent, the athlete must be immediately evaluated by a physician.

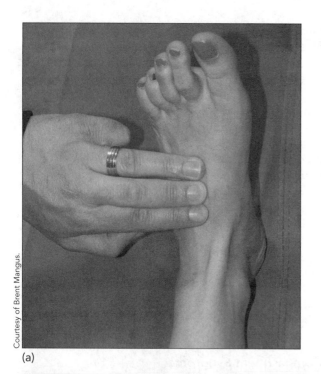

(a)

FIGURE 16.13 Some soccer players wear shin guards that are too small.

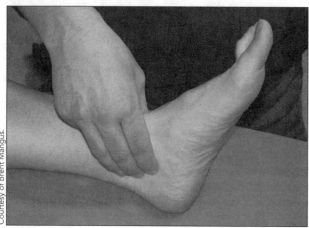

(b)

FIGURE 16.12 Checking the pulse of the dorsalis pedis (a) and the posterior tibial arteries (b).

Many soccer athletes tend to want to wear shin guards that are small (**Figure 16.13**). The athletes contend that large shin guards inhibit their play, so they don't like to wear them. When athletes wear shin guards that are too small, however, they run the risk of not having appropriate preventative padding if they are kicked in the lower leg (**Figure 16.14**). Fortunately for the athlete shown in Figure 16.14, the kick was to the medial side of the leg, which allowed the hematoma to be controlled and reduced in a short time. Being kicked on the lateral side of the leg could have resulted in excessive anterior compartment pressure and loss of blood flow and/or function requiring immediate medical attention.

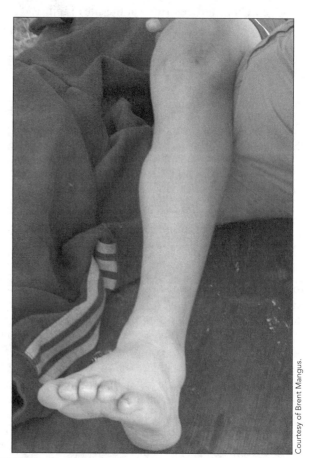

FIGURE 16.14 Severe contusion with hematoma formation on the medial aspect of the lower leg.

Signs and symptoms of compartment syndrome include the following:

- Pain and swelling in the lower leg.
- The athlete may complain of chronic or acute injury to the area.
- There may be a loss of sensation or motor control to the lower leg and/or foot.
- There can be a loss of pulse to the foot.
- Inability to extend the great toe or dorsiflex the foot.

First aid care of compartment syndrome involves the following:

1. Apply ice and elevate. Do not apply compression because the area is already compromised with too much pressure.
2. If the foot becomes numb, there is loss of movement, or there is loss of pulse to the foot, seek medical help immediately.
3. Seek proper medical advice early because these problems can worsen very quickly.

Shin Splints

Another very common disorder of the lower leg is "shin splints," a term used to describe exercise-induced leg pain. Shin splints are also labeled as medial tibial stress syndrome (MTTS), tibial stress injury (TSI), or chronic exertional compartment syndrome (CECS), all of which can describe a wide variety of exercise-induced lower leg disorders. This is a dubious disorder that does not have definite parameters to follow for determining the exact problem causing pain in the lower leg. Over time, medical professionals have attempted to rename this problem using the descriptive terms (i.e., MTTS, TSI, CECS) rather than shin splints, but they are merely a description rather than a diagnosis of the problem (Brewer & Gregor, 2012; Hubbard, Carpenter, & Cordova, 2009; Moen et al., 2012). The types of activities that produce this problem and the manifestations of the injury vary depending on the athlete. However, to date there has not been a positive link between any one specific cause and the resulting leg pain. Moreover, it is generally accepted that with rest the pain will subside and the athlete will be able once again to participate.

Signs and symptoms of shin splints include the following:

- Lower leg pain either medially or posteromedially.
- Typically, the athlete reports a chronic problem that gets progressively worse.

- The pain and discomfort can be bilateral or unilateral.

First aid care of shin splints involves the following:

1. Apply ice and have the athlete rest.
2. Nonsteroidal anti-inflammatory medications may help.

To help the athlete work through shin splints, suggest a change in workout routine. Recommend that the athlete run in water, reduce running, or eliminate the irritating stimulus altogether and use another type of exercise until there is an improvement. The athlete may also want to have his or her gait analyzed to look for biomechanical deficiencies such as overpronation. Myriad related problems can exacerbate the pain and discomfort associated with shin splints. If the problem worsens, the athlete must seek professional medical advice so that long-term complications do not arise. An athletic trainer can assist the athlete with shin splints through preventive taping procedures and some therapies. However, long-term treatment with adhesive tape is not advised: The skin of the lower leg will become irritated, and often this does not alleviate the initial problem causing the pain and discomfort. Each athlete responds differently to taping and therapy; therefore, a controlled progression of alternative taping procedures and a well planned and implemented approach to the rehabilitation program are important in determining which factor the athlete is responding to during the healing process.

Foot Disorders

The foot contains many bones, joints, ligaments, muscles, and other tissues. It is important to remember that athletes participating in different sports will have

 WHAT IF?

A high school gymnast has just struck the front of her lower left leg on the lower bar of the uneven bars. She immediately grabs her leg and complains loudly of extreme pain. On further examination, you note that she has swelling and discoloration directly over the muscles of the anterior compartment. In addition, she states that she is unable to extend her big toe. What is the likely cause of these signs and symptoms? What would be the most appropriate first aid for this injury?

Athletic Trainers SPEAK Out

Courtesy of Dale Mildenberger, ATC-L, Utah State University.

The most common injuries to the lower leg, often minimized by athletes and coaches, are traumatic contusions, which may progress to compartment syndrome. These injuries are commonly caused by kicks to the anterior lateral lower leg. Due to the anatomical compartments of the lower leg, there is little room for expansion caused by hemorrhage.

An improperly recognized or treated contusion can result in increased pressure to nerves and blood vessels. This is especially true with injuries to the anterior compartment of the lower leg. These injuries can become lifelong disabilities if not properly recognized and treated. As the effusion increases pressure, the area may need to be surgically decompressed. All athletic trainers need to be aware of and concerned about the possibility of compartment syndrome when treating trauma to the lower leg. This is one area of the body where external pressure from elastic wraps should not be used as a method for control of swelling. The wrap may only increase the internal pressure and further hasten the symptoms of compartment syndrome.

—Dale Mildenberger, MS, ATC-L

Dale Mildenberger is head athletic trainer for Utah State University.
Courtesy of Dale Mildenberger, ATC-L, Utah State University.

---

different injuries associated with the foot. Some injuries are more common to specific sports.

Plantar Fasciitis

The plantar fascia is a dense collection of tissues, including muscles and tendons, that traverses from the plantar aspect of the metatarsal heads to the calcaneal tuberosity. If this collection of tissues becomes tight or inflamed by overuse or trauma, it can produce pain and disability in the bottom of the foot, known as plantar fasciitis. A change in shoes, training technique, activity, or other factors may be precipitating factors to this injury. People who spend most of the week at a desk and then try to get in as much exercise as possible on the weekend are more susceptible to this problem than are full-time athletes. Plantar fasciitis in the young athlete typically is a combined problem with calcaneal apophysitis (Omey & Micheli, 1999). It is important to remember in the adolescent athlete that this condition may also include medial arch and/or heel pain (Omey & Micheli, 1999). To determine whether the condition is plantar fasciitis, the examiner must take a thorough history. Ask the athlete if he or she experiences almost unbearable pain in the plantar aspect of the foot with the first steps taken on getting out of bed in the morning and whether the pain eases with each of the following steps. Also inquire

if there is point tenderness on the plantar aspect of the calcaneal tuberosity. If both of these symptoms exist, there is a high probability that plantar fasciitis is the problem.

Treatment of plantar fasciitis is typically conservative; it includes rest, anti-inflammatories, and the use of cold and heat alternatively to enhance healing. A heel pad and stretching the Achilles tendon complex can assist in recovery and resolution. The use of semi-rigid orthoses has also been shown to be effective in recovering from plantar fasciitis; however, many athletes find it difficult to participate in sports with such an orthotic in their shoes. Athletes will be tempted to continue exercising with this injury. However, the more the injury is aggravated by further insult to the same area, the longer it will take to heal, even when the healing process is being augmented with assorted therapeutic agents.

Heel Spurs

Heel spurs can also be related to plantar fasciitis: Sometimes with chronic cases of inflammation there is ossification at the site of the muscular attachment on the plantar aspect of the calcaneus. This results in long-term disability for many athletes because the heel spur can become problematic at any time during the exercise or activity program. Additionally, these small ossifications can occur on the posterior aspect of the calcaneus just below the attachment of the Achilles tendon. These too can become disabling to an athlete. The athlete needs to consult a physician to determine the proper treatment plan if these spurs become too incapacitating. Doughnut-shaped pads placed beneath the heel and some therapeutic interventions may assist the athlete to participate fully, but rarely do they ameliorate the problem.

Morton's Foot

Morton's foot typically involves either a shortened first metatarsal bone or an elongated second metatarsal bone. The result is that the majority of weight bearing is done on the second metatarsal instead of along the first metatarsal and spreading out to the remainder of the foot. This problem can result in pain throughout the foot and difficulty in ambulation. The use of padding can help the athlete, but, to have the problem correctly addressed, the athlete should see a physician so that the proper treatment can be prescribed.

Also associated with this area is a condition called Morton's neuroma. This is a problem with the nerve, usually between the third and fourth metatarsal heads. As a result, pain radiates to the third and fourth toes. A neuroma is an abnormal growth on the nerve itself. Tight-fitting shoes have been blamed for irritation of the nerve in many cases of Morton's neuroma. Consequently, going barefoot is one of the best methods of pain relief for this problem. This condition is most often taken care of by a medical doctor, who should always be consulted regarding the early detection of foot problems.

Arch Problems

Athletes can experience several problems associated with the arches of the foot (Figures 16.1 and 16.2). Essentially, arch problems can be classified into two categories: pes planus (an abnormally flat foot) and pes cavus (an abnormally high arch in the foot). Both problems present difficulties to some athletes. Others with similar foot conditions may never complain of problems associated with arches.

Athletes with flat feet may have too much foot pronation, causing difficulties with or around the navicular bone. This leads to generalized discomfort around the foot and ankle. A low-cost alternative and potential method of determining if the athlete could benefit from an orthotic (**Figure 16.15**) or some other type of augmentation for flat feet is to begin with an arch-taping procedure. Several taping procedures have been developed to augment the arch in athletes. How long the effects of taping enhance the arch has been evaluated by at least one research team, whose findings were

FIGURE 16.15 Soft orthotics can be placed in athletes' shoes to assist with some foot problems.

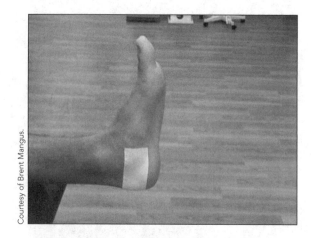

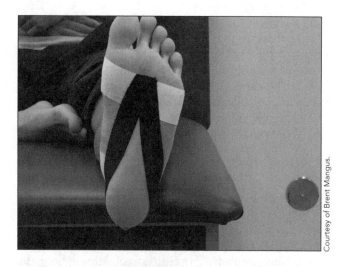

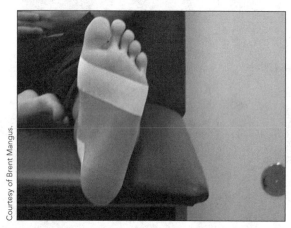

FIGURE 16.16 After an adhesive is applied, begin with anchor strips on the heel and base of the toes.

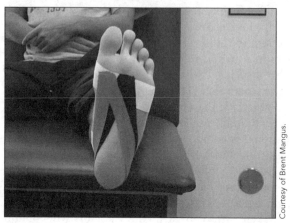

FIGURE 16.17 Apply support strips starting from medial moving to lateral as demonstrated.

consistent with those for ankle-taping procedures. There seems to be limited effectiveness in adhesive-strapping techniques for the person who walks for a minimum of 10 minutes continuously (Lohkamp et al., 2009). However, it may be worth trying to tape the arch(es) with the intent to determine if the application provides any benefit for the athlete during practice (**Figures 16.16** through **16.18**). A Board of Certification, Inc. (BOC)–certified athletic trainer can assist in providing direction in this taping procedure. Coaches should not attempt to apply adhesive tape to an athlete until they have received the proper training. Many athletes with flat feet can be helped in the long term by orthotics and proper shoe selection. It should be noted, however, that there is no evidence that the flat-footed athlete is a slower runner or has less motor ability than the athlete with a regular or high arch.

From time to time an athlete may feel one or both feet experiencing a generalized soreness or weakness due to fatigue. As mentioned earlier, orthotics may be necessary to assist the athlete on a long-term basis,

but for the short-term arch support taping may assist the athlete to get through a practice or game. In some athletes, support taping for one or both arches can help reduce this feeling of sore or weak feet during participation.

In many cases, the athlete with an excessively high arch also has foot problems. There are research reports outlining the abnormal forces placed on the high-arch foot suggesting a potential for injury (Carson et al., 2012). A foot with too much arch is often associated with plantar fasciitis and clawing of the toes. There have also been cases of athletes with too much arch having generalized discomfort about the foot and ankle because of the inability of the foot to absorb forces owing to the tightness of joints there. These athletes can also benefit from some orthotic help and proper shoe selection. As with the athlete with flat feet, the height of an athlete's arch need not hinder athletic performance.

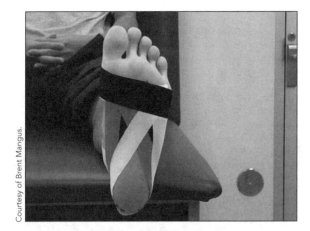

Courtesy of Brent Mangus.

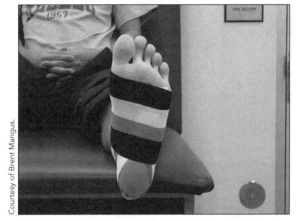

Courtesy of Brent Mangus.

FIGURE 16.18 Finish by alternating strips around the foot to maintain and stabilize the arch tape.

Bunions

Bunions are not very common in athletes at the high school and college levels. Bunions can be simply a matter of inflamed bursae, or they can involve complicated bone and joint deformities. Many times bunions are caused by improperly fitting footwear. By getting the athlete into correctly fitting shoes, the early signs of a bunion should resolve. If an athlete has had a bunion for an extended period of time (weeks to months), then the athlete should seek the advice of a physician in the care of this condition.

Blisters and Calluses

Blisters and calluses are very common formations on athletes' feet. Excessive amounts of movement can produce a great deal of friction between the layers of skin in the foot and the shoe, resulting in the formation of either a blister or callus. When the athlete starts to experience this abnormal friction (termed a "hot spot") the application of padding or some lubricant to the localized spot will avert the formation of a blister. If a blister forms, the layers of skin have been separated, and the friction has built up a fluid deposit. Always observe the color of the fluid within a blister. Most often the fluid is clear, but on occasion it will be dark, which means there is blood in this small cavity. Frequently, the pain and discomfort from a blister prevent the athlete from participating in sports. If the blister is large, the fluid should be drained and the area padded well to prevent further friction and blister formation. When a blister is drained, it is best to leave the top layer of skin in place until a new layer develops, thereby reducing the possibility of introducing infection into the area. In addition, place a doughnut-shaped pad made of felt or a large pad of thin adhesive directly over the blister to reduce friction. In case the blister opens inadvertently (the top flap tears off for some reason), care needs to be taken to ensure that the area is clean and the possibility of infection is reduced. Anytime the blister opens there is a possibility of infection entering the body. If the skin over the top of the blister tears, it is important to try to maintain the torn flap and keep it in contact with the blister if possible. This maintains a little protection for the area. Apply an antibacterial ointment to the area and cover it as necessary.

When draining a blister, be sure to follow the recommended precautions regarding human immunodeficiency virus (HIV) and hepatitis B:

1. Always use sterile instruments and keep the environment sterile.
2. Use latex gloves or some other barrier so that body fluids are not contacted.

The following procedures should be followed when caring for a blister:

1. Initially wash the area with soap and warm water and sterilize the area with rubbing alcohol.
2. Using a sterile needle, puncture the base of the blister and gently drain by applying light pressure. This may need to be repeated several times in the first 24 hours. Do not remove the top of the blister; apply antibiotic ointment to the top of the blister and cover with a sterile dressing.
3. Check the area daily for redness or pus to determine if infection is occurring at the site.
4. After 3 to 7 days, gently remove the top of the blister, apply an antibiotic ointment, and cover with a sterile dressing.
5. Watch the area closely for signs of infection such as redness or pus and pad the area well with gauze pads or moleskin. This allows for healing to occur without further irritation.

If the blister is small, padding the area to prevent further friction usually suffices until the blister heals. Athletes should be encouraged to report the formation of any new hot spots or blisters as soon as possible so that padding and protection can be provided. It is definitely best to help prevent blisters by having properly fitted footwear and giving new shoes a short break-in period before using them in practice or competition.

In addition to blisters, excessive tissue can build up on the bottom of the feet, which is commonly known as a callus. Calluses tend to build up over a bony area of the foot and should not be allowed to become large and extremely thick. If this happens, the callus can begin to move with the shoe and not with the foot. This creates an area of friction between the callus and layers of skin, causing a blister to form between the callus and the next lower layer of skin. This can cause problems because the blister is difficult to drain and can be very painful to the athlete. To prevent this from happening, a callus should be shaved regularly to allow for only a small amount of buildup, which then acts as a padding for the area. If a callus gets too large, the athlete will begin to complain of pain and discomfort in the area.

Toe Injuries

The toes can also be injured during sports participation. In some sports, the toes can be stepped on, resulting in torn-off nails or hematoma formation under the nail (**Figure 16.19**). This collection of blood under a nail needs to be released. Numerous techniques to remove this blood exist. Commercially available nail drills bore a small hole in the nail and allow the trapped blood to be released. This provides a great deal of relief to the athlete because this injury can produce a great deal

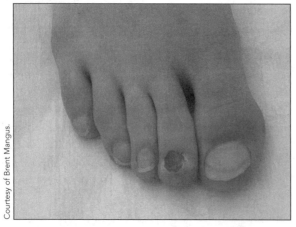

FIGURE 16.19 Players can get their toes stepped on, resulting in hematoma formation under the toenail; in some instances, as here, the nail can be torn off.

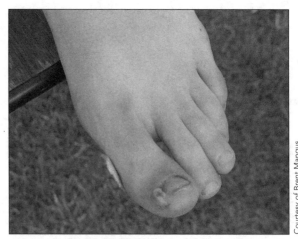

FIGURE 16.20 Shoes that are too tight can lead to ingrown toenails in the athlete.

of pain. If an athlete wears shoes that are too tight or small, this can also create a situation in which a toenail is smashed and blood collects under the nail. Shoes that are too small or too tight can also result in an ingrown toenail (**Figure 16.20**). Ingrown toenails need to be treated early because delaying care can result in infection and serious problems. The ingrown nail can produce an open sore on the toe, and when the foot is placed in the sport shoe, bacteria can enter this open sore and result in further problems. Ingrown toenails should be treated by soaking them in a warm antibacterial solution. The nail needs to be elevated so that it will grow in a normal direction. This can be done by placing a small cotton roll under the affected part and leaving it there as the nail grows. It is important to address the situation that led up to the ingrown toenail. If the athlete is wearing shoes that are too small or too tight, he or she needs to get a shoe that has a more comfortable fit. Another prevention technique for ingrown toenails is to have the athlete trim the nail straight across, which will encourage the nail to grow out normally.

With the advent of artificial playing surfaces, there has been in increase in the number of injuries to the toe, which has been termed "turf toe" in the athletic population. Turf toe is essentially a hyperextension sprain to the ligaments of the great toe and can include an inflammatory process to the sesamoid bones located just under the first metatarsal joint. Athletes will either push off in an explosive move or be tackled and the foot moves but the great toe for some reason remains on the turf. In the case of an immediate-onset injury, athletes will report they heard a "pop" and felt a sharp pain in their great toe. In chronic cases, the symptoms of pain and inflammation in the big toe area are progressive over time. This is an injury that typically occurs on artificial turf, but can

Courtesy of Brent Mangus.

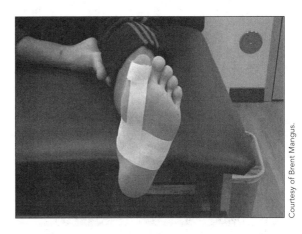

Courtesy of Brent Mangus.

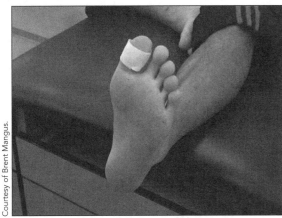

Courtesy of Brent Mangus.

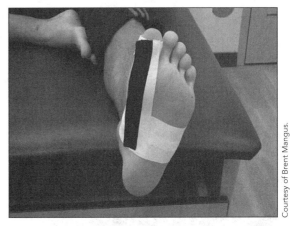

Courtesy of Brent Mangus.

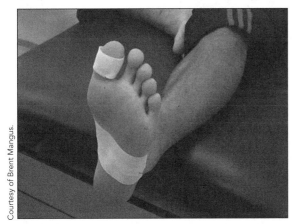

Courtesy of Brent Mangus.

Courtesy of Brent Mangus.

FIGURE 16.21 After an adhesive is applied, begin with a toe and foot anchor strip.

FIGURE 16.22 Apply stabilizing strips as demonstrated.

occur on other surfaces. Care for turf toe is similar to other sprains: Ice, compression, and elevation should be implemented. Often athletes do not want to rest this injury, and in some cases turf toe taping is helpful to allow the athlete to continue to participate during the recovery period (**Figures 16.21** through **16.24**).

Preventive Ankle Taping

Applying preventive ankle taping to athletes is a popular practice among many high school, collegiate, and professional athletic trainers. Athletes commonly have their ankles taped as a routine procedure before practice or competition to prevent or reduce ankle injuries.

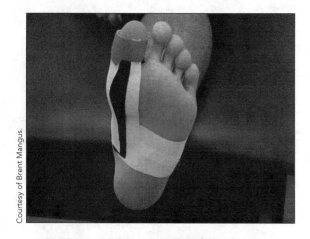

Courtesy of Brent Mangus.

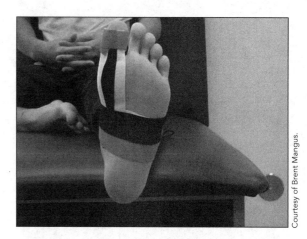

Courtesy of Brent Mangus.

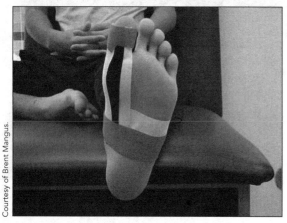

Courtesy of Brent Mangus.

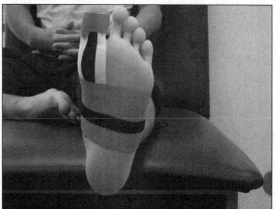

Courtesy of Brent Mangus.

FIGURE 16.23 Lock down the stabilizing strips at the toe and foot.

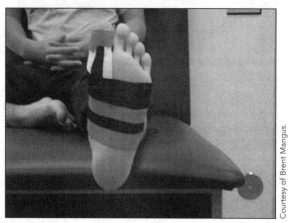

Courtesy of Brent Mangus.

FIGURE 16.24 Complete the turf toe taping by adding finishing strips.

The advantages and disadvantages of preventive ankle taping have been discussed widely, and a continuum of recommendations—from not using taping as a preventive measure to always taping both ankles when participating in any sport—is advocated by various athletic trainers.

Some athletic trainers promote the use of lace-up and other rigid braces rather than preventive taping. Recent research concludes that ankle braces are just as effective, if not more so, as preventive taping in reducing inversion ankle sprains (McGuire et al., 2011; McGuire et al., 2012). This concept has been verified by research demonstrating that ankle bracing can reduce inversion ankle sprains in volleyball players (Pedowitz et al., 2008) and assists in the stabilization of the lower extremity (Zinder et al., 2009). It has also been demonstrated that ankle braces do not detract from an athlete's ability to run, jump, or perform other skills as necessary during athletic competition.

This then creates an interesting decision matrix for coaches and athletic trainers when determining which preventive measures should be implemented to reduce inversion ankle sprains in athletes. Realizing the probability that preventive ankle taping can result in a reduction in efficacy of the tape reducing inversion movement over time (Fleet, Galen, & Moore, 2009), the athletic training and coaching staff need to determine the most efficient means of preventing ankle sprains in the athletic population of their school. There is a time- and cost-benefit analysis that should be evaluated by the staff personnel in making this decision. Some coaches believe that taping the ankles is more efficient when it is done on a semi-regular basis, for example, once or twice a week. From a cost analysis, if a player is going to be taped multiple times a day or week, it may be less expensive to use prophylactic braces that the athlete can put on him- or herself before each practice or game.

There are many factors—for example, athlete comfort—that must be analyzed when deciding to use tape or braces for the athletes. Some athletes feel like the braces are bulky and do not let them move normally. Some athletes contend that the ability to wear them with the proper shoes for practice and games is compromised by the size of the brace. Some sports require shoes that are tight and are not conducive to fitting the foot and the brace in the shoe. Braces are hardware; they do wear out and their effectiveness diminishes over time. The cost of the braces is an upfront cost and sometimes is expensive for the athlete or the school to purchase. These are just some of the issues that must be taken into consideration when deciding how to prevent inversion ankle injuries in athletes at a specific location.

Preventive ankle taping is an important skill that must be learned properly, practiced until a level of mastery is gained, and then applied in an athletic team setting. Taping is an art and a science, and each strip of tape has its own function. The following preventive taping outline is intended to provide the beginning student with the theoretical basis for the reasons the tape is applied. If students are interested in developing taping skills, it is recommended that they work under the direct supervision of a BOC-certified athletic trainer to learn and practice the art of taping.

As shown in **Figure 16.25**, the use of prewrap and anchoring strips is important in starting the taping procedure correctly. An adherent is used to help the prewrap to stay in place. If an adherent is not used, the tape will, in most situations, loosen and slide, diminishing the effectiveness of the taping procedure. The use of stirrups (**Figures 16.25** to **16.28**) is intended to maintain the foot in a normal or slightly everted position. Stirrups are combined with horseshoe strips, which help to hold the stirrups in place and reduce the gaps in the tape on the posterior portion of the foot. **Figures 16.29** to **16.33** demonstrate the use of heel locks, which assist in stabilizing the subtalar joint. Heel locks are followed by the use of figure-eights (**Figures 16.34** to **16.36**), which are intended to help stabilize the talocrural joint and the transverse tarsal joint. From this point on, the procedure involves using finishing strips to make sure there are no gaps or holes between strips of tape, securing the tape at the bottom, and using a final covering to ensure that tape ends do not get rolled or wrinkled as the athlete puts on socks and shoes (**Figures 16.37** and **16.38**).

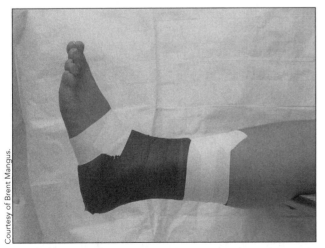

FIGURE 16.25 The application of prewrap and anchoring strips starts the ankle-taping procedure.

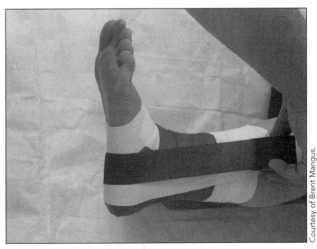

FIGURE 16.26 Stirrups are used to maintain a normal or slightly elevated foot position.

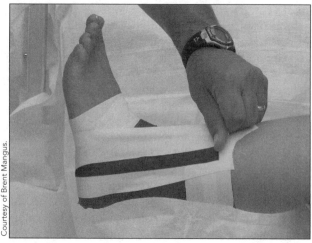

FIGURE 16.27 Overlapping stirrups, starting posteriorly and moving anteriorly.

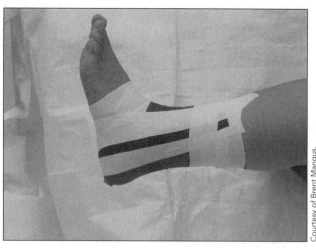

FIGURE 16.28 Stirrups are completed and anchored.

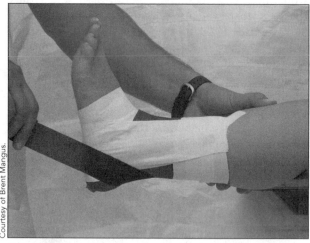

FIGURE 16.29 Applying the heel locks requires practice to perform correctly.

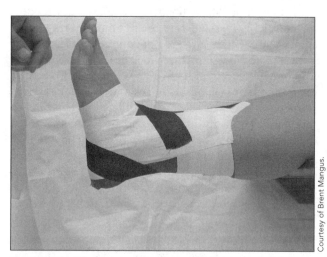

FIGURE 16.30 One heel lock completed (side view).

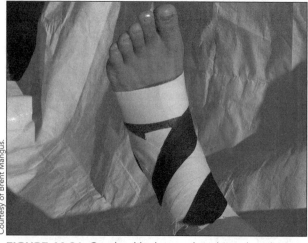

FIGURE 16.31 One heel lock completed (overhead view).

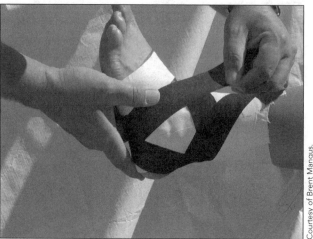

FIGURE 16.32 Second heel lock being applied.

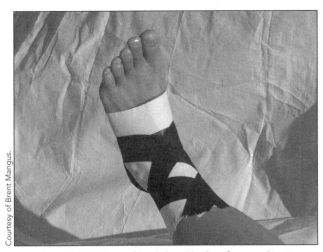

FIGURE 16.33 View of both heel locks after application.

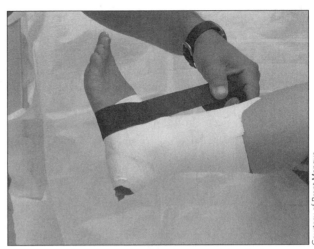

FIGURE 16.34 Starting the figure-eights also takes practice and proper direction of pull on the tape to be performed correctly.

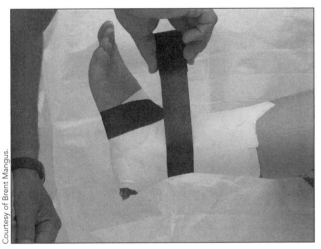

FIGURE 16.35 Completing the figure-eight procedure.

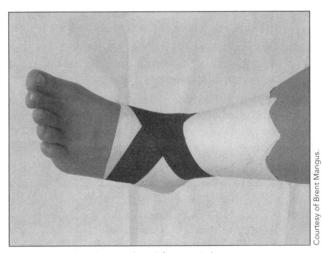

FIGURE 16.36 A completed figure-eight.

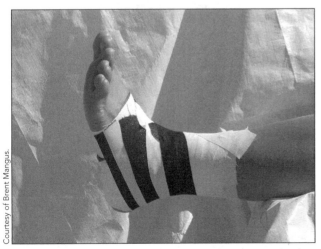

FIGURE 16.37 Finishing horseshoe stirrups are applied, alternating from distal to proximal.

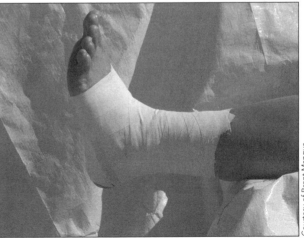

FIGURE 16.38 The completed ankle taping procedure.

REVIEW QUESTIONS

1. Name the two bones located in the lower leg.

2. Explain where the fibula is located and approximately how much body weight is supported by this bone.

3. What is the technical name for the ankle joint?

4. Name the strongest and largest of the ankle ligaments.

5. Draw or outline the compartments of the lower leg and describe the actions that the muscles in each compartment have on the foot.

6. Which compartment of the lower leg presents the most problems with fluid accumulation?

7. Outline the signs and symptoms of a fracture of the lower leg.

8. True or false: An inversion ankle sprain is more common than an eversion ankle sprain.

9. Explain which type of ankle sprain is more severe.

10. Describe where the Achilles tendon attaches, and describe the signs, symptoms, and treatment of Achilles tendinitis.

11. Explain the possible long-term complications if problems with anterior compartment syndrome are left untreated.

12. Explain what types of changes (e.g., biomechanical, training) an athlete may need to make to alleviate and prevent further episodes of shin splints.

13. Outline the key signs and symptoms of plantar fasciitis and explain how heel spurs are associated with this condition.

14. What structures are involved in Morton's foot?

15. Explain the difference between pes cavus and pes planus.

16. Explain the difference between a blister and a callus.

17. Outline how a blister should be cared for when it is drained.

18. Explain how blisters can be prevented.

19. True or false: It is not possible for a callus to form over a blister.

20. True or false: Callus formation on the plantar aspect of the foot should be trimmed regularly to reduce friction.

REFERENCES

Alt W, Lohrer H, Gollhofer A. (1999). Functional properties of adhesive ankle taping: Neuromuscular and mechanical effects before and after exercise. *Foot Ankle Int.* 20:238–245.

Babins EM. (2012). Lace-up ankle braces reduced acute ankle injuries in high school basketball players. *Clin J Spts Med.* 22(4):377–380.

Brewer RB, Gregory AJM. (2012). Chronic lower leg pain in athletes: A guide for the differential diagnosis, evaluation, and treatment. *Sports Health.* 4(2):121–127.

Carson DW, Myer GD, Hewett TE, Heidt Jr. RS, Ford KR. (2012). Increased plantar force and impulse in American football players with high arch compared to normal arch. *The Foot.* 22:310–314.

Del Buono A, Aweid O, Coco M, Maffulli N. (2012). Ankle instability: What do we know and what is the future? *FuB & Sprunggelenk.* 11(1):3–8.

Ferrin NA, Maffulli N. (2010). Epidemiology of sprains of the lateral ankle ligament complex. *Foot Ankle Clin.* 11:659–662.

Fleet K, Galen S, Moore C. (2009). Duration of strength retention of ankle taping during activities of daily living. *Injury, Int J Care Injured.* 40:333–336.

Gray H. (1974). *Anatomy, Descriptive and Surgical.* Philadelphia, Pa: Running Press.

Hall S, Lundeen G, Shahin A. (2012). Not just a sprain: 4 foot and ankle injuries you may be missing. *J Fam Pract.* 61(4):198–204.

Hubbard TJ, Carpenter EM, Cordova ML. (2009). Contributing factors to medial tibial stress syndrome: A perspective investigation. *Med Sci Sports Exerc.* 41(3):490–496.

Hubscher M, et al. (2010). Neuromuscular training for sports injury prevention: A systematic review. *Med Sci Sports Exerc.* 42(3):413–421.

Kaplan Y. (2011). Prevention of ankle sprains in sport: A systematic literature review. *Br J Sports Med.* 4:355.

Knapik JJ, Spiess A, Swedler DI, Grier TL, Darakjy SS, Jones BH. (2010). Systematic review of the parachute ankle brace. Injury risk reduction and cost effectiveness. *Am J Prev Med.* 38(1S):S182–188.

Lohkamp M, Craven S, Walker-Johnson C, Greig M. (2009). The influence of ankle taping on changes in postural stability during soccer specific activity. *J Sport Rehabil.* 18(2):482–492.

Lohrer H, Alt W, Gollhofer A. (1999). Neuromuscular properties and functional aspects of taped ankles. *Am J Sports Med.* 27:69–75.

Longo UG, Loppini M, Berton A, Marinozzi A, Maffulli N, Denaro V. (2012). The FIFA 11+ program is effective in preventing injuries in elite male basketball players. *Am J Sports Med.* 40(6):996–1005.

Mangus BC, Hoffman MA, Parry SA. (1999). Management of tibiofibular syndesmosis injuries. *Athl Ther Today.* 4(5):47–50.

McGuire TA, Brooks A, Hetzel S. (2011). The effect of lace-up ankle braces on injury rates in high school basketball players. *Am J Spts Med.* 39(9):1840–1848.

McGuire TA, Hetzel S, Wilson J, Brooks A. (2012). The effect of lace-up ankle braces on injury rates in high school football players. *Am J Spts Med.* 40(1):49–57.

Moen MH, Holtslag L, Bakker E, Barten C, Weir A, Tol JL, Backx F. (2012). The treatment of medial tibial stress syndrome in athletes; a randomized clinical trial. *Sports Med Arthrosc Rehab Ther Technol.* 4(12):1–8.

Moore K, Dalley AF, Aqur AM. (2013). *Clinically Oriented Anatomy* (7th ed.). Philadelphia, Pa: Lippincott, Williams and Wilkins.

Omey ML, Micheli LJ. (1999). Foot and ankle problems in the young athlete. *Med Sci Sport Ex Suppl.* S470–486.

Pedowitz D, et al. (2008). Prophylactic bracing decreases ankle injuries in collegiate female volleyball players. *Am J Sports Med.* 36(2):324–327.

Ricard MD, Schulties SS, Saret JJ. (2000a). Effects of high-top and low-top shoes on ankle inversion. *J Athl Train.* 35(1):38–43.

Ricard MD, Schulties SS, Saret JJ. (2000b). Effects of tape and exercise on dynamic ankle inversion. *J Athl Train.* 35(1):31–37.

Shindle MK, Yoshimi Endo E, Warren RF, Lane JM, Helfet DL, Schwartz EN, Ellis SJ. (2012). Stress fractures about the tibia, foot, and ankle. *J Am Acad Ortho Surg.* 20(3):167–176.

Verhagen EALM, Bay K. (2010). Optimizing ankle sprain prevention: A critical review and practical appraisal of the literature. *Br J Sports Med.* 44:1082–1088.

Waterman BR, Owens BD, Davey S, Zacchilli MA, Belmont PJ Jr. (2010). The epidemiology of ankle sprains in the United States. *J Bone Joint Surg Am.* 92(13):2279–2284.

Zafer MS, Mahmood A, Mafulli N. (2009). Basic science and clinical aspects of Achilles tendinopathy. *Sports Med Arthrosc Rev.* 17:190–197.

Zinder SM, Granata KP, Shultz SJ, Gansneder BM. (2009). Ankle bracing and the neuromuscular factors influencing joint stiffness. *J Athl Train.* 44(4):363–369.

Skin Conditions in Sports

17

go.jblearning.com/PfeifferCWS

For a full suite of assignments and additional learning activities (indicated by the icons throughout the text), use the access code found in the front of your text. If you do not have an access code, you can obtain one at go.jblearning.com/PfeifferCWS.

MAJOR CONCEPTS

The skin, the largest organ of the human body, is often involved in sports injuries, which range from simple wounds to a variety of bacterial, fungal, and viral infections. This chapter discusses the basic anatomy of the skin and describes the categories of wounds and their care. Obviously, the risk of the human immunodeficiency virus (HIV) and hepatitis B (HBV) infection must be considered whenever a potential exposure to blood exists. The chapter presents the latest guidelines available for the prevention of accidental exposure to human blood.

Next, the chapter covers skin conditions related to excessive exposure to ultraviolet light, with an emphasis on prevention and safety precautions. Any number of microorganisms, ranging from minute viruses and bacteria to relatively large fungi, can produce skin infections. The chapter introduces the reader to the common types of skin infections in sports, with descriptions of signs and symptoms and recommended treatment and prevention protocols. The National Collegiate Athletic Association (NCAA) guidelines on wrestling and skin infections are included, along with a listing of conditions to be considered. This section also covers a related group of skin conditions resulting from allergic reactions to plant toxins and other materials.

The skin, or common integument, represents the largest organ of the human body. As shown in **Figure 17.1**, two major layers of tissues, the epidermis and dermis, combine to form this complex organ, which has a total surface area of 3000 square inches on the average adult (American Academy of Orthopaedic Surgeons [AAOS], 1991). Located immediately beneath the skin is a layer of subcutaneous fat that helps to insulate the body from the external environment. Skin thickness varies regionally on the body: Thicker skin covers areas subject to pressure, such as the soles of the feet and palms of the hands; thinner skin covers areas where joint mobility is essential.

The skin serves a variety of purposes, not the least of which is protecting the body from the environment. It is also essential for controlling fluid balance within the body, protecting the body from disease organisms, and regulating body temperature. Furthermore, it houses nerves of sensation that register touch, temperature, and pressure. In addition, specialized cells within the skin produce vitamin D (AAOS, 1991).

The skin can be damaged in a variety of ways during participation in sports. External trauma can cause wounds, and damage can result from exposure to ultraviolet rays (sunlight) and burning or freezing temperatures. Skin infections can arise from a variety of organisms, including viruses, **bacteria**, and fungi. In addition, allergies can also affect the skin; these may be related to contact with plants or clothing and equipment that contain chemicals to which the athlete is sensitive.

Wounds

Sports injuries can cause many types of wounds, ranging from abrasions (scrapes, burns, and strawberry) to lacerations (cuts and gashes), all of which might result in infection and cosmetic complications (American Medical Association [AMA], 1968). The primary goals of initial wound care are control of bleeding followed by prevention of infection through cleaning and bandaging. A primary concern when rendering first aid care for any wound is to avoid contact with whole blood that may transmit infectious organisms such as the human immunodeficiency virus (**HIV**) or hepatitis B virus (**HBV**). The majority of wounds seen in sports are abrasions caused by rubbing, scraping, and burning; lacerations produced by a blunt object tearing the skin; and incisions caused by sharp objects. A special type of abrasion, known as turf burn, has been associated with playing surfaces in stadiums made of artificial turf. Turf burns are the result of falls sustained on artificial turf that produce friction and heat.

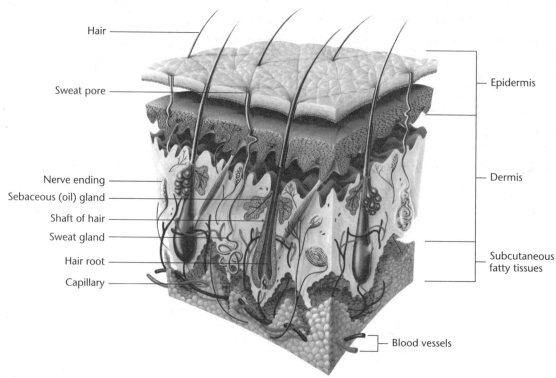

FIGURE 17.1 A cross section of human skin.

Treatment

Treatment of open wounds in sports can be considered as a two-phase process. Initial first aid care is designed to control bleeding to prevent additional blood loss, to protect others from exposure, and to protect the area from further injury. This is followed later with ongoing protection of the area so that return to participation is possible while healing takes place. As previously stated, an important aspect of wound care is protection of fellow athletes, coaches, and other personnel from exposure to whole blood, which can result in the transmission of HIV and HBV organisms. Risk of exposure involves not only the wound itself, but also blood-soaked clothing and any blood that may be on playing surfaces.

Guidelines for the initial treatment of open wounds are as follows (Anderson, Hall, & Martin, 2005; National Safety Council, 1993):

1. Before rendering first aid, precautions should be taken against the possible transmission of HIV and HBV. Wear latex gloves and dispose of all waste in a storage container for biohazardous materials. In cases of profuse bleeding or bleeding involving the airway (nose, mouth, etc.), eye protection is recommended.

2. Remove clothing and/or equipment covering the wound. Clean the wound and the area around the wound with an antiseptic solution.

3. Control bleeding with direct pressure over the wound site by applying some type of sterile dressing. Commercial sterile gauze pads are available in an array of sizes and work well in these situations.

4. If dressing becomes soaked with blood, add more dressing on top. Do not remove blood-soaked dressings.

5. Although rare in sports, severe bleeding may not respond to direct pressure. In such cases, combine direct pressure with elevation.

6. Increased hemorrhage control can be achieved via the application of a pressure bandage to a point over either the brachial or femoral arteries, depending on location of the wound. Once pressure is applied to either of these points, it should not be released until the athlete is under the care of a physician.

7. Tourniquets should be applied only as a last resort; they are rarely needed in first aid for sports-related wounds.

8. If more than 5 years have lapsed since an athlete's last tetanus booster, refer the athlete to a physician.

9. All materials used to treat the wound—gauze pads, towels, and paper towels—should be stored for later disposal or cleaning in a container properly identified as containing biohazardous materials.

At the time of initial first aid, a decision must be made about whether the athlete will be allowed to return to participation. Obviously, the health and safety of the athlete must be the first priority; however, the majority of sports-related wounds are not life-threatening occurrences. Another consideration is protection of other participants, coaches, and personnel from exposure to whole blood from any wound. In sports such as wrestling, tackle football, and basketball, wounds must be dealt with in such a way to protect other athletes and the coaching staff from incidental exposure. Although research indicates the risk of transmission of HIV and HBV in such situations is remote, the possibility does exist (Calabrese, Haupt, & Hartman, 1993).

Once the initial bleeding is arrested, a commercially made dressing should be applied to the wound and held in place with an adhesive bandage. Small wounds are usually treatable by simply applying a bandage; larger wounds, such as a strawberry on the thigh or arm may require a large sterile gauze pad that is held in place with adhesive tape. Such bandages should be rechecked periodically during participation to ensure that they remain in proper position and bleeding has not resumed.

Lacerations and incisions, particularly those to the scalp or face, merit special attention because of their potential cosmetic impact. Such wounds should be referred to a physician for evaluation and possibly for stitches. As a general rule, any wound going below the dermal layer that is more than a centimeter in length—especially if it is on the face—should be seen by a physician for evaluation.

The National Safety Council (1993) provides the following guidelines for cleaning wounds:

1. Personnel rendering first aid should protect themselves from direct exposure to whole blood by wearing latex gloves.

bacteria Plural of bacterium. A Schizomycetes, unicellular microorganism that can either be parasitic or free-living and has a wide range of biochemical, often pathogenic, properties.

2. Wash the wound with a sterile gauze pad saturated with soap and water. Hydrogen peroxide (3% solution) may be used to bubble away blood clots and related debris. This is especially helpful when treating abrasions containing significant amounts of dirt and other foreign material.

3. Flush the wound with large amounts of water; then dry the area with a sterile gauze pad.

4. Use isopropyl rubbing alcohol to clean the skin adjacent to the wound site; however, do not apply the alcohol directly to the wound.

5. Do not apply chemicals such as merbromin (Mercurochrome), thimerosal (Merthiolate), or iodine to wounds; their effectiveness is minimal, and they may cause an allergic reaction.

6. Apply a sterile, dry dressing and hold it in place with some type of bandage. For smaller wounds, Band-Aid bandages are effective; for larger wounds, sterile gauze pads held in place with elastic adhesive tape are recommended. By definition, a **dressing** is a sterile material, usually gauze, used to cover a wound to control bleeding and prevent contamination. A **bandage** is used to hold the dressing in place. Bandages need not be anything more than a folded cravat, strips of cloth, or commercially made elastic adhesive tape that can be directly applied to the skin and holds well even near a moving joint.

7. Severe wounds should be treated for control of bleeding and referred immediately for medical evaluation.

HIV/HBV and the Athlete

Although the majority of national spotlight regarding these two viral infections has focused primarily on HIV, HBV has been on the increase as well. It is estimated that 300,000 new HBV infections occur each year. In 1981, the first diagnosed case of acquired immune deficiency syndrome (AIDS) was reported. In 1986 there were approximately 2000 people infected with HIV in the United States; recent data from the Centers for Disease Control and Prevention (CDC, 2012) indicate that at the end of 2009 there were an estimated 1,148,200 diagnosed cases of HIV in the United States.

Virtually anyone who is sexually active, including athletes, is at risk of contracting HIV. Athletes who inject anabolic steroids may also be at risk of infection, especially when sharing needles (Calabrese, 1989). The virus is spread primarily through intimate sexual contact or blood-to-blood exposure, which can easily occur when sharing needles during intravenous drug use. HBV is a bloodborne pathogen and is most easily spread via blood-to-blood contact with an infected person. Both HIV and HBV are carried within the blood of infected persons; therefore, anytime such individuals sustain a bleeding wound, the possibility of transmission exists. This is especially true if another athlete who also has an open wound comes into contact with the blood of an infected person.

Although the chance of such an occurrence may be remote, some precautions are necessary, especially in sports in which external bleeding is likely. The Occupational Safety and Health Administration (**OSHA**) developed a comprehensive set of guidelines for healthcare workers regarding prevention of exposure to HIV and HBV (U.S. Department of Labor & U.S. Department of Health and Human Services, 1991). These guidelines have subsequently been updated and are available online (U.S. Department of Labor, n.d.). Although coaching personnel are not commonly thought of as healthcare providers, virtually all coaches find themselves dealing on a regular basis with open wounds on some of their athletes. Coaches and athletes are routinely exposed to blood-contaminated towels, water bottles, playing surfaces, and blood-soaked bandaging materials. As a result, the prudent coach should make every effort to follow the basic preventive guidelines for HIV and HBV transmission that have been outlined by OSHA.

Athletes participating in wrestling, tackle football, and boxing frequently sustain bleeding wounds. It is advised that coaches and officials remove players from participation when excessive bleeding is evident. Furthermore, those persons providing first aid care for such injuries should protect themselves by wearing latex gloves and perhaps even eye protection when treating a bleeding wound. In addition, athletes should be cautioned about sharing water bottles or blood-stained towels with fellow athletes (Calabrese, 1989). Athletes, coaches, and healthcare providers should wash hands and skin as soon as possible after being exposed to the blood of an injured athlete. Conversely, coaches and healthcare providers with open wounds should protect athletes from possible infection by wearing latex gloves or bandages and practicing good personal hygiene.

Education of athletes, coaches, and parents about the transmission and prevention of HIV and HBV is essential. While participation in organized sports presents a very low risk for contraction of the viruses, prudence dictates that precautions be implemented, as sports participation does carry some risk to all parties involved—athletes, coaches, and sports medicine personnel.

Other Skin Conditions

Ultraviolet Light–Related Skin Problems

Outdoor sports played during the summer can result in exposure of large areas of the body to harmful rays of the sun. Typically, summer sportswear does not cover the arms and legs; in some sports, such as swimming and diving, major portions of the skin are unprotected. Medical evidence is substantial that even minor sunburn can be harmful to the skin; it may lead to serious, even lethal, complications such as skin-related carcinomas and melanomas (Reichel & Laub, 1992). Two different wavelengths of ultraviolet light are involved in the sunburn process: ultraviolet A (UVA) and ultraviolet B (UVB). UVB is a shorter wavelength than UVA and seems more related to the development of skin problems (Rustad, 1992).

Some individuals are at a higher risk for damage from sunlight exposure, especially those with lighter skin, red hair, and freckles (Reichel & Laub, 1992). Exposure to sunlight at any time of day can result in sunburn; however, the most dangerous time is between 10:00 a.m. and 2:00 p.m.

Sunburn has two clinical phases. The first, known as the immediate erythema phase, involves reddening of the skin, which occurs during exposure to sunlight. The second phase, called the delayed erythema phase, normally develops within a few hours of exposure and peaks at 24 hours (Reichel & Laub, 1992). Although most cases of sunburn result in mild discomfort, with symptoms diminishing within a day or two, more severe cases can include the formation of blisters associated with chills and gastrointestinal distress.

The primary concern should be on protection of exposed skin when an athlete is participating in outdoor sports. Certain body areas may require special protection with a commercially prepared sunscreen—particularly the outer ear, nose, lips, back of the neck, forehead, and (if not covered by clothing) the forearms and hands. Though many sunscreen products are available, athletes should use only those rated with at least a sun protection factor (SPF) of 15. The SPF rating is derived by determining the sunscreen's ability to absorb harmful ultraviolet light over time. Thus, athletes using a product with an SPF rating of 15 will receive the same amount of ultraviolet light to the skin in 15 hours outdoors as they would have in 1 hour of unprotected exposure. Sunblocks are also available; they contain chemicals that block all light from reaching the skin. These products contain zinc oxide or titanium dioxide. Sunscreen products may contain a variety of chemicals that either absorb or reflect UVA and UVB light;

these include para-aminobenzoic acid (**PABA**), cinnamates, salicylates, benzophenone-3, 3% avobenzone, and dibenzoylmethane (Rustad, 1992). For best results, sunscreens should be applied in advance of exposure to sunlight. Although many products are advertised as waterproof or water-resistant, athletes who perspire heavily or who are involved in water sports should periodically (every 60 minutes) reapply the product to maintain adequate protection.

Treatment of sunburn involves application of a commercially made topical anesthetic and a skin lotion to help relieve burning and dryness. In severe cases, medical attention may be warranted, and treatment may include the administration of anti-inflammatory medications.

Skin Infections

A variety of organisms can cause infections of the skin—including fungi, bacteria, and viruses. Although a detailed discussion of sports dermatology is beyond the scope of this text, some of the more common afflictions—along with their signs, symptoms, and treatment—are presented. It should also be remembered that many apparent skin infections can be symptoms of more serious infectious and/or allergic conditions, including Lyme disease, herpes, or contact dermatitis, and should be referred to a doctor for evaluation. Skin infections in athletes are a major and persistent concern within the sports medicine community. All stakeholders need to work collectively to prevent and control these infections. Given the nature of athletic participation, the likelihood of passing a skin infection to a fellow athlete is high. One recent study of infectious diseases in athletes reported that 56% of infections involved the skin (Tuberville, Cowan, & Greenfield, 2006). In recent years, this topic has taken on a new urgency with the arrival of drug-resistant strains of common bacteria such as *Staphylococcus aureus*. This particular organism has become a major health concern, because it is now resistant to antibiotics including methicillin, thus the label methicillin-resistant *Staphylococcus aureus* (MRSA). As such, everyone, including the athletes,

dressing Covering, either protective or supportive, that is applied to an injury or wound.
bandage Material used to cover a wound.
OSHA Occupational Safety and Health Administration.
PABA Para-aminobenzoic acid; the common active ingredient in sunscreen products.

parents, coaches, athletic trainers, and support personnel such as custodians, must remain vigilant. The National Athletic Trainers' Association (NATA, 2010) has published an extensive Position Statement on skin diseases, which can be used as an additional resource.

Tinea (Ringworm)

Tinea, commonly known as ringworm, is an infection of the skin caused by a group of fungi (**Figure 17.2**). In athletes, the common locations for tinea include the groin region (tinea cruris, commonly known as jock itch) and the feet and toes (tinea pedis). Tinea infections are common in these body areas because moisture and warmth make them ideal for fungal growth. Tinea can affect other parts of the body as well, including the scalp (tinea capitis) and the extremities. Although tinea infections are not serious, if left untreated they may persist and lead to secondary bacterial infections that can be cosmetically displeasing.

Signs and symptoms of tinea infections include the following:

- Small, superficial, brownish-red, elevated lesions that tend to be circular in shape.

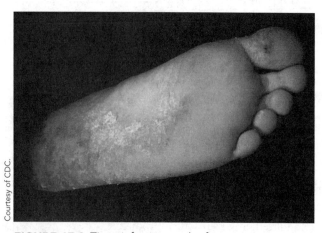

Courtesy of CDC.

FIGURE 17.2 Tinea infection on the foot.

- When infections involve the toes, lesions may include cracking between toes associated with oozing and crusting.
- Itching and pain are associated with tinea pedis and tinea cruris.
- Scaling of the skin over the lesions may also be noted.

Treatment of tinea infections—according to Rustad (1992)—involves the following:

1. Vigilant cleaning of the involved areas, followed by drying
2. Applying an over-the-counter topical treatment such as tolnaftate (Tinactin)
3. Applying a moisture-absorbing powder to the area
4. Wearing clothing made of natural fibers such as cotton

Tinea Versicolor (TV)

This particular fungal infection is considered to be the most common warm-weather-related skin problem among teenagers and young adults (Rustad, 1992). **Tinea versicolor** gets its name from the symptoms it produces on the skin of the affected person. This infection is characterized by the appearance of lesions that are of a different color than the adjacent, normal skin. It is usually confined to the upper trunk, neck, and upper abdomen (AMA, 1968).

Signs and symptoms of tinea versicolor include the following:

- Circular lesions that appear either lighter or darker than adjacent skin.
- Skin may appear white, in contrast to adjacent unaffected skin, after exposure to sunlight.
- Lesions are normally found on the trunk.

Treatment of tinea versicolor involves the following:

- Prescription drugs, either oral or topical.

Treatment may require weeks or even months to be effective.

Bacterial Infections

Bacterial infections of the skin are relatively common in sports that involve close physical contact between participants. Known collectively as **pyoderma** (pus-producing infection of the skin), these infections are normally caused by two common bacteria, *Staphylococcus aureus* and *Streptococcus*. The former is related to conditions such as furuncles, carbuncles, and folliculitis; the latter causes impetigo (**Figure 17.3**) and cellulitis.

All of these conditions are characterized by infected, **purulent** (pus-producing) lesions on the skin. For example, in folliculitis the lesions are located at the base of a hair follicle. Furuncles are similar in appearance; however, they form large nodules around the hair follicles and may burst as the infection develops. Impetigo

is similar in appearance, but may develop in areas with little or no hair.

Signs and symptoms of furuncles, carbuncles, and folliculitis include the following:

- The underlying symptom of all forms of pyoderma is a lesion, regardless of location, that is producing pus.
- Folliculitis involves lesions located at the base of a hair follicle.
- Furuncles, commonly called "boils," are lesions that form large nodules around the base of a hair follicle and may burst as the infection develops.
- Boils can appear anywhere, but are more common on the arms, armpits, neck and chest, buttocks, and groin (Booher & Thibodeau, 2000).
- Carbuncles are essentially a collection of boils that together form a weeping, pus-producing lesion typically found around the posterior neck and upper trunk regions.

tinea Group of fungi-related skin infections, commonly called ringworm, which can affect various parts of the body—groin (tinea cruris), feet and toes (tinea pedis), and scalp (tinea capitis).

tinea versicolor Fungus infection resulting in the formation of circular skin lesions that appear either lighter or darker than adjacent skin.

pyoderma Pus-producing infection of the skin.

purulent Consisting of, or forming, pus.

Courtesy of CDC.

FIGURE 17.3 Impetigo on the ankle.

TIME OUT 17.1

Official Statement from the National Athletic Trainers' Association on Community-Acquired MRSA (CA-MRSA) Infections

In an effort to educate the public about the potential risks of the emergence of community-acquired methicillin-resistant *Staphylococcus aureus* (CA-MRSA) infection, the National Athletic Trainers' Association (NATA) recommends that healthcare personnel and physically active participants take appropriate precautions with suspicious lesions and talk with a physician.

According to the CDC, approximately 25% to 30% of the population is colonized in the nose with *Staphylococcus aureus*, often referred to as "staph," and approximately 1% of the population is colonized with MRSA.*

Cases have developed from person-to-person contact, shared towels, soaps, improperly treated whirlpools, and equipment (mats, pads, surfaces, etc.). Staph or CA-MRSA infections usually manifest as skin infections, such as pimples, pustules, and boils, which present as red, swollen, painful, or have pus or other drainage. Without proper referral and care, more serious infections may cause pneumonia, bloodstream infections, or surgical wound infections.

Maintaining good hygiene and avoiding contact with drainage from skin lesions are the best methods for prevention.

Proper prevention and management recommendations may include, but are not limited to, the following:

1. Keep hands clean by washing thoroughly with soap and warm water or using an alcohol-based hand sanitizer routinely.

2. Encourage immediate showering following activity.
3. Avoid whirlpools or common tubs with open wounds, scrapes, or scratches.
4. Avoid sharing towels, razors, and daily athletic gear.
5. Properly wash athletic gear and towels after each use.
6. Maintain clean facilities and equipment.
7. Inform or refer to appropriate healthcare personnel for all active skin lesions and lesions that do not respond to initial therapy.
8. Administer or seek proper first aid.
9. Encourage healthcare personnel to seek bacterial cultures to establish a diagnosis.
10. Care and cover skin lesions appropriately before participation.

*CA-MRSA Information for the Public. Centers for Disease Control and Prevention. Available online at: http://www.cdc.gov/ncidod/hip/aresist/ca_mrsa_public.htm.

Reproduction of the Official statement from the National Athletic Trainers' Association on community acquired MRSA infections. Reprinted with permission.

Signs and symptoms of impetigo and cellulitis include the following:

- The underlying symptom of all forms of pyoderma is a lesion, regardless of location, that is producing pus.

- Often seen on the face, impetigo presents groups of raised skin lesions that are honey-colored and crusty in appearance.

- Cellulitis also is a skin infection; however, it affects the deeper layer of skin known as the dermis (Figure 17.1). The skin will appear red and warmer than adjacent skin and, in addition, will be painful to the touch.

Regardless of the specific condition, all pyodermal infections share a common characteristic—the presence of lesions that are obviously infected and associated with drainage and pus formation. Any athlete demonstrating such signs and/or symptoms as described should be removed from participation and referred for medical evaluation. If pyoderma is the diagnosis, the precautions outlined in **Time Out 17.1** should be immediately instituted.

Viral Infections

Two of the more common virus-related skin problems in sports are plantar warts and herpes gladiatorum. As a skin problem, warts are quite common in the general population and occur as the result of infection by a specific group of viruses known collectively as the human papillomavirus (**HPV**), of which more than 55 specific types have been identified. The majority of plantar warts are caused by two types: HPV-1 and HPV-4. The infection is contagious; however, some individuals seem more susceptible, with an **incubation period** ranging from 1 to 20 months (Ramsey,

1992). The most well known characteristic of a wart is the abnormal buildup of epidermis around the region of actual infection; warts can vary in size from 1 millimeter in diameter to as large as 1 centimeter or more.

Plantar Warts

Plantar warts are simply warts that occur on the plantar surfaces of the feet. Although warts elsewhere generally rise up from the skin, the pressure of bearing weight drives the plantar wart inward on the bottom of the feet, often resulting in annoying if not painful symptoms.

Signs and symptoms of plantar warts include the following:

- The warts are usually first noticed when they become painful as an athlete is walking or running because they are located on a weight-bearing surface.
- Small, thickened areas of skin may be noticeable, with tiny black or dark red dots appearing within the area (Ramsey, 1992).
- Contrary to popular myth, these small dark spots are not seeds, but rather are small capillaries that have been destroyed within the wart.
- Sometimes a group of warts will develop, causing a relatively large area to become involved. This is referred to as a mosaic wart.

Treatment of plantar warts ranges from the application of chemicals designed to dissolve the wart to surgical removal, although the latter is not recommended by the medical community. A variety of prescription products are available, most of which contain salicylic, pyruvic, and lactic acids. These compounds soften and erode the wart (the process is known technically as keratolysis); the ultimate goal is complete removal of the growth. Other treatment options exist, including the use of chemicals designed to stop the growth of the wart. Sometimes liquid nitrogen is applied to freeze the affected tissue; this is followed by surgical removal. A form of **laser** surgery has also been developed for use on plantar warts (Ramsey, 1992).

Interestingly, in many athletes plantar warts terminate on their own with no long-term symptoms. Athletes who find plantar warts to be detrimental to participation in sports should consult a doctor to determine the best course of treatment. Coaches and athletes should not attempt treatment, as this may result in a worsening of the condition, infection, and even permanent scarring.

Herpes Gladiatorum

Herpes gladiatorum is the name given to herpes infections among athletes such as wrestlers. This virus, herpes simplex virus type 1 (**HSV-1**), is well known as the causative agent of the common cold sore or fever blister, which typically occurs on the outer lip area. Lesions are often associated with physical trauma, sunburn, emotional disturbances, fatigue, or infection (AMA, 1968). A unique aspect of herpes infection is its ability to remain dormant for long periods, sometimes months or even years, between active periods when lesions reappear. The infection is most contagious when open lesions are present. Once exposed to the virus, the incubation period may be as long as 2 weeks.

Signs and symptoms of herpes gladiatorum include the following:

- Development of a lesion, often on the face, which is characterized by blistering associated with a red, infected area of skin.
- Open, draining lesions may persist for a few days; afterward they become crusted and begin to heal.
- General fatigue, body aches, and inflammation of lymph glands associated with tenderness (White, 1992).

Outbreaks of herpes must be controlled, or the infection can be devastating in a sport such as wrestling, in which acute outbreaks can involve many athletes. Coaches and athletes must be educated about the early signs and symptoms of HSV-1 infections. Moreover, any type of open lesion must be evaluated to rule out the possibility of infection. Athletes with active infections must be removed from participation until lesions have healed, a process that may take up to 5 days. It has been noted that once the crust of the lesion has come off, it is safe to resume activity (Olerud, 1989). Drugs are available for control of the infection; however, they must not be used without the supervision of a physician. In addition to drug therapy, athletes known to have an HSV-1 infection should wear sunscreen when exposed to sunlight, include foods high in lysine in their diets, and apply ice to lesions when they first appear (Olerud, 1989).

HPV   Human papillomavirus; approximately 55 specific types of these viruses have been identified, at least two of which are related to plantar warts.

incubation period   The time between an exposure to an infectious agent and the appearance of symptoms of that infection.

laser   A device that concentrates high energies into a narrow beam of visible monochromatic light.

HSV-1   Herpes simplex virus type 1; related to infections in athletes commonly known as herpes gladiatorum.

Wrestling and Skin Infections

Due to the nature of the sport of wrestling, participation with an active skin infection presents special hazards to the athletes involved. At the collegiate level, it has been reported that 17% of practice time-loss injuries are related to skin infections (NCAA, 2012). Common sense should prevail in such situations, and any open sore or skin lesion that cannot be covered adequately should be grounds for removal from participation until the infection subsides. The NCAA has published specific criteria for disqualification because of skin infections among wrestlers (NCAA, 2012). The NCAA recommends that any infected area that cannot be protected adequately should be considered as cause for disqualification from practice and/or competition. The NCAA (2012) has included all of the following as infections worth considering under their recommendations:

- Bacterial skin infections
  - Impetigo
  - Erysipelas
  - Carbuncle
  - Staphylococcal disease, MRSA
  - Folliculitis (generalized)
  - Hidradenitis suppurativa
- Parasitic skin infections
  - Pediculosis
  - Scabies
- Viral skin infections
  - Herpes simplex
  - Herpes zoster (chicken pox)
  - Molluscum contagiosum
- Fungal skin infections
- Tinea corporis (ringworm)

Allergic Reactions

Allergic skin reactions can be caused by exposure to any number of chemical agents from a variety of sources. For those susceptible, contact with the offending chemical

WHAT IF?

A member of the cross-country team asks you to examine a strange rash he has developed on his legs. He reports that it developed about 12 to 24 hours after he used a topical analgesic with a wintergreen odor. What is a likely cause of this condition and what would you recommend to this athlete?

results in a condition known as **contact dermatitis**. Plants such as poison ivy, poison oak, and poison sumac contain potent chemicals that cause reactions in susceptible people. Certain types of sports equipment and related clothing may also contain compounds causing allergic reactions.

According to the National Safety Council (1993), allergies to poison ivy, poison oak, and poison sumac result in skin reactions in 90% of adults. The sap of the plant contains the offending chemical; therefore, any direct contact with the plant can cause sap to be deposited onto the skin.

Contact with contaminated clothing or other materials can also result in reactions. The average time period between exposure and development of symptoms is 24 to 48 hours; the earliest symptoms include itching and redness in the affected area. These symptoms are followed by the development of blisters, which often break open and subsequently become crusted. Healing takes place within 1 to 2 weeks from the time of the initial reaction.

Athletes who know they are allergic to poison ivy, poison oak, or poison sumac should learn to recognize the plants to avoid contact with them when participating in outdoor activities. Organizers of events that may place athletes in areas where these plants grow should alert participants to the potential problem. A good example is cross-country running, a traditional autumn sport in high schools across the nation. It is common for training runs and races to take the runners through areas where plants such as poison ivy flourish. Obviously, these athletes need to be able to recognize such vegetation. Coaches and organizers should also make every effort to keep courses well away from areas where such plants may grow.

Allergies related to chemicals contained in sports equipment or clothing have been receiving increased attention in sports medicine literature. It has been reported that products containing rubber, topical analgesics (pain relievers), resins found in athletic tape, and epoxy used in face gear are associated with allergic reactions in sensitive athletes. The chemicals initiating the allergic reaction are called sensitizers. They can produce classic symptoms of contact dermatitis—swelling and redness of the skin (erythema) followed by the development of pimple- or blister-like lesions. Symptoms normally occur approximately 7 days after the initial exposure. In athletes with a history of previous allergic reactions, repeat exposures may yield symptoms within 24 hours (Fisher, 1993).

Major sensitizers include synthetic rubber additives commonly found in certain brands of tennis shoes, swim caps, swim goggles, nose clips, and earplugs as well as topical analgesics containing either salicylates or menthol. Adhesive athletic tapes made with formaldehyde resins and face gear and helmets made with epoxy resins can also initiate allergic reactions (Fisher, 1993). For athletes with known allergies to any of these products, it is essential that alternative gear be identified if possible.

An athlete suspected of having allergic contact dermatitis should be referred to a dermatologist for specific diagnosis and treatment, which includes identification of the sensitizer and treatment of symptoms with anti-inflammatory drugs.

contact dermatitis Inflammation of the skin that is nonallergenic.

REVIEW QUESTIONS

1. Review the primary goals of initial wound care.
2. List the precautions that should be taken when treating an athlete with an open wound to avoid possible transmission of HIV and HBV.
3. Describe and differentiate between a wound dressing and a bandage.
4. True or false: With respect to the types of sunlight causing sunburn, evidence suggests that UVB is more connected with the development of skin-related problems.
5. Discuss the two clinical phases of sunburn as described in the chapter.
6. Define the acronym PABA.
7. True or false: The term *pyoderma* implies a pus-producing infection of the skin.
8. Describe the recommended treatment(s) for plantar warts.
9. True or false: There is no evidence that synthetic materials such as tennis shoes, swim caps, and swim goggles can cause allergic skin reactions.
10. True or false: The first case of AIDS was reported in the United States in 1981.

REFERENCES

Anderson MK, Hall SJ, Martin M. (2005). *Foundations of Athletic Training: Prevention, Assessment, and Management.* Philadelphia, Pa: Lippincott Williams & Wilkins.

American Academy of Orthopaedic Surgeons (AAOS). (1991). *Athletic Training and Sports Medicine.* Park Ridge, Ill: American Academy of Orthopaedic Surgeons.

American Medical Association (AMA). (1968). *Standard Nomenclature of Athletic Injuries.* Chicago, Ill: American Medical Association.

Booher JM, Thibodeau GA. (2000). *Athletic Injury Assessment* (2nd ed.). Boston, Mass: McGraw-Hill.

Calabrese LH. (1989). AIDS and athletes. *Phys Sportsmed.* 17(1):127–132.

Calabrese LH, Haupt HA, Hartman L. (1993). HIV in sports: What is the risk? *Phys Sportsmed.* 21:172–180.

Centers for Disease Control and Prevention (CDC). (2012). Monitoring selected national HIV prevention and care objectives by using HIV surveillance data—United States and 6 U.S. dependent areas—2010. *HIV Surveillance Supplemental Report.* 17(No. 3, part A). Available: http://www.cdc.gov/hiv/statistics/basics/.

Fisher AA. (1993). Allergic contact dermatitis: Practical solutions for sports-related rashes. *Phys Sportsmed.* 21(3):65–72.

National Athletic Trainers' Association. (2010). National Athletic Trainers' Association position statement: Skin diseases. *J Athl Train.* 45(4):411–428. Available: http://www.nata.org/sites/default/files/position-statement-skin-disease.pdf.

National Collegiate Athletic Association (NCAA). (2012). *2012–13 Sports Medicine Handbook* (23rd ed.). Indianapolis, Ind: NCAA. Available: http:// NCAA.org/health-safety.

National Safety Council. (1993). *First Aid and CPR* (2nd ed.). Boston, Mass: Jones and Bartlett.

Olerud, J. (1989). Common skin problems. In: Smith N (ed.), *Common Problems in Pediatric Sports Medicine.* Chicago, Ill: Year Book Medicine Publishers.

Ramsey ML. (1992). Plantar warts: Choosing treatment for active patients. *Phys Sportsmed.* 20(11):69–88.

Reichel M, Laub DA. (1992). From acne to black heel: Common skin injuries in sports. *Phys Sportsmed.* 20(2):111–118.

Rustad OJ. (1992). Outdoors and active: Relieving summer's siege on skin. *Phys Sportsmed.* 20(5):163–176.

Tuberville SD, Cowan LD, Greenfield RA. (2006). Infectious disease outbreaks in competitive sports: A review of the literature. *Am J Sports Med.* 34(11):1860–1865.

U.S. Department of Labor. (n.d.). Bloodborne Pathogens. Available: http://www.osha.gov/pls/oshaweb/owasrch.search_form?p_doc_type=PREAMBLES&p_toc_level=1&p_keyvalue=Bloodborne~Pathogens.

U.S. Department of Labor, U.S. Department of Health and Human Services. (1991). Joint Advisory Notice Protection Against Occupational Exposure to Hepatitis B (HBV) and Human Immunodeficiency Virus (HIV). *Federal Register.* 56:235.

White J. (1992). Vigilance vanquishes herpes gladiatorum. *Phys Sportsmed.* 20(1):56.

Thermal Injuries

MAJOR CONCEPTS

Sports and athletic events are staged under a wide range of environmental conditions, including indoors and a nearly infinite variety of outdoor settings. This chapter explores the body's response to extremes of heat and cold, with particular attention given to life-threatening conditions. It is critical to note that a significant percentage of the deaths directly attributable to sports today result from heat-related problems. In addition, the chapter discusses cold-related problems, including hypothermia, frostbite and frostnip, and a relatively unknown condition called cold urticaria.

go.jblearning.com/PfeifferCWS

For a full suite of assignments and additional learning activities (indicated by the icons throughout the text), use the access code found in the front of your text. If you do not have an access code, you can obtain one at go.jblearning.com/PfeifferCWS.

WHAT IF?

During practice in late August, one of your football players, an offensive lineman, suddenly staggers away from the blocking sled, falls to the ground, and is unable to get to his feet. During your initial assessment, you note that he is semiconscious and that his skin is dry, reddish in color, and hot to the touch. He is able to tell you that he is thirsty and that he has not had any water for more than an hour. It is 95°F out, approximately 78% humidity, and there is little wind. Given this scenario, what is most likely the problem? If you are correct, what is the appropriate first aid for this athlete?

Because of the great range of environmental conditions within which sports take place, a variety of temperature-related health emergencies occur each year; some result in death. To emphasize this point, from 1995 to 2010, 35 football players died from heat-related (exertional) illness in the United States (Mueller & Colgate, 2010). The majority, if not all, of these deaths could be prevented if coaches, athletes, and administrators would take the time to consider the environmental conditions prior to allowing an event to begin.

Normal metabolism can be maintained within only a very narrow range of body **core temperatures**, between 98.0°F and 98.6°F when measured orally (Guyton, 1986). Heat is a natural product of metabolism; during exercise, the metabolic rate can increase significantly, resulting in elevations of body temperature to 104°F. Excess heat must be eliminated from the body during exercise, or the body temperature can rise to dangerous levels in a short period of time. The body can rid itself of excess heat by taking advantage of basic physics through a complex process known as thermoregulation. Thermoregulation is controlled primarily by the temperature-regulating centers within the hypothalamus of the brain (Binkley et al., 2002; Wilmore & Costill, 1988). A variety of neurologic sensors throughout the body, in the deep tissues and the skin, provide information regarding body temperature to the hypothalamus (Guyton, 1986; McArdle, Katch, & Katch, 2010).

Excess heat can be lost through **radiation** (via infrared light), **conduction** (absorbed into surrounding objects), **convection** (moving air currents), and evaporation (sweating). Each of these methods is effective, although during most exercise on dry land, evaporation is the most efficient. Its effectiveness as a form of thermoregulation

can be severely compromised by extremes in relative humidity. Relative humidity represents the amount of water vapor suspended in the air, and it determines how much water can effectively evaporate from the skin during exercise. The higher the relative humidity, the less ability the surrounding air has to absorb fluid (sweat) from the skin surface. As a result, the higher the relative humidity the greater the potential for heat-related problems. In cases of outdoor activity during times of both extremely high temperatures and high humidity, coaches need to make modifications in the demands of the exercise session or consider delaying activity until conditions improve.

Athletes need to be given adequate time to adjust their systems to a major change in temperature. This process, known as **acclimatization** (**Time Out 18.1**), can take from 1 to 6 weeks, or longer, and occurs naturally when a person is exposed to continuous and significant climatic changes. As a general rule, those with a higher level of fitness tend to acclimatize more quickly;

TIME OUT 18.1

Physiologic Responses After Heat Acclimatization Relative to Nonacclimatized State

Physiologic Variable	After Acclimatization (10–14 Days) Exposure
Heart rate	Decreases
Stroke volume	Increases
Body core temperature	Decreases
Skin temperature	Decreases
Sweat output/rate	Increases
Onset of sweat	Earlier in training
Evaporation of sweat	Increases
Salt in sweat	Decreases
Work output	Increases
Subjective discomfort (rating of perceived exertion [RPE])	Decreases
Fatigue	Decreases
Capacity for work	Increases
Mental disturbance	Decreases
Syncopal response	Decreases
Extracellular fluid volume	Increases
Plasma volume	Increases

Reproduced from Binkley HM, et al. (2002). National Athletic Trainers' Association position statement: Exertional Heat Illnesses. *J Athl Train.* 37(3):337. Reprinted with permission.

...

Exertional Heat Illnesses

Exertional heat illnesses (EHI) can involve any one of the following forms: dehydration, heat cramps, heat exhaustion, and exertional heatstroke (Hubbard & Armstrong, 1989; McArdle et al., 2010). A recently published study of high school sports found that boys' football had the highest rate of EHI across all participants, accounting for 74.4% of all reported cases. Football was followed by girls' swimming and diving and then girls' soccer as having the second and third highest rates (Kerr et al., 2013). All forms of EHI are presented here in the order of severity from least to most, beginning with dehydration.

Dehydration

Given the very nature of physical activity and the metabolic processes associated with muscle contraction, a certain amount of dehydration is unavoidable. However, as long as the amount of dehydration is minimal (i.e., less than 2% body weight lost), the effects will not compromise performance or health. However, if dehydration is allowed to progress to a point of more than 2% body weight, performance and thermoregulation can be negatively affected.

Signs and symptoms of dehydration include the following (National Athletic Trainers' Association [NATA], 2003a):

- Dry mouth
- Thirst
- Irritability or crankiness
- Headache
- Seeming bored or disinterested
- Dizziness
- Cramps
- Excessive fatigue
- Not able to run as fast or play as well as usual

core temperature Internal body temperature as opposed to shell or peripheral temperature.
radiation Emission and diffusion of rays of heat.
conduction Heating through direct contact with a hot medium.
convection Heating indirectly through another medium such as air or liquid.
acclimatization The adaptation of the body to a different environment.
heatstroke Excessive heat buildup within the body resulting in the body's inability to cool itself, with core temperatures exceeding 106°F.

FIGURE 18.1 During hot-weather activity, adequate hydration is essential.

adolescents, obese individuals, and those with certain metabolic disorders take longer to readjust their systems.

As a result of proper acclimatization, the sweating mechanism can yield 1.5 to 3.0 liters (L) of sweat per hour, to as much as 12 L/day (Binkley et al., 2002; Guyton, 1986; McArdle et al., 2010). During times of high ambient temperature, athletes need to consume (rehydrate) from 4 to 10 L of fluids per day to avoid dehydration (Montain, Maughan, & Sawka, 1996). (See **Figure 18.1.**) Another way to gauge effectiveness of rehydration is to weigh athletes before exercise and after with the goal of keeping post-exercise weight loss at less than 2% of body weight (Binkley et al., 2002).

Athletes, regardless of geographic region, can be susceptible to temperature-related disorders. For example, temperature extremes at both ends of the scale are common in the northern climates depending on time of year. Conversely, participants living in the southern states, particularly the southeastern United States, are routinely exposed to the combination of high temperature and high humidity. A typical scenario might involve a high school football player who has lost fitness over the summer and begins practices twice daily in August, when the temperature is 96°F and the relative humidity is 90%. Under such conditions, athletes are at an elevated risk for heat-related disorders such as heat cramps, heat exhaustion, or, in a worst-case scenario, exertional **heatstroke**. Specific guidelines for heat acclimatization for youth sports participants have been developed to avoid heat disorders (these are presented later in this chapter). It is critical to note that the process of heat acclimatization does not decrease the body's fluid needs; in fact, fluid needs are increased as the rate of sweating increases with improved fitness (Montain et al., 1996).

Management of dehydration involves the following:

1. Remove the athlete from the game or practice and move him or her to a cool location.
2. Rehydrate the athlete with either water or sports drinks, preferably at a temperature of between 50°F and 59°F (Casa et al., 2000).
3. If dehydration is minor (less than 2% body weight) and the athlete's symptoms are relieved, he or she may be returned to participation (NATA, 2003a).
4. If the athlete's symptoms persist after rehydration, seek medical attention.

Heat Cramps

Heat cramps generally develop within the muscles being exercised (e.g., the leg muscles in runners or the shoulder muscles in swimmers). The physiology of heat cramps is not clear; however, they are thought to occur as a result of water and mineral loss caused by sweating. As previously stated, air temperature and relative humidity work together to increase the likelihood of heat-related problems in athletes. The body rids itself of excess heat primarily through the evaporation of sweat from the skin surface. Under conditions of high relative humidity, however, the evaporation process becomes less effective, thereby contributing to elevations in body temperature. As shown in **Table 18.1**, apparent air temperature can vary significantly depending on the relative humidity.

Signs and symptoms of heat cramps include the following:

- Severe muscle cramps in the arms or legs, not related to muscle strain.
- Muscle cramping may occur in the abdominal muscles.
- Profuse sweating.

TABLE 18.1

HEAT INDEX

Temperature (°F)

Relative Humidity (%)	80	82	84	86	88	90	92	94	96	98	100	102	104	106	108	110
40	80	81	83	85	88	91	94	97	101	105	109	114	119	124	130	136
45	80	82	84	87	89	93	96	100	104	109	114	119	124	130	137	
50	81	83	85	88	91	95	99	103	108	113	118	124	131	137		
55	81	84	86	89	93	97	101	106	112	117	124	130	137			
60	82	84	88	91	95	100	105	110	116	123	129	137				
65	82	85	89	93	98	103	108	114	121	128	136					
70	83	86	90	95	100	105	112	119	126	134						
75	84	88	92	97	103	109	116	124	132							
80	84	89	94	100	106	113	121	129								
85	85	90	96	102	110	117	126	135								
90	86	91	98	105	113	122	131									
95	86	93	100	108	117	127										
100	87	95	103	112	121	132										

Likelihood of Heat Disorders with Prolonged Exposure or Strenuous Activity

☐ Caution   ☐ Extreme Caution   ☐ Danger   ■ Extreme Danger

Reproduced from the National Weather Service.

Management of heat cramps involves the following:

1. Immediate cessation of exercise.
2. Consumption of fluids, either water or sports drinks.
3. Static stretching of the involved muscles.

Heat Exhaustion

Heat exhaustion, as the term implies, involves generalized fatigue that occurs during exercise when excessive body fluids have been lost through sweating and are not adequately replaced. Though not in itself a life-threatening condition, heat exhaustion can be a precursor to heatstroke, which is a true medical emergency. The prudent coach should constantly monitor athletes for the signs and symptoms of heat exhaustion when they must practice and compete in extreme climatic conditions of high heat and/or high humidity.

Signs and symptoms of heat exhaustion can include any of the following (Binkley et al., 2002):

- Moist, clammy skin
- Profuse sweating
- Persistent muscle cramps
- Nausea
- Dizziness
- Severe thirst
- Headache
- Increased respiratory rate and rapid pulse
- Body temperature ranging from 97°F to 104°F
- Chills

For a more complete listing of signs and symptoms of heat exhaustion refer to Binkley and colleagues (2002).

Management of heat exhaustion involves the following:

1. Immediate cessation of exercise.
2. If the athlete is not nauseous, give fluids immediately—preferably cool water or a commercial sports drink.
3. Move the athlete to a cool place.
4. Place the athlete in a supine position, with legs elevated 8 to 12 inches.
5. Loosen clothing and cool the athlete with wet towels or ice packs.
6. If the athlete is not fully recovered within 30 minutes, seek immediate medical attention.
7. Do not allow the athlete to return to participation for the remainder of that day.

Exertional Heatstroke

Exertional heatstroke involves the body's inability to cool itself, with subsequent radical elevations in body temperature, sometimes exceeding 106.7°F (McArdle et al., 2010). Exertional heatstroke is a life-threatening condition that is typically associated with high-intensity exercise in a warm and/or humid environment. It is usually related to excessive fluid loss resulting from heavy sweating combined with a lack of adequate evaporation-related cooling. In essence, exertional heatstroke results from a combination of increased metabolic heat related to exercise and the body's inability to dissipate that heat effectively as a result of high ambient temperatures and/or high relative humidity. It is this latter set of environmental conditions that reduces the effectiveness of sweating to carry away heat from the skin surface. If unchecked, this condition can degenerate, leading to a loss of thermoregulatory control, which, as already stated, can ultimately be fatal (McArdle et al., 2010). It is critical to remember that exertional heatstroke is a true medical emergency and must be treated accordingly.

Signs and symptoms of exertional heatstroke can include any of the following (Binkley et al., 2002):

- Sweating may or may not be present (Hubbard & Armstrong, 1989).
- Hot and wet or dry skin.
- Confusion.
- Loss of consciousness.
- Vomiting.
- Weakness.
- Tachycardia (100–120 heartbeats per minute).
- Body core temperature is higher than 104°F (athletic healthcare team should be trained to ascertain rectal core body temperature).

For a more complete listing of signs and symptoms of heat exhaustion, refer to Binkley and colleagues (2002).

It must be emphasized that exertional heatstroke can result in permanent damage to the central nervous system and other systems in the body. Death can result if the body temperature is not controlled quickly; therefore, correct initial management of heatstroke is critical.

heat cramps Muscle spasms related to excessive heat buildup within the body.
heat exhaustion Generalized fatigue related to excessive heat buildup within the body; may be a precursor to heatstroke.

Management of exertional heatstroke involves the following:

1. If emergency medical services (EMS) personnel, an athletic trainer, or a physician is present, the athlete can be immediately cooled by using cold-water immersion, which is recommended to return body core temperature (measured rectally) to 101°F to 102°F. This can best be accomplished by removing the athlete's clothing and equipment and placing him or her into a tub of cold water (35°F to 59°F; Binkley et al., 2002; NATA, 2003b).

2. If they are not already on site, summon EMS as per the emergency plan.

3. If cold-water immersion is not possible, move the athlete to a cool, humidity-controlled environment.

4. Wrap the athlete in wet sheets or towels or place cold packs in areas with abundant blood supply (e.g., neck, armpits, head, groin).

5. Treat for shock and monitor temperature, not allowing it to drop below 102°F. Remove the athlete from the water once the rectal temperature reaches 102°F (Binkley et al., 2002).

6. Keep the athlete in a semi-seated position.

Prevention of Exertional Heat Illnesses

Heat-related illness causing death among athletes is a totally preventable problem. Application of a few simple guidelines and a dose of common sense are all that is needed to avoid possible tragedy. NATA published a position statement titled "Fluid Replacement for Athletes" with the objective "to present recommendations to optimize the fluid replacement practices of athletes" (Casa et al., 2000). More recently, additional guidelines were published detailing heat-acclimatization recommendations for secondary school athletes (Casa & Csillan, 2009). All personnel involved with the supervision of young athletes should review the entire NATA document and make every effort to incorporate the recommendations.

To prevent heat disorders, athletes, coaches, and parents should comply with the following guidelines:

1. Utilize a weight chart. To determine whether an athlete is consuming enough fluids during training, record body weight daily, before and after practice/competition, throughout the season. The pre-exercise weight is a good indicator of the athlete's rehydration over 24 hours, whereas post-exercise weight provides an indication of the athlete's ability to drink adequate amounts of fluid during workouts, and how much fluid needs to be

---

Athletic Trainers SPEAK Out

Courtesy of Christine Stopka, University of Florida.

A far too common type of injury is heat illness. This must be recognized in its early stages so that it can be easily managed. Refusing to recognize the signs and symptoms can quickly lead to heatstroke, which is a medical emergency and causes the most deaths among high school athletes. As a student athletic trainer, I experienced several situations in which aggressive treatment was prohibited by a well meaning but ignorant coaching staff. We were often not allowed to administer assistance to the athletes until they dropped or lost consciousness. We were scolded for touching them to help break their falls as they fainted. These athletes fortunately did recover but had to be hospitalized for 3 to 7 days. The coaching staff was also replaced before the end of the academic year. [This problem] can be entirely avoided with proper preventive measures and aggressive management of those suspected of manifesting early signs and symptoms of heat stress.

—Christine Stopka, PhD, ATC, LAT, CSCS, CAPE, MTAA

Dr. Stopka is a professor with the Department of Health Education and Behavior at the University of Florida.

Courtesy of Christine Stopka, University of Florida.

consumed after exercise to rehydrate adequately. A weight chart can be easily developed on a computer, with the weight being recorded by the coach or team manager. It is important that the same scale be used for all weighing. Coaches and athletic trainers can use a program such as Microsoft Excel to make the calculations of the percentage of body mass lost after exercise and how much fluid the athlete needs to consume to get back to an adequate level of hydration.

To determine how much fluid the athlete needs to drink after practice/competition, calculate that for every pound (lb) of weight loss, 24 ounces (oz) of fluid should be consumed (Gatorade Sports Science Institute, 1997). For example, a soccer player who weighs 165 lbs at the beginning of practice and weighs 160 lbs after practice has lost 5 lbs, or nearly 3% of body weight in fluid. This indicates a need to consume approximately 120 oz of fluid to attain normal hydration. Post-exercise rehydration should take place within 4 to 6 hours after the practice/competition (Casa et al., 2000). Such a weight change also indicates that this athlete is not consuming enough fluid during exercise. Coaches should monitor body weight throughout the season, noting any significant changes. The scale should be located in an easily accessible area, and coaches must require that athletes comply with the daily weight-monitoring protocols.

2. Consume fluids (17–20 oz) 2 to 3 hours preceding activity and an additional 7 to 10 oz 10 to 20 minutes prior to activity (Casa et al., 2000).

3. Consume fluids and avoid dehydration when participating in activities in warm and humid environments. Experts recommend the consumption of 7 to 10 oz of fluids every 10 to 20 minutes during activity (Casa et al., 2000).

4. Avoid heavy exertion during times of extreme environmental conditions, especially when the temperature is above 95°F and there is high humidity.

5. Remember that restrictive garments can impair circulation of air, thus reducing the evaporation of sweat. Be aware that dark colors on uniforms and helmets may facilitate heat buildup.

6. Remember that fitness has a positive effect on the ability to function in extreme conditions. The process of developing a tolerance to extremes of climate, or acclimatization, normally requires a period of weeks.

As mentioned previously, specific guidelines describing the recommended acclimatization protocol to be used with secondary school athletes have been developed (Casa & Csillan, 2009). These guidelines are based on a 14-day duration model that can be implemented during the typical preseason in late summer for sports such as tackle football, field hockey, and others. The recommendations are listed in **Table 18.2**.

Obviously, prevention of heatstroke must be a top priority for all those involved in organized sports. The legal community has shown little tolerance for coaching personnel who are found to be negligent in the implementation of prudent heatstroke-prevention procedures. All personnel should be well versed in the major risk factors for heatstroke; these are listed in **Table 18.3**.

Cold-Related Health Problems

Just as extremes in heat and humidity can create problems for athletes, so can temperatures that are significantly lower than the body's core temperature. Exposure to cold can result in several conditions, including hypothermia, which can be a life-threatening situation.

Hypothermia

Hypothermia, another aspect of thermal-related injury, has to do with losing body heat too rapidly, resulting in total body cooling. Clinically, hypothermia involves a lowering of the body core temperature significantly below the norm of 98.6°F. Mild hypothermia begins to occur when core temperature drops to 95°F. Historically, the study of hypothermia has been limited to military personnel in the North Sea and those taking part in expeditions in extremely cold environments (Thornton, 1990). Recently, however, cases of clinical hypothermia have been documented in athletes involved in outdoor aerobic events such as long-distance runs. Participants with the greatest risk are extremely lean athletes who have very little insulating body fat to help conserve heat. Surprisingly, hypothermia can occur at temperatures well above freezing. The combination of wind and moisture can cause rapid heat loss and the onset of hypothermia, during which the hypothalamus induces shivering in the skeletal muscles to generate heat. If this is unsuccessful, shivering ceases at around 87°F to 90°F; then, uncontrolled body cooling occurs.

hypothermia A body temperature below 33.3°C (95°F).

TABLE 18.2

RECOMMENDATIONS FOR THE 14-DAY HEAT ACCLIMATIZATION PERIOD

1. Days 1 through 5 of the heat-acclimatization period consist of the first 5 days of formal practice. During this time, athletes may not participate in more than 1 practice per day.
2. If a practice is interrupted by inclement weather or heat restrictions, the practice should recommence once conditions are deemed safe. Total practice time should not exceed 3 hours in any 1 day.
3. A 1-hour maximum walkthrough is permitted during days 1–5 of the heat-acclimatization period. However, a 3-hour recovery period should be inserted between the practice and walkthrough (or vice versa).
4. During days 1–2 of the heat-acclimatization period, in sports requiring helmets or shoulder pads, a helmet should be the only protective equipment permitted (goalies, as in the case of field hockey and related sports, should not wear full protective gear or perform activities that would require protective equipment). During days 3–5, only helmets and shoulder pads should be worn. Beginning on day 6, all protective equipment may be worn and full contact may begin.
   - Football only: On days 3–5, contact with blocking sleds and tackling dummies may be initiated.
   - Full-contact sports: 100% live contact drills should begin no earlier than day 6.
5. Beginning no earlier than day 6 and continuing through day 14, double-practice days must be followed by a single-practice day. On single-practice days, 1 walkthrough is permitted, separated from the practice by at least 3 hours of continuous rest. When a double-practice day is followed by a rest day, another double-practice day is permitted after the rest day.
6. On a double-practice day, neither practice should exceed 3 hours in duration, and student athletes should not participate in more than 5 total hours of practice. Warmup, stretching, cool-down, walkthrough, conditioning, and weight-room activities are included as part of the practice time. The two practices should be separated by at least 3 continuous hours in a cool environment.
7. Because the risk of exertional heat illnesses during the preseason heat-acclimatization period is high, it is strongly recommended that an athletic trainer be on site before, during, and after all practices.

Reproduced from Casa DJ, Csillan D. (2009). Preseason heat-acclimatization guidelines for secondary school athletics. *J Athl Train.* 44(3):332–333. Reprinted with permission.

TABLE 18.3

FACTORS THAT INCREASE THE RISK OF HEATSTROKE

Drugs	Drugs such as cocaine or speed tend to increase physical activity and reduce the awareness of fatigue.
Alcohol	Decreases cardiac output and can cause hyperthermia. Causes electrolyte disturbances in skeletal muscle. Causes dehydration.
Illness	Particularly dangerous when fever is present. Athletes are often reluctant to report illness for fear of losing their position on the team or being seen as a shirker.
Prescription Medications	Some cold medications act like amphetamines and increase heat production. Antihistamines interfere with body cooling by reducing sweat production. Many drugs for suppressing nausea or diarrhea also reduce sweating. So do many tranquilizers. Diuretics are associated with loss of salt, potassium, and water.
Lack of Physical Conditioning	Poor physical condition predisposes an athlete to heatstroke. Poor condition leads to inefficient performance that results in more heat production per unit of work performed.
Inappropriate Clothing	Being overdressed prevents the evaporation of sweat from the skin.
Environmental Factors	High temperature, high humidity, no breeze. Physical exertion in the sun during the hottest part of the day.
Genetics	Obesity, or large, heavy physique. Male gender. Sickle-cell trait.

Reproduced from Knochel JP. (1996). Management of heat conditions. *Athl Ther Today.* 1(4):30–35. Reprinted with permission from Human Kinetics (Champaign, Ill.).

Signs and symptoms of hypothermia—according to the National Safety Council (1997) and Thornton (1990)—include the following:

- In mild cases, the athlete will display shivering, loss of motor control, slurring of speech, and mental problems such as confusion and loss of memory.
- In severe cases, shivering will cease, and muscles will become stiff, giving the appearance of rigor mortis. Skin will become blue, and respiration and pulse rates will decrease. The athlete will be semiconscious or unconscious.

Management of mild hypothermia involves the following:

1. Move the athlete to a source of heat and out of the cold environment.
2. Remove any clothing that may be wet.
3. Wrap the athlete in warm, dry clothing or blankets.
4. Use an electric blanket or hot packs placed around the head and neck, armpits, groin, and chest. Avoid rewarming the extremities because doing so may cause vasodilation resulting in cooled blood from the extremities returning to the core and lowering the core temperature, a condition known as "after-drop" (Cappaert et al., 2008).

Management of severe hypothermia involves the following (body temperature below 90°F):

1. Transport the athlete immediately to a healthcare facility.
2. Prevent further heat loss by moving the athlete to a warm environment and gently removing cold, wet clothing.
3. Treat the athlete gently because cardiac-related problems are likely at low body temperatures.
4. Monitor vital signs and be prepared to administer artificial respiration or cardiopulmonary resuscitation (CPR).

As is the case with heat-related disorders, the best approach to the treatment of hypothermia is prevention. This can be accomplished in the majority of cases by following a few simple rules.

To prevent hypothermia, athletes should comply with the following guidelines:

1. Assess the risk by learning to use the windchill chart shown in **Table 18.4**. As shown, even on days when the temperature is moderate, the windchill factor can significantly increase the risk of hypothermia.
2. Do not embark on an outdoor activity of long duration, such as running or cycling, alone. Train with a friend or at least tell someone where you are going and when you plan to return.
3. Learn to recognize the early warning signs of hypothermia. If you have uncontrolled shivering in conjunction with loss of motor control, get to a warmer environment immediately.
4. Dress with appropriate cold-weather clothing. The synthetic materials now available allow body moisture to be wicked away from the skin surface while retaining body heat. It is also advised that you carry extra dry clothing whenever possible. When practical, keep your hands, feet, and head protected with extra insulation.
5. Make sure you remain properly hydrated and keep sufficient calories in your system to generate body heat. It is best to consume food and drink at regular intervals during long outdoor exposures. Also, avoid drugs such as alcohol, which creates the illusion of warmth but in fact contributes to heat loss.

Personnel rendering first aid to a victim of hypothermia should be versed in assessing body core temperature rectally. Oral thermometers are of little practical value when dealing with this form of medical emergency.

Frostbite and Frostnip

Exposure to extremely cold temperatures can result in skin-related problems, known commonly as frostbite and frostnip. The American Academy of Orthopaedic Surgeons (1991) defines frostbite as "freezing of tissues from excessive exposure to cold." Symptoms of frostbite include an initial feeling of burning and pain, followed by progressive loss of sensation. Damage in frostbite is caused by actual freezing of tissues and lack of blood (oxygen) supply to the tissues as a result of clotting. **Frostnip** is generally considered less severe than frostbite and involves freezing of only outer layers of skin, without damage to underlying tissue. Both of these conditions can occur when the nose, ears, fingers, and

frostnip Less severe form of frostbite.

TABLE 18.4

WIND CHILL CHART

Wind Chill Chart

Effective 11/01/01

Wind (mph) \ Calm	40	35	30	25	20	15	10	5	0	-5	-10	-15	-20	-25	-30	-35	-40	-45
5	36	31	25	19	13	7	1	-5	-11	-16	-22	-28	-34	-40	-46	-52	-57	-63
10	34	27	21	15	9	3	-4	-10	-16	-22	-28	-35	-41	-47	-53	-59	-66	-72
15	32	25	19	13	6	0	-7	-13	-19	-26	-32	-39	-45	-51	-58	-64	-71	-77
20	30	24	17	11	4	-2	-9	-15	-22	-29	-35	-42	-48	-55	-61	-68	-74	-81
25	29	23	16	9	3	-4	-11	-17	-24	-31	-37	-44	-51	-58	-64	-71	-78	-84
30	28	22	15	8	1	-5	-12	-19	-26	-33	-39	-46	-53	-60	-67	-73	-80	-87
35	28	21	14	7	0	-7	-14	-21	-27	-34	-41	-48	-55	-62	-69	-76	-82	-89
40	27	20	13	6	-1	-8	-15	-22	-29	-36	-43	-50	-57	-64	-71	-78	-84	-91
45	26	19	12	5	-2	-9	-16	-23	-30	-37	-44	-51	-58	-65	-72	-79	-86	-93
50	26	19	12	4	-3	-10	-17	-24	-31	-38	-45	-52	-60	-67	-74	-81	-88	-95
55	25	18	11	4	-3	-11	-18	-25	-32	-39	-46	-54	-61	-68	-75	-82	-89	-97
60	25	17	10	3	-4	-11	-19	-26	-33	-40	-48	-55	-62	-69	-76	-84	-91	-98

Frostbite Times: 30 minutes, 10 minutes, 5 minutes

Wind Chill (°F) = $35.74 + 0.6215T - 35.75(V^{0.16}) + 0.4275T(V^{0.16})$

Where, T=Air Temperature (°F) V=Wind Speed (mph)

feet are exposed to temperatures below 32°F for a long enough time period for freezing to occur. Skin temperatures must range between 28°F and 21°F for tissue freezing to occur. A temperature of 20°F is required for total freezing of exposed areas (Deivert, 1996). Medical evidence indicates that the most severe damage related to frostbite occurs when the frozen tissue thaws and then refreezes prior to medical treatment.

Fortunately, the risk of frostbite is minimal in most organized outdoor activities such as team sports. Typically, such activities are held near school or community facilities so that participants can return to a warm environment before any significant freezing takes place. The probability of frostnip occurring is quite high, however, even under such circumstances because participants may not realize the severity of tissue cooling taking place. During activities in extreme conditions in which temperatures are below freezing and windchill is a factor, athletes should be instructed by coaching personnel to watch closely for the early warning signs of frostbite and frostnip. Remember, the early signs of these problems are often noted by someone other than the victim.

The National Safety Council (1997) has published criteria to aid in the treatment of frostbite and frostnip; its guidelines are listed in **Time Out 18.2**. Tissue freezing can be categorized as either superficial or deep, depending on the duration and extent of exposure.

Cold Urticaria

Another related problem of the skin associated with exposure to cold temperatures is **cold urticaria**, which involves a skin reaction of localized **edema** (fluid accumulation) associated with severe itching. The areas involved are usually those directly exposed to the cold or those not well protected by clothing. The exact mechanism of cold urticaria is unknown but appears to be an

TIME OUT 18.2

Frostnip and Frostbite Care

Care for a Frostnip Victim

1. Gently warm the affected area by placing it against a warm body part (for example, put bare hands under the armpits or on the stomach) or by blowing warm air on the area. After rewarming, the affected area can be red and tingling.
2. Do not rub the affected area.

Care for a Frostbite Victim

All frostbite injuries require the same first aid treatment. Seek medical care immediately. Rewarming of frostbite should seldom be attempted outside a medical facility.

1. Get the victim out of the cold and to a warm place.
2. Remove any wet clothing or constricting items such as rings that could impair blood circulation.
3. Seek immediate medical care.
4. If the affected part is partially thawed or the victim is in a remote or wilderness situation (more than 1 hour from a medical facility), and you have warm water, use the following wet, rapid rewarming method. Place the frostbitten part in warm (102°F to 105°F) water. If you do not have a thermometer, pour some of the water over the inside of your arm or put your elbow into it to test that it is warm, not hot. Maintain water temperature by adding warm water as needed. Rewarming usually takes 20 to 40 minutes or until the tissues are soft. To help control the severe pain during rewarming, give the victim aspirin (adults only) or ibuprofen. For ear or facial injuries, apply warm, moist cloths, changing them frequently.
5. After thawing:
   - If the feet are affected, treat the victim as a stretcher case—the feet will be impossible to use after they are rewarmed.
   - Protect the affected area from contact with clothing and bedding.
   - Place dry, sterile gauze between the toes and the fingers to absorb moisture and keep them from sticking together.
   - Slightly elevate the affected part to reduce pain and swelling.
   - Apply aloe vera gel to promote skin healing.
   - Provide aspirin (adults only), ibuprofen, or acetaminophen to limit pain and inflammation.

Signs and symptoms of superficial freezing include the following:

- Skin color is white or grayish yellow.
- Pain may occur early and later subside.
- Affected part may feel very cold and numb. There may be a tingling, stinging, or aching sensation.
- Skin surface will feel hard or crusty, and underlying tissue will be soft when depressed gently and firmly.

Signs and symptoms of deep freezing include the following:

- Affected part feels hard, solid, and cannot be depressed.
- Blisters appear in 12 to 36 hours.
- Affected part is cold with pale, waxy skin.
- A painfully cold part suddenly stops hurting.

---

allergic reaction to cold temperatures. Some individuals are more susceptible, including people with mononucleosis, syphilis, varicella (chickenpox), and hepatitis. In addition, those using certain drugs, such as penicillin and oral contraceptives, demonstrate a higher incidence of cold urticaria (Escher & Tucker, 1993).

Fortunately, symptoms of cold urticaria tend to be self-limiting, with the acute symptoms resolving within a few hours after rewarming of the affected areas. For athletes who repeatedly suffer such symptoms, medical referral may be warranted. Treatment may include taking drugs such as antihistamines to control edema and itching. Athletes may also find certain types of outdoor clothing to be more effective in protecting the skin.

cold urticaria A condition in which the skin reacts to exposure to cold with localized edema associated with severe itching.

edema Swelling caused by the collection of fluid in connective tissue.

REVIEW QUESTIONS

1. Describe the normal range for body core temperature.

2. Explain how the body rids itself of excess heat.

3. What is the relationship between relative humidity and the process of evaporation?

4. True or false: Heat exhaustion is potentially more serious than exertional heatstroke is.

5. True or false: Heat cramps may be managed with rest, consumption of fluids, and static stretching of the involved muscles.

6. What is the recommended fluid intake during physical activity?

7. What is the fluid ounce equivalent of 4 L?

8. A fluid loss of from 2% to 6% can impair physical performance by how much?

9. At what core temperature does hypothermia begin?

10. At what body temperature does the shivering response cease?

11. What is the relationship between hypothermia and cardiac function?

12. Describe the signs and symptoms of cold urticaria.

13. Compute the fluid deficiency of an athlete who weighs 5.5 lbs less after practice than he did prior to practice.

REFERENCES

American Academy of Orthopaedic Surgeons. (1991). *Athletic Training and Sports Medicine*. Park Ridge, Ill: American Academy of Orthopaedic Surgeons.

Binkley HM, Beckett J, Casa DJ, Kleiner DM, Plummer PE. (2002). National Athletic Trainers' Association position statement: Exertional heat illnesses. *J Athl Train*. 37(3):329–343.

Cappaert TA, Stone JA, Castellani JW, Krause BA, Smith D, Stephens BA. (2008). National Athletic Trainers' Association position statement: Environmental cold injuries. *J Athl Train*. 43(6):640–658.

Casa DJ, Armstrong LE, Hillman SK, Montain SJ, Reiff RV, Rich BSE, Roberts WO, Stone JA. (2000). National Athletic Trainers' Association position statement: Fluid replacement for athletes. *J Athl Train*. 35(2):212–224.

Casa DJ, Csillan D. (2009). Preseason heat-acclimatization guidelines for secondary school athletics. *J Athl Train*. 44(3):332–333.

Deivert RG. (1996). Adverse environmental conditions and athletes. *Athl Ther Today*. 1(4):5–10.

Escher S, Tucker A. (1993). Preventing, diagnosing, and treating cold urticaria. *Phys Sportsmed*. 21:125–133.

Gatorade Sports Science Institute. (1997). Dehydration and heat injuries: Identification, treatment, and prevention. Gatorade Sports Science Institute.

Guyton AC. (1986). *Textbook of Medical Physiology*. Philadelphia, Pa: W. B. Saunders.

Hubbard RW, Armstrong LE. (1989). Hyperthermia: New thoughts on an old problem. *Phys Sportsmed*. 16(6): 97–113.

Kerr ZY, Casa DJ, Marshall SW, Comstock RD. (2013). Epidemiology of exertional heat illness among U.S. high school athletes. *Am J Prev Med*. 44(1):8–14.

Knochel JP. (1996). Management of heat conditions. *Athl Ther Today*. 1(4):30–35.

McArdle WD, Katch FL, Katch VL. (2010). *Exercise Physiology: Nutrition, Energy, and Human Performance*. Philadelphia, Pa: Lippincott Williams & Wilkins.

Montain SJ, Maughan RJ, Sawka MN. (1996). Fluid replacement strategies for exercise in hot weather. *Athl Ther Today*. 1(4):24–27.

Mueller F, Colgate B. (2011). Annual survey of football injury research, 1931–2010. National Center for Catastrophic Sports Injury Research: University of North Carolina at Chapel Hill. Available: http://www.unc.edu/depts/nccsi/.

National Athletic Trainers' Association. (2003a). How to recognize, prevent and treat exertional heat illnesses. *NATA news release*. Available: http://nata.org/NR07242003b.

National Athletic Trainers' Association. (2003b). Inter-Association Task Force on Exertional Heat Illnesses consensus statement. *NATA News*, 24–29.

National Safety Council. (1997). *First Aid and CPR* (3rd ed.). Sudbury, Mass: Jones and Bartlett Publishers.

Thornton JS. (1990). Hypothermia shouldn't freeze out cold-weather athletes. *Phys Sportsmed*. 18(1):109–113.

Wilmore JH, Costill DL. (1988). *Training for Sport and Activity: The Physiological Basis of the Conditioning Process*. Dubuque, Ia: Wm. C. Brown.

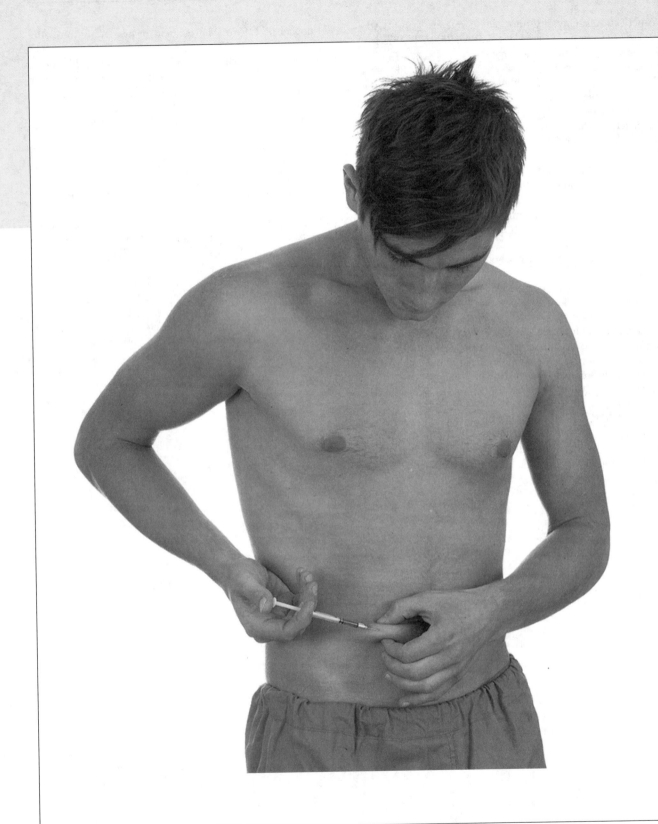

Other Medicinal Concerns

Athletes, like everyone else, occasionally become ill with infections that involve the respiratory and/or gastrointestinal systems. This chapter provides participation guidelines along with examples of typical signs and symptoms of the more common types of infections. Increases in cases of Lyme disease and methicillin-resistant *Staphylococcus aureus* (MRSA) within the athletic community have spurred growing concern over the last few years. These are bacterial infections and can have serious short-term and long-term implications for athletes. The chapter outlines early and late signs and symptoms, plus tips on how to avoid exposure to Lyme disease and MRSA.

Next, the chapter examines several illnesses caused by viruses, including infectious mononucleosis and infectious strains of hepatitis A and B. All of these conditions pose a serious health risk to athletes; their signs and symptoms can assist the coach in identification.

The chapter concludes with a discussion of the current thinking regarding sports participation by athletes suffering from exercise-induced asthma (EIA), sickle cell trait, diabetes, or epilepsy. The emphasis is on identification of the major signs and symptoms of each of these conditions and on management and special precautions related to sports participation.

go.jblearning.com/PfeifferCWS

For a full suite of assignments and additional learning activities (indicated by the icons throughout the text), use the access code found in the front of your text. If you do not have an access code, you can obtain one at go.jblearning.com/PfeifferCWS.

Exercise and Infectious Disease

Infectious disease is illness caused by some type of microorganism: viruses, bacteria, fungi, or protozoa. Although it is generally thought that physical activity helps to improve one's resistance to common infections, athletes remain vulnerable to the same illnesses as the general population. Exercise is purported to have some modulation effects on stress hormones, immune system dynamics, and possibly immune function (Karacabey et al., 2005; Pedersen & Hoffman-Goetz, 2000). However, the nature of the interactions is very complex and may include a variety of mechanisms including changes in recruitment and alterations in cell division. Research is ongoing in an effort to better identify the effects of exercise on the immune system (Karacabey et al., 2005; Pedersen & Hoffman-Goetz, 2000). This focuses on several infectious conditions affecting athletes that involve the respiratory, gastrointestinal, skin, or hepatic systems.

Respiratory Infections

According to Afrasiabi and Spector (1991), respiratory infections can be categorized as upper respiratory infections (**URI**) involving the nose, throat, ears and sinuses, tonsils, and associated lymph glands, or lower respiratory infections (**LRI**) involving the lungs, bronchi, and larynx. The majority of upper and lower respiratory infections in athletes are caused by viruses.

Upper Respiratory Infections

Upper respiratory infections produce classic symptoms of the common cold or **rhinitis**—sore throat, stuffy nose, mild cough, mild fatigue, and fever. As a general rule, these infections are self-limited and last only a few days. Because the infection is related to a virus, antibiotic therapy will have no effect on the organism causing the illness. Athletes with colds should be cautioned not to borrow drugs such as antibiotics from a friend or parent, as this could result in drug-related poisoning or allergic reactions.

Athletes with URI can normally participate in competitive sports when symptoms are mild or there are no specific symptoms that place them at obvious risk. Several symptoms including fever, **vertigo**, and **myalgia** are of particular concern and should restrict an athlete from practice or competition if they exist. If an athlete has a fever, then the athlete will have decreased heat tolerance (increased risk of heat illness) and increased fluid losses, thereby increasing cardiopulmonary effort and reducing maximal exercise capacity (Purcell, 2007; Rice, 2008). A fever may also be a sign of **myocarditis**, which makes usual exercise very dangerous (Rice, 2008). If an athlete has an ear infection, then the vestibular system is often affected and vertigo (loss of balance) is a result; therefore, it may be unwise to allow participation in a sport demanding a high degree of balance, such as figure skating, gymnastics, or diving (Nelson, 1989). Scientific evidence regarding the effects of viral infections on **endurance** and **muscular strength** are equivocal. Eichner (1993) found that athletes with viral infections suffered decreases in endurance and muscular strength. Weidner and associates found that URI did not negatively affect athletic performance (Weidner et al., 1997). Athletes involved in national or international events also must be warned not to treat themselves with over-the-counter medications such as decongestants or analgesics, as many of these drugs have been banned by sports regulatory organizations.

Infections of the upper respiratory system that persist for more than 1 week might be related to bacterial infections such as streptococci. There are no key symptoms that determine the difference between a viral and bacterial infection, but symptoms of such infections are generally more pronounced, with visible lesions in the back of the throat (strep throat), severe sore throat, extended fever and chills, general discomfort and malaise, and swollen lymph glands in the neck and lower jaw. Medical evaluation is essential; it usually includes a physical assessment, throat culture (to identify the infectious agent), and, in some cases, a prescription for an antibiotic medication. Proper diagnosis is necessary before treatment. Taking antibiotics without a firm diagnosis of a bacterial infection is dangerous and may lower a person's resistance to future infections. URIs are common and do take time to resolve, so athletes demonstrating any symptoms should not be allowed to participate, especially in team sports in which they are in close contact with other athletes, because such infections are routinely contagious. The athlete should be advised to rest and drink plenty of nonalcoholic fluids until the major symptoms begin to subside. Return to activity can usually occur within a few days when signs and symptoms reduce and there is no fever or significant fatigue.

Lower Respiratory Infections

Infections of the lower respiratory system can impair performance for periods ranging up to several weeks. Normally related to a viral infection of the bronchi, the symptoms include cough, fever, and **malaise** (general discomfort). Obviously, athletes involved in aerobic sports—running, swimming, cycling, or cross-country skiing—will be directly and negatively affected by such an infection. As is the case with upper respiratory infections, athletes with lower respiratory infections should be isolated from their peers and referred to a physician for complete evaluation and treatment. Such cases are normally treated with rest and medication designed to control coughing and to relieve the associated aches and pains. More serious types of infections in the lower respiratory system include bacterial infections such as bronchitis and pneumonia (inflammation of the lungs), the latter of which can sometimes be life threatening. Symptoms of bronchitis include fever, coughing, and general feelings of illness. In addition the cough may yield sputum that appears greenish-yellow in color (Leaver-Dunn, Robinson, & Laubenthal, 2000). The symptoms of pneumonia are more profound and also include coughing up of discolored sputum (American Academy of Orthopaedic Surgeons [AAOS], 1991). A physician must make a diagnosis of either bronchitis or pneumonia, neither of which is determined by the color of the sputum. Treatment includes rest, medication (antibiotics), and, in severe cases, hospitalization. Decisions regarding when to return to activity should be made on the advice of the attending physician and by the athlete (or parents in the case of a minor). Clearly, there should be no residual signs and symptoms, especially myalgia or malaise, because the stress of exercise might lead to unnecessary musculoskeletal injury.

Gastrointestinal Infections

Illnesses of the gastrointestinal (**GI**) system are typically related to viral, bacterial, or protozoan infections. Known collectively as **gastroenteritis** (inflammation of the stomach and intestines), these infections produce similar symptoms. Symptoms include abdominal cramping, nausea (often associated with vomiting), fever and chills, and diarrhea. When such symptoms occur, the best approach is to remove the athlete from participation, monitor the symptoms for 24 hours, and then make a decision regarding medical referral. Any athlete complaining of severe diarrhea or bloody stools should be referred immediately for a complete medical evaluation. Gastroenteritis, usually self-limiting within 1 to 3 days, is a generic problem that can be the result of a number of causes, including pathogens such as viruses, bacteria, or protozoa. In addition, such symptoms can be the result of food allergies, food poisoning, and even psychological stress. The athlete should be encouraged to drink plenty of nonalcoholic fluid because dehydration can occur when vomiting and/or diarrhea persist. If symptoms continue for more than a few days, the athlete should consult a physician. Related conditions that may be more serious are caused by bacteria (in the case of typhoid fever) and protozoa (in the case of giardiasis). As a general rule, an athlete with

GI symptoms—including severe (explosive or bloody) diarrhea, fever, extreme dehydration, and chills—should be referred to a physician for a complete physical evaluation and diagnosis.

A large and diverse number of problems of the gastrointestinal system can produce the symptoms of gastroenteritis. Evidence suggests that in some athletes the stress of physical activity may be the causative mechanism (Anderson, 1992). Other research has documented the reduction of GI symptoms in groups of athletes involved in aerobic activity (Halvorsen et al., 1990). Common GI-related problems include **gastritis** (inflammation of the stomach lining), **colitis** (inflammation of the colon), and **colic** (intra-abdominal pain). As with any recurrent and persistent clinical symptoms, referral to a physician is the prudent choice of action.

Other Infectious Diseases

Several other types of infections can affect athletes, and all present special problems with respect to identification, management, and prevention. Two infectious diseases that have increased in the athletic population are Lyme disease and methicillin-resistant *Staphylococcus aureus* (MRSA). Lyme disease is rarely a life-threatening illness; however, MRSA can lead to complications that can result in death. Both severely limit one's ability to

URI Upper respiratory infection.
LRI Lower respiratory infection.
rhinitis The common cold.
vertigo Type of dizziness that causes a perception of motion and includes a loss of balance.
myalgia General muscle pain.
myocarditis Infection of the heart with inflammation and damage to the heart muscle.
endurance The ability of the body to engage in prolonged physical activity.
muscular strength The maximal force that can be applied by a muscle during a single maximal contraction.
malaise Discomfort and uneasiness caused by an illness.
GI Gastrointestinal.
gastroenteritis Inflammation of the stomach and intestines.
gastritis Inflammation of the stomach lining.
colitis Inflammation of the colon.
colic Intra-abdominal pain.

participate in sports due to symptoms (Lyme disease) or the risk of infecting others (MRSA). Others infectious diseases include infectious mononucleosis and hepatitis A (HAV) and hepatitis B (HBV), which are extremely dangerous conditions.

Lyme Disease

Lyme disease is a bacterial (*Borrelia burgdorferi*) infection transmitted by the common deer tick (sometimes called bear tick in the western United States), which is widespread throughout the United States. Lyme disease gets its name from one of the towns where the first cases were identified in 1975: Lyme, Old Lyme, and East Haddam, Connecticut (Pinger, Hahn, & Sharp, 1991). Since that time Lyme disease has surpassed Rocky Mountain spotted fever as the most prevalent tick-borne infectious disease in the United States.

The disease is transmitted via a tick bite. Once a person is infected, initial symptoms may appear as early as 3 days later; however, symptoms may be absent for as long as 1 month after the bite. Regardless of the time period, the early symptom is the development of a circular area of reddened skin at the site of the bite. This is technically known as erythema chronicum migrans (ECM) and signifies the first stage of the infection. ECM will continue to develop for days; it can vary in size from a few inches to a foot or more. Additional symptoms include chills, fever, general aches and pains (malaise), and general fatigue. Most cases of Lyme disease that are caught early can be treated successfully with a few weeks of antibiotics; however, in prolonged cases drug therapy has been ineffective (Centers for Disease Control and Prevention [CDC], 2013b). If left untreated, the disease will become systemic and can affect the joints, heart, and central nervous system. In the majority of untreated cases, arthritis will develop, with the knee being the most commonly affected joint (Pinger, Hahn, & Sharp, 1991). Symptoms may appear together or separately and can be accompanied by a repeated appearance of ECM. It is important to note that untreated Lyme disease can persist for years in the body and produce symptoms of a variety of disorders, thereby making recognition and diagnosis difficult (CDC, 2013b).

The best approach is prevention of the disease by avoiding an infectious tick bite. Sports organizations that promote outdoor activities during the summer months in wooded areas should check with local medical authorities regarding reports of tick activity. Every effort should be made to hold events in areas where the likelihood of tick exposure is minimal. Athletes who are involved in outdoor sports held in wooded areas are at risk of exposure to infected ticks and they should be taught how to perform a thorough inspection of their bodies for the presence of a tick. They may require assistance when inspecting hard-to-see areas, such as the hairline at the back of the neck, behind the ears, and the posterior torso. Prevention may also include wearing repellent containing at least 20% DEET or **permethrin**-treated clothing (CDC, 2013b).

Ticks are very small—about the size of a pinhead in the nymph stage, which is the time it is best able to transmit the disease. If a tick is found, it should be removed immediately because it has been found that length of attachment plays a role in likelihood of infection. **Time Out 19.1** outlines recommended procedures for removal of a tick.

Methicillin-Resistant *Staphylococcus aureus*

Methicillin-resistant *Staphylococcus aureus* (MRSA) is a bacterium that is resistant to many antibiotics. Most MRSA infections are skin infections that occur at sites of skin trauma like cuts and abrasions. They are also common in the groin, armpit, or back of the neck,

---

TIME OUT 19.1

Guidelines for Tick Removal

Do not use the following methods of tick removal:

- Petroleum jelly
- Fingernail polish
- Rubbing alcohol
- A hot match

Pull the tick off, employing the following methods:

1. Use tweezers or, if you have to use your fingers, protect your skin by using a paper towel or disposable tissue. Although few people ever encounter ticks infected with a disease, the person removing the tick may become infected by germs entering through breaks in the skin.
2. Grasp the tick as close to the skin surface as possible and pull away from the skin with a steady pressure or lift the tick slightly upward and pull parallel to the skin until the tick detaches. Do not twist or jerk the tick because this may result in incomplete removal.
3. Wash the bite site and your hands well with soap and water. Apply alcohol to further disinfect the area. Then, apply a cold pack to reduce pain. Calamine lotion might aid in relieving any itching. Keep the area clean.

because these areas of the body are covered by hair, making them common sites for hair follicle irritation. An infected site often looks like just a bump that is red, swollen, and painful; however, it progresses to a pustule or boil that may have pus or other drainage. MRSA can cause life-threatening bloodstream infections, cardiomyopathies, and pneumonia if it is not recognized and treated correctly (CDC, 2013a).

Cases of MRSA have developed in athletic populations due to shared towels, soaps, and clothing and person-to-person contact and improperly cleaned whirlpools or equipment (e.g., mats, surfaces, protective pads). Cleaning or sanitizing equipment is of the utmost importance, but disinfection is the only way to inactivate germs like MRSA. Although proper cleaning and sanitizing procedures using typical cleaning agents are great at lifting dirt and germs off the surface, in order to truly reduce the risk of a MRSA infection, the equipment must be disinfected. Disinfectants effective against *Staphylococcus aureus* (staph) are usually effective against MRSA, and these products are readily available from retail stores. Before using, check the back of the label to determine the germs that the disinfectant can destroy and also confirm the product is registered by the Environmental Protection Agency (EPA). Registration by EPA is signified with a registration number (CDC, 2013a).

The first step in protection from MRSA is prevention. The best methods for prevention are teaching and maintaining good hygiene and avoiding contact with drainage from any skin lesions. **Time Out 19.2** presents a list of recommended actions for the prevention of MRSA in an athletic environment (National Athletic Trainers' Association [NATA], 2005). The next step is appropriate referral and treatment. As a coach or physical educator, you must refer athletes with possible infections to a team physician, athletic trainer, school nurse, or primary care doctor, and if the athlete is younger than 18 years old, be sure to notify parents or guardians (CDC, 2013a). Typical treatment involves incision, drainage, cleaning, and sometimes packing of the wound plus culturing of pus or drainage for confirmation of infectious bacteria. Because MRSA is resistant to typical antibiotics used for other staph infections, antibiotic treatment should be guided by the culture results and the patient's response to immediate treatment. Healthcare providers should also discuss a follow-up plan, because MRSA skin infections can develop into more serious infections; therefore, any overall body symptoms (fever or malaise) or worsening of local skin symptoms (redness, pus, swelling) should be immediately reported (CDC, 2013a). The final step is appropriate return to sport and/or community exposure. Athletes with active infections or open wounds should not use swimming pools or other common-use water facilities and they should not use therapy pools (whirlpools) that are not cleaned between each athlete's use (CDC, 2013a; NATA, 2005). Currently, the recommendation for return to sports participation is a "qualified yes," if the infection area can properly be covered and there is no risk of spreading the infection to other persons or equipment (Rice, 2008). However, for the safety of all concerned, if the activity poses a risk of injury to the infected area, then the athlete should be held from participation even if the lesion can be properly covered (CDC, 2013a).

Infectious Mononucleosis

Infectious mononucleosis (IM) is extremely common in the United States among young people and is caused by the Epstein-Barr virus, which is in the family of viruses responsible for herpes infections. The reported incidence in the general population is very high; 3% of college students contract IM per year (Eichner, 1996; McKeag & Kinderknecht, 1989). The initial symptoms of the infection are similar to the common cold—sore throat, fever, chills, and enlarged lymph nodes in the neck and jaw region. Infected persons often complain of extreme fatigue as well and may first notice the problem when they find it difficult to participate in sports. As the disease progresses, other organs may become involved, including the liver and spleen.

Transmission of the disease usually occurs via contact with discharge from an infected person's mouth (airway). Once exposed, the incubation period is variable; however, it usually ranges between 2 and 6 weeks (AAOS, 1991). Once the illness develops, its duration ranges from 5 to 15 days, with recovery beginning thereafter. Treatment is essentially symptom control once the diagnosis is made by a physician; the emphasis is on rest and pain control with some type of analgesic drug. Fortunately, infectious mononucleosis is a self-limited disease with no long-term effects.

A major concern with IM, however, is its effect on the spleen. It has been well documented that acute cases result in enlargement of the spleen (splenomegaly)—40% to

Lyme disease Bacterial infection transmitted by the black-legged tick (deer tick).

permethrin Broad-spectrum insecticide that can be infused in clothes to prevent insect bites.

infectious mononucleosis Viral infection characterized by general fatigue and enlargement of organs such as the spleen.

TIME OUT 19.2

MRSA Prevention and Management Recommendations

Personal hygiene and care of open wounds:

1. Keep hands clean by washing thoroughly with soap and warm water or use an alcohol-based hand sanitizer routinely.
2. Shower immediately following activity.
3. Wash athletic gear and towels after each use using proper techniques including hot/warm water and detergent.
4. Administer or seek proper first aid for any active skin lesions.
5. Alert appropriate staff (coaches or healthcare personnel) of any lesions that do not respond to typical treatment.

Preventing community exposure:

1. Do not share towels, razors, and daily athletic gear.
2. Do not use whirlpools or common tubs with open wounds, scrapes, or scratches.
3. Maintain a clean facility and equipment by using EPA-approved products for disinfection of surfaces.
4. Before participation, care for and cover all skin lesions.

Data from: Official Statement from the National Athletic Trainers' Association on Community-Acquired MRSA Infections (CA-MRSA). NATA. March 1, 2005; Centers for Disease Control (2013). Methicillin-resistant Staphylococcus aureus (MRSA) infections. Available at: http://www.cdc.gov/mrsa/.

60% of all cases (McKeag & Kinderknecht, 1989). When the spleen experiences an episode of blunt trauma, as is common in many contact sports, splenomegaly predisposes this organ to rupture. Data regarding rupture are sparse; however, the available information indicates the incidence of rupture in the infected population to be approximately 1 per 1000 cases (Eichner, 1996). Therefore, the attending physician is faced with the dilemma of determining when it is safe for an athlete to return to participation after recovering from infectious mononucleosis. It has been documented that most spleen ruptures occur between the 4th and 21st day of the illness; consequently, athletes never should be allowed to participate during this period (McKeag & Kinderknecht, 1989). The coach, athlete, and parents must rely on the attending physician regarding the best time to resume participation.

Prevention of the spread of infectious mononucleosis is difficult when dealing with athletes involved in team sports in which they are in close contact with one another on a daily basis. Athletes should know that the major mode of transmission of this disease involves coming into contact with an infected person's saliva. Preventive steps include advising athletes not to share water bottles or any other beverage containers and not to engage in kissing with potentially infected individuals. As a general precaution, towels and jerseys should not be shared by the athletes, because such items may be contaminated with respiratory discharge containing the virus. In addition, athletes should be taught the importance of reporting any

symptoms of illness to the coach so he or she can decide a given athlete's participation status.

Hepatitis Infection

Hepatitis infection, either HAV or HBV, is serious, although HBV or serum hepatitis is considered to be the more serious and potentially life-threatening variety. HAV is transmitted via feces and is a serious problem among food handlers who fail to wash their hands after going to the bathroom. Serum hepatitis is transmitted through the blood and sexual fluids of an infected person; it is routinely transmitted among intravenous drug users or accidentally by healthcare workers working with contaminated needles. It is also possible that transmission of HBV may occur during blood transfusions from infected persons.

Once a person is infected, the incubation period for HAV is 15 to 50 days; for HBV it is 45 to 160 days (Benenson, 1975). Symptoms of HAV and HBV infection are varied, but symptoms of both strains include nausea, abdominal pain, vomiting, fever, and malaise. If untreated, both strains will begin to affect the liver, resulting in jaundice (yellowing of the skin). This indicates liver involvement; in severe cases this vital organ may be severely damaged, leading in some cases to death. Treatment for either form of hepatitis infection is limited, thus prevention is essential. For HBV prevention, all athletes should receive hepatitis B vaccination before participation, any skin lesions should be covered properly, and athletic personnel should use universal

Athletic Trainers SPEAK Out

Courtesy of Ronnie P. Barnes, New York Giants.

Just recently I spoke to a mother of a 19-year-old who died participating in college football practice because of an unknown cardiac condition. Although non-traumatic deaths associated with sport and vigorous exercise in athletes under the age of 25 are rare, they do occasionally occur in individuals as young as 12 years of age.

It is important that a preparticipation physical examination, including individual and family history and Marfan's screening, be performed annually in all sports. Parents, coaches, and youth sports administrators should be aware that there are inherent risks in sports. A study done by Dr. Barry Maron revealed 25 deaths due to cardiac arrest in youths between the ages of 3 and 19. These deaths included 24 males and one female. All of these deaths occurred after receiving an unexpected blow to the chest in various sports. Deaths have also been reported in athletes after vigorous exercise without trauma. None of us can forget the death of Flo Hyman during an international volleyball competition or Hank Gathers during a basketball game or Reggie Lewis or Pete Maravich during pickup basketball games.

These deaths are rare and this should not detract from the positive benefits of sports participation, but it should heighten our awareness of the importance of the preseason physical examination in sports.

—Ronnie P. Barnes

Ronnie P. Barnes is Head Athletic Trainer for the New York Giants.
Courtesy of Ronnie P. Barnes, New York Giants.

precautions when handling blood or body fluids with visible blood (Rice, 2008). For HAV prevention, vaccination is available and should be used if teams are travelling to countries that might have low food quality standards. In treating for HAV, it appears that immediate inoculation with immune serum globulin (ISG) may confer passive immunity. There is some evidence that this also may be effective in treating cases of HBV exposure. Obviously, an athlete with HAV or HBV infection should be removed from participation and given prompt medical treatment. There is an apparent minimal risk of infection to others when sanitary procedures and universal precautions are followed; therefore, all sports may be played as an athlete's state of health allows, but because of the vulnerability of the liver during hepatitis infection, all decisions regarding return to participation for recovering athletes should be made by the attending physician (Rice, 2008).

WHAT IF?

You are coaching track at a small college in the Midwest. Your best miler has been suffering from an upper respiratory infection for several days and, worse, the regional qualifying meet is in 3 days. What would you recommend to this young athlete and, further, what would you caution regarding over-the-counter medication?

Exercise-Induced Asthma

Exercise-induced asthma (EIA) has been defined as a constriction of the airway resulting in the typical symptoms associated with asthma (wheezing, chest tightness, dyspnea) resulting from participation in strenuous exercise (Miller et al., 2005). A less severe condition known as exercise-induced bronchospasm (EIB) is also associated with an exercise-induced restriction in the airways but does not result in asthmatic symptoms (Weiler, 1996). The highest incidence of EIA is found, not surprisingly, among chronic asthmatics: About 90%

will develop an attack during exercise (Lacroix, 1999). However, EIA afflicts 15% to 25% of the general population as well (Miller et al., 2005).

The typical scenario for the onset and symptoms of EIA begins with exercise of sufficient magnitude to be considered intense, typically 70% to 85% maximal heart rate (Mayers & Rundell, n.d.). Activities like basketball, cycling, soccer, and distance running are significantly intense to elicit an attack (Lacroix, 1999). Sports that occur in cold air (hockey, speed skating, ice skating) or in outdoor arenas with high pollution levels are likely to elicit attacks, whereas sports that occur in an indoor humid environment are less likely to elicit attacks. During exercise the airway will typically dilate; however, on cessation of exercise, airway restriction or bronchospasm will occur within minutes. EIA has been found to be more common among athletes engaging in continuous exercise lasting at least 6 to 8 minutes and less common among athletes involved in intermittent forms of exercise typical of team sports, such as football or baseball (Lemanske & Henke, 1989). Although the exact cause of EIA is unknown, the two most accepted theories are (1) the water-loss theory—rapid respiration results in a drying of the mucus of the airway, and because more is inhaled through the mouth than the nose, this results in bronchoconstriction due to dry air irritating the lower airways—and (2) the heat-exchange theory—immediately after exercise the air in the lower airway is cooler, so the blood vessels dilate in an attempt to send warm blood to the area. As a result of blood vessel dilation, there is a decrease in space within the airways for air to flow, which might lead to difficulty breathing (Lacroix, 1999).

Signs and symptoms of EIA include the following:

- Coughing and tightness in the chest.
- Shortness of breath and inability to catch one's breath.
- Fatigue and stomachache (in children).
- Use of accessory muscles to breathe (abdominal muscles).
- Some athletes may become alarmed and anxious.
- Bluish skin or mucous membranes.

Management of EIA generally involves the use of any one of a variety of drugs that prevent airway restriction or bronchospasm. However, immediate treatment can include opening the airways by encouraging an open chest position and providing for the inhalation of warm, humid air (breathing through scarf, muffler, or hand). Effective drugs are available and can be administered either with an inhaler or orally. There are two basic types of drugs used to treat EIA: rescue inhalers and long-term anti-inflammatories (inhaler or oral). For the coach or physical educator, the rescue inhaler is the most important tool in treatment and management of EIA. The most common drugs used are inhaled beta-2 agonists, which include albuterol, terbutaline sulfate, and salmeterol. The administration of choice is by way of a rescue inhaler called a metered-dose inhaler (MDI), a device that is held approximately 1.5 inches from the mouth that releases an aerosol form of the drug that is then inhaled slowly. Coaches should be aware of any athlete on their roster who suffers from EIA and who uses medication to control symptoms. Having an asthma action plan for these athletes and being able to help an athlete retrieve and use medications including rescue inhalers are in the scope of a coach's duties (Lacroix, 1999). Athletes who have more than two episodes a week of EIA and need immediate use of a rescue inhaler to resolve symptoms are not well controlled and should be directed to a healthcare professional. If the athlete is under 18 years of age, then parents/guardians should be notified (Miller et al., 2005).

It is important to note that certain drugs have been banned by some major sports-regulating agencies, including the National Collegiate Athletic Association (NCAA) and the International Olympic Committee (IOC). The NCAA continues to allow athletes with diagnosed EIA to self-treat with beta-2 agonists by way of an MDI. The IOC has prohibited the use of beta-2 agonists with the exception of albuterol, albuterol/ipratropium, salmeterol, and terbutaline, and these can only be administered via an inhaler. In addition, the athlete must have submitted written notification from his or her personal physician to the IOC (Lacroix, 1999).

Highly susceptible individuals may be required to avoid certain activities such as high intensity and low rest activities, or at least be cognizant of environmental conditions and avoid such activity on cold, dry, or polluted days. Sports involving short bursts of activity followed by periods of rest are excellent alternatives for high-risk athletes. For outdoor activities on cold, dry days, wearing a mask or scarf has been recommended (Lacroix, 1999). Warm-up exercises have also been found to help reduce the likelihood of an attack (Lemanske & Henke, 1989). The National Athletic Trainers' Association (Miller et al., 2005) has published a comprehensive position statement on the management of asthma in athletes (it is available online at http://www.nata.org/sites/default/files/MgmtOfAsthmaInAthletes.pdf).

The appropriate steps in the management of an athlete suffering an acute attack of EIA are shown in **Figure 19.1**.

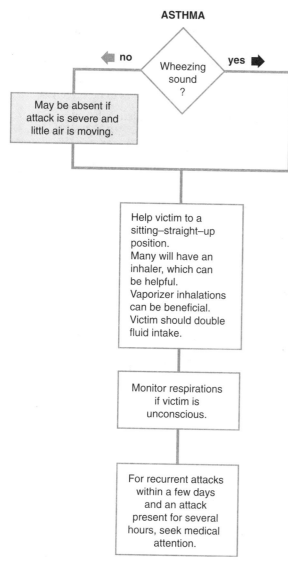

ASTHMA

Wheezing sound ?

no → May be absent if attack is severe and little air is moving.

yes →

Help victim to a sitting–straight–up position.
Many will have an inhaler, which can be helpful.
Vaporizer inhalations can be beneficial.
Victim should double fluid intake.

Monitor respirations if victim is unconscious.

For recurrent attacks within a few days and an attack present for several hours, seek medical attention.

FIGURE 19.1 First aid procedures for asthma victims.

The Athlete with Sickle Cell Trait

Sickle cell trait (SCT) is not a disease and will not turn into sickle cell anemia. It is a genetic trait where the individual has inherited one gene for normal hemoglobin and one gene for sickle hemoglobin (Martin, 2011; NCAA, 2012). SCT occurs in about 8% of the African American population and rarely in the Caucasian population. It is also common in individuals with ancestors from Africa, South or Central America, the Caribbean, Mediterranean countries, India, and Saudi Arabia (Martin, 2011; NCAA, 2012). Currently, the NCAA (2012) mandates SCT testing of all Division I and II athletes and is considering it at other levels. SCT is not a deterrent to athletic participation or outstanding

performances and many athletes compete at the high school, collegiate, and professional levels without any complications. However, the reason that individuals with SCT need to be identified is that intense exercise, especially in hot and humid conditions and/or at high altitudes, can predispose an athlete to a sickling collapse, which can result in death. A sickling collapse can mimic heat illness, asthma, or overall exhaustion, but it must be treated differently including immediate activation of emergency services; if a healthcare provider is present, then supplemental oxygen should be delivered.

A sickling crisis occurs during intense exertion because red blood cells, which deliver oxygen, can change from their typical donut-shaped appearance to a "sickle" or a quarter-moon shape (Martin, 2011). The change in shape causes less efficiency in oxygen delivery, and the sickle cells can also stick together and block blood flow to organs and tissues. Because there is less blood flow and oxygen delivery during a sickling crisis, an athlete can experience intense pain in the legs and low back, weakness, shortness of breath, and extremity swelling. Unfortunately, these signs and symptoms can also be seen in other conditions and may be missed initially. However, in athletes with SCT, these signs and symptoms can turn lethal due to the lack of blood flow to the kidneys and spleen (Martin, 2011). Conditions like gross hematuria (blood in urine), splenic infarction (spleen lesions), exertional rhabdomyolysis (skeletal muscle breakdown), Splenic infarction, and rhabdomyolysis can be lethal (NCAA, 2012). Dehydration, altitude, and uncontrolled asthma can predispose SCT athletes to experiencing a crisis situation (Martin, 2011).

For coaches and physical educators, prevention and recognition are the primary goals if SCT athletes are practicing and competing under their supervision. Several training techniques can be used to minimize the possibility of a sickling crisis. They include allowing SCT athletes to set their own pace, to be excused from all-out exertion drills, to have longer rest periods, to maintain adequate hydration, to control asthma symptoms, and to stop any activity if signs and symptoms appear (Martin, 2011; NCAA, 2012). The common signs and symptoms of a pending sickle cell crisis include the following (Martin, 2011):

- Athlete appears dazed or confused.
- Athlete may experience sudden collapse, but remain conscious.
- Athlete appears weak, fatigued, and is not keeping up with other team members.
- Athlete experiences shortness of breath.
- Athlete experiences significant muscle pain and/or cramping that is not easily resolved.

A sickling crisis is a medical emergency and must be treated immediately via activation of emergency medical services (EMS). Ideally, healthcare providers would be available and supplemental oxygen can also be delivered. However, when the athlete is conscious, cooling and rehydration are essential. While waiting for EMS, basic first aid techniques—monitoring vitals and preventing shock—are acceptable.

The Athlete with Diabetes

The American Diabetes Association (ADA; n.d.) defines diabetes as "a group of diseases characterized by high blood glucose levels that result from defects in the body's ability to produce and/or use insulin." The two most common forms of diabetes are (1) **juvenile-onset diabetes (type 1)**, which requires an external source of insulin to control blood glucose levels, and (2) **adult-onset diabetes (type 2)**, which involves the body becoming resistant to the insulin produced by the pancreas. Blood glucose levels in an athlete with diabetes may fluctuate widely, ranging from excessive levels of blood glucose (**hyperglycemia**) to exceedingly low levels (**hypoglycemia**). Though a detailed explanation of the specific mechanisms for controlling levels of blood glucose is beyond the scope of this text, suffice it to say that the ability to either manufacture insulin or utilize the insulin produced naturally is not possible for the athlete with either form of diabetes. An athlete has unique challenges in regard to managing blood glucose, because both diet and exercise intensity can have profound effects on the blood glucose levels.

Exercise is now generally considered to be beneficial for children and adults with diabetes; therefore, coaches and physical educators are likely to come into contact with individuals who have diabetes. However, certain problems can arise if exercise intensity, diet, and insulin dosage are not carefully monitored. Proper regulation of blood glucose is best accomplished by working with a physician prior to the beginning of the competitive season. Because the health status of a person with diabetes can change rapidly, it is important that athletic personnel be aware of the following three general reactions that are possible in the athlete with diabetes who initiates an exercise session (Robbins & Carleton, 1989):

1. The athlete anticipates correctly the amount of insulin needed to keep levels of blood glucose between 100 and 200 milligrams per deciliter. In this situation, glucose utilization in muscles is equal to that produced by the liver.

2. If the athlete does not take into account the effects of exercise and starts working out with a low level of insulin and elevated blood glucose, liver glucose production may actually increase. This may lead to a dangerously elevated level of blood glucose, a condition known as hyperglycemia.

3. In some cases, an athlete who begins exercising with a high or normal level of insulin may react just the opposite to the preceding scenario. Liver glucose production may decrease, whereas muscle glucose demand increases, causing dangerously low levels of blood glucose and leading to a condition known as hypoglycemia.

Research has shown that the intensity of exercise, the timing of exercise after insulin injection, and the environment may also determine what type of insulin and blood glucose response will occur (Horton, 1989; Jimenez et al., 2007). It has been found that sustained exercise of moderate intensity results in maintenance of, or even a decrease in, levels of blood glucose. Therefore, it is recommended that diabetic athletes involved in long-duration, moderate-intensity exercise, such as triathlons or marathons, decrease their insulin levels and increase caloric intake before a race or training session. Interestingly, brief bouts of high-intensity exercise (80% or greater VO_2max) result in increases in blood glucose levels. So, athletes participating in high-intensity sports, such as tackle football, soccer, and basketball, must be monitored to ensure they do not develop hyperglycemia and its complications. In general, exercise should be delayed until at least 1 hour after insulin injection and sometimes up to 4 hours depending on the type of insulin (fast-acting or long-acting) injected and the area to which it is delivered. The ambient temperature may also affect insulin absorption. Extreme temperatures below 36°F (2°C) or above 86°F (30°C) will reduce insulin action (Jimenez et al., 2007). In addition to ambient temperature, athletes should be cautioned about applying hot or cold modalities to the injection site, because heat will increase absorption rate and cold will slow absorption rate (Jimenez et al., 2007).

For proper monitoring, athletes with diabetes must learn how to monitor blood glucose levels; this is most easily accomplished through a test involving a finger-sticking technique. Periodic monitoring of blood glucose levels allows the athlete to adjust caloric and insulin intake prior to, during, and after exercise. Athletes should learn to estimate the caloric content of foods and the caloric demands of a given exercise session. With this information, the athlete can adjust diet prior to an event to compensate for the typical abnormal metabolic response seen in diabetics.

Coaches, physical educators, parents, and fellow athletes need to be versed in the early recognition and first aid treatment of hypoglycemia and hyperglycemia. Although both conditions present unique signs and symptoms, either condition can become life threatening. Hyperglycemia (high blood sugar) can lead to a condition known as **diabetic coma** or **ketoacidosis**. This occurs when fatty acids are metabolized to provide energy and yield ketones, which make the blood more acidic. Hypoglycemia occurs when too little sugar is available or too much insulin has been introduced into the body. In either case, the body has too little glucose, and **insulin shock** can occur.

Signs and symptoms of hyperglycemia include the following:

- Symptoms develop slowly.
- Fruity odor on the breath (indicates ketoacidosis).
- The athlete will complain of extreme thirst and will have the urge to urinate frequently.
- Nausea and/or vomiting.
- Loss of consciousness.

Management of hyperglycemia involves the following:

1. Summon emergency medical services.
2. Treat for shock and monitor vital signs.

Signs and symptoms of hypoglycemia include the following:

- Symptoms develop quickly.
- The athlete may demonstrate unusual behavior—for example, aggression or confusion followed by loss of consciousness.
- Profuse perspiration.
- Loss of motor coordination.
- Extreme hunger.

Management of hypoglycemia involves the following:

1. If the athlete is conscious, immediately administer a food or beverage containing sugar—for example, soda or fruit juice.
2. If the athlete does not improve within minutes, summon emergency medical services, treat for shock, and monitor vital signs.

A management flowchart covering the major treatment approaches for diabetic-related emergencies is shown in **Figure 19.2**.

WHAT IF?

You are coaching high school softball. During practice one afternoon your right fielder comes to you complaining of extreme hunger and acting strangely. You notice during your conversation that she is perspiring heavily although it is a cool, cloudy afternoon. You know from her preseason physical evaluation that she has diabetes. What condition would these signs and symptoms indicate? What would be the appropriate first aid for this young athlete?

Epilepsy and Sports Participation

Epilepsy is a disorder of the brain associated with a wide variety of symptoms. The most well known symptom is a **seizure**—a sudden episodic change in behavior or internal psychic state associated with an abrupt paroxysmal

juvenile-onset diabetes (type 1) Insulin-dependent type of diabetes mellitus usually occurring in children and adolescents. The body does not produce insulin.

adult-onset diabetes (type 2) Non-insulin-dependent type of diabetes. The body does not produce enough insulin or the body does not use insulin properly.

hyperglycemia Excessively high level of blood sugar.

hypoglycemia Low level of blood sugar.

diabetic shock Shock resulting from abnormally high sugar content in the blood and low insulin levels.

ketoacidosis Metabolic processes that occur in the absence of insulin. Fatty acids are used to provide energy and metabolism creates ketones. Result is disorientation and fruity breath smell.

insulin shock Shock resulting from an abnormally low sugar content in the blood and higher insulin levels.

epilepsy A chronic disorder characterized by sudden attacks of brain dysfunction, including altered consciousness, abnormal motor activity, sensory phenomena, and/or inappropriate behavior.

seizure Sudden onset of uncoordinated muscular activity and changes in consciousness lasting an unpredictable time.

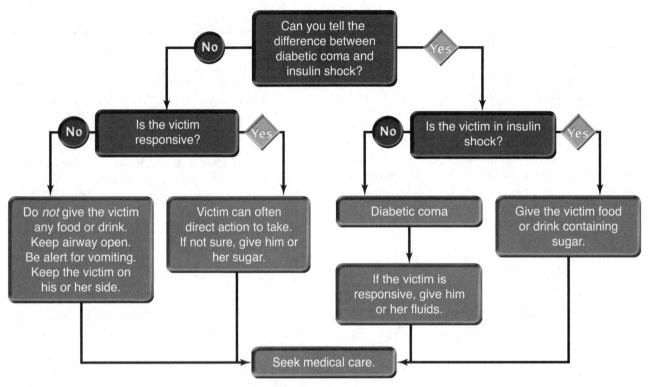

FIGURE 19.2 First aid procedures for diabetic emergencies.

discharge of electrical activity in the brain (Gates, 1991). Seizures take many forms and may involve motor systems, perceptions, and even the mood of the athlete. Epilepsy is not as common as popularly believed; it affects only 5 out of every 1000 among the general population (van Linschoten et al., 1990).

There are three forms of epileptic seizure the coach or physical educator is likely to encounter among athletes (Gates, 1991). The first, a generalized tonic-clonic seizure known as the grand mal seizure, involves perhaps the most dramatic symptoms (Dubow & Kelly, 2003). This seizure is characterized by generalized convulsions involving a fall to the ground and uncontrolled shaking of the arms and legs plus body twitching. During the seizure, the person is unconscious, but the eyes may be open, thereby creating the illusion that the person is awake. The typical generalized tonic-clonic (grand mal) seizure lasts from 2 to 5 minutes. The second type is called an absence attack, previously known as a petit mal seizure (Dubow & Kelly, 2003). The classic symptoms are sudden loss of awareness of immediate surroundings associated with a blank stare that lasts for a few seconds. Immediately following the seizure, the person will recover and may not know one has occurred. The third form is known as a complex partial seizure

(Dubow & Kelly, 2003). An athlete suffering this type of seizure will suddenly lose contact with surroundings and demonstrate any number of unusual behaviors, including mumbling, picking at or removing clothing, or walking around in an apparently random fashion. This type of seizure may last for up to 5 minutes, after which time the athlete will recover but will remain confused and disoriented, possibly for a considerable time. The athlete will have no memory of activity during the seizure.

From the coach's standpoint, two major concerns must be addressed regarding an athlete with epilepsy—safety in the chosen activity and proper first aid care should a seizure occur. Many questions have been raised within the lay and medical communities regarding what activities may pose a risk for the athlete with epilepsy. With the advent of anticonvulsant drugs, the vast majority of these athletes can control seizures. It has been reported that over half of epileptics taking antiseizure medication can remain free from seizures; another 30% will have infrequent attacks (Gates, 1991). The prevailing medical evidence suggests that high-risk activities for athletes afflicted with epilepsy include aquatic sports, sports in which falling is possible, and contact and collision sports (Gates, 1991; van Linschoten et al., 1990).

Obviously, a seizure occurring while an athlete is in the water carries the risk of drowning; therefore, athletes who may suffer seizures should always swim with a buddy and alert pool personnel of their condition. However, it is generally advised that the benefits to a young athlete with epilepsy who is interested in water sports, such as competitive swimming, far outweigh any risks.

Athletes interested in sports capable of producing a dangerous fall, such as cycling, ice-skating or speed skating, skydiving, and horseback riding, should be discouraged from participating (Dubow & Kelly, 2003). In such activities the risks of injury related to a seizure exceed whatever benefits may be derived from participation. A persistent myth has been that athletes with epilepsy should not be involved in contact and collision sports, as the potential jarring of the brain may increase the likelihood of seizure. Research, however, does not support this premise; in fact, it appears that athletes with epilepsy have no more risk from participation in such sports than does anyone else (Dubow & Kelly, 2003; Gates, 1991). The personal physician, parents, and athlete should collaborate to make reasonable decisions about participation. Of course, athletes with epilepsy involved in contact sports should take the same safety precautions as other athletes by wearing helmets, facemasks, and mouth guards.

There is no reason why any youngster with epilepsy should be excluded from most school or community sports programs. In fact, such children can benefit a great deal from participation, particularly with regard to their self-esteem and overall physical fitness (Dubow & Kelly, 2003). It is important for coaching personnel to educate all participants about epilepsy in the event that an athlete suffers from a seizure. In this way, fear and anxiety on the part of teammates can be minimized.

First aid care for epileptic seizures is determined by the type of seizure and the immediate circumstances. Obviously, a generalized tonic-clonic seizure that takes place in the water will require quite different first aid than a complex partial seizure that occurs in the wrestling arena. For the most part, first aid for any type of seizure involves protection of the athlete from self-injury followed by psychological support. The appropriate first aid care for an athlete suffering an epileptic seizure is provided in **Time Out 19.3**.

TIME OUT 19.3

First Aid Care for Epileptic Seizure in an Athlete (Generalized Tonic-Clonic Seizure)

- Coaching staff should know who on their team has epilepsy, the specific type of the disorder, and any related medications the athlete is taking.
- Note the approximate time, to the minute, that the seizure began, because this is very important information to relay to patient and any advanced medical care providers.
- If the seizure occurs in an aquatic setting, the priority must be to remove the victim from the water immediately and maintain the airway.
- Ask other athletes to move away from the victim and to resume their practice and/or game-related activities.
- Do not attempt to restrain the athlete during the seizure.
- Do not put anything in the person's mouth. Efforts to hold the tongue down can injure the teeth or jaw. Seizure victims will not swallow their tongue.
- Remove any restricting clothing around the neck that might restrict breathing.
- Move potentially harmful objects away from the immediate area of the athlete.
- If the athlete is not wearing some type of helmet (football, lacrosse, hockey, etc.), place something soft under the head of the athlete.
- As the seizure passes, place the athlete onto his or her side, sometimes called the "recovery position."
- As the athlete regains consciousness be sure to provide psychological support and treat for any injuries incurred or signs or symptoms of shock.
- Initiate the emergency plan, including contacting emergency medical services if:
  - The seizure lasts more than 5 minutes.
  - The victim is having trouble breathing.
  - Another seizure occurs.
  - Injuries were obtained and need advanced treatment.
  - Victim remains unconscious after seizure has ended.

REVIEW QUESTIONS

1. Define the acronyms URI and LRI.
2. What types of organisms are related to respiratory infections?
3. Define the term *gastroenteritis*.
4. Describe briefly the history of Lyme disease in the United States.
5. What is the mode of transmission for Lyme disease?
6. Describe the major signs and symptoms of Lyme disease.
7. True or false: Lyme disease is caused by a virus.
8. Describe the major signs and symptoms of MRSA.
9. True or false: MRSA does not spread from person to person.
10. True or false: All cleaners are acceptable to clean athletic surfaces and equipment when trying to protect against MRSA transmission.
11. What is the causative agent of infectious mononucleosis?
12. What is the risk related to collision sports and mononucleosis?
13. Describe the common signs and symptoms of EIA.
14. What can a coach do to assist an athlete suffering from EIA?
15. Which ethnicities are likely to carry the sickle cell trait (SCT)?
16. What conditions are likely to cause a sickle cell crisis?
17. Describe several ways you can prevent a sickling crisis in athletes with SCT.
18. What are the recommended levels of blood glucose for the athlete with diabetes?
19. List the signs and symptoms of hyperglycemia.
20. List the signs and symptoms of hypoglycemia.
21. What is the difference between in-field management for the preceding two conditions?
22. Define epilepsy.
23. What are the management guidelines for an athlete suffering an epileptic seizure?

REFERENCES

Afrasiabi R, Spector SL. (1991). Exercise-induced asthma. *Phys Sportsmed.* 19(5):49–60.

American Academy of Orthopaedic Surgeons (AAOS). (1991). *Athletic Training and Sports Medicine.* Park Ridge, Ill: American Academy of Orthopaedic Surgeons.

American Diabetes Association. (n.d.). Diabetes basics. Available: http://www.diabetes.org/diabetes-basics/?loc=GlobalNavDB.

Anderson CR. (1992). A runner's recurrent abdominal pain. *Phys Sportsmed.* 20:81–83.

Benenson AS (ed.). (1975). *Control of Communicable Diseases in Man.* Washington, DC: American Public Health Association.

Centers for Disease Control and Prevention. (2011). First aid for seizures. Available: http://www.cdc.gov/epilepsy/basics/first_aid.htm.

Centers for Disease Control and Prevention. (2013a). Methicillin-resistant *Staphylococcus aureus* (MRSA) infections. Available: http://www.cdc.gov/mrsa/.

Centers for Disease Control and Prevention. (2013b). Tickborne diseases of the United States: A reference manual for health care providers. Available: http://www.cdc.gov/lyme/resources/TickborneDiseases.pdf.

Dubow J, Kelly J. (2003). Epilepsy in sports and recreation. *Sports Med.* 33(7):499–516.

Eichner ER. (1993). Infection, immunity, and exercise: What to tell patients? *Phys Sportsmed.* 21:125–133.

Eichner ER. (1996). Infectious mononucleosis—recognizing the condition, reactivating the patient. *Phys Sportsmed.* 24:49–54.

Gates JR. (1991). Epilepsy and sports participation. *Phys Sportsmed.* 19:98–104.

Halvorsen FA, Lyng J, Glomsaker T, Ritland S. (1990). Gastrointestinal disturbances in marathon runners. *Br J Sports Med.* 24:266–268.

Horton ES. (1989). Exercise and diabetes in youth. In: Gisolfi CV, Lamb DR (eds.), *Perspectives in Exercise Science and Sports Medicine, Vol. 2: Youth Exercise and Sport* (pp. 97–113). Indianapolis, Ind: Benchmark Press.

Jimenez C, Corcoran M, Crawley J, Hornsby, Jr WG, Peer K, Philbin R, Riddell M. (2007). National Athletic Trainers' Association Position Statement: Management of the athlete with type 1 diabetes mellitus. *J Athl Train.* 42(4):536–545.

Karacbey K, Saygin O, Ozmerdivenli R, Zorba E, Godekmerdan A, Bulut V. (2005). The effects of exercise on the immune system and stress hormones in sportswomen. *Neuro Endocrinol Lett.* 26(4):361–366.

Lacroix VJ. (1999). Exercise-induced asthma. *Phys Sportsmed.* 27(12):75.

Leaver-Dunn D, Robinson JB, Laubenthal J. (2000). Assessment of respiratory conditions in athletes. *Athletic Therapy Today.* 5(6):14–19.

Lemanske RF, Henke KG. (1989). Exercise-induced asthma. In: Gisolfi CV, Lamb DR (eds.), *Perspectives in Exercise Science and Sports Medicine, Vol. 2: Youth Exercise and Sport* (pp. 465–596). Indianapolis, Ind: Benchmark Press.

Martin D. (2011). Sickle cell trait. In: *National Federation of State High School Associations Sports Medicine Handbook* (4th ed., pp. 113–115). Indianapolis, Ind: National Federation of State High School Associations.

Mayers LB, Rundell KW. (n.d.) Exercise induced asthma. *ACSM Current Comment.* Available: http://www.acsm.org.

McKeag DB, Kinderknecht J. (1989). A basketball player with infectious mononucleosis. In: Smith NJ (ed.), *Common Problems in Pediatric Sports Medicine* (pp. 191–203). Chicago, Ill: Year Book Medical Publishers.

Miller M, Weiler J, Baker R, Collins J. (2005). National Athletic Trainers' Association Position Statement: Management of asthma in athletes. *J Athl Train.* 40(3):224–245.

National Athletic Trainers' Association. (2005). Official Statement from the National Athletic Trainers' Association on Community-Acquired MRSA Infections (CA-MRSA). Available: http://www.nata.org/sites/default/files/MRSA.pdf.

National Collegiate Athletic Association. (2012). *Sports Medicine Handbook* (2012–2013). Indianapolis, Ind: National Collegiate Athletic Association.

Nelson MA. (1989). A young gymnast with an acute upper respiratory infection. In: Smith NJ (ed.), *Common Problems in Pediatric Sports Medicine* (pp. 204–209). Chicago, Ill: Year Book Medical Publishers.

Pedersen B, Hoffman-Goetz L. (2000). Exercise and the immune system: Regulation, integration, and adaptation. *Physiol Rev.* 80(3):1055–1081.

Pinger RR, Hahn DB, Sharp RL. (1991). The role of the athletic trainer in the detection and prevention of Lyme disease in athletes. *Athletic Training.* 26:324–331.

Purcell L. (2007). Exercise and febrile illnesses. *Paediatr Child Health.* 12(10):885–887.

Rice S. (2008) Medical conditions affecting sports participation. *Pediatrics.* 121(4):841–848.

Robbins DC, Carleton S. (1989). Managing the diabetic athlete. *Phys Sportsmed.* 17(12):45–54.

van Linschoten R, et al. (1990). Epilepsy in sports. *Sports Med.* 10:10–19.

Weidner TG, Anderson BN, Kaminsky LA, Dick EC, Schurr T. (1997). Effect of rhinovirus caused upper respiratory illness on pulmonary function test and exercise response. *Med Sci Sports Exerc.* 29(5):604–609.

Weiler JM. (1996). Exercise-induced asthma: A practical guide to definitions, diagnosis, prevalence and treatment. *Allergy Asthma Proc.* 17(6):315–325.

The Adolescent Athlete: Special Medical Concerns

MAJOR CONCEPTS

Approximately 35 million youths between the ages of 5 and 18 years participate in a wide array of organized sports nationwide (Statistic Brain, 2013). Sixty percent of boys and 47% of girls are on sports teams by the age of 6 years. An additional 7.6 million children are involved in secondary school-sponsored activities. With that large number of participants has come rather startling injury data. It is estimated that approximately 3.5 million injuries occur annually during sports participation among children and adolescents. Before puberty, girls and boys suffer the same risk of sports injuries. During puberty, boys suffer more injuries more severely than girls. Recent injury data show 2.7 million kids under 20 were treated for sports and recreation injuries and 21% of all traumatic brain injuries were related to sports and recreation.

Though young athletes suffer the greatest number of injuries of all sports participants, they often receive limited medical care. The availability and expertise of sports medicine providers, including physicians, Board of Certification, Inc. (BOC)–certified athletic trainers, and physical therapists, increases as athletes reach more elite levels of competition. Accordingly, the relatively small number of athletes competing at the Olympic and professional levels have unlimited access to specialty medical care. Collegiate athletes usually have the services of a full-time athletic trainer and one or more active team physicians. The situation changes drastically at the high school level, as a minority of schools employ athletic trainers to care for the millions of sports participants. At the youth sports level, there is rarely any involvement by trained medical personnel. As a result, coaches and parents are often left to provide initial care for injured athletes.

go.jblearning.com/PfeifferCWS

For a full suite of assignments and additional learning activities (indicated by the icons throughout the text), use the access code found in the front of your text. If you do not have an access code, you can obtain one at go.jblearning.com/PfeifferCWS.

Youth Sports in America

Organized youth sports have been a part of American culture for more than a century. As 19th-century America became increasingly industrialized and urbanized, local schools and churches formed youth sports organizations to help "build character" through physical activity. In the 1890s, the YMCA first began offering young men the opportunity to compete against each other. The founding of New York City's Public School Athletic League in 1903 ushered in the explosion of organized sports participation in the first half of the 20th century, which culminated with the birth of Little League Baseball in 1939. The 1970s then saw an influx of girls and young women entering the traditionally male-dominated youth sports culture as barriers were overcome both legally and socially (Title IX Info, 2013). However, there were some backlashes against youth sports throughout the years; many educational leaders opposed competition, citing its potentially harmful psychological effects. Educators also observed a corresponding decrease in free play activities as children immersed themselves in organized sports. They feared "premature specialization" in certain sports would lead to injuries and interfere with the normal physical and mental development of childhood. Formal school budgets have been cut, causing physical education to be removed from the curriculum. Based on these examples, many formal elementary school athletic programs were disbanded, beginning a shift in philosophy that has had repercussions in youth sports for many years. Physical educators and other teachers started to play a diminishing role in coaching school-sponsored sports for young participants, thereby allowing thousands of parents and other volunteers to take their places. Unfortunately, the majority of these well-meaning volunteers have had no formal training in coaching or in child developmental phases. As a result, concerns have continued to be raised about the potential for young athletes to suffer physical and emotional harm from sports competition. In response to such concerns, for example, many youth baseball and soccer leagues have stopped keeping score or recording wins and losses, Little League Baseball established pitch counts, and many athletes are encouraged not to specialize too early. However, despite these oppositions, youth sports have never been more popular. In a recent survey, 34% of girls and 61% of boys say that sports are a big part of their lives (Kelley & Carchia, 2013).

Factors in Youth Sports Participation

Why do children and adolescents play organized sports? There are a variety of answers. Not surprisingly, the primary motivating factor for many young athletes is having fun. Other often-cited rationales have been making friends through team involvement, developing skills, and improving physical fitness (Pommering, n.d.). Researchers at Michigan State University have also found that preadolescent boys in urban settings can benefit from sports involvement because gang involvement may reduce because sports involvement provides other role models to look up to (ISYS, 2013).

Eventually, almost half of young athletes who go out for sports will discontinue participation prior to the end of their season. Unfortunately, the reasons for doing so are relatively few. Fear of injury was found to be the most common factor in withdrawing from sports among high school students. Lack of playing time, overemphasis on competition, and dislike of the coach were also cited by high school students. Sadly, attrition among boys and girls results from an "absence of fun" (Kelley & Carchia, 2013).

Epidemic of Youth Sports Injury

Injuries can span the gamut from catastrophic injuries to injuries that result in very little time loss from practice or competition. Catastrophic injuries are typically categorized as fatal (death), nonfatal (life-altering complications), and serious (significant time loss) injuries (Mueller & Cantu, 2012). Mueller and Cantu reported 22 catastrophic injuries in high school football in 2010—2 fatalities, 10 nonfatalities, and 10 serious injuries with recovery. In comparison, female high school cheerleaders suffered one nonfatal injury in 2010–2011; however, in 2005–2006 there was 1 fatality and 10 serious cheerleading injuries. Overall for the time period from fall 1982 to spring 2011, there were 128 (fatal, nonfatal, and serious) direct catastrophic injuries for high school females and only 51 direct catastrophic injuries for college females (Mueller & Cantu, 2012). Much of this is attributed to less regulation, inexperienced athletes and coaches, and lack of proper access to health care in the high school setting versus the collegiate setting.

Noncatastrophic injuries also occur commonly in high school athletes and there seem to be timing (practice vs. competition) and team- and gender-specific factors that contribute to different injury rates. During one year, nine boys' and girls' sports demonstrated a higher rate of injury per 1000 athlete-exposures in competition (4.63) than in practice (1.69) (Rechel, Yard, & Comstock, 2008). Over a 3-year period from 2008–2011, approximately 10% of high school injuries were fractures, with the highest rate being in boys' sports (football and hockey) rather than girls' sports and in competition rather than practice (Swenson et al., 2012). Over a 1-year period, among high school athletes approximately 53% of injuries were acute lower extremity injuries. Football had the highest rate for boys and soccer the highest for girls. Girls had 1.5 times the proportion of season-ending lower extremity injuries than boys (Fernandez, Yard, & Comstock, 2007). Acute injuries were not the only types of injuries suffered; overuse or repetitive trauma injuries represented approximately 50% of pediatric sports-related injuries (Valovich McLeod et al., 2011). These data can be used by healthcare providers, coaches, physical educators, and parents to safeguard young athletes during sports participation.

Two recent alliances have been established in an effort to educate the public about the rate and types of injuries that happen in youth sports. The overall purposes of these alliances are to increase knowledge about sports injury prevention, recognition, and treatment so sporting careers and even lives can be saved. The Youth Sports Safety Alliance (http://www.youthsportssafetyalliance.org/) and STOP (Sports Trauma Overuse and Prevention) Sports Injuries (http://www.stopsportsinjuries.org/) both offer websites full of valuable information that can be downloaded about different sports and the role that coaches, parents, and athletes can all play in guaranteeing safe participation. The Youth Sports Safety Alliance was started by the National Athletic Trainers' Association (NATA) and has brought together more than 100 other organizations that care about youth athletes. In particular, the alliance commits to several calls to action listed in **Time Out 20.1**. STOP Sports Injuries

was initiated by the American Orthopaedic Society for Sports Medicine (AOSSM) in 2007 and has been joined by several other medical or athletic societies.

The Growing Athlete
Puberty

Before proceeding with a discussion of common injury patterns, an understanding of the uniqueness of the growing athlete is required. It has often been said that children are not just "little adults." Nowhere does this saying apply more than in athletics. Emotionally and physically, children and adolescents respond far differently to the rigors of sports activity than do their adult counterparts.

Prior to reaching physical maturity, the young athlete's body is in a dynamic state. Change is constant as growth and development take place. Puberty is defined as the time when children develop secondary sexual characteristics, experience an increase in the rate of linear growth, and add muscle mass. Puberty usually begins at an average age of 10 years in girls and is signaled by the onset of breast development. At around the age of 12 years, boys will begin puberty, with an increase in testicular volume being the first physical sign. Growth during puberty may account for up to 20% of final adult height. The average boy will see a doubling of his total muscle mass between the ages of 10 and 17 years. Puberty may last for 3 to 6 years.

Longitudinal growth accelerates during early puberty, with peak height velocity being attained at an average of age 12 years in girls and 14 years in boys. In young women, this timeframe typically corresponds to just

---

TIME OUT 20.1
Calls to Action for Youth Sports Safety Alliance

- Ensure that youth athletes have access to qualified healthcare professionals.
- Educate the public about the signs and symptoms of sports injuries and conditions.
- Assure preparticipation exams and appropriate baseline testing be performed for all athletes.
- Ensure that sports equipment, uniforms, playing surfaces, and environmental conditions are checked for safety and best conditions.
- Insist that research into youth sports injuries be supported and published.
- Support a national registry of sports-related catastrophic injuries and fatalities.

- Request that appropriate emergency action plans and safety protocols and procedures are at every sporting event and facility.
- Eliminate the culture of "playing through pain" without assessment.
- Ensure that general and sports-specific safety education be a priority for every administrator, coach, parent, and player.

Modified from The Youth Sports Safety Alliance Call to Action. http://www.youthsportssafetyalliance.org/call-to-action. Accessed: September 28, 2013. Used with permission.

prior to the onset of menses. On average, menarche occurs 2 years after breast development begins. Most girls will see no more than 5 centimeters of height added after menarche. Boys attain peak height velocity later in puberty than do girls, corresponding to Tanner stage 3 or 4 of sexual maturity (near adult pubic hair distribution and genital development) (Morris & Udry, 1980). Peak height velocity may result in linear growth rates of almost 10 centimeters per year.

Growth

The longitudinal growth of bones arises from the physis (growth plate) located near the ends of long bones. Though a rather complex structure, the physis is basically an anatomic framework where rows of a cartilaginous matrix are progressively laid down to allow for longitudinal growth. Each layer undergoes a series of physiologic transformations, culminating in complete ossification (new bone formation). All bones continually lengthen beginning with embryonic development, but puberty signals a particularly rapid phase of bone growth. Bone growth ends once the physis closes, signaling the attainment of skeletal maturity. The average age of full skeletal development is approximately 14 years for girls and 16 years for boys, but there may be much variation (Micheli, 1991).

The physes, apophyses, and articular surfaces of long bones are three key anatomic structures susceptible to injury in the young athlete (**Figure 20.1**). All three share the presence of growth cartilage. The apophysis represents the site at which large muscle–tendon units attach

to bones. Similar in structure to the physis, these tendon sites typically mature and completely ossify prior to the closure of the physes. The articular cartilage may be more susceptible to stress injury in young athletes, because the surface and underlying matrix have not yet achieved maturity. Therefore, it is likely unable to attenuate stress as well as the adult tissue can.

Skeletal muscle has no corresponding "growth center" to that found in long bones. In fact, muscles grow in length in a similar manner as they grow in size—they respond to increasing forces. The progressive lengthening of the bone stimulates the muscles to correspondingly become longer. Therefore, muscles lag behind bones in length, setting up the potential for injury, particularly at times of rapid growth (Micheli, 1991).

Injury Mechanisms

Macrotrauma and microtrauma (overuse) events are the two basic injury categories seen in sports. Macrotrauma results from a single, high-force traumatic event. Examples include compound and comminuted fractures, joint dislocations, and tendon or ligament ruptures. Though young athletes may suffer these injuries, they are more likely to suffer trauma to the growth plate (physis) than to tear a ligament or fracture the shaft of a long bone. As with any structure, the weakest point is the most susceptible to damage when subjected to a force. The growth cartilage within the physis offers less resistance than the correspondingly stronger bones and joints (Micheli, 1991). There is no evidence that organized sports cause more macrotraumatic injuries than does free play or other recreational activities. Microtrauma or overuse injuries result from chronic, repetitive stress to local tissues. Overuse injuries are increasingly common in children and adolescents and represent the majority of injuries seen in young athletes. They often result from repetitive activities or chronic submaximal loading of tissues that occurs in activities like throwing, swimming, and distance running. Multiple factors, including training errors, improper technique, excessive training, inadequate rest, early specialization, and muscle weaknesses and imbalances, can lead to these injuries (Valovich McLeod et al., 2011). Many of these factors are discussed in more detail throughout the chapter.

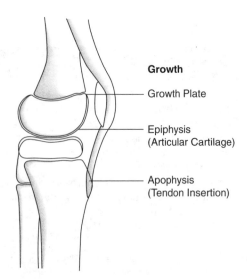

FIGURE 20.1 Long bone, showing physis, articular cartilage, and apophysis.

Ligament Injuries

Severe ligamentous injuries are less common in adolescent athletes than in adults, but they still do occur.

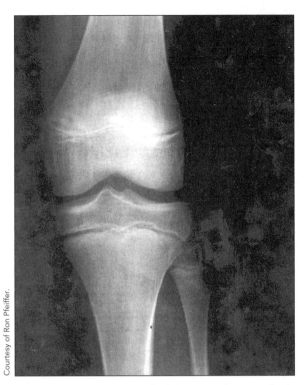

Courtesy of Ron Pfeiffer.

FIGURE 20.2 Stress X-ray of a fracture at the growth plate of a tibia in a skeletally immature athlete. Without the stress applied to the fracture by the radiology technologist to the medial aspect of the tibia, it would be difficult to visualize the fracture.

An increased laxity of the ligaments prior to skeletal maturity and the relative plasticity of the long bones contribute to this. As previously discussed, the physis offers less resistance to force than the ligaments and in many instances is the site of injury. The physis may act to absorb more of the forces. For example, if a young athlete suffers a lateral blow to the knee, the valgus force will more likely result in a distal femoral or proximal tibial physis fracture than in the medial collateral ligament sprain often seen in skeletally mature athletes (**Figure 20.2**).

However, an increasing body of evidence supports the fact that prior to puberty, ligamentous injuries may occur more commonly than previously thought. Prior to the pubertal growth spurt, the physis and its attachment site to the underlying bone may actually be stronger than the ligaments (Adirim & Cheng, 2003). When evaluating potential ligament injuries in adolescents, the basic principle of comparing the injured joint with the contralateral joint must always be remembered. The examiner may initially suspect ligamentous disruption owing to the increased laxity of immature joints. Similar laxity in the contralateral joint confirms a normal finding.

TABLE 20.1	
COMMON SITES OF APOPHYSITIS	
Anatomic Site	**Condition**
Tibial tubercle	Osgood-Schlatter disease
Inferior pole of patella	Sinding-Larsen Johansson disease
Calcaneus	Sever's disease
Medial distal humerus	Little League elbow
Fifth metatarsal base	Iselin's disease
Iliac crest	Iliac apophysitis
Ischial tuberosity	Ischial apophysitis

Tendon Injuries

Chronic, microtraumatic injuries to the immature apophysis and the resultant inflammation have long been recognized. In 1903, Osgood and Schlatter each described traction injury at the tibial tubercle and named the condition Osgood-Schlatter's disease (Osgood, 1903). Other commonly involved sites include the calcaneus (Sever's disease) and medial humerus (Little League elbow) (**Table 20.1**). Apophyseal injuries provide excellent examples of the multiple factors that lead to injury in the growing athlete. As discussed, muscles lengthen in response to bone growth. Therefore, a susceptible period exists when the muscle is shorter than necessary for optimal function in relation to the bone. The result is constant tension on the apophysis, which is exacerbated by repetitive activity. With repeated traction placed on the apophysis, there may be some weakening within the growth cartilage matrix, culminating in inflammation, pain, and loss of function (Adirim & Cheng, 2003).

Young athletes are more susceptible to **apophysitis** during times of rapid bone growth, but overtraining, poor technique, and chronic misuse all may inflict damaging forces across joints and contribute to injury (Valovich McLeod et al., 2011). Infrequently, macrotraumatic injuries can also occur at the apophysis. High-force injuries may result in the complete disunion of the apophyseal growth cartilage, the adolescent equivalent of a complete tendon avulsion. Initial treatment of apophyseal injuries is similar to the treatment of other musculoskeletal injuries. Stretching of

apophysitis Inflammation of an apophysis.

the involved muscle groups, changes in activity level, and anti-inflammatory medications may also help. Calcaneal apophysitis (Sever's disease) is often particularly amenable to the placement of a heel lift in the shoe of the involved foot. The heel lift acts to functionally shorten the pull of the gastrocnemius and soleus muscles, lessening the tension at the calcaneal apophysis.

Growth Plate Injuries

Injuries to the physis may result from microtrauma and macrotrauma. In the 1960s, Salter and Harris (1963) classified five injury patterns seen after trauma to the physis. The Salter-Harris type I fracture is by far the most common physis injury and represents a "separation" of the cartilaginous zone from the bone (Figure 20.2). The diagnosis is most often made based on physical exam findings, because radiographs are typically normal. Such an injury should always be suspected when the athlete presents with a joint injury, but with tenderness predominantly over the distal or proximal portion of the bone and a normal joint examination. Injuries to the distal fibula and distal radius are most often seen. Treatment consists of casting for 4 to 6 weeks, and complications are rare.

Injuries in the Salter-Harris classification system become progressively more serious as the corresponding type number increases. Types III and IV involve fractures of the bone's articular surface and usually require surgical repair. Type V injuries represent a compression of the growth plate and carry the highest incidence of premature closure and growth arrest. Over the years another type of growth plate injury has been recognized. Chronic, repetitive axial loading of a physis may lead to microvascular injury and resultant growth arrest. This injury is most commonly seen in gymnasts, who present with radial deviation of their hands secondary to overgrowth of the ulna as compared with the shortened radius.

Over the past several decades, a number of physeal injury classification systems have arisen. While the Salter-Harris system has stood the test of time and remains the most commonly used system, it does not adequately describe all possible fracture variants. Therefore, two additional physeal injuries deserve special mention. Rang and Ogden (1981) described an injury that may occur at the perichondral region of the physis (**Figure 20.3**). In the early 1990s, Peterson (1994) proposed a classification system with many similarities to the Salter-Harris scheme. His main addition was that of the Peterson type I fracture—a transverse fracture of the metaphysis with a longitudinal extension into the physis, often seen in the distal radius (**Figure 20.4**).

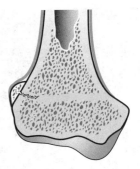

FIGURE 20.3 Rang-Ogden type IV injury.

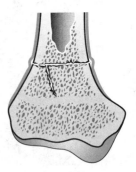

FIGURE 20.4 Peterson type I injury.

Growth Cartilage

The articular surfaces of all bones are covered with cartilage. Immature growth cartilage differs biomechanically and biologically from that found in adults. In addition to providing a low-friction articulating surface, cartilage acts to absorb and disperse forces in weight-bearing joints. Growth cartilage may be somewhat softer than

WHAT IF?

A 15-year-old tackle football player, a linebacker, limps severely toward the sideline after having been involved in a tackle during a scrimmage. He reports having felt his knee twist severely, and that he experienced a popping, or "letting go" feeling, when the injury occurred. He notes tenderness along the top of the tibia bone along his knee joint line. This pain was made worse by asking him to simply stand on the injured leg. Based on the information presented in this chapter, what would you conclude are possible injuries given this athlete's injury history, signs, and symptoms?

Athletic Trainers SPEAK Out

Courtesy of Elicia Leal, MEd, ATC, LAT, McKinney North High School, McKinney, TX.

Why is it so important to have athletic trainers in the secondary school setting?

With the rising number of young adults participating in contact and collision sports and the increasing prevalence of concussions, having an athletic trainer in the secondary setting is invaluable and no longer a luxury but a necessity. As an allied healthcare professional I not only assess concussions but I am a strong advocate for the student-athlete in the classroom by educating teachers on the signs and symptoms of concussion and modifications needed for a full recovery. As an athletic trainer at the secondary setting I am able to provide daily assessments, treatments, and rehabilitation of a variety of athletic injuries; I communicate with the parents, educate them on injuries, and provide home care instructions or physician referral if needed. By providing daily prevention and care I help keep down the number of insurance claims filed, physical therapy visits, and physician referrals, thus saving the school district and family money. Due to the rising cost of health care and the low socioeconomic status of many of our student-athletes, I often become the first or only option of being seen by a healthcare provider. As a school employee I also serve as a Sports Medicine instructor, where I'm able to expose students to the profession of Athletic Training and Sports Medicine. These classes serve as a gateway for many of our Athletic Training students to attend college and pursue Athletic Training as a career. It also exposes them to other healthcare professions which they may not have even considered as a career path.

People often ask me why I work at the secondary setting when I have so many years of experience and have worked the Olympic Games. It's because I feel that this is where I can make the greatest impact on young athletes' lives by educating and mentoring them regarding the prevention and care of athletic injuries. These are the developmental stages and it's when they are forming habits and making decisions regarding their health care. Most often their first exposure to injures, health care, or athletic trainers is in the secondary setting; I try to make it a positive and impacting experience by providing an educational and all-encompassing means of health care.

—Elicia Leal, MEd, ATC, LAT

Elicia Leal is the Head Girls' Athletic Trainer at McKinney North High School in McKinney, Texas.

Courtesy of Elicia Leal, MEd, ATC, LAT, McKinney North High School, McKinney, TX.

---

its adult equivalent and subjects the underlying tissues to damage. Though less common than the two injury patterns mentioned earlier, injuries do occur. The primary example is osteochondritis of the radial head capitellum, found in Little League elbow. Such injuries may impart long-term damage to the articular cartilage.

Contributors to Injury

Sports medicine specialists nationwide are in agreement that sports-related injuries among adolescents and children have risen dramatically since the 1990s.

Multiple factors are responsible for the rise and are most easily categorized as intrinsic and extrinsic contributors to injury. Intrinsic factors are individual biologic and psychosocial characteristics associated with internal factors like age, ability, strength, or flexibility, whereas extrinsic factors are associated with external factors like the playing field or the environment (Caine et al., 2008). Though multiple factors exist, this discussion focuses on those believed to be most important and amenable to change. It must also be remembered that many injuries are the result of a combination of factors rather than a single entity.

Intrinsic Factors

The most important intrinsic factor involved in youth sports injuries is the growing body itself. The suscep-tibility to injury of growth cartilage, bone, and the muscle–tendon unit represents factors that are under only limited control. During the pubescent growth spurt where the peak height velocity is occurring, the bone is temporarily more porous and more prone to injury like epiphyseal fractures (Caine et al., 2008). However, several other intrinsic factors have been iden-tified as predisposing pediatric athletes to overuse inju-ries. In particular, previous injury and associated laxity or instability to joints and overall experience with sport techniques play very important roles. Previous injury may result in tissue changes including fibrosis that may cause limited range of motion and function (Caine et al., 2008). For example, a high school cross-country runner has a four- to fivefold increased likelihood of reinjury at the same body site (Rauh et al., 2005). Also, young males with taller stature, thinner body structure, less strength, decreased muscle flexibility, and high degrees of ligamentous laxity are particularly prone to overuse injuries. Young males with thinner body structures and less strength are more likely to suffer overuse injuries when paired in repeated contests with larger male ath-letes of the same age because of the constant wear and tear applied to weaker joints and muscles (Caine et al., 2008). Young females with taller and thinner body structures are also prone to overuse injuries and their decreased muscle flexibility will often contribute to genu valgum or overpronation of feet (Valovich McLeod et al., 2011). For example, biomechanical malalignment at the knees and feet may lead to increased incidence of medial tibial stress syndrome (shin splints) and stress fractures (Valovich McLeod et al., 2011).

Extrinsic Factors

Cultural Deconditioning

Despite record numbers of youngsters involved in orga-nized sports, obesity among youths continues to rise. Twenty percent of girls and 17% of boys ages 6–11 years are considered obese (Kelley & Carchia, 2013). The degree of obesity in children and adolescents has been directly correlated to the amount of television watched by kids in the past; video games and computers have only worsened this trend. Concomitantly, free play, the spontaneous physical activity of childhood, has con-tinued to decline. Along with the decrease in free play, simple activities such as walking to school or bicycling from one destination to another have also declined. Less than 31% of children get 60 minutes or more of physical

activity 7 days a week (Kelley & Carchia, 2013). At the time of its origin, organized youth activity was intended to be an adjunct to free play. Unfortunately, organized sports have become the basis of physical activity for most children. Therefore, we now see young athletes enter into sports with no underlying base of physical fit-ness or skill in sports, leaving them prone to acute and chronic injury.

Training Errors or Improper Technique

An important figure in the life of any young athlete is his or her coach. Unfortunately, there is a nationwide short-age of qualified individuals to fulfill these vital roles; the need for coaches has quadrupled since the 1990s. More than three-quarters of all youth sports coaches have no formal training. As a result, many young athletes are never taught proper preseason conditioning methods, nor do they learn the basic fundamentals vital to their sport. In addition, athletes and coaches alike fall prey to the "more is better" philosophy of training, attempt-ing to accomplish too much, too soon in an attempt to improve, but setting the stage for injury instead.

Formally trained or not, many coaches simply do not have the requisite knowledge base for instructing young athletes on the principles of sport techniques or condi-tioning. Volunteers without formal training often base their coaching style and teaching of fundamentals on personal experiences. Even trained coaches will likely have learned many of the technical aspects of their job by observing and listening to other coaches. Both of these styles of acquiring knowledge are prone to misin-formation, with improper theory being perpetuated for years. Weight training (discussed in further detail later in the chapter) is a particularly important area where improper training can lead to serious injury.

Excessive Training, Inadequate Rest, and Early Specialization

A recent position statement on overuse injuries in pediatric athletes developed by the National Ath-letic Trainers' Association (Valovich McLeod et al., 2011) identifies several recommendations in regard to excessive training, inadequate rest, and early special-ization. These are merely recommendations, and the authors note that more research is needed to clarify their validity; however, they are a place to start in an effort to prevent overuse injuries in young athletes. Valovich McLeod and colleagues (2011) recommend the following:

- Pediatric athletes should have at least 1 to 2 days off per week from competitive practices, compe-titions, and sport-specific training.

- Progression of training intensity, load, time, and distance should only increase by 10% each week to allow for adequate adaptation.

- Pediatric athletes should participate on only one team of the same sport per season and practice/play no more than 5 days per week.

- Pediatric athletes should take time off between sport seasons and up to 2 to 3 nonconsecutive months away from one specific sport.

- If pediatric athletes do participate in simultaneous or consecutive seasons, then it is important to follow guidelines on the cumulative amount of specific activities (e.g., pitch counts, miles run, meters swimming).

The STOP Sports Injuries (Oates et al., 2011) website also provides valuable information on the prevention of overuse injuries by limiting overtraining and unneeded specialization that can be downloaded for free (see http://www.stopsportsinjuries.org/resources/coaches-curriculum-toolkit/overuse-injuries.aspx).

Equipment

Although less important than the factors previously discussed, athletic equipment can play a role in injury. Football helmets must be up to current standards and fit properly. Shoulder pads also must be of the correct size and fit. Proper footwear can play a significant role in lower extremity injuries among young distance runners. Footwear should be inspected for the quality of the impact absorption material, good fit, and ability to compensate for alignment changes, particularly during heel strike.

Playing Surfaces

The condition of athletic fields at the high school and youth sports levels may range from near professional quality to abysmal. All playing surfaces should be inspected prior to events to search for potential hazards such as sprinkler heads, holes, and other hazardous objects.

Injury Imitators

Any discussion of adolescent musculoskeletal injuries must include a review of pathologic conditions that may initially present with similar physical findings to common injuries. An old medical axiom is that "common illnesses happen commonly." However, we must always consider common presentations of uncommon conditions. This section briefly reviews some serious

 WHAT IF?

> A 14-year-old female cross-country runner has been complaining to you for the past week about hip pain. She reports that these symptoms started shortly after the team began running high-intensity practices that included extremely explosive sprints with emphasis placed on driving the knees as high as possible. When asked to point to where the pain is most severe, she points to the area of the anterior superior iliac spine on her right hip. In addition, she reports that simply raising up her right leg, as if to bring her knee toward her face, causes considerable pain at that same site. Based on the information presented in this chapter, what would you conclude are possible injuries given this athlete's injury history, signs, and symptoms?

medical conditions that may be initially confused with musculoskeletal trauma. When evaluating injured adolescents, one must bear in mind three principles regarding such conditions:

1. *Physical findings inconsistent with injury history*: In general, the extent of the physical findings should be comparable to the severity of the injury described by the athlete or witnessed by others. Finding a complete rupture of the anterior talofibular ligament following an ankle inversion is consistent. Severe tenderness, edema, and erythema of the entire foot 2 to 3 days after a similar injury does not make sense. Additionally, absence of any trauma history coupled with physical exam findings consistent with injury (swelling, erythema, tenderness) should especially raise concerns for a more serious underlying pathologic process.

2. *Unusual local symptoms*: Exquisite tenderness, erythema, or pain out of proportion to the injury mechanism should all raise suspicion for other pathology. Severe night pain and pain on awakening in the morning are also unusual aspects of typical musculoskeletal injuries that should be further investigated.

3. *Systemic symptoms*: A young athlete with musculoskeletal complaints coupled with any combination of fevers, weight loss, night sweats, nausea, or vomiting requires urgent medical attention and a thorough evaluation.

Oncologic

Adolescence is the peak age for occurrence of long bone tumors. Such tumors are rare, yet their onset is typically insidious and the symptoms may be mistaken for a traumatic etiology early on in the course of illness. Unfortunately, delay in treatment can decrease chances for survival. Bone tumors often result in local pain, tenderness, edema, and night pain. Other complaints may include fever and weight loss. Osteosarcomas most commonly arise in the metaphyses of the femur, tibia, and humerus. Ewing's sarcoma is typically found in the midshaft of long bones, but also may arise in the pelvis. Diagnosis is made by plain radiographs and confirmed by biopsy. Treatment for each consists of tumor excision and intensive chemotherapy. Five-year survival rates are near 80%.

Rheumatologic

When an athlete presents with complaints of pain or swelling in more than one joint, particularly in the absence of trauma, a diagnosis of juvenile rheumatoid arthritis (JRA) must be considered. Pauciarticular JRA presents with involvement of only a few joints, typically of the lower limbs. Affected individuals initially complain of pain and stiffness on awakening in the morning, with symptoms improving with increased activity. Symptoms are progressive. There may also be inflammation of the sacroiliac joint. Though a thorough review of JRA is beyond the scope of our discussion, it may result in severe low back and lower extremity pain, disability, and additional systemic symptoms (fever, rash). Diagnosis is made by clinical history and blood testing.

Infectious

Variations in the blood supply to the joints and physes make young athletes more susceptible to bone and joint infections than their adult counterparts. Bone infections (**osteomyelitis**) may present similarly to bone tumors, with fevers being more common in infection. Plain radiographs are normal early in the course, with diagnosis typically made by bone scan or magnetic resonance imaging (MRI). Infections are treated with 4 to 6 weeks of antibiotics, usually intravenously. Adolescents are also at risk for localized muscle infections. **Pyomyositis** results from bacterial invasion of the muscle tissue. Symptoms include fever, pain, and local tenderness. Diagnosis may be made by MRI. Treatment typically requires surgical drainage and 4 to 6 weeks of intravenous antibiotics. Lyme disease, a bacterial infection, may also present with joint involvement and other systemic symptoms, and methicillin-resistant *Staphylococcus aureus* (MRSA) can also present with systemic symptoms, but a skin lesion characterizes it.

Neurovascular

Reflex neuropathic dystrophy (RND) merits discussion, because early intervention and treatment greatly aid in the resolution of symptoms. Though the exact pathogenesis is unknown, there is usually some degree of psychogenic overlay. Most common in girls between the ages of 9 and 16 years, RND is preceded by minor injury about half of the time and usually involves the lower extremities. Severe pain and dysfunction are the predominant presenting complaints. Physical findings include marked tenderness (**hyperesthesia**) and signs of local autonomic dysfunction, which may include cyanosis, coolness, diffuse edema, or increased perspiration. Laboratory tests are usually inconclusive. Once the diagnosis is made, patients are placed in an aggressive physical therapy program to regain function of the affected extremity. Treatment may also include individual or family counseling.

Psychologic

All members of the sports medicine team are familiar with athletes who malinger or seek secondary gain from their injuries. However, coaches and athletic trainers must also watch for the subtle signs of depression. Athletes presenting with a continuum of seemingly minor, yet troublesome, injuries should be further questioned about sleep habits, activities, and mood. An athlete's endorsement of symptoms such as poor sleep, early awakening, abandonment of pleasurable activities (**anhedonia**), and feelings of worthlessness indicate potential depression, and referral to a physician, psychologist, or school counselor is mandatory.

Strength Training

Adolescent strength training has become increasingly popular in recent years. Long thought of as being unnecessary, or even harmful, weight training for adolescents and preadolescents has come under a new focus with concentration on benefits, safety, and the appropriate age at which to begin participation (Faigenbaum, 2013; Lavallee, 2002). Studies examining the incidence and types of injuries incurred while weight training have shown varying results. High injury rates are typically attributed to improper supervision in combination with the nature of the lifting technique—Olympic lifts or single lifts with maximum weight.

A concern in adolescent weight training is that skeletal immaturity may allow for growth plate injuries to occur. Although there have been reports of growth plate injury caused by weight training, many of these injuries were felt to be caused primarily by unsupervised training programs and the need to lift maximal weights. Because of this potential risk, the American Academy of Pediatrics (AAP) issued rather restrictive guidelines for adolescent weight training (Sallis & Patrick, 1994). The guidelines called for close supervision by knowledgeable coaches and medical professionals for children and adolescents who strength train; however, they also advised that adolescents reach Tanner stage 5 of sexual maturity before participating in vigorous weight training.

Besides being overly cautious, the AAP guidelines present a potential obstacle. For many coaches and strength specialists, attempting to determine whether or not an athlete has reached Tanner stage 5 can be confusing and possibly present legal concerns. There is a large body of literature supporting the initiation of resistance training at much younger stages of development with little or no risk of injury (Faigenbaum, 2013). Therefore, a simpler approach should be employed. Children should begin a strength-training program if they have the desire to do so, are receptive to coaching, and can follow instructions. If a child is not coachable or loses interest in strength training, the program should be discontinued.

As with any sport, potential risks do exist, but strength training can be beneficial for children and adolescents. Before puberty, many of the gains achieved through strength training are attributable to neuromuscular adaptations. These adaptations may allow the young athlete to achieve greater and faster hypertrophy in the postpubertal stages because of the learning that occurred in the prepubertal stages.

Can strength training prevent injury? As mentioned earlier, strength training increases neuromuscular coordination and muscle mass and strength. Assuming all other variables are equal, these neuromuscular adaptations may allow young athletes to perform better at their chosen sports. Also, these adaptations may make the young athlete less susceptible to the microtrauma of overuse injuries. Strength training should not be expected to prevent all serious acute injuries that are inherent in sports, but it may lessen the athlete's risk for injury.

Safety

Safety should be the focus of all adolescent weight-training programs. The main way to avoid injury is to provide young athletes with proper supervision and guidelines. Other possible strategies may include, but are not limited to, eliminating use of single-repetition maximum lifts, limiting the use of Olympic and powerlifting techniques, and offering safer alternative techniques for lifting.

One area of concern with the adolescent population and strength training is the obsession with the measurement of strength. The predominant way to measure strength is through the use of the one-repetition maximum lift (1 RM). This technique is commonly used in squatting, the bench press, and other Olympic or powerlifting lifts. The 1 RM consists of a one-time maximal exertion of force used to move the weight. This one-time effort requires near perfect execution of form and puts an inordinate amount of stress on the body. In adult populations this may be a valid and accurate way to assess strength, but not for adolescents (Faigenbaum, 2013). Their limited amount of training with regard to maintaining appropriate technique, combined with skeletal immaturity, predisposes them to injury while performing the 1 RM.

There are better and safer ways to assess an adolescent's strength. One such technique is to use a 1-RM equivalent. This allows the athlete to estimate/assess maximum strength without the increased chance of injury. It can be calculated as follows:

$$(\text{weight lifted} \times \text{number of repetitions} \times 0.03) + \text{weight lifted} = 1\ RM$$

Although this technique is not precise with regard to Olympic or powerlifting standards, it does provide a safer alternative for assessing strength in adolescent populations.

Another way to limit injury is to avoid placing the body in positions that may put the joints and limbs at a mechanical disadvantage, which increases the risk for injury. The following are four examples of common lifting mistakes with a description of the proper and safe lifting techniques to avoid them.

osteomyelitis Infection of bone or bone marrow with associated inflammation.

pyomyositis Bacterial infection of muscles resulting in pus-filled abscesses.

hyperesthesia Nonpainful touch stimuli becomes painful.

anhedonia No longer experiencing pleasure from activities that once were enjoyable.

Lat Pull Down

Problem

When the weight is pulled behind the neck, the neck is placed in excessive flexion, and the shoulder joints are loaded at the extreme of external rotation. Also, the line of pull with relation to the bar and the latissimus muscle is such that this position does not oppose the latissimus dorsi, thus not providing quality resistance.

Solution

A safer way to perform this exercise is to sit down with the bar directly overhead. Grabbing the bar with the hands approximately shoulder width apart, the athlete should lean back slightly so the bar just passes in front of the head, pulling the bar straight down in front of the head to chin level. This will allow for a more optimal line of pull on the latissimus dorsi and decrease stress on the shoulder joint. The torso should not rock back and forth while performing this exercise to avoid low back injury.

Bench Press

Problem

Hyperextension of the shoulders (dropping the bar to the chest or the elbows behind the plane of the body) puts the pectoralis major at a mechanical disadvantage, contributes to shoulder instability, and puts excessive stress on the acromioclavicular joint.

Solution

A safer way to perform this exercise is to keep the elbows even with the plane of the body (do not drop elbows beyond the level of the chest walls). This will decrease stress on the shoulder joint and allow for a better mechanical advantage, thus providing better resistance for the muscle. To ensure proper depth of the elbows, the use of a partner to watch elbow depth is beneficial. Once proper depth has been achieved, a towel placed on the chest may be used as a reminder. As the bar touches the towel, the push phase of the movement begins. When performing the chest press (or any exercise), control of the weight must be maintained. The bar should never be bounced off the chest.

Military Press

Problem

Extreme shoulder external rotation and abduction during a behind-the-neck military press puts stress on the shoulder capsule, contributing to shoulder instability.

Solution

A safer way to perform this exercise and eliminate these stresses is to do the military press in the front of the head. Also, by not allowing the shoulder to drop below 60° abduction, the deltoid muscle moves the weight through the range of motion without putting undue stress on the rotator cuff.

Squats

Problem

When performing a squat in which the thighs are parallel to or lowered to the floor, there is an excessive amount of shear force on the knee in a position where the articular cartilage is thinnest.

Solution

When weight training, the individual should avoid deep squats and maintain lumbar spine stability. Alternative lifts to the squat may include the leg press and the box squat. When employing the box squat, the box must only be used as a guide for appropriate depth of movement. The box itself should never be used to drop down to and rest on or bounce off of to gain momentum. When performing the leg press, the depth of the movement should entail not allowing the knees to be bent at greater than a 90° angle.

Adolescent weight training, like any activity, has the potential to result in musculoskeletal injury. However, the rate of injury does not seem to be any higher than that of other activities adolescents participate in on a daily basis. Through proper teaching, close supervision, adherence to suggested guidelines, and avoidance of one-repetition maximums, the low rate of injuries can be further reduced. Strength training is a safe and beneficial means of exercise for adolescent populations.

Prevention of Injury

Though all sports activities carry an inherent risk of injury, certain principles can be applied that will help decrease the number of injuries sustained. Strength and conditioning techniques have already been covered, and multiple studies show the benefits of such training for athletes of all ages. Other important areas of intervention include the following.

Preparticipation Physical Examination

All athletes should have a complete evaluation prior to their entry into organized sports. The preparticipation physical examination (PPE) is not intended to be a comprehensive medical examination but should be focused on sports participation. Particular attention should be paid to previous musculoskeletal injuries, as there is a high rate of recurrence if they have not been properly rehabilitated. Ideally, a physician with training and specific knowledge in the adolescent athlete population should conduct the exam. Though much attention has been placed on the detection of cardiovascular conditions that may result in sudden cardiac death, the American Heart Association does not endorse the routine use of echocardiograms or echocardiography as screening tools unless indicated by history or physical examination (Maron et al., 1996).

Treatment and Rehabilitation of Injuries

The relative lack of medical care for young athletes has resulted in injuries going undiagnosed and in diagnosed injuries not being properly rehabilitated. In 2009, only 42% of secondary schools had access to athletic trainers (NATA, 2009). Fortunately, as of 2013 approximately 60% of secondary schools now have access to athletic trainers; however, this rate is still too low when it comes to protecting the young athletic population. First, injuries that are undiagnosed can lead to serious health complications. Second, when an athlete is injured, he or she is highly susceptible to reinjury of that limb or joint over the next several years. In the end, improperly treated first time injuries or reinjury might eventually limit participation in physical activity later in life, thereby leading to other health complications (Valovich McLeod et al., 2011). New evidence also suggests that improperly rehabilitated knee and wrist injuries may increase the risk for osteoarthritis years after the initial insult (Maffulli et al., 2010). Many of these "old injuries" can be assessed during the PPE, but coaches and athletic trainers must ensure that all injuries receive proper initial and follow-up care.

Stretching Programs

As previously discussed, muscles lengthen in response to longitudinal bone growth. Therefore, to improve overall flexibility, stretching and flexibility exercises should be a routine part of all conditioning programs prior to and during the sports season. Major muscle groups, including the quadriceps, hamstrings, and low back, should typically be targeted. However, all sports involve specific muscles and movements, thus flexibility exercises should be geared to the muscles and movements most commonly performed. Stretching protocols can be valuable in improving range of motion (ROM) right after their application, but there

is limited evidence that the application of brief stretching bouts prior to activity can actually improve ROM over the long term. However, stretching activities were determined to reduce the risk of bothersome soreness (Jamtvedt et al., 2010) when compared to exercisers who did not stretch as a part of their activity plan. Therefore, stretching activities before and after sports participation should be continued; however, their limitations in preventing sports injury must be understood.

Coaching Techniques

Coaches can play a valuable role in the prevention of acute and chronic injuries among their young athletes. However, they must be knowledgeable in the fundamental techniques of their sport and know the proper principles of strength and conditioning. A basic understanding of the anatomic variations of young athletes is also helpful.

The overall training load and the progression toward more intense training early in the course of a sports season are major determinants in the development of overuse injuries, along with other factors previously discussed. In addition to placing increased stress on the muscles and joints, the body is more likely to fatigue, thus compromising form and technique. This increases the risk of injury even more. As discussed earlier, an increase in total training volume or intensity of no more than 10% per week has been suggested to provide coaches with a model of how to limit injury risk. For example, a young distance runner who begins the week running 3 miles per day would increase that to no more than 3.3 miles the next week. The same principle can be applied to young pitchers, swimmers, or gymnasts in regard to the overall length of their training sessions.

Female Athletes

At the time of the PPE, or if appropriate for a specific injury or complaint, a detailed menstrual history should be obtained from all female athletes. Any history of primary amenorrhea (absence of menses by age 16) or secondary amenorrhea (absence of menses for more than three consecutive cycles after regular monthly cycles have become established) should be further explored. Many female athletes believe that menstrual irregularities (absent menses or scant flow) during their competitive season are normal and will not perceive them as a problem unless specifically questioned. Such irregularity is typically indicative of poor nutritional intake, often the result of burning more calories than are being consumed. This energy (calorie) deficit may be unintentional (poor eating habits) or intentional (disordered eating).

Female athletes with a history of primary or secondary amenorrhea should be evaluated by a physician. Nutrition education or referral to a nutritionist may also be appropriate. Any history of previous stress fractures should also prompt a thorough training history (overload, poor technique, "too much, too soon") and a review of menstrual history and nutritional intake, because such injuries should raise suspicion for the presence of the female athlete triad (anorexia, amenorrhea, and osteoporosis).

Prescription Stimulant Medications

The increasing use of stimulant medications for the treatment of attention deficit hyperactivity disorder (ADHD) is an emerging area of uncertainty in the sports medicine field. The majority of ADHD medications (methylphenidate [Ritalin], dextroamphetamine [Dexedrine], amphetamine plus dextroamphetamine [Adderall]) are amphetamine derivatives and, therefore, are banned by the National Collegiate Athletic Association and International Olympic Committee. In addition to the benefits seen in the classroom, when given appropriate medication young athletes with ADHD also show increased ability to concentrate on tasks during athletic practices, along with improvements in balance and coordination (perhaps secondary to improved concentration) (Hickey & Fricker, 1999). The ergogenic effects of these medications on this population are not known. Currently, athletes with ADHD should continue to take their medications as prescribed, regardless of athletic activity. Unfortunately, it seems likely that over time the potential for performance enhancement may lead to abuse of these medications. Future research should further define the ergogenic potency of these medications within the ADHD population.

REVIEW QUESTIONS

1. What are the rates for lower extremity injury in females and in males?

2. What does research indicate is the primary motivating factor for children to engage in organized sports?

3. What is the most common cause reported for withdrawing from sports among high school students?

4. On average, boys will see how much of an increase in muscle mass between the ages of 10 and 17 years?

5. What is the anatomic term for the point on a long bone where large muscle–tendon units attach?

6. True or false: Changes in bone length occur more slowly than length changes in muscle–tendon structures.

7. What is the technical term for a growth plate?

8. Where can you find reliable and valid information regarding adolescents and injury?

9. True or false: Severe ligament injuries are more common in children than in adults.

10. The term *Salter-Harris fracture* refers to a type of fracture classification of what specific anatomic structure?

11. According to the text, what is the most important intrinsic factor related to youth sports injuries?

12. Define the term *cultural deconditioning* and describe how it contributes to sports injury.

13. What are the recommended steps to help reduce overtraining, inadequate rest, and early specialization?

14. True or false: Most youth sports coaches have no formal training.

15. Define the terms *osteomyelitis* and *pyomyositis*.

16. Explain briefly the guidelines on adolescent strength training in children that are presented by the American College of Sports Medicine (Faigenbaum).

17. Using the 1-RM equivalent equation presented in the text, calculate the 1-RM equivalent for 120 pounds lifted for 10 repetitions on the bench press.

SUGGESTED READINGS

Abbassi V. (1998). Growth and normal puberty. *Pediatrics.* 102:507–511.

Faigenbaum AD, Micheli LJ. (2000). Preseason conditioning for the preadolescent athlete. *Pediatr Annals.* 29:156–161.

Koester MC. (2000). Youth sports: A pediatrician's perspective on coaching and injury prevention. *J Ath Training.* 35:466–470.

Micheli LJ. (1994). The child and adolescent. In: Harries M, Williams C, Stanish WD, Micheli LJ (eds.), *Oxford Textbook of Sports Medicine* (pp. 646–652). New York, NY: Oxford University Press.

Risser WL, Risser JM, Preston D. (1990). Weight-training injuries in adolescents. *Am J Dis Child.* 144:1015–1017.

Szer IS. (1996). Musculoskeletal pain syndromes that affect adolescents. *Arch Pediatr Adolesc Med.* 150:740–747.

Webb D. (1990). Strength training in children and adolescents. *Pediatr Clin North Am.* 37:1187–1207.

REFERENCES

Adirim T, Cheng T. (2003). Overview of injuries in the young athlete. *Sports Med.* 33(1):7–581.

Caine D, Maffulli N, Caine C. (2008) Epidemiology of injury in child and adolescent sports: Injury rates, risk factors, and prevention. *Clin Sports Med.* 27:19–50.

Faigenbaum AD. (2013). Youth Strength Training: Facts and Fallacies. American College of Sports Medicine. Available: http://www.acsm.org/access-public-information/articles/2012/01/13/youth-strength-training-facts-and-fallacies.

Fernandez W, Yard E, Comstock R. (2007). Epidemiology of lower extremity injuries among U.S. high school athletes. *Acad Emerg Med.* 14(7):641–645.

Hickey G, Fricker P. (1999). Attention deficit hyperactivity disorder, CNS stimulants and sport. *Sports Med.* 27(1):11–21.

Institute for the Study of Youth Sports (ISYS). (2013). Reducing youth gang involvement through sport. Available: http://edwp.educ.msu.edu/isys/2013/wingate-university-lecture-isys-and-detroit-pal-partnership-and-reducing-youth-gang-involvement/.

Jamtvedt G, Herbert RD, Flottorp S, Odgaard-Jensen J, Håvelsrud K, Barratt A, Mathieu E, Burls A, Oxman D. (2010). A pragmatic randomised trial of stretching before and after physical activity to prevent injury and soreness. *Br J Sports Med.* 44:1002–1009.

Kelley B, Carchia C. (2013). "Hey, data data...swing!" The hidden demographics of youth sports. *ESPN The Magazine.* Available: http://espn.go.com/espn/story/_/id/9469252/hidden-demographics-youth-sports-espn-magazine.

Lavallee M. (2002). Strength training in children and adolescents. *ACSM Current Comment.* Available: http://www.acsmlearning.org/acsmweb/pdf_library/view/currentcomments/stretrai122602.pdf.

Maffulli N, Longo UG, Gougoulias N, Loppini M, Denaro V. (2010). Long-term health outcomes of youth sports injuries. *Br J Sports Med.* 44:21–25.

Maron BJ, Thompson PD, Puffer JC, McGrew CA, Strong WB, Douglas PS, Clark LT, Mitten MJ, Crawford MH,

Atkins DL, Driscoll DJ, Epstein AE. (1996). Cardiovascular preparticipation screening of competitive athletes. *Circulation.* 94(4):850–856.

Micheli L. (1991). The child athlete. In: R Cantu, L Micheli (eds.), *ACSM's Guidelines for the Team Physician* (pp. 228–241). Philadelphia: Lea & Febiger.

Morris N, Udry J. (1980). Validation of a self-administered instrument to assess stage of adolescent development. *J Youth Adolescence.* 9(3):271–280.

Mueller F, Cantu R. (2012). Catastrophic sports injury research. Twenty-ninth annual report (Fall 1982-Spring 2011). Available: http://www.unc.edu/depts/nccsi/2011Allsport.pdf.

National Athletic Trainers' Association. (2009). Athletic trainers fill a necessary niche in secondary schools. Available: http://www.nata.org/NR031209.

Oates W, Barlow C, McGrattan C, Batista V. (2011). *An Injury Prevention Curriculum for Coaches.* Available: http://www.stopsportsinjuries.org/files/coaches_curriculum_toolkit/AOS-103%20Coaches%20Curriculum%20Toolkit%20%28nm%29%202.8%5B1%5D.pdf.

Osgood RB. (1903). Lesions of the tibial tubercle occurring during adolescence. *Boston Med Surg J.* 148:114–117.

Peterson HA. (1994). Physeal fractures. Part 3. Classification. *J Pediatr Orthop.* 14:439.

Pommering TL. (n.d.). Allowing youth sports to be child's play. Available: http://www.nationwidechildrens.org/allowing-youth-sports-to-be-childs-play.

Rang M, Ogden JA. (1981). Injury to the growth mechanism of the immature skeleton. *Skeletal Radiol.* 6:237.

Rauh MJ, Koepsell TD, Rivera FP, et al. (2005). Epidemiology of musculoskeletal injuries among high school cross-country runners. *Am J Epidemiol.* 163:151–159.

Rechel J, Yard E, Comstock R. (2008). An epidemiologic comparison of high school sports injuries sustained in practice and competition. *J Athl Train.* 43(2):197–204.

Sallis JF and Patrick K. (1994). Physical activity guidelines for adolescents: Consensus statement. *Pediatric Exercise Science.* 6:302–314.

Salter RB, Harris WR. (1963). Injuries involving the epiphyseal plate. *J Bone Joint Surg.* 45A:587–622.

Statistic Brain. (2013). Youth Sports Statistics. Available: http://www.statisticbrain.com/youth-sports-statistics/.

Swenson D, Henke N, Collins C, Fields S, Comstock R. (2012). Epidemiology of United States high school sports-related fractures, 2008-09 to 2010-11. *Am J Sports Med.* 40(9):2078–2084.

Title IX Info. (2013). The living law. Available: http://www.titleix.info/History/The-Living-Law.aspx.

Valovich McLeod T, Decoster L, Loud K, Micheli L, Parker J, Sandrey M, White C. (2011). National Athletic Trainers' Association position statement: Prevention of pediatric overuse injuries. *J Athl Train.* 46(2):206–220.

Appendix 1

National Athletic Trainers' Association Position Statement: Preventing Sudden Death in Sports

Douglas J. Casa, PhD, ATC, FNATA, FACSM* (co-chair); Kevin M. Guskiewicz, PhD, ATC, FNATA, FACSM† (co-chair); Scott A. Anderson, ATC‡; Ronald W. Courson, ATC, PT, NREMT-I, CSCS§; Jonathan F. Heck, MS, ATC||; Carolyn C. Jimenez, PhD, ATC¶; Brendon P. McDermott, PhD, ATC#; Michael G. Miller, PhD, EdD, ATC, CSCS**; Rebecca L. Stearns, MA, ATC*; Erik E. Swartz, PhD, ATC, FNATA††; Katie M. Walsh, EdD, ATC‡‡

*Korey Stringer Institute, University of Connecticut, Storrs; †Matthew Gfeller Sport-Related Traumatic Brain Injury Research Center, University of North Carolina at Chapel Hill; ‡University of Oklahoma, Norman; §University of Georgia, Athens; ||Richard Stockton College, Pomona, NJ; ¶West Chester University, PA; #University of Tennessee at Chattanooga; **Western Michigan University, Kalamazoo; ††University of New Hampshire, Durham; ‡‡East Carolina University, Greenville, NC

Objective: To present recommendations for the prevention and screening, recognition, and treatment of the most common conditions resulting in sudden death in organized sports.

Background: Cardiac conditions, head injuries, neck injuries, exertional heat stroke, exertional sickling, asthma, and other factors (eg, lightning, diabetes) are the most common causes of death in athletes.

Recommendations: These guidelines are intended to provide relevant information on preventing sudden death in sports and to give specific recommendations for certified athletic trainers and others participating in athletic health care.

Key Words: asthma, cardiac conditions, diabetes, exertional heat stroke, exertional hyponatremia, exertional sickling, head injuries, neck injuries, lightning safety

Sudden death in sports and physical activity has a variety of causes. The 10 conditions covered in this position statement are

- Asthma
- Catastrophic brain injuries
- Cervical spine injuries
- Diabetes
- Exertional heat stroke
- Exertional hyponatremia
- Exertional sickling
- Head-down contact in football
- Lightning
- Sudden cardiac arrest

(Order does not indicate rate of occurrence.)

Reprinted from Journal of Athletic Training 2012:47(1):96–118 © by the National Athletic Trainers' Association, Inc www.nata.org/jat.

Recognizing the many reasons for sudden death allows us to create and implement emergency action plans (EAPs) that provide detailed guidelines for prevention, recognition, treatment, and return to play (RTP). Unlike collegiate and professional teams, which usually have athletic trainers (ATs) available, nearly half of high schools as well as numerous other athletic settings lack the appropriate medical personnel to put these guidelines into practice and instead rely on the athletic director, team coach, or strength and conditioning specialist to do so.

To provide appropriate care for athletes, one must be familiar with a large number of illnesses and conditions in order to properly guide the athlete, determine when emergency treatment is needed, and distinguish among similar signs and symptoms that may reflect a variety of potentially fatal circumstances. For the patient to have the best possible outcome, correct and prompt emergency care is critical; delaying care until the ambulance arrives may result in permanent disability or death. Therefore, we urgently advocate training coaches in first aid, cardiopulmonary resuscitation (CPR), and automated external defibrillator (AED) use, so that they can provide treatment until a medical professional arrives; however, such training is inadequate for the successful and complete care of the conditions described in this position statement. Saving the life of a young athlete should not be a coach's responsibility or liability.

For this reason, we also urge every high school to have an AT available to promptly take charge of a medical emergency. As licensed medical professionals, ATs receive thorough training in preventing, recognizing, and treating critical situations in the physically active. Each AT works closely with a physician to create and apply appropriate EAPs and RTP guidelines.

Throughout this position statement, each recommendation is labeled with a specific level of evidence based on the Strength of Recommendation Taxonomy (SORT).[1] This taxonomy takes into account the quality, quantity, and consistency of the evidence in support of each recommendation: Category A represents consistent good-quality evidence, B represents inconsistent or limited-quality or limited-quantity evidence, and C represents recommendations based on consensus, usual practice, opinion, or case series.

The following rules apply to every EAP:

1. Every organization that sponsors athletic activities should have a written, structured EAP. *Evidence Category: B*

2. The EAP should be developed and coordinated with local EMS staff, school public safety officials, onsite first responders, school medical staff, and school administrators. *Evidence Category: B*

3. The EAP should be specific to each athletic venue. *Evidence Category: B*

4. The EAP should be practiced at least annually with all those who may be involved. *Evidence Category: B*

Those responsible for arranging organized sport activities must generate an EAP to directly focus on these items:

1. Instruction, preparation, and expectations of the athletes, parents or guardians, sport coaches, strength and conditioning coaches, and athletic directors.

2. Health care professionals who will provide medical care during practices and games and supervise the execution of the EAP with respect to medical care.

3. Precise prevention, recognition, treatment, and RTP policies for the common causes of sudden death in athletes.

The EAP should be coordinated and supervised by the onsite AT. A sports organization that does not have a medical supervisor, such as an AT, present at practices and games and as part of the medical infrastructure runs the risk of legal liability. Athletes participating in an organized sport have a reasonable expectation of receiving appropriate emergency care, and the standards for EAP development have also become more consistent and rigorous at the youth level. Therefore, the absence of such safeguards may render the organization sponsoring the sporting event legally liable.

The purpose of this position statement is to provide an overview of the critical information for each condition (prevention, recognition, treatment, and RTP) and indicate how this information should dictate the basic policies and procedures regarding the most common causes of sudden death in sports. Our ultimate goal is to guide the development of policies and procedures that can minimize the occurrence of catastrophic incidents in athletes. All current position statements of the National Athletic Trainers' Association (NATA) are listed in the Appendix.

Asthma

Recommendations

Prevention and Screening

1. Athletes who may have or are suspected of having asthma should undergo a thorough medical history and physical examination.[2] *Evidence Category: B*

2. Athletes with asthma should participate in a structured warmup protocol before exercise or sport activity to decrease reliance on medications and minimize asthmatic symptoms and exacerbations.[3] *Evidence Category: B*

3. The sports medicine staff should educate athletes with asthma about the use of asthma medications as prophylaxis before exercise, spirometry devices, asthma triggers, recognition of signs and symptoms, and compliance with monitoring the condition and taking medication as prescribed. *Evidence Category: C*

Recognition

4. The sports medicine staff should be aware of the major asthma signs and symptoms (ie, confusion, sweating, drowsiness, forced expiratory volume in the first second [FEV_1] of less than 40%, low level of oxygen saturation, use of accessory muscles for breathing, wheezing, cyanosis, coughing, hypotension, bradycardia or tachycardia, mental status changes, loss of consciousness, inability to lie supine, inability to speak coherently, or agitation) and other conditions (eg, vocal cord dysfunction, allergies, smoking) that can cause exacerbations.[4,5] *Evidence Category: A*

5. Spirometry tests at rest and with exercise and a field test (in the sport-specific environment) should be conducted on athletes suspected of having asthma to help diagnose the condition.[2,6] *Evidence Category: B*

6. An increase of 12% or more in the FEV_1 after administration of an inhaled bronchodilator also indicates reversible airway disease and may be used as a diagnostic criterion for asthma.[7]

Treatment

7. For an acute asthmatic exacerbation, the athlete should use a short-acting β_2-agonist to relieve symptoms. In a severe exacerbation, rapid sequential administrations of a β_2-agonist may be needed. If 3 administrations of medication do not relieve distress, the athlete should be referred promptly to an appropriate health care facility.[8] *Evidence Category: A*

8. Inhaled corticosteroids or leukotriene inhibitors can be used for asthma prophylaxis and control. A long-acting β_2-agonist can be combined with other medications to help control asthma.[9] *Evidence Category: B*

9. Supplemental oxygen should be offered to improve the athlete's available oxygenation during asthma attacks.[10] *Evidence Category: B*

10. Lung function should be monitored with a peak flow meter. Values should be compared with baseline lung volume values and should be at least 80% of predicted values before the athlete may participate in activities.[11] *Evidence Category: B*

11. If feasible, the athlete should be removed from an environment with factors (eg, smoke, allergens) that may have caused the asthma attack. *Evidence Category: C*

12. In the athlete with asthma, physical activity should be initiated at low aerobic levels and exercise intensity gradually increased while monitoring occurs for recurrent asthma symptoms. *Evidence Category: C*

Background and Literature Review

Definition, Epidemiology, and Pathophysiology. In 2009, asthma was thought to affect approximately 22 million people in the United States, including approximately 6 million children.[4] *Asthma* is a disease in which the airways become inflamed and airflow is restricted.[4] Airway inflammation, which may lead to airway hyperresponsiveness and narrowing, is associated with mast cell production and activation and increased number of eosinophils and other inflammatory cells.[2,3] Cellular and mediator events cause inflammation, bronchial constriction via smooth muscle contraction, and acute swelling from fluid shifts. Chronic airway inflammation may cause remodeling and thickening of the bronchiolar walls.[12,13]

Clinical signs of asthma include confusion, sweating, drowsiness, use of accessory muscles for breathing, wheezing, coughing, chest tightness, and shortness of breath. Asthma may be present during specific times of the year, vary with the type of environment, occur during or after exercise, and be triggered by respiratory infections, allergens, pollutants, aspirin, nonsteroidal anti-inflammatory drugs, inhaled irritants, exposure to cold, and exercise.[5]

Prevention. Athletes suspected of having asthma should undergo a thorough health history examination and preparticipation physical examination. Unfortunately, the sensitivity and specificity of the medical history are not known, and this evaluation may not be the best method for identifying asthma.[14]

Performing warmup activities before sport participation can help prevent asthma attacks. With a structured warmup protocol, the athlete may experience a refractory period of as long as 2 hours, potentially decreasing the risk of an exacerbation or decreasing reliance on medications.[6] In addition, the sports medicine team should provide education to assist the athlete in recognizing asthma signs and symptoms, understanding how to use medication as prescribed (including potential adverse effects and barriers to taking medications, which can include failure to recognize the importance of controlling asthma, failure to recognize the potential severity of the condition, medication costs, difficulty obtaining medications, inability to integrate treatment of the disease with daily life, and distrust of the medical establishment), and using spirometry equipment correctly.[2,4,5]

Recognition. Athletes with asthma may display the following signs and symptoms: confusion, sweating, drowsiness, FEV$_1$ of less than 40%, low level of oxygen saturation, use of accessory muscles for breathing, wheezing, cyanosis, coughing, hypotension, bradycardia or tachycardia, mental status changes, loss of consciousness, inability to lie supine, inability to speak coherently,

or agitation.[2,4,5] Peak expiratory flow rates of less than 80% of the personal best or daily variability greater than 20% of the morning value indicate lack of control of asthma. The sports medicine staff should consider testing all athletes with asthma using a sport-specific and environment-specific exercise challenge protocol to assist in determining triggers of airway hyperresponsiveness.[6]

Treatment. Treatment for those with asthma includes recognition of exacerbating factors and the proper use of asthma medications (**Figure 1**). A short-acting β$_2$-agonist should be readily available; onset of action is typically 5 to 15 minutes, so the medication can be readministered 1 to 3 times per hour if needed.[10] If breathing difficulties continue after 3 treatments in 1 hour or the athlete continues to have any signs or symptoms of acute respiratory distress, referral to an acute or urgent care facility should ensue. For breathing distress, the sports medicine team should provide supplemental oxygen to help maintain blood oxygen saturation above 92%.[10]

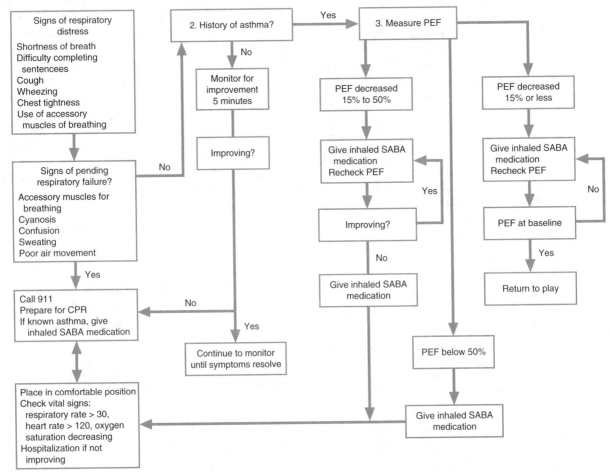

FIGURE 1 Asthma pharmacologic management. Abbreviations: CPR, cardiopulmonary resuscitation; PEF, peak expiratory flow; SABA, short-acting β$_2$-agonist. Casa DJ, *Preventing Sudden Death in Sport and Physical Activity*, 2012: Jones & Bartlett Learning, Sudbury, MA. www.jblearning.com. Reprinted with permission.

Proper use of inhaled corticosteroids can decrease the frequency and severity of asthma exacerbations while improving lung function and reducing hyperresponsiveness and the need for short-acting β_2-agonists.[15,16] Leukotriene modifiers can be used to control allergen-, aspirin-, or exercise-induced bronchoconstriction and decrease asthma exacerbations.[17]

Return to Play. No specific guidelines describe RTP after an asthma attack in an athlete. However, in general, the athlete should first be asymptomatic and progress through graded increases in exercise activity. Lung function should be monitored with a peak flow meter and compared with baseline measures to determine when asthma is sufficiently controlled to allow the athlete to resume participation.[11] Where possible, the sports medicine staff should identify and treat asthmatic triggers, such as allergic rhinitis, before the athlete returns to participation.

Catastrophic Brain Injuries

Recommendations

Prevention

1. The AT is responsible for coordinating educational sessions with athletes and coaches to teach the recognition of concussion (ie, specific signs and symptoms), serious nature of traumatic brain injuries in sport, and importance of reporting concussions and not participating while symptomatic. *Evidence Category: C*

2. The AT should enforce the standard use of certified helmets while also educating athletes, coaches, and parents that although such helmets meet a standard for helping to prevent catastrophic head injuries, they do not prevent cerebral concussions. *Evidence Category: B*

Recognition

3. The AT should incorporate the use of a comprehensive objective concussion assessment battery that includes symptom, cognitive, and balance measures. Each of these represents only one piece of the concussion puzzle and should not be used in isolation to manage concussion. *Evidence Category: A*

Treatment and Management

4. A comprehensive medical management plan for acute care of an athlete with a potential intracranial hemorrhage or diffuse cerebral edema should be implemented. *Evidence Category: B*

5. If the athlete's symptoms persist or worsen or the level of consciousness deteriorates after a concussion, the patient should be immediately referred to a physician trained in concussion management. *Evidence Category: B*

6. Oral and written instructions for home care should be given to the athlete and to a responsible adult. *Evidence Category: C*

7. Returning an athlete to participation after a head injury should follow a graduated progression that begins once the athlete is completely asymptomatic. *Evidence Category: C*

8. The athlete should be monitored periodically throughout and after these sessions to determine whether any symptoms develop or increase in intensity. *Evidence Category: C*

Background and Literature Review

Definition, Epidemiology, and Pathophysiology. Cerebral concussion is classified as mild traumatic brain injury and often affects athletes in both helmeted and nonhelmeted sports.[18,19] The Centers for Disease Control and Prevention estimated that 1.6 to 3.8 million sport-related concussive injuries occur annually in the United States.[20] Although they are rare, severe catastrophic traumatic brain injuries, such as subdural and epidural hematomas and malignant cerebral edema (ie, second-impact syndrome), result in more fatalities from direct trauma than any other sport injury. When these injuries do occur, brain swelling or pooling of blood (or both) increases intracranial pressure; if this condition is not treated quickly, brainstem herniation and respiratory arrest can follow. Catastrophic brain injuries rank second only to cardiac-related injuries and illnesses as the most common cause of fatalities in football players.[21] However, the National Center for Catastrophic Sport Injury Research reported that fatal brain injuries have occurred in almost every sport, including baseball, lacrosse, soccer, track, and wrestling.[22] For a catastrophic brain injury such as second-impact syndrome, which has a mortality rate approaching 50% and a morbidity rate nearing 100%, prevention is of the utmost importance.

Prevention. Preventing catastrophic brain injuries in sports, such as skull fractures, intracranial hemorrhages, and diffuse cerebral edema (second-impact syndrome), must involve the following: (1) prevention and education about traumatic brain injury for athletes, coaches, and parents; (2) enforcing the standard use of sport-specific and certified equipment (eg, National Operating Committee on Standards for Athletic Equipment [NOCSAE] or Hockey Equipment Certification Council, Inc [HECC]–certified helmets); (3) use of comprehensive, objective baseline and postinjury assessment measures; (4) administration of home care and referral instructions emphasizing the monitoring and management of deteriorating signs and symptoms; (5) use of systematic and monitored graduated RTP progressions; (6) clearly documented records of the evaluation and management of the injury to help guide a sound RTP decision; and (7) proper preparedness for on-field medical management of a serious head injury.

Prevention begins with education. The AT is responsible for coordinating educational sessions with athletes and coaches to teach the recognition of concussion (ie, specific signs and symptoms), serious nature of traumatic brain injuries in sport, and importance of reporting their injuries and not participating while symptomatic. During this process, athletes who are at risk for subsequent concussion or catastrophic injury should be identified and counseled about the risk of subsequent injury.

As recommended in the NATA position statement on management of sport-related concussion,[23] the AT should enforce the standard use of helmets for preventing catastrophic head injuries and reducing the severity of cerebral concussions in sports that require helmet protection (eg, football, men's lacrosse, ice hockey, baseball, softball). The AT should ensure that all equipment meets NOCSAE, HECC, or American Society for Testing and Materials (ASTM) standards. A poorly fitted helmet is limited in the amount of protection it can provide, and the AT must play a role in enforcing the proper fit and use of the helmet. Protective sport helmets are designed primarily to help prevent catastrophic injuries (eg, skull fractures and intracranial hematomas) and not concussions. A helmet that protects the head from a skull fracture does not adequately prevent the rotational and shearing forces that lead to many concussions,[24] a fact that many people misunderstand.

Recognition. The use of objective concussion measures during preseason and postinjury assessments helps the AT and physician accurately identify deficits associated with the injury and track recovery. However, neuropsychological testing is only one component of the evaluation process and should not be used as a standalone tool to diagnose or manage concussion or to make RTP decisions after concussion. Including objective measures of cognitive function and balance prevents premature clearance of an athlete who reports being symptom free but has persistent deficits that are not easily detected through the clinical examination.

The concussion assessment battery should include a combination of tests for cognition, balance, and self-reported symptoms known to be affected by concussion. Because many athletes (an estimated 49% to 75%)[25,26] do not report their concussions, this objective assessment model is important. The sensitivity of this comprehensive battery, including a graded symptom checklist, computerized neuropsychological test, and balance test, reached 94%,[27] which is consistent with previous reports.[28,29]

Multiple concussion assessment tools are available, including low-technology and high-technology balance tests, brief paper-and-pencil cognitive tests, and computerized cognitive tests. As of 2010, the National Football League, National Hockey League, and National Collegiate Athletic Association require an objective assessment as part of a written concussion management protocol. By using objective measures, which were endorsed by the Third International Consensus Statement on Concussion in Sport (Zurich, 2008),[30,31] ATs and physicians are better equipped to manage concussion than by relying solely on subjective reports from the athlete. Additionally, the often hidden deficits associated with concussion and gradual deterioration that may indicate more serious brain trauma or postconcussion syndrome (ie, symptoms lasting longer than 4 weeks) may be detected with these tools.

Treatment. Once the athlete has been thoroughly evaluated and identified as having sustained a concussion, a comprehensive medical management plan should be implemented. This begins with making a determination about whether the patient should be immediately referred to a physician or sent home with specific observation instructions. Although this plan should include serial evaluations and observations by the AT (as outlined earlier), continued monitoring of postconcussion signs and symptoms by those with whom the athlete lives is both important and practical. If symptoms persist or worsen or the level of consciousness deteriorates after a concussion, the athlete should be immediately referred to a medical facility. To assist with this, oral and written instructions for home care should be given to the athlete and to a responsible adult (eg, parents or roommate) who will observe and supervise the athlete during the acute phase of the concussion while at home or in the dormitory. The AT and physician should agree on a standard concussion home instruction form similar to the one presented in the NATA position statement[23] and Zurich guidelines.[30,31]

The proper preparedness for on-field and sideline medical management of a head injury becomes paramount if the athlete has a more serious and quickly deteriorating condition. If the athlete presents with a Glasgow coma score of less than 8 or other indications of more involved brain or brainstem impairment appear (eg, posturing, altered breathing pattern), the AT or other members of the sports medicine team must be prepared to perform manual ventilations through either endotracheal intubation or bag-valve-mouth resuscitation. These procedures should be initiated if the athlete is not oxygenating well (ie, becoming dusky or blue, ventilating incompletely and slower than normal at 12 to 15 breaths per minute).[32]

Normal end tidal carbon dioxide partial pressure of 35–45 mm Hg usually result from a bagging rate of 12 breaths per minute. Hyperventilation may be indicated if the athlete demonstrates obvious signs of brainstem herniation (eg, "blown" pupil or posturing). In the event of impending cerebral herniation, increasing the rate to about 20 breaths per minute will achieve the objective of reducing the end tidal carbon dioxide partial pressure below the recommended 35 mm Hg. Additionally, the sports medicine team should aim to reduce intracranial pressure by elevating the head to at least 30° and ensuring that the head and neck are maintained in the midline position to optimize venous outflow from the brain. Intravenous (IV) diuretics such as mannitol (0.5 to 1.0 g/kg) may also decrease intracranial pressure but would typically be administered in a controlled medical environment by personnel trained in these techniques.[32] Obviously, being prepared for immediate transfer to a medical facility is extremely important under these conditions.

Return to Play. Returning an athlete to participation should follow a graduated RTP progression (**Table 1**). If the exertional activities do not produce acute symptoms, he or she may progress to the next step. No more than 2 steps should be performed on the same day, which allows monitoring of both acute (during the activity) and delayed (within 24 hours after the activity) symptoms. The athlete may advance to step 5 and return to full participation once he or she has remained asymptomatic for 24 hours after step 4 of the protocol. The athlete should be monitored periodically throughout and after these sessions with objective assessment measures to determine whether an increase in intensity is warranted. If the athlete's symptoms return at any point during the RTP progression, at least 24 hours without symptoms must pass before the protocol is reintroduced, beginning at step 1.

Although some state concussion laws have allowed provisions for allied health care professionals to make the RTP decision, it is recommended that a physician with training and experience in concussion management be involved in a structured team approach. A concussion management policy outlining the roles and responsibilities of each member of the sports medicine team should

TABLE 1	
GRADUATED RETURN-TO-PLAY SAMPLE PROTOCOL	
Exertion Step	**Activities**
1.	20-min stationary bike at 10–14 mph (16–23 kph)
2.	Interval bike: 30-s sprint at 18–20 mph (29–32 kph), 30-s recovery × 10 repetitions; body weight circuit: squats, push-ups, sit-ups × 20 s × 3 repetitions
3.	60-yd (55-m) shuttle run × 10 repetitions with 40-s rest, plyometric workout: 10-yd (9-m) bounding, 10 medicine ball throws, 10 vertical jumps × 3 repetitions; noncontact, sport-specific drills × 15 min
4.	Limited, controlled return to practice with monitoring for symptoms
5.	Full sport participation in practice

be adopted. At a minimum, the AT should document all pertinent information surrounding the evaluation and management of any suspected concussions, including (a) mechanism of injury; (b) initial signs and symptoms; (c) state of consciousness; (d) findings on serial testing of symptoms, neuropsychological function, and balance (noting any deficits compared with baseline); (e) instructions given to the athlete, parent, or roommate; (f) recommendations provided by the physician; (g) graduated RTP progression, including dates and specific activities involved in the athlete's return to participation; and (h) relevant information on the player's history of prior concussion and associated recovery patterns.[23] This level of detail can help prevent a premature return to participation and a catastrophic brain injury such as second-impact syndrome.

Cervical Spine Injuries

Recommendations

Prevention

1. Athletic trainers should be familiar with sport-specific causes of catastrophic cervical spine injury and understand the physiologic responses in spinal cord injury. *Evidence Category: C*

2. Coaches and athletes should be educated about the mechanisms of catastrophic spine injuries and pertinent safety rules enacted for the prevention of cervical spine injuries. *Evidence Category: C*

3. Corrosion-resistant hardware should be used in helmets, helmets should be regularly maintained throughout a season, and helmets should undergo regular reconditioning and recertification.[33] *Evidence Category: B*

4. Emergency department personnel should become familiar with proper athletic equipment removal, seeking education from sports medicine professionals regarding appropriate methods to minimize motion. *Evidence Category: C*

Recognition

5. During initial assessment, the presence of any of the following, alone or in combination, requires the initiation of the spine injury management protocol: unconsciousness or altered level of consciousness, bilateral neurologic findings or complaints, significant midline spine pain with or without palpation, or obvious spinal column deformity.[34–39] *Evidence Category: A*

Treatment and Management

6. The cervical spine should be in neutral position, and manual cervical spine stabilization should be applied immediately.[40,41] *Evidence Category: B*

7. Traction must not be applied to the cervical spine.[42,43] *Evidence Category: B*

8. Immediate attempts should be made to expose the airway. *Evidence Category: C*

9. If rescue breathing becomes necessary, the person with the most training and experience should establish an airway and begin rescue breathing using the safest technique.[44,45] *Evidence Category: B*

10. If the spine is not in a neutral position, rescuers should realign the cervical spine.[46,47] However, the presence or development of any of the following, alone or in combination, is a contraindication to realignment[45,48]: pain caused or increased by movement, neurologic symptoms, muscle spasm, airway compromise, physical difficulty repositioning the spine, encountered resistance, or apprehension expressed by the patient. *Evidence Category: B*

11. Manual stabilization of the head should be converted to immobilization using external devices such as foam head blocks.[47,49] Whenever possible, manual stabilization[50] is resumed after the application of external devices. *Evidence Category: B*

12. Athletes should be immobilized with a long spine board or other full-body immobilization device.[51,52] *Evidence Category: B*

Equipment-Laden Athletes

13. The primary acute treatment goals in equipment-laden athletes are to ensure that the cervical spine is immobilized in neutral and vital life functions are accessible. Removal of helmet and shoulder pads in any equipment-intensive sport should be deferred[53–56] until the athlete has been transported to an emergency medical facility except in 3 circumstances[57]: the helmet is not properly fitted to prevent movement of the head independent of the helmet, the equipment prevents neutral alignment of the cervical spine, or the equipment prevents airway or chest access.[53,54,58] *Evidence Category: C*

14. Full face-mask removal using established tools and techniques[59–61] is executed once the decision has been made to immobilize and transport. *Evidence Category: C*

15. If possible, a team physician or AT should accompany the athlete to the hospital. *Evidence Category: C*

16. Remaining protective equipment should be removed by appropriately trained professionals in the emergency department. *Evidence Category: C*

Background and Literature Review

Definition, Epidemiology, and Pathophysiology. A catastrophic cervical spinal cord injury occurs with structural distortion of the cervical spinal column and is associated with actual or potential damage to the spinal cord.[62] The spinal injury that carries the greatest risk of immediate sudden death for the athlete occurs when the damage is both severe enough and at a high enough level in the spinal column (above C5) to affect the spinal cord's ability to transmit respiratory or circulatory control from the brain.[63,64] The priority in these situations is simply to support the basic life functions of breathing and circulation. Unfortunately, even if an athlete survives the initial acute management phase of the injury, the risk of death persists because of the complex biochemical cascade of events that occurs in the injured spinal cord during the initial 24 to 72 hours after injury.[64] Because of this risk, efficient acute care, transport, diagnosis, and treatment are critical in preventing sudden death in a patient with a catastrophic cervical spine injury.

Treatment and Management. A high level of evidence (ie, prospective randomized trials) on this topic is rare, and technology, equipment, and techniques will continue to evolve, but the primary goals offered in the NATA position statement on acute management of the cervical spine—injured athlete[65] remain the same: create as little motion as possible and complete the steps of the EAP as rapidly as is appropriate to facilitate support of basic life functions and prepare for transport to the nearest emergency treatment facility.

Additional complications can affect the care of the spine-injured athlete in an equipment-intensive sport when rescuers may need to remove protective equipment that limits access to the airway or chest. Knowing how to deal properly with protective equipment during the immediate care of an athlete with a potential catastrophic cervical spine injury can greatly influence the outcome. Regardless of the sport or the equipment, 2 principles should guide management of the equipment-laden athlete with a potential cervical spine injury:

1. Exposure and access to vital life functions (eg, airway, chest for CPR, or use of an AED) must be established or easily achieved in a reasonable and acceptable manner.

2. Neutral alignment of the cervical spine should be maintained while allowing as little motion at the head and neck as possible.

Return to Play. Return to play after cervical spine injury is highly variable and may be permitted only after complete tissue healing, neurologic recovery, and clearance by a physician. Factors considered for RTP include the level of injury, type of injury, number of levels fused for stability, cervical stenosis, and activity.[66]

Diabetes Mellitus

Recommendations

Prevention

1. Each athlete with diabetes should have a diabetes care plan that includes blood glucose monitoring and insulin guidelines, treatment guidelines for hypoglycemia and hyperglycemia, and emergency contact information. *Evidence Category: C*

2. Prevention strategies for hypoglycemia include blood glucose monitoring, carbohydrate supplementation, and insulin adjustments. *Evidence Category: B*

3. Prevention strategies for hyperglycemia are described by the American Diabetes Association (ADA) and include blood glucose monitoring, insulin adjustments, and urine testing for ketone bodies.[67] *Evidence Category: C*

Recognition

4. Hypoglycemia typically presents with tachycardia, sweating, palpitations, hunger, nervousness, headache, trembling, or dizziness; in severe cases, loss of consciousness and death can occur. *Evidence Category: C*

5. Hyperglycemia can present with or without ketosis. Typical signs and symptoms of hyperglycemia without ketosis include nausea, dehydration, reduced cognitive performance, feelings of sluggishness, and fatigue. *Evidence Category: C*

6. Hyperglycemia with ketoacidosis may include the signs and symptoms listed earlier as well as Kussmaul breathing (abnormally deep, very rapid sighing respirations characteristic of diabetic ketoacidosis), fruity odor to the breath, unusual fatigue, sleepiness, loss of appetite, increased thirst, and frequent urination. *Evidence Category: C*

Treatment and Management

7. Mild hypoglycemia (ie, the athlete is conscious and able to swallow and follow directions) is treated by administering approximately 10–15 g of carbohydrates (examples include 4–8 glucose tablets or 2 tablespoons of honey) and reassessing blood glucose levels immediately and 15 minutes later. *Evidence Category: C*

8. Severe hypoglycemia (ie, the athlete is unconscious or unable to swallow or follow directions) is a medical emergency, requiring activation of emergency medical services (EMS) and, if the health care provider is properly trained, administering glucagon. *Evidence Category: C*

9. Athletic trainers should follow the ADA guidelines for athletes exercising during hyperglycemic periods. *Evidence Category: C*

10. Physicians should determine a safe blood glucose range to return an athlete to play after an episode of mild hypoglycemia or hyperglycemia. *Evidence Category: C*

Background and Literature Review

Definition, Epidemiology, and Pathophysiology. Diabetes mellitus is a chronic metabolic disorder characterized by hyperglycemia, caused by either absolute insulin deficiency or resistance to the action of insulin at the cellular level, which results in the inability to regulate blood glucose levels within the normal range of 70–110 mg/dL. Type 1 diabetes is an autoimmune disorder stemming from a combination of genetic and environmental factors. The autoimmune response is often triggered by an environmental event, such as a virus, and it targets the insulin-secreting beta cells of the pancreas. When beta cell mass is reduced by approximately 80%, the pancreas is no longer able to secrete sufficient insulin to compensate for hepatic glucose output.[67,68]

Prevention. Although the literature supports physical activity for people with type 1 diabetes, exercise training and competition can result in major disturbances to blood glucose management. Extreme glycemic fluctuations (severe hypoglycemia or hyperglycemia with ketoacidosis) can lead to sudden death in athletes with type 1 diabetes mellitus.[69–71] Prevention of these potentially life-threatening events begins with the creation of the diabetes care plan by a physician. The plan should identify blood glucose targets for practices and games, including exclusion thresholds; strategies to prevent exercise-associated hypoglycemia, hyperglycemia, and ketosis; a list of medications used for glycemic control; signs, symptoms, and treatment protocols for hypoglycemia, hyperglycemia, and ketosis; and emergency contact information.[72]

Preventing hypoglycemia relies on a 3-pronged approach of frequent blood glucose monitoring, carbohydrate supplementation, and insulin adjustments. The athlete should check blood glucose levels 2 or 3 times before, every 30 minutes during, and every other hour up to 4 hours after exercise. Carbohydrates should be eaten before, during, and after exercise; the quantity the athlete ingests depends on the prevailing blood glucose level and exercise intensity. Finally, some athletes may use insulin adjustments to prevent hypoglycemia. These adjustments vary depending on the method of insulin delivery (insulin pump versus multiple daily injections), prevailing blood glucose level, and exercise intensity.[67,68,73,74]

Athletes with type 1 diabetes may also experience hyperglycemia, with or without ketosis, during exercise. Hyperglycemia during exercise is related to several factors, including exercise intensity[75,76] and the psychological stress of competition.[77] When the insulin level is adequate, these episodes of hyperglycemia are transient. However, when the insulin level is insufficient, ketosis

can occur. Exercise is contraindicated when ketones are present in the urine. Athletic trainers should know the ADA guidelines for athletes exercising during an episode of hyperglycemia.[67] In addition, the athlete's physician should determine the need for insulin adjustments during hyperglycemic periods.

Recognition. Signs and symptoms of hypoglycemia typically occur when blood glucose levels fall below 70 mg/dL (3.9 mmol/L). Early symptoms include tachycardia, sweating, palpitations, hunger, nervousness, headache, trembling, and dizziness. These symptoms are related to the release of epinephrine and acetylcholine. As the glucose level continues to fall, symptoms of brain neuronal glucose deprivation occur, including blurred vision, fatigue, difficulty thinking, loss of motor control, aggressive behavior, seizures, convulsions, and loss of consciousness. If hypoglycemia is prolonged, severe brain damage and even death can occur. Athletic trainers should be aware that the signs and symptoms of hypoglycemia are individualized and be prepared to act accordingly.[78–80]

Although the signs and symptoms of hyperglycemia may vary from one athlete to another, they include nausea, dehydration, reduced cognitive performance, slowing of visual reaction time, and feelings of sluggishness and fatigue. The signs and symptoms of hyperglycemia with ketoacidosis may include those listed earlier as well as Kussmaul breathing, fruity odor to the breath, sleepiness, inattentiveness, loss of appetite, increased thirst, and frequent urination. With severe ketoacidosis, the level of consciousness may be reduced. Athletic trainers should also be aware that some athletes with type 1 diabetes intentionally train and compete in a hyperglycemic state (above 180 mg/dL [10 mmol/L]) to avoid hypoglycemia. Competing in a hyperglycemic state places the athlete at risk for dehydration, reduced athletic performance, and possibly ketosis.[67,81]

Treatment and Management. Treatment guidelines for mild and severe cases of hypoglycemia are shown in **Table 2**.[82,83] The ADA provides guidelines for exercise during hyperglycemic periods. If the fasting blood glucose level is ≥250 mg/dL (≥13.9 mmol/L), the athlete should test his or her urine for the presence of ketones. If ketones are present, exercise is contraindicated. If the blood glucose value is ≥300 mg/dL (≥16.7 mmol/L) and without ketones, the athlete may exercise with caution and continue to monitor blood glucose levels. Athletes should work with their physicians to determine the need for insulin adjustments for periods of hyperglycemia before, during, and after exercise.[67]

Return to Play. The literature does not address specific RTP guidelines after hypoglycemic or hyperglycemic events. Therefore, RTP for an athlete varies with the individual and becomes easier as the AT works with the athlete

TABLE 2

TREATMENT GUIDELINES FOR MILD AND SEVERE HYPOGLYCEMIA[76,77]

Mild Hypoglycemia

1. Give 10–15 g of fast-acting carbohydrate. Example: 4–8 glucose tablets, 2 Tbsp honey.
2. Measure blood glucose level.
3. Wait 15 min and remeasure blood glucose level.
4. If blood glucose level remains low, administer another 10–15 g of fast-acting carbohydrate.
5. Recheck blood glucose level in 15 min.
6. If blood glucose level does not return to normal after second dose of carbohydrate, activate EMS.
7. Once blood glucose level normalizes, provide a snack (eg, sandwich, bagel).

Severe Hypoglycemia

1. Activate EMS.
2. Prepare glucagon for injection, following directions in glucagon kit.
3. Once athlete is conscious and able to swallow, provide food.

Abbreviation: EMS, emergency medical services. Revised with permission from Jimenez CC, Corcoran MH, Crawley JT, et al. National Athletic Trainers' Association position statement: management of the athlete with type I diabetes mellitus. *J Athl Train*. 2007;42(4):536–545.

on a regular basis and learns how his or her blood glucose reacts to exercise and insulin and glucose doses. The athlete should demonstrate a stable blood glucose level that is within the normal range before RTP. Athletic trainers working with new athletes should seek guidance from the athlete, athlete's physician, and athlete's parents to gain insight on how the athlete has been able to best control the blood glucose level during exercise.

Exertional Heat Stroke

Recommendations

Prevention

1. In conjunction with preseason screening, athletes should be questioned about risk factors for heat illness or a history of heat illness. *Evidence Category: C*

2. Special considerations and modifications are needed for those wearing protective equipment during periods of high environmental stress. *Evidence Category: B*

3. Athletes should be acclimatized to the heat gradually over a period of 7 to 14 days. *Evidence Category: B*

4. Athletes should maintain a consistent level of euhydration and replace fluids lost through sweat during games and practices. Athletes should have free access to readily available fluids at all times, not only during designated breaks. *Evidence Category: B*

5. The sports medicine staff must educate relevant personnel (eg, coaches, administrators, security guards, EMS staff, athletes) about preventing exertional heat stroke (EHS) and the policies and procedures that are to be followed in the event of an incident. Signs and symptoms of a medical emergency should also be reviewed. *Evidence Category: C*

Recognition

6. The 2 main criteria for diagnosis of EHS are (1) core body temperature of greater than 104° to 105°F (40.0° to 40.5°C) taken via a rectal thermometer soon after collapse and (2) CNS dysfunction (including disorientation, confusion, dizziness, vomiting, diarrhea, loss of balance, staggering, irritability, irrational or unusual behavior, apathy, aggressiveness, hysteria, delirium, collapse, loss of consciousness, and coma). *Evidence Category: B*

7. Rectal temperature and gastrointestinal temperature (if available) are the only methods proven valid for accurate temperature measurement in a patient with EHS. Inferior temperature assessment devices should not be relied on in the absence of a valid device. *Evidence Category: B*

Treatment

8. Core body temperature must be reduced to less than 102°F (38.9°C) as soon as possible to limit morbidity and mortality. Cold-water immersion is the fastest cooling modality. If that is not available, cold-water dousing or wet ice towel rotation may be used to assist with cooling, but these methods have not been shown to be as effective as cold- water immersion. Athletes should be cooled first and then transported to a hospital unless cooling and proper medical care are unavailable onsite. *Evidence Category: B*

9. Current suggestions include a period of no activity, an asymptomatic state, and normal blood enzyme levels before the athlete begins a gradual return-to-activity progression under direct medical supervision. This progression should start at low intensity in a cool environment and slowly advance to high-intensity exercise in a warm environment. *Evidence Category: C*

Background and Literature Review

Definition, Epidemiology, and Pathophysiology. Exertional heat stroke is classified as a core body temperature of greater than 104° to 105°F (40.0° to 40.5°C) with associated CNS dysfunction.[84–87] The CNS dysfunction may present as disorientation, confusion, dizziness, vomiting, diarrhea, loss of balance, staggering, irritability, irrational or unusual behavior, apathy, aggressiveness, hysteria, delirium, collapse, loss of consciousness, and coma. Other signs and symptoms that may be present are dehydration, hot and wet skin, hypotension, and hyperventilation. Most athletes with EHS will have hot, sweaty skin as opposed to the dry skin that is a manifestation of classical EHS.[84,85,88,89]

Although it is usually among the top 3 causes of death in athletes, EHS may rise to the primary cause during the summer.[89] The causes of EHS are multifactorial, but the ultimate result is an overwhelming of the thermoregulatory system, which causes a buildup of heat within the body.[84,90–92]

Prevention. Exercise intensity can increase core body temperature faster and higher than any other factor.[85] Poor physical condition is also related to intensity. Athletes who are less fit than their teammates must work at a higher intensity to produce the same outcome. Therefore, it is important to alter exercise intensity and rest breaks when environmental conditions are dangerous.[93]

As air temperature increases, thermal strain increases, but if relative humidity increases as well, the body loses its ability to use evaporation as a cooling method (the main method used during exercise in the heat).[87,94–97] Adding heavy or extensive protective equipment also increases the potential risk, not only because of the extra weight but also as a barrier to evaporation and cooling. Therefore, extreme or new environmental conditions should be approached with caution and practices altered and events canceled as appropriate.

Acclimatization is a physiologic response to repeated heat exposure during exercise over the course of 10 to 14 days.[90,98] This response enables the body to cope better with thermal stressors and includes increases in stroke volume, sweat output, sweat rate, and evaporation of sweat and decreases in heart rate, core body temperature, skin temperature, and sweat salt losses.[90] Athletes should be allowed to acclimatize to the heat before stressful conditions such as full equipment, multiple practices within a day, or performance trials are implemented.[91,93]

Hydration can help reduce heart rate, fatigue, and core body temperature while improving performance and cognitive functioning.[96–98] Dehydration of as little as 2% of body weight has a negative effect on performance and thermoregulation.[87] Caution should be taken to ensure that athletes arrive at practice euhydrated (eg, having reestablished their weight since the last practice) and maintain or replace fluids that are lost during practice.

Assessment. The 2 main diagnostic criteria for EHS are CNS dysfunction and a core body temperature of greater than 104° to 105°F (40.0° to 40.5°C).[99–101] The only accurate measurements of core body temperature are via rectal thermometry or ingestible thermistors.[102] Other devices, such as oral, axillary, aural canal, and temporal artery thermometers, are inaccurate methods of assessing body temperature in an exercising person. A delay in accurate temperature assessment must also be considered during diagnosis and may explain body temperatures that are lower than expected. Lastly, in some cases of EHS, the patient has a lucid interval during which he or she is cognitively normal, followed by rapidly deteriorating symptoms.[86]

Due to policy and legal concerns in some settings, obtaining rectal temperature may not be feasible. Because immediate treatment is critical in EHS, it is important to not waste time by substituting an invalid method of temperature assessment. Instead, the practitioner should rely on other key diagnostic indicators (eg, CNS dysfunction, circumstances of the collapse). If EHS is suspected, cold-water immersion should be initiated at once. The evidence strongly indicates that in patients with suspected EHS, prompt determination of rectal temperature followed by aggressive, whole-body cold-water immersion maximizes the chances for survival. Practitioners in settings in which taking rectal temperature is a concern should consult with their administrators in advance. Athletic trainers, in conjunction with their supervising physicians, should clearly communicate to their administrators the dangers of skipping this important step and should obtain a definitive ruling on how to proceed in this situation.

Treatment. The goal for any EHS victim is to lower the body temperature to 102°F (38.9°C) or less within 30 minutes of collapse. The length of time body temperature is above the critical core temperature (~105°F [40.5°C]) dictates any morbidity and the risk of death from EHS.[103] Cold-water immersion is the most effective cooling modality for patients with EHS.[104,105] The water should be approximately 35°F (1.7°C) to 59°F (15.0°C) and continuously stirred to maximize cooling. The athlete should be removed when core body temperature reaches 102°F (38.9°) to prevent overcooling. If appropriate medical care is available, cooling should be completed before the athlete is transported to a hospital. Although cooling rates with cold-water immersion will vary for numerous reasons (eg, amount of body immersed, body type, temperature of water, amount of stirring), a general rule of thumb is that the cooling rate will be about 0.2°C/min (0.37°F/min) or about 1°C every 5 minutes (or 1°F every 3 minutes) when considering the entire immersion period from postcollapse to 39°C (102°F).[86,105] If cold-water immersion is not available, other modalities, such as wet ice towels rotated and placed over the entire body or cold-water dousing with or without fanning, may be used but are not as effective. Policies and procedures for cooling athletes before transport to the hospital must be explicitly clear and shared with potential EMS responders, so that treatment by all medical professionals involved with a patient with EHS is coordinated.

Return to Play. Structured guidelines for RTP after EHS are lacking. The main considerations are treating any associated sequelae and, if possible, identifying the cause of the EHS, so that future episodes can be prevented. Many patients with EHS are cooled effectively and sent home the same day; they may be able to resume modified activity within 1 to 3 weeks. However, when treatment is delayed, patients may experience residual complications for months or years after the event. Most guidelines suggest that the athlete be asymptomatic with normal blood work (renal and hepatic panels, electrolytes, and muscle enzyme levels) before a gradual return to activity is initiated.[106] Unfortunately, no evidence-based tools are available to determine whether the body's thermoregulatory system is fully recovered. In summary, in all cases of EHS, after the athlete has completed a 7-day rest period and obtained normal blood work and

physician clearance, he or she may begin a progression of physical activity, supervised by the AT, from low intensity to high intensity and increasing duration in a temperate environment, followed by the same progression in a warm to hot environment. The ability to progress depends largely on the treatment provided, and in some rare cases full recovery may not be possible. If the athlete experiences any side effects or negative symptoms with training, the progression should be slowed or delayed.

Exertional Hyponatremia

Recommendations

Prevention

1. Each physically active person should establish an individualized hydration protocol based on personal sweat rate, sport dynamics (eg, rest breaks, fluid access), environmental factors, acclimatization state, exercise duration, exercise intensity, and individual preferences. *Evidence Category: B*

2. Athletes should consume adequate dietary sodium at meals when physical activity occurs in hot environments. *Evidence Category: B*

3. Postexercise rehydration should aim to correct fluid loss accumulated during activity. *Evidence Category: B*

4. Body weight changes, urine color, and thirst offer cues to the need for rehydration. *Evidence Category: A*

5. Most cases of exertional hyponatremia (EH) occur in endurance athletes who ingest an excessive amount of hypotonic fluid. Athletes should be educated about proper fluid and sodium replacement during exercise. *Evidence Category: C*

Recognition

6. Athletic trainers should recognize EH signs and symptoms during or after exercise, including overdrinking, nausea, vomiting, dizziness, muscular twitching, peripheral tingling or swelling, headache, disorientation, altered mental status, physical exhaustion, pulmonary edema, seizures, and cerebral edema. *Evidence Category: B*

7. In severe cases, EH encephalopathy can occur and the athlete may present with confusion, altered CNS function, seizures, and a decreased level of consciousness. *Evidence Category: B*

8. The AT should include EH in differential diagnoses until confirmed otherwise. *Evidence Category: C*

Treatment and Management

9. If an athlete's mental status deteriorates or if he or she initially presents with severe symptoms of EH, IV hypertonic saline (3% to 5%) is indicated. *Evidence Category: B*

10. Athletes with mild symptoms, normal total body water volume, and a mildly altered blood sodium level (130 to 135 mEq/L; normal is 135 to 145 mEq/L) should restrict fluids and consume salty foods or a small volume of oral hypertonic solution (eg, 3 to 5 bouillon cubes dissolved in 240 mL of hot water). *Evidence Category: C*

11. The athlete with severe EH should be transported to an advanced medical facility during or after treatment. *Evidence Category: B*

12. Return to activity should be guided by a plan to avoid future EH episodes, specifically an individualized hydration plan, as described earlier. *Evidence Category: C*

Background and Literature Review

Definition, Epidemiology, and Pathophysiology. Exertional hyponatremia is a rare condition defined as a serum sodium concentration less than 130 mEq/L.[107] Although no incidence data are available from organized athletics, the condition is seen in fewer than 1% of military athletes[108] and up to 30% of distance athletes.[107,109] Signs and symptoms of EH include overdrinking, nausea, vomiting, dizziness, muscular twitching, peripheral tingling or swelling, headache, disorientation, altered mental status, physical exhaustion, pulmonary edema, seizures, and cerebral edema. If not treated properly and promptly, EH is potentially fatal because of the encephalopathy. Low serum sodium levels are identified more often in females than in males and during activity that exceeds 4 hours in duration.[107,110] Two common, often additive scenarios occur when an athlete ingests hypotonic beverages well beyond sweat losses (ie, water intoxication) or an athlete's sweat sodium losses are not adequately replaced.[111–114] Water intoxication causes low serum sodium levels because of a combination of excessive fluid intake and inappropriate body water retention. Insufficient sodium replacement causes low serum sodium levels when high sweat sodium content leads to decreased serum sodium levels (which may occur over 3 to 5 days). In both scenarios, EH causes intracellular swelling due to hypotonic intravascular and extracellular

fluids. This, in turn, leads to potentially fatal neurologic and physiologic dysfunction. When physically active people match fluid and sodium losses, via sweat and urine, with overall intake, EH is prevented.[94,115] Successful treatment of EH involves rapid sodium replacement in sufficient concentrations via foods containing high levels of sodium (minor cases) or hypertonic saline IV infusion (for moderate or severe cases).

Prevention. Exertional hyponatremia is most effectively prevented when individualized hydration protocols are used for the physically active, including hydration before, during, and after exercise.[94,115] This strategy should take into account sweat rate, sport dynamics (eg, rest breaks, fluid access), environmental factors, acclimatization state, exercise duration, exercise intensity, and individual preferences. The strategy should guide hydration before, during, and after activity to approximate sweat losses but ensure that fluids are not consumed in excess. This goal can be achieved by calculating individual sweat rates (sweat rate = preexercise body weight – postexercise body weight + fluid intake + urine volume/exercise time, in hours) for a representative range of environmental conditions and exercise intensities. Suggestions for expediting this procedure can be found in the NATA position statement on fluid replacement.[94] Sweat rate calculation is the most fundamental consideration when establishing a rehydration protocol. Average sweat rates from the scientific literature or other athletes vary from 0.5 L/h to more than 2.5 L/h.[115]

Dietary sodium is important for normal body maintenance of fluid balance and can help prevent muscle cramping, heat exhaustion, and EH.[91] The AT should encourage adequate dietary sodium intake, especially when athletes are training in a hot environment and as a part of daily meals.[116] Sport drinks generally contain low levels of sodium relative to blood and do little to attenuate decreases in whole-body sodium levels. Instead, athletes should consume foods that are high in sodium (eg, canned soups, pretzels) during meals before and after exercise. Including sodium in fluid-replacement beverages should be considered under the following conditions: inadequate access to meals, physical activity exceeding 2 hours in duration, and during the initial days to weeks of hot weather.[94,115] Under these conditions, adding salt in amounts of 0.3 to 0.7 g/L can offset salt losses in sweat and minimize medical events associated with electrolyte imbalances.

Postexercise hydration should aim to correct the fluid loss accumulated during activity.[94,115] Ideally completed within 2 hours, rehydration fluids should contain water, carbohydrates to replenish glycogen stores, and electrolytes to speed rehydration. When rehydration must be rapid (within 2 hours), the athlete should compensate for obligatory urine losses incurred during the rehydration process and drink about 25% more than sweat losses to ensure optimal hydration 4 to 6 hours after the event.[117] However, athletes should not drink enough to gain weight beyond pre-exercise measurements.[94,115,116]

Body weight changes, urine color, and thirst offer cues to the need for rehydration.[118] When preparing for an event, an athlete should know his or her sweat rate and pre-exercise hydration status and develop a rehydration plan (discussed in detail in the recommendations).[94,115] If the athlete's specific needs are unknown, the athlete should not drink beyond thirst.

Recognition. The AT should recognize and the physically active should be educated on EH signs and symptoms during exercise.[113,114,116] After an exercise bout or competition, symptoms of EH may appear immediately or gradually progress over several hours. The most efficient method of diagnosing EH onsite is the use of a handheld analyzer, which can identify the serum sodium concentration within minutes.[113,114] Athletic trainers should work with physicians and EMS to maximize access to these analyzers when EH is likely.

A collapsed, semiconscious, or unconscious athlete should be evaluated for all potential causes of sudden death in sport. The key to the differential diagnosis of EH is serum sodium assessment, which should be conducted when EH is suspected.[113,114] If a portable serum sodium analyzer is not available, it is then necessary to rule out other conditions that may warrant onsite treatment (eg, EHS) before emergency transport.[91]

Treatment. If the athlete's mental status deteriorates or if he or she initially presents with severe symptoms, IV hypertonic saline (3% to 5%) is indicated.[91,113,114] Intravenous hypertonic saline rapidly corrects the symptoms of EH and decreases intracellular fluid volume. Serial measures of blood sodium should be obtained throughout treatment (after every 100 mL of IV fluid). To avoid complications, hypertonic saline administration should be discontinued when the serum sodium concentration reaches 128 to 130 mEq/L.[114] Normal saline (0.9% NaCl) IV fluids should not be provided to patients without prior serum sodium assessment.[113,114] Ideally, the ATs have discussed with EMS in the off-season the importance of having a portable sodium analyzer available and being ready to administer hypertonic saline during transport.

Athletes with mild symptoms, normal total body water volume, and a mildly altered blood sodium concentration (130 to 135 mEq/L) should restrict fluids and consume salty foods or a small volume of oral hypertonic solution (eg, 3 to 5 bouillon cubes dissolved in 240 mL of hot water). This can be continued until diuresis and correction of the blood sodium concentration occur; such management may take hours to complete, but it is successful in stable patients.[114]

The patient with severe EH should be transported to an advanced medical facility during or after treatment. Once the patient arrives at the emergency department, a plasma osmolality assessment is performed to identify hypovolemia or hypervolemia. Patients with persistent hypovolemia despite normal serum sodium values should receive 0.9% NaCl IV until euvolemia is reached. The progress of symptoms and blood sodium levels determines the follow-up care.[119]

Return to Play. When EH is treated appropriately with IV hypertonic saline, chronic morbidity is rare. Literature documenting the expected time course of recovery after EH is lacking, but recovery seems to depend on the severity and duration of brain swelling. Rapid recognition and prompt treatment reduce the risk of CNS damage.[120]

Return to activity should be guided by a plan to avoid future EH episodes, specifically an individualized hydration plan (documented earlier).[94,115] This plan should also be based on the history and factors that contributed to the initial EH episode.

Exertional Sickling

Recommendations

Prevention

1. The AT should educate coaches, athletes, and, as warranted, parents about complications of exertion in the athlete with sickle cell trait (SCT). *Evidence Category: C*

2. Targeted education and tailored precautions may provide a margin of safety for the athlete with SCT. *Evidence Category: C*

3. Athletes with known SCT should be allowed longer periods of rest and recovery between conditioning repetitions, be excluded from participation in performance tests such as mile runs and serial sprints, adjust work-rest cycles in the presence of environmental heat stress, emphasize hydration, control asthma (if present), not work out if feeling ill, and have supplemental oxygen available for training or competition when new to a high-altitude environment. *Evidence Category: B*

Recognition

4. Screening for SCT, by self-report, is a standard component of the preparticipation physical evaluation

(PPE) monograph. Testing for SCT, when included in the PPE or conducted previously, confirms SCT status. *Evidence Category: A*

5. The AT should know the signs and symptoms of exertional sickling, which include muscle cramping, pain, swelling, weakness, and tenderness; inability to catch one's breath; and fatigue, and be able to differentiate exertional sickling from other causes of collapse. *Evidence Category: C*

6. The AT should understand the usual settings for and patterns of exertional sickling. *Evidence Category: C*

Treatment

7. Signs and symptoms of exertional sickling warrant immediate withdrawal from activity. *Evidence Category: C*

8. High-flow oxygen at 15 L/min with a nonrebreather face mask should be administered. *Evidence Category: C*

9. The AT should monitor vital signs and activate the EAP if vital signs decline. *Evidence Category: C*

10. Sickling collapse should be treated as a medical emergency. *Evidence Category: C*

11. The AT has a duty to make sure the athlete's treating physicians are aware of the presence of SCT and prepared to treat the metabolic complications of explosive rhabdomyolysis. *Evidence Category: B*

Background and Literature Review

Prevention. No contraindications to participation in sport exist for the athlete with SCT.[121–123] Recognition of the athlete's positive SCT status must be followed with targeted education and tailored precautions because deaths have been tied to lapses in education and inadequate precautions.[124] The athlete with SCT should be informed that SCT is consistent with a normal, healthy life span, although associated complications may occur. Education should include genetic considerations with respect to family planning and questioning about any past medical history of sickling events. Athletes and staff should be educated about the signs, symptoms, and settings of exertional sickling and precautions for the athlete with SCT.[123]

The premise behind the suggested precautions is that exertional sickling can be brought about through intense, sustained activity with modifiers that increase the intensity.[125] One precaution that can mitigate exertional sickling is a slow, paced training progression that allows longer periods of rest and recovery between repetitions.[123,125] Strength and conditioning programs may increase preparedness but must be sport specific. Athletes with SCT should be excluded from participation in performance tests, such as mile runs and serial sprints, because several deaths have occurred in this setting.[124] Cessation of activity with the onset of symptoms is essential to avoid escalating a sickling episode (eg, muscle cramping, pain, swelling, weakness, and tenderness; inability to catch one's breath; fatigue).[123,125] In general, when athletes with SCT set their own pace, they seem to do well.[123,125] Therefore, athletes with SCT who perform repetitive high-speed sprints, distance runs, or interval training that induces high levels of lactic acid as a component of a sport-specific training regimen should be allowed extended recovery between repetitions because this type of conditioning poses special risks to them.[123,125]

Factors such as ambient heat stress, dehydration, asthma, illness, and altitude predispose the athlete with SCT to a crisis during physical exertion, even when exercise is not all-out.[123,125] Extra precautions are warranted in these conditions. These precautions may include the following:

- Work-rest cycles should be adjusted for environmental heat stress.
- Hydration should be emphasized.
- Asthma should be controlled.
- The athlete with SCT who is ill should not work out.
- The athlete with SCT who is new to a high-altitude environment should be watched closely. Training should be modified and supplemental oxygen should be available for competitions.

One last precaution is to create an environment that encourages athletes with SCT to immediately report any signs or symptoms such as leg or low back cramping, difficulty breathing, or fatigue. Such signs and symptoms in an athlete with SCT should be assumed to represent sickling.[123]

Recognition. The PPE monograph[14] recommends screening for SCT with the question, "Do you or [does] someone in your family have SCT or disease?" Small numbers of affected athletes limit the collection of sufficient evidence to support testing for SCT in the PPE. However, because PPE medical history form answers are highly suspect[126] and deaths can be tied to a lack of awareness about SCT, the argument for testing to confirm trait status remains strong. The National Collegiate Athletic Association currently mandates testing for SCT. Irrespective of testing, the AT should educate staff, coaches, and athletes on the potentially lethal nature of this condition.[123] Education and precautions work best when targeted at the athletes most at risk. Incidence rates of SCT are approximately 8% in African Americans, 0.5% in Hispanics, and 0.2% in whites (but more common in those from the Mediterranean, the Middle East, and India).[127]

Not all athletes who experience sickling present the same way. The primary limiting symptoms are leg or low back cramps or spasms, weakness, debilitating low back pain,[128] difficulty recovering ("I can't catch my breath"), and fatigue. Sickling often lacks a prodrome, so these symptoms in an athlete with SCT should be treated as exertional sickling.[123]

Sickling collapse has been mistaken for cardiac collapse or heat illness.[129] However, unlike sickling collapse, cardiac collapse tends to be instantaneous, is not associated with cramping, and results in the athlete hitting the ground without any protective reflex mechanism and being unable to talk. Also unlike sickling collapse, heat illness collapse often occurs after a moderate but still intense bout of exercise, usually more than 30 minutes in duration. In addition, the athlete will have a core body temperature >104°F (40.0°C). Alternatively, sickling collapse typically occurs within the first half hour on the field, and core temperature is not greatly elevated.[129,130]

Sickling is often confused with heat cramping but may be differentiated by the following:

- Heat cramping often has a prodrome of muscle twinges; sickling has none.

- Heat-cramping pain is more excruciating and can be pinpointed, whereas sickling cramping is more generalized but still strong.

- Those with heat cramps hobble to a halt with "locked-up" muscles, whereas sickling athletes slump to the ground with weak muscles. Many times, sickling athletes push through several instances of collapse before being unable to continue.

- Those with heat cramps writhe and yell in pain; their muscles are visibly contracted and rock hard. Those who are sickling lie fairly still, not yelling in pain, with muscles that look and feel normal to the observer.

Certain factors are common in severe or fatal exertional sickling collapses. These cases tend to be similar in setting and syndrome and are characterized by the following:

- Sickling athletes may be on the field only briefly before collapsing, sprinting only 800 to 1600 meters, often early in the season.

- Sickling can occur during repetitive running of hills or stadium steps, during intense, sustained strength training; if the tempo increases toward the end of intense 1-hour drills; and at the end of practice when athletes run "gassers." Sickling occurs rarely in competition, most often in athletes previously exhibiting symptoms in training for sport.[123]

Severe to fatal sickling cases are not limited to football players. Sickling collapse has occurred in distance racers and has killed or nearly killed several collegiate and high school basketball players (including 2 women) in training, typically during "suicide sprints" on the court, laps on a track, or a long training run.[123]

The harder and faster athletes with SCT work, the earlier and greater the sickling. Sickling can begin after only 2 to 3 minutes of sprinting––or any all-out exertion––and can quickly increase to grave levels if the athlete struggles on or is urged on by the coach.[124]

Athletes react in different ways. Some stoic athletes simply stop and say, "I can't go on." When the athlete rests, sickle red cells regain oxygen in the lungs; most sickle cells then revert to normal shape, and the athlete soon feels good again and ready to continue. This self-limiting feature surely saves lives.

Treatment. Complaints or evidence of exertional sickling signs and symptoms in a working athlete with SCT should be assumed to represent the onset of sickling and first managed by cessation of activity. A sickling collapse is treated as a medical emergency. Immediate action can save lives[123]:

1. Check vital signs.

2. Administer high-flow oxygen, 15 L/min (if available), with a nonrebreather face mask.

3. Cool the athlete if necessary.

4. If the athlete is obtunded or if vital signs decline, call 911, attach an AED, and quickly transport the athlete to the hospital.[125,129] Appropriate medical personnel should start an IV.

5. The AT should inform treating physicians of the athlete's trait status so that they are prepared to treat explosive rhabdomyolysis and associated metabolic complications.[124,125,129,131,132]

6. Proactively prepare by having an EAP and appropriate emergency equipment available.

Return to Play. After nonfatal sickling, the athlete may return to sport the same day or be disqualified from further participation. Athletes whose conditions are identified quickly and managed appropriately may return the same day as symptoms subside. Others have self-limiting myalgia from myonecrosis in moderate rhabdomyolysis and may need 1 to 2 weeks of recovery with serial assessments.[122] Patients with severe rhabdomyolysis necessitating dialysis and months of hospitalization[133] may not RTP due to diminished renal function, muscle lost to myonecrosis, or neuropathy from compartment syndrome.[121] As with any RTP after a potential deadly incident, it is imperative that the physician, AT, coach, and athlete work in concert to ensure the athlete's safety and minimize risk factors that may have caused the initial incident.

Head-Down Contact in Football

Recommendations

Prevention

1. Axial loading is the primary mechanism for catastrophic cervical spine injury. *Head-down contact*, defined as initiating contact with the top or crown of the helmet, is the only technique that results in axial loading. *Evidence Category: A*

2. *Spearing* is the intentional use of a head-down contact technique. Unintentional head-down contact is the inadvertent dropping of the head just before contact. Both head-down techniques are dangerous and may result in axial loading of the cervical spine and catastrophic injury. *Evidence Category: A*

3. Football helmets and other standard football equipment do not cause or prevent axial-loading injuries of the cervical spine. *Evidence Category: A*

4. Injuries that occur as a result of head-down contact are technique related and are preventable to the extent that head-down contact is preventable. *Evidence Category: C*

5. Making contact with the shoulder or chest while keeping the head up greatly reduces the risk of serious head and neck injury. With the head up, the player can see when and how impact is about to occur and can prepare the neck musculature. Even if head-first contact is inadvertent, the force is absorbed by the neck musculature, the intervertebral discs, and the cervical facet joints. This is the safest contact technique. *Evidence Category: C*

6. The game can be played as aggressively with the head up and with shoulder contact but

FIGURE 2 Initiating contact with the shoulder while keeping the head up reduces the risk of head and neck injuries.

with much less risk of serious injury (**Figure 2**). However, the technique must be learned, and to be learned, it must be practiced extensively. Athletes who continue to drop their heads just before contact need additional coaching and practice time. *Evidence Category: C*

7. Initiating contact with the face mask is a rule violation and must not be taught. If the athlete uses poor technique by lowering his head, he places himself in the head-down position and at risk of serious injury. *Evidence Category: C*

8. The athlete should know, understand, and appreciate the risk of head-down contact, regardless of intent. Formal team education sessions (conducted by the AT, team physician, or both with the support of the coaching staff) should be held at least twice per season. One session should be conducted before contact begins and the other at the midpoint of the season. Recommended topics are mechanisms of head and neck injuries, related rules and penalties, the incidence of catastrophic injury, the severity of and prognosis for these injuries, and the safest contact positions. The use of videos such as *Heads Up: Reducing the Risk of Head and Neck Injuries in Football*[134] and *Tackle Progression*[135] should be mandatory. Parents of high school athletes should be given the opportunity to view these videos. *Evidence Category: C*

Recognition

9. Attempts to determine a player's intent regarding intentional or unintentional head-down

contact are subjective. Therefore, coaching, officiating, and playing techniques must focus on decreasing all head-down contact, regardless of intent. *Evidence Category: C*

10. Officials should enforce existing helmet contact rules to further reduce the incidence of head-down contact. A clear discrepancy has existed between the incidence of head-down or head-first contact and the level of enforcement of the helmet contact penalties. Stricter officiating would bring more awareness to coaches and players about the effects of head-down contact. *Evidence Category: B*

Background and Literature Review

Definition and Pathophysiology. Sudden death from a cervical spine injury is most likely to occur in football from a fracture-dislocation above C4. Axial loading is accepted as the primary cause of cervical spine fractures and dislocations in football players.[136,137] Axial loading occurs secondary to head-down contact, whether intentional or unintentional, when the cervical vertebrae are aligned in a straight column. Essentially, the head is stopped at contact, the trunk keeps moving, and the spine is crushed between the two. When maximum vertical compression is reached, the cervical spine fails,[138] resulting in damage to the spinal cord.

Although the football helmet has been successful in reducing the number of catastrophic brain injuries, it is neither the cause nor the solution for cervical spine fractures, primarily because with head-first impact, the head, neck, and torso decelerate nonuniformly. Even after the head is stopped, the body continues to accelerate, and no current football helmet can effectively manage the force placed on the cervical spine by the trunk.[139–141] As identified in the 1970s, contact technique remains the critical factor in preventing axial loading.

Prevention. Initiating contact with the shoulder while keeping the head up is the safest contact position.[142–148] With the head up, the athlete can see when and how impact is about to occur and can prepare the neck musculature accordingly. This guideline applies to all position players, including ball carriers. The game can be played just as aggressively with this technique but with much less risk of serious head or neck injury. Tacklers can still deliver a big hit, and ball carriers can still break tackles.[149]

A top priority for prevention is player education. Athletes have to know, understand, and appreciate the risks of head-first contact in football.[150,151] The videos

Heads Up: Reducing the Risk of Head and Neck Injuries in Football[134] and *Tackle Progression*[135] are excellent educational tools. Parents of high school players should also be given the opportunity to view these videos. Coaches have a responsibility to spend adequate time teaching and practicing correct contact techniques with all position players. The goal should be not merely to discourage head-down contact but to eliminate it from the game.[139]

Recognition. Coaches have stated that although they have taught players to tackle correctly, the players still tended to lower their heads just before contact.[143,144] It seems that players have learned to approach contact with their head up, but they need to maintain this position during contact.[146,149] Instinctively, players protect their eyes and face from injury by lowering their heads at impact.[144,146,149] Therefore, coaches must allocate enough practice time to overcome this instinct. Players who drop their heads at the last instant are demonstrating that they need additional practice time with correct contact techniques in game-like situations. In addition to teaching correct contact in the beginning of the season, coaches should reinforce the technique regularly throughout the season.[144]

The increase in catastrophic cervical spine injuries in the early 1970s was attributed to coaches teaching players to initiate contact with their face masks.[136,150] Players did not execute maneuvers as they were taught, often unintentionally, and they lowered their heads just before impact, resulting in increased exposure to axial loading and cervical spine fractures. The teaching of face-first contact remains a rule violation at the high school level and is a concern at all levels of football.

Adequate enforcement of the helmet contact rules will further reduce the risk of catastrophic injuries.[142–144,152–154] Both the National Collegiate Athletic Association and the National Federation of State High School Associations have changed their helmet contact penalties multiple times in the past 5 years[155] to resolve the dilemma for officials trying to distinguish between intentional and unintentional helmet contact. The current rules for both organizations are now more complete and concise.

A discrepancy has existed between enforcement of the helmet contact penalties and the incidence of head-down contact. Contact with the top of the helmet has been observed in 40% of plays[146] and 18% of helmet collisions in 2007.[156] In contrast, NCAA Division I officials called 1 helmet contact penalty in every 75 games in 2007.[157] If illegal helmet contact is not penalized, the message is that the technique is acceptable.[158] Therefore, football officials must continue to improve the enforcement of these penalties.

Lightning Safety

Recommendations

Prevention

1. The most effective means of preventing lightning injury is to reduce the risk of casualties by remaining indoors during lightning activity. When thunder is heard or lightning seen, people should vacate to a previously identified safe location.[159–161] *Evidence Category: A*

2. Establish an EAP or policy specific to lightning safety.[161,162] *Evidence Category: C*

3. No place outdoors is completely safe from lightning, so alternative safe structures must be identified. Sites that are called "shelters" typically have at least one open side and therefore do not provide sufficient protection from lightning injury. These sites include dugouts; picnic, golf, or rain shelters; tents; and storage sheds.[160,163,164] Safe places to be while lightning occurs are structures with 4 substantial walls, a solid roof, plumbing, and electric wiring–structures in which people live or work.[160,164] *Evidence Category: B*

4. Buses or cars that are fully enclosed and have windows that are completely rolled up and metal roofs can also be safe places during a lightning storm.[165] *Evidence Category: B*

5. People should remain entirely inside a safe building or vehicle until at least 30 minutes have passed since the last lightning strike or the last sound of thunder.[166,167] *Evidence Category: A*

6. People injured by lightning strikes while indoors were touching electric devices or using a landline telephone or plumbing (eg, showering). Garages with open doors and rooms with open windows do not protect from the effects of lightning strikes.[159,161,168–170] *Evidence Category: B*

Treatment and Management

7. Victims are safe to touch and treat, but first responders must ensure their own safety by being certain the area is safe from imminent lightning strikes.[171,172] *Evidence Category: A*

8. Triage first lightning victims who appear to be dead. Most deaths are due to cardiac arrest.[171,173,174]

Although those who sustain a cardiac arrest may not survive due to subsequent apnea, aggressive CPR and defibrillation (if indicated) may resuscitate these patients. *Evidence Category: A*

9. Apply an AED and perform CPR as warranted.[174] *Evidence Category: A*

10. Treat for concussive injuries, fractures, dislocations, and shock.[14,164] *Evidence Category: A*

Background and Literature Review

Definition. Lightning is a natural phenomenon that most people observe within their lifetimes. One of the most dangerous natural hazards encountered, it causes more than 60 fatalities and hundreds of injuries annually in the United States.[169,175] Lightning occurs with greater frequency in the southeastern United States, the Mississippi and Ohio river valleys, the Rocky Mountains, and the Southwest,[175] but no location is truly safe from the hazard of lightning. Lightning is most prevalent from May through September, with most fatalities and trauma reported in July.[169,175,176] Most deaths and injuries are recorded between 10:00 AM and 7:00 PM, when many people are engaged in outdoor activities.[159,169,177]

Lightning can occur from cloud to cloud or cloud to ground. Injuries and deaths are often attributed to cloud-to-ground lightning, but compared with cloud-to-cloud lightning, it occurs only 30% of the time. Negatively charged ionized gas builds up in clouds and seeks objects on the earth (eg, people, houses, trees) that have positively charged regions. When the 2 channels meet, lightning is produced, and an audible repercussion is created; we know this as thunder.[170,178] The lightning channel has an average peak current of 20000 A and is 5 times hotter than the surface of the sun.[170,178]

Prevention. Prevention of lightning injury is simple: Avoid the risk of trauma by staying completely indoors in a substantial building where people live and work.[160,162] A proactive lightning-specific safety policy is paramount to preventing lightning-specific injury. The policy should identify a weather watcher whose job is to look for deteriorating conditions. The weather watcher must have the unchallengeable authority to clear a venue when conditions are unsafe.[161] In addition to onsite observations for deteriorating conditions, use of federal weather monitoring Web sites is encouraged. Safe buildings must be identified before outdoor activity begins.[161,162,179] The lightning safety plan must allow sufficient time to safely move people to the identified building, and this time frame should be adjusted according to the number of people being moved. For example, moving a soccer team to safety takes less time than moving a football team. It is also critical to remain wholly within the safe building for at least 30 minutes after the last sighting of lightning and sound of thunder.[166,168]

Treatment. People who have been struck by lightning are safe to touch and treat and do not carry an electric charge. However, rescuers themselves are vulnerable to a lightning strike while treating victims during active thunderstorms. Treatment of lightning strike patients includes establishing and maintaining normal cardiorespiratory status.[161,162,171,173,174] Patients may present in asystole, pulseless, and with fixed and dilated pupils. Therefore, CPR should be continued even when defibrillation with an AED is not indicated (eg, asystole). Advanced cardiac life support, medications, intubation, and continued CPR may resuscitate these victims. People with a Glasgow Coma Scale score as low as 5 have survived after aggressive resuscitation.[180] After a lightning strike, many patients present with symptoms resembling a concussion. Some may have temporary paralysis, hearing loss, or skin markings, yet true burns are rare. Patients should be assessed and treated for concussion, fractures, dislocations, and shock.[174]

Return to Play. Lightning strike patients are eligible to return to previous activities upon release by a qualified physician. Many never seek treatment and do not need hospitalization. If orthopaedic injuries are present, recovery follows the typical protocols. More often than not, however, patients experience neurologic sequelae and have difficulty returning to their preinjury levels.[175,181] They may never fully return to desired levels, and they need consistent and perhaps multidisciplinary medical and psychological follow-up.[174,181]

Sudden Cardiac Arrest

Recommendations

Prevention

1. Access to early defibrillation is essential. A goal of less than 3–5 minutes from the time of collapse to delivery of the first shock is strongly recommended. *Evidence Category: B*

2. The preparticipation physical examination should include the completion of a standardized history form and attention to episodes of exertional syncope or presyncope, chest pain, a personal or family history of sudden cardiac arrest or a family history of sudden death, and exercise intolerance. *Evidence Category: C*

Recognition

3. Sudden cardiac arrest (SCA) should be suspected in any athlete who has collapsed and is unresponsive. A patient's airway, breathing, circulation, and heart rhythm (using the AED) should be assessed. An AED should be applied as soon as possible for rhythm analysis. *Evidence Category: B*

4. Myoclonic jerking or seizure-like activity is often present after collapse from SCA and should not be mistaken for a seizure. Occasional or agonal gasping should not be mistaken for normal breathing. *Evidence Category: B*

Management

5. Cardiopulmonary resuscitation should be provided while the AED is being retrieved, and the AED should be applied as soon as possible. Interruptions in chest compressions should be minimized by stopping only for rhythm analysis and defibrillation. Treatment should proceed in accordance with the updated American Heart Association guidelines,[182] which recommend that health care professionals follow a sequence of chest compressions (C), airway (A), and breathing (B). *Evidence Category: B*

Background and Literature Review

Definition, Epidemiology, and Pathophysiology. Sudden cardiac death (SCD) is the leading cause of death in exercising young athletes.[183,184] The underlying cause of SCD is usually a structural cardiac abnormality. Hypertrophic cardiomyopathy and coronary artery anomalies are responsible for approximately 25% and 14% of SCD, respectively, in the United States.[183] Commotio cordis accounts for approximately 20% of SCD in young athletes; caused by a blunt, nonpenetrating blow to the chest, it induces ventricular arrhythmia in an otherwise normal heart.[183] Other structural anomalies that can cause SCD include myocarditis, arrhythmogenic right ventricular dysplasia, Marfan syndrome, valvular heart disease, dilated cardiomyopathy, and atherosclerotic coronary artery disease. In 2% of athletes with SCD, a postmortem examination fails to identify a structural abnormality. These deaths may result from inherited arrhythmia syndromes and ion channel disorders or familial catecholaminergic polymorphic ventricular tachycardia.[183]

The incidence of SCD in high school athletes is estimated to be 1:100000 to 1:200000.[184,185] In collegiate athletes, this incidence is slightly higher, with estimates ranging from 1:65000 to 1:69000.[184,186] A recent report[185] described the incidence of SCD in National Collegiate Athletic Association student-athletes as 1:43000, with higher rates in black athletes (1:1700) and male basketball players (1:7000). Unfortunately, because we have no mandatory national reporting system, the true incidence of SCD is unknown and probably underestimated. The reports demonstrating the greatest incidence have estimated up to 110 deaths each year in young athletes, equating to 1 death every 3 days in the United States.[187]

Prevention. Preparticipation screening is one strategy available to prevent SCD, but the best protocol to screen athletes is highly debated, and some methods lack accuracy. As many as 80% of patients with SCD are asymptomatic until sudden cardiac arrest occurs,[188,189] suggesting that screening by history and physical examination alone may have limited sensitivity to identify athletes with at-risk conditions. Further research is needed to understand whether additional tests such as electrocardiograms and echocardiograms improve sensitivity and can be performed with acceptable cost-effectiveness and an acceptable false-positive rate. Detection of asymptomatic conditions should be improved with standardized history forms and attention to episodes of exertional syncope or presyncope, chest pain, a personal or family history of sudden cardiac arrest or a family history of sudden death, or exercise intolerance; selective use of electrocardiograms in high-risk athletes; and a stronger knowledge base for health care professionals.

In 2007, the American Heart Association released a helpful 12-point preparticipation cardiovascular screen for competitive athletes based on the medical history and physical examination (**Table 3**).

TABLE 3

THE 12-ELEMENT AHA RECOMMENDATIONS FOR PREPARTICIPATION CARDIOVASCULAR SCREENING OF COMPETITIVE ATHLETES

Medical history[a]

Personal history
1. Exertional chest pain/discomfort
2. Unexplained syncope/near-syncope[b]
3. Excessive exertional and unexplained dyspnea/fatigue, associated with exercise
4. Prior recognition of a heart murmur
5. Elevated systemic blood pressure

Family history
6. Premature death (sudden and unexpected, or otherwise) before age 50 years due to heart disease, in ≥1 relative
7. Disability from heart disease in a close relative <50 years of age
8. Specific knowledge of certain cardiac conditions in family members: hypertrophic or dilated cardiomyopathy, long-QT syndrome or other ion channelopathies, Marfan syndrome, or clinically important arrhythmias

Physical examination
9. Heart murmur[c]
10. Femoral pulses to exclude aortic coarctation
11. Physical stigmata of Marfan syndrome
12. Brachial artery blood pressure (sitting position)[d]

---

[a] Parental verification is recommended for high school and middle school athletes.
[b] Judged not to be neurocardiogenic (vasovagal); of particular concern when related to exertion.
[c] Auscultation should be performed in both supine and standing positions (or with Valsalva maneuver), specifically to identify murmurs of dynamic left ventricular outflow tract obstruction.
[d] Preferably taken in both arms (Kaplan NM, Gidding SS, Pickering TG, Wright JT Jr. Task Force 5: systemic hypertension. *J Am Coll Cardiol.* 2005;45(8):1346–1348).

Reprinted with permission from Maron BJ, Thompson PD, Ackerman MJ, et al. Recommendations and considerations related to preparticipation screening for cardiovascular abnormalities in competitive athletes: 2007 update. Circulation. 2007;115(12):1643–1655.

Emergency Preparedness. Preparation is the key to survival once SCA has occurred. Public access to AEDs and established EAPs greatly improve the likelihood of survival. All necessary equipment should be placed in a central location that is highly visible and accessible; multiple AEDs may be needed for larger facilities. An EAP should be in place and specific to each athletic venue and should include an effective communication system, training of likely first responders in CPR and AED use, acquisition of the necessary emergency equipment, a coordinated and practiced response plan, and access to early defibrillation. It should identify the person or group responsible for documentation of personnel training, equipment maintenance, actions taken during the emergency, and evaluation of the emergency response.[192] The EAP should be coordinated with the local EMS agency and integrated into the local EMS system. It should also be posted at every venue and near appropriate telephones and include the address of the venue and specific directions to guide EMS personnel.

Assessment. Differential diagnosis of nontraumatic exercise-related syncope or presyncope includes sudden cardiac arrest, EHS, heat exhaustion, hyponatremia, hypoglycemia, exercise-associated collapse, exertional sickling, neurocardiogenic syncope, seizures, pulmonary embolus, cardiac arrhythmias, valvular disorders, coronary artery disease, cardiomyopathies, ion channel disorders, and other structural cardiac diseases. In any athlete who has collapsed in the absence of trauma, suspicion for sudden cardiac arrest should be high until normal airway, breathing, and circulation are confirmed. Agonal respiration or occasional gasping should not be mistaken for normal breathing and should be recognized as a sign of SCA[193]; myoclonic jerking or seizure-like activity shortly after collapse should also be treated as SCA until proven otherwise.[194,195] If no pulse is palpable, the patient should be treated for SCA, and CPR should be initiated.

Treatment. In any athlete who has collapsed and is unresponsive, SCA should be suspected. If normal breathing and pulse are absent, CPR should be started immediately and EMS activated. The CPR should be performed in the order of CAB (chest compressions, airway, breathing) by medical professionals (hands-only CPR is now recommended for lay responders) while waiting for arrival of the AED and stopped only for rhythm analysis and defibrillation. This should continue until either advanced life support providers take over or the victim starts to move.[193,194,196,197] Early detection, prompt CPR, rapid activation of EMS, and early defibrillation are vital to the athlete's survival. For any athlete who has collapsed and is unresponsive, an AED should be applied as soon as possible for rhythm analysis and defibrillation if indicated. The greatest factor affecting survival after SCA arrest is the time from arrest to defibrillation.[195,196] Survival rates have been reported at 41%–74% if bystander CPR is provided and defibrillation occurs within 3 to 5 minutes of collapse.[186,194,196–207]

Certain weather situations warrant special consideration. In a rainy or icy environment, AEDs are safe and do not pose a shock hazard. However, a patient lying on a wet surface or in a puddle should be moved. A patient lying on a metal conducting surface (eg, stadium bleacher) should be moved to a nonmetal surface. If lightning is ongoing, rescuers must ensure their safety by moving the patient indoors if possible.

Acknowledgments

We gratefully acknowledge the efforts of Gianluca Del Rossi, PhD, ATC; Jonathan Drezner, MD; John MacKnight, MD; Jason Mihalik, PhD, ATC; Francis O'Connor, MD, MPH; and the Pronouncements Committee in the preparation of this document.

Disclaimer

The NATA publishes its position statements as a service to promote the awareness of certain issues to its members. The information contained in the position statement is neither exhaustive nor exclusive to all circumstances or individuals. Variables such as institutional human resource guidelines, state or federal statutes, rules, or regulations, as well as regional environmental conditions, may impact the relevance and implementation of these recommendations. The NATA advises its members and others to carefully and independently consider each of the recommendations (including the applicability of same to any particular circumstance or individual). The position statement should not be relied upon as an independent basis for care but rather as a resource available to NATA members or others. Moreover, no opinion is expressed herein regarding the quality of care that adheres to or differs from NATA's position statements. The NATA reserves the right to rescind or modify its position statements at any time.

Appendix. National Athletic Trainers' Association Statements[a]

Topic (Year)	Citation	URL
Safe weight loss and maintenance practices in sport and exercise (2011)	Sammarone Turocy P, DePalma BF, Horswill CA, et al. National Athletic Trainers' Association position statement: safe weight loss and maintenance practices in sport and exercise. J Athl Train. 2011;46(3):322–336.	http://www.nata.org/sites/default/files/JAT-46-3-16-turocy-322-336.pdf
Prevention of pediatric overuse injuries (2011)	Valovich McLeod TC, Decoster LC, Loud KJ, et al. National Athletic Trainers' Association position statement: prevention of pediatric overuse injuries. J Athl Train. 2011;46(2):206–220.	http://www.nata.org/sites/default/files/Pediatric-Overuse-Injuries.pdf
Skin diseases (2010)	Zinder SM, Basler RSW, Foley J, Scarlata C, Vasily DB. National Athletic Trainers' Association position statement: skin diseases. J Athl Train. 2010;45(4):411–428.	http://www.nata.org/sites/default/files/position-statement-skin-disease.pdf
Acute management of the cervical spine-injured athlete (2009)	Swartz EE, Boden BP, Courson RW, et al. National Athletic Trainers' Association position statement: acute management of the cervical spine-injured athlete. J Athl Train. 2009;44(3):306–331.	http://www.nata.org/sites/default/files/acutemgmtofcervicalspineinjuredathlete.pdf
Preventing, detecting, and managing disordered eating in athletes (2008)	Bonci CM, Bonci LJ, Granger LR, et al. National Athletic Trainers' Association position statement: preventing, detecting, and managing disordered eating in athletes. J Athl Train. 2008;43(1):80–108.	http://www.nata.org/sites/default/files/PreventingDetectingAndManagingDisorderedEating.pdf
Environmental cold injuries (2008)	Cappaert TA, Stone JA, Castellani JW, Krause BA, Smith D, Stephens BA. National Athletic Trainers' Association position statement: environmental cold injuries. J Athl Train. 2008;43(6):640–658.	http://www.nata.org/sites/default/files/EnvironmentalColdInjuries.pdf
Sickle cell trait and the athlete (2007)	Anderson S, Eichner ER. Consensus statement: sickle cell trait and the athlete.[b]	http://www.nata.org/sites/default/files?SickleCellTraitAndTheAthlete.pdf
Emergency preparedness and management of sudden cardiac arrest in high school and college athletic programs (2007)	Drezner JA, Courson RW, Roberts WO, Mosesso VN, Link MS, Maron BJ. Inter-Association Task Force Recommendations on emergency preparedness and management of sudden cardiac arrest in high school and college athletic programs: a consensus statement. J Athl Train. 2007;42(1):143–158.	http://www.nata.org/sites/default/files/sudden-cardiac-arrest-consensus-statement.pdf
Management of the athlete with type I diabetes mellitus (2007)	Jimenez CC, Corcoran MH, Crawley JT, et al. National Athletic Trainers' Association position statement: management of the athlete with type I diabetes mellitus. J Athl Train. 2007;42(4):536–545.	http://www.nata.org/sites/default/files/MgmtOfAthleteWithType1DiabetesMellitus.pdf
Management of asthma in athletes (2005)	Miller MG, Weiler JM, Baker R, Collins J, D'Alonzo G. National Athletic Trainers' Association position statement: management of asthma in athletes. J Athl Train. 2005;40(3):224–245.	http://www.nata.org/sites/default/files/MgmtOfAsthmaInAthletes.pdf
Head-down contact and spearing in tackle football (2004)	Heck JF, Clarke KS, Peterson TR, Torg JS, Weis MP. National Athletic Trainers' Association position statement: head-down contact and spearing in tackle football. J Athl Train. 2004;39(1):101–111.	http://www.nata.org/sites/default/files/HeadDownContactAndSpearingInTackleFB.pdf
Management of sport-related concussion (2004)	Guskiewicz KM, Bruce SL, Cantu RC, et al. National Athletic Trainers' Association position statement: management of sport-related concussion. J Athl Train. 2004;39(3):280–297.	http://www.nata.org/sites/default/files?MgmtOfSportRelatedConcussion.pdf
Emergency planning in athletics (2002)	Andersen JC, Courson RW, Kleiner DM, McLoda TA. National Athletic Trainers' Association position statement: emergency planning in athletics. J Athl Train. 2002;371(1):99–104.	http://www.nata.org/sites/default/files/EmergencyPlanningInAthletics.pdf
Exertional heat illness (2002)	Binkley HM, Beckett J, Casa DJ, Kleiner DM, Plummer PE. National Athletic Trainers' Association position statement: exertional heat illnesses. J Athl Train. 2002;37(3):329–342.	http://www.nata.org/sites/default/files/ExternalHeatIllnesses.pdf
Fluid replacement for athletes (2000)	Casa DJ, Armstrong LE, Hillman SK, et al. National Athletic Trainers' Association position statement: fluid replacement for athletes. J Athl Train. 2000; 35(2):212–224.	http://www.nata.org/sites/default/files/FluidReplacementsForAthletes.pdf
Lightning safety for athletics and recreation (2000)	Walsh KM, Bennett B, Cooper MA, Holle RL, Kithil R, Lopez RE. National Athletic Trainers' Association position statement: lightning safety for athletics and recreation. J Athl Train. 2000;35(4):471–477.	http://www.nata.org/sites/default/files/LightningSafety4AthleticsRec.pdf

[a]Updated position statements are posted at www.nata.org. Readers should check the Web site for the most current versions.
[b]Available online only.

REFERENCES

1. Ebell MH, Siwek J, Weiss BD, et al. Strength of recommendation taxonomy (SORT): a patient-centered approach to grading evidence in the medical literature. *Am Fam Physician.* 2004;69(6): 548–556.

2. Weiler JM. Exercise-induced asthma: a practical guide to definitions, diagnosis, prevalence, and treatment. *Allergy Asthma Proc.* 1996;17(6):315–325.

3. Reiff DB, Choudry NB, Pride NB, Ind PW. The effect of prolonged sub-maximal warm-up exercise on exercise-induced asthma. *Am Rev Respir Dis.* 1989;139(2):479–484.

4. National Heart Lung and Blood Institute. *What Is Asthma?* http://www.nhlbi.nih.gov/health/dci/Diseases/Asthma/Asthma_WhatIs.html. Accessed February 22, 2010.

5. National Institutes of Health, National Heart, Lung, and Blood Institute. *Global Strategy for Asthma Management and Prevention.* Bethesda, MD: National Institutes of Health, National Heart, Lung, and Blood Institute; 2002. No. 02-3659.

6. Rundell KW, Wilber RL, Szmedra L, Jenkinson DM, Mayers LB, Im J. Exercise-induced asthma screening of elite athletes: field versus laboratory exercise challenge. *Med Sci Sports Exerc.* 2000;32(2):309–316.

7. Lung function testing: selection of reference values and interpretative strategies. American Thoracic Society. *Am Rev Respir Dis.* 1991;144(5):1202–1218.

8. Allen TW. Sideline management of asthma. *Curr Sports Med Rep.* 2005;4(6):301–304.

9. Boulet LP. Long versus short-acting beta 2-agonists: implications for drug therapy. *Drugs.* 1994;47(2): 207–222.

10. Dennis RJ, Solarte I, Fitzgerald M. Asthma in adults. In: *BMJ Clinical Evidence Handbook.* London, England; BMJ Publishing Group: 2008; 502–503.

11. *National Asthma Education and Prevention Program. Expert Panel Report II: Guidelines for the Diagnosis and Management of Asthma.* Bethesda, MD: National Institutes of Health; 1997. No. 97-4051:12–18.

12. de Magalhaes Simoes S, dos Santos MA, da Silva Oliveira M, et al. Inflammatory cell mapping of the respiratory tract in fatal asthma. *Clin Exp Allergy.* 2005;35(5):602–611.

13. Hamid Q, Song Y, Kotsimbos TC, et al. Inflammation of small airways in asthma. *J Allergy Clin Immunol.* 1997;100(1):44–51.

14. Bernhardt DT, Roberts WO. *Preparticipation Physical Evaluation.* 4th ed. Elk Grove Village, IL: American Academy of Pediatrics; 2010.

15. Haahtela T, Jarvinen M, Kava T, et al. Comparison of a beta 2-agonist, terbutaline, with an inhaled corticosteroid, budesonide, in newly detected asthma. *N Engl J Med.* 1991;325(6):388–392.

16. Barnes PJ, Pedersen S, Busse WW. Efficacy and safety of inhaled corticosteroids. New developments. *Am J Respir Crit Care Med.* 1998;157(3 pt 2):S1–S53.

17. Leff JA, Busse WW, Pearlman D, et al. Montelukast, a leukotriene-receptor antagonist, for the treatment of mild asthma and exercise-induced bronchoconstriction. *N Engl J Med.* 1998;339(3):147–152.

18. Hootman JM, Dick R, Agel J. Epidemiology of collegiate injuries for 15 sports: summary and recommendations for injury prevention initiatives. *J Athl Train.* 2007;42(2):311–319.

19. Lincoln AE, Caswell SV, Almquist JL, Dunn RE, Norris JB, Hinton RY. Trends in concussion incidence in high school sports: a prospective 11-year study. *Am J Sports Med.* 2011;39(5):958–963.

20. Langlois JA, Rutland-Brown W, Wald MM. The epidemiology and impact of traumatic brain injury: a brief overview. *J Head Trauma Rehabil.* 2006;21(5):375–378.

21. Mueller F, Cantu R, eds. *Football Fatalities and Catastrophic Injuries: 1931–2008.* Durham, NC: Carolina Academic Press; 2010.

22. National Center for Catastrophic Sport Injury Research. http://unc.edu/depts/nccsi. Accessed October 6, 2011.

23. Guskiewicz KM, Bruce SL, Cantu RC, et al. National Athletic Trainers' Association position statement: management of sport-related concussion. *J Athl Train.* 2004;39(3):280–297.

24. Halstead DP. Performance testing updates in head, face, and eye protection. *J Athl Train.* 2001;36(3):322–327.

25. McCrea M, Hammeke T, Olsen G, Leo P, Guskiewicz K. Unreported concussion in high school football players: implications for prevention. *Clin J Sport Med.* 2004;14(1):13–17.

26. Register-Mihalik JK, Guskiewicz KM, Marshall SW, et al. *Knowledge, Attitudes, and Behaviors Concerning Concussion Among High School Athletes* [dissertation]. The University of North Carolina at Chapel Hill;2010.

27. Broglio SP, Macciocchi SN, Ferrara MS. Sensitivity of the concussion assessment battery. *Neurosurgery.* 2007;60(6):1050–1058.

28. McCrea M, Guskiewicz KM, Marshall SW, et al. Acute effects and recovery time following concussion in collegiate football players: the NCAA Concussion Study. *JAMA.* 2003;290(19):2556–2563.

29. Guskiewicz KM, Ross SE, Marshall SW. Postural stability and neuropsychological deficits after concussion in collegiate athletes. *J Athl Train.* 2001;36(3):263–273.

30. McCrory P, Meeuwisse W, Johnston K, et al. Consensus statement on concussion in sport: the 3rd International Conference on Concussion in Sport held in Zurich, November 2008. *J Athl Train.* 2009;44(4):434–448.

31. McCrory P, Meeuwisse W, Johnston K, et al. Consensus statement on concussion in sport: the 3rd International Conference on Concussion in Sport held in Zurich, November 2008. *Clin J Sport Med.* 2009;19(3):185–200.

32. Guha A. Management of traumatic brain injury: some current evidence and applications. *Postgrad Med J.* 2004;80(949):650–653.

33. Swartz EE, Decoster LC, Norkus SA, Cappaert TA. The influence of various factors on high school football helmet face mask removal: a retrospective, cross-sectional analysis. *J Athl Train.* 2007;42(1):11–20.

34. Crosby E. Airway management after upper cervical spine injury: what have we learned? *Can J Anaesth.* 2002;49(7):733–744.

35. Sanchez AR II, Sugalski MT, LaPrade RF. Fieldside and prehospital management of the spine-injured athlete. *Curr Sports Med Rep.* 2005;4(1): 50–55.

36. Domeier RM, Frederiksen SM, Welch K. Prospective performance assessment of an out-of-hospital protocol for selective spine immobilization using clinical spine clearance criteria. *Ann Emerg Med.* 2005;46(2):123–131.

37. Domeier RM, Swor RA, Evans RW, et al. Multicenter prospective validation of prehospital clinical spinal clearance criteria. *J Trauma.* 2002;53(4): 744–750.

38. Holly LT, Kelly DF, Counelis GJ, Blinman T, McArthur DL, Cryer HG. Cervical spine trauma associated with moderate and severe head injury: incidence, risk factors, and injury characteristics. *J Neurosurg.* 2002;96(3 suppl):285–291.

39. Iida H, Tachibana S, Kitahara T, Horiike S, Ohwada T, Fujii K. Association of head trauma with cervical spine injury, spinal cord injury, or both. *J Trauma.* 1999;46(3):450–452.

40. Crosby ET. Airway management in adults after cervical spine trauma. *Anesthesiology.* 2006;104(6): 1293–1318.

41. Lennarson PJ, Smith DW, Sawin PD, Todd MM, Sato Y, Traynelis VC. Cervical spinal motion during intubation: efficacy of stabilization maneuvers in the setting of complete segmental instability. *J Neurosurg.* 2001;94(2 suppl):265–270.

42. Turner LM. Cervical spine immobilization with axial traction: a practice to be discouraged. *J Emerg Med.* 1989;7(4):385–386.

43. Bivins HG, Ford S, Bezmalinovic Z, Price HM, Williams JL. The effect of axial traction during orotracheal intubation of the trauma victim with an unstable cervical spine. *Ann Emerg Med.* 1988;17(1):25–29.

44. Aprahamian C, Thompson BM, Finger WA, Darin JC. Experimental cervical spine injury model: evaluation of airway management and splinting techniques. *Ann Emerg Med.* 1984;13(8):584–587.

45. Gabbott DA, Baskett PJ. Management of the airway and ventilation during resuscitation. *Br J Anaesth.* 1997;79(2):159–171.

46. Cantu RC. Head and spine injuries in the young athlete. *Clin Sports Med.* 1988;7(3):459–472.

47. De Lorenzo RA, Olson JE, Boska M, et al. Optimal positioning for cervical immobilization. *Ann Emerg Med.* 1996;28(3):301–308.

48. De Lorenzo RA. A review of spinal immobilization techniques. *J Emerg Med.* 1996;14(5):603–613.

49. Chandler DR, Nemejc C, Adkins RH, Waters RL. Emergency cervical-spine immobilization. *Ann Emerg Med.* 1992;21(10):1185–1188.

50. Gerling MC, Davis DP, Hamilton RS, et al. Effects of cervical spine immobilization technique and laryngoscope blade selection on an unstable cervical spine in a cadaver model of intubation. *Ann Emerg Med.* 2000;36(4):293–300.

51. Johnson DR, Hauswald M, Stockhoff C. Comparison of a vacuum splint device to a rigid

backboard for spinal immobilization. *Am J Emerg Med.* 1996;14(4):369–372.

52. Luscombe MD, Williams JL. Comparison of a long spinal board and vacuum mattress for spinal immobilisation. *Emerg Med J.* 2003;20(5): 476–478.

53. Donaldson WF III, Lauerman WC, Heil B, Blanc R, Swenson T. Helmet and shoulder pad removal from a player with suspected cervical spine injury: a cadaveric model. *Spine (Phila Pa 1976).* 1998;23(16):1729–1733.

54. Prinsen RK, Syrotuik DG, Reid DC. Position of the cervical vertebrae during helmet removal and cervical collar application in football and hockey. *Clin J Sport Med.* 1995;5(3):155–161.

55. Metz CM, Kuhn JE, Greenfield ML. Cervical spine alignment in immobilized hockey players: radiographic analysis with and without helmets and shoulder pads. *Clin J Sport Med.* 1998;8(2): 92–95.

56. Tierney RT, Mattacola CG, Sitler MR, Maldjian C. Head position and football equipment influence cervical spinal-cord space during immobilization. *J Athl Train.* 2002;37(2):185–189.

57. Sherbondy PS, Hertel JN, Sebastianelli WJ, Milton S. The effect of protective equipment on cervical spine alignment in collegiate lacrosse players. *Am J Sports Med.* 2006;34(10):1675–1679.

58. Mihalik JP, Beard JR, Petschauer MA, Prentice WE, Guskiewicz KM. Effect of ice hockey helmet fit on cervical spine motion during an emergency log roll procedure. *Clin J Sport Med.* 2008;18(5):394–398.

59. Copeland AJ, Decoster LC, Swartz EE, Gattie ER, Gale SD. Combined tool approach is 100% successful for emergency football face mask removal. *Clin J Sport Med.* 2007;17(6):452–457.

60. Gale SD, Decoster LC, Swartz EE. The combined tool approach for face mask removal during on-field conditions. *J Athl Train.* 2008;43(1):14–20.

61. Toler JD, Petschauer MA, Mihalik JP, Oyama S, Halverson SD, Guskiewicz KM. Comparison of 3 airway access techniques during suspected spine injury management in American football. *Clin J Sport Med.* 2010;20(2):92–97.

62. Banerjee R, Palumbo MA, Fadale PD. Catastrophic cervical spine injuries in the collision sport athlete, part I: epidemiology, functional anatomy, and diagnosis. *Am J Sports Med.* 2004;32(4):1077–1087.

63. Clark CR, Ducker TB, Cervical Spine Research Society. *The Cervical Spine.* 3rd ed. Philadelphia, PA: Lippincott-Raven; 1998:xx, 1003.

64. Hulsebosch CE. Recent advances in pathophysiology and treatment of spinal cord injury. *Adv Physiol Educ.* 2002;26:238–255.

65. Swartz EE, Boden BP, Courson RW, et al. National Athletic Trainers' Association position statement: acute management of the cervical spine-injured athlete. *J Athl Train.* 2009;44(3):306–331.

66. Ellis JL, Gottlieb JE. Return-to-play decisions after cervical spine injuries. *Curr Sports Med Rep.* 2007;6(1–4):56–61.

67. Zinman B, Ruderman N, Campaigne BN, Devlin JT, Schneider SH. Physical activity/exercise and diabetes. *Diabetes Care.* 2004;27(suppl 1):S58-S62.

68. Riddell MC, Perkins BA. Type 1 diabetes and exercise, part I: applications of exercise physiology to patient management during vigorous activity. *Can J Diabetes.* 2006;30(1):63–71.

69. The Diabetes Control and Complications Trial Research Group. The effect of intensive treatment of diabetes on the development and progression of long-term complications in insulin-dependent diabetes mellitus. *N Engl J Med.* 1993;329(14):977–986.

70. Ludvigsson J, Nordfeldt S. Hypoglycaemia during intensified insulin therapy of children and adolescents. *J Pediatr Endocrinol Metab.* 1998;11(suppl 1):159–166.

71. The Diabetes Control and Complications Trial Research Group. Hypoglycemia in the Diabetes Control and Complications Trial. *Diabetes.* 1997;46(2):271–286.

72. American Diabetes Association. Care of children with diabetes in the school and day care setting. *Diabetes Care.* 1999;22(1):163–166.

73. Berger M. Adjustments of insulin and oral agent therapy. In: Ruderman N, Devlin JT, Schneider SH, Kriska A, eds. *Handbook of Exercise in Diabetes.* Alexandria, VA: American Diabetes Association; 2002:365–376.

74. Wright DA, Sherman WM, Dernbach AR. Carbohydrate feedings before, during, or in combination improve cycling endurance performance. *J Appl Physiol.* 1991;71(3):1082–1088.

75. Marliss EB, Vranic M. Intense exercise has unique effects on both insulin release and its roles in glucoregulation: implications for diabetes. *Diabetes.* 2002;51(suppl 1):S271-S283.

76. Mitchell TH, Abraham G, Schiffrin A, Leiter LA, Marliss EB. Hyperglycemia after intense exercise in IDDM subjects during continuous subcutaneous

insulin infusion. *Diabetes Care.* 1988;11(4): 311–317.

77. Hargreaves M, Angus D, Howlett K, Conus NM, Febbraio M. Effect of heat stress on glucose kinetics during exercise. *J Appl Physiol.* 1996;81(4):1594–1597.

78. Cryer PE, Davis SN, Shamoon H. Hypoglycemia in diabetes. *Diabetes Care.* 2003;26(6):1902–1912.

79. Bolli GB. How to ameliorate the problem of hypoglycemia in intensive as well as nonintensive treatment of type 1 diabetes. *Diabetes Care.* 1999;22(suppl 2):B43–B52.

80. McAulay V, Deary IJ, Frier BM. Symptoms of hypoglycaemia in people with diabetes. *Diabet Med.* 2001;18(9):690–705.

81. Hornsby WG Jr, Chetlin RD. Management of competitive athletes with diabetes. *Diabetes Spectrum.* 2005;18(2):102–107.

82. American Diabetes Association. Hypoglycemia (low blood glucose). http://www.diabetes.org/type-1-diabetes/hypoglycemia.jsp. Accessed September 13, 2011.

83. American Diabetes Association. Living with diabetes. http://www.dia betes.org/living-with-diabetes/treatment-and-care/blood-glucose-control/tight-diabetes-control.html. Accessed September 13, 2011.

84. American College of Sports Medicine, Armstrong LE, Casa DJ, et al. Exertional heat illnesses during training and competition. *Med Sci Sports Exerc.* 2007;39(3):556–572.

85. Mora-Rodriguez R, Del Coso J, Estevez E. Thermoregulatory responses to constant versus variable-intensity exercise in the heat. *Med Sci Sports Exerc.* 2008;40(11):1945–1952.

86. Casa DJ, Armstrong LE, Ganio MS, Yeargin S. Exertional heat stroke in competitive athletes. *Curr Sports Med Rep.* 2005;4(6):309–317.

87. Montain SJ, Coyle EF. Influence of graded dehydration on hyperthermia and cardiovascular drift during exercise. *J Appl Physiol.* 1992;73(4): 1340–1350.

88. Hubbard RW, Armstrong LE. The heat illness: biochemical, ultrastructural, and fluid-electrolyte considerations. In: Pandolf KB, Sawka N, Gonzalez RR. *Human Performance Physiology and Environment Medicine at Terrestrial Extremes.* Indianapolis, IN: Benchmark Press; 1988: 305–359.

89. Bergeron MF, McKeag DB, Casa DJ, et al. Youth football: heat stress and injury risk. *Med Sci Sports Exerc.* 2005;37(8):1421–1430.

90. Armstrong LE, Maresh CM. The induction and decay of heat acclimatisation in trained athletes. *Sports Med.* 1991;12(5):302–312.

91. Binkley HM, Beckett J, Casa DJ, Kleiner DM, Plummer PE. National Athletic Trainers' position statement: exertional heat illnesses. *J Athl Train.* 2002;37(3):329–343.

92. Casa DJ, Almquist J, Anderson S. Inter-Association Task Force on Exertional Heat Illnesses consensus statement. *NATA News.* June 2003;24–29.

93. Casa DJ, Csillan D; Inter-Association Task Force for Preseason Secondary School Athletics Participants. Preseason heat-acclimatization guidelines for secondary school athletics. *J Athl Train.* 2009;44(3):332–333.

94. Casa DJ, Armstrong LE, Hillman SK, et al. National Athletic Trainers' Association position statement: fluid replacement for athletes. *J Athl Train.* 2000;35(2):212–224.

95. Casa DJ, Stearns RL, Lopez RM, et al. Influence of hydration on physiological function and performance during trail running in the heat. *J Athl Train.* 2010;45(2):147–156.

96. Castellani J. Physiology of heat stress. In: Armstrong LE, ed. *Exertional Heat Illnesses.* Champaign, IL: Human Kinetics; 2003:1–15.

97. Sawka MN, Latzka WA, Matott RP, Montain SJ. Hydration effects on temperature regulation. *Int J Sports Med.* 1998;19(suppl 2):S108–S110.

98. Casa DJ, Clarkson PM, Roberts WO. American College of Sports Medicine roundtable on hydration and physical activity: consensus statements. *Curr Sports Med Rep.* 2005;4(3):115–127.

99. Epstein Y, Roberts WO. The pathophysiology of heat stroke: an integrative view of the final common pathway. *Scand J Med Sci Sports.* In press.

100. Bouchama A, Knochel JP. Heat stroke. *N Engl J Med.* 2002;346(25):1978–1988.

101. McDermott BP, Casa DJ, Yeargin SW, Ganio MS, Armstrong LE, Maresh CM. Recovery and return to activity following exertional heat stroke: considerations for the sports medicine staff. *J Sport Rehabil.* 2007;16(3):163–181.

102. Casa DJ, Becker SM, Ganio MS, et al. Validity of devices that assess body temperature during outdoor exercise in the heat. *J Athl Train.* 2007;42(3):333–342.

103. Costrini A. Emergency treatment of exertional heatstroke and comparison of whole body cooling techniques. *Med Sci Sports Exerc.* 1990;22(1):15–18.

104. Casa DJ, Anderson JM, Armstrong LE, Maresh CM. Survival strategy: acute treatment of exertional heat stroke. *J Strength Cond Res.* 2006;20(3):462.

105. Casa DJ, McDermott BP, Lee EC, Yeargin SW, Armstrong LE, Maresh CM. Cold water immersion: the gold standard for exertional heatstroke treatment. *Exerc Sport Sci Rev.* 2007;35(3):141–149.

106. O'Connor FG, Casa DJ, Bergeron MF, et al. American College of Sports Medicine roundtable on exertional heat stroke: return to duty/return to play. Conference proceedings. *Curr Sports Med Rep.* 2010;9(5):314–321.

107. Almond CSD, Shin AY, Fortescue EB, et al. Hyponatremia among runners in the Boston Marathon. *N Engl J Med.* 2005;352(15):1550–1556.

108. Armed Forces Health Surveillance Center. Update: exertional hyponatremia, active component, U.S. Armed Forces, 1999–2010. *MSMR.* 2011;18(3):12–15.

109. Hoffman MD, Stuempfle JK, Rogers IR, Wescheler LB, Hew-Butler T. Hyponatremia in the 2009 161-km Western States Endurance Run. *Int J Sports Physiol Perform.* In press.

110. Casa DJ, Roberts WO. Considerations for the medical staff in preventing, identifying and treating exertional heat illnesses. In Armstrong LE, ed. *Exertional Heat Illnesses.* Champaign, IL: Human Kinetics; 2003:169–195.

111. Armstrong LE, Epstein Y. Fluid-electrolyte balance during labor and exercise: concepts and misconceptions. *Int J Sport Nutr.* 1999;9(1):1–12.

112. Armstrong LE, Curtis WC, Hubbard RW, Francesconi RP, Moore R, Askew W. Symptomatic hyponatremia during prolonged exercise in the heat. *Med Sci Sports Exerc.* 1993;25(5):543–549.

113. Hew-Butler T, Ayus JC, Kipps C, et al. Statement of the Second International Exercise-Associated Hyponatremia Consensus Development Conference, New Zealand, 2007. *Clin J Sport Med.* 2008;18(2):111–121.

114. Speedy DB, Noakes TD, Schneider C. Exercise-associated hyponatremia: a review. *Emerg Med (Fremantle).* 2001;13(1):17–27.

115. American College of Sports Medicine, Sawka MN, Burke LM, et al. American College of Sports Medicine position stand: exercise and fluid replacement. *Med Sci Sports Exerc.* 2007;39(2):377–390.

116. Armstrong LE. Exertional hyponatremia. In: Armstrong LE, ed. *Exertional Heat Illnesses.* Champaign, IL: Human Kinetics; 2003:103–135.

117. Shirreffs SM, Taylor AJ, Leiper JB, Maughan RJ. Post-exercise rehydration in man: effects of volume consumed and drink sodium content. *Med Sci Sports Exerc.* 1996;28(10):1260–1271.

118. Armstrong LE. Assessing hydration status: the elusive gold standard. *J Am Coll Nutr.* 2007;26(suppl 5):S575–S584.

119. Armstrong LE, McDermott BP. Symptomatic exertional hyponatremia. In: Casa DJ, ed. *Preventing Sudden Death in Sport and Physical Activity.* Burlington, MA: Jones and Bartlett; 2012:185–200.

120. Ayus JC, Krothapalli RK, Arieff AI. Treatment of symptomatic hyponatremia and its relation to brain damage: a prospective study. *N Engl J Med.* 1987;317(19):1190–1195.

121. Diggs LW, Flowers E. High school athletes with the sickle cell trait (Hb A/S). *J Natl Med Assoc.* 1976;68(6):492–493, 479.

122. Murphy JR. Sickle cell hemoglobin (Hb AS) in black football players. *J Am Med Assoc.* 1973:225(8):981–982.

123. National Athletic Trainers' Association. Sickle cell trait and the athlete. http://www.nata.org/consensus-statements. Accessed September 13, 2011.

124. Anzalone ML, Green VS, Buja M, Sanchez LA, Harrykissoon RI, Eichner ER. Sickle cell trait and fatal rhabdomyolysis in football training: a case study. *Med Sci Sports Exerc.* 2010;42(1):3–7.

125. Eichner ER. Sickle cell trait in sports. *Curr Sports Med Rep.* 2010;9(6):347–351.

126. Carek PF, Futrell M, Hueston WJ. The preparticipation physical examination history: who has the correct answers? *Clin J Sport Med.* 1999;9(3):124–128.

127. Bonham VL, Dover GJ, Brody LC. Screening student athletes for sickle cell trait: a social and clinical experiment. *N Engl J Med.* 2010;363(11):997–999.

128. Schnebel B, Eichner ER, Anderson S, Watson C. Sickle cell trait and lumbar myonecrosis as a cause of low back pain in athletes [abstract]. *Med Sci Sports Exerc.* 2008;40(suppl 5):S537.

129. Eichner ER. Sickle cell trait. *J Sport Rehabil.* 2007;16(3):197–203.

130. Gardner JW, Kark JA. Fatal rhabdomyolysis presenting as mild heat illness in military training. *Mil Med.* 1994;159(2):160–163.

131. Helzlsouer KJ, Hayden FG, Rogol AD. Severe metabolic complications in a cross-country runner with sickle cell trait. *JAMA.* 1983;249(6):777–779.

132. West SA, Ciccolella ME. Issues in the standard of care for certified athletic trainers. *J Legal Asp Sport.* 2004;14(1):63–74.

133. Hale MH, Clugston JR, Prine BR, Pass AN, Gupta A. Severe low back pain in a football player. Poster presented at: American Medical Society for Sports Medicine 17th Annual Meeting; March 25–29, 2008; Las Vegas, NV.

134. National Athletic Trainers' Association. *Heads Up: Reducing the Risk of Head and Neck Injuries in Football* [DVD]. Dallas, TX: National Athletic Trainers' Association; 2006.

135. USA Football. *Tackle Progression.* Indianapolis, IN. http://videos.usafootball.com/video/Tackle-Progression-Level-of-C-2. Accessed October 3, 2011.

136. Torg JS, Truex R Jr, Quedenfeld TC, Burstein A, Spealman A, Nichols CE III. The National Football Head and Neck Injury Registry: report and conclusions, 1978. *JAMA.* 1979;241(14):1477–1479.

137. Torg JS, Vegso JJ, O'Neill MJ, Sennett B. The epidemiologic, pathologic, biomechanical, and cinematographic analysis of football-induced cervical spine trauma. *Am J Sports Med.* 1990;18(1):50–57.

138. Torg JS, Quedenfeld TC, Burstein A, Spealman AD, Nichols CE III. National Football Head and Neck Injury Registry: report on cervical quadriplegia, 1971 to 1975. *Am J Sports Med.* 1979;7(2):127–132.

139. Bishop PJ. Factors related to quadriplegia in football and the implications for intervention strategies. *Am J Sports Med.* 1996;24(2):235–239.

140. Bishop PJ, Wells RP. The inappropriateness of helmet drop tests in assessing neck protection in head-first impacts. *Am J Sports Med.* 1990;18(2):201–205.

141. Burstein AH, Otis JC, Torg JS. Mechanics and pathomechanics of athletic injuries to the cervical spine. In: Torg JS, ed. *Athletic Injuries to the Head, Neck, and Face.* Philadelphia, PA: Lea & Febiger; 1982:139–154.

142. Cantu RC, Mueller FO. Catastrophic football injuries: 1977–1998. *Neurosurgery.* 2000;47(3):673–675.

143. Mueller FO, Blyth CS. Fatalities from head and cervical spine injuries occurring in tackle football: 40 years' experience. *Clin Sports Med.* 1987;6(1):185–196.

144. Heck JF. The incidence of spearing by high school football ball carriers and their tacklers. *J Athl Train.* 1992;27(2):120–124.

145. Hodgson VR, Thomas LM. Play head-up football. *Natl Fed News.* 1985;2:24–27.

146. Heck JF. The incidence of spearing during a high school's 1975 and 1990 football seasons. *J Athl Train.* 1996;31(1):31–37.

147. National Federation of State High School Associations. *Official Football Rules.* Indianapolis, IN: National Federation of State High School Associations; 2002.

148. Kleiner DM, Almquist JL, Bailes J, et al. *Prehospital Care of the Spine-Injured Athlete.* Dallas, TX: Inter-Association Task Force for Appropriate Care of the Spine-Injured Athlete; 2001.

149. Heck JF. Re-examining spearing: the incidence of cervical spine injury hides the risks. *Am Football Coach.* 1999;5(8):52–54.

150. Clarke KS. Cornerstones for future directions in head/neck injury prevention in sports. In: Hoerner EF, ed. *Head and Neck Injuries in Sports: ASTM STP 1229.* Philadelphia, PA: American Society for Testing and Materials; 1994(1229):3–9.

151. Heck JF, Weis MP, Gartland JM, Weis CR. Minimizing liability risks of head and neck injuries in football. *J Athl Train.* 1994;29(2):128–139.

152. Centers for Disease Control. Football-related spinal cord injuries among high school players: Louisiana, 1989. *MMWR Morb Mortal Wkly Rep.* 1990;39(34):586–587.

153. Drake GA. Research provides more suggestions to reduce serious football injuries. *Natl Fed News.* November/December 1994;18–21.

154. Peterson TR. Roundtable: head and neck injuries in football. Paper presented at: American Society for Testing and Materials International Symposium on Head and Neck Injuries in Sports; May 1993; Atlanta, GA.

155. Heck J. Helmet contact penalties and historical changes. http://www.jonheck.com/hdc/penalties.htm. Accessed July 11, 2010.

156. Mihalik JP, Bell DR, Marshall SW, Guskiewicz KM. Measurement of head impacts in collegiate football players: an investigation of positional and

event-type differences. *Neurosurgery.* 2007;61(6): 1229–1235.

157. Heck J. NCAA helmet-contact penalty data: major Division I football, 2000–2007. http://www.jonheck.com/hdc/enforcement.htm. Accessed September 28, 2011.

158. National Federation of State High School Associations. *Official Football Rules.* Indianapolis, IN: National Federation of State High School Associations; 1988.

159. National Lightning Safety Institute. Multiagency recommendations for lightning safety. http://www.lightningsafety.com/nlsi_pls/multi_recommendation.html. Accessed September 13, 2011.

160. Holle RL. Lightning-caused deaths and injuries in and near dwellings and other buildings. Paper presented at: 4th Conference on the Meteorological Applications of Lightning Data; January 11–15, 2009; Phoenix, AZ.

161. Bennett B, Holle R, Lopez R. Lightning safety guidelines. In: Klossner D, ed. *National Collegiate Athletic Association Sports Medicine Handbook, 2010–2011.* Overland Park, KS: National Collegiate Athletic Association; 2010:13–15.

162. Walsh KM, Bennett B, Cooper MA, Holle RL, Kithil R, Lopez REL. National Athletic Trainers' Association position statement: lightning safety for athletics and recreation. *J Athl Train.* 2000;35(4):471–477.

163. Rakov VA. Lightning protection of structures and personal safety. Paper presented at: International Lightning Detection Conference; November 7–8, 2000; Tucson, AZ.

164. Roeder WP, Vavrek RJ. Lightning safety for schools: an update. National Oceanic and Atmospheric Administration. http://www.lightningsafety.noaa.gov/resources/ASSE-Schools.pdf. Accessed September 13, 2011.

165. Holle RL. Lightning-caused deaths and injuries in the vicinity of vehicles. Paper presented at: 3rd Conference on Meteorological Applications of Lightning Data; January 19–23, 2008; New Orleans, LA.

166. Cherington M. Lightning injuries in sports: situations to avoid. *Sports* Med. 2001;31(4):301–308.

167. Lengyel MM, Brooks HE, Holle RL, Cooper MA. Lightning casualties and their proximity to surrounding cloud-to-ground lightning. Paper presented at: American Meteorological Society annual meeting; January 9–13, 2005; San Diego, CA.

168. Holle RL, Lopez RE, Howard KW, Vavrek J, Allsopp J. Safety in the presence of lightning. *Semin Neurol.* 1995;15(4):375–380.

169. Duclos PJ, Sanderson LM. An epidemiological description of lightning-related deaths in the United States. *Int J Epidemiol.* 1990;19(3):673–679.

170. Uman M. *All About Lightning.* New York, NY: Dover Publications; 1986.

171. Cooper MA. Lightning prognostic signs for death. *Ann Emerg Med.* 1980;9(3):134–138.

172. Cooper MA. Myths, miracles, and mirages. *Semin Neurol.* 1995;15(4):358–361.

173. Cooper MA. Emergent care of lightning and electrical injuries. *Semin Neurol.* 1995;15(3):268–278.

174. Cooper MA. Lightning injuries. eMedicine. http://emedicine.medscape.com/article/770642. Accessed September 13, 2011.

175. Holle RL, Cummins KL, Demetriades NWS. Monthly distributions of NLDN and GLD360 cloud-to-ground lightning. Paper presented at: International Lightning Detection Conference; April 21–22, 2010; Orlando, FL.

176. Lopez RE, Holle RL, Heitkamp TA, Boyson M, Cherington M, Langford K. The underreporting of lightning injuries and deaths in Colorado. *Bull Am Meterol Soc.* 1993;74(11):2171–2178.

177. Lopez RE, Holle RL. Demographics of lightning casualties. *Semin Neurol.* 1995;15(3):286–295.

178. Rakov V, Uman M. *Lightning: Physics and Effects.* Cambridge, England: Cambridge University Press; 2003.

179. American Meteorological Society. Lightning safety awareness statement. http://ametsoc.org/policy/lightningpolicy_2002.html. Accessed September 15, 2011.

180. Steinbaum S, Harviel JD, Jaffin JH, Jordan MH. Lightning strike to the head: a case report. *J Trauma.* 1994;36(1):113–115.

181. Cherington M. Neurological manifestations of lightning strikes. *Neurology.* 2003;60(2):182–185.

182. Field JM, Hazinski MF, Sayre MR, et al. Part I: executive summary. 2010 American Heart Association guidelines for cardiopulmonary resuscitation and emergency cardiovascular care. *Circulation.* 2010;122(18, suppl 3):S640–S656.

183. Maron BJ. Sudden death in young athletes. *N Engl J Med.* 2003;349(11):1064–1075.

184. Van Camp SP, Bloor CM, Mueller FO, Cantu RC, Olson HG. Nontraumatic sports death in high

school and college athletes. *Med Sci Sports Exerc.* 1995;27(5):641–647.

185. Harmon K, Asif I, Klossner D, Drezner J. Incidence of sudden cardiac death in NCAA athletes. *Circulation.* 2011;123(15):1594–1600.

186. Drezner JA, Rogers KJ, Zimmer RR, Sennett BJ. Use of automated external defibrillators at NCAA Division I universities. *Med Sci Sports Exerc.* 2005;37(9):1487–1492.

187. Maron BJ, Doerer JJ, Haas TS, Tierney DM, Mueller FO. Profile and frequency of sudden death in 1463 young competitive athletes: from a 25 year U.S. national registry, 1980–2005. Paper presented at: American Heart Association Scientific Sessions; November 12–15, 2006; Chicago, IL.

188. Maron BJ, Shirani J, Poliac LC, Mathenge R, Roberts WC, Mueller FO. Sudden death in young competitive athletes: clinical, demographic, and pathological profiles. *JAMA.* 1996;276(3): 199–204.

189. Basso C, Maron BJ, Corrado D, Thiene G. Clinical profile of congenital coronary artery anomalies with origin from the wrong aortic sinus leading to sudden death in young competitive athletes. *J Am Coll Cardiol.* 2000;35(6):1493–1501.

190. Maron BJ, Thompson PD, Puffer JC, et al. Cardiovascular preparticipation screening of competitive athletes: a statement for health professionals from the Sudden Death Committee (clinical cardiology) and Congenital Cardiac Defects Committee (cardiovascular disease in the young), American Heart Association. *Circulation.* 1996;9(4):850–856.

191. Maron BJ, Douglas PS, Graham TP, Nishimura RA, Thompson PD. Task Force 1: preparticipation screening and diagnosis of cardiovascular disease in athletes. *J Am Coll Cardiol.* 2005;45(8): 1322–1326.

192. Andersen J, Courson RW, Kleiner DM, McLoda TA. National Athletic Trainers' Association position statement: emergency planning in athletics. *J Athl Train.* 2002;37(1):99–104.

193. Emergency Care Committee, Subcommittees and Task Forces of the American Heart Association. 2005 American Heart Association guidelines for cardiopulmonary resuscitation and emergency cardiovascular care, part 3: overview of CPR. *Circulation.* 2005;112(suppl 24):IV12–IV18.

194. Drezner JA, Rao AL, Heistand J, Bloomingdale MK, Harmon KG. Effectiveness of emergency response planning for sudden cardiac arrest in United States high schools with automated external defibrillators. *Circulation.* 2009;120(6):518–525.

195. Drezner JA, Courson RW, Roberts WO, Mosesso VN Jr, Link MS, Maron BJ. Inter-association Task Force recommendations on emergency preparedness and management of sudden cardiac arrest in high school and college athletic programs: a consensus statement. *J Athl Train.* 2007; 42(1):143–158.

196. Emergency Care Committee, Subcommittees and Task Forces of the American Heart Association. 2005 American Heart Association guidelines for cardiopulmonary resuscitation and emergency cardiovascular care, part 4: adult basic life support. *Circulation.* 2005;112(suppl 24):IV19–IV34.

197. Emergency Care Committee, Subcommittees and Task Forces of the American Heart Association. 2005 American Heart Association guidelines for cardiopulmonary resuscitation and emergency cardiovascular care, part 5: electrical therapies. Automated external defibrillators, defibrillation, cardioversion, and pacing. *Circulation.* 2005; 112(suppl 24):IV35–IV46.

198. The American Heart Association in collaboration with the International Liaison Committee on Resuscitation. Guidelines 2000 for cardiopulmonary resuscitation and emergency cardiovascular care, part 4: the automated external defibrillator. Key link in the chain of survival. *Circulation.* 2000;102(suppl 8):I60–I76.

199. Caffrey SL, Willoughby PJ, Pepe PE, Becker LB. Public use of automated external defibrillators. *N Engl J Med.* 2002;347(16):1242–1247.

200. Hallstrom AP, Ornato JP, Weisfeldt M, et al. Public-access defibrillation and survival after out-of-hospital cardiac arrest. *N Engl J Med.* 2004;351(7): 637–646.

201. Page RL, Joglar JA, Kowal RC, et al. Use of automated external defibrillators by a U.S. airline. *N Engl J Med.* 2000;343(17):1210–1216.

202. Valenzuela TD, Roe DJ, Nichol G, Clark LL, Spaite DW, Hardman RG. Outcomes of rapid defibrillation by security officers after cardiac arrest in casinos. *N Engl J Med.* 2000;343(17):1206–1209.

203. Weaver WD, Hill D, Fahrenbruch CE, et al. Use of the automatic external defibrillator in the management of out-of-hospital cardiac arrest. *N Engl J Med.* 1988;319(11):661–666.

204. White RD, Asplin BR, Bugliosi TF, Hankins DG. High discharge survival rate after out-of-hospital

ventricular fibrillation with rapid defibrillation by police and paramedics. *Ann Emerg Med.* 1996;28(5):480–485.

205. Myerburg RJ, Fenster J, Velez M, et al. Impact of community-wide police car deployment of automated external defibrillators on survival from out-of-hospital cardiac arrest. *Circulation.* 2002;106(9):1058–1064.

206. White RD, Bunch TJ, Hankins DG. Evolution of a community-wide early defibrillation programme experience over 13 years using police/fire personnel and paramedics as responders. *Resuscitation.* 2005;65(3):279–283.

207. Mosesso VN Jr, Davis EA, Auble TE, Paris PM, Yealy DM. Use of automated external defibrillators by police officers for treatment of out of-hospital cardiac arrest. *Ann Emerg Med.* 1998;32(2):200–207.

Address correspondence to National Athletic Trainers' Association, Communications Department, 2952 Stemmons Freeway, Dallas, TX 75247.

Appendix 2

National Athletic Trainers' Association Position Statement: Safe Weight Loss and Maintenance Practices in Sport and Exercise

Paula Sammarone Turocy, EdD, ATC (Chair)*; Bernard F. DePalma, MEd, PT, ATC†; Craig A. Horswill, PhD‡; Kathleen M. Laquale, PhD, ATC, LDN§; Thomas J. Martin, MD‖; Arlette C. Perry, PhD¶; Marla J. Somova, PhD#; Alan C. Utter, PhD, MPH, FACSM**

*Duquesne University, Pittsburgh, PA; †Cornell University, Ithaca, NY; ‡University of Illinois at Chicago and Trinity International University, Deerfield, IL; §Bridgewater State University, MA; ‖Hershey Medical Center, PA; ¶University of Miami, FL; #Carlow University, Pittsburgh, PA; **Appalachian State University, Boone, NC

Objective: To present athletic trainers with recommendations for safe weight loss and weight maintenance practices for athletes and active clients and to provide athletes, clients, coaches, and parents with safe guidelines that will allow athletes and clients to achieve and maintain weight and body composition goals.

Background: Unsafe weight management practices can compromise athletic performance and negatively affect health. Athletes and clients often attempt to lose weight by not eating, limiting caloric or specific nutrients from the diet, engaging in pathogenic weight control behaviors, and restricting fluids. These people often respond to pressures of the sport or activity, coaches, peers, or parents by adopting negative body images and unsafe practices to maintain an ideal body composition for the activity. We provide athletic trainers with recommendations for safe weight loss and weight maintenance in sport and exercise. Although safe weight gain is also a concern for athletic trainers and their athletes and clients, that topic is outside the scope of this position statement.

Recommendations: Athletic trainers are often the source of nutrition information for athletes and clients; therefore, they must have knowledge of proper nutrition, weight management practices, and methods to change body composition. Body composition assessments should be done in the most scientifically appropriate manner possible. Reasonable and individualized weight and body composition goals should be identified by appropriately trained health care personnel (eg, athletic trainers, registered dietitians, physicians). In keeping with the American Dietetics Association (ADA) preferred nomenclature, this document uses the terms *registered dietitian* or *dietician* when referring to a food and nutrition expert who has met the academic and professional requirements specified by the ADA's Commission on Accreditation for Dietetics Education. In some cases, a *registered nutritionist* may have equivalent credentials and be

Reprinted from Journal of Athletic Training 2011:46(3):322–336 © by the National Athletic Trainers' Association, Inc www.nata.org/jat.

the commonly used term. All weight management and exercise protocols used to achieve these goals should be safe and based on the most current evidence. Athletes, clients, parents, and coaches should be educated on how to determine safe weight and body composition so that athletes and clients more safely achieve competitive weights that will meet sport and activity requirements while also allowing them to meet their energy and nutritional needs for optimal health and performance.

Key Words: body composition, body fat, diet, hydration, metabolism, sport performance

---

Weight classifications in sport (eg, youth football, wrestling, rowing, boxing) were designed to ensure healthy, safe, and equitable participation[1]; however, not all sports or activities in which weight might play a role in performance use a weight classification system. In activities such as dance, distance running, gymnastics, and cycling, weight and body composition are believed to influence physical performance and the aesthetics of performance. Yet the governing organizations of these activities have no mandated weight control practices. In 2005, the American Academy of Pediatrics[2] published a general weight control practice guide for children and adolescents involved in all sports.

In addition to the potential performance benefits of lean body mass and lower levels of body fat, long-term health benefits include decreased cardiovascular risk factors, reduced triglyceride concentration, possible increases in cardioprotective high-density lipoprotein cholesterol concentration, increased fibrinolysis, reduced resting blood pressure, reduced resting glucose and insulin, and increased insulin sensitivity.[3] In females, lower body fat may also protect against breast and other reproductive cancers.[4] Although lean body mass has been associated with positive health benefits, negative health outcomes are associated with excessive loss or gain of body mass.[5]

Recommendations

Based on the current research and literature, the National Athletic Trainers' Association (NATA) suggests the following safe weight loss and weight maintenance strategies for participants in all sports and physical activities. These recommendations are built on the premise that scientific evidence supports safe and effective weight loss and weight management practices and techniques, regardless of the activity or performance goals. The recommendations are categorized using the Strength of Recommendation Taxonomy criterion scale proposed by the American Academy of Family Physicians[6] on the basis of the level of scientific data found in the literature. Each recommendation is followed by a letter describing the level of evidence found in the literature supporting the recommendation: *A* means there are well-designed experimental, clinical, or epidemiologic studies to support the recommendation; *B* means there are experimental, clinical, or epidemiologic studies that provide a strong theoretical rationale for the recommendation; and *C* means the recommendation is based largely on anecdotal evidence at this time.

Assessing Body Composition and Weight

1. Body composition assessments should be used to determine safe body weight and body composition goals. *Evidence Category: B*

2. Body composition data should be collected, managed, and used in the same manner as other personal and confidential medical information. *Evidence Category: C*

3. The body composition assessor should be appropriately trained and should use a valid and reliable body composition assessment technique (**Table 1**). *Evidence Category: C*

4. Body weight should be determined in a hydrated state. *Evidence Category: B*

5. When determining goal weight, body weight should be assessed relative to body composition. This assessment should occur twice annually for most people, with no less than 2 to 3 months between measurements (**Tables 2, 3**). *Evidence Category: C*

6. To track a person's progress toward a weight or body composition goal, private weigh-ins and body composition assessments should be scheduled at intervals that provide information to guide and refine progress, as well as to establish reinforcement and reassessment periods. *Evidence Category: C*

TABLE 1

BODY COMPOSITION ASSESSMENT TECHNIQUES[7]

Model	Assessment Technique	Standard Error of Estimate, %
2 Compartment	Hydrodensitometry	±2.5
	Air displacement plethysmography	±2.2–3.7[a]
	Skinfold measurements	±3.5[b]
	Near-infrared interactance	±5[b]
3 Compartment	Bioelectric impedance	±3.5–5[b]
	Dual-energy x-ray absorptiometry	±1.8[a]
Multiple compartment	Computed tomography or magnetic resonance imaging	Not fully developed[a]

[a]More research is needed.
[b]Differs with each equation.

TABLE 2

BODY FAT STANDARDS (%) BY SEX AND AGE

Body Fat Standard	Males	Females
Lowest reference body fat (adults)[5,8–11]	5	12
Lowest reference body fat (adolescents)[2,12]	7	14
Healthy body fat ranges[13]	10–22	20–32

TABLE 3

DETERMINING GOAL WEIGHT FROM BODY COMPOSITION

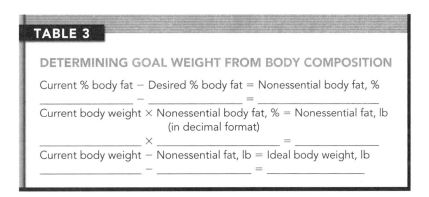

Current % body fat − Desired % body fat = Nonessential body fat, %

_____ − _____ = _____

Current body weight × Nonessential body fat, % = Nonessential fat, lb
(in decimal format)

_____ × _____ = _____

Current body weight − Nonessential fat, lb = Ideal body weight, lb

_____ − _____ = _____

7. When hydration is a concern, regular or more frequent (or both) assessments of body weight are indicated. *Evidence Category: C*

8. Active clients and athletes in weight classification sports should not gain or lose excessive amounts of body weight at any point in their training cycles. *Evidence Category: C*

9. Management of body composition should include both diet and exercise. *Evidence Category: B*

10. Total caloric intake should be determined by calculating the basal metabolic rate (BMR) and the energy needs for activity. *Evidence Category: B*

11. Caloric intake should be based on the body weight goal (**Table 4**). *Evidence Category: C*

12. A safe and healthy dietary plan that supplies sufficient energy and nutrients should be maintained throughout the year (**Table 5**). *Evidence Category: B*

13. The U.S. Department of Agriculture's Food Pyramid Guide is one of the methods that can be used to ensure adequate nutrient intake. *Evidence Category: C*

14. The metabolic qualities of the activity should be considered when calculating the need for each

---

TABLE 4

DETERMINING TOTAL CALORIC NEEDS

Harris-Benedict[14]
Female basal metabolic rate = 655.1 + (9.6 × weight [kg]) + (1.9 × height [cm]) − (4.7 × age [y]) + Activity needs
Male basal metabolic rate = 66.5 + (13.8 × wt [kg]) + (5 × ht [cm]) − (6.8 × age [y]) + Activity needs

Activity needs
Sedentary (mostly sitting): add 20%–40% of basal metabolic rate
Light activity (sitting, standing, some walking): add 55%–65% of basal metabolic rate
Moderate activity (standing and some exercise): add 70%–75% of basal metabolic rate
Heavy activity: add 80%–100% of basal metabolic rate

Mifflin–St. Jeor[15]
Female basal metabolic rate = (10 × wt [kg]) + (6.25 × ht [cm]) − (5 × age [y]) − 161
Male basal metabolic rate = (10 × wt [kg]) + (6.25 × ht [cm]) − (5 × age [y]) + 5

TABLE 5

DETERMINING ENERGY-PRODUCING NUTRIENT INTAKE

Protein intake
a. Calculation of protein needs based on activity levels:
BW, kg × g/kg BW = g of protein/kg BW
_____ × _____ = _____

b. Convert the g of protein into kcal needed:
_____ g protein × 4 = _____ kcal from protein

c. % Protein needed of total caloric intake:
_____ kcal from protein ÷ _____ total kcal = _____%

Carbohydrate intake
a. Calculation of CHO needs based on activity levels:
BW in kg × grams/kg BW = g of CHO/kg BW
_____ × _____ = _____

b. Convert the g of CHO into kcal needed:
_____ g CHO × 4 = _____ kcal from CHO

c. Convert % kcal into actual number of calories:
_____ kcal from CHO divided by _____ total kcal = _____%

Fat intake
a. Based on the remaining number of calories needed, calculate the fat intake needed:
CHO, kcal + protein, kcal = kcal from CHO and protein
_____ + _____ = (A) _____

b. Total caloric need − value A = fat needed, kcal
_____ − _____ = (B) _____

c. Value B ÷ 9 = fat, g
_____ ÷ 9 = _____

Abbreviations: BW, body weight; CHO, carbohydrate

TABLE 6

ENERGY-PRODUCING NUTRIENTS

Nutrient	General Population Requirement
Carbohydrates	5–7 g/kg of body weight per d
Proteins	0.8–1 g/kg of body weight per d
Fats	15%–35% of total caloric intake per d

TABLE 8

PROTEIN INTAKE[5,8,14,17,18]

Athlete Type	Recommendation
Strength athletes	1.7–1.8 g/kg of body weight (maximum = 2 g)
Endurance athletes	1.2–1.4 g/kg of body weight
General population	0.8–1 g/kg of body weight
Vegetarians	0.9–1 g/kg of body weight

energy-producing nutrient in the diet (**Tables 6–8**). *Evidence Category: B*

15. Safe and appropriate aerobic exercise will facilitate weight and body fat loss. *Evidence Category: C*

16. Body composition adjustments should be gradual, with no excessive restrictions or use of unsafe behaviors or products. *Evidence Category: C*

17. Combining weight management and body composition goals with physical conditioning periodization goals will assist athletes or clients in reaching weight goals. *Evidence Category: C*

18. Education on safe dietary and weight management practices should be communicated on a regular and planned basis. *Evidence Category: C*

19. Individual body composition or dietary needs should be discussed privately with appropriately trained nutrition and weight management experts. *Evidence Category: C*

20. Ergogenic and dietary aids should be ingested cautiously and under the advisement of those knowledgeable of the requirements of sports and other governing organizations. *Evidence Category: C*

Background and Literature Review

Weight management and nutrition is a multibillion-dollar industry that has become pervasive in almost every aspect of modern life. Diet and exercise have always affected sports and physical activity, but with the intensity of competition increasing at all levels has come a renewed interest in controlling the factors that influence performance and health. Diet, exercise, body composition, and weight management now play larger roles in an active person's life and performance. Because athletic trainers (ATs) and other members of the health care team have regular contact and ongoing relationships with athletes and clients engaged in active lifestyles, they are frequently asked for assistance in achieving personal and performance goals. These goals often include diet, exercise, and weight management. Some AT-client relationships and their shared body composition goals are formalized, as with weight-class sport athletes; others are not.

Weight Management in Weight-Class Sports

Many safe and effective methods are available to achieve and maintain goal weight and body composition. However, although published and widely accepted weight and body composition standards exist,[9] there are few published or mandated weight or body composition management requirements. Even within sports with weight-class systems (eg, boxing, lightweight crew, sprint football, wrestling), only wrestling and sprint

TABLE 7

CARBOHYDRATE INTAKE[5,16]

Activity Type	Recommendation
Optimal glycogen storage for single term or single event	7–10 g/kg of body weight per d
Carbohydrate for moderate-intensity or intermittent exercise >1 h	0.5–1 g/kg of body weight per h (30–60 g/h)
Daily recovery and fuel for aerobic athlete (1–3 h moderate-intensity to high-intensity exercise)	7–10 g/kg of body weight per d
Daily recovery and fuel for extreme exercise program (>4–5 h moderate-intensity to high-intensity exercise)	10–12 + g/kg of body weight per d

football consider the components of an athlete's weight and body composition, as well as the safety considerations for achieving and maintaining that body size.[19,20]

Since 1997, specific rules and guidelines have been implemented to ensure that weight control practices in wrestling are safe, applied early in the competitive season, and conducted on a regular and planned schedule around competitions and do not include dehydration as a means of weight loss.[1] These weight management and dehydration prevention regulations are effective in reducing unhealthy "weight-cutting" behaviors and promoting equitable competition.[21]

In 2006, the National Federation of State High School Associations adopted similar standards (ie, body composition, weigh-in procedures, and hydration status) for determining minimum body weights in high school wrestlers, but the body fat minimums were higher ($\geq$7% in males, $\geq$12% in females) than the levels for collegiate athletes determined by the National Collegiate Athletic Association (NCAA).[21] These differences were implemented to address growth needs in adolescents and sex differences. The National Federation of State High School Associations standards have not been accepted or enforced universally in the United States. Therefore, universally safe or effective weight management practices in high school wrestling are not assured.

Sprint football is a collegiate sport sponsored by 6 teams in the Collegiate Sprint Football League: Cornell University, Mansfield University, Princeton University, University of Pennsylvania, U.S. Military Academy at West Point (Army), and U.S. Naval Academy (Navy). Sprint football has the same rules as NCAA football but also has a weight limit for players of 172.0 lb (78 kg), which is far lower than the weights typically seen in NCAA football players.[20] To the previously required minimum body composition of 5% body fat, sprint football in 2008 added compulsory assessment of body composition and playing weight in a hydrated state with a urine specific gravity of <1.020.[20]

In 1997, collegiate lightweight crew and rowing athletes began using U.S. Rowing weight classifications and a 5% minimum body fat guideline to determine a safe rowing weight. Unlike wrestling, the revised 2007 crew weight requirements did not take into account the athlete's body composition or hydration status in determining minimum body weight. Although some institutions have adopted weight certification guidelines similar to those in wrestling, no formal rules are in place. Today's standards stipulate that male lightweight rowers must not exceed 160 lb (73 kg), and female lightweight rowers must not exceed 130 lb (59 kg). Minimum weights are in place only for coxswains. All crew members must be weighed once a day, between 1 and 2 hours before the scheduled time of the first race, each day that the athlete competes.[22]

Sport Performance and Aesthetics

Practices of weight manipulation and body fat control are not exclusive to sports with weight-class requirements. Participants in other activities requiring speed and aesthetics also use weight manipulation to improve performance. Leaner athletes in sports such as middle-distance and long-distance running, cycling, and speed skating are often perceived by coaches and peers to perform better.[10]

Although body fat contributes to weight, it does not always contribute to energy in the muscular contractions needed for exercise and sport. A disproportionately greater amount of muscle mass and smaller amount of body fat are needed by participants in activities that may be influenced by body size. In sports such as the broad jump or vertical jump, in which the body must be propelled through space, generating power is essential. More power can be achieved by a body with a higher ratio of muscle to fat than one of the same mass with a lower ratio of muscle to fat. In swimming, although body fat allows for greater buoyancy in water, which reduces drag, athletes with a greater proportion of muscle mass to fat can produce more speed.

Similarly, in sports such as ski jumping, a lean, slight build was once thought desirable to reduce air resistance and to allow the athlete to stay airborne as long as possible and to cover a greater distance before landing.[10] This performance standard also holds true for activities such as dance, figure skating, gymnastics, and diving. The aesthetic aspect of performance is also a consideration for weight management practices in these activities. Leaner participants are viewed as more attractive and successful[23,24] and perceived to demonstrate better body symmetry, position, and fluidity of motion.

Because no scientific or health principles support weight management for the purpose of aesthetics in performance, we will address this topic only in its association with body composition and weight management. Many considerations for aesthetic performance activities are related to the body composition of female participants, but research[25,26] also recognizes the effect of similar social pressures on male body images.

Pressures on participants to control weight stem from various sources, including society, family,[25,27–29] peers,[3] and coaches,[30–33] as well as the judging criteria used in some activities.[34] These pressures may place participants at higher risk for developing unrealistic weight goals and problematic weight control behaviors. Most aesthetic performance activities require fit body types for success, and these requirements may trigger an unhealthy preoccupation with weight.[35] Generally, participants in competitive activities that emphasize leanness for the sake of performance or aesthetic enhancement are at the highest risk for developing dysmorphia, eating disorders, and disordered eating.[36–40]

Because of the need to control all factors that may affect performance, perfectionism is a common psychological trait among athletes. Along with the desire to look thin and the belief that decreased weight enhances performance, perfectionism increases the risk of developing an eating disorder.[41–43] Perfectionism is typically associated with setting high goals and working hard to attain them, which enables athletes to succeed.[40,44] People who are aware of concerns about their weight from coaches, parents, teammates, friends, or significant others are more likely to develop subclinical eating disorders.[45]

In general, women in non–weight-class activities identify their ideal body sizes and shapes as smaller than their actual bodies, whereas men tend to want to be larger (ie, more muscular) and are more concerned with shape than with weight.[46–49] The demands of a male's activity determine whether desirable body size or weight (or both) is smaller (eg, gymnastics) or larger (eg, football). Because the topic of dysmorphia has been addressed more comprehensively in the NATA's position statement on preventing, detecting, and managing disordered eating in athletes,[50] it is addressed here only in the context of weight management practices.

Regardless of the rationale to support weight management practices, goal weights and body compositions for athletes and active clients must be determined and maintained in a safe and effective manner. The purposes of this position statement are to identify safe methods by which goal weight can be determined and maintained and to discuss unsafe weight management practices and the effects of those practices on performance and overall health.

Body Composition

To fully understand the topic of body composition, it is essential to understand how body composition is assessed. Using the most common description of body composition, the 2-compartment (2-C) model is a quantifiable measure that can be divided into 2 structural components: fat and fat-free mass (FFM). Fat-free mass consists primarily of muscle, bone, water, and remainder elements.[9] In the general population, excess body fat is associated with adverse health consequences, which include cardiovascular disease,[51] diabetes,[52]

gallstones,[53] orthopaedic problems,[54] and certain types of cancer.[55] Although active people have a lower incidence of these conditions, excess body fat combined with a family history of cardiovascular or metabolic diseases and inactivity can reverse the benefits of acquired health associated with an active, healthy lifestyle.

To develop a method for determining the risks associated with excess body fat, the body mass index (BMI) assessment was created. The original purpose of the BMI assessment was to predict the potential for developing the chronic diseases associated with obesity.[9] Body mass index may be an appropriate method for determining body size in the general population, but this technique does not assess fat mass and FFM. Therefore, BMI assessment is less accurate for athletes and active clients who have higher levels of FFM.[14] Even though a sedentary person and an active person may have the same height and weight, their fat to FFM ratios may be very different. When applied to the BMI formula, the active person's additional FFM skews the assessment of body composition, resulting in a BMI evaluation that is inaccurate as a predictor of increased risk for chronic diseases. More individualized body weight and body composition assessments are needed for active people with high levels of lean body mass to accurately evaluate the effect of body weight on the risk of developing chronic diseases (**Table 9**).

Body Weight, Fat, and FFM

Fat mass can be categorized as essential fat, sex-specific fat, and storage fat.[9] Essential fat, which averages 3% of total fat, makes up the bone marrow, heart, lungs, liver, spleen, kidneys, intestines, muscles, and lipid-rich tissues of the central nervous system.[9] In women, essential fat also may include sex-specific fat (eg, breasts, hips, pelvis) and averages 12%.[5,8–11] Storage fat, which averages 12% in men and 12% to 15% in women, is layered

TABLE 9

BODY MASS INDEX (BMI)[a] CLASSIFICATIONS[7]

BMI	Classification
<18.5	Underweight
18.5–24.99	Average (normal)
25.0–29.9	Overweight
30.0–34.9	Grade I obesity
35.0–39.9	Grade II obesity
≥40	Grade III extreme obesity

[a]BMI = weight, kg/height^2, m.

subcutaneously; it is stored by the body to provide an energy substrate for metabolism.[9] When essential fat is added to storage fat, men average 15% total body fat, whereas women average 20% to 27% total body fat. Low-reference body fat composition is 5% in men and 12% in women.[5,8–11] Low-reference body fat composition, which is necessary to maintain normal reproductive health and hormone function, is 7% in adolescent males and 14% in adolescent females.[2,12] Lower levels of fat have been associated with good health and normal body function.[5,8–11] Although no maximum body fat requirements exist, the highest safe weights should not exceed the body fat ranges considered satisfactory for health: 10% to 22% and 20% to 32% in physically mature adolescent males and females, respectively.[13]

Body fat is distributed in sex-specific patterns. Typically, women distribute more body fat in the gluteofemoral region in a gynoid fat distribution pattern, sometimes referred to as "pear shaped." Women also store more fat in the extremities than men. In contrast, men distribute more fat in the abdominal region in an android or "apple" pattern and have greater subscapular to triceps skinfold thickness than do women.[56] The android fat distribution has been related to more significant health consequences associated with cardiovascular disease, including diabetes, hypertension, and hyperlipidemia,[7,57] and may contribute more to increased disease risk than does obesity alone.[58]

Assessment of Body Composition

Several methods are available to measure body composition, but most research on assessment in athletes has focused on densitometry, indirect measurement of body density using a 2-C model consisting of fat mass and FFM. Body density is the ratio of body weight to body volume (Table 1).

Total body volume is typically measured by hydrostatic (underwater) weighing[59] with a correction for pulmonary residual lung volume.[60] Most other body composition techniques have been validated in comparison with hydrostatic weighing because of its lower standard error of the estimate. Similar to hydrostatic weighing, air displacement plethysmography is a newer densitometric method that measures mass and volume to calculate body density.[61]

Multicompartment models, in which FFM is divided into 2 or more components, have been validated with hydrostatic weighing methods in athletes.[59–65] Some authors[66–68] suggested that these multicompartment models may be more appropriate for the athletic population; however, these findings are not widely accepted. Two-compartment models demonstrated a significant

overestimation for air displacement plethysmography in collegiate football players[69] but close agreement between hydrostatic weighing and air displacement plethysmography in collegiate wrestlers.[70]

Some concerns have been raised about selecting the appropriate conversion formula when using the 2-C model to assess body composition in active people. The Schutte equation[71] is commonly used to estimate fat and FFM from body density in black males, but with multicompartment models, recent researchers[72–74] found that using race-specific equations to estimate percentage of fat from bone density was inappropriate. For adolescent and high school athletes, the adult conversion formulas of Siri[75] and Brozek et al[76] are generally accepted.

Dual-energy x-ray absorptiometry (DXA) has been reported[63,64] to slightly underestimate body fat in some athletic populations when compared with multicompartment models. Other authors[54,56] have noted strong agreement between DXA and multicompartment models in various athletic groups. Athletes generally have greater bone mineral content, bone mineral density, and FFM and a lower percentage of body fat than nonathletes.[77] Considering that DXA also measures bone mineral composition and density, it may be preferable to either hydrostatic or air displacement plethysmography 2-C models as a reference method for assessing body composition in athletes and active people.[78]

Clinical Methods Used to Assess Body Composition

Skinfold thickness, which has been validated with hydrostatic weighing, is the most frequently used and easily accessible clinical method to estimate body composition. Although skinfold measures are easy to obtain, the importance of developing a skillful measuring technique cannot be overstated. Standardized skinfold sites and measurement techniques are described in the *Anthropometric Standardization Reference Manual*.[79] An extensive number of prediction equations are available for estimating bone density from skinfold measures in different athletic populations (Durnin and Womersley, Katch and McArdle, Jackson-Pollock), but selected equations have been recognized for broad applicability to both male and female athletic populations. In addition to these equations, the generalized Lohman equation[80] is recommended for both high school and collegiate wrestlers.[78] Based on the referenced validity studies, ready availability of equipment, and ease of use, skinfold prediction is highly recommended as a body composition assessment technique for athletes and active clients.

The accuracy of bioelectric impedance analysis (BIA), another method used to assess body composition, is highly dependent on testing under controlled conditions. Skin temperature, strenuous exercise, dehydration, and glycogen depletion significantly affect impedance values.[81,82] Population-specific and generalized BIA equations, developed for the average population, do not accurately estimate the FFM of athletic men and women.[83–86] Some researchers[65,87,88] reported that the skinfold method is a better predictor of body fat percentage in athletes than the BIA method, which is a more effective tool for obtaining group data on athletes than for detecting small changes in individual athletes' body fat.[89]

Another body fat measuring technique, near-infrared interactance (NIR), provides optical density values for estimating body fat. The manufacturer's prediction equation systematically underestimated body fat in both active men and collegiate football players.[83,90,91] Limited research is available on the validity of NIR among female athletes in various sports. A few authors[92,93] used optical density values to develop prediction equations in athletic populations. The NIR prediction equations were slightly better than the skinfold method in estimating body composition and minimal wrestling weight in high school–aged wrestlers.[94]

Fat and FFM should be assessed by an AT or other trained body-composition assessor using one of the validated methods available (eg, hydrostatic weighing, air displacement plethysmography, skinfold measures). All manual measurement techniques (eg, skinfold calipers) should follow standardized protocols and be performed at least 3 times by the same assessor to ensure reliability.[79] The body size needs of the activity and the typical body composition of the participants in that activity should be considered, as well as the minimum body composition standards when available.

Body Composition and Hydration Assessment

Body composition and weight assessments should always be conducted on hydrated people. Criterion (ie, total body water and plasma markers) and field methods (ie, acute body mass change, urine and saliva markers, bioelectric impedance) can be used to assess hydration status. The gold standard for determining hydration status is measurement of total body water. Repeated measurements of water content before and after rapid weight reduction reflect the absolute change in fluid content. The FFM of adult bodies contains approximately 72% water,[94] a value slightly less than in children (75%) and adolescents (73%).[94,95]

Plasma markers, or a comparison of blood indices of hydration status with laboratory standards, also may be used to determine hydration status. Plasma osmolality of the blood, sodium content, and hemoglobin and hematocrit levels are typically elevated when the plasma volume is reduced because of dehydration. The plasma osmolality of a hydrated person ranges between 260 and 280 mOsm/kg. A plasma osmolality above 290 mOsm/kg indicates dehydration.[96] Hemoglobin and hematocrit levels can also be used to assess relative changes in plasma volume based on loss of fluid from the vascular space. However, this technique has many limitations and does not always reflect changes in hydration.[97,98]

The acute body-mass change field method is one of the simplest ways to assess changes in hydration. Assessing body weight before and after a period of exercise or heat exposure can provide data reflecting hydration. Immediate weight loss after exercise results from dehydration and should be addressed using the guidelines described in the NATA position statement on hydration.[99] Using weight-tracking charts to evaluate these changes during exercise can help to determine the hydration status of an active person.

Urine markers are another noninvasive method to determine the hydration status of the blood.[100–104] When the body has a fluid deficit, urine production decreases, and the urine becomes more concentrated. The total volume of urine produced during a specified period is lower than expected (normal is approximately 100 mL/h).[96] Simultaneously, urine specific gravity, osmolality, and conductivity increase due to a greater number of solids in the urine and the conservation of body fluid. Urine color also may serve as a gross predictor of hydration state.[102]

Urine specific gravity and osmolality respond to acute changes in hydration status. However, changes in these markers may be delayed or insensitive to low levels of acute dehydration (1% to 3% of body weight).[100] In addition, these markers may be no more effective in detecting dehydration than assessing urine protein content via the dipstick method.[105] Ease of collection and measurement, at least for urine specific gravity and color, make the dipstick method practical for self-assessment of hydration status in most settings.[99]

Similar to those of urine, characteristics of saliva change as the hydration level changes.[106] Because the salivary glands produce saliva using plasma, a decrease in plasma volume due to dehydration affects the concentration of substances found in saliva. Although a saliva sample is easy to obtain, the analysis for osmolality and total protein content requires instrumentation beyond the scope of most practice settings. Saliva flow rate is collected with a dental swab but requires an analytical balance for precise measurement of the change in swab weight after saliva collection.

Recently, BIA and bioelectric impedance spectroscopy have been proposed[104,107] for measuring total body water and the compartments within the total body water, respectively. These methods provide reasonable measurements of body composition and total body water for groups of individuals, but whether they can track changes in hydration status and an individual's hydration level is unknown. Several investigators[108,109] found that bioelectric impedance analysis and bioelectric impedance spectroscopy failed to accurately predict reductions in total body water after rapid dehydration. Some of this inaccuracy may result from other factors (eg, increased core temperature and skin blood flow) that may influence the reactance and resistance measurements on which these techniques rely.

To ensure adequate hydration, an average adult's water intake should be 3.7 L/d for men and 2.7 L/d for women. Athletes, active clients, and those who are exposed to hot environments need higher intakes of total water.[110] To maintain adequate hydration, a person should drink 200 to 300 mL of fluid every 10 to 20 minutes during exercise. Pre-exercise and postexercise fluid intake should be consistent with the recommendations provided in the NATA position statement on fluid replacement.[99]

As noted previously, body weight and body composition should be assessed with the person in a hydrated state. Those who fail to meet the minimum hydration levels (urine specific gravity of less than 1.020 or urine color less than or equal to 4)[111] should not be assessed until hydration standards are met and no sooner than 24 hours after the first hydration status failure.

Body Composition and Determining Body Weight

No single source offers normative body composition data for athletes. Therefore, ATs and other health care personnel involved in body composition assessment should become familiar with data sources specific to their athlete or client populations. They should take into consideration the safe ranges and the body composition needs of the sport and then individualize weight and body composition goals.

The lowest safe weight should be calculated at no lower than the weight determined by the low-reference body fat composition delineated by sex and age. The *lowest safe weight* can be defined operationally as the lowest weight, sanctioned by the governing body, at which a competitor may compete. When no standard exists, participants should be required to remain above

a certain minimum body fat. Highest safe weight should be calculated using a value no higher than the highest end of the range considered satisfactory for health: 10% to 22% body fat in males and 20% to 32% in females (Table 2).[13]

The AT should work closely with the team physician or medical supervisor to develop a plan for the collection and management of body composition data and related information.[112] This information should be restricted to those who need it to provide care for the athlete or client. The AT should fully disclose to the athlete or client who will have access to personal body composition information.[113] If the body composition or other nutritional and weight management findings indicate a potentially harmful or high-risk behavior, the AT is responsible for informing the athlete or client of the risk[113] and the team physician or medical supervisor of the medical concern.[114]

Body composition measurements to determine goal weights should be assessed twice annually,[115] with no less than 2 to 3 months between measurements[50] for most people. These regular measurements will allow ATs and other health professionals to alter weight goals based on decreases in body fat and increases in lean muscle mass. Caution should always be taken to ensure that an athlete's or client's body composition never falls below the lowest or rises above the highest safe weight or body fat level. To track an athlete's or client's progress toward a weight or body composition goal, private weight and body composition assessments should be scheduled at more frequent intervals to guide and refine progress and to establish reinforcement and reassessment periods.

Measurement intervals should be identified in consultation with the physician and other members of the health care team involved in the athlete's or client's care. This team should include an AT, licensed mental health care provider, physician, and registered dietitian.[116] If weight control practices are a concern, collaboration and education should occur early and frequently in the process.

Monitoring Body Weight

During preseason activities that involve equipment that could increase sweat loss or prevent adequate cooling in warmer and more humid climates, body weight should be reassessed at least daily because of the increased risk of dehydration and heat-related illness. Daily weigh-ins, before and after exercise, can help identify excessive weight loss due to dehydration.

Active clients and athletes in weight classification sports should not gain or lose excessive amounts of body weight at any point in their training cycles. Athletes and clients should attempt to maintain levels that are close to their weight and body composition goal when not competing and maintain their goal weight and body composition during competition. Excessive fluctuations in body weight or body composition (or both) can negatively affect the body, including but not limited to changes in metabolic activity, fluctuations in blood glucose levels, and muscle wasting.[14] Athletes in weight classification sports should have individual monitoring plans, such as assessments at least once per month in the off-season and at regular intervals, not to exceed once per week, to monitor for weight fluctuations.[115]

Body Composition and Dietary Intake

Caloric and nutrient intake should be based on lean body mass, desired body composition, goal weight, and sport or activity requirements. Intake that is too high or too low to support the desired lean body mass will negatively affect metabolic function and body composition. Metabolic function is more efficient in those with greater amounts of lean body mass. Metabolic function and oxygen utilization can be measured or estimated with predictive equations that take into consideration body size, fat mass, FFM, age, sex, and the expenditure of energy for activity.[12,117] The Harris-Benedict[14] and Mifflin-St. Jeor[15] estimation formulas, which account for height, weight, age, and sex to determine the BMR, are commonly recommended methods for indirectly estimating total caloric need; however, other methods are also appropriate. One drawback to the use of estimation formulas is that muscular tissue uses more energy than does nonmuscular tissue. Therefore, estimation formulas may underestimate the daily caloric needs of athletes or clients who are very muscular (Table 4).

A healthy diet or meal plan should provide adequate calories to achieve body weight goals, supply essential nutrients, and maintain hydration. To ensure effective performance, energy intake must come from an appropriate balance of the 3 essential energy-producing nutrients (ie, protein, carbohydrates, and fats). In addition, appropriate intake of non–energy-producing essential nutrients (eg, vitamins, minerals, water) is needed to facilitate energy creation and maintain other body processes.[8] Carbohydrates should provide 55% to 70% of the total caloric need of athletes and active people and may be as high as 12 g or more per kilogram of body weight.[5,10,16] Muscle glycogen (stored glucose) and blood glucose, derived from carbohydrates, are the primary energy substrates for working muscle.[17,18,118] Therefore, the more aerobic the activity, the greater the carbohydrate need (Tables 6, 7).

To determine needed protein intake, it is important to identify the type of exercise and the intensity level of that exercise.[5,10,17,18] Protein assists with many bodily functions, but most athletes and clients are interested in building and repairing muscle contractile and connective tissue. Protein provides 8% to 10% of the body's total energy needs. In events lasting longer than 60 to 70 minutes, amino acid oxidation increases, thereby increasing the use of protein to support the greater energy demands. Strength athletes and those whose goals are to build FFM need the most protein in the diet. For those who are not interested in developing a great deal of FFM but want to meet the needs of an aerobic activity, more moderate amounts of protein are desirable. Protein intake in excess of the body's physical requirements increases hydration needs, overburdens the liver and kidneys, and interferes with calcium absorption; in addition, excess protein can be broken down and used as components of other molecules, including stored fat (Table 6).[14]

Finally, dietary fats are essential to a healthy diet because they provide energy, assist in the transport and use of fat-soluble vitamins, and protect the essential elements of cells.[12] Fat metabolism provides a portion of the energy needed for low- to moderate-intensity exercise, and the use of fat for energy metabolism increases as aerobic metabolism increases. Fats can be used to spare both readily available glucose and stored muscle glycogen. Although the average intake of fat in athletes is approximately 30% of total caloric intake,[10,14] the commonly held consensus is that 20% to 25% of total caloric intake should come from fats.[12] To maximize performance, athletes should take in no less than 15% of total caloric intake from dietary fats.[12,17] Fat intake should minimize partially hydrogenated, unsaturated (trans) fats and saturated fats[17]; total fat intake should be equally divided among polyunsaturated, monounsaturated, and trans or saturated fats.

Maintaining Body Composition and Weight with Diet and Exercise

Diet. Management of body composition should include both diet and exercise. To maintain good health and stave off disease, a regular exercise program should be combined with a dietary plan. The dietary plan should be developed to address the athlete's or client's specific body composition, body weight, and activity goals. Individual body composition and dietary needs should be discussed privately with appropriately trained nutrition and weight management experts. Athletic trainers and other health professionals, such as registered dietitians, should provide nutritional information to athletes and clients. A Board-Certified Sports Dietitian (CSSD) is a registered dietitian who has earned the premier professional sports nutrition credential from the American Dietetic Association. Coaches, peers, and family members should not provide information on diet, body composition, weight, or weight management practices and should refrain from making comments on or participating in the monitoring of body composition and weight.[50]

Total caloric intake should be determined by calculating BMR and the energy needs for activity. Many methods are available to determine total caloric need, including assessments of metabolic function and oxygen utilization, but equations that estimate metabolic function are more plausible options for clinicians. These metabolic estimation equations take into consideration body size, fat mass and FFM, age, sex, and the expenditure of energy for activity.[12,117] One drawback to the use of estimation formulas is that muscular tissue uses more energy than does nonmuscular tissue; therefore, estimation formulas that are not adjusted for lean muscle mass may underestimate the daily caloric needs for athletes or clients who are very muscular.

Caloric intake should be based on the body weight goal. A person should consume a total number of calories based on body composition and weight goals. Caloric intake that is too high or too low to support the desired lean body mass will negatively affect metabolic function and body composition. Metabolic function is more efficient in those with greater amounts of lean body mass. When BMR is calculated based on the body composition and weight goals, this formula provides an important estimate of the energy needed to meet activity requirements.

A safe and healthy dietary plan that supplies sufficient energy and nutrients should be maintained throughout the year. A healthy diet or meal plan provides adequate calories to achieve body weight goals, supply essential nutrients, and maintain hydration. The U.S. Department of Agriculture's Food Pyramid Guide is one method that can be used to ensure adequate nutrient intake. Athletes and clients should identify the appropriate Food Guide Pyramid (www.mypyramid.gov)[119] that describes food groups and the recommended number of daily servings per group adults and children need to consume for essential nutrients. The AT or other trained health care professional can also use the appropriate Food Guide Pyramid to calculate the recommended caloric intake level based on the individual's goal weight. The guidelines at www.mypyramid.gov are consistent with recommendations by organizations such as the American Heart Association and the American Cancer Society to control diabetes, heart

disease, cancer, and other chronic and debilitating diseases.[120] Even though this method may underestimate the protein and carbohydrate needs of athletes or clients, it can be used to correctly guide a person's eating needs for vitamin and mineral intake and overall caloric intake.

The metabolic qualities of the activity should be used to calculate the need for each energy-producing nutrient in the diet. To determine specific dietary needs and adjustments, an analysis of the metabolic characteristics (eg, anaerobic or aerobic) with consideration for the performance, body composition, weight, and personal goals of the athlete or client (eg, build muscle mass, lose fat) must be performed.

Ergogenic and dietary aids should be ingested with caution and under the advice of those knowledgeable about the requirements of sports and other governing organizations. The NCAA, U.S. Olympic Committee, and International Olympic Committee regulate supplements approved for use by athletes. By-law 16.52 g of the NCAA states that an institution may provide only non–muscle-building nutritional supplements to a student-athlete at any time for the purpose of providing additional calories and electrolytes, as long as the supplements do not contain any substances banned by the NCAA.[19] Athletes and clients should be educated against taking any dietary or other nutritional supplements without first checking with the AT or another health care provider who is familiar with the competitive regulations.

Exercise. The exercise program should not only train the person for his or her activity but should also help the person maintain overall physical fitness and wellness. Body weight and composition may be maintained by pursuing an exercise regimen that matches a person's needs. The American College of Sports Medicine recommends 30 minutes of exercise, 5 days per week to remain healthy[7]; however, if the goals are to facilitate weight and body fat loss, a safe and appropriate aerobic exercise program will facilitate that loss. To maximize the metabolism of excess fat, one must participate in continuous, rhythmic aerobic exercise for a minimum of 30 minutes per exercise bout but no longer than 60 to 90 minutes, for at least 150 minutes per week.[118,119,121] Although interval exercise for 30 minutes burns the same number of calories, the metabolism of fat is less. If the person is unfit or has not exercised at this level previously, a graded-progression approach should be used to achieve the exercise goals.[14] Target heart rate for this aerobic activity must be above 50% VO_2max to initiate lipolysis, with the most efficient fat metabolism occurring between 60% and 70% VO_2max (approximately 55% to 69% of maximum heart rate).[5,118] Caution should be used in those with orthopaedic or other health conditions that may warrant changes in exercise protocols. Non–weight-bearing or limited–weight-bearing aerobic exercises are recommended for those with orthopaedic conditions.

Body composition adjustments should be gradual, with no excessive restrictions or unsafe behaviors or products. On average, weight loss goals should be approximately 1 to 2 lb (0.5 to 0.9 kg) per week but should not exceed 1.5% of body weight loss per week.[1,122] A higher rate of weight loss indicates dehydration or other restrictive or unsafe behaviors that will negatively affect performance and health. One pound (0.5 kg) of fat is equal to 3500 kilocalories of energy; therefore, increases or decreases in calories to the level needed to maintain ideal lean mass will help to achieve body fat goals. Few authors have studied plans for weight gain goals in active people, but a process similar to that for weight loss may be used. The AT should work closely with the other members of the health care team to assist in this determination.

Combining weight management and body composition goals with physical conditioning periodization goals will assist athletes and clients in reaching weight goals. Periodization involves manipulating training intensity and volume to yield specific performance outcomes. The best time for adjustments in weight and body composition is during the preparatory period, which occurs outside competition.[115] The main emphasis of the competitive period should be on performing the sport or activity with the body nearing its highest level of physical fitness. During the competitive period, less time is available for physical conditioning and more time is spent on strength, power, and increased training intensity specifically related to sport performance. During the different phases of the preparatory period, physical conditioning goals can be used to achieve body composition goals. During the hypertrophy or endurance phase, the emphasis is on developing lean body mass, aerobic capacity, and muscular endurance, which can provide a physiologic environment to assist in decreasing body fat. During the basic strength and strength-power phases, the emphasis is on developing strength and speed and involves increasing levels of anaerobic activity.[123] An AT or other trained health care professional should be consulted for assistance in manipulating these phases of the periodization plan to meet training goals.

Education on safe dietary and weight management practices should be conducted on a regular and planned basis. The AT and other health care professionals should be involved in educating athletes or clients and monitoring their diets. The initial team meeting or client interview is an opportune time to communicate information on healthy eating habits and the effect of proper nutrition and hydration on performance.

Common Unsafe Weight Management Practices

Athletes and active people regularly seek methods to maximize performance, and many of the common methods involve managing diet, weight, or body composition (or a combination of these). Although many safe methods exist to achieve goal weight or the lowest safe weight, unsafe practices involve self-deprivation techniques that lead to dehydration, self-starvation, and disordered eating. In field studies and experimental research on weight-class athletes, the most common unsafe methods are a mixture of dehydration and other methods, including food restriction or improper dieting to reduce body fat. Therefore, the results of studies examining the physiologic and performance effects of rapid weight reduction may not reflect only dehydration. Studies selected for this summary are those that focused primarily on dehydration techniques and involved short-term, rapid weight reduction.

Dehydration and Weight Management

Since the late 1930s and as recently as 2003, authors[124,125] have reported that athletes used voluntary dehydration as a method of rapid weight loss to reach a lower body weight for competition. Several rapid weight loss methods involve rapid fluid loss; these methods use active, passive, diet-induced, pharmacologic-induced, and blood reinfusion techniques to achieve a desired weight. The active method involves increasing metabolic rate through exercise to increase the rate of heat production in active skeletal muscle.[126] At least 1 L of fluid may be lost through sweat evaporation during exercise[127] when an active person abstains from drinking fluid during activity. To ensure continued sweating, exercise is often combined with excessive clothing, which diminishes the evaporative effects of sweating and increases insulation and core temperature.[128,129] At one time, dehydration was a common method used by wrestlers,[130–132] but a survey[127] indicated that this method has become less popular because of changes in the weigh-in procedures (ie, assessments of hydration status) of sport governing bodies. These active methods may be enhanced by combining the active technique with environmental changes that increase the passive sweat rate, resulting in higher levels of dehydration, or the training facility may be artificially heated to ensure a higher passive sweat rate with less physical effort.[130–134] Recent changes in sport guidelines appear to have reduced the extent to which collegiate wrestlers use passive dehydration.[125]

Athletes who use passive dehydration methods also may restrict food intake for weight loss or may purposefully consume foods that promote diuresis for fluid loss. A combined high-protein, low-carbohydrate diet may promote dehydration through several mechanisms. Meals high in protein and devoid of carbohydrate may modestly stimulate urine production. As the body is deprived of carbohydrates, fat oxidation is increased, promoting additional fluid loss in the urine. With a high protein intake, the person may further induce diuresis from the increased nitrogen metabolism and urea excreted via the kidneys.[14]

Some researchers[135] suggested that total body water is elevated with the consumption of a high-carbohydrate diet, forcing muscle glycogen to be stored along with water, which can increase body weight. As dietary carbohydrate intake is restricted, glycogen resynthesis may be limited, thereby avoiding the increase in body weight caused by water storage.[135] However, this dietary strategy does not provide optimal energy stores for a competitive athlete,[136,137] and performance may suffer.[98,138,139]

Ingesting medications that stimulate urine production (eg, diuretics) may have a greater influence on body weight than does altering the diet. Diuretics appropriately prescribed for hypertensive therapy or to reduce edema have been misused by athletes seeking rapid weight loss for competition. Fortunately, the misapplication of pharmacologic agents was uncommon in weight-class athletes who were surveyed[23,132]; however, this practice has not been fully eradicated.

Finally, one report[140] and other anecdotal stories from athletes indicate that some athletes at international competitions have had blood removed intravenously before the required weigh-in. The blood is then reinfused after the athlete "makes weight" for competition. Other than the lone report, no formal information is available about this method or the extent to which it has been practiced or is currently used.

Effects of Dehydration on Performance

Dehydration results in suboptimal performance when the dehydration is ≥1% in children and ≥2% in adults.[140,141] In children, 1% dehydration causes a reduction in aerobic performance[142] and an increase in core temperature.[143] In adults, 2% to 3% dehydration causes decreased reflex activity, maximum oxygen consumption, physical work capacity, muscle strength, and muscle endurance and impairs temperature regulation.[144,145] At 4% to 6% dehydration, further deterioration occurs

in maximum oxygen consumption, physical work capacity, muscle strength, and endurance time; temperature regulation is severely impaired.[111] These physiologic effects of dehydration are discussed in depth in 2 NATA position statements[99,111] and will not be discussed further here.

Most athletes who participate in weight-class sports need short-duration, high-intensity efforts that demand rates of energy production at or above the peak oxygen uptake. For single efforts, whether performance is affected by dehydration before performance is unclear. Dehydration does not appear to reduce phosphagen energy stores (adenosine triphosphate, creatine phosphate),[137] although some of the weight reduction found in this study occurred with diet manipulation and not dehydration alone. People involved in activities that use weight manipulation to improve performance appear to be more profoundly affected by hydration status. Efforts that are sustained at intensities below peak oxygen uptake are notably affected by prior dehydration. Dehydration induced with the use of pharmacologic diuretics increases frequency of muscle twitches, a potential risk factor for muscle cramps, more so than does exercise- or sauna-induced dehydration.[132]

Dietary Caloric Restriction and Weight Management

Dietary restriction is another common method used to maintain weight. Very low-calorie diets affect the cardiovascular system and can produce myofibrillar damage, orthostatic hypotension, bradycardia, low QRS voltage, QT-interval prolongation, ventricular arrhythmias, and sudden cardiac death.[146–149] Sudden death may be caused by the ventricular arrhythmias or hypokalemia associated with caloric restriction.[14] Very low-calorie diets can also result in a marked blunting of the normal heart rate increase and blood pressure response to exercise.[149] In addition to these physiologic changes, dietary restrictions cause deficits in recall, understanding visuospatial information,[150] working-memory capacity, recall on the phonologic loop task, and simple reaction time.[151] They also affect planning time.[152]

Low-calorie diets also affect the endocrine system. Levels of growth hormone and insulin-like growth factor (IGF) binding protein 2 are increased. The growth hormone response to growth hormone–releasing hormone is increased; however, levels of IGF I and IGF binding protein 3 are decreased.[153–155] The decrease in IGF I, an anabolic factor, limits growth and muscle development.[153] With improved nutrition, growth "catchup" occurs but is inadequate; children, in particular, will never achieve their potential genetic height.[156,157] Also, lower levels of IGF I are associated with poor muscle development, and thus potential maximum strength is never realized.[153] Lower levels of IGF I are associated with lower bone mineral densities.[153] Urinary excretion of cross-links, a marker of bone absorption, is increased, and serum osteocalcin, a marker for bone formation, is lower than normal in patients with low BMIs.[154] These findings indicate that more bone is being absorbed and less bone is being produced than normal, potentially leading to osteoporosis[154] and stress fractures.

Changes in thyroid function also occur as a result of low-calorie diets. Total thyroxine (T_4) and triiodothyronine (free T_3) decrease, and reverse triiodothyronine (rT_3) increases.[155] The response of thyroid-stimulating hormone (TSH) to thyrotropin-releasing hormone (TRH) is diminished,[155] and the BMR is lowered. The adrenal glands produce an increased amount of free cortisol, and serum cortisol levels are elevated, without associated changes in adrenocorticotropic hormone.[155] Gonadotropin-releasing hormone (GnRH) from the hypothalamus is reduced,[158] leading to decreased levels of luteinizing hormone (LH) and follicle-stimulating hormone (FSH) from the anterior pituitary.[159] Estrogen production is low, contributing significantly to osteoporosis[159] and menstrual dysfunction.[15]

Dietary restrictions affect the immune system by significantly impairing cell-mediated immunity, phagocyte function, the complement system, secretory immunoglobulin A levels, cytokinase production,[160–163] haptoglobin production, orosomucoid production,[164] T-lymphocyte response, and production of Th_2 cytokine; Th_1 cytokinase production increases.[162] These immunologic abnormalities may lead to an increased number of infections during the period of inadequate dietary intake.[165]

Eating Disorders, Disordered Eating, and Weight Management

Disordered eating behaviors have been identified in both male and female athletes.[131,166] A total of 10% to 15% of boys who participate in weight-sensitive sports practice unhealthy weight loss behaviors.[131,166] Eleven percent of wrestlers have been found to have eating disorders or disordered eating,[166] and up to 45% of wrestlers were at risk of developing an eating disorder.[129,167,168] Several studies[169–171] revealed a high prevalence of eating disorders in female athletes involved in weight-sensitive sports. Sixty percent of average-weight girls and 18% of underweight girls involved in swimming were attempting to lose weight.[172] Thus, both males and females may develop dysmorphia, disordered eating, and eating disorders as a consequence of their efforts to lose weight for their activities. The female athlete triad is a relationship among disordered eating, altered menstrual function, and abnormal bone mineralization.[160,173,174] Amenorrhea occurs as a result of decreased pulsatile release of GnRH from the hypothalamus,[157] which leads to fewer LH and FSH pulses from the anterior pituitary.[175] Osteoporosis can result from decreased estrogen or IGF I[153,154] and from excess cortisol production.[155]

Athletes competing in aesthetic sports had the highest indicators of eating disorders.[176] Those who participated in weight-matched sports also showed higher levels of disordered eating than did athletes in non–weight-restricted sports.[175–177] Athletes whose bodies differ from the "ideal" physique of the sport may also be at higher risk for developing disordered eating.[20] Some experts have surmised that the demands of the athletic subculture may involve inherent risk for the development of unhealthy weight control behaviors. Subclinical eating disorders in athletes have been associated with dieting to enhance appearance or improve health or dieting because someone (eg, coach, peer) recommended it.[45]

The spectrum of disordered eating behaviors ranges from the very benign and mild to the very severe.[50] In athletes, disordered eating may affect up to 62% of the population and is reportedly highest in weight-class events, such as boxing and wrestling, and aesthetic activities, such as dance and gymnastics, in which low body weight and leanness are emphasized.[178,179]

Disordered eating in the mild and earliest stages may start simply as a dietary plan to achieve a better aesthetic appearance or better performance. A common "diet" involves caloric restrictions, but when these restrictions are taken to the extreme, there is reason for concern. Often, athletes seek weight loss or dieting advice from friends or teammates or simply follow the suggestions of others without fully understanding the importance of maintaining an adequate energy balance. Other times, athletes may adhere to the recommendations made by coaches without understanding the nutritional requirements of the sport.[50] The health care team should be in place to help athletes and active clients address disordered eating behaviors and to assist in providing accurate and appropriate advice. The topics of disordered eating, eating disorders, and dysmorphia are addressed more comprehensively in the NATA position statement on disordered eating.[50]

Acknowledgments

We gratefully acknowledge the efforts of Leslie J. Bonci, MPH, RD, LDN; Matthew Doyle, ATC; Dan Foster,

PhD, ATC; Gregory L. Landry, MD; Margot Putukian, MD; James Thornton, MS, ATC; and the Pronouncements Committee in the preparation of this document.

Disclaimer

The NATA publishes its position statements as a service to promote the awareness of certain issues to its members. The information contained in the position statement is neither exhaustive not exclusive to all circumstances or individuals. Variables such as institutional human resource guidelines, state or federal statutes, rules, or regulations, as well as regional environmental conditions, may impact the relevance and implementation of these recommendations. The NATA advises its members and others to carefully and independently consider each of the recommendations (including the applicability of same to any particular circumstance or individual). The position statement should not be relied upon as an independent basis for care but rather as a resource available to NATA members or others. Moreover, no opinion is expressed herein regarding the quality of care that adheres to or differs from NATA's position statements. The NATA reserves the right to rescind or modify its position statements at any time.

REFERENCES

1. National Collegiate Athletic Association Wrestling Rules Committee. Rule 8: weight management. In: Bubb RG, ed. *2008–2009 Wrestling Rules.* Indianapolis, IN: National Collegiate Athletic Association Publications; 2008:WR81–WR92.

2. American Academy of Pediatrics Committee on Sports Medicine and Fitness. Policy statement: promotion of healthy weight control practices in young athletes. *Pediatrics.* 2005;116(6): 1557–1564.

3. Fletcher GF, Blair SN, Blumenthal J, et al. Statement on exercise: benefits and recommendations for physical activity programs for all Americans: a statement for health professionals by the Committee on Exercise and Cardiac Rehabilitation of the Council on Clinical Cardiology, American Heart Association. *Circulation.* 1992;86(1):340–344.

4. Frisch RE, Hubinont PO. *Adipose Tissue and Reproduction: Progress in Reproductive Biology and Medicine.* Basel, Switzerland: S. Karger AG; 1990:14.

5. Berning JR, Steen SN. *Nutrition for Sport and Exercise.* Gaithersburg, MD: Aspen Publishers Inc; 1998:23–25, 49, 50, 54, 65, 163.

6. Ebell MH, Siwek J, Weiss BD, et al. Strength of recommendation taxonomy (SORT): a patient-centered approach to grading evidence in the medical literature. *Am Fam Physician.* 2004;69(3): 548–556.

7. Ehrman JK, ed. *ACSM's Resource Manual for Guidelines for Exercise Testing and Prescription.* 6th ed. Philadelphia, PA: Lippincott Williams & Wilkins; 2010:266, 277.

8. Clark N. *Nancy Clark's Sport Nutrition Guidebook.* 3rd ed. Champaign, IL: Human Kinetics; 2003:22, 163, 164, 182.

9. McArdle WD, Katch FI, Katch VL. *Exercise Physiology, Energy, Nutrition, and Human Performance.* 6th ed. Baltimore, MD: Lippincott Williams & Wilkins; 2007:776, 779, 783–785, 793–796, 812–813.

10. McArdle WD, Katch FI, Katch VL. *Sports and Exercise Nutrition.* 3rd ed. Baltimore, MD: Lippincott Williams & Wilkins; 2009:247, 402, 403, 429, 430, 462.

11. Behnke AR, Wilmore JH. *Evaluation and Regulation of Body Build and Composition.* Englewood Cliffs, NJ: Prentice Hall; 1974.

12. American College of Sports Medicine, American Dietetic Association, Dietitians of Canada. Joint position statement: nutrition and athletic performance. *Med Sci Sports Exerc.* 2000:32(12):2130–2145.

13. Thompson WR, ed. *ACSM's Guidelines for Exercise Testing and Prescription.* 8th ed. Philadelphia, PA: Lippincott Williams & Wilkins; 2010:71.

14. Byrd-Bredbenner C, Beshgetoor D, Moe G, Berning J. *Wardlaw's Perspectives in Nutrition.* 8th ed. New York, NY: McGraw Hill; 2009:247–248, 302, 320, 378–383.

15. Seagle HM, Strain GW, Makris A, Reeves RS; American Dietetic Association. Position of the American Dietetic Association: weight management. *J Am Diet Assoc.* 2009;109(2):330–346.

16. Burke LM, Cox GR, Culmmings NK, Desbrow B. Guidelines for daily carbohydrate intake: do athletes achieve them? *Sports Med.* 2001;31(4):267–299.

17. Rosenbloom C. Fueling athletes: facts versus fiction on feeding athletes for peak performance. *Nutr Today.* 2006;41(5):227–232.

18. Lambert EV, Goedecke JH. The role of dietary macronutrients in optimizing endurance performance. *Curr Sports Med Rep.* 2003;2(4):194–201.

19. National Collegiate Athletic Association. Bylaw 16.52.g. In: *NCAA Bylaws and Regulations Division I Handbook.* Indianapolis, IN: National Collegiate Athletic Association; 2008:199.

20. Collegiate Spring Football League. CSFL weight certification procedures. http://www.sprintfootball.com/p4_league_information.jsp. Accessed March 1, 2009.

21. Oppliger RA, Utter AC, Scott JR, Dick RW, Klossner D. NCAA rule change improves weight loss among national championship wrestlers. *Med Sci Sports Exerc.* 2006;38(5):963–970.

22. US Rowing Rules of Rowing. Article IV, rules 4-106, 4-110. http://www.rci.rutgers.edu/~ronchen/ruleindx.htm. Accessed June 7, 2004.

23. Eating, body weight, and performance in athletes: an introduction. In: Brownell KD, Rodin J, Wilmore JH, eds. *Eating, Body Weight and Performance in Athletes: Disorders of Modern Society.* Philadelphia, PA: Lea & Febiger; 1992:1–16.

24. Johnson A, Steinberg R, Lewis W. Bulimia. In: Clark K, Parr R, Castelli W, eds. *Evaluation and Management of Eating Disorders, Anorexia, Bulimia and Obesity.* Champaign, IL: Life Enhancement Publications; 1988:187–227.

25. McCabe MP, Ricciardelli LA. Sociocultural influences on body image and body changes among adolescent boys and girls. *J Soc Psychol.* 2003;143(1):5–26.

26. Cohane GH, Pope HG Jr. Body image in boys: a review of the literature. *Int J Eat Disord.* 2001;29(4):373–379.

27. Benedikt R, Wertheim EH, Love A. Eating attitudes and weight-loss attempts in female adolescents and their mothers. *J Youth Adolesc.* 1998;27(1):43–57.

28. Paxton SJ, Wertheim EH, Gibbons K, Szmukler GL, Hillier L, Petrovich JL. Body image satisfaction, dieting beliefs, and weight loss behaviors in adolescent girls and boys. *J Youth Adolesc.* 1991;20(3):361–379.

29. Dixon R, Adair V, O'Connor S. Parental influences on the dieting beliefs and behaviors of adolescent females in New Zealand. *J Adolesc Health.* 1996;19(4):303–307.

30. Berry TR, Howe BL. Risk factors for disordered eating in female university athletes. *J Sport Behav.* 2000;23(3):207–218.

31. Rosen LW, Hough DO. Pathogenic weight control behaviors of female college gymnasts. *Phys Sportsmed.* 1988;16(9):141–146.

32. Neumark-Sztanier D, Beutler R, Palti H. Personal and socioenvironmental predictors of disordered eating among adolescent females. *J Nutr Educ.* 1996;28(4):195–201.

33. Griffin J, Harris MB. Coaches' attitudes, knowledge, experiences, and recommendations regarding weight control. *Sport Psychol.* 1996;10(2):180–194.

34. Beals KA, Manore MM. The prevalence and consequences of subclinical eating disorders in female athletes. *Int J Sports Nutr.* 1994;4(2):175–195.

35. Gill KS, Overdorf VG. Body image, weight and eating concerns, and use of weight control methods among high school female athletes. *Women Sport Phys Act J.* 1994;3(2):69.

36. Brooks-Gunn J, Burrow C, Warren MP. Attitudes toward eating and body weight in different groups of female adolescents. *Int J Eat Disord.* 1988;7(6):749–757.

37. Davis C, Cowles M. A comparison of weight and diet factors among female athletes and non-athletes. *J Psychosom Res.* 1989;33(5):527–536.

38. Fulkerson JA, Keel PK, Leon GR, Dorr T. Eating-disordered behaviors and personality characteristics of high school athletes and nonathletes. *Int J Eat Disord.* 1999;26(1):73–79.

39. Garner DM, Garfinkel PE, Rochert W, Olmsted MP. A prospective study of eating disturbances in the ballet. *Psychother Psychosom.* 1987;48(1–4):170–175.

40. Sundgot-Borgen J. Prevalence of eating disorders in elite female athletes. *Int J Sport Nutr.* 1993;3(1):29–40.

41. Johnson MD. Disordered eating in active and athletic women. *Clin Sports Med.* 1994;13(2):355–369.

42. Leichner P. Anorexia nervosa, bulimia, and exercise. *Coach.* March/April 1986;66–68.

43. Taub D, Blinde EM. Eating disorders among adolescent female athletes: influence of athletic participation and sport team membership. *Adolescence.* 1992;27(108):833–848.

44. Hewitt PL, Flett GL. Perfectionism in the self and social contexts: conceptualization, assessment, and association with psychopathology. *J Pers Soc Psychol.* 1991;60(3):456–470.

45. Williams PL, Sargent RG, Durstine LJ. Prevalence of subclinical eating disorders in collegiate female athletes. *Women Sport Phys Act J.* 2003;12(2):127.

46. Andersen AE, DiDomenico L. Diet vs. shape content of popular male and female magazines: a dose-response relationship to the incidence of eating disorders. *Int J Eat Disord.* 1992;11(3):283–287.

47. Furnham A, Badmin N, Sneade I. Body-image dissatisfaction: gender differences in eating attitudes, self-esteem, and reasons for exercise. *J Psychol.* 2002;136(6):581–596.

48. Raudenbush B, Meyer B. Muscular dissatisfaction and supplement use among male intercollegiate athletes. *J Sport Exerc Psychol.* 2003;25(2):161–170.

49. Silberstein LR, Striegel-Moore RH, Timko C, Rodin J. Behavioral and psychological implications of body dissatisfaction: do men and women differ? *Sex Roles.* 1988;19(3–4):219–232.

50. Bonci CM, Bonci LJ, Granger LR, et al. National Athletic Trainers' Association position statement: preventing, detecting, and managing disordered eating in athletes. *J Athl Train.* 2008;43(1):80–108.

51. Health implications of obesity: National Institutes of Health consensus development conference statement. *Ann Intern Med.* 1985;103(6, pt 2):1073–1077.

52. Mokdad AH, Ford ES, Bowman BA, et al. Prevalence of obesity, diabetes, and obesity-related health risk factors, 2001. *JAMA.* 2003;289(1):76–79.

53. Maclure KM, Hayes KC, Colditz GA, Stampfer MJ, Speizer FE, Willett WC. Weight, diet, and the risk of symptomatic gallstones in middle-aged women. *N Engl J Med.* 1989;321(9):563–569.

54. Manninen P, Riihimaki H, Heliovaara M, Makela P. Overweight, gender, and knee osteoarthritis. *Int J Obes Relat Metab Disord.* 1996;20(6):595–597.

55. Calle EE, Rodriguez C, Walker-Thurmond K, Thun MJ. Overweight, obesity, and mortality from cancer in a prospectively studied cohort of U.S. adults. *N Engl J Med.* 2003;348(17):1625–1638.

56. Baumgartner RN, Roche AF, Guo S, Lohman T, Boileau RA, Slaughter MH. Adipose tissue distribution: the stability of principal components by sex, ethnicity and maturation stage. *Hum Biol.* 1986;58(5):719–735.

57. Brown CD, Higgins M, Donato KA, et al. Body mass index and the prevalence of hypertension and dyslipidemia. *Obes Res.* 2000;8(9):605–619.

58. Durstine JL, Moore GE, Painter PL, Roberts SO, eds. *ACSM's Exercise Management for Persons with Chronic Diseases and Disabilities.* 3rd ed. Champaign, IL: Human Kinetics; 2009:194.

59. Akers R, Busrkirk ER. An underwater weighing system utilizing "force cube" transducers. *J Appl Physiol.* 1969;26(5):649–652.

60. Wilmore JH. A simplified method for determination of residual lung volume. *J Appl Physiol.* 1969;27(1):96–100.

61. Dempster P, Aitkens S. A new air displacement method for the determination of human body composition. *Med Sci Sports Exerc.* 1995;27(12):1692–1697.

62. Penn IW, Wang ZM, Buhl KM, Allison DB, Burastero SE, Heymsfeld SB. Body composition and two-compartment model assumptions in male long distance runners. *Med Sci Sports Exerc.* 1994;26(3):392–397.

63. van der Ploeg GE, Brooks AG, Withers RT, Dollman J, Leaney F, Chatterton BE. Body composition changes in female bodybuilders during preparation for competition. *Eur J Clin Nutr.* 2001;55(4):268–277.

64. Arngrimsson SA, Evans EM, Saunders MJ, Ogburn CL III, Lewis RD, Cureton KJ. Validation of body composition estimates in male and female distance runners using estimates from a four-component model. *Am J Hum Biol.* 2000;12(3):301–314.

65. Clark RR, Bartok C, Sullivan JC, Schoeller DA. Minimum weight prediction methods cross-validated by the four-component model. *Med Sci Sports Exerc.* 2004;36(4):639–647.

66. Modlesky CM, Cureton KJ, Lewis RD, Prior BM, Sloniger MA, Rowe DA. Density of the fat-free mass and estimates of body composition in male weight trainers. *J Appl Physiol.* 1996;80(6):2085–2096.

67. Prior BM, Cureton KJ, Modlesky CM, et al. In vivo validation of whole body composition estimates from dual-energy x-ray absorptiometry. *J Appl Physiol.* 1997;83(2):623–630.

68. Bunt JC, Going SB, Lohman TG, Heinrich CH, Perry CD, Pamenter RW. Variation in bone mineral content and estimated body fat in young adult females. *Med Sci Sports Exerc.* 1990;22(5):564–569.

69. Collins MA, Millard-Stafford ML, Sparling PB, et al. Evaluation of the BOD POD for assessing body fat in collegiate football players. *Med Sci Sports Exerc.* 1999;31(9):1350–1356.

70. Utter AC, Goss FL, Swan PD, Harris GS, Robertson RJ, Trone GA. Evaluation of air displacement for assessing body composition of collegiate wrestlers. *Med Sci Sports Exerc.* 2003;35(3):500–505.

71. Schutte JE, Townsend EJ, Hugg J, Shoup RF, Malina RM, Blomqvist CG. Density of lean body mass is greater in blacks than in whites. *J Appl Physiol.* 1984;56(6):1647–1649.

72. Millard-Stafford ML, Collins MA, Modlesky CM, Snow TK, Rosskopf LB. Effect of race and resistance training status on the density of fat-free mass and percent fat estimates. *J Appl Physiol.* 2001;91(3):1259–1268.

73. Visser M, Gallagher D, Deuenberg P, Wang J, Pierson RN Jr, Heymsfield SB. Density of fat-free mass: relationship with race, age, and level of body fatness. *Am J Physiol.* 1997;272(5, pt 1): E781–E787.

74. Collins MA, Millard-Stafford ML, Evans EM, Snow TK, Cureton KJ, Rosskopf LB. Effect of race and musculoskeletal development on the accuracy of air plethysmography. *Med Sci Sports Exerc.* 2004;36(6):1070–1077.

75. Siri WE. Body composition from fluid spaces and density: analysis of methods. In: Brozek J, Henschel A, eds. *Techniques for Measuring Body Composition.* Washington, DC: National Academy of Sciences; 1961:223–244.

76. Brozek J, Grande F, Anderson JT, Keys A. Densitometric analysis of body composition: revision of some quantitative assumptions. *Ann N Y Acad Sci.* 1963;110:113–140.

77. Evans EM, Prior BM, Arngrimsson SA, Modlesky CM, Cureton KJ. Relation of bone mineral density and content to mineral content and density of the fat-free mass. *J Appl Physiol.* 2001;91(5): 2166–2172.

78. Heyward VH, Wagner DR. *Applied Body Composition Assessment.* 2nd ed. Champaign, IL: Human Kinetics; 2004.

79. Lohman TG, Roche AF, Martorell R, ed. *Anthropometric Standardization Reference Manual.* Champaign, IL: Human Kinetics; 1988.

80. Lohman TG. Skinfolds and body density and their relation to body fatness: a review. *Hum Biol.* 1981;53(2):181–225.

81. Caton JR, Molé PA, Adams WC, Heustis DS. Body composition analysis by bioelectrical impedance: effect of skin temperature. *Med Sci Sports Exerc.* 1988;20(5):489–491.

82. Deurenberg P, Weststrate JA, Paymans I, van der Kooy K. Factors affecting bioelectrical impedance measurements in humans. *Eur J Clin Nutr.* 1988;42(12):1017–1022.

83. Hortobágyi T, Israel RG, Houmard JA, O'Brien KF, Johns RA, Wells JM. Comparison of four methods to assess body composition in black and white athletes. *Int J Sport Nutr.* 1992;2(1):60–74.

84. Oppliger RA, Nielsen DH, Shetler AC, Crowley ET, Albright JP. Body composition of collegiate football players: bioelectrical impedance and skinfolds compared to hydrostatic weighing. *J Orthop Sports Phys Ther.* 1992;15(4):187–192.

85. Williams CA, Bale P. Bias and limits of agreement between hydrodensitometry, bioelectrical impedance and skinfold calipers measures of percentage body fat. *Eur J Appl Physiol Occup Physiol.* 1998;77(3):271–277.

86. Colville BC, Heyward VH, Sandoval WM. Comparison of two methods for estimating body composition of bodybuilders. *J Appl Sport Sci Res.* 1989;3(3):57–61.

87. Houtkoopr LB, Mullins VA, Going SB, Brown CH, Lohman TG. Body composition profiles of elite American heptathletes. *Int J Sport Nutr Exerc Metab.* 2001;11(2):162–173.

88. Stewart AD, Hannan WJ. Prediction of fat and fat-free mass in male athletes using dual X-ray absorptiometry as the reference method. *J Sports Sci.* 2000;18(4):263–274.

89. Segal KR. Use of bioelectrical impedance analysis measurements as an evaluation for participating in sports. *Am J Clin Nutr.* 1996;64(suppl 3): 469S–471S.

90. Israel RG, Houmard JA, O'Brien KF, McCammon MR, Zamora BS, Eaton AW. Validity of a near-infrared spectrophotometry device for estimating human body composition. *Res Q Exerc Sport.* 1989;60(4):379–383.

91. Houmard JA, Israel RG, McCammon MR, O'Brien KF, Omer J, Zamora BS. Validity of near-infrared device for estimating body composition in a collegiate football team. *J Appl Sport Sci Res.* 1991;5(2):53–59.

92. Fornetti WC, Pivarnik JM, Foley JM, Fiechtner JJ. Reliability and validity of body composition

measures in female athletes. *J Appl Physiol.* 1999; 87(3):1114–1122.

93. Oppliger RA, Clark RR, Nielsen DH. New equations improve NIR prediction of body fat among high school wrestlers. *J Orthop Sports Phys Ther.* 2000;30(9):536–543.

94. Boileau RA, Lohman TG, Slaughter MH, Ball TE, Going SB, Hendrix MK. Hydration of the fat-free body in children during maturation. *Hum Biol.* 1984;56(4):651–666.

95. Boileau RA, Lohman TG, Slaughter MH. Exercise and body composition of children and youth. *Scand J Sports Sci.* 1985;7:17–27.

96. Girandola RN, Wisewell RA, Romero G. Body composition changes resulting from fluid ingestion and dehydration. *Res Q.* 1977;48(2):299–303.

97. Hayes PM, Lucas JC, Shi X. Importance of post-exercise hypotension in plasma volume restoration. *Acta Physiol Scand.* 2000;169(2):115–124.

98. Horswill CA, Hickner RC, Scott JR, Costill DL, Gould D. Weight loss, dietary carbohydrate modifications and high intensity, physical performance. *Med Sci Sports Exerc.* 1990;22(4):470–476.

99. Casa DJ, Armstrong LE, Hillman SK, et al. National Athletic Trainers' Association position statement: fluid replacement for athletes. *J Athl Train.* 2000;35(2):212–224.

100. Popowski LA, Oppliger RA, Lambert GP, Johnson RF, Johnson AK, Gisolf CV. Blood and urinary measures of hydration status during progressive acute dehydration. *Med Sci Sports Exerc.* 2001;33(5):747–753.

101. Armstrong LE, Soto JA, Hacker FT Jr, Casa DJ, Kavouras SA, Maresh CM. Urinary indices during dehydration, exercise, and rehydration. *Int J Sport Nutr.* 1998;8(4):345–355.

102. Armstrong LE, Maresh CM, Castellani JW, et al. Urinary indices of hydration status. *Int J Sport Nutr.* 1994;4(3):265–279.

103. Francesconi RP, Hubbard RW, Szlyk PC, et al. Urinary and hematologic indexes of hypohydration. *J Appl Physiol.* 1987;62(3):1271–1276.

104. Kavouras SA. Assessing hydration status. *Curr Opin Clin Nutr Metab Care.* 2002;5(5):519–524.

105. Bartok C, Schoeller DA, Sullivan JC, Clark RR, Landry GL. Hydration testing in collegiate wrestlers undergoing hypertonic dehydration. *Med Sci Sports Exerc.* 2004;36(3):510–517.

106. Walsh NP, Montague JC, Callow N, Rowlands AV. Saliva flow rate, total protein concentration and osmolality as potential markers of whole body hydration status during progressive acute dehydration in humans. *Arch Oral Biol.* 2004;49(2):149–154.

107. Armstrong LE, Kenefick RW, Castellani JW, et al. Bioimpedance spectroscopy technique: intra-, extracellular, and total body water. *Med Sci Sports Exerc.* 1997;29(12):1657–1663.

108. Bartok C, Schoeller DA, Clark RR, Sullivan JC, Landry GL. The effect of dehydration on wrestling minimum weight assessment. *Med Sci Sports Exerc.* 2004;36(1):160–167.

109. Petrie H, Osterberg KL, Horswill CA, Murray R. Reliability of bioelectrical impedance spectroscopy (BIS) use in athletes after exercise-induced dehydration. *Med Sci Sports Exerc.* 2004;36(suppl 5):S239.

110. Institute of Medicine of the National Academies of Science. *Dietary Reference Intakes: Water, Potassium, Sodium, Chloride, and Sulfate.* Washington, DC: Institute of Medicine; 2004.

111. Binkley HM, Beckett J, Casa DJ, Kleiner DM, Plummer PE. National Athletic Trainers' Association position statement: exertional heat illnesses. *J Athl Train.* 2002;37(3):329–343.

112. Rankin JM, Ingersoll CD. *Athletic Training Management, Concepts and Applications.* 3rd ed. Boston, MA: McGraw-Hill; 2006:118.

113. Ray R. *Management Strategies in Athletic Training.* 2nd ed. Champaign, IL: Human Kinetics; 2000:247, 250.

114. Schlabach GA, Peer KS. *Professional Ethics in Athletic Training.* St. Louis, MO: Mosby-Elsevier; 2008:169.

115. National Collegiate Athletic Association. Guideline 2e: assessment of body composition. In: *NCAA Sports Medicine Handbook 2008–09.* Indianapolis, IN: National Collegiate Athletic Association; 2008: 34–38.

116. Johnson M. The female athlete triad: 1994 update (disordered eating, amenorrhea, and osteoporosis). Paper presented at: 41st Annual Meeting of the American College of Sports Medicine; June 1, 1994; Indianapolis, IN.

117. Manore MM. Dietary recommendations and athletic menstrual dysfunction. *Sports Med.* 2002; 32(14):887–901.

118. Jakicic JM, Clark K, Coleman E, et al. American College of Sports Medicine position stand: appropriate intervention strategies for weight loss and prevention of weight regain for adults. *Med Sci Sports Exerc.* 2001;33(12):2145–2156.

119. United States Department of Agriculture. Food pyramid. http://www.mypyramid.gov/pyramid/. Accessed March 1, 2009.

120. Krebs-Smith SM, Kris-Etherton P. How does MyPyramid compare to other population-based recommendations for controlling chronic disease? *J Am Diet Assoc.* 2007;107(5):830–837.

121. Carey DG. Quantifying differences in the "fat burning" zone and the aerobic zone: implications for training. *J Strength Cond Res.* 2009;23(7):2090–2095.

122. Horswill CA. The 1.5%-per-week rule: part 1, fat loss. http://www.nwcaonline.com/articles/percentage_part1.pdf. Accessed March 15, 2009.

123. Baechle TR, Earle RW, eds. *Essentials of Strength Training and Conditioning.* 3rd ed. Champaign, IL: Human Kinetics; 2008:509–514.

124. Kenney HE. The problem of weight making for wrestling meets. *J Health Phys Educ.* 1930;1(24): 24–25, 49.

125. Oppliger RA, Steen SA, Scott JR. Weight loss practices of college wrestlers. *Int J Sport Nutr Exerc Metab.* 2003;13(1):29–46.

126. Nadel ER. Temperature regulation and prolonged exercise. In: Lamb DR, Carmel MR, eds. *Perspectives in Exercise Science and Sports Medicine: Prolonged Exercise.* Indianapolis, IN: Benchmark Press Inc; 1988:125–151.

127. Astrand PO, Rodahl K. *Textbook of Work Physiology.* New York, NY: McGraw-Hill Book Co; 1977.

128. Kenny GP, Reardon FD, Thoden JS, Giesbrecht GG. Changes in exercise and post-exercise core temperature under different clothing conditions. *Int J Biometeorol.* 1999;43(1):8–13.

129. Shapiro Y, Pandolf KB, Goldman RF. Predicting sweat loss response to exercise, environment, and clothing. *Eur J Appl Physiol Occup Physiol.* 1982;48(1):83–96.

130. Steen SN, Brownell KD. Patterns of weight loss and regain in wrestlers: has tradition changed? *Med Sci Sports Exerc.* 1990;22(6):762–768.

131. Weissenger E, Housh TJ, Johnson GO, Evans SA. Weight loss behavior in high school wrestling: wrestler and parent perceptions. *Ped Exerc Sci.* 1991;3(1):64–73.

132. Tipton CM, Tcheng TK. Iowa Wrestling Study: weight loss in high school students. *JAMA.* 1970;214(7):1269–1274.

133. Caldwell JE, Ahonen E, Nousiainen U. Diuretic therapy, physical performance, and neuromuscular function. *Phys Sportsmed.* 1984;(6)12:73–85.

134. Fogelholm M. Effects of bodyweight reduction on sports performance. *Sports Med.* 1994;18(4): 249–267.

135. Olsson KE, Saltin B. Variation in total body water with muscle glycogen changes in man. *Acta Physiol Scand.* 1970;80(1):11–18.

136. Tarnopolsky M, Cipriano N, Woodcroft C, et al. The effects of rapid weight loss and wrestling on muscle glycogen concentration. *Clin J Appl Physiol.* 1994;6(2):78–84.

137. Houston ME, Marrin DA, Green HJ, Thomson JA. The effect of rapid weight loss on physiological functions in wrestlers. *Phys Sportsmed.* 1981;9(11):73–78.

138. Walberg JL, Leidy MK, Sturgill DJ, Hinkle DE, Ritchey SJ, Sebolt DR. Macronutrient content of a hypoenergy diet affects nitrogen retention and muscle function in weight lifters. *Int J Sports Med.* 1988;9(4):261–266.

139. Buschschluter S. Games blood-letting. *Swim Tech.* 1977;13:99.

140. Nagii MR. The significance of water in sport and weight control. *Nutr Health.* 2000;14(2):127–132.

141. Cheuvront SN, Carter R III, Sawka MN. Fluid balance and endurance exercise performance. *Curr Sports Med Rep.* 2003;2(4):202–208.

142. Wilks B, Yuxiu H, Bar-Or O. Effect of body hypohydration on aerobic performance of boys who exercise in the heat. *Med Sci Sports Exerc.* 2002;34(suppl 5):S48.

143. Bar-Or O, Blimkie CJR, Hay JA, MacDougall JD, Ward DS, Wilson WM. Voluntary dehydration and heat intolerance in cystic fibrosis. *Lancet.* 1992;339(8795):696–699.

144. Montain SJ, Coyle EF. Influence of graded dehydration on hyperthermia and cardiovascular drift during exercise. *J Appl Physiol.* 1992;73(4): 1340–1350.

145. Sawka MN, Pandolf KB. Effects of body water loss in physiological function and exercise performance. In: Lamb DR, Gisolfi CV, eds. *Perspectives in Exercise Science and Sports Medicine: Fluid Homeostasis During Exercise.* Indianapolis, IN: Benchmark Press; 1990:1–38.

146. Ahmed W, Flynn MA, Alpert MA. Cardiovascular complications of weight reduction diets. *Am J Med Sci.* 2001;321(4):280–284.

147. Stevens A, Robinson DP, Turpin J, Groshong T, Tobias JD. Sudden cardiac death of an adolescent during dieting. *South Med J.* 2002;95(9):1047–1049.

148. Swenne I, Larsson PT. Heart risk associated with weight loss in anorexia nervosa and eating disorders: risk factors for QTc interval prolongation and dispersion. *Acta Paediatr.* 1999;88(3):304–309.

149. Schocken DD, Holloway JD, Powers PS. Weight loss and the heart: effects of anorexia nervosa and starvation. *Arch Intern Med.* 1989;149(4):877–881.

150. Mathias JL, Kent PS. Neuropsychological consequences of extreme weight loss and dietary restriction in patients with anorexia nervosa. *J Clin Exp Neuropsychol.* 1998;20(4):548–564.

151. Kretsch MJ, Green MW, Fong AK, Elliman NA, Johnson HL. Cognitive effects of a long-term weight reducing diet. *Int J Obes Relat Metab Disord.* 1997;21(1):14–21.

152. Green MW, Rogers PJ. Impairments in working memory associated with spontaneous dieting behavior. *Psychol Med.* 1998;28(5):1063–1070.

153. Snow CM, Rosen CJ, Robinson TL. Serum IGF-1 is higher in gymnasts than runners and predicts bone and lean mass. *Med Sci Sports Exerc.* 2000;32(11):1902–1907.

154. Hotta M, Fukuda I, Sato K, Hizuka N, Shibasaki T, Takano K. The relationship between bone turnover and body weight, serum insulin-like growth factor (IGF) I and serum IGF binding protein in patients with anorexia nervosa. *J Clin Endocrinol Metab.* 2000;85(1):200–205.

155. Douyon L, Schteingart DE. Effect of obesity and starvation on thyroid hormone, growth hormone, and cortisol secretion. *Endocrinol Metab Clin North Am.* 2002;31(1):173–189.

156. Lantzouni E, Frank GR, Golden NH, Shenker RI. Reversibility of growth stunting in early onset anorexia nervosa: a prospective study. *J Adolesc Health.* 2002;31(2):162–165.

157. Lanes R, Soros A. Decreased final height of children with growth deceleration secondary to poor weight gain during late childhood. *J Pediatr.* 2004;145(1):128–130.

158. Joy EA, MacIntyre JG. Women in sports. In: Mellion MB, Walsh WM, Madden C, Putukian M, Shelton GL, eds. *The Team Physician's Handbook.* 3rd ed. Philadelphia, PA: Hanley and Belfus Inc; 2002:77–83.

159. Nattiv A, Loucks AB, Manore MM, Sanborn CF, Sundgot-Borgen J, Warren MP. American College of Sports Medicine position stand: the female athlete triad. *Med Sci Sport Exerc.* 2007;39(10):1867–1882.

160. Chandra RK. Nutrition and the immune system from birth to old age. *Eur J Clin Nutr.* 2002;56(suppl 3):S73–S76.

161. Vaisman N, Hahn T, Dayan Y, Schattner A. The effect of different nutritional states on cell-mediated cytotoxicity. *Immunol Lett.* 1990;24(1):37–41.

162. Marcus A, Valela P, Toro O, et al. Interaction between nutrition and immunity in anorexia nervosa: a 1-y follow-up study. *Am J Clin Nutr.* 1997;66(2):485S–490S.

163. Lord GM, Matares G, Howard JK, Baker RJ, Bloom SR, Lechler RI. Leptin modulates the T-cell immune response and reverses starvation-induced immunosuppression. *Nature.* 1998;394(6696):897–901.

164. Palmblad J, Cantell K, Holm G, Norberg R, Strander H, Sunblad L. Acute energy deprivation in man: effect on serum immunoglobulins antibody response, complement factors 3 and 4, acute phase reactants and interferon-producing capacity of blood lymphocytes. *Clin Exp Immunol.* 1977;30(1):50–55.

165. Bishop NC, Blannin AK, Walsh NP, Robson PJ, Gleeson M. Nutritional aspects of immunosuppression in athletes. *Sports Med.* 1999;28(3):151–176.

166. Garner DM, Rosen LW, Barry D. Eating disorders among athletes: research and recommendations. *Child Adolesc Psychiatr Clin N Am.* 1998;7(4):839–857.

167. Perriello VA Jr. Aiming for healthy weight in wrestlers and other athletes. *Contemp Pediatr.* September 1, 2001;18:55–74.

168. Perriello VA Jr, Almquist J, Conkwright D Jr, et al. Health and weight control management among wrestlers: a proposed program for high school athletes. *Va Med Q.* 1995;122(3):179–185.

169. Brownell KD, Rodin J. Prevalence of eating disorders in athletes. In: Brownell KD, Rodin J, Wilmore JH, eds. *Eating, Body Weight and Performance in Athletes: Disorders of Modern Society.* Philadelphia, PA: Lea & Febiger; 1992.

170. Rosen LW, McKeag DB, Hough DO, Curley V. Pathogenic weight-control behavior in female athletes. *Phys Sportsmed.* 1986;14(1):79–86.

171. Johnson MD. Disordered eating in active and athletic women. *Clin Sports Med.* 1994;13(2):355–369.

172. Dummer GM, Rosen LW, Heusner WW, Roberts PJ, Counsilman JE. Pathogenic weight control behaviors of young competitive swimmers. *Phys Sportsmed.* 1987;15(5):75–86.

173. Kazis K, Iglesias E. The female athlete triad. *Adolesc Med.* 2003;14(1):87–95.

174. Otis CL. The female athlete triad. In: Sallis RE, Massimino F, eds. *Essentials of Sports Medicine 1997.* St. Louis, MO: Mosby–Year Book; 1997: 202–205.

175. Hausenblas HA, Carron AV. Eating disorder indices and athletes: an integration. *J Sport Exerc Psychol.* 1999;21(3):230–258.

176. Stoutjesdyk D, Jevne R. Eating disorders among high performance athletes. *J Youth Adolesc.* 1993; 22(3):271–282.

177. Sundgot-Borgen J. Prevalence of eating disorders in elite female athletes. *Int J Sport Nutr.* 1993;3(1): 29–40.

178. Sundgot-Borgen J. Risk and trigger factors for the development of eating disorders in female elite athletes. *Med Sci Sports Exerc.* 1994;26(4): 414–419.

179. Steen SN, Bernadot D, Englebert-Fenton K, Freeman K, Hartsough C. Roundtable #18: eating disorders in athletes: the dietician's perspective. *Gatorade Sports Sci Inst.* 1994;5(4):2.

Address correspondence to National Athletic Trainers' Association, Communications Departments, 2952 Stemmons Freeway, Dallas, TX 75247.

Glossary

A

abrasion Rubbing or scraping off of skin. (Chapter 9)

acclimatization The adaptation of the body to a different environment. (Chapter 18)

acromioclavicular (AC) joint Articulation (arthrodial) formed by the distal end of the clavicle and the acromion process. (Chapter 11)

acute injury Characterized by rapid onset, resulting from a traumatic event. (Chapter 1)

adjustment disorders A disorder in which mild depressive or anxiety symptoms occur in response to specific events. (Chapter 5)

adult-onset diabetes (type 2) Non-insulin-dependent type of diabetes. The body does not produce enough insulin or the body does not use insulin properly. (Chapter 19)

agonistic muscles Muscles in a state of contraction as related to opposing muscles. (Chapter 15)

amenorrhea Absence or suppression of menstruation. (Chapter 5)

analgesic Agent that relieves pain without causing a complete loss of sensation. (Chapter 8)

anatomic Pertaining to anatomy. (Chapter 15)

angiogenesis Formation of capillaries, which interconnect, resulting in the formation of new vessels. (Chapter 8)

anhedonia No longer experiencing pleasure from activities that once were enjoyable. (Chapter 20)

anisocoria Rare but naturally occurring condition where the pupils are of unequal size, not related to any acute condition such as head injury. (Chapter 9)

anorexia nervosa A disorder characterized by a pattern of self-starvation with a concomitant obsession with being thin and an overwhelming fear of being fat. (Chapter 5)

antagonistic muscles Muscles that counteract the action of agonistic muscles. (Chapter 15)

anterior Before or in front of. (Chapter 1)

anterograde amnesia Inability to recall events that have occurred since the injury. (Chapter 9)

anti-inflammatories Drugs designed to prevent swelling. Two basic categories are currently in use: steroidal and nonsteroidal. (Chapter 8)

antipyretic Agent that relieves or reduces fever. (Chapter 8)

apophysis Bony outgrowth to which muscles attach. (Chapter 1)

apophysitis Inflammation of an apophysis. (Chapter 20)

apoptosis Process of programmed cell death. Biochemical events can lead to changes in cell characteristics thereby causing cell death. (Chapter 8)

arachidonic acid Chemical released when cells are damaged that serves as a precursor to the formation of other inflammatory chemicals including leukotrienes and prostaglandins. (Chapter 8)

athletic energy deficit When sustained activity is not balanced with a proportional increase in nutrition, so the calories out balances with the calories in. (Chapter 6)

avascular necrosis Death of tissue caused by the lack of blood supply. (Chapter 15)

avulsion Forcible tearing away or separation. (Chapter 1)

avulsion Forcible tearing away or separation. (Chapter 16)

B

bacteria Plural of bacterium. A *Schizomycetes*, unicellular microorganism that can either be parasitic or free-living and has a wide range of biochemical, often pathogenic, properties. (Chapter 17)

ballistic stretching Stretching technique that uses repetitive bouncing motions. (Chapter 4)

bandage Material used to cover a wound. (Chapter 17)

basal metabolic rate (BMR) The amount of energy needed at to sustain functioning at rest. (Chapter 6)

411

Bennett's fracture Fracture and/or dislocation of the first metacarpal bone away from the greater multangular bone of the wrist. (Chapter 12)

biomechanical The effect of external and internal forces on the anatomic tissues and the movements of the body. (Chapter 15)

biomechanics Branch of study that applies the laws of mechanics, internal or external, to the living body. (Chapter 5)

bipolar disorder A manic-depressive illness that involves cycling mood swings from major depression to mania where individuals feel full of energy. (Chapter 5)

boutonnière deformity Buttonhole deformity whereby the proximal interphalangeal joint of the finger is forced through the central band of the tendon of the extensor digitorum muscle. (Chapter 12)

boxer's fracture Fracture of the proximal fourth and/or fifth metacarpal bones. (Chapter 12)

bradykinin Inflammatory chemical released when tissues are damaged; it results in increased pain in the area and may play a role in the production of other inflammatory chemicals such as prostaglandins. (Chapter 8)

bulimia nervosa A disorder characterized by repeated bouts of binge eating followed by some form of purging, such as vomiting, use of laxatives, fasting, and vigorous and excessive exercise. (Chapter 5)

bursa Small synovial sac typically located over bony prominences that assists in cushioning and reducing friction. (Chapter 12)

bursitis Inflammation of a bursa. (Chapter 11)

C

carpal tunnel Anatomic region of the wrist where the median nerve and the majority of the tendons of the forearm pass into the hand. (Chapter 12)

carpal tunnel syndrome A complex of symptoms resulting from pressure on the median nerve as it passes through the carpal tunnel of the wrist, causing soreness and numbness. (Chapter 12)

catastrophic injury Injury involving damage to the brain and/or spinal cord that presents a potentially life-threatening situation or the possibility of permanent disability. (Chapter 1)

cerebral contusion Bruising of the brain tissue. (Chapter 9)

chondromalacia Abnormal softening of cartilage, typically noted between the patella and femur. (Chapter 15)

chronic injury Characterized by a slow, insidious onset, implying a gradual development of structural damage. (Chapter 1)

chronic traumatic encephalopathy A condition that can only be identified after death with a brain autopsy. It is a degenerative disease characterized by a distinct collection of tau proteins in several areas of the brain that affect function. (Chapter 9)

CNS Central nervous system. (Chapter 9)

cold urticaria A condition in which the skin reacts to exposure to cold with localized edema associated with severe itching. (Chapter 18)

colic Intra-abdominal pain. (Chapter 19)

colitis Inflammation of the colon. (Chapter 19)

collagen The major protein of connective tissue. (Chapter 8)

Colles' fracture Transverse fracture of the distal radius. (Chapter 12)

commission A legal liability arising when a person commits an act that is not legally his or hers to perform. (Chapter 3)

complement system Part of the immune system. It is innate and complements the antibodies and cleaning cells to clear pathogens from damaged tissue. (Chapter 8)

concentric contraction Occurs when a muscle shortens and there is movement at the joint accompanied by contraction against resistance. (Chapter 11)

conduction Heating through direct contact with a hot medium. (Chapter 18)

connective tissue The most common tissue in the body; includes ligaments, bones, retinaculum, joint capsules, cartilage, fascia, and tendons. (Chapter 8)

contact dermatitis Inflammation of the skin that is nonallergenic. (Chapter 17)

contusion Bruise or injury to soft tissue that does not break the skin. (Chapter 1)

convection Heating indirectly through another medium such as air or liquid. (Chapter 18)

core temperature Internal body temperature as opposed to shell or peripheral temperature. (Chapter 18)

crepitation Crackling sound heard during the movement of a broken bone. (Chapter 1)

critical force Magnitude of a single force by which an anatomic structure is damaged. (Chapter 1)

cryotherapy Therapeutic use of cold. (Chapter 8)

CSF Cerebrospinal fluid. (Chapter 9)

D

de Quervain's disease Inflammation of sheaths surrounding the extensor tendons of the thumb. (Chapter 12)

diabetic shock Shock resulting from abnormally high sugar content in the blood and low insulin levels. (Chapter 19)

diplopia Double vision. (Chapter 9)

dislocation The displacement of contiguous surfaces of bones comprising a joint. (Chapter 1)

distal interphalangeal (DIP) joint The joint formed by the articulation between the intermediate and distal phalanges of the digits (hinge type of joint). (Chapter 12)

dorsiflexion Bending toward the dorsum or rear; the opposite of plantar flexion. (Chapter 16)

dressing Covering, either protective or supportive, that is applied to an injury or wound. (Chapter 17)

dynamic stretching A voluntary stretching technique that uses full-range, sport-like motions to warm up. (Chapter 4)

dysesthesia Impairment of the sense of touch. (Chapter 9)

dysthymia Characterized by nondisabling depressive symptoms that are chronic but do not cause changes in usual functioning. (Chapter 5)

E

eccentric contraction The simultaneous processes of muscle contraction and stretching of the muscle–tendon unit by an extrinsic force. (Chapter 1)

ecchymosis Black-and-blue discoloration of the skin caused by hemorrhage. (Chapter 1)

edema Abnormal accumulation of fluid in the interstitial tissue between the skin and body cavities. Homeostasis of fluid mechanics is disturbed. (Chapter 8)

edema Swelling caused by the collection of fluid in connective tissue. (Chapter 18)

endurance The ability of the body to engage in prolonged physical activity. (Chapter 19)

environmental The aggregate of surrounding things, conditions, or influences. (Chapter 15)

epicondylitis Inflammatory response at the epicondyle. (Chapter 12)

epidemiology The study of the distribution of disease or injury within a population and its environment. (Chapter 1)

epidural hematoma Bleeding between the dura and the cranial bones. (Chapter 9)

epilepsy A chronic disorder characterized by sudden attacks of brain dysfunction, including altered consciousness, abnormal motor activity, sensory phenomena, and/or inappropriate behavior. (Chapter 19)

epiphysis Cartilaginous growth region of a bone. (Chapter 1)

epistaxis Nosebleed. (Chapter 9)

ergogenic aids Foods or beverages that have the potential to increase the work output of the person using them. (Chapter 6)

erythema Red discoloration of the skin. (Chapter 8)

eversion of the foot To turn the foot outward. (Chapter 16)

exercise-induced asthma (EIA) Acute, reversible, self-limiting bronchospasm occurring during or after exercise. (Chapter 7)

exostosis Bony outgrowths that protrude from the surface of a bone where there is not a typical bony formation. (Chapter 12)

F

fascia Fibrous membrane that covers, supports, and separates muscles. (Chapter 1)

fibroblast Immature, fiber-producing cells of connective tissue that can mature into one of several different cell types. (Chapter 8)

flexibility The range of motion (ROM) in a given joint or combination of joints. (Chapter 4)

fracture A break or crack in a bone. (Chapter 1)

fracture-dislocation An injury resulting in both the fracture of a bone and dislocation at the joint. (Chapter 12)

friction Heat producing. (Chapter 1)

frostnip Less severe form of frostbite. (Chapter 18)

G

gamekeeper's thumb Sprain of the ulnar collateral ligament of the metacarpophalangeal joint of the thumb. (Chapter 12)

ganglion Herniation of the synovium surrounding a tendon and subsequent filling of the area with synovial fluid, resulting in a visible bump seen through the skin. (Chapter 12)

gastritis Inflammation of the stomach lining. (Chapter 19)

gastroenteritis Inflammation of the stomach and intestines. (Chapter 19)

GI Gastrointestinal. (Chapter 19)

glenohumeral (GH) joint Articulation (spheroid) formed by the head of the humerus and the glenoid fossa of the scapula. (Chapter 11)

golfer's elbow Medial humeral epicondylitis related to incorrect golf technique. (Chapter 12)

H

hamstrings The three muscles that make up the posterior thigh: biceps femoris, semimembranosus, and semitendinosus. (Chapter 15)

heat cramps Muscle spasms related to excessive heat buildup within the body. (Chapter 18)

heat exhaustion Generalized fatigue related to excessive heat buildup within the body; may be a precursor to heatstroke. (Chapter 18)

heatstroke Excessive heat buildup within the body resulting in the body's inability to cool itself, with core temperatures exceeding 106°F. (Chapter 18)

hematoma A localized collection of extravasated blood, usually clotted, that is confined within an organ, tissue, or space. (Chapter 1)

hemorrhage Injury involving muscles and tendons or the junction between the two, commonly known as the musculotendinous junction. (Chapter 1)

hernia Protrusion of a part of an organ or tissue through an abnormal opening. (Chapter 14)

hip pointer Contusion and associated hematoma to the superior/anterior portion of the iliac crest. (Chapter 14)

histamine Powerful inflammatory chemical that causes an increase in vascular permeability and vasodilation. (Chapter 8)

hormones Various internally secreted compounds formed in endocrine glands that affect the functions of specifically receptive organs or tissues. (Chapter 15)

HPV Human papillomavirus; approximately 55 specific types of these viruses have been identified, at least two of which are related to plantar warts. (Chapter 17)

HSV-1 Herpes simplex virus type 1; related to infections in athletes commonly known as herpes gladiatorum. (Chapter 17)

humeroradial joint Articulation (arthrodial) formed by the proximal end of the radius and the distal end of the humerus, specifically the capitellum. (Chapter 12)

humeroulnar joint Articulation (ginglymus) formed by the proximal end of the ulna, specifically the trochlear notch, with the distal end of the humerus, specifically the trochlea. (Chapter 12)

hyperesthesia Nonpainful touch stimuli becomes painful. (Chapter 20)

hyperglycemia Excessively high level of blood sugar. (Chapter 19)

hypertrophy Enlargement of a part caused by an increase in the size of its cells. (Chapter 4)

hypoglycemia Low level of blood sugar. (Chapter 19)

hypothermia A body temperature below 33.3°C (95°F). (Chapter 18)

hypovolemic shock Inability of the cardiovascular system to maintain adequate circulation to all parts of the body. (Chapter 7)

I

ICE Ice, compression, and elevation. (Chapter 12)

idiopathic Cause of a condition is unknown. (Chapter 15)

incubation period The time between an exposure to an infectious agent and the appearance of symptoms of that infection. (Chapter 17)

infectious mononucleosis Viral infection characterized by general fatigue and enlargement of organs such as the spleen. (Chapter 19)

injury Act that damages or hurts. (Chapter 1)

insidious Slow onset or signs and symptoms occur with no obvious mechanism. (Chapter 9)

insulin shock Shock resulting from an abnormally low sugar content in the blood and higher insulin levels. (Chapter 19)

intracerebral hematoma Bleeding within the brain tissues. (Chapter 9)

intracranial injury Head injury characterized by disruption of blood vessels, either veins or arteries, resulting in the development of a hematoma or swelling within the confines of the cranium. (Chapter 9)

inversion of the foot To turn the foot inward; inner border of the foot lifts. (Chapter 16)

iontophoresis Using an electrical current to drive a chemical directly through the skin. (Chapter 8)

J

joint capsule Saclike structure that encloses the ends of bones in a diarthrodial joint. (Chapter 1)

juvenile-onset diabetes (type 1) Insulin-dependent type of diabetes mellitus usually occurring in children and adolescents. The body does not produce insulin. (Chapter 19)

K

Kehr's sign Pain radiating into the left shoulder that is normally associated with an injury to the spleen. (Chapter 13)

Ketoacidosis Metabolic processes that occur in the absence of insulin. Fatty acids are used to provide energy and metabolism creates ketones. Result is disorientation and fruity breath smell. (Chapter 19)

L

laser A device that concentrates high energies into a narrow beam of visible monochromatic light. (Chapter 17)

leukocytes White blood cells. (Chapter 8)

Little League elbow Condition related to excessive throwing that results in swelling of the medial epicondyle of the elbow, that is, medial humeral epicondylitis. (Chapter 1)

locus of control People's belief, or lack thereof, of being in control of events occurring in their lives. (Chapter 5)

LRI Lower respiratory infection. (Chapter 19)

luxation Complete dislocation of a joint. (Chapter 1)

Lyme disease Bacterial infection transmitted by the black-legged tick (deer tick). (Chapter 19)

lysosomes Cellular organelles that contain enzymes that break down waste materials and cellular debris. (Chapter 8)

M

major depression Characterized by a combination of five or more symptoms and noticeable changes in usual functioning like sleep, eating, work, or school. (Chapter 5)

malaise Discomfort and uneasiness caused by an illness. (Chapter 19)

malfeasance An act of commission where conduct is performed that is wholly unlawful. (Chapter 3)

mallet finger Deformity of the distal interphalangeal joint of the finger caused by an avulsion of the tendon of the extensor digitorum muscle from the distal phalanx. (Chapter 12)

menisci Fibrocartilaginous structures that are between the hyaline cartilage surfaces in some synovial joints (e.g., the knee). (Chapter 15)

metaphysis That portion of growing bone located between the shaft and the epiphysis. (Chapter 1)

misfeasance An act of commission where lawful conduct is performed but done improperly. (Chapter 3)

modalities Physical agents that help create an optimal healing environment. (Chapter 8)

muscular strength The maximal force that can be applied by a muscle during a single maximal contraction. (Chapter 19)

myalgia General muscle pain. (Chapter 19)

myelin Performs an insulating function to the axon of a nerve. Composed of fats and proteins. (Chapter 9)

myocarditis Infection of the heart with inflammation and damage to the heart muscle. (Chapter 19)

myositis Inflammation of muscle. (Chapter 12)

myositis ossificans Myositis marked by ossification within a muscle. (Chapter 1)

N

negligence The failure to do what a reasonably careful and prudent person would have done under the same or like circumstances, or doing something that a reasonably careful and prudent person would not have done under the same or like circumstances. (Chapter 3)

neuromuscular Pertaining to the nervous intervention of the muscles. (Chapter 15)

NSAID Nonsteroidal anti-inflammatory drug. (Chapter 8)

O

omission A legal liability arising when a person does not perform an action that ought to be taken. (Chapter 3)

orthopedic surgeon Physician who corrects deformities of the musculoskeletal system. (Chapter 2)

Osgood-Schlatter disease Epiphyseal inflammation of the tibial tubercle. (Chapter 15)

OSHA Occupational Safety and Health Administration. (Chapter 17)

osteitis pubis Inflammation of the bones in the region of the symphysis pubis. (Chapter 14)

osteoblasts Cells that synthesize bone. Function in groups of connected cells. (Chapter 8)

osteochondritis dissecans Condition in which a fragment of cartilage and underlying bone are detached from the articular surface. (Chapter 12)

osteoclasts Bone cells that remove bone tissue by breaking up the organic bone. (Chapter 8)

osteomyelitis Infection of bone or bone marrow with associated inflammation. (Chapter 20)

P

PABA Para-aminobenzoic acid; the common active ingredient in sunscreen products. (Chapter 17)

palpation The act of feeling with the hands for the purpose of determining the consistency of the part beneath. (Chapter 7)

passive stretching Movement of a joint through its ROM by someone other than the athlete. (Chapter 4)

patellofemoral joint Articulation (saddle) formed by the posterior surface of the patella and the anterior surface of the femoral condyles. (Chapter 15)

pathogenic Causing disease. (Chapter 5)

periodization The organization of training into a cyclical structure to attain the optimal development of an athlete's performance capacities. (Chapter 4)

permethrin Broad-spectrum insecticide that can be infused in clothes to prevent insect bites. (Chapter 19)

phagocytosis Destruction of injurious cells or particles by phagocytes (white blood cells). (Chapter 8)

phalanges Anatomic name for the bones of both the fingers and/or toes. (Chapter 12)

phonophoresis Introduction of ions of soluble salt into the body through ultrasound. (Chapter 8)

physical exam Checking a victim of an emergency for signs and symptoms associated with injury and/or illness. (Chapter 7)

plaintiff The individual who was injured and brings the lawsuit. (Chapter 3)

PNS Peripheral nervous system. (Chapter 9)

point tenderness Pain produced when an injury site is palpated. (Chapter 7)

proprioceptive neuromuscular facilitation (PNF) Stretching techniques that involve combinations of alternating contractions and stretches. (Chapter 4)

prostaglandins Perhaps some of the most powerful chemicals produced in the body; related to the inflammatory process, they cause a variety of effects including vasodilation, increased vascular permeability, pain, fever, and clotting. (Chapter 8)

proximal interphalangeal (PIP) joint The joint formed by the articulation between the proximal and intermediate phalanges of the digits (hinge type of joint). (Chapter 12)

purulent Consisting of, or forming, pus. (Chapter 17)

pyoderma Pus-producing infection of the skin. (Chapter 17)

pyomyositis Bacterial infection of muscles resulting in pus-filled abscesses. (Chapter 20)

Q

Q angle Angle made by the rectus femoris and the patellar tendon as they attach to the tibial tubercle. (Chapter 15)

quadriceps Four muscles of the anterior thigh: rectus femoris, vastus medialis, vastus intermedius, and vastus lateralis. (Chapter 15)

R

radiation Emission and diffusion of rays of heat. (Chapter 18)

radiocarpal joint Articulation (ellipsoidal) formed by the distal end of the radius and three bones of the wrist: navicular, lunate, and triquetral. (Chapter 12)

radioulnar joints Two articulations (pivot) formed by the proximal and distal radius and ulna, known commonly as the proximal and distal radioulnar joints. (Chapter 12)

regeneration Damaged tissue is replaced by some cells of the same type along with scar tissue, and it retains most of its original structure. (Chapter 8)

repair Original tissue is replaced by scar tissue and the structure and function are lost. (Chapter 8)

resolution Complete healing where dead cells and cellular debris are removed and the tissue is left functionally the same. (Chapter 8)

retrograde amnesia Inability to recall events that occurred just prior to an injury. (Chapter 9)

rhinitis The common cold. (Chapter 19)

risk factor Causative agent in a sports injury. (Chapter 1)

rotator cuff Group of four muscles of the glenohumeral joint: subscapularis, supraspinatus, infraspinatus, and teres minor. (Chapter 11)

S

Salter-Harris fracture A category of fractures that involves the growth plate. (Chapter 1)

secondary enzymatic injury Indirect result of tissue trauma. Healthy tissues surrounding primary injury die due to aggressive eating of healthy tissue within area of original injury. Waste products also damage cell membranes of healthy cells causing cell death. (Chapter 8)

secondary metabolic injury Indirect result of tissue trauma. Healthy tissues surrounding primary injury die due to lack of blood flow and lack of metabolic supplies. The energy needed exceeds that of the energy available. (Chapter 8)

seizure Sudden onset of uncoordinated muscular activity and changes in consciousness lasting an unpredictable time. (Chapter 19)

self-concept The image of the self that is constructed from the beliefs one holds about oneself. (Chapter 5)

shoulder pointer Contusion and subsequent hematoma in the region of the acromioclavicular joint. (Chapter 11)

sign Objective evidence of an abnormal situation within the body. (Chapter 7)

soft tissue Includes muscles, fascia, tendons, joint capsules, ligaments, blood vessels, and nerves. (Chapter 1)

spearing A practice in tackle football whereby a player performs either a tackle or a block using the head as the initial point of contact. (Chapter 1)

sports medicine Branch of medicine concerned with the medical aspects of sports participation. (Chapter 2)

sprain Injury to a joint and the surrounding structures, primarily ligaments and/or joint capsules. (Chapter 1)

static stretching Passively stretching an antagonistic muscle by placing it in a maximal stretch and holding it there. (Chapter 4)

sternoclavicular (SC) joint Articulation (arthrodial) formed by the union of the proximal clavicle and the manubrium of the sternum. (Chapter 11)

stress fracture Small crack or break in a bone related to excessive, repeated overloads; also known as overuse fracture or march fracture. (Chapter 1)

stressor Anything that affects the body's physiological or psychological condition and upsets the homeostatic balance. (Chapter 5)

subdural hematoma Bleeding below the dura mater. (Chapter 9)

subluxation Partial or incomplete dislocation of an articulation. (Chapter 1)

subtalar joint Articulation (arthrodial) formed by the inferior surface of the talus and the superior surface of the calcaneus. (Chapter 16)

symptom Subjective evidence of an abnormal situation within the body. (Chapter 7)

syndrome Group of typical symptoms or conditions that characterize a deficiency or disease. (Chapter 11)

T

tackler's exostosis Formation of a benign growth projecting from the humerus that is caused by repeated blows to the upper arm region; common in tackle football. (Chapter 12)

talocrural joint Articulation (ginglymus) formed by the distal tibia and fibula with the superior surface (dome) of the talus. (Chapter 16)

team physician A medical doctor who agrees to provide at least limited medical coverage to a particular sports program or institution. (Chapter 2)

tendinitis Inflammation of a tendon. (Chapter 11)

tenosynovitis Inflammation of the sheath of a tendon. (Chapter 12)

thermotherapy Therapeutic use of heat. (Chapter 8)

tibiofemoral joint Articulation (bicondylar) formed by the medial and lateral femoral condyles and the medial and lateral tibial condyles. (Chapter 15)

tinea Group of fungi-related skin infections, commonly called ringworm, which can affect various parts of the body—groin (tinea cruris), feet and toes (tinea pedis), and scalp (tinea capitis). (Chapter 17)

tinea versicolor Fungus infection resulting in the formation of circular skin lesions that appear either lighter or darker than adjacent skin. (Chapter 17)

TMJ Temporomandibular joint. (Chapter 9)

tort A private wrong or injury, suffered by an individual as a result of another person's conduct. (Chapter 3)

trait anxiety A general disposition or tendency to perceive certain situations as threatening and to react with an anxiety response. (Chapter 5)

trauma Wound or injury. (Chapter 8)

tunnel of Guyon Anatomic region formed by the hook of the hamate bone and the pisiform bone, whereby the ulnar nerve passes into the hand. (Chapter 12)

U

URI Upper respiratory infection. (Chapter 19)

V

valgus Position of a body part that is bent outward. (Chapter 12)

varus Position of a body part that is bend inward. (Chapter 12)

vasoconstriction Decrease in the diameter of a blood vessel resulting in a decreased blood flow. (Chapter 8)

vasodilation Increase in the diameter of a blood vessel resulting in an increased blood flow. (Chapter 8)

vertigo Type of dizziness that causes a perception of motion and includes a loss of balance. (Chapter 19)

Volkmann's contracture Contracture of muscles of the forearm related to a loss of blood supply caused by a fracture and/or dislocation of either of the bones in the forearm or the humerus. (Chapter 12)

Index

Note: Page numbers followed by *f* or *t* indicate material in figures or tables, respectively.

A

AAFP. *See* American Academy of Family Physicians
AAP. *See* American Academy of Pediatrics
AAS. *See* anabolic androgenic steroids
abdominal region. *See also* thorax and abdomen injuries
    anatomy, 224–225, 225*f*
    muscle strains, 227
    pain in, 232–233
abdominal rigidity, 113
abnormal patellofemoral configuration, 258
abrasions, 165
absence attack, 332
Academy of Nutrition and Dietetics (2009), 78
acclimatization, 308, 309
acetabulum, 238, 238*f*
acetylsalicylic acid, 130
Achilles tendinitis, 278
Achilles tendon, 4, 5*f*, 271, 278
    complex, 282
ACL. *See* anterior cruciate ligament
ACL Research Retreat of 2012, 262
acromioclavicular (AC) joint, 10, 180, 180*f*, 181, 185–186
acromion process, 185
ACSM. *See* American College of Sports Medicine
Act of God, 36, 37
active assisted exercise, 131
active exercise, 131
acute appendicitis, 232
acute fracture symptoms, 8
acute injuries, 4, 5, 339
    pain and, 125–126
ADA. *See* American Diabetes Association
Adderall (amphetamine and dextroamphetamine), 100, 350
adductor muscles, 239, 240
ADHD. *See* attention deficit hyperactivity disorder
adhesive strapping techniques, 284
adjustment disorders, 65
adolescent fractures, hip/pelvis, 241
adolescent medical concerns, 337

American youth sports, 338
    coaching techniques, 349
    cultural deconditioning, 344
    equipment, 345
    extrinsic factors, 344–345
    female athletes, 349–350
    growth, 340
    growth cartilage, 342–343
    growth plate injuries, 342
    infectious imitators, 346
    injury contributors, 343–345
    injury imitators, 345–346
    injury mechanisms, 340–343
    injury prevention, 348–350
    intrinsic factors, 344
    ligament injuries, 340–341
    neurovascular imitators, 346
    oncologic imitators, 346
    playing surfaces, 345
    PPE, 348–349
    prescription stimulant medication, 350
    psychologic imitators, 346
    puberty, 339–340
    rehabilitation of previous injuries, 349
    rheumatologic imitators, 346
    safety, 347
    sports participation factors, 338
    strength training, 346–348
    stretching programs, 349
    tendon injuries, 341–342
    training error, 344
adult-onset diabetes, 330
AEDs. *See* automated external defibrillators
aerobic dance and congenital heart disorders, 12
aerobic fitness/aerobic power, 51
aerosol coolants, 127
afterdrop, 315
agonistic muscles, 254, 255
airway assessment, 110
airway obstructions, 27, 108, 226
albuterol, 328
alcohol detoxification, 231
alertness assessment, 109
ALES. *See* Athletic Life Experience Survey
allergic reactions, 304–305
AMA. *See* American Medical Association
AMA House of Delegates, 30

amenorrhea, 72, 73, 350
American Academy of Family Physicians (AAFP), 40, 48–50
American Academy of Orthopaedic Surgeons (AAOS)
    continuing education courses, 27
    frostbite, 315
    initial check, 109
American Academy of Pediatrics (AAP), 50
    adolescent weight training, 347
    boxing, 12
    PPE guidelines, 40
    sports categories based on contact, 12
American Association of Oral and Maxillofacial Surgeons, 160
American College of Sports Medicine (ACSM), 89
American Diabetes Association (ADA), 330
American Heart Association, 107
    BOC certification courses, 27
    CPR and AED courses, 39
    PPE recommendations, 349
American Journal of Sports Medicine, 185
American Medical Association (AMA), 7
American Medical Society for Sports Medicine, 40, 48
American Orthopaedic Society for Sports Medicine, 40
American Osteopathic Academy of Sports Medicine, 40, 48
American Red Cross, 27, 39
American Society for Testing and Materials (ASTM), 162
amino acids, 83, 94, 96*t*, 99
ammonia capsules, 145
amphetamine (Adderall), 100, 350
anabolic androgenic steroids (AAS), 229–230
anabolic steroids, 100
anaerobic fitness, 51–52
analgesics, 127
anatomic rationale, 262, 263
anatomic snuffbox, palpation in, 209, 209*f*
anatomy
    abdominal region, 224–225
    arm/wrist/hand injuries, 196
    hip/pelvis injuries, 238–240
    internal organs, 225

anatomy *(Continued)*
  lower leg/ankle/foot, 270–273
  lumbar spine, 173, 173f
  shoulder, 180–183, 180f
  thigh/knee/leg injuries, 250–252
  thoracic spine, 170, 170f
  thorax, 224–225
anconeus, 196
androstenedione (andro), 96t, 99
angiogenesis, 124, 125
anhedonia, 66, 346, 347
anisocoria, 146, 147
ankle joint, 270
  ligaments of, 271f
ankle sprains, 275
ankle taping, 277
  preventive, 287–291
  procedure, 291f
ankles
  anatomy, 270–273
  fractures, 273–274
  injuries, 274–278. *See also* lower leg,
    ankle, and foot injuries
  skeletal injuries, 273–274
  soft-tissue injuries, 274–281
  taping/bracing, 284
  tendon injuries, 278–279
annular ligament of elbow, 196, 196f
annulus, 176
anorexia nervosa, 70–71
anoxia, 140
antagonistic muscles, 254, 255
anterior, 16, 17
anterior compartment, muscles of, 270
anterior cruciate ligament (ACL), 251, 261
  injuries, 50
  osteoarthritis in knee and, 15
  soccer, 18
anterior dislocation of GH joint, 186, 186f
anterior longitudinal ligaments, 173
anterior muscles, 250
anterior shoulder pain, 16
anterior talofibular, 270
  ligaments, 274
anterograde amnesia, 141
anti-inflammatory drugs, 127
anticonvulsant drugs, 332
antihistamines, 317
antipyretic effects, 130
apophyseal injuries, 341
apophysis, 16, 17, 340, 340f
apophysitis, 202, 204, 341
  common sites of, 341t
apoptosis, 124, 125
appendix, rupture, 232
Appropriate Medical Care for the
  Secondary School-Aged Athlete
  (NATA), 40
aquatic sports and epilepsy, 332
arachidonic acid, 123, 130
arachnoid, 136f, 137
arch problems, 283–285
arch taping procedure, 283
arm injuries
  anatomy, 196

elbow fractures, 203–204
myositis ossificans traumatica, 197–198
osteochondritis dissecans of elbow,
  205–206
triceps injuries, 198–199
upper arm fractures, 199–201
upper arm soft tissue injuries, 196–199
arnica, 96t
arteries of arm, 184f
articular cartilage, 124, 340
articular surfaces of long bones, 340
articulation between vertebrae, 173
artificial turf, 296
aspirin, 130
assessment of injuries, 109–114
  airway, 109, 110, 226
  alertness, 109
  breathing, 110
  circulation, 111
  coach's responsibility, 108
  evaluation process, 108–109
  head injuries, 145
  hemorrhage, 111
  medical history, 112–113
  palpation, 113–114
  physical exam, 112–114
  responsiveness, 109–110
  shock, 114
Association for Applied Sport
  Psychology, 67
assumption of risk, 37
ASTM. *See* American Society for Testing
  and Materials
ATHENA. *See* Athletes Targeting Healthy
  Exercise and Nutrition Alternatives
athlete exposure, 3
athletes
  diabetes, 330–331
  dietary guidelines for
    during competition, 93
    daily maintenance, 91–92
    for post exercise, 93
    precompetition diets, 92–93
  diets, 78, 90
  ergogenic substances used by, 96t–97t
  growing
    bone growth, 340
    puberty, 339–340
  injured, 94
  nutritional knowledge of, 86–87
  oral/injectable steroids, 100
  SCT, 329–330
  tape/braces for, 289
Athletes Targeting Healthy Exercise and
  Nutrition Alternatives (ATHENA),
  73, 91
athletic energy deficit, 88
athletic health care team (AHCT), 23–30
  athletic training settings, 27–30
  BOC-certified trainers, 29–30
  key team members, 25–27
  professional content, 27
  secondary school setting, 28–29
  sports medicine, defined, 24–25
Athletic Life Experience Survey (ALES), 64

Athletic Medicine Unit, 30. *See also* athletic
  health care team (AHCT)
athletic trainers. *See also* Board of
  Certification (BOC)-certified
  athletic trainers
  certification subjects, 27
  heat illnesses, 312
  injury prevention and, 6
  job settings, 27
  mental preparation, 192
  professional sports, 27–28
  salary ranges, 28
  for secondary schools, 28–30
athletic training settings, 28–30
atlantoaxial joint, 138
attention deficit hyperactivity disorder
  (ADHD), 350
  stimulants, 100
auricula, 163
auricular hematoma, 163
automated external defibrillators
  (AEDs), 228f
  BOC certification training, 27
  coach training/certification in, 25, 39
  coaches' training in, 109
  commotio cordis, 228
  and CPR, 228
  emergency plans and, 106, 107
avascular necrosis, 253
avoidance behaviors, 69
AVPU scale, 109
avulsion, 8, 273
  tooth, 159
avulsion fractures, 204
  hip/pelvis, 244
  tendon-bone strain, 8
axial loading of cervical spine, 151

B

bacteria, defined, 296, 297
bacterial infections, 346
  skin, 300–302
badminton
  GH joint impingement
    syndrome, 190
  non-contact sport, 12
balanced diet, 92
ball-and-socket joint, 238, 238f
ballistic stretching, 54, 55
bandage, 298, 299
bands of extensor tendons, 217, 218f
barrier devices, 27
basal metabolic rate (BMR), 79
baseball
  catastrophic injuries, 6, 12
  contusions, 8
  head/face injuries, 15
  injury data, 2, 3, 15
  injury rates by gender, 3
  as limited contact sport, 12
  Little League elbow, 16, 16f
  protective chest equipment, 229
baseball finger. *See* mallet finger
bases, types of, 47

basketball, 14–15
  catastrophic injuries, 12
  collision sports, 12
  commotio cordis, 228
  contusions, 8
  GH joint impingement syndrome, 190
  injury rates by gender, 14–15
  knee ligament sprains, 15
  lower-extremity injuries, 14, 14*f*
  protective chest equipment, lack of, 229
batting cages, 47
bench press, 348
Bennett's fracture, 213, 214*f*
beta-2 agonists, 328
beta-hydroxy beta-methylbutyrate
      (HMB), 99
β-alanine, 99
biceps brachii, 16, 196
  muscle tendon, 191, 191*f*
biceps femoris muscle, 240, 250
biceps tendon, 191
biomechanical deficiencies, 281
biomechanical rationale, 262, 263
biomechanics of sport, 69
bipolar disorder, 65
black eye, 161
bladder injuries, 231–232
blisters and calluses, 285–286
blood
  blood glucose levels, 80, 330
  exposure to, 159
  transfusions and HBV, 329
  in urine, 231
bloodborne pathogens, 111, 159
BMR. *See* basal metabolic rate
Board of Certification (BOC)-certified
      athletic trainers, 78
  as AHCT members, 25
  ankle taping procedure, 284
  benefits for school, 28–29
  CAATE accreditation, 27
  injury recognition, 11
  rehabilitative exercise and, 131
  secondary schools, 28–29
BOC Exam Candidate Handbook, 26
body composition, 54–55, 95
body image, 73
body weight management, nutrition and,
      94–95, 97
boils, 301
bone infections, 346
bone scans, 9
bones of hand and wrist, 213*f*
boutonnière deformity, 217–218, 218*f*
bowling, 12
boxer's fracture, 214, 215
boxing
  bleeding wounds, 298
  participation not recommended
      by AAP, 12
brachial plexus, 152, 154*f*, 181, 184*f*
brachialis, 196
bradykinin, 121
brain contusions, 8
brain stem, 137

breach of duty, 36, 37
breast injuries, 227
breathing assessment, 110, 145
buddy taping, 214
budgetary constraints, 47
bulimia nervosa, 70–71
bunions, 285
burners, 152
bursa, 206, 207
bursitis, 189

C

CA-MRSA. *See* community-acquired
      methicillin-resistant *Staphylococcus
      aureus*
CAATE. *See* Commission on Accreditation
      of Athletic Training Education
caffeine, 98
calcaneal apophysitis, 342
calcaneofibular ligaments, 274
calcium, 85–86
calf muscles, 270
calluses (fracture healing), 9, 124, 125*f*, 286
  blisters and, 285–286
calories, 79
Canadian Standards Association (CSA), 162
capsular ligaments, 180*f*, 186
carbohydrates (CHO), 79–81, 94
carbuncles, 300, 301
cardiac contusion, 228, 231
cardiac issues
  cardiac arrest, 145
  pathology, 228
  sudden death, 228
cardiac medical history, 48
cardiopulmonary resuscitation (CPR)
  after circulation assessment, 111, 145
  athletic trainers and, 27
  coach's training in, 14, 25, 109
  emergency care training, 107, 108*f*
  emergency plans and, 106, 107, 108*f*
  sudden cardiac arrest, 228
carpal tunnel, 210, 211, 211*f*
  syndrome, 210, 211
carrdiac issues
  cardiac arrest, 108
  cardiogenic shock, 114
Carroll, Michael, 115
cartilage, 251
case-series studies, 11
catastrophic injuries, 6–7, 140, 150,
      151*t*, 338
categories of sports by AAP, 12
cauda equina, 238
cauliflower ear, 17, 163
causative factors in injury, 46
caution, 66
cellulitis, 300, 302
cellulose, 79
Center for Epidemiological Studies Depres-
      sion Scale Revised (CESD-R), 66
Centers for Disease Control and
      Prevention, 298
central nervous system (CNS), 109, 137, 311

cerebellum, 137
cerebral contusion, 143
cerebral edema, 142
cerebral meninges, 137, 137*f*
cerebrospinal fluid (CSF), 137
cerebrum, 137
Certificate of Added Qualifications in
      Sports Medicine (CAQ), 25
certified athletic trainers (ATs), 78
certified strength and conditioning
      specialists (SCSs), 78
cervical protrusions, 146
cervical spine injuries, 149–151
  brachial plexus injuries, 152
  fractures and dislocations, 153–154
  guidelines for appropriate care of, 157
  ice hockey, 152
  mechanisms of injury, 151–152
  sprains, 152–153
  strains, 153
cervical vertebras, 138
CESD-R. *See* Center for Epidemiological
      Studies Depression Scale Revised
CEUs. *See* continuing education programs
checklist, symptom-scale, 148
cheerleading, 139–140
chemical allergies, 304
chemical cold-packs, 127
chemotactic factors, 123
chemotaxis, 123
chest protector, 229
chickenpox, 317
chondromalacia, 259
ChooseMyPlate.gov, 92*f*
chronic Achilles tendinitis, treatment for,
      278
chronic exertional compartment syndrome
      (CECS), 281
chronic GH joint subluxation, 187
chronic injuries, 4, 5
chronic obstructive pulmonary disease, 233
chronic traumatic encephalopathy (CTE),
      142, 143
circulation assessment, 111, 145
classifications of injury, 7–11
clavicle, 180, 183–185
CNS. *See* central nervous system
coaches
  advice for, 73
  AHCT responsibilities, 25
  first contact with injured student, 34, 34*f*
  legal protections, 39
  liability insurance coverage, 39
  limitations, 115–116
  negligent actions, 38
  nutrition for athletes, 90–91
  nutritional knowledge of, 86–87
  responsibility, 108
  and student team leaders, 91
coaching personnel, 64
coaching techniques, 349
coccygeal plexus, 238
coccyx, 173, 175, 238
cold-related health problems, 313–316
cold treatment for inflammation, 127

cold urticaria, 316–317
colic, 323
colitis, 323
collagen, 125, 131
collateral ligaments, 215, 216, 260
  injuries, 260–261
Colles' fracture, 206, 207, 208f
collision sports, 12
comminuted fractures, 8, 9f
commission, 36, 37
  act of, 36
Commission on Accreditation of Athletic
  Training Education (CAATE),
  26–27
Committee on the Medical Aspects
  of Sports, 7
common integument, 296
commotio cordis, 228
communication skills, 172
community-acquired methicillin-resistant
  Staphylococcus aureus
  (CA-MRSA), 302
comparative negligence, 37
compartment syndrome, 279–281
competition, environment, 47
competitive stress, 66–68
complement system, 123
complete proteins, 83
complex carbohydrates, 79
complex partial seizure, 332
compound fractures, 8
compression, 119, 120f, 127, 128, 128f
computerized neurocognitive
  assessment, 149
concentric contraction, 189
concussion (mild traumatic brain injury),
  19, 140–141
concussion education, 149
conduction, 308, 309
condyloid joint, 214
congenital heart disorders, 12
connective tissue, 120, 121
conoid ligaments, 185
Consumer Product Safety Commission
  (CPSC), 19
contact ACL injuries, 261
contact/collision category, 12
contact/collision sports and epilepsy, 332
contact dermatitis, 304, 305
contact lens problems, 162
contact sports, 12
continuing education programs (CEUs), 27
contrecoup injury, 140
contributory negligence, 37
contusions, 8, 9
  cardiac, 228
  cerebral, 143
  defined, 8
  of elbow, 206
  pulmonary, 230–231
  shoulder, 191–192
  testicular/scrotal, 244
convection, 308, 309
coracoacromial arch, 190, 190f
coracoclavicular ligament, 180f, 185

coracohumeral ligament, 180f, 186
coracoid process, 191
core exercises, 53
core temperature, 308, 309, 315
coronal plane MRI of a torn ACL, 260f
corporate athletic trainers, 27
cortisone, 129
costochondral joint, 224
costochondral separation, 226
costoclavicular ligaments, 188
CPR. *See* cardiopulmonary resuscitation
CPSC. *See* Consumer Product Safety
  Commission
cranial injury, 144
cranium, 136, 136f
creatine, 96t, 99
crepitation, 8, 9
crepitus, 113
critical force, 4, 5, 120
cross-country running, heatstroke, 6
cross-country skiing, catastrophic injuries, 12
cruciate ligaments, 250
  injuries, 261–263
cryotherapy, 127–129
CSA. *See* Canadian Standards Association
CSF. *See* cerebrospinal fluid
CTE. *See* chronic traumatic encephalopathy
cultural deconditioning, 344
cup protector, 244, 247
cycling
  clavicle fractures, 183
  hypothermia, 315
cystic fibrosis, 233

D

daily fiber intake, 80
date rape drug, 101
de Quervain's disease, 212, 213
deformity
  as acute fracture symptom, 8
  as dislocation symptom, 10–11
degenerative enzymes, 123
degradation effect, 123
dehydration, symptoms and treatment,
  309–310
dehydroepiandrosterone (DHEA), 96t, 99
delayed erythema phase, 299
deltoid muscle, 181f, 225
dental injuries, 159–160
depressed skull fractures, 144
depression, 65–66, 346
dermis, 296, 302
detached retina, 161, 162
dexamethasone, 129
dexedrine, 100, 350
dextroamphetamine, 100
DHEA. *See* dehydroepiandrosterone
diabetes, 330–331
diabetic coma, 331
diabetic shock, 331
diaphragm, 225
  irritation, 225
diathermy, 127
  machines, 47

dietary carbohydrates, 79–80
dietary fats, 82
dietary fiber, 79
dietary guidelines for athletes
  during competition, 93
  daily maintenance, 91–92
  for post exercise, 93
  precompetition diets, 92–93
dietary nitrate, 96t
dietary plan, safe and healthy, 79
dietary protein, 83
Dietary Supplement Health and Education
  Act (DSHEA), 98
diets
  post exercise, 93
  precompetition, 92–93
DIP joint. *See* distal interphalangeal joint
diplopia, 162, 163
direct catastrophic injuries, 6
disaccharides, 79
disk protrusion at level L-5/S-1, 176f
dislocated hip, 243
dislocations, 10, 11
  cervical, 153
  defined, 10, 11
  of elbow, 202, 202f
  fracture, 213
  of hand, 214–218
  of jaw, 164
  manubrium, 226
  wrist, 209–210
disordered eating. *See* eating disorders
displaced fractures, 226
distal forearm fractures, 207
distal interphalangeal (DIP) joint, 216, 217
diving, 164
doctrine of sovereign immunit, 37
documentation of injuries, 40–41
dorsal radiocarpal ligament, 209, 210f
dorsalis pedis, pulse of, 280f
dorsiflexion, 156, 270, 271
doughnut-shaped pads, 283
downhill skiing, 12
dressing for wounds, 298, 299
drills, 54
DSHEA. *See* Dietary Supplement Health
  and Education Act
dugout locations, 47
duodenal ulcer, 232
dura mater, 137
dynamic flexibility, 53
dynamic stretching, 54, 55
dysesthesia, 156, 157
dyspnea, 172, 173
dysthymia, 65

E

EAPs. *See* emergency action plans
ear injuries, 163–164
eardrum, 163
Eating Attitude Test (EAT-26), 88
eating disorders, 69–70, 349
  anorexia nervosa and bulimia nervosa,
  70–71

prevention of, 73
research, 71
sport specificity and, 72–73
treatment of, 73
ECC. *See* emergency cardiac care
eccentric contractions, 5, 120, 189
ecchymosis, 8–9
echinacea, 97t
echocardiogram/echocardiography, 232
ECM. *See* erythema chronicum migrans
edema, 124, 125, 316, 317
EIA. *See* exercise-induced asthma
EIB. *See* exercise-induced bronchospasm
elbow dislocation, 202, 202f
elbow injuries, 201–202
  contusions, 206
  epicondylitis, 204–205
  fractures, 203–204
  ODC, 205–206
  splinting of, 202, 203f
  sprains and dislocations, 202–203
elbow joint, 196, 196f
  epicondylitis of, 204–205, 204f
elbow sprains, 202
electrolyte imbalances, 72
electrotherapies, 127
elevation of injury, 128
emergency action plans (EAPs), 106,
    115, 228
  airway assessment, 109, 110
  breathing assessment, 110
  circulation assessment, 111
  circulatory system, 111–112
  coach's limitations, 115–116
  coach's responsibility, 108
  elements, 106–107
  emergency care training, 107–108
  evaluation process, 108–109
  first aid training, 107
  hemorrhage assessment, 111
  initial assessment of injuries, 109–112
  injury evaluation procedures, 108–109
  medical history, 112–113
  palpation, 113–114
  physical exam, 112–114
  practices for athletics, 107
  removal from field/court, 114
  respiratory system, 110
  responsiveness of athlete, 109–110
  return to play condition, 114–115
  shock, 114
emergency cardiac care (ECC), 27
Emergency Care and Safety Institute, 107
emergency care training, 107–108
emergency medical services (EMS),
    105, 330
  access routes, 47
  availability, 154
emergency plans, 39, 105
emergency team, 107
empty calorie foods, 79
EMS. *See* emergency medical services
encephalon, 136, 137
endurance, 322, 323
  sports, nutrition and, 88

energy
  athletic energy deficit, 88
  and fat-containing food composition, 82t
enlarged spleen, 231
environmental bases, 262, 263
ephedra, 96t, 98–99
epicondylitis, 201
  of elbow joint, 204–205, 204f
epidemiology, 11
  of sports injuries, 11–12
epidermis, 296
epidural hematoma, 143
epigastric pain, 232
epilepsy, 113, 331
epiphysis, 10, 11
epistaxis, 162, 163
epithelial tissue, 120
epoxy resin allergies, 304
Epstein-Barr virus, 325
equilibrium and inner ear, 163
equipment fitting, injury prevention
    and, 345
equipment inspections, 41
erector spinae muscles, 175, 175f
ergogenic aids, 96t–97t, 97–98, 350
  anabolic-androgenic products, 100–101
  nutritional supplements, 98–100
ergonomics, 28
Erwin, John, 67
erythema, 121
erythema chronicum migrans (ECM), 324
erythropoietin (EPO), 100
esophageal problems, 232
essential amino acids, 83
estrogen inhibitors, 96t
ETAP. *See* exercise-related transient
    abdominal pain
ethics of sports-injury care, 35
ethyl chloride, 127, 128
etiology of spondylolisthesis, 174, 175
evaluation process in injury assessment,
    108–109
evaporation, 308
eversion of foot, 270, 271
Ewing's sarcoma, 346
exercise, 81
  post exercise diet, 93
  water during, 86
exercise-induced asthma (EIA), 113
exercise-induced bronchospasm (EIB), 327
exercise order, 53
exercise rehabilitation, 131–132
exercise-related transient abdominal pain
    (ETAP), 232
exercise selection, 53
exertional heat illnesses, 309–313
  heat stroke, 311–312
exostosis, 197
explosive power training, 53
extensor/supinator forearm muscles,
    196, 198f
extensor tendons, bands of, 217, 218f
external acoustic meatus, 163
external ear, 163
external locus of control, 63

external oblique muscles, 225
extracellular fluids, 86
extrinsic factors, 46, 47
extrinsic overuse injuries, 5
eyes
  anatomy, 160f
  injuries, 160–162, 162f
  protection, 15, 16

F

face
  anatomy, 138
  fractures, 164
  wounds, 164–165
facemask removal, 157, 158f
facilities, 47
  inspections, 41
false ribs, 224
Family Educational Rights and Privacy Act
    (FERPA), 50
fascia, 6, 7
fast foods, 90f
fat-soluble vitamins, 84
fatalities
  from cardiac problems, 228, 230
  cheerleading, 139
  heat-related, 311
  in soccer, 19
fats, 81–82, 82t
fatty acid, 82
FDP muscle. *See* flexor digitorum
    profundus muscle
Federation Internationale de Football, 19
female athlete triad, 350
female athletes, 85, 88, 349–350
  contact ACL injuries, 261
  knee injuries in basketball, 14
  noncontact ACL injury, 261
  sports participation growth, 2, 2f, 3
femoral fractures, 252–253
  of right leg, 252f
femoral hernias, 245
femoral neck stress fracture, 241
FERPA. *See* Family Educational Rights and
    Privacy Act
fibrin, 83
fibrinogen, 83
fibroblastic repair phase, 124
fibroblasts, 124, 125
fibula, fracture of, 274f
fibular (lateral) collateral ligament, 250
field hockey, catastrophic injuries, 12
finger-sweep method, 110, 111f
first aid care
  AC joint sprains, 186
  of Achilles tendon, 279
  asthma victims, 328, 329f
  avulsion fractures, 244
  biceps tendon problems, 191
  boutonnière deformity, 218
  of brachial plexus injury, 152
  cardiac/pulmonary contusion, 231
  certification, 39
  cervical fractures, 153–154

first aid care *(Continued)*
cervical spine strains, 153
clavicle fracture, 184–185
of compartment syndrome, 281
costochondral separation, 226
de Quervain's disease, 212
diabetic emergencies, 331, 332f
dislocated hip, 243
distal forearm fractures, 207
elbow
fractures, 204
sprains and dislocations, 202–203
epicondylitis/apophysitis, 205
epileptic seizures, 333
femoral fractures, 253
gamekeeper's thumb, 216
ganglion, 213
GH joint dislocation, 187
hand fractures, 214
herniated disk, 176
hip pointer, 241
humeral fractures, 201
inflamed bursa, 257
jersey finger, 217
jumper's knee, 258
knee ligaments, 263
of lateral ankle sprain, 275
lower leg/foot fracture, 274
lumbar sprains/strains, 176
mallet finger, 217
muscle strains, 255
muscular contusion, 254
nerve injuries to wrist, 211–212
ODC, 206, 256
olecranon bursitis, 206
Osgood-Schlatter disease, 258
patellar dislocation/subluxation, 257
pelvis fractures, 240
rib fractures, 171
rotator cuff injuries, 189
SC joint injuries, 189
of shin splints, 281
shoulder contusions, 192
SLAP, 187–188
of sprains, 153
sternum/rib fracture, 226
testicular/scrotal contusions, 245
of tib/fib syndesmosis sprain, 276
torn meniscus, 260
training, 14, 25
emergency action plans, 107
triceps muscle, 199
upper arm contusions, 198
vertebral fractures, 171
wrist
fractures, 209
sprains and dislocations, 210
first-degree sprains/strains, 7
first responders, 108
fitness components, 50
fixed-base contact, 15
flail chest, 226
flexibility, 53–54
flexor carpi ulnaris, 210

flexor digitorum profundus (FDP) muscle, 217, 218
flexor/pronator forearm muscles, 196, 199f
floating ribs, 224
Flores, Doris E., 172
"Fluid Replacement for Athletes," 312
folliculitis, 301
foot disorders, 281–282
foot injuries. *See* lower leg, ankle, and foot injuries
football
bleeding wounds, 298
brain/spinal cord injuries, 14
catastrophic injuries, 12
cervical spine injuries, 12
commotio cordis, 228
contact/collision category, 12
contusions, 8
injury rates, 3
liver injury, 231
myositis ossificans traumatica, 197
neck fractures, 6
pelvis fractures, 240
spearing, 11
spondylolisthesis, 174
thoracic strains, 172
forearm injuries
axial loading of, 206
wrist injuries and, 206–207, 207f, 208f
fractures, 208–209
nerve injuries, 210–212
sprains and dislocations, 209–210
tendon problems, 212–213
forearm muscles, 196, 198f, 199f
foreseeability, 36, 39
formaldehyde resin allergies, 304
fracture-dislocation, 213
fractures, 8, 226, 273–274
elbow, 203–204
hand, 213–214
scaphoid bone, 208, 208f
sternal, 226
stress X-ray of, 341f
types, 8, 9f. *See also* specific bones and sports
upper arm, 199–201
wrist, 208–209
free play decline, 344
friction burns, 17
frostbite/frostnip, 315–316
fructose, 80
functional activities, 132
functional knee braces, 265, 266, 266f
functional loss and return to play, 115
furuncles, 300, 301

G

galea aponeurotica, 136
gamekeeper's thumb, 214–216, 215f
gamma-hydroxybutyrate (GHB), 96t, 101
ganglion of wrist, 212, 212f, 213
gastritis, 323
gastrocnemius, 271
gastroenteritis, 323

gastrointestinal infections (GI), 323
gemelli muscles, 239
gender-based injury rates, 3
general conditioning programs, 51
getting one's bell rung, 115
GH joint. *See* glenohumeral joint
GHB. *See* gamma-hydroxybutyrate
GI. *See* gastrointestinal infections; glycemic index
ginseng, 97t
glenohumeral (GH) joint, 10, 50, 180, 181, 186–188
glenohumeral joint–related impingement syndrome, 190–191
glenoid fossa, 180, 186, 186f, 188, 196
glenoid labrum, 16, 180
glucocorticoids, 129
gluteus minimus muscle, 238
glycemic index (GI), 80, 81t
glycerol, 82
glycogen, 79, 93
loading, 80–81
golf, 12
golfer's elbow, 205
Good Samaritan law, 37, 39
gracilis muscle, 239f, 240
graduate student/athletic trainer, 28
grand mal seizure, 332
greater multangular (trapezium) bone, 214
greenstick fractures, 8, 9f, 183, 226
groin injuries, 254
groin pulls, 254
groin strains, prevention of, 246
growth cartilage, 342–343
growth in adolescents, 340
growth plates, 342
guarana, 97t, 98, 99
gymnastics, 88, 160
catastrophic injuries, 6, 12
GH joint impingement syndrome, 190
kyphosis, 171
microvascular injury, 342
spondylolisthesis, 174

H

Hageman factor (XIIa), 123
hamstring muscles, 239f, 240, 250, 251
hand fractures, 213–214
hand injuries, 213
fractures, 213–214
sprains and dislocations, 214–218
HAV. *See* hepatitis A virus
HBV. *See* hepatitis B virus
HCM. *See* hypertrophic cardiomyopathy
head, neck, and face injuries
anatomy, 136–138
background information for head injuries, 138–140
brachial plexus injuries, 152
breathing assessment, 145
central nervous system, 137
cervical spine injuries, 149–154
circulation assessment, 145
concussion, 140–141

contact lens problems, 162
cranial injury, 144
dislocations, 153–154
ear injuries, 163–164
eye injuries, 160–162
face, 138, 164–165
football emergency procedures for treatment, 156–158
fractures, 153–154
initial check, 145
intracranial injury, 143–144
maxillofacial region injuries, 158
    dental injuries, 159–160
    eye injuries, 160–162
    face injury, 164–165
    nose injuries, 162–164
mechanism of, 140
meninges, 137, 137f
neck (cervical spine), 138, 154–158
nose injuries, 162–163
peripheral nervous system, 138
physical exam, 145–149
post-concussive syndrome, 141–142
second impact syndrome, 142, 143f
sideline assessment, 147
skull, 136
sprains, 152–153
strains, 153
treatment guidelines, 144–149, 154–156
head-tilt/chin-lift technique, 110, 110f
healing process, acute phase of, 279
Health Insurance Portability and Accountability Act (HIPPA), 41, 50
heart
    injuries, 228–229
    murmurs/arrhythmias, 233
heat cramps, 310, 311
heat exhaustion, 311
heat-related issues
    acclimatization, 312
    heat cramps, 310–311
    heat exhaustion, 12, 311–312
    heat index, 310, 310t
    heatstroke, 6, 12, 311–312, 314t
heat treatment for inflammation, 127
heatstroke, 309
heel spurs, 282–283
helmets, 156f
    baseball, 15
    cervical spine injuries and, 12
    removal dangers, 110, 146, 157
hematoma formation, 8–9, 121
    intracerebral, 143
    under nail, 286, 286f
    severe contusion with, 280, 280f
hematuria, 175, 231
hemorrhage, 7
    assessment, 111
    sprains and, 7
hemothorax, 171, 226
hepatitis A virus (HAV), 326
hepatitis B virus (HBV), 296, 326
hepatitis infection, 326–327
herbal supplements, 96t–97t, 100
hernias, 245

herniated disk, 176, 177
herniation of synovium, 212
herpes
    herpes gladiatorum, 302
    HSV-1, 303
    wrestling and, 17
herpes simplex virus type 1 (HSV-1), 303
"high ankle sprain," 276
high-force injuries, 341
High School Reporting Information Online (RIO), 12
hip/pelvis injuries
    adolescent fractures, 241
    anatomy, 238–240
    avulsion fractures, 244
    femoral neck stress fracture, 241
    hernias, 245
    hip dislocation, 243
    hip pointer, 241
    male genitalia injuries, 244–245
    nerve problems, 245
    osteitis pubis, 243
    other hip problems, 241–243
    pelvis fractures, 240–241
    prevention of, 246–247
    sacroiliac joint injury, 243
    skeletal injuries, 240–243
    slipped capital femoral epiphysis, 241
    soft-tissue injuries, 244–246
    sports-related injuries, 240–246
HIPAA. See Health Insurance Portability and Accountability Act
histamine, 121
history of injury, 8, 112, 112f
HIV. See human immunodeficiency virus
HMB. See hydroxymethylbutyrate
hockey
    commotio cordis, 228
    pelvis fractures, 240
hormones, 263
    effect of sex, 262
horseshoe-shaped pad, 275, 276f
horseshoe stirrups, 291f
hospital-based sports medicine outpatient services, 28
HPV. See human papillomavirus
human immunodeficiency virus (HIV), 296
human papillomavirus (HPV), 302, 303
humeroradial joint, 196, 197
humeroulnar joint, 196, 197
humerus bone, humeral head, 186, 189
Hummel, Chris H., 150
hydration techniques, 78
hydrocollator packs, 127
hydrocortisone, 129
hydrogen peroxide, 298
hydroxymethylbutyrate (HMB), 96t
hyoid, 138
hyperesthesia, 346, 347
hyperextension, 174, 175
    of cervical spine, 152
hyperflexion of cervical spine, 151, 152
hyperglycemia, 330, 331
hyperosmolality, 93
hypersomnia, 66

hypertrophic cardiomyopathy (HCM), 228, 229f, 233
hypertrophy/endurance phase (periodization), 55
hyphema, 162
hypoglycemia, 330, 331
hypothalamus, 308, 313
hypothenar eminence, 211
hypothermia, 313, 315
hypovolemic shock, 111

I

ice, compression, and elevation (ICE), 207
ice hockey
    catastrophic injuries, 6, 12
    contact/collision category, 12
    SAD and, 66
    thoracic strains, 172
idiopathic nature, 258, 259
IFS. See interferential stimulation
iliac artery/vein, 238
iliacus muscle, 239, 239f
iliocostalis muscles, 224
iliopsoas group, 239
iliotibial band, 214
IM. See infectious mononucleosis
immediate erythema phase, 299
immediate-onset injury, 286
immune serum globulin (ISG), 327
impacted fractures, 8, 9f
impetigo, 300, 301f
impingement syndrome, 190
incubation period, 302, 303
indirect catastrophic injuries, 6
industrial/corporate athletic trainers, 28
infections, skin, 299–303
infectious imitators, 346
infectious mononucleosis (IM), 325–326
inferior nasal concha bones, 138
inflamed bursae, 256–257
inflammatory process, 121, 122f
inflammatory response phase, 121–124
infraspinatus muscles, 181, 181f, 183
ingrown toenail, 286f
inguinal hernias, 245
initial assessment of injuries, 109–112
initial check, injury
    dental injuries, 159
    eye, 161–162
    head, 145
    nose, 163
injuries, 4
    acute/chronic, 4, 4f, 5
    contributors, 343–345
    data, 2–3
    defined, 3
    evaluation procedures, 108–109
    imitators, 345–346
    mechanisms, 340–343
    recognition, 11
injury prevention, 57, 348–350
injury process, 119–132
    cryotherapy, 127–129
    exercise rehabilitation, 131–132

injury process *(Continued)*
  fibroblastic repair phase, 124
  inflammatory process, 121, 122*f*
  inflammatory response phase,
    121–124
  intervention procedures, 126–131
  mechanical forces, 120, 121*f*
  nonsteroidal anti-inflammatory drugs,
    130–131, 130*t*
  pain and acute injury, 125–126
  pharmacologic agents, 129–131
  physics of injury, 120
  physiology of injury, 120–125
  prevention, 126
  remodeling phase, 124–125
  steroidal anti-inflammatory drugs,
    129–130
  thermotherapy, 127–129
injury rehabilitation, 57
injury-specific exercise, 132
Injury Surveillance System (ISS), 3
inner ear and equilibrium, 163
innominate bones, 238
insidious, 162, 163
insulin, 80, 330
insulin shock, 331
intercarpal joints, 209
interclavicular ligaments, 188
intercostal muscles, 172, 224
interferential stimulation (IFS), 127
internal hemorrhaging, 111
internal injuries, thorax/abdomen,
    227–233
internal locus of control, 63
internal oblique muscles, 225
internal organs, 225
  injury with fracture, 175
International Olympic Committee (IOC),
    328, 350
interstitial spaces, 121
intervention procedures, 126–131
intervention strategies
  extrinsic factors, 47
  intrinsic factors, 48–50
intervertebral joints, 224
intra-articular cartilaginous disk, 185
intracellular fluids, 86
intracerebral hematoma, 143
intracranial injury, 143–144
intracranial pressure, 140
intrinsic factors, 46, 48–50
intrinsic overuse injuries, 5
intrusive thoughts, 69
inversion ankle sprains, 288
inversion of foot, 270, 271
invertebral disk injuries, 172
IOC. *See* International Olympic
    Committee
iodine, 298
iontophoresis, 129–131
iron, 85
ischium, 238
ISG. *See* immune serum globulin
isopropyl rubbing alcohol, 298
ISS. *See* Injury Surveillance System

J

jaw-thrust technique, 110, 110*f*
jersey finger, 217, 217*f*
jock itch, 300
joint capsules, 6, 7
joint dysfunction, as dislocation
    symptom, 10
joint mice. *See* osteochondritis dissecans
    (OCD)
Journal of Athletic Training, 24
JRA. *See* juvenile rheumatoid arthritis
jumper's knee, 257–258
juvenile-onset diabetes (type I), 330
juvenile rheumatoid arthritis (JRA), 346

K

Kehr's sign, 231
keratolysis, 303
ketoacidosis, 331
kidneys
  contusions, 8
  heat susceptibility, 231
  injuries, 231
kinesiology, 189
knee bracing, 265–266
knee injuries
  ligaments of, 260–263
  participation of athletes with, 264*t*
  preventing, 263
knee joint, 249, 259
  ligaments of, 252*f*
kyphosis, 171

L

labyrinth, 163
lacerated spleen, 231
lacrimal bones, 138
lacrosse
  catastrophic injuries, 12
  collision sports, 12
  commotio cordis, 228
lactose, 79
laser surgery, 303
lat pull down, 348
lateral ankle sprain, 276
lateral flexion of cervical spine, 152
latex gloves, 163
latissimus dorsi muscle, 181, 181*f*, 224–225
law and sports injury, 33–42
  actions when sued, 42
  coach's liability, 37–39
  coach's protections, 39
  ethics of sports-injury care, 35
  Good Samaritan law, 37, 39
  state regulation of athletic training, 42
  torts, 35–37
lean body weight (LBW), 95
LEQ. *See* Life Event Questionnaire
LESA. *See* Life Event Scale for Adolescents
LESCA. *See* Life Event Survey for Collegiate
    Athletes
leukocytes, 123, 124
leukotrienes, 123

levator scapulae muscle, 180, 181*f*
Leverenz, Larry J., 227
liability insurance coverage, 39
Life Event Questionnaire (LEQ), 64
Life Event Scale for Adolescents
    (LESA), 64
Life Event Survey for Collegiate Athletes
    (LESCA), 64
ligaments, 196
  of ankle joint, 271*f*
  damage categories, 185
  injuries, 340–341
  of knee joint, 252*f*
lighting, 47
limited contact category, 12
lipids, 81–82
liquid nitrogen, 303
litigation. *See also* law and sports injury
    coach liability, 11
Little League Baseball in 1939, 338
Little League elbow, 16, 16*f*, 17, 204–205,
    343
liver injuries, 231
load-volume, 52
local symptoms, unusual, 345
locus of control, 63
long bone tumors, 346
long-distance running, hypothermia, 313
long-term treatment with adhesive
    tape, 281
longissimus muscle, 224
lordosis, 171
low back pain, 232
low-cost alternative method, 283
low glycemic index carbohydrates, 80
lower extremity biomechanics, 262
lower-extremity injuries, 14, 14*f*
lower leg, ankle, and foot injuries
  anatomy, 270–273
  ankle taping, preventive, 287–291
  sports injuries
    ankle injuries, 274–278
    arch problems, 283–285
    blisters and calluses, 285–286
    bunions, 285
    compartment syndrome,
      279–281
    foot disorders, 281–282
    heel spurs, 282–283
    Morton's foot, 283
    plantar fasciitis, 282
    shin splints, 281
    skeletal injuries, 273–274
    soft-tissue injuries, 274
    tendon-related injuries, 278–279
    toe injuries, 286–287
lower respiratory infections (LRI),
    322–323
lumbar disk injuries, 176–177
lumbar plexus, 238, 238*f*
lumbar vertebrae, 173
lung injuries, 230–231
luxation, 10–11
lyme disease, 299, 323, 324, 326, 346
lysosomes, 123

M

macrocycle, 55
macronutrients, 78
macrophages, 123, 124, 129
macrotrauma, 340, 342
magnetic resonance imaging (MRI), 9, 346
major depression, 65
major minerals, 85*t*
malaise, 322, 323
male genitalia injuries, 244–245
malfeasance, 36, 37
mallet (baseball) finger, 216–217, 216*f*
malocclusion, 164
maltose, 79
mandible, 138, 159
mandibular condyle, 164
mandibular fossa, 164
manubrium of sternum, 188
Marfan syndrome, 230
martial arts, 12
maturation phase, 124–125
maxilla, 138, 159
maxillofacial region injuries, 158
    dental injuries, 159–160
    eye injuries, 160–162
    face injury, 164–165
    nose injuries, 162–164
mechanical dysfunction, 258–259
mechanical forces of injury, 120, 121*f*
mechanisms of injury
    cervical spine, 151–152
    head, 140
medial epicondylitis, 205
medial tibial stress syndrome (MTTS), 281
mediastinum, 225
medical history of injury assessment, 112–113
melanomas, 299
meninges, 137, 137*f*
menisci injuries, 251, 259–260
menstruation, 350
merthiolate, 298
mesocycles, 55
metabolic activity of inflammatory agents, 129
metabolic emergencies, 113
metacarpal bones, 213, 214
metacarpophalangeal (MP) joint, 214
metaphysis, 10, 11
methicillin-resistant *staphylococcus aureus* (MRSA), 17, 302, 323–325
    prevention and management recommendations, 326
methylphenidate (Ritalin), 100
microcycle, 55
micronutrients, 84
microtrauma, 273, 340, 342
microvascular injury, 342
mid-shaft humeral fractures, 199, 200*f*
middle ear, 163
mild traumatic brain injury, 140–141
Mildenberger, Dale, 282
military press, 348
minerals, 85–86, 85*t*

minimal competitive weight, 95, 97
Minnesota study, history/symptoms in PPE, 232
misfeasance, 36, 37
missing organs, 50
modalities for pain, 126, 127, 127*t*
monocytes, 123, 124
mononucleosis, 231, 317
monosaccharides, 79, 80
monounsaturated fats, 82
Morton's foot, 283
mosaic wart, 303
mouth guards, 15, 160
movable soccer goals, 19
MRI. *See* magnetic resonance imaging
MRSA. *See* methicillin-resistant *Staphylococcus aureus*
MTJ. *See* musculotendinous junction
multivitamin supplement, 85
muscle endurance, 52–53
muscle power, 52–53
muscle protein, 83
muscle strength, 52–53
muscles, 198, 200
    activity/innervation, 224, 225
    of arm, 196, 197*f*
    strains, 226
muscular strength, 322, 323
muscular tissue, 120
musculotendinous junction (MTJ), 7, 120
myalgia, 322, 323
myelin, 137
myocarditis, 322, 323
myositis ossificans, 8, 9, 253–254
myositis ossificans traumatica, 197–198

N

NAIRS. *See* National Athletic Injury/Illness Reporting System
nasal bones, 138
NATA. *See* National Athletic Trainers' Association
National Association of Anorexia Nervosa and Associated Disorders (ANAD), 2013, 70–71
National Athletic Injury/Illness Reporting System (NAIRS), 12
National Athletic Trainers' Association (NATA), 78, 94, 157, 339
    AHCT description, 24
    BOC certification, 27
    Career Center placement service, 29–30
    football injury survey, 13
    heat-related illness, 312
    injury definitions, 3
    MRSA, 302
    position statement, 79
    recognition/treatment, 228
    volleyball injury survey, 18
National Center for Catastrophic Sports Injury Research (NCCSIR), 6, 12
National Collegiate Athletic Association (NCAA), 64, 91, 139, 160, 162, 328
    banned drugs, 350

    contact ACL injuries, 261
    deaths in athlete population, 228
    guideline (medical evaluations, immunizations, and records), 48
    noncontact ACL injury, 261
    soccer goal construction, 19
    sports injury definitions, 3
    wrestling/skin infection guidelines, 304
National Collegiate Athletic Association Injury Surveillance System (NCAA-ISS), 12, 15, 69
National Federation of State High School Associations (NFHS), 13, 19, 48, 89
National Football League (NFL), 12, 152, 261
National Hockey League (NHL), 12
National Institute for Mental Health (NIMH), 66
National Safety Council
    CPR and AED training, 39, 107
    fracture symptoms, 8
    frostbite/frostnip, 316
    hypothermia, 315
    initial check, 109
    poison ivy, poison oak, and poison sumac, 304
    wound treatment guidelines, 297
National Strength and Conditioning Association (NSCA), 52, 100
NCAA. *See* National Collegiate Athletic Association
NCAA-ISS. *See* National Collegiate Athletic Association Injury Surveillance System
NCCSIR. *See* National Center for Catastrophic Sports Injury Research
neck (cervical spine), 138
    injuries
        football emergency procedures for treatment, 156–158
        treatment guidelines for, 154–156
negative body image, 73
negative pressure, 230*f*
negligence, 34–37
nerves, 238
    CNS, 311
    injuries to wrist, 210–212
    problems, 245
nervous tissue, 120
neural arch, 173, 174*f*
neurocognitive function, 19
neurogenic shock, 114
neuroma, 283
neuromuscular activity, 262, 263
neuromuscular electrical stimulation (NMES), 127
neuropsychological testing, 40
neurotrauma, 14
neurovascular imitators, 346
neutrophils, 123
New York City Public School Athletic League, 338
NFHS. *See* National Federation of State High School Associations
NFL. *See* National Football League

NIMH. *See* National Institute for Mental Health
nipple irritation, 227
nitric oxide (NO), 99–100
NMES. *See* neuromuscular electrical stimulation
NO. *See* nitric oxide
nonathlete's diet, 91
noncatastrophic injuries, 338
noncontact ACL injury, 261
noncontact category, 12
nonsteroidal anti-inflammatory drugs (NSAIDs), 130–131, 130*t*
nose injuries, 162–163
NSAIDs. *See* nonsteroidal anti-inflammatory drugs
NSCA. *See* National Strength and Conditioning Association
nucleus pulposus, 176
nutrition
    body composition and, 55
    body weight management, 94–95, 97
    for coach's athletes, 90
    dietary guidelines for athletes
        during competition, 93
        daily maintenance, 91–92
        for post exercise, 93
        precompetition diets, 92–93
    education, 90–91
    endurance sports, 88
    female athletes, 88
    and injury recovery, 93–94
    nutrients overview
        caloric intake, 78–79
        CHO, 79–81
        fats, 81–82, 82*t*
        minerals, 85–86, 85*t*
        proteins, 83–84, 84*t*
        vitamins, 84–85, 84*f*
        water, 86
    nutritional knowledge, 86–87
    supplements, 97–100
    wrestling, 88–89
nutritional calorie, 78–80

O

obesity in children and adolescents, 344
oblique fractures, 8, 9*f*
oblique muscles, 225
observation of injury, 112, 113
Occupational Safety and Health Administration (OSHA), 298, 299
OCD. *See* osteochondritis dissecans
omega-3 fatty acids, 94
omega-6 fatty acids, 94
omission, 36, 37
oncologic imitators, 346
1-RM equivalent, 347
one-repetition maximum lift (1 RM), 347
oral contraceptives, 317
orthopedic surgeons, 24, 25, 252
Osgood-Schlatter disease, 257–258, 341
OSHA. *See* Occupational Safety and Health Administration

ossification, 340
osteitis pubis, 243
    prevention of, 246
osteoarthritis, 15
osteoblasts, 124, 125
osteochondritis dissecans (OCD), 205–207, 256
osteoclasts, 124, 125
osteomyelitis, 346, 347
osteoporosis, 72, 350
osteosarcomas, 346
OTC sale. *See* over the counter sale
oval window rupture, 164
over the counter (OTC) sale, 99
overlapping stirrups, 290*f*
overuse injuries, 4, 340, 344, 345
oxidative energy conversion, 51

P

PABA. *See* para-aminobenzoic acid
pain, 8
    and acute injury, 125–126
palatine bones, 138
palmar radiocarpal ligament, 209, 209*f*
palpation
    in anatomic snuffbox, 209, 209*f*
    injury assessment, 112–114, 114*f*
    thoracic strains, 172
para-aminobenzoic acid (PABA), 299
parasitic skin infections, 304
paratroopers, braces in, 277
parental consent forms, 39–40
pars interarticularis, 173, 175
passive exercise, 131
passive stretching, 55
patella
    dislocation/subluxation, 257
    fractures, 253
    patellar tendon, 4, 5*f*
    patellar tracking, 258
patellofemoral conditions, 258–259
patellofemoral joint, 250, 251
    injuries, 256–258
pathogenic eating behaviors, 69–70
PCS. *See* post-concussive syndrome
pectineus muscle, 240
pectoral muscles, strains in, 226
pectoral region, muscles of, 182*f*
pectoralis major/minor muscles, 180, 181, 181*f*, 224
pelvis, 173, 174*f*
    fractures, 240–241
penetrating eye injuries, 161
penicillin, 317
periodization, 51, 55–56
periosteum of cranial bone, 136
peripheral mechanical stabilization, 263
peripheral nervous system (PNS), 138, 139
permethrin, 324, 326
peroneus brevis, 273
personal responsibility for healing, 69
personality variables, 62–64
pes anserinus group, 240
pes cavus, 283

pes planus, 283
Peterson type I injury, 342, 342*f*
petit mal seizure, 332
phagocytosis, 123
phalanges, 213
    fractures of, 214
pharmacologic agents, 127, 129–131
phase 1, 57
    stress model, 68
phase 2, 57
    stress model, 68
phase 3, 57
    stress model, 68
phonophoresis, 129
phospholipids, 123
physes, 340
physical exam during injury assessment, 112–114, 145–149
    computerized neurocognitive assessment, 149
    concussion education, 149
    home instructions, 148
    return to play, 148–149, 148*t*
    sideline assessment, 147–148
physical findings inconsistent with injury history, 345
physics of sports injury, 120
physiology of sports injury, 120–125
pia mater, 137, 137*f*
PIP joint. *See* proximal interphalangeal joint
piriformis muscle, 238–239
plaintiff, 36, 37
plantar fasciitis, 282
plantar flexion, 270, 271
plantar warts, 302, 303
plasma proteins, 123
platelets, 123
playing surfaces, 47, 345
pleural sac, 225, 230
pneumothorax, 171, 172*f*, 226, 230, 230*f*, 231
PNF. *See* proprioceptive neuromuscular facilitation
PNS. *See* peripheral nervous system
point tenderness, 112, 113
pole-vaulting, pelvis fractures, 240
polycarbonate, 162
polymorphs, 124
polysaccharides, 79
polyunsaturated fats, 82
PONY football league injuries, 14
popliteus muscle, 271
post-concussive syndrome (PCS), 141–142
post-traumatic amnesia (PTA), 141
posterior cruciate ligament, 251
posterior longitudinal ligaments, 173
posterior rib fracture, 171
posterior SC dislocation, 188
posterior talofibular ligaments, 274
posterior tibial artery, 273
postexercise rehydration, 313
postexercise weight loss, 309
postgraduate classes, 41
postural problems, 49
postural stability testing, 40

power phase (periodization), 56
PPE. *See* preparticipation physical examination/evaluation
practice/competition environment, 47
"Pre-hospital Care of the Spine-Injured Athlete," 157
precompetition diets, 92–93
prednisolone, 129
prednisone, 129
premature specialization, 338
preparticipation physical examination/ evaluation (PPE), 40, 48
  by coordinated medical team, 49
  females' menstrual history, 349
  as requirement, 40
  sports classifications and, 12
  Veneto, Italy/Minnesota comparison study, 232–233
prepatellar bursitis, 256, 257
prescription stimulant medication, 350
preseason conditioning, 50, 344
preventive ankle taping, 289
  advantages and disadvantages of, 288
prewrap, application of, 289, 289*f*
primary amenorrhea, 349
professional sports settings, 27–30
pronator forearm muscles, 196
prophylactic adhesive-taping procedure, 277
prophylactic knee brace, 265, 265*f*
proprioception training exercises, 277
proprioceptive neuromuscular facilitation (PNF), 54, 55
prostaglandins, 121, 123, 130
protection, rest, ice, compression, and elevation (PRICE), 127
protective cup, 244, 247
protective equipment, 47
  heart/lung injury, 229
  padding, 47
protective eyewear, 162
protein supplementation, 83–84
protein supplements, 83
proteins, 83–84, 84*t*, 94
  consumption after exercise, 93
proteoglycans, 124
proximal interphalangeal (PIP) joint, 217
proximal musculotendinous junction (MTJ), 120
proximate cause, 36
psoas muscles, 239
psychogenic shock, 114
psychologic imitators, 346
psychological stress, 62
psychology of injury, 61–62
  competitive stress and child/adolescent, 66–68
  eating disorders, 69–70
    anorexia nervosa and bulimia nervosa, 70–71
    prevention of, 73
    research, 71
    sport specificity and, 72–73
    treatment of, 73
  personality variables, 62–64

psychosocial variables, 64–65
  depression, 65–66
  SAD, 66
  recommendations, 69
psychometric tests, 64
psychosocial variables of injury, 64–65
  depression, 65–66
  SAD, 66
PTA. *See* post-traumatic amnesia
puberty, 339–340
pubic bones, 238
pubis, 238
pulmonary contusion, 230–231
purulent lesions, 301
pyoderma, 300, 301
pyomyositis, 346, 347

Q

Q angle, 258, 259*f*
quadriceps, 250, 251
quadriceps muscles, 239, 239*f*, 250*f*, 254

R

radiation, 308, 309
radiocarpal joint, 196, 197
radioulnar joints, 196, 197
Rang-Ogden type IV injury, 342, 342*f*
range of motion (ROM), 53
  factors determining, 54
  rehabilitative exercise for, 131–132
recovery (rest) periods, 52
rectus abdominis muscles, 225
rectus femoris muscle, 239, 250
referred pain, 232
reflex neuropathic dystrophy (RND), 346
refractometer, 95
regeneration, 121
rehabilitation
  of previous injuries, 349
  programs, 281
rehabilitative exercises, 125, 131–132
rehearsal of emergency plan, 107
rehydration, 309, 312
relative humidity, 308
remodeling phase, 124–125
removal from activity area, 114
renal failure, 231
repair, 121
repetition maximum (RM), 52
repolarization phase of contracting heart, 228
rescue breathing, 108
research, athlete, 71
resistance training, 52–53
resistive exercise, 132
resolution, 121
respiratory infections
  LRI, 322–323
  URI, 322
respiratory system
  injury assessment, 110
  respiratory arrest, 108, 145
responsiveness of athlete, 109
rest, ice, compression, and elevation (RICE), 171

rest periods, 53
retinaculum, 206
retrograde amnesia, 141
return to play condition, 114–115, 148–149, 148*t*
rheumatologic imitators, 346
rhinitis, 322, 323
rhodiola, 97*t*
rhomboid muscle, 180, 181*f*, 224–225
rib fractures, 171–172, 226
rib joints, 224
RICE. *see* rest, ice, compression, and elevation
Richards, Skylar, 57
rigid ankle brace, 278*f*
ringworm, 17, 300
risk factors, 11
  identification of, 11, 12
Ritalin (methylphenidate), 100, 350
RM. *See* repetition maximum
RND. *See* reflex neuropathic dystrophy
ROM. *See* range of motion
room dimensions, 47
rotation of cervical spine, 152
rotational deformity, 214
rotator cuff, 4, 5*f*, 183, 188–189, 189*f*
running. *See also* cross-country running; long-distance running
  chronic injuries, 4, 4*f*
  non-contact sports, 12
  snapping hip syndrome, 242
ruptured eardrum, 164
ruptured rectus femoris muscle, 255, 255*f*
  case study of, 255

S

sacral plexus, 238, 238*f*
sacroiliac (SI) joints, 173, 238, 243
sacrum, 173, 238
SAD. *See* seasonal affective disorder
safe weight loss and management, 94
safety fences, 47
sagittal plane MRI of a torn ACL, 261*f*
salmeterol, 328
Salter-Harris fractures, 10, 10*f*, 11, 342
sanitation facility location, 47
SARRS. *See* Social and Athletic Readjustment Rating Scale
sartorius muscle, 239–240
saturated fats, 82
SC joint. *See* sternoclavicular joint
scalp, 136*f*
scaphoid bone, fracture of, 208, 208*f*
scapula, 180, 185
scar tissue, 121, 125
Scheuermann's disease, 171
sciatic nerve, 238, 245
scoliosis, 171
scrotal contusions, 244–245
seasonal affective disorder (SAD), 64, 66
second-degree sprains/strains, 7
second impact syndrome (SIS), 142, 143*f*
second-user CPR, 27
secondary amenorrhea, 349, 350

secondary enzymatic injury, 124, 125
secondary metabolic injury, 124, 125
secondary school setting, 28–29
secondary sexual characteristics, 339
seizure, 331
self-concept as risk factor, 63
self-help strategies, 65, 66
semi-rigid orthoses, 282
semicircular fibrocartilaginous disks, 251
semimembranosus muscle, 240
sensitizers, 304
septal hematoma, 163
septal injuries, 163
serratus anterior muscle, 180, 181f
serum hepatitis (HBV), 296
Sever's disease, 342
shear forces, 120, 120f
shin splints, 8, 281
Shingles, Rene Revis, 255
shock in injury assessment, 114
shoes, 246
shoulders
    acromioclavicular joint injuries, 185–186
    anatomy, 180–183
    biceps tendon, 191
    contusions, 191–192
    fractured clavicle, 183–185
    fractured scapula, 185
    girdle muscles, 50, 180, 181f, 182f
        actions, and innervations of, 182–183
    glenohumeral joint injuries, 186–188
    joint, 180
    muscles, 180, 181f, 182f
    pointer, 191
    rotator cuff, 188–189
    skeletal injuries, 183–185
    soft-tissue injuries, 185–192
    sternoclavicular joint injuries, 188
    strains, 189
    subluxation, 113
    tip pain, 232
SI joint. *See* sacroiliac joints
sickle cell trait, 329
side aches, 232
sidearm pitching, 16
sideline assessment, head injuries, 147
sign, defined, 112, 113
signs and symptoms
    AC joint sprains, 186
    Achilles tendon, 279
    biceps tendon problems, 191
    boutonnière deformity, 218
    brachial plexus injury, 152
    cervical spine sprains, 153
    cervical spine strains, 153
    clavicle fracture, 184
    coccyx fracture, 175
    compartment syndrome, 281
    concussion (mild head injury), 141
    de Quervain's disease, 212
    dehydration, 309–310
    dental injuries, 159
    distal forearm fractures, 207
    ear injuries, 163
    EIA, 328

elbow fractures, 203–204
elbow sprains and dislocations, 202
epicondylitis/apophysitis, 205
exertional heatstroke, 311
eye injuries, 161
femoral fractures, 253
frostbite (deep freezing), 317
frostnip (superficial freezing), 317
furuncles, carbuncles, and
    folliculitis, 301
gamekeeper's thumb, 216
ganglion, 213
GH joint injuries, 186, 187
hand fractures, 214
heat cramps, 310–311
heat exhaustion, 311
herniated disk, 176
herpes gladiatorum, 303
humeral fractures, 200
hyperglycemia, 331
hypoglycemia, 331
hypothermia, 315
impetigo and cellulitis, 302
impingement syndrome, 190
inflamed bursa, 257
injuries to triceps muscle, 199
jersey finger, 217
jumper's knee, 258
knee ligaments, 263
lateral ankle sprain, 275
lower leg/foot fracture, 274
lumbar sprains/strains, 175
mallet finger, 216–217
muscle strains, 254
muscular contusion, 253
nerve injuries to wrist, 211
ODC, 206
olecranon bursitis, 206
Osgood-Schlatter disease, 258
osteochondritis dissecans, 256
patellar dislocation/subluxation, 257
plantar warts, 303
rotator cuff injuries, 189
SC joint injuries, 188
shin splints, 281
shoulder contusions, 191–192
sickle cell trait, 329
SLAP, 187
tib/fib syndesmosis sprain, 276
tinea infection, 300
tinea versicolor, 300
torn meniscus, 259
upper arm contusions, 197–198
vertebral fractures, 171
wrist fractures, 209
wrist sprains and dislocations, 210
zygomatic bone fracture, 164
silver fork deformity, 207, 208f
simple carbohydrates, 80
simple fats, 82
SIS. *See* second impact syndrome
skeletal injuries, 6, 170–172, 252–253,
    273–274
    hip/pelvis, 240–243
    shoulder, 183–185

skin
    allergic reactions, 304–305
    bacterial infections, 300–302
    infections, 17, 299–303
    MRSA, 17, 302
    plantar warts, 303
    ringworm, 300
    tinea versicolor, 300
    ultraviolet light and, 299
    viral infections, 302–303
    wounds, 296–298
    wrestling and skin infections, 304
skull anatomy, 136, 136f
slipped capital femoral epiphysis, 241
SNAI. *See* Standard Nomenclature of Ath-
    letic Injuries
snapping hip syndrome, 242
soccer
    catastrophic injuries, 12
    collision sports, 12
    data, 18
    injury rates, 2, 3, 18
    jumping and pelvic avulsion, 244
    osteitis pubis, 243
Social and Athletic Readjustment Rating
    Scale (SARRS), 64
social physique anxiety, 70
Social Readjustment Rating Scale (SRRS), 64
social support, psychological recovery and, 69
soft orthotics, 283f
soft tissue, defined, 6, 7
soft tissue injuries, 274
    avulsion fractures, 244
    hernias, 245
    male genitalia injuries, 244–245
    nerve problems, 245
    shoulder, 185–192
    to thigh, 253–255
    to upper arm, 196–199
softball
    anterior shoulder pain, 16
    catastrophic injuries, 12
    fixed-based contact injuries, 15
    game *vs.* practice injury rates, 15
    injury data, 2, 15
    limited contact sport, 12
    protective chest equipment, 229, 229f
soleus muscles, 271
Solley, Troyce, 126
sovereign immunity, 37
spearing, 11, 151
spheroidal articulation, 186
spinal curvature, 171
spinal nerves, 138
spinalis muscle, 224
spine
    lumbar disk injuries, 176–177
    lumbar spine
        anatomy, 173
        sprains, 175
        strains, 175
    rib fractures, 171
    skeletal injuries, 170–172
    spinal curvature, 171
    spondylolisthesis, 173–175

spondylolysis, 173–175
strains, thoracic spine, 172
thoracic cage, 170, 170f
thoracic spine anatomy, 170, 170f
traumatic fractures, 175
vertebral fractures, 171
spine boards, 155f
spleen injuries, 231
splinting
  of elbow injury, 202, 203f
  techniques, 214, 215f
spondylolisthesis, 173–175, 174f
spondylolysis, 173–175, 174f
spontaneous pneumothorax, 230
sport environment, 70
sport specificity and eating disorders, 72–73
sport task, 70
sports bras, 227
sports classifications, 12
sports hernias, 245, 246f
sports injury, concept of, 1–19, 106
  ankle, 274–278
  baseball/softball, 15–16
  basketball, 14–15
  classifications of injury, 7–11
  contusions, 8
  defined, 3–7
  dislocations, 10–11
  epidemiology, 11–12
  fractures, 8–10
  injury recognition, 11
  knee ligament, 260–263
  lower leg
    arch problems, 283–285
    blisters and calluses, 285–286
    bunions, 285
    compartment syndrome, 279–281
    foot disorders, 281–282
    heel spurs, 282–283
    Morton's foot, 283
    plantar fasciitis, 282
    shin splints, 281
    tendon-related injuries, 278–279
    toe injuries, 286–287
  lumbar disk, 176–177
  menisci, 259–260
  patellofemoral conditions, 258–259
  patellofemoral joint, 256–258
  physics of, 120
  physiology of, 120–125
  Salter-Harris fractures, 10, 11
  skeletal, 183–185, 252–253, 273–274
  soccer, 18–19
  soft-tissue, 185–192, 274
    to thigh, 253–255
  spondylolisthesis, 173–175
  spondylolysis, 173–175
  sports classifications, 12
  sprains, 7, 175–176
  strains, 7–8, 175–176
  stress fractures, 8–9
  tackle football, 13–14
  traumatic fractures, 175
  volleyball, 18
  wrestling, 16–18

sports injury prevention
  aerobic fitness, 51
  body composition, 54–55
  causitive factors, 46–47
  extrinsic factors, 47
  flexibility, 53–54
  heat illnesses, 312–313
  intervention strategies, 47–50
  intrinsic factors, 48–50
  muscle strength, power, and endurance,
    52–53
  nutrition, 55
  periodization, 55–56
  prevention and conditioning, 50–56
sports medicine, 24, 25
  clinic, 27, 28f
  defined, 24–25
  fellowships, 25
  specialists involved in, 25
sports nutrition programs, 91
sprains, 7, 274
  cervical spine, 152–153
  defined, 7
  dislocations as, 10
  elbow, 202
  of hand, 214–218
  lumbar spine, 175
  softball, 15
  thoracic spine, 172
  wrist, 209–210
sprinting and pelvic avulsion fracture, 244
squash, 190
squats, 348
"squeeze" test, 276, 276f
SRRS. See Social Readjustment Rating
    Scale
stabilization of head and neck, 145f, 146
standard ankle-taping procedure, 277
Standard Nomenclature of Athletic Injuries
    (SNAI), 7
standing toe touch, 54
Staphylococcus aureus, 300
starch, 79
state regulation of athletic training, 42
static flexibility, 53
static stretching, 54, 55
sternal fracture, 226
sternoclavicular (SC) joint, 180, 180f, 181,
    188, 224
sternocostal joints, 224
steroidal anti-inflammatory drugs,
    129–130
steroids, 100, 231, 298
stingers, 152
stirrups, 289, 289f, 290f
  horseshoe, 291f
  overlapping, 290f
stitch in the side, 232
STOP Sports Injuries, 339
strains, 7
  abdominal muscle, 227
  cervical spine, 153
  defined, 7
  injuries, prevention of, 263
  lumbar spine, 175

  muscle, 226–227
  thoracic spine, 172
strength phase (periodization), 55
strength training, 346–348
Streptococcus, 300
stress fractures, 8–9, 273
stress-injury model, 64
stress process, 68f
stress X-ray of fracture, 341f
stressful life events, 64
stressor, 68, 69
stretching exercises, 54, 349
student athletic trainer program, 29
subacromial space, 190
subclavian artery, 181
subclavius muscle, 180, 181f
subcutaneous fat, 94
subdural hematoma, 143
subluxations, 10, 11, 191, 226
subscapularis muscles, 181, 181f, 183
subsequent ankle sprains, control of, 277
subsyndromal SAD, 66
subtalar joint, 270, 271
sucrose, 79
sudden death, 228
sugars, 79
sunburn protection, 299
superior dislocation of SC joint, 188
supinator forearm muscles, 196
Supplement 411, 98
supplementation, protein, 83–84
supracondylar fractures, 203
supraglenoid tubercle, 191
supraorbital regions, 138
supraspinatus muscle tendon, 5, 181,
    181f, 183, 190
surgically implanted fixation, 214
surveillance systems for risk factors, 12
suture joints, 136
suturing, 165
sweat evaporation process, 86
swelling as acute fracture symptom, 8
swimming
  catastrophic injuries, 12
  congenital heart disorders, 12
  GH joint–related impingement
    syndrome, 190
sympathetic eye movement, 161
symphysis pubis joint, 238, 243
symptomatic SAD, 66
symptoms, defined, 112, 113
syndesmosis sprain, 276
syndrome, 190
synovial fluid, 212
synoviated articulation, 185, 188
synthetic rubber additive allergies, 304
syphilis, 317
systemic symptoms, 345

T

table tennis, GH joint impingement
    syndrome, 190
tackler's exostosis, 197
talocrural joint, 270, 271

Tanner stages of sexual maturity, 347
taping
    ankles, 284
    wrist and thumb, 218, 219f–220f
teacher as athletic trainer, 28
team dynamics, 65
team physicians, 25–26
temporomandibular joint (TMJ), 160, 164,
        164f, 165
tenderness, complaints of, 8
tendinitis, 189, 191, 210
tendons
    finger, 216f
    injuries, 269, 278–279, 341–342
    muscles, 252
    problems of wrist, 212–213
    thumb, 212f
Tennessee Self-Concept Scale (TSCS), 63
tennis
    catastrophic injuries, 12
    GH joint impingement syndrome, 190
    and pelvic avulsion fracture, 244
    rotator cuff injuries, 5f
tennis elbow, 205
tenosynovitis, 212, 213
TENS. See transcutaneous electrical nerve
        stimulation
tensile forces, 120, 120f
tensor fasciae latae muscle, 238, 239
terbutaline sulfate, 328
teres major/minor muscles, 181, 181f, 183
terrible-triad injury, 263
testicle injuries, 245
testicular contusion, 244, 245
testosterone precursors, 99
therapeutic exercise, 131–132
therapeutic heat, 127
thermal injuries, 307–317
    cold-related health problems, 313–316
    cold urticaria, 316–317
    dehydration, 309–310
    exertional heat illnesses, 309–313
    exertional heat stroke, 311–312
    frostbite/frostnip, 315–316
    heat cramps, 310–311
    heat exhaustion, 311
    hypothermia, 313, 315
    indoor activities and, 47
    prevention, heat illnesses, 312–313
thermoregulation, 86, 308
thermotherapy, 127–129
thigh, knee, and leg injuries
    anatomy, 250–252
    knee ligament, 260–263
    ligaments, 2, 15
    menisci injuries, 259–260
    patellofemoral conditions, 258–259
    patellofemoral joint, 256–258
    prevention, 263–266
    skeletal, 252–253
    soft-tissue injuries to thigh, 253–255
third-degree sprains/strains, 7
thoracic cage, 170, 170f, 171
thorax and abdomen injuries, 223–233
    abdominal pain, 232–233

anatomy, 224–225
bladder injuries, 231–232
breast injuries, 227
external injuries, 226–227
fractures, 226
heart injuries, 228–229
internal injuries, 227–223
internal organs, 225, 225f
kidney injuries, 231
liver injuries, 231
lung injuries, 230–231
spleen injuries, 231
thorax/chest injuries in baseball/softball, 16
thumb taping, wrist and, 218, 219f–220f
tib/fib syndesmosis sprain, 275, 276
tibia, fracture of, 274f
tibial (medial) collateral ligament, 250
tibial stress injury (TSI), 281
tibiofemoral joint, 250, 251
    dislocation of, 253
time lost as injury definition, 4
Tinactin, 300
tinea, 300, 300f, 301
tinea versicolor (TV), 300, 301
tissue, types of, 120
TMJ. See temporomandibular joint
toe injuries, 286–287
tonic-clonic seizure, 332
tooth avulsion, 159
tooth enamel erosion, 72
topical analgesic allergies, 304
torn meniscus, 259
tort, 35–37
trace minerals, 85t
track and field, GH joint impingement
        syndrome, 190
training
    error, 344
    recommended carbohydrate intake, 81t
training frequency, 53
training intensity, 51, 52
training volume, 52
trait anxiety, 63
trait theory, 62
trait variables, 63
transcutaneous electrical nerve stimulation
        (TENS), 127
transition phase in training cycle, 55, 56
transport device, 114
transverse carpal ligaments, 206
transverse fractures, 8, 9f
transverse humeral ligament, 191
trapezium bone, 214
trapezius muscle, 180, 180f, 225
trapezoid ligaments, 185
trauma, 120
traumatic fractures, 175
traumatic injuries, 273
traveling teams, 2
treatment guidelines
    dehydration, 309–310
    dental injuries, 159
    exercise-induced asthma, 328
    exertional heatstroke, 312
    eye injuries, 161–162

head injury, 144–149
heat cramps, 311
heat exhaustion, 311
hypothermia, 315
for neck injuries, 154–156
nose injury, 163
plantar warts, 303
tinea infection, 300
triamcinolone, 129
triceps injuries, 198–199
trochanteric bursitis, 242
true ribs, 224
TSCS. See Tennessee Self-Concept Scale
tunnel of Guyon, 210, 211
turf burn, 296
turf toe, 286
    taping, 288f
Turocy, Paula Sammarone, 87
tympanic membrane, 163
type I (juvenile-onset/insulin-dependent)
        diabetes, 330
type II (adult-onset) diabetes, 330
typical physical exams, 49

U

ulnar collateral ligaments, 216
ulnar nerve, 202, 210
ultrasound diathermy, 127
ultrasound therapies, 47
ultraviolet A (UVA) light rays, 299
ultraviolet B (UVB) light rays, 299
uncus of temporal lobes, 142
unilateral spondylolysis, 174
University of North Carolina, 6
unresponsive to any stimulus assessment,
        109
unsafe weight management practices, 94
unsaturated fats, 82
upper arm. See arm injuries
upper extremities, 46
upper respiratory infections (URI), 322,
        323
urine dipstick method, 95
U.S. Anti-Doping Agency (USADA), 98
U.S. Food and Drug Administration
        (FDA), 83, 98
U.S. National Registry of Sudden Death in
        Young Athletes, 228
U.S. Olympic Committee, 160
U.S. society, 48
USADA. See U.S. Anti-Doping Agency
UVA light rays. See ultraviolet A light rays

V

valgus forces, 202, 203
varicella, 317
varus forces, 202, 203
vascular engorgement of brain tissue, 142
vasoactive substances, 123
vasoconstriction, 121, 123
vasodilation, 121, 315
ventricular fibrillation, 228
vertebral fractures, 171
vertebral joints, 224

vertigo, 322, 323
vestibulocochlear nerve, 163
violent force injures, 259
violent trauma, 253, 273
viral infections, skin, 302–303
vitamins, 84–85, 84*f*
Volkmann's contracture, 203, 203*f*
volleyball
 catastrophic injuries, 12
 data, 18
 GH joint impingement syndrome, 190
 limited contact sport, 12
vomer, 138

W

WADA. *See* World Anti-Doping Agency
waist, 208
Walsh, Katie, 192
warmup exercises, 54
water
 body weight, 94
 as nutrient, 86
water polo, 12
water-soluble vitamins, 84
weight chart, 312
weight cutting, 89
weight gain, in injured athletes, 94
weight lifting, spondylolisthesis, 174

weight loss, 89
weight management, nutrition and, 94–95, 97
weight-training exercises, 52
whiplash injuries, 140, 153
whirlpool bath safety risks, 47
windchill chart, 315, 316*t*
WMWP. *See* Wrestling Minimum Weight Project
World Anti-Doping Agency (WADA), 98
wounds, skin, 296–298
wrestling, 16–18
 AC joint injuries, 183
 bleeding wounds, 298
 catastrophic injuries, 12
 contact/collision category, 12
 GH joint injuries, 183
 herpes gladiatorum, 303
 nutrition and, 88–89
 skin problems, 301, 304
 takedowns/escapes, 17, 17*f*
 thoracic strains, 172
Wrestling Minimum Weight Project (WMWP), 89
wrist dislocations, 209–210
wrist fractures, 208–209
wrist injuries
 and forearm, 206–207, 207*f*, 208*f*
 fractures, 208–209

nerve injuries, 210–212
 sprains and dislocations, 209–210
 tendon problems, 212–213
nerve injuries to, 210–212
sprains, 209–210
tendons problems of, 212–213
and thumb taping, 218, 219*f*–220*f*
written contracts, 39

X

X-ray diagnoses of stress fractures, 9, 10*f*

Y

YMCA, 338
youth sports
 in America, 338
 growing athlete
  growth, 340
  puberty, 339–340
 injury, epidemic of, 338–339
 participation, factors in, 338
Youth Sports Safety Alliance, 339

Z

zingiberis rhizoma, 97*t*
zygomatic bones, 138
 fracture, 164